PROBLEMS IN THE
OF ANCIENT GREECE

PROBLEMS IN THE HISTORY OF ANCIENT GREECE

SOURCES AND INTERPRETATION

Donald Kagan

Yale University

and

Gregory F. Viggiano

Sacred Heart University

Prentice Hall

Boston   Columbus   Indianapolis   New York   San Francisco   Upper Saddle River
Amsterdam   Cape Town   Dubai   London   Madrid   Milan   Munich   Paris   Montreal   Toronto
Delhi   Mexico City   Sao Paulo   Sydney   Hong Kong   Seoul   Singapore   Taipei   Tokyo

Editorial Director: Leah Jewell
Executive Editor: Charles Cavaliere
Editorial Assistant: Lauren Aylward
Director of Marketing: Brandy Dawson
Production Manager: Wanda Rockwell
Creative Director: Jayne Conte
Cover Designer: Bruce Kenselaar
Manager, Visual Research: Beth Brenzel
Manager, Rights and Permissions: Zina Arabia
Image Permission Coordinator: Annette Linder
Manager, Cover Visual Research & Permissions: Karen Sanatar
Cover Art: Studio Kontos Photostock
Full-Service Project Management: Integra Software Services, Ltd.
Printer/Binder: Hamilton Printing Co.
Cover Printer: DPC
Cover Source: Vanni/Art Resource, NY

Library of Congress Cataloging-in-Publication Data

Kagan, Donald.
    Problems in the history of ancient Greece : sources and interpretation /
Donald Kagan and Gregory F. Viggiano.
        p. cm.
    Includes bibliographical references and index.
    ISBN-13: 978-0-13-614045-0 (alk. paper)
    ISBN-10: 0-13-614045-9 (alk. paper)
    1. Greece—History—To 146 B.C.—Historiography.   2. Greece—History—To
146 B.C.—Sources.   I. Viggiano, Gregory.   II. Title.
DF211.K34 2010
938.0072—dc22

                                                                    2009029805

10 9 8 7 6 5 4 3 2 1

Prentice Hall
is an imprint of

www.pearsonhighered.com

ISBN 13: 978-0-13-614045-0
ISBN 10:   0-13-614045-9

BRIEF CONTENTS

CONTENTS

PREFACE

This collection of contested problems in the history of Ancient Greece aims to enhance and deepen the experience of college students beginning the study of that subject. It is meant to be used in conjunction with a narrative history or some suitable substitute. Together with such a narrative account, it provides material for instructive and, if our experience as teachers is typical, exciting discussions. Each chapter is a self-contained unit that presents a problem of continuing interest to historians. In each case there is a selection of pertinent ancient sources in translation, with a number of modern viewpoints also presented. In this way, the beginner may experience immediately the nature of the historian's craft: the excitement of weighing and evaluating sources, the problem of posing meaningful and enlightening questions, the need to change hypotheses in light of new evidence or new insights, and the necessity, in some cases, of suspending judgment. This method aims at reproducing in some small measure the actual conditions of historical investigation and making the results available to the neophyte.

The problems have been selected on the basis of several criteria: First, they attempt to span the chronological period usually covered by courses in ancient Greek history in a reasonably representative way; second, they are all real problems that continue to excite interest among scholars, and in almost every case they have been the subject of relatively recent study; finally, they are meant to be sufficiently varied in topic and approach to expose the student to a variety of historical methods and techniques. Each problem, along with an accompanying narrative text, is sufficient for a week's work, but teachers will be able to assign the material to meet their own needs. We hope that the sampling of the ancient authors offered here will provide an irresistible stimulus for the student to read them in their entirety. The authors have developed the text as a course pack over several semesters with remarkable success. Gregory Viggiano has enjoyed excellent results in his upper-division class at Sacred Heart University. The book has also worked very well in the discussion sections of Donald Kagan's large lower-division lecture course at Yale.

We also thank Charles Cavaliere for supporting our project and seeing it through to completion. We are grateful to Jonathan Perry, University of South Florida; Kathryn Simonsen, Memorial University of Newfoundland; and Carol Thomas, University of Washington who reviewed the manuscript and whose insightful suggestions improved it. All errors and omissions are of course ours alone.

New Haven
April 2009

ABOUT THE AUTHORS

Donald Kagan is Sterling Professor of History and Classics at Yale University, where he has taught since 1969. He received the A.B. degree in history from Brooklyn College, the M.A. in classics from Brown University, and the Ph.D. in history from Ohio State University. During 1958–1959 he studied at the American School of Classical Studies as a Fulbright Scholar. He has received three awards for undergraduate teaching at Cornell and Yale. He is the author of a history of Greek political thought, *The Great Dialogue* (1965); a four-volume history of the Peloponnesian War, *The Origins of the Peloponnesian War* (1969); *The Archidamian War* (1974); *The Peace of Nicias and the Sicilian Expedition* (1981); *The Fall of the Athenian Empire* (1987); a biography of Pericles, *Pericles of Athens and the Birth of Democracy* (1991); *On the Origins of War* (1995); and *The Peloponnesian War* (2003). He is coauthor, with Frederick W. Kagan, of *While America Sleeps* (2000). With Brian Tierney and L. Pearce Williams, he is the editor of *Great Issues in Western Civilization*, a collection of readings. He was awarded the National Humanities Medal for 2002 and was chosen by the National Endowment for the Humanities to deliver the Jefferson Lecture in 2004.

Gregory Viggiano received his Ph.D. in Classics from Yale University. He is an assistant professor in the history department at Sacred Heart University, where he teaches courses on ancient Greece and Rome, and Western civilization. He is currently coediting a book on ancient Greek hoplite warfare with Donald Kagan.

PROBLEMS IN THE HISTORY
OF ANCIENT GREECE

INTRODUCTION TO THE ANCIENT SOURCES

THE FIRST PROBLEM any student of ancient Greek history confronts is the nature of the sources historians must use in reconstructing and interpreting the events. There are certain difficulties that the historian of ancient Greece must face. First, most of the evidence that survives is literary and late, often written centuries after the events in question. Second, even when there is material available for the time period in question, it was often not composed for historical purposes. For example, the most valuable testimony for the Dark Age is Homer's epics but these were not created to aid the historian. A third problem, which is related to the first two, involves the controversy that surrounds the verisimilitude of the surviving sources. There is great disagreement among historians about how to treat late sources. In any case, the problem is unavoidable. A brief sketch of the nature of the evidence for the first five chapters in this book is given below.

Following the collapse of the Aegean Bronze society in the twelfth century, the art of writing was lost in the Greek world until the eighth century. And it was not until the mid-fifth century that Herodotus invented history in the West and wrote the first continuous historical prose narrative. Therefore, almost all knowledge about the centuries from the Late Bronze Age to the Persian Wars of the fifth century derives from the later tradition and from authors who were not necessarily historians. It is also common for these authors to pay little attention to even relative chronology and to combine myth with history in a manner that obscures the facts. On the positive side, these later writers often had access to credible source material, including official archives, which no longer survive. In the very least, they tell us what the Greeks thought about their past. Historians can also draw upon archaeology and epigraphy for material to compare with the literary accounts and to develop their arguments. The study of works of representational art and monumental architecture is the core of classical archaeology. Chapter 2 on early hoplite warfare demonstrates the significance of vase paintings for that topic. Epigraphy involves the study of inscriptions on permanent materials such as wood, bronze, and stone and has become central to the work of the ancient historian. Chapter 5 features the controversy over one of the most famous inscriptions from classical Greece, the decree of Themistocles. Inscriptions have a preeminent place in the various debates concerning the nature of the Athenian empire as well (see Chapter 9).

AUTHORS

1. Homer. Scholars most often discuss the epic poems the ancient world attributed to Homer, the *Iliad* and *Odyssey*, as the earliest and greatest works of Greek literature. Historians, on the other hand, take special interest in the poems due to their cultural significance for the Greeks. Many also believe that the poems reflect something of the social and political institutions and the military customs of early Greece.

Research into what scholars call the Homeric Question has shown how complex the task of the historian becomes when he or she wants to treat the poems as historical testimony.

THE HOMERIC QUESTION

The problem of the first two chapters relates to the Homeric Question: Was there a monumental poet named Homer who composed the *Iliad* and *Odyssey* in something like their present form? The ancient Greeks (and Romans, for that matter) had no doubt that a single genius, Homer, was responsible for both epics. This view of antiquity went unchallenged for many centuries. However, in the seventeenth century, the abbé d'Aubignac reacted against the reverence for Homer in his own day. He protested that the poems handed down in Homer's name were merely a collection of the works of various men. From the polemic of d'Aubignac, the modern form of the Homeric Question originated. Throughout the nineteenth century, debate raged about the composition of the Homeric epics between two schools of thought, the Unitarians and the Analysts. The Unitarians argued that a single poet was responsible for the creation of both the *Iliad* and *Odyssey*. The Analysts, for their part, saw in the poems distinct layers of composition or combinations of earlier poems that one individual or group of authors had patched together. The idea of a single creative genius disappears.

The ideas of both the Unitarians and the Analysts assumed some text or texts were originally by Homer, which had been fixed in writing. Prior to the debate of the Unitarians and the Analysts, Friedrich August Wolf, in his *Prolegomena ad Homerum* of 1795, had argued that Homer had lived in a time before the alphabet was in use. Wolf, though, gave no indication how Homer might have composed the *Iliad* and *Odyssey* without writing. The work of Parry and Lord, however, suggested that Homer had composed his epics through a technique of oral improvisation similar to that of the bards they had observed in the Balkans. Thus, however the epics reached their final form, they represent the culmination of a long tradition of oral poetry, which took generations of singers to produce. For Lord, the poet is at the same time both a creator and the tradition, which is a product of the culture and older than any written literature. The question still remains how the texts of the *Iliad* and *Odyssey* became fixed following the introduction of writing in eighth-century Greece.

Recent scholars have argued that a written text of Homer was produced around the time of the invention of Greek writing, a monumental achievement that occurred in the early to mid-eighth century BC. The Greek alphabet, the first writing system to include vowels, was invented by adaptation from the existing Phoenician alphabet. Barry Powell contends that the "adaptor" created Greek writing specifically to record the *Iliad* and *Odyssey* of Homer. He imagines that poems of Homer were written down by the scribe to whom the great poet himself dictated. Richard Janko also thinks a fixed written text was produced by Homer. He uses linguistic analysis of the poems to posit that Homer dictated both poems, each a unified creation, in the second half of the eighth century.

On the other hand, Gregory Nagy, a former student of Albert Lord, argues for a living oral tradition that continued well past the time of the eighth century. He envisions the epics moving from relatively more fluid to more static phases of oral tradition. Nagy puts less emphasis on the creative genius of one singer than on the dynamic nature of the tradition that produced the poetry. One of the essential ideas for Nagy is that composition occurs in performance. Therefore, the singer has no need of writing to create. Instead, Nagy proposes that the poems continued to evolve as oral compositions for centuries after the invention of Greek writing. The early diffusion of the *Iliad* and *Odyssey* in the archaic period of Greece caused the relatively fluid oral tradition to become more rigid. The sixth century, during the rule of the Peisistratid tyrants in Athens, marks the next stage in the process of the epics becoming even more stable. It was at the Panathenaia, the seasonal pan-Hellenic festival at Athens, that the tyrants established by law the performance of fixed "texts" of the *Iliad* and *Odyssey* by rhapsodes. However, Nagy argues that the Peisistratids did not establish a fixed written text for the Homeric poems but a set order for the episodes, which would be recited in succession by the various competing rhapsodes in relay. For Nagy, writing does not become a significant factor in fixing the texts of the tradition until the rise of the book trade at Athens in the late fifth century.

A definitive answer to the Homeric Question seems unlikely at this point. But this brief discussion suggests some of the difficulties involved in using the epics as historical documents for the world of Homer.

2. Hesiod was a poet who many scholars believe lived in Boeotia and composed two epic poems, the *Theogony* and the *Works and Days*, at around 700 BC. However, the work of Hesiod and the identity of the author have been the subject of the same type of analysis as that of Homer.

3. Tyrtaeus was an elegiac poet contemporary with the Second Messenian War in the seventh century BC. The fragments of his poems that survive are a major source of our knowledge of the early history of Sparta. Ancient writers credited Tyrtaeus with leading the Spartans to victory in war and contributing to their system of education.

4. Semonides (not to be confused with the fifth-century poet Simonides) was a Greek iambic poet who composed in the mid-seventh century BC.

5. Solon was a sixth-century Athenian lawgiver credited with wide-ranging political and economic reforms. Despite the importance of his work, there is no extant written account of Solon's legislation and constitutional reforms earlier than the mid-fifth century BC. Fortunately, Solon was not only a great statesman but also an accomplished poet, who used his poems to comment on the events in which he played a leading role. The surviving fragments come from a variety of sources and shed light on how Solon viewed the nature and significance of his political actions. The poems also reveal the characteristic moderation and moral fortitude that earned him a place among the Seven Wise Men.

6. Herodotus of Halicarnassus, universally regarded as "the father of history," lived in the fifth century BC and wrote the definitive account of the Persian Wars. His work was the first not just to chronicle historical events but to inquire (the root meaning of history) into their causes (*aitia*) and to provide a complete account of why they happened. In the process, Herodotus not only invented history but also created the first great work of Western prose literature. His narrative explains why the Greeks and Persians fought and includes many digressions, which have earned Herodotus at least as great a reputation for being a storyteller as a historian. For Herodotus, dreams, oracles, the gods, and the supernatural in general play a role in shaping history. His belief in divine intervention, his love of telling a good story, and the fact that he describes events that happened generations before his time have since antiquity cast doubt on the truthfulness of Herodotus. On the other hand, modern research into the nature of oral traditions has proven the reliability of such information. The finds of archaeologists and the knowledge of languages he could not read have vindicated much of what Herodotus says and have increased his stature as a historian.

7. Thucydides (c. 460–399 BC) wrote the history of the war fought between Athens and Sparta in the last third of the fifth century (431–404 BC), known as the Peloponnesian War. Scholars recognize him as the greatest historian of antiquity and as the most modern in his approach to the subject. Thucydides is often cited for the objective and scientific character of his work. In contrast to Herodotus, he believed that it was only worthwhile to write about contemporary events at which the historian could either himself be present or have access to eye-witness reports. Thucydides took pride in not accepting the first account he heard about an event but cross-examining numerous witnesses to determine the truth. The strong influence of the fifth-century sophists (teachers of rhetoric) is seen in one of the most prominent features of his work: the speeches he reports and for which he claims to give "the general sense of what was actually said." Like the medical writers (e.g., Hippocrates), he rejects the supernatural in explaining human affairs. In his famous descriptions of the horrible plague that struck Athens at the start of the war and during the brutal civil war (*stasis*) at Corcyra, he draws a parallel between the pathology of the sickness and a polis infected with *stasis*. On the one hand, Herodotus had sought to write a memorial of the great deeds of the Greeks and barbarians (*kleos andrón*). On the other hand, Thucydides aimed at producing an eternal possession (*ktéma es aiei*) to instruct future generations. His idea was that given the constancy of human nature, the basic patterns of history remain the same.

8. The "Old Oligarch" (Pseudo-Xenophon) is the name assigned to an anonymous author of a pamphlet on the Athenian constitution, which has come down to us among the works of Xenophon. Internal evidence places the date of the treatise toward the beginning of the Peloponnesian War (c. 425 BC). The author was thus, like Thucydides the historian, a contemporary of Pericles. His views, though different from those of Thucydides, are not to be dismissed.

9. Sophocles (497/6–406 BC) was probably the greatest Athenian tragic playwright. He wrote more than 120 plays and won first prize at least 20 times. Sophocles was also one of the treasurers of Athena in 443–442 BC and served as general with Pericles in 441/0 during the revolt of Samos.

10. Euripides (c. 485–406 BC) was one of the three greatest writers of Attic tragedy during the fifth century. Nineteen of his ninety plays survive.

11. Aristophanes (c. 450–386 BC) was the greatest poet of the Old Attic Comedy. Eleven of his forty plays survive, including the *Clouds*, which parodies Socrates as a sophist and natural scientist. Historians take special interest in the plays Aristophanes wrote during the Peloponnesian War for the light they shed on the political scene in Athens at the time.

12. Lysias was an Attic orator (459/8–c. 380 BC) who wrote speeches for litigants of the courts in Athens.

13. Xenophon (c. 430–354 BC) was an Athenian who was exiled and lived much of his life in the Peloponnesus. He fought in the Spartan army as a mercenary under King Agesilaus, whose friend and admirer he was. A prolific writer, Xenophon's works include *Hellenica*, a history of Greek affairs from 411 to 362, and his *Constitution of the Spartans*. Xenophon was a contemporary of Plato's and also an admirer and associate of Socrates. In his own brief *Apology of Socrates* and in his *Memorabilia* or "Recollections," however, he presents a very different picture of the philosopher.

14. Plato (427–347 BC) was a student and admirer of Socrates and one of the greatest philosophers in antiquity. His dialogues and his *Apology* are the primary source for the life and ideas of his teacher, Socrates, who left no writings. His most famous dialogue, the *Republic*, inspired Whitehead's celebrated remark that "the

European philosophical tradition…consists of a series of footnotes to Plato." Plato's work has great significance for the historian in understanding Greek political and moral thought, as well as Greek culture in the fifth and fourth centuries.

15. Isocrates (436–338 BC) was a leading Athenian rhetorician. His written speeches give important commentary on the great political issues of the fourth century. After the Peloponnesian War, Isocrates repeatedly called on the Greeks to launch an invasion of the Persian Empire to solve their economic and social problems.

16. Aristotle (384–322 BC) was a student of Plato and, along with his teacher and Socrates, the greatest philosopher in antiquity. His output was vast and includes scientific works on physics, biology, and zoology, as well as on philosophy and even a *Poetics*. Aristotle's *Politics* and *Athenian Constitution* (see below) hold particular interest for historians. Unlike Plato, who wrote his dialogues in a high literary style, the extant works of Aristotle resemble lecture notes in form. His writings systematize the entire Greek tradition and are noted for their frequent disagreements with Plato. A Macedonian himself, Aristotle was tutor for the young Alexander III, later known as Alexander the Great.

17. The *Athenian Constitution* (i.e., *Athenaion Politeia* or *A.P.*) is one of the works on the constitutions of 158 Greek poleis credited to Aristotle. The *Athenian Constitution* comprises two sections; the first two-thirds (Chapters 1–41) give a history of the constitution from its origins to the restoration of the democracy after the suppression of the Thirty Tyrants in 403 BC. This section derives from a variety of sources and contains much valuable information, which does not survive in any other texts. The final third (42–69) discusses the working of the constitution in Aristotle's own time. The work may not have been written by the master but by one of his students. In any case, it represents the research of the school of Aristotle, who must have approved of its contents.

18. Polybius (c. 200–c. 118 BC) was a Greek historian whose work, a universal history in 40 books, attempted to explain how the Romans conquered the Mediterranean world.

19. Diodorus Siculus was a Sicilian Greek who lived in the time of Caesar and Augustus. Between 60 and 30 BC he wrote a world history in 40 volumes from the earliest times to Caesar's Gallic War (54 BC). His work is based on that of earlier writers and rarely on primary evidence. His chronology is often confused and his general reliability is debated. His greatest value is in preserving the works of historians now lost to us, especially Ephorus of Cyme, a writer of the fourth century BC.

20. Strabo (64 BC–c. AD 21) was the author of a *Geographia* in 17 books. The work, by far the most important source for ancient geography, contains important material from lost authors.

21. Plutarch, the Greek biographer of the first and second century AD, is renowned for his *Parallel Lives*, which pairs the lives of famous Greeks and Romans, and his *Moralia*. Although writing biography many centuries after the events he describes, Plutarch is an important source for ancient historians, not least because he had access to many contemporary sources now lost (e.g., the Aristotelian *Laconian Constitution*). His intention was primarily moral and he did not intend to provide a detailed historical account, but his library was superb and he has preserved much material that would otherwise have been lost. Plutarch's sources included the works of the comic poets, historians, political theorists, and documentary inscriptions.

22. Pausanias (fl. c. AD 150) wrote *Description of Greece*, an account of his travels, in which he claims to describe "all things Greek." The work focuses on the monuments of the archaic and classical periods and their historical context.

23. Scholia comes from the Greek word *scholion*, which means "interpretation" or "comment." The term refers to notes of various lengths placed on a text, from a single word to an extended commentary. Commentators from antiquity placed these notes in the margins or between the lines of manuscripts of ancient authors for explanatory or critical purposes.

24. Stobaeus, an author, probably writing in the early fifth century AD, who composed an *Anthology* of excerpts from poets and prose writers to instruct his son Septimius.

25. The Suda: The word *Suda* or *Suidas* refers to a lexicon, not an author, and means *Fortress* or *Stronghold*. The work is a historical lexicon compiled at the end of the tenth century AD.

26. Demosthenes (384–322 BC) was the greatest Athenian orator. Demosthenes delivered his famous *Philippics* to warn the Athenians of the threat he perceived in Philip of Macedon and to gather military support against him.

27. Arrian (c. AD 86–160) was one of the leading writers of an intellectual movement of the Roman Empire known as the Second Sophistic, during which he achieved fame as a philosopher. He saw himself as a second Xenophon. His *Anabasis of Alexander*, a history of Alexander the Great in seven books, is the leading work that survives on the subject.

CHAPTER 1
THE WORLD OF HOMER

❧

IN ANTIQUITY, FEW GREEKS doubted either the historicity of the Trojan War or the existence of a former Age of Heroes that Homer describes in his *Iliad* and *Odyssey*. Even Thucydides, renowned for the rational and scientific character of his work, reconstructed early Greek history from the testimony of Homer's epics. The Romans also accepted the core of epic legend concerning the events and heroes of ancient Troy. These beliefs held firm throughout the Middle Ages and into the Renaissance. In modern times, however, scholars started to question whether a Trojan War took place or if individuals such as Agamemnon and Achilles ever existed. For example, George Grote, one of the most eminent historians of the nineteenth century, began his great *History of Greece* (1846–1856) with the first Olympiad (776 BC), for he considered the myths of the Bronze Age unusable for the historian. Homer was merely fiction.

The excavations by Heinrich Schliemann in the 1870s brought about a dramatic shift in the thinking of scholars on the value of Homer for the historian. Digging on the high plateau of Hisarlik in modern-day Turkey, Schliemann uncovered the remains of an ancient city that he believed was Homer's Troy. Further excavations at Hisarlik and at Mycenae, on the mainland of Greece, seemed to confirm that the Greek myths about an age of heroes had a historical basis.

Even if Homer's epics contained knowledge of Bronze Age centers, there remained the question of how such knowledge could have been preserved without writing in the Dark Age. During the 1930s, Milman Parry and his student, Albert Lord, compared the living traditions of South Slavic oral poetry with Homer. Their work showed that Homer may have composed his epics using techniques similar to those of the singers they studied in the Balkans. Scholars could now understand how bards might have preserved traditional tales for centuries and composed poetry on the scale of the *Iliad* without the use of writing. Both archaeological finds and theories of oral composition convinced many that the type of society Homer depicted once existed in the Greece of the Late Bronze Age.

In 1939, Carl Blegen found more than a thousand inscribed clay tablets at the Bronze Age palace of Pylos on the mainland of Greece. The writing was identical to the script of many of the tablets that Arthur Evans had discovered on the island of Crete a generation earlier. Michael Ventris' 1952 decipherment of this script, named Linear B by Evans, challenged the historical accuracy of Homer as a witness to Mycenaean Greece. The Linear B tablets proved that the world of the Bronze Age palaces was a Greek one, but they describe a monarchic society that is highly bureaucratic and not at all "heroic." Certain objects described by Homer and many Homeric personal names do seem to come from a poetic tradition originating in the time of the shaft graves of Mycenae, but the omissions of the poet are telling. Homer appears ignorant of the type of society that the tablets reveal. In fact, most scholars now agree that the points of contact between the world of Homer and that of Late Bronze Age Greece are few and superficial in comparison to the many and great differences. On the other hand, scholars are still far from agreement on what world, if any, Homer describes.

Although historians and archaeologists debate both the scope and the significance of the event, there is now a general agreement that something resembling a Trojan War had taken place toward the end of the Bronze Age (c. 1200 BC). Between the time of the war and the composition of Homer's epics, many generations of bards performed songs they had heard about the events surrounding the siege of Priam's city. The singers, however, did not simply repeat the tales they inherited but amplified the traditional themes, and centuries of innovation and development may have altered the original story in profound ways. On the other hand, certain words, objects, episodes, and ideas found in Homer originated deep in the Bronze Age and became fixed in traditional formulae. These formulae consist of the stock phrases that the poet uses under certain metrical conditions. They form the building blocks, so to speak, in a system of traditional oral poetry. Examples of Bronze Age survivals include the huge tower shield of the Greek hero Ajax and the boar's-tusk helmet given to Odysseus. These objects became part of the legends later told about the Trojan War. So, despite the belief of many scholars that Homer's epics—either as written texts or as oral songs—reached some stage of completion by about the end of the eighth century, the following questions remain: When did the world of Homer exist? When did Greek society resemble the material culture; the political, legal, and social institutions; as well as the moral values of Homer's heroes? Hence, how far back we date the institutions of Homer affects how early we can date many of the developments characteristic of the rising Greek city-state, the polis.

The three scholars featured in this chapter show a remarkable range of opinions. Moses Finley argues for a ninth- or tenth-century date for the world of Homer. Finley bases his claim on the conservative nature of traditional oral poetry and the absence of the institutions historians associate with the polis. Anthony Snodgrass examines the archaeological evidence to contend that Homer's world never existed at any single time; what the poet describes is a conflation of the many societies that existed between the time of the Trojan War and Homer's own day. Barry Strauss uses the most recent excavations to argue that Homer is a faithful witness to the Bronze Age city of Troy. He argues that the Trojan War and the historicity of Homer's characters are plausible as the poet describes them.

Ancient Sources

1. Homer, *Iliad*, THE QUARREL OF ACHILLES AND AGAMEMNON 1.1–303
2. Homer, *Iliad*, ODYSSEUS AND THERSITES 2.53–278
3. Homer, *Iliad*, THE SHIELD OF ACHILLES 18.478–508
4. Homer, *Odyssey*, KINGSHIP AT ITHACA 1.365–424
5. Homer, *Iliad*, HECTOR AND ANDROMACHE 6.440–502
6. Homer, *Iliad*, THE EMBASSY TO ACHILLES 9.307–429
7. Homer, *Iliad*, GLAUCON AND SARPEDON 12.310–328

Opinions of Modern Scholars

1. From Moses Finley, *The World of Odysseus*
2. From Anthony Snodgrass, "An Historical Homeric Society?"
3. From Barry Strauss, *The Trojan War: A New History*

The citadel of Mycenae, a major center of the Greek civilization of the Bronze Age, was built of enormously heavy stones. The lion gate at its entrance was built in the thirteenth century BCE.

ANCIENT SOURCES FOR HOMERIC SOCIETY

The *Iliad* and *Odyssey* were translated by Samuel Butler and revised by Timothy Power and Gregory Nagy. Gregory Nagy, the Francis Jones Professor of Classical Greek Literature and Professor of Comparative Literature at Harvard University and Director of the Harvard Center for Hellenic Studies in Washington DC, has generously provided all of the Homer translations.

Pearson's publication of them is nonexclusive; they are published by Harvard's Center for Hellenic Studies, Washington, DC, under a Creative Commons Attribution Share-Alike license (http://creativecommons.org/licenses/by-sa/3.0/).

1. THE QUARREL OF ACHILLES AND AGAMEMNON

In the beginning of the *Iliad,* Homer describes the quarrel that took place between the leader of the Greek expedition to Troy, Agamemnon, and the poem's greatest warrior, Achilles. Besides setting forth the plot for the epic, the poet also provides a graphic illustration of and raises questions about the nature of kingship in early Greek aristocratic society. *Iliad* 1.1–303

[1] Anger [*mēnis*], sing it, O goddess, [the anger] of Achilles son of Peleus, which brought countless pains [*algos* pl.] upon the Achaeans. Many a brave soul [*psukhē*] did it send hurrying down to Hadēs, and them[1] it left as a prey to dogs

[5] and birds, and the Will [*boulē*] of Zeus was fulfilled—starting from the day on which the son of Atreus, king [*(w)anax*][2] of men, and great Achilles, first quarreled with one another. And which of the gods was it that set them on to quarrel? It was the son of Zeus and Leto; for he was angry with the king [*basileus*]

[10] and sent a pestilence upon the host of warriors to plague the people, because the son of Atreus had dishonored Khrysēs his priest. Now Khrysēs had come to the ships of the Achaeans to free his daughter, and had brought with him a great ransom [*apoina*]: moreover he bore in his hand the scepter of Apollo wreathed with a suppliant's wreath

[15] and he besought the Achaeans, but most of all the two sons of Atreus, who were their chiefs. "Sons of Atreus," he cried, "and all other Achaeans, may the gods who dwell in Olympus grant you to destroy the city of Priam, and to reach your homes in safety;

[20] but free my daughter, and accept a ransom [*apoina*] for her, in reverence to Apollo, son of Zeus." At this the rest of the Achaeans with one voice were for respecting the priest and taking the ransom that he offered; but not so Agamemnon,

[25] who spoke fiercely to him and sent him roughly away. "Old man," said he, "let me not find you tarrying about our ships, nor yet coming hereafter. Your scepter of the god and your wreath shall profit you nothing. I will not free her. She shall grow old

[30] in my house at Argos far from her own home, busying herself with her loom and visiting my bed; so go, and do not provoke me or it shall be the worse for you." The old man feared him and obeyed. Not a word he spoke, but went by the shore of the sounding sea

[35] and prayed apart to King Apollo whom lovely Leto had borne. "Hear me," he cried, "O god of the silver bow, you who protect Khrysē and holy Killa and rules Tenedos with your might, hear me O Sminthian Apollo. If I have ever decked your temple with garlands,

[40] or burned your thigh-pieces in fat of bulls or goats, grant my prayer, and let your arrows avenge these my tears upon the Danaans." Thus did he pray,

---

[1] The bodies, not the "souls" [*psukhai*], of the heroes are their selves.

[2] Scholars have determined that the w-sound, which most classical dialects (c. 750–350 BC) and the language of Homer had lost, was still present in early Greek (c. 1500 BC). Therefore, the form "wanax" shows up in the Linear B tablets in reference to the kings of the Late Bronze Age, but the same term appears as "anax" in the *Iliad* and *Odyssey*. We present the reconstructed form here to encourage comparison between the roles of the (w)anax in Homer and the extensive, if not absolute, civil and military and religious powers of the Mycenaean wanax.

and Apollo heard his prayer. He came down furious from the summits of Olympus,

[45] with his bow and his quiver upon his shoulder, and the arrows rattled on his back with the rage that trembled within him. He sat himself down away from the ships with a face as dark as night, and his silver bow rang death as he shot his arrow in the midst of them.

[50] First he smote their mules and their hounds, but presently he aimed his shafts at the people themselves, and all day long the pyres of the dead were burning. For nine whole days he shot his arrows among the people, but upon the tenth day Achilles called them together in assembly—

[55] moved to do so by Hera, who saw the Achaeans in their death-throes and had compassion upon them. Then, when they were assembled, he rose and spoke among them. "Son of Atreus," said he, "I deem that we should now

[60] turn roving home if we would escape destruction, for we are being cut down by war and pestilence at once. Let us ask some priest or prophet [*mantis*], or some reader of dreams (for dreams, too, are of Zeus) who can tell us why Phoebus Apollo is so angry, and say

[65] whether it is for some vow that we have broken, or hecatomb that we have not offered, and whether he will accept the savor of lambs and goats without blemish, so as to take away the plague from us." With these words he sat down, and Kalkhas son of Thestor, wisest of seers,

[70] who knew things past, present, and to come, rose to speak. He it was who had guided the Achaeans with their fleet to Ilion, through the prophecies with which Phoebus Apollo had inspired him. With all sincerity and goodwill he addressed them thus: "Achilles, dear to Zeus, you bid me tell you about the

[75] anger [*mēnis*] of King [*(w)anax*] Apollo, I will therefore do so; but consider first and swear that you will stand by me heartily in word and deed, for I know that I shall offend one who rules the Argives with might, to whom all the Achaeans are in subjection.

[80] A plain man cannot stand against the anger of a king [*basileus*], who even if he swallows his displeasure now, will yet nurse revenge till he has taken it. Consider, therefore, whether or not you will protect me." And Achilles answered,

[85] "Fear not, but speak as it is given to you by the gods. I swear by Apollo, Kalkhas, to whom you pray, and whose oracles you reveal to us, that not a Danaan at our ships shall lay his hand upon you, while I yet live to look upon the face of the earth—

[90] no, not even if you name Agamemnon himself, who is by far the foremost of the Achaeans." At that the seer [*mantis*] spoke boldly. "The god," he said, "is not angry about either a vow or a hecatomb, but for his priest's sake, whom Agamemnon has dishonored,

[95] in that he would neither free his daughter nor take a ransom [*apoina*] for her; therefore has he sent these pains [*algos* pl.] upon us, and will yet send others. He will not deliver the Danaans from this pestilence till Agamemnon has restored the girl without fee or ransom [*apoina*] to her father, and has sent a holy hecatomb

[100] to Khrysē. Thus we may perhaps appease him." With these words he sat down, and Agamemnon rose in anger. His heart was black with rage, and his eyes flashed fire

[105] as he scowled at Kalkhas and said, "Seer [*mantis*] of evil, you never yet prophesied good things concerning me, but have always loved to foretell that which was evil. You have brought me neither comfort nor performance; and now you come prophesying among the Danaans, and saying

[110] that Apollo has plagued us because I would not take a ransom [*apoina*] for this girl, the daughter of Khrysēs. I have set my heart on keeping her in my own house, for I prefer her to my own wife Clytemnestra, whom I courted when young, whose peer she is in

[115] both form and feature, in intelligence and accomplishments. Still I will give her up if I must, for I want the people to live, not die; but you must find me a prize [*geras*] instead, or I alone among the Argives shall be without one. This is not well;

[120] for you see, all of you, that my prize [*geras*] is to go elsewhere." And Achilles answered, "Most noble son of Atreus, covetous beyond all humankind, how shall the Achaeans find you another prize [*geras*]? We have no common store from which to take one.

[125] Those we took from the cities that have been divided up; we cannot disallow the awards that have been made already. Give this girl, therefore, to the god, and if ever Zeus grants that we destroy the city of Troy we will requite you three and fourfold."

[130] Then Agamemnon said, "Achilles, valiant though you be, you shall not thus get the better of me in matters of the mind [*noos*]. You shall not overreach and you shall not persuade me. Are you to keep your own prize [*geras*], while I sit tamely under my loss and give up the girl at your bidding?

[135] Let the Achaeans find me a prize [*geras*] in fair exchange to my liking, or I will come and take your own, or that of Ajax or of Odysseus; and to whomsoever I may come shall regret my coming.

[140] But of this we will take thought hereafter; for the present, let us draw a ship into the sea, and find a crew for her expressly; let us put a hecatomb on board, and let us send Khrysēis also; further, let some chief [*arkhos*] man among us be in command,

[145] either Ajax, or Idomeneus, or yourself, son of Peleus, mighty warrior that you are, that we may offer sacrifice and appease the anger of the god." Achilles scowled at him and answered, "You are steeped in insolence and lust of gain.

[150] With what heart can any of the Achaeans do your bidding, either on foray or in open fighting? I came to make war here not because the Trojans are responsible [*aitioi*] for any wrong committed against me. I have no quarrel with them. They have not raided my cattle nor my horses,

[155] nor cut down my harvests on the rich plains of Phthia; for between me and them there is a great space, both mountain and sounding sea. We have followed you, shameless one, for your pleasure, not ours—to gain satisfaction [*timē*] from the Trojans for you—you with the looks of a dog—and for Menelaos.

[160] You forget this, and threaten to rob me of the prize [*geras*] for which I have toiled, and which the sons of the Achaeans have given me. Never when the Achaeans destroy any rich city of the Trojans do I receive so good a prize [*geras*] as you do,

[165] though it is my hands that do the better part of the fighting. When the sharing comes, your share is far the largest, and I must go back to my ships, take what I can get and be thankful, when my labor of fighting is done. Now, therefore, I shall go back to Phthia; it will be much better

[170] for me to return home with my ships, for I will not stay here dishonored to gather gold and substance for you." And Agamemnon answered, "Leave if you will, I shall make you no entreaties to stay you. I have others here

[175] who will do me honor, and above all Zeus, the lord of counsel. There is no king [*basileus*] here so hateful to me as you are, for you are ever quarrelsome and ill affected. So what if you are strong? Was it not a god that made you so? Go home, then, with your ships and comrades

[180] to lord it over the Myrmidons. I care neither for you nor for your anger [*kotos*]; and thus will I do: since Phoebus Apollo is taking Khrysēis from me, I shall send her with my ship and my followers, but I shall come to your tent and

[185] take your own prize Brisēis, that you may learn how much stronger I am than you are, and that

another may fear to set himself up as equal or comparable with me." The son of Peleus felt grief [*akhos*], and the heart within his shaggy breast was divided

[190] whether to draw his sword, push the others aside, and kill the son of Atreus, or to restrain himself and check his anger [*kholos*]. While he was thus of two minds, and was drawing his mighty sword from its scabbard, Athena came down

[200] from the sky (for Hera had sent her in the love she bore for them both), and seized the son of Peleus by his golden hair, visible to him alone, for of the others no man could see her. Achilles turned in amazement, and by the fire that flashed from her eyes at once knew that she was

[200] Athena. "Why are you here," said he, "daughter of aegis-bearing Zeus? To see the outrage [*hubris*] of Agamemnon, son of Atreus? Let me tell you—and it shall surely be—

[205] he shall pay for this insolence with his life." And Athena said, "I come from the sky, if you will hear me, to bid you stay your anger [*menos*]. Hera has sent me, who cares for both of you alike.

[210] Cease, then, this quarreling, and do not draw your sword; rail at him if you will, with words, and your railing will not be vain, for I tell you—and it shall surely be—that you shall hereafter receive gifts three times as splendid by reason of this present outrage [*hubris*]. Hold, therefore, and obey."

[215] "Goddess," answered Achilles, "whatever anger [*kholos*] a man may have, he must do as you two command him. This will be best, for the gods ever hear the prayers of him who has obeyed them." He stayed his hand on the silver hilt of his sword,

[220] and thrust it back into the scabbard as Athena bade him. Then she went back to Olympus among the other gods [*daimones*], and to the house of aegis-bearing Zeus. But the son of Peleus again began railing at the son of Atreus, for he had not yet desisted from his anger [*kholos*].

[225] "Wine-bibber," he cried, "you with the looks of a dog and the heart of a deer, you never dare to go out with the host of warriors in fight, nor yet with our chosen (best of the Achaeans) men in ambuscade. You shun this as you do death itself. You had rather go round and

[230] rob his prizes from any man who contradicts you. You devour your people, for you are king [*basileus*] over a feeble folk; otherwise, son of Atreus, from now on you would insult no man. Therefore I say, and swear it with a great oath—by

this my scepter which shall sprout neither leaf nor shoot,

[235] nor bud anew from the day on which it left its parent stem upon the mountains—for the axe stripped it of leaf and bark, and now the sons of the Achaeans bear it as judges and guardians of the decrees [*themis* pl.] of the gods—so surely and solemnly do I swear

[240] that hereafter they shall look fondly for Achilles and shall not find him. In the day of your distress, when your men fall dying by the murderous hand of Hector, you shall not know how to help them, and shall rend your heart with rage for the hour when you offered insult to the best [*aristos*] of the Achaeans."

[245] With this the son of Peleus dashed his gold-studded scepter on the ground and took his seat, while the son of Atreus was beginning fiercely from his place upon the other side. Then up rose smooth-tongued Nestor, the facile speaker of the Pylians, and the words fell from his lips sweeter than honey.

[250] Two generations of men born and bred in Pylos had passed away under his rule, and he was now reigning over the third. With all sincerity and good-will, therefore, he addressed them thus: "Truly," he said, "a great grief [*penthos*] has befallen the Achaean land.

[255] Surely Priam with his sons would rejoice, and the Trojans be glad at heart if they could hear this quarrel between you two, who are so excellent in fight and counsel [*boulē*]. I am older than either of you; therefore be guided by me.

[260] Moreover I have been the familiar friend of men even greater than you are, and they did not disregard my counsels. Never again can I behold such men as Perithoös and Dryas, shepherd of his people, or as Kaineus, Exadios, godlike Polyphemus,

[265] and Theseus son of Aegeus, peer of the immortals. These were the mightiest men ever born

upon this earth: mightiest were they, and when they fought the fiercest tribes of mountain savages they utterly overthrew them. I came from distant Pylos, and went about among them,

[270] for they would have me come, and I fought as it was in me to do. Not a man now living could withstand them, but they heard my words, and were persuaded by them. So be it also with yourselves, for this is the more excellent way.

[275] Therefore, Agamemnon, though you be strong [*agathos*], take not this girl away, for the sons of the Achaeans have already given her to Achilles; and you, Achilles, strive not further with the king [*basileus*], for no man who by the grace of Zeus wields a scepter has like honor [*timē*] with Agamemnon.

[280] You are mighty, and have a goddess for your mother; but Agamemnon is mightier than you, for he has more people under him. Son of Atreus, check your anger [*menos*], I implore you; end this quarrel with Achilles, who in the day of battle is a tower of strength to the Achaeans."

[285] And Agamemnon answered, "Sir, all that you have said is true, but this man wants to become our lord and master: he must be lord of all, king of all, and chief of all, and this shall hardly be.

[290] Granted that the gods have made him a great warrior, have they also given him the right to speak with railing?" Achilles interrupted him. "I should be a coward and a good-for-nothing," he cried, "if I were to give in to you in all things.

[295] Order other people about, not me, for I shall obey no longer. Furthermore I say—and lay my saying to your heart—I shall fight neither you nor any man about this girl, for those that take were those also that gave.

[300] But of all else that is at my ship you shall carry away nothing by force. Try, that others may see; if you do, my spear shall be reddened with your blood."

Questions

1. **Does the figure of Agamemnon more closely resemble a wanax from Late Bronze Age Mycenae or a basileus of Dark Age Greece? Why?**
2. **If Agamemnon is the sceptered king, why can Achilles abuse him with impunity?**
3. **What do the words of Nestor tell us about the values of heroic society?**
4. **Why does Nestor care to reconcile the two warriors?**

2.   ODYSSEUS AND THERSITES

In the Second Book of the *Iliad,* Agamemnon—after being visited by a dream from Zeus promising that Agamemnon would take Troy—calls a Council of Elders to discuss the matter. Then, in a meeting of the assembly, he tests the spirit of his troops by suggesting that they give up the siege of Troy and return home; his plan fails when the men run to their ships. The scene gives a glimpse of the political structures of Dark Age Greece. *Iliad* 2.53–278

The goddess Dawn now wended her way to vast Olympus that she might herald day to Zeus and to the other immortals,

[50] and Agamemnon sent the criers round to call the people in assembly; so they called them and the people gathered thereon. But first he summoned a meeting of the elders at the ship of Nestor king [*basileus*] of Pylos,

[55] and when they were assembled he laid a cunning counsel [*boulē*] before them. "My friends," said he, "I have had a divine dream in the dead of night, and the dream's face and figure resembled none but Nestor's. It hovered over my head and said,

[60] 'You are sleeping, son of Atreus; one who has the welfare of his host of warriors [*boulēphoros*] and so much other care upon his shoulders should dock his sleep. Hear me at once, for I am a messenger from Zeus, who, though he be not near, yet takes thought for you and pities you.

[65] He bids you get the Achaeans instantly under arms, for you shall take Troy. There are no longer divided counsels among the gods; Hera has brought them over to her own mind, and woe betides the Trojans

[70] at the hands of Zeus. Remember this.' The dream then vanished and I awoke. Let us now, therefore, arm the sons of the Achaeans. But it will be the right thing [*themis*] that I should first sound them, and to this end I will tell them to flee with their ships;

[75] but do you others go about among the host of warriors and prevent their doing so." He then sat down, and Nestor the prince [*(w)anax*] of Pylos with all sincerity and goodwill addressed them thus: "My friends," said he, "princes and councilors of the Argives,

[80] if any other man of the Achaeans had told us of this dream we should have declared it false, and would have had nothing to do with it. But he who has seen it is the foremost [*aristos*] man among us; we must therefore set about getting the people under arms." With this he led the way from the assembly [*boulē*],

[85] and the other sceptered kings [*basileis*] rose with him in obedience to the word of Agamemnon; but the people pressed forward to hear. They swarmed like bees that come forth from some hollow cave and flit in countless throng among the spring flowers,

[90] bunched in knots and clusters; even so did the mighty multitude pour from ships and tents to the assembly [*agora*], and range themselves upon the wide-watered shore, while among them ran Wildfire Rumor, messenger of Zeus, urging them ever to the fore.

[95] Thus they gathered [*agora*] in a pell-mell of mad confusion, and the earth groaned under the tramp of men as the people sought their places. Nine heralds went crying about among them to stay their tumult and bid them listen to the kings [*basileis*], till at last they were got into their several places and ceased their clamor.

[100] Then King Agamemnon rose, holding his scepter. It was the work of Hephaistos, who gave it to Zeus the son of Kronos. Zeus gave it to Hermes, slayer of Argos, guide and guardian. King [*(w)anax*] Hermes gave it to Pelops, the mighty charioteer, and

[105] Pelops to Atreus, shepherd of his people. Atreus, when he died, left it to Thyestes, rich in flocks, and Thyestes in his turn left it to be borne by Agamemnon, that he might be lord of all Argos and of the isles. Leaning, then, on his scepter, he addressed the Argives.

[110] "My friends," he said, "heroes, attendants [*therapontes*] of Ares, Zeus the son of Kronos has tied me down with *atē*. Cruel, he gave me his solemn promise that I should destroy the city of Priam before returning, but he has played me false, and is now bidding me

[115] go ingloriously [*dus+kleos*] back to Argos with the loss of much people. Such is the will of Zeus, who has laid many a proud city in the dust, as he will yet lay others, for his power is above all. It will be a sorry tale hereafter that an

[120] Achaean host of warriors, at once so great and valiant, battled in vain against men fewer in

number than themselves; but as yet the end is not in sight. Think that the Achaeans and Trojans have sworn to a solemn covenant, and that they have each been numbered—

[125] the Trojans by the counting of their house-holders, and we by companies of ten; think further that each of our companies desired to have a Trojan house-holder to pour out their wine; we are so greatly more in number that full many a company would have to go without its cup-bearer.

[130] But they have in the town allies from other places, and it is these that hinder me from being able to destroy the rich city of Ilion. Nine of Zeus' years are gone;

[135] the timbers of our ships have rotted; their tackling is sound no longer. Our wives and little ones at home look anxiously for our coming, but the work that we came here to do has not been done. Now, therefore, let us all do as I say:

[140] let us sail back to our own land, for we shall not take Troy." With these words he moved the hearts of the multitude, so many of them as knew not the cunning counsel of Agamemnon. They surged to and fro like the waves

[145] of the Icarian Sea [*pontos*], when the east and south winds break from celestial clouds to lash them; or as when the west wind sweeps over a field of wheat and the ears bow beneath the blast, even so were they [the *agora*] swayed as they flew with loud cries

[150] towards the ships, and the dust from under their feet rose skyward. They cheered each other on to draw the ships into the sea; they cleared the channels in front of them; they began taking away the stays from underneath them, and the sky rang with their glad cries, so eager were they to return.

[155] Then surely the Argives would have had a return [*nostos*] after a fashion that was not fated. But Hera said to Athena, "Alas, daughter of aegis-bearing Zeus, the one who cannot be worn down, shall the Argives flee home to their own land over the broad sea,

[160] and leave Priam and the Trojans the glory of still keeping Helen, for whose sake so many of the Achaeans have died at Troy, far from their homes? Go about at once among the host [*laos*] of warriors, and speak fairly to them, man by man,

[165] that they draw not their ships into the sea." Athena was not slack to do her bidding. Down she darted from the topmost summits of Olympus, and in a moment she was at the ships of the Achaeans. There she found Odysseus, peer of Zeus in counsel,

[170] standing alone. He had not as yet laid a hand upon his ship, for he felt grief [*akhos*] and was sorry; so she went close up to him and said, "Odysseus, noble son of Laertes,

[175] are you going to fling yourselves into your ships and be off home to your own land in this way? Will you leave Priam and the Trojans the glory of still keeping Helen, for whose sake so many of the Achaeans have died at Troy, far from their homes? Go about at once among the host [*laos*] of warriors,

[180] and speak fairly to them, man by man, that they draw not their ships into the sea." Odysseus knew the voice as that of the goddess: he flung his cloak from him and set off to run. His attendant Eurybates, a man of Ithaca, who waited on him, took charge of the cloak,

[185] whereon Odysseus went straight up to Agamemnon and received from him his ancestral, imperishable staff. With this he went about among the ships of the Achaeans. Whenever he met a king or chieftain, he stood by him and spoke to him fairly.

[190] "Sir," said he, "this flight is cowardly [*kakos*] and unworthy. Stand by your post, and bid your peo-ple also keep their places. You do not yet know the full mind [*noos*] of Agamemnon; he was sounding us, and before long will visit the Achaeans with his dis-pleasure. We were not all of us at the council [*boulē*] to hear what he then said;

[195] see to it lest he be angry and do us harm; for the honor [*timē*] of kings [*basileis*] is great, and the hand of Zeus is with them." But when he came across some man from some locale [*dēmos*] who was making a noise, he struck him with his staff and rebuked him, saying,

[200] "What kind of *daimōn* has possessed you? Hold your peace, and listen to better men than your-self. You are a coward and no warrior; you are nobody either in fight or council [*boulē*]; we cannot all be kings; it is not well [*agathos*] that there should be many masters [*polukoiraniē*]; one man must be supreme—

[205] one king [*basileus*] to whom the son of scheming Kronos has given the scepter and divine laws to rule over you all." Thus masterfully did he go about among the host of warriors, and the people hurried back to the council [*agora*] from their tents and ships with a sound as the thunder of surf when it comes crashing down upon the shore,

[210] and all the sea [*pontos*] is in an uproar. The rest now took their seats and kept to their own sev-eral places, but Thersites still went on wagging his unbridled tongue—a man of many words, and those

unseemly; a monger of sedition, a railer against all who were in authority [*kosmos*], who cared not what he said,

[215] so that he might set the Achaeans in a laugh. He was the ugliest man of all those that came before Troy—bandy-legged, lame of one foot, with his two shoulders rounded and hunched over his chest. His head ran up to a point, but there was little hair on the top of it.

[220] He was hateful to Achilles and Odysseus most of all, for it was with them that he used to wrangle the most; now, however, with a shrill squeaky voice he began heaping his abuse on Agamemnon. The Achaeans were angry and disgusted, but nevertheless he kept on brawling and bawling at the son of Atreus.

[225] "Agamemnon," he cried, "what ails you now, and what more do you want? Your tents are filled with bronze and with fair women, for whenever we take a town we give you the pick of them. Would you have yet more gold,

[230] which some Trojan is to give you as a ransom for his son, when I or another Achaean has taken him prisoner? or is it some young girl to hide and lie with? It is not well that you, the ruler [*arkhos*] of the Achaeans, should bring them into such misery.

[235] Weakling cowards, women rather than men, let us sail home, and leave this man here at Troy to stew in his own prizes of honor, and discover whether or not we were of any service to him. Achilles is a much better man than he is, and see how he has treated him—

[240] robbing him of his prize and keeping it himself. Achilles takes it meekly and shows no fight; if he did, son of Atreus, you would never again insult him." Thus railed Thersites, but Odysseus at once went up to him

[245] and rebuked him sternly. "Check your glib tongue, Thersites," said be, "and babble not a word further. Chide not princes [*basileis*] when you have no one to back you. There is no viler creature that has come to Troy with the sons of Atreus.

[250] Drop this chatter about kings [*basileis*], and neither revile them nor keep harping about homecoming [*nostos*]. We do not yet know how things are going to be, nor whether the Achaeans are to return with good success or evil. How dare you berate Agamemnon

[255] because the Danaans have awarded him so many prizes? I tell you, therefore—and it shall surely be—that if I again catch you talking such nonsense, I will either forfeit my own head

[260] and be no longer called father of Telemakhos, or I will take you, strip you stark naked to reveal your shame [*aidōs*], and whip you out of the assembly [*agora*] till you go blubbering back to the ships."

[265] At this he beat him with his staff about the back and shoulders till he dropped and fell weeping. The golden scepter raised a bloody welt on his back, so he sat down frightened and in pain, looking foolish as he wiped the tears from his eyes.

[270] The people were sorry for him, but they laughed heartily, and one man would turn to his neighbor saying, "Odysseus has done many a good thing before now in fight and council, but he never did the Argives a better turn

[275] than when he stopped this man's mouth from barking any further. He will give the kings [*basileis*] no more of his insolence." Thus said the people...

Questions

1. **How do the values Odysseus expresses compare with the political order of Mycenaean society, as found in the Linear B tablets?**
2. **How does the above passage reflect the political structures of Dark Age Greece?**
3. **Why do the common soldiers accept the beating of Thersites as just?**
4. **What is the purpose of Homer's extended description of this scene?**

---

3. THE SHIELD OF ACHILLES

In Book XVIII of the *Iliad*, the smith of the gods, Hephaestus, fashions a new shield for Achilles with portrayals of several scenes of the life of Homeric society. The following passage describes an aspect of political life. *Iliad* 18.478–508

[478] First he shaped the shield so great and strong, adorning it all over and binding it round with

[480] a gleaming circuit in three layers; and the baldric was made of silver. He made the shield in five thicknesses, and with many a wonder did his cunning hand enrich it. He crafted the earth, the sky, and the sea; the moon also at her full and the untiring sun,

[485] with all the signs that glorify the face of the sky—the Pleiades, the Hyades, huge Orion, and the Bear, which men also call the Wain and which turns round ever in one place, facing Orion, and alone never dips into the stream of Okeanos.

[490] He wrought also two cities [*poleis*], fair to see and busy with the hum of men. In the one were weddings and wedding-feasts, and they were going about the city [*astu*] with brides whom they were escorting by torchlight from their chambers. Loud rose the cry of Hymen, and the youths danced to the music

[495] of reed and lyre, while the women stood each at her house door to see them. Meanwhile the people were gathered in assembly [*agora*], for there was a quarrel [*neikos*], and two men were wrangling about the blood-price [*poinē*] for a man who had died. The one made a claim [*eukheto*] to pay back in full,

[500] declaring publicly to the district [*dēmos*], but the other was refusing to accept anything. Each was trying to make his own case good, and the people [*laos*] took sides, each man backing the side that he had taken; but the heralds kept them back, and the elders sat on their seats of stone in a solemn circle,

[505] holding the scepters which the heralds had put into their hands. Then they rose and each in his turn gave judgment, and there were two talents of gold laid down, to be given to him whose judgment [*dikē*] should be deemed the straightest.

Questions

1. **How does this portrayal of justice in Homer compare with the laws and courts of the polis?**
2. **Who determines the laws in the polis?**
3. **Compare this situation with that in the world of Homer.**

---

4. KINGSHIP AT ITHACA

In the First Book of the *Odyssey,* Telemachus calls an assembly to address the problems of Ithaca, and especially those of his family. The discussion reveals much about the nature of Homeric kingship. *Odyssey* 1.365–424

[365] But the suitors were clamorous throughout the covered halls, and prayed each one that he might be her bedmate. Then Telemakhos spoke, "You suitors of my mother," he cried, "you with your overweening insolence [*hubris*], let us feast at our pleasure now, and let there be no

[370] brawling, for it is a rare thing to hear a man with such a divine voice as Phemios has; but in the morning meet me in full assembly [*agora*] that I may give you formal notice to depart, and feast at one another's houses,

[375] turn and turn about, at your own cost. If on the other hand you choose to persist in sponging upon one man, may the gods help me, but Zeus shall reckon with you in full,

[380] and when you fall in my father's house there shall be no man to avenge you." The suitors bit their lips as they heard him, and marveled at the boldness of his speech. Then, Antinoos, son of Eupeithes, said, "The gods seem to have given you lessons

[385] in bluster and tall talking; may Zeus never grant you to be chief [*basileus*] in Ithaca as your father was before you." Telemakhos answered, "Antinoos, do not chide with me, but,

[390] god willing, I will be chief too if I can. Is this the worst fate you can think of for me? It is no bad thing [*kakos*] to be a chief, for it brings both riches and honor. Still, now that Odysseus is dead there are many great men in Ithaca [*basileus*]

[395] both old and young, and some other may take the lead among them; nevertheless I will be chief [*(w)anax*] in my own house, and will rule those whom Odysseus has won for me." Then Eurymakhos, son of Polybos, answered,

[400] "It rests with the gods to decide who shall be chief [*basileus*] among us, but you shall be master in your own house and over your own possessions; no one while there is a man in Ithaca shall do you violence [*biē*] nor rob you.

[405] And now, my good man, I want to know about this stranger. What country does he come from? Of what family is he, and where is his estate? Has he brought you news about the return of your father, or was he on business of his own?

[410] He seemed a well-to-do man, but he hurried off so suddenly that he was gone in a moment before we could get to know him." "The homecoming [*nostos*] of my father is dead and gone," answered Telemakhos, "and even if some rumor reaches me I put no more faith in it now.

[415] My mother does indeed sometimes send for a soothsayer and question him, but I give his prophesying no heed. As for the stranger, he was Mentes, son of Ankhialos, chief of the Taphians, an old friend [*xenos*] of my father's."

[420] But in his heart he knew that it had been the goddess. The suitors then returned to their singing and dancing until the evening; but when night fell upon their pleasuring they went home to bed each in his own abode.

Questions

1. Why is Telemachus not the king of Ithaca if Odysseus is presumed dead?
2. Where is the father of Odysseus, Laertes?
3. Why is Laertes not the king?
4. How come the most powerful suitor does not simply seize the throne of Ithaca by force?

---

5.   HECTOR AND ANDROMACHE

It is important to consider the values of the world of Homer to determine what society the poet depicts. The speeches of Hector to Andromache, Achilles to Ajax, Odysseus, and Phoenix, and Sarpedon to Glaucus in *Iliad* Books IV, IX, and XII respectively are essential to the discussion of Homeric ethics.

In Book VI, Hector's wife Andromache begs her husband not to return to the battlefield and face near-certain death at the hands of Achilles. Instead she instructs him to draw up the men where the city is most vulnerable to attack and to fight from within the walls of Troy. Hector's response is perhaps the finest expression of the heroic code in the entire epic. *Iliad* 6.440–494

[440] And Hector answered, "Wife, I too have thought upon all this, but with what face should I look upon the Trojans, men or women, if I shirked battle like a coward [*kakos*]? I cannot do so: I know nothing save

[445] to fight bravely in the forefront of the Trojan host of warriors and win fame [*kleos*] alike for my father and myself. Well do I know that the day will surely come when mighty Ilion shall be destroyed with Priam and Priam's people,

[450] but I grieve for none of these—not even for Hecuba, nor King Priam, nor for my brothers many and brave who may fall in the dust before their foes—for none of these do I grieve as for yourself when the day shall come on which some one of the Achaeans

[455] shall rob you forever of your freedom, and bear you weeping away. It may be that you will have to ply the loom in Argos at the bidding of a mistress, or to fetch water from the springs Messeis or Hypereia, treated brutally by some cruel task-master; then will one say who sees you weeping,

[460] 'She was wife to Hector, the bravest warrior [an *aristeus*] among the Trojans during the war before Ilion.' At this your tears will break forth anew for him who would have put away the day of captivity from you. May I lie dead under the tomb that is heaped over my body

[465] before I hear your cry as they carry you into bondage." He stretched his arms towards his child, but the boy cried and nestled in his nurse's bosom, scared at the sight of his father's armor,

[470] and at the horse-hair plume that nodded fiercely from his helmet. His father and mother laughed to see him, but Hector took the helmet from his head and laid it all gleaming upon the ground. Then he took his darling child, kissed him, and dandled him in his arms,

[475] praying over him the while to Zeus and to all the gods. "Zeus," he cried, "grant that this my child may be even as myself, chief among the Trojans; let him be not less excellent [*agathos*] in strength, and let him rule Ilion with his might. Then may one say of him as he comes from battle, 'The son is far better than the father.'

[480] May he bring back the bloodstained spoils of him whom he has laid low, and let his mother's heart be glad.'" With this he laid the child again in the arms of his wife, who took him to her own soft bosom, smiling through her tears. As her husband watched her his heart yearned towards her

[485] and he caressed her fondly, saying, "My own wife, do not take these things too bitterly to heart. No one can hurry me down to Hadēs before my time, but if a man's hour is come, be he brave or be he coward, there is no escape for him when he has once been born.

[490] Go, then, within the house, and busy yourself with your daily duties, your loom, your distaff, and the ordering of your servants; for war is man's matter, and mine above all others of them that have been born in Ilion."

Questions

1. **Is Hector foolish in rejecting Andromache's advice? Why or why not?**
2. **For whom does Hector feel the most responsibility?**

---

6. THE EMBASSY TO ACHILLES

In Book IX of the *Iliad*, Agamemnon admits his error in dishonoring Achilles and attempts to persuade him to return to the fighting by offering gifts. Achilles' reply to the ambassadors sent to him by Agamemnon includes an illuminating critique of the heroic system. *Iliad* 9.307–424

[305] Achilles answered, "Odysseus, noble son of Laertes, I should give you formal notice plainly

[310] and in all fixity of purpose that there be no more of this cajoling, from whatsoever quarter it may come. As hateful [*ekhthros*] to me as the gates of Hadēs is one who says one thing while he hides another in his heart; therefore I will say what I mean.

[315] I will be appeased neither by Agamemnon son of Atreus nor by any other of the Danaans, for I see that I have no thanks [*kharis*] for all my fighting. He that fights fares no better than he that does not; coward [*kakos*] and hero are held in equal honor [*timē*],

[320] and death deals like measure to him who works and him who is idle. I have taken nothing by all my hardships—with my life [*psukhē*] ever in my hand; as a bird when she has found a morsel takes it to her nestlings, and herself fares hardly,

[325] even so many a long night have I been wakeful, and many a bloody battle have I waged by day against those who were fighting for their women. With my ships I have taken twelve cities, and eleven round about Troy have I stormed with my men by land;

[330] I took great store of wealth from every one of them, but I gave all up to Agamemnon son of Atreus. He stayed where he was by his ships, yet of what came to him he gave little, and kept much himself. "Nevertheless he did distribute some prizes of honor among the chieftains and kings [*basileis*],

[335] and these have them still; from me alone of the Achaeans did he take the woman in whom I delighted—let him keep her and sleep with her. Why, pray, must the Argives fight the Trojans? What made the son of Atreus gather the host [*laos*] of warriors and bring them? Was it not for the sake of Helen?

[340] Are the sons of Atreus the only men in the world who love their wives? Any man of common right feeling [an *agathos*] will love and cherish her who is his own, as I this woman, with my whole heart, though she was but the prize [*geras*] of my spear. Agamemnon has taken her from me; he has played me false;

[345] I know him; let him tempt me no further, for he shall not move me. Let him look to you, Odysseus, and to the other princes [*basileis*] to save his ships from burning. He has done much without me already. He has built a wall; he has dug a trench

[350] deep and wide all round it, and he has planted it within with stakes; but even so he stays not the murderous might of Hector. So long as I fought the Achaeans Hector did not let the battle range far from the city walls; he would come to the Scaean gates and to the oak tree, but no further.

[355] Once he stayed to meet me and hardly did he escape my onset: now, however, since I am in no mood to fight him, I will tomorrow offer sacrifice to Zeus and to all the gods; I will draw my ships into the water and then victual them duly; tomorrow morning, if you care to look, you will see

[360] my ships on the Hellespont, and my men rowing out to sea with might and main. If great Poseidon grants me a fair passage, in three days I shall be in Phthia. I have much there that I left behind me when I came here

[365] to my sorrow, and I shall bring back still further store of gold, of red copper, of fair women, and of iron, my share of the spoils that we have taken; but one prize [*geras*], he who gave has insolently taken away. Tell him all as I now bid you,

[370] and tell him in public that the Achaeans may hate him and beware of him should he think that he can yet dupe others for his effrontery never fails him. "As for me, hound that he is, he dares not look me in the face. I will take no counsel with him, and will undertake nothing in common with him.

[375] He has wronged me and deceived me enough, he shall not cozen me further; let him go his own way, for Zeus has robbed him of his reason. His presents are hateful [*ekhthra*] to me, and for him I care not a bit. He may offer me ten or even twenty times

[380] what he has now done, nay—not though it be all that he has in the world, both now or ever shall have; he may promise me the wealth of Orkhomenos or of Egyptian Thebes, which is the richest city in the whole world, for it has a hundred gates through each of which two hundred men may drive at once with their chariots and horses;

[385] he may offer me gifts as the sands of the sea or the dust of the plain in multitude, but even so he shall not move me till I have been revenged in full for the bitter wrong he has done me. I will not marry his daughter; she may be fair as Aphrodite,

[390] and skilful as Athena, but I will have none of her: let another take her, who may be a good match for her and who rules a larger kingdom. If the gods spare me to return home, Peleus will find me a wife;

[395] there are Achaean women in Hellas and Phthia, daughters of kings that have cities under them; of these I can take whom I will and marry her. Many a time was I minded when at home in Phthia to woo and wed a woman who would make me a suitable wife,

[400] and to enjoy the riches of my old father Peleus. My life [*psukhē*] is more to me than all the wealth of Ilion while it was yet at peace before the Achaeans went there, or than all the treasure that lies on the stone floor

[405] of Apollo's temple beneath the cliffs of Pytho [Delphi]. Cattle and sheep are to be had by raiding, and a man can buy both tripods and horses if he wants them, but when his life [*psukhē*] has once left him it can neither be bought nor raided back again.

[410] "My mother Thetis tells me that there are two ways in which I may meet my end [*telos*]. If I stay here and fight, I shall not have a return [*nostos*] alive but my glory [*kleos*] will be unwilting [*aphthiton*]: whereas if I go home

[415] my glory [*kleos*] will perish, but it will be long before the end [*telos*] shall take me. To the rest of you, then, I say, 'Go home, for you will not take Ilion.' Zeus

[420] has held his hand over her to protect her, and her people [*laos*] have taken heart. Go, therefore, as in duty bound, and tell the princes of the Achaeans the message that I have sent them; tell them to find some other plan for the saving of their ships and people…

Questions

1. **Why does Achilles reject the gifts of Agamemnon and the entreaties of his friends?**
2. **Is Achilles being childish and selfish in ignoring the needs of his men? Explain.**
3. **Should Achilles have returned to the fighting at this point? Why or why not?**

7. GLAUCON AND SARPEDON

The speech of Sarpedon to *Glaucus*, in Book XII of *Iliad*, as the two Trojan warriors march into battle reveals an important aspect of Homeric society. *Iliad* 12.310–328

[310] "Glaukos, why in Lycia do we receive especial honor as regards our place at table? Why are the choicest portions served us and our cups kept brimming, and why do men look up to us as though we were gods? Moreover we hold a large estate by the banks of the river Xanthos, fair with orchard lawns and wheat-growing land;

[315] it becomes us, therefore, to take our stand at the head of all the Lycians and bear the brunt of the fight, that one may say to another, our princes [*basileis*] in Lycia eat the fat of the land

[320] and drink best of wine, but they are fine men; they fight well and are ever at the front in battle. My good friend, if, when we were once out of this fight, we could escape old age and death thenceforward and forever, I should neither press forward myself

[325] nor bid you do so, but death in ten thousand shapes hangs ever over our heads, and no man can elude him; therefore let us go forward and either win glory for ourselves, or yield it to another."

Questions

1. **How do the values expressed by Sarpedon represent the heroic code?**
2. **Are the ideals of Sarpedon consistent with those of Hector and Achilles? Explain.**

OPINIONS OF MODERN SCHOLARS

1. In his famous book *The World of Odysseus*, Moses Finley argues that Homer is no witness to the thirteenth-century Bronze Age society revealed by the Linear B tablets. He thinks, however, that the essential consistency of Homer's epics points to a real social system dating to the tenth- or ninth-century Dark Age of Greece. M. I. Finley was Professor of Ancient History at University of Cambridge.

FROM MOSES FINLEY, *THE WORLD OF ODYSSEUS*

THAT THERE HAD ONCE BEEN A TIME OF HEROES few Greeks, early or late, ever doubted. They knew all about them: their names, their genealogies, and their exploits. Homer was their most authoritative source of information, but by no means the only one. Unfortunately, neither Homer nor Hesiod had the slightest interest in history as we might understand the notion. The poets' concern was with certain "facts" of the past not with their relationship to other facts, past or present, and, in the case of Homer, not even with the consequences of those facts. The outcome of the Trojan War, the fall and destruction of Troy and the fruits of Greek victory, would have been of prime importance to a

historian of the war. Yet the poet of the *Iliad* was indifferent to all that, the poet of the *Odyssey* scarcely less so. Similarly with the ages of man. In the Zoroastrian version there is a mathematical precision: each age was of 3,000 years, and law and morality declined by one-fourth in each. In Hesiod there is not even a whisper about date or duration, just as Homer gives no indication of the date of the Trojan War other than "once upon a time."

Later Greeks made up the chronology in detail. Although they did not reach entire agreement, few departed very far from a date equivalent to 1200 B.C. for the war with Troy and a period of four generations as the age of the heroes. Homer, they decided, lived four hundred years later, and Hesiod was his contemporary—in one version even his cousin.

Heroes are ubiquitous, of course. There are always men called heroes; and that is misleading, for the identity of label conceals a staggering diversity of substance. In a sense, they always seek honour and glory, and that too may be misleading without further definition of the contents of honour and the road to glory. Few of the heroes of history, or of literature from the Athenian drama of the fifth century B.C. to our own time, shared the single-mindedness of their Homeric counterparts. For the latter everything pivoted on a single element of honour and virtue: strength, bravery, physical courage, prowess. Conversely, there was no weakness, no unheroic trait, but one, and that was cowardice and the consequent failure to pursue heroic goals.

"0 Zeus and the other gods," prayed Hector, "grant that this my son shall become as I am, most distinguished among the Trojans, as strong and valiant, and that he rule by might in Ilion. And then may men say, 'He is far braver than his father'; as he returns from war. May he bring back spoils stained with the blood of men he has slain, and may his mother's heart rejoice." There is no social conscience in these words, no trace of the Decalogue, no responsibility other than familial, no obligation to anyone or anything but one's own prowess and one's own drive to victory and power.

The age of heroes, then, as Homer understood it, was a time in which men exceeded subsequent standards with respect to a specified and severely limited group of qualities. In a measure, these virtues, these values and capacities, were shared by many men of the period, for otherwise there could have been no distinct age of heroes between the bronze and the iron. Particularly in the *Odyssey* the word "hero" is a class term for the whole aristocracy, and at times it even seems to embrace all the free men. "Tomorrow," Athena instructed Telemachus, "summon the Achaean heroes to an assembly" (1.272), by which she meant "call the regular assembly of Ithaca." That in fact there had never been a four-generation heroic age in Greece, in the precise, self-contained sense of Homer, scarcely requires demonstration. The serious problem for the historian is to determine whether, and to what extent, there is anything in the poems that relates to social and historical reality; how much, in other words, of the world of Odysseus existed only in the poet's head and how much outside, in space and time. The

prior question to be considered is whence the poet took his picture of that world and his stories of its wars and its heroes' private lives.

* * *

Despite these differences, however, the *Iliad* and *Odyssey* stand together as against the poems of Hesiod, particularly his *Works and Days*. For all his use of the language and the formulas, Hesiod does not belong with the heroic poets. Whenever he treats of matters that are not obvious myth, when he deals with human society and human behaviour, he is always personal and contemporary in his outlook. Neither heroes nor ordinary mortals of a past age are his characters, but Hesiod himself, his brother, his neighbours, his overlords. Hesiod is wholly a part of the iron age of the present, specifically of the archaic Greek world of the eighth and early seventh centuries B.C.

Not so the *Iliad or Odyssey*. They look to a departed era, and their substance is unmistakably old. The *Odyssey* in particular encompasses a wide field of human activities and relationships: social structure and family life, royalty, aristocrats and commoners, banqueting and ploughing and swineherding. These are things about which we know a little as regards the period in which the *Odyssey* was apparently composed, and what we know and what the *Odyssey* relates are simply not the same. It is enough to point to the *polis* (city-state) form of political organization, widespread in the Hellenic world by then, at least in recognizably embryonic form. Yet neither poem has any trace of a *polis* in its political sense. *Polis* in Homer means nothing more than a fortified site, a town. The poets of the *Iliad* and *Odyssey,* unlike Hesiod, were basically neither personal nor contemporary in their reference.

The historian's verdict, obviously, can rest neither on faith in the divine origin of the poems nor on the once common notion that sufficient antiquity *is* a proper warrant of truth—"we have the certainty that old and wise men held them to be true," says the preface to the *Heimskringla,* the saga of the Norse kings. The historian, having established the point that neither the *Iliad* nor the *Odyssey* was essentially contemporary in outlook, must then examine their validity as pictures of the past. Was there ever a time in Greece when men lived as the poems tell (after they are stripped of supernatural intervention and superhuman capacities)? But first, was there a Trojan War?

Everyone knows the exciting story of Heinrich Schliemann, the German merchant with a vision and a love for the language of Homer, who dug in the soil of Asia Minor and rediscovered the city of Troy. Some three miles from the Dardanelles, at a place now called Hissarlik, there was one of the mounds that are the almost certain signs of ancient habitation. By careful analysis of topographical detail in ancient writings, Schliemann concluded that under this mound were the remains of the city of Ilion, which later Greeks had established on what they thought was the site of Troy and which outlived the Roman Empire. When he tunnelled into the mound he found layers of ruins, the oldest of which, we now know, dates from about 3000 B.C., and two bore unmistakable signs of violent destruction. One of these layers, the seventh according to more recent excavators, was no doubt the city of Priam and Hector. The historicity of the Homeric tale had been demonstrated archaeologically.

Schliemann's achievements were epoch-making. Nevertheless, despite the claims, the unassailable fact is that nothing he or his successors have found, not a single scrap, links the destruction of Troy VIIa with Mycenaean Greece, or with an invasion from any other source. Nor does anything known from the archaeology of Greece and Asia Minor or from the Linear B tablets fit with the Homeric tale of a great coalition sailing against Troy from Greece. No appropriate motive comes to mind. Troy VIIa turns out to have been a pitiful poverty-stricken little place, with no treasure, without any large or imposing buildings, with nothing remotely resembling a palace. It is not mentioned in any contemporary document in Hittite or any other language, nor is a "Trojan War." And there are other archaeological difficulties with the tale, notably in the chronology.

More interesting than the disappearance of the city is the total disappearance of the Trojans themselves. To begin with, as a nationality in the *Iliad* they are without distinguishing characteristics. True, the poet denigrates them in small, but subtle, ways that easily escape the modern reader. The Trojan hosts, but never the Achaeans, are compared to a flock of sheep or a swarm of locusts. Or, in the repeated battle incidents, a Trojan sometimes strikes a Greek with his spear, fails to pierce the armour, tries to withdraw but is slain by another warrior. Greeks also miss, but not once do the two succeeding steps follow in their case. Despite these touches, however, the Trojans are as Greek and as heroic in deeds and values as their opponents in every respect. If the opening line of the Iliad introduces Achilles, the closing line bids farewell to Hector the chief Trojan hero: "Thus they performed the funeral rites for Hector, tamer of horses."

Hector is a Greek name (found in the Linear B tablets along with Tros and other characteristically "Trojan" names), and as late as the middle of the second century after Christ travellers who came to Thebes in Boeotia on the Greek mainland were shown his tomb, near the Fountain of Oedipus, and were told how his bones had been brought from Troy at the behest of the Delphic oracle. This typical bit of fiction must *mean* that there was an old Theban hero Hector, a Greek, whose myths antedated the Homeric poems. Even after Homer had located Hector in Troy for all time, the Thebans held on to their hero, and the Delphic oracle provided the necessary sanction.

Among the Trojan allies there were peoples who were certainly non-Greek. It was for one of them, the Carians, that the poet reserved the epithet *barbarophonoi* (barbarous-talking, that is, unintelligible). The Carians are well known historically; the tomb of their fourth-century king, Mausolus, gives us our word "mausoleum." Other Trojan allies are also historically identifiable, and that serves to underscore the curious fact that the Trojans themselves, like Achilles' Myrmidons, have vanished so completely. Even if we were to accept the ancient explanation for the disappearance of the city, that it was so thoroughly demolished by the Victors that "there is no certain trace of walls" (Euripides, *Helen,* 108)—which would involve us in new difficulties with Schliemann and his successors, who found walls—it is hard to discover a parallel for the mysterious failure of the people themselves to leave any traces.

On the Greek side there is some correlation between the important place-names given in the *Iliad* and the centres of the so-called Mycenaean civilization rediscovered by modern archaeologists, although the poverty of the finds in Odysseus's Ithaca is one of the notable exceptions. This civilization flourished in Greece in the period 1400 to 1200 B.C., and here the name of Schliemann as the first discoverer must remain unchallenged. But again Homer and archaeology part company quickly. On the whole, he knew where the Mycenaean civilization flourished, and his heroes lived in great palaces unknown in Homer's own day (but unlike the Mycenaean, or any other, palaces). And that is virtually all he knew about Mycenaean times, for the catalogue of his errors is very long. His arms bear a resemblance to the armour of his time, quite unlike the Mycenaean, although he persistently casts them in antiquated bronze, not iron. His gods had temples and the Mycenaeans built none, whereas the latter constructed great vaulted tombs in which to bury their chieftains and the poet cremates his. A neat little touch is provided by the battle chariots. Homer had heard of them, but he did not really visualize what one did with chariots in a war. So his heroes normally drove from their tents a mile or less away, carefully dismounted, and then proceeded to battle on foot.

The contrast between the world of the poems and the society revealed by the Linear B tablets is no less complete. The very existence of the tablets is decisive: not only was the Homeric world without writing or record-keeping, but it was one in which the social system was too simple and the operations too restricted, too small in scale, to require either their inventories or the controls recorded on the tablets. Something like one hundred different agricultural and industrial occupations have been identified on the tablets; Homer knew of only a dozen or so, and it was no problem for the swineherd Eumaeus to keep them all in his head, along with Odysseus's livestock inventory. Parallels for the Mycenaean bureaucracy and its management of every facet of life are to be found in the contemporary kingdoms of the Near East, not in the Greek world at any time from Homer until after the eastern conquests of Alexander the Great.

Homer, we too easily forget, had no notion of a Mycenaean Age, or of the sharp break between it and the new age that followed its destruction. The Mycenaean Age is a purely modern construct; what the poet believed he was singing about was the heroic past of his own, Greek world, a past that was known to him through oral transmission by the bards who preceded him. The raw materials of the poems were the mass of inherited formulas and episodes, and as they passed through generations of bards they underwent change after change, partly by deliberate act of the poets, whether for artistic reasons or from more prosaic political considerations, and partly by carelessness or indifference to historical accuracy, compounded by the errors that are inevitable in a world without writing. That there was a Mycenaean kernel in the *Iliad* and *Odyssey* cannot be doubted, but it was small and what little there was of it was distorted beyond sense or recognition. Often the material was self-contradictory, yet that was no bar to its use. Poetic convention demanded traditional formulas, and neither the bard nor his audience checked the details. The man who started it all by abducting Helen is named both Alexander, which is Greek, and Paris, which is not (just as his city had two names, Ilion and Troy); he is both an easy-going sensualist and a warrior. As usual, later generations began to seek explanations, but not the poet of the *Iliad*.

We may take it for granted that there was a "Trojan War" in Mycenaean times; more correctly, that there were many "Trojan" wars. War was normal in that world. But a ten-year war, or a war of any smaller number of years, is out of the question. "Would that I were in the prime of youth and my might as steadfast as when a quarrel broke out between us and the Eleans over a cattle raid…Exceedingly abundant was then the booty we drove out of the plain together, fifty herds of cattle, as many flocks of sheep, as many droves of swine, as many herds of goats, and a hundred and fifty bays, all mares…And Neleus was glad at heart that so much booty fell to me the first time I went to war" (*Iliad*, 670–84).

This was a typical "war" as narrated by Nestor, a raid for booty. Even if repeated year after year, these wars remained single raids. There is a scene in the third book of the *Iliad* in which Helen sits alongside Priam on the battlement of Troy and identifies Agamemnon, Odysseus and a few other Achaean heroes for the old king. That could make sense at the beginning of the war; it can make none in the tenth year (unless we are prepared to believe that the poet could find no better device by which to introduce some details of little importance). It could also make sense in a brief war, and perhaps this is an illustration of the way in which one traditional piece of the story was retained after the war had ballooned into ten years and the piece had become rationally incongruous. While the war was growing, furthermore, the bards neglected to make proper arrangements for recruits to replace the fallen men, for the feeding of besiegers and besieged, *or for* the establishment of some sort of communication between the battlefield and the home bases of the Greeks.

The glorification of insignificant incidents is common in heroic poetry. The French *Song of Roland* tells of a great battle at Roncevaux in the year A.D. 778, between the hosts of Charlemagne and the Saracens. Like Homer, the poet of the French epic is unknown, but he certainly lived in the twelfth century, at the time of the Crusades. Unlike Homer, he could read and he had access to chronicles, which he explicitly says he used. But the facts are these: the actual battle of Roncevaux was a minor engagement in the Pyrenees between a small detachment of Charlemagne's army and some Basque raiders. It was neither important nor crusade-like. The twelve Saracen chieftains of the poem and their army of 400,000 are pure invention, with German, Byzantine or made-up names; there is even a strong case for dismissing Roland himself as an imaginary person. The *Song of Roland* can be checked against written records. The *Iliad* and the *Odyssey* cannot, and, in so far as historical detail is concerned, there is no way of reversing the process of distortion and re-establishing the original kernel.

The *Song of Roland* shares another negative with the *Iliad* and *Odyssey.* It is not contemporary in its social conditions, its politics or its details of war and warriors. Not that it lacks realism. On the contrary, it is of the essence of heroic poetry that, "since heroes move in what is assumed to be a real world, their background and their circumstances must be depicted" always "with realism and objectivity." Specifically, the background of Roland is the France of about a century before the poet's own time. The key to this chronological "aberration" lies in the formulas, which have the necessary flexibility for both moving the substance along with changes in the world itself and, at the same time, restraining it from excessive contemporaneity, a limit imposed by the need to retain the "once upon a time" image. For Homer, technical linguistic analysis has now shown that formulas were continually being lost, elaborated, and replaced, always with a certain logic. Thus, the language for the sea was ancient and stable, whereas the diction for helmets or shields remained fluid.

The world of Odysseus was not the Mycenaean Age *five* or six or seven hundred years earlier, but neither was it the world of the eighth or seventh centuries B.C. The list of exclusions of contemporary institutions and practices is very long and very fundamental—no Ionia, no Dorians to speak of, no writing, no iron weapons, no cavalry in battle scenes, no colonization, no Greek *traders,* no communities without kings. If, then, the world of Odysseus is to be placed in time, as everything we know from the comparative study of heroic poetry says it must, the most likely centuries seem to be the tenth and ninth. By then the catastrophe that brought *down* Mycenaean civilization and made itself felt all over the eastern Mediterranean had been forgotten. Or rather, it had been converted into a "memory" of a no longer existent age of heroes, proper Greek heroes. The history of the Greeks as such had begun.

Essentially the picture offered by the poems of the society *and* its system of values *is* a coherent one. Anachronistic fragments cling to it in spots, some too ancient and some, particularly in the *Odyssey,* too recent, a reflection of the poet's own time. For historical study,

the institutional and psychological accuracy is easily separable from the demonstrable inaccuracy of palaces and similar material elements of the culture, and of the episodes and the narrative detail, the action. "Homer," wrote Aristotle (*Poetics* 24.13) "is praiseworthy in many respects, and especially because he alone of poets perceives the part he should take himself. The poet should speak as little as possible in his own person…" But this technical virtue, become a vice to poets of another world, should not mislead us, as it did no less gifted a critic than Coleridge. "There is no subjectivity whatever in the Homeric poetry," was the judgement of Coleridge romantic, neither the "*subjectivity of* the poet, as of Milton, who is himself before himself in everything he wrote," nor the "subjectivity of the *persona,* or dramatic character, as in all Shakespeare's great creations."

This standing at a distance *from* his characters and their behaviour, which is a mark of Homeric technique, had nothing to do with indifference, with disinterest, [and] with an unwillingness to become involved. The poet transmitted his inherited background materials with a deceptively cool precision. That enables us to treat his materials as the raw materials for the study of a real world of real men, a world of history and not of fiction. But it also besets our analysis with traps, for the temptation is ever present to ignore the implications in the poet's selectivity, conscious and unconscious, and to brush aside apparent confusions and contradictions in social or political matters (as distinct from narrative incidents) as nothing more than the carelessness of a bard who did not care. Real societies are never tidy: Homeric confusions in this respect are a better warrant than absolute coherence and consistency of the historicity of the picture.

Of course, there must be something of a historian's licence in pinning down the world of Odysseus to the tenth and ninth centuries before Christ. And that licence must extend still further. There are sections in the poems, such as the tale of the adultery of Ares and Aphrodite or the *scene* in Hades in the eleventh book of the *Odyssey,* which may have a later origin in the oral tradition than other sections. By licence, we here ignore the distinction for the most part, just as we sometimes speak of one Homer, as if the *Iliad* and *Odyssey* were the products of one man's creation. Some distortion results, but the margin of error can be held to a rather acceptable minimum, because the patterns we draw rest on an overall analysis of the poems, not on any one single verse, segment or narrative incident; because all parts, early or late, were built so much from formulas; and because later

Greek history and the *study* of other societies together offer a great measure of control. No poet (or "poetic tradition"), for example, could have invented and described with such formal precision the institution of gift-exchange which modern anthropology has been able to parallel from regions and continents.

It is convenience, finally, rather than licence, that suggests retention of the ten-year war, and of Achilles and Hector and Odysseus and all the other famous names, as useful labels for unknown King X and Chieftain Y.

2. Anthony Snodgrass, Laurence Professor Emeritus of Classical Archaeology, University of Cambridge, sees too many inconsistencies in the social life of the Homeric world to believe that its culture existed at any single historical period. Instead, the *Iliad* and *Odyssey* form an amalgamation of elements spanning the centuries of their composition.

FROM ANTHONY SNODGRASS, "A HISTORICAL HOMERIC SOCIETY?"

THOSE WHO MAINTAIN THAT HOMERIC SOCIETY is unitary and historical are bound to ask themselves the question, to what time and place that society belongs. The two answers which might seem, *prima facie,* to be the likeliest, can be shown to be improbable on other grounds: namely the historical period in which the story of the poems is ostensibly set, the later Mycenaean age, and the period in which the poems reached their final form and in which the historical Homer most probably lived, the eighth century B.C. A fully Mycenaean setting is rendered almost impossible by the evidence of the Linear B tablets, whose picture has been shown, by Finley more than anyone else, to be quite inconsistent with Homer, especially in the field of social and political structure. A purely contemporary origin, though it may not be excluded by the ubiquitous and pervasive presence of formulae, affecting social life as much as other aspects, would surely be in utter conflict with the other evidence that we have for eighth-century society, from Hesiod and from archaeological sources. It is a surprise to encounter such primitive features as bride-price and polygamy in Homer at all; that they should have been taken, as normal features, from the Greek society of his own day is almost unthinkable. This means that, if one is set on an historical explanation, the likely models are narrowed down to two periods, the "Age of Migrations" between the fall of the Mycenaean citadels around 1200, and a lower date in the region of 1000; and the ensuing two centuries, a more settled period which in my view forms the central part of the Dark Age.

In inclining as he does towards tenth- and ninth-century Greece as the historical basis for the world of Odysseus, Finley makes a telling point. "If it is to be placed in time," he writes, "as *everything we know about heroic poetry says it must…*" (my italics), and so on. I concede the general truth of this. Finley's favoured comparisons are with the *Chanson de Roland* and the *Nibelungenlied,* of which this is evidently true; and to these one could add a parallel not used by him, the "Ulster Cycle" of prose epic about which my Edinburgh colleague Professor K. H. Jackson has written with such authority. "This whole picture of the ancient Irish heroic way of life," he concludes, "as it is seen in the oldest tales is self-consistent, of a very marked individuality, and highly circumstantial. One can hardly doubt that it represents a genuine tradition of a society that once existed." This is independent and striking confirmation for Finley's view. But there is a well-tried counter to such analogy between Homer and other Epic: this is to say that the qualitative distinction between Homeric and most other, perhaps all other Epic is such as to invalidate these analogies. The argument may perhaps be too well-worn today to carry the conviction that it once did, without detailed substantiation of a kind that I am not competent to provide. Nevertheless I firmly believe that it is soundly based. In support of this whole position, I wish now to draw some analogies, not outside but within the Homeric Epic, that is with topics other than the social system.

Inevitably, it is with the material aspects of culture that we have the most secure external evidence. I wish to discuss briefly certain aspects—specifically, metal-usage, burial-practices, military equipment and temples—which figure in the cultural background of the poems, and which may provide valid analogies with the social features.

For metal-working, it should be generally appreciated...that Homer's picture is a very curious one. His exclusive use of bronze, for every sword and every spearhead mentioned in both poems, is the point of greatest significance; for these are the two supreme weapons of the Epic. There is no period of Greek history or prehistory, later than the first half of the eleventh century B.C., of which such a picture would be representative. Professor Kirk rightly observes that afterwards bronze continued to be used "often enough, for spear-and arrowheads and even for axes." But for Homer, arrowheads and axes are of secondary importance; and for Homer bronze is used for the two prime offensive weapons, not "often enough" but always. Such a culture never existed after the end of the Bronze Age; the formulae on which the picture is based—although the language is not exclusively formulaic—can only have originated in either the full Mycenaean period or its immediate aftermath. But this simple assertion at once faces us with the other aspects of Homer's metallurgy which conflict utterly with this: first and foremost, that iron is not only known to Homer as a working metal and a trading commodity, but is actually the normal metal for his agricultural and industrial tools. Historically, iron for tools was adopted, if anything, rather later than iron for weapons; it follows therefore that no historical society, at least in the relevant part of the ancient world, ever showed even fleetingly the combination of metal usages found in Homer. The central era of the Dark Age, the tenth and the ninth centuries, is in some ways the least appropriate of all periods to look to for an historical setting for Homer's metallurgy, for at this time the dependence on iron reached its peak, to recede a little in the eighth and seventh centuries and give way to that partial recourse to bronze which prompted Professor Kirk's statement quoted above.

On burial practices, there is no unanimity today, any more than in the past. To quote two very recent books, Professor Finley in his *Early Greece* still holds that "The *Iliad* and *Odyssey* remain firmly anchored in the earlier Dark Age on this point (*sc.* burial rite)"; while Dr Kurtz and Mr Boardman are equally sure that Homer's picture "is almost wholly in keeping with

Geometric and later Greek practice," which is not at all the same thing. My own view, predictably, is that Homer's burial practices are not firmly anchored in, nor wholly in keeping with, anything. His heroes cremate each other, maybe, because that was the rite with which Homer was most familiar. But from this point on, historical verisimilitude disappears. For it is not true that at any one period all Greece, nor even all Ionia, cremated. In Homer, the heroes are cremated singly or *en masse* according to the dictates of the story. When, as regularly happens, a tumulus is erected over a single cremation (whereas historically the tumulus almost always contains a multiple burial) we may again suspect that the requirements of the plot are the overriding factors. A few elements of the funerary practice may be culled from the Bronze Age: the fairly lavish provision of possessions for the deceased, the occasional use of horse-sacrifice, the idea of cenotaphs, possibly the funerary games. Although it is agreed that the great Homeric funerals are among the most magnificent set-pieces in the poems, it seems certain that no Greek ever witnessed in real life the precise sequence of events narrated in Patroklos' funeral. Life may imitate art, but it cannot match it.

What need be said about Homeric fighting-equipment beyond the fact, today I hope accepted, that it is composite and shows internal inconsistency? To illustrate this, it may be enough to recall that the same hero repeatedly sets out to fight with a pair of throwing-spears and is then found in action with a single heavy thrusting-spear. But there is another conclusion to be drawn from Homeric weaponry and armour: this is, that whatever conspicuous item of equipment we choose to focus our attention on—the fairly common bronze corslets, bronze greaves, and bronze helmets, the pair of throwing-spears which is clearly the hero's regular armament, the occasionally metal-faced shield, the silver-studded sword-hilt—argument may rage as to whether their historical origin lies in the Mycenaean period or in the improved equipment of the poet's own day, the eighth century; but the one period at which virtually no evidence for their existence is to be found is the tenth and ninth centuries, and it could be added that there is but slight indication of their presence in the preceding Age of Migrations.

Something of a pattern may thus be emerging from the categories of material culture that we have been considering. The historical models for each feature can be looked for either early (that is in the full Bronze Age) or late (that is in the poet's own times). They show a remarkable reluctance to reveal themselves in the intervening four centuries, between about 1200 and 800. The same lesson is provided by the study of the Homeric temple. There are now free-standing religious buildings, worthy of the name *neos* and conforming to the Homeric references, known from Bronze Age Greece. *I would* cite the structure found by Professor Caskey at Ayia Irini on Keos, and the temples of Mycenaean date at Kition in Cyprus which Dr Karageorghis has recently excavated. There is also the smaller shrine which Lord William Taylour has uncovered at Mycenae. At the other end of the time-scale, the revival of the temple in historical times, in the light of the latest chronological evidence, can barely if at all be traced back before 800 B.C. on any Greek site. Of the earlier so-called temples that have been claimed, either the identification as a temple, or the ascription to the ninth century (occasionally the tenth) is doubtful—sometimes both.

This archaeological evidence has, I fear, been rather summarily presented here. But my aim is the fairly limited one of showing that, in certain aspects of the material world he portrays, Homer, besides in some cases combining features from different historical eras, also displays certain tendencies in the choice of those eras. The reasons for these tendencies may be of the simplest kind—perhaps that the poet's desire is to portray a materially impressive culture, and that this inevitably leads to the choice of either the Mycenaean world which had been impressive in this way, or to the contemporary world which was becoming so, but to avoid the less well-endowed intervening periods. But a question remains: would similar factors operate in the more intangible world of social relations?

Professor Finley again has a ready answer to such suggestions: "The comparative study of heroic poetry shows, I think decisively, that the society portrayed tends to be relatively (though not entirely) 'modern,' for all the pretence of great antiquity and for all the archaism of the armour and the political geography." *I* would disagree with him over one point: what we have in Homer is surely not just archaism in material culture, but artificial conflations of historical practices, a few features such as the provision of twin spears being, probably of decidedly recent origin. But this must not be allowed to distract us from the fundamental question: is it possible to have social institutions operating quite independently of material culture in a literary world? I wish to argue, not that it is quite impossible, but that it is unlikely to have happened with Homer.

For consider certain of the characteristics of Homeric society that Finley and Adkins have described

so well. It is strongly success-orientated and strongly materialistic; among its most pervasive features are the ceremonial exchange of gifts in a wide variety of situations, in which it insists on the actual exchange value and not merely *the* aesthetic or sentimental value of the *gifts,* and also the equally ceremonial feasting. These are activities whose successful operation demands quite a high material standard of living: for kings to exchange mean gifts is not merely unheroic from a literary point of view, it is socially ineffective in real life; for a host to entertain an uninvited group of long-term guests on skimpy fare is, equally, not merely unheroic but historically improbable. A society that cannot afford to perform such ceremonial lavishly will nor practise it at all. Now all the evidence yielded by the archaeology of the settlements and graves of the earlier Dark Age suggests that here, at any rate, was a society that could afford nothing of the kind. Precious metals are for long totally unknown; bronze utensils and other large metal objects are exceedingly rare; while in one particular field, that of the funerary feasts, we are luckily able to make a precise comparison between Homer and archaeology. We find differences not only in degree, but in kind. The quantities of animal bones found beside Dark Age graves are relatively modest, and represent cut joints of meat rather than Homer's whole carcasses; furthermore, the beef and pork so prominent in Homer are far eclipsed by the cheaper mutton and goat's meat. If challenged on the validity of archaeological evidence in such contexts, I would point not only to the obvious contrast with Mycenaean Greece, but to the example of a contemporary society in another part of Europe, the Urnfield Culture *of* East Central Europe, whose cemetery-sites produce evidence of just such a lavish society as we would expect from Homer's description: graves with quantities of elaborate bronzework, and with the accoutrements of feasting and of war particularly conspicuous. Another instance could be found in the rich tombs of the eighth century at Salamis in Cyprus. Clearly, therefore, it is possible for archaeological evidence to match up to a literary picture thus far.

If, on the other hand, the objection were made that Homer's picture, though glorified by poetic licence, is yet fundamentally rooted in the historical society of the Dark Age, then one could indicate other qualities in the archaeological record of the period, which would have required Homer not merely to exaggerate but positively to contradict. There are, for instance, signs of drastic depopulation, and of the interrupted communications which naturally accompanied this. Homeric society does not admit of either circumstance.

Another point about the centuries of the Dark Age is that their memory was not retained, let alone treasured, by any Greek writer of whom we know. Hesiod regarded the era as one of unrelieved disaster; later Greeks found themselves embarrassed by their total ignorance of these years. It is fair to ask how this happened if Greek society of that period possessed anything resembling the striking qualities of Homeric society, its self-reliance, its extreme competitiveness, its prodigious acquisitiveness and generosity, [and] the functional simplicity of its ethics. If such a society had flourished at so relatively recent a time, would not its ideals and values have inevitably seeded themselves more widely in early Greek thought?

In the later part of this paper I have concentrated on one particular period, roughly the tenth and ninth centuries B.C., in order to assess its claim to have provided the model for Homeric society. It may be felt that the preceding Age of *Migrations,* for example, has escaped scrutiny in this connection. But I hope to have made clear that some at least of these arguments apply to any identification, of whatever period, of an historical society which might be faithfully reflected in Homer. For *it* seems to me that such identifications involve, in one respect, a certain derogation from Homer's artistic standing. If Homer really preserved, like a faded sepia photograph, a faithful image of a real society that belonged, not to his own times nor to the period which had provided such historical background as there was for the actual events he described, but to the period which happened to be most influential in the formation of this aspect of the Epic tradition; then indeed he was on a footing with the forgotten and anonymous authors of the *Chanson de Roland* or the *Cattle Raid of Cooley*

or any one of the numerous epics and sagas of normal type. For an oral poet who adopts, entire, from his predecessors of a certain period, something as pervasive as a social framework, becomes in my view not merely traditional but derivative. To an important extent, he can make his characters behave in the way that people actually behaved at that time, and in no other way. The scope for creative contributions is sharply inhibited. If he does extend this social pattern himself, he must do it with such scrupulous care as to obliterate his own tracks completely. This is no doubt one reason why no author's name has survived for the *Nibelungenlied,* the Ulster Cycle, the Icelandic sagas and those others of even the finest non-Homeric epics in which such social and historical verisimilitude is to be found. By contrast, a poet who is also traditional, and ultimately just as indebted to predecessors, but who depends on predecessors of *many* periods, and admits elements from his own experience and imagination into the bargain, is far freer. He can select, he can conflate, he can idealise. Unless he is pedantically careful, minor inconsistencies will creep in, of the kind we have been discussing; but his scope for creativity, even though the picture he paints is not truly fictional, will be greater. This is a subjective argument to end with, but the fact that the Homeric poems are attached to a name, and that, even if we doubt the existence of an eighth-century poet called Homer, we are nevertheless aware, in reading the *Iliad* and *Odyssey,* of being at least intermittently in the presence of poetic genius, is a strong hint that Homeric Epic conforms to the second of the two pictures sketched above, and not the first. At all events, I offer this as a further argument against the existence of an historical Homeric society.

3. In his 2007 book, *The Trojan War*, Barry Strauss, Professor of History and Classics at Cornell University, gives Homer's *Iliad* and *Odyssey* a fresh reading in light of the latest archaeological research. He argues for the essential historicity of the Trojan War and Homer's tale. Strauss's central thesis challenges the trend of the last generation of Homeric scholarship that seeks to divorce the epics from their alleged Bronze Age setting. Moreover, he demonstrates how the new evidence might revise previous notions of the Trojan War.

FROM BARRY STRAUSS, *THE TROJAN WAR: A NEW HISTORY*

TROY INVITES WAR. Its location, where Europe and Asia meet, made it rich and visible. At Troy, the steel-blue water of the Dardanelles Straits pours into the Aegean and opens the way to the Black Sea. Although

the north wind often blocked ancient shipping there, Troy has a protected harbor and so it beckoned to merchants—and marauders. Walls, warriors, and blood were the city's lot.

People had already fought over Troy for two thousand years by the time Homer's Greeks are said to have attacked it. Over the centuries since then, armies have swept past Troy's ancient walls, from Alexander the Great to the Gallipoli Campaign of 1915.

And then there are the archaeologists. In 1871 Heinrich Schliemann amazed the world with the announcement that a mound near the entrance to the Dardanelles contained the ruins of Troy. Schliemann, who relied on preliminary work by Frank Calvert, was an inspired amateur if also something of a fraud. But the trained archaeologists who have followed him by the hundreds in the 130 years since have put the excavations on a firm and scientific basis. And they all came to Troy because of the words of a Greek poet.

But are those words true? Granted that ancient Troy really existed, was it anything like the splendid city of Homer's description? Did it face an armada from Greece? Did the Trojan War really happen?

Spectacular new evidence makes it likely that the Trojan War indeed took place. New excavations since 1991 constitute little less than an archaeological revolution, proving that Homer was right about the city. Twenty years ago, it looked as though Troy was just a small citadel of only about half an acre. Now we know that Troy was, in fact, about seventy-five acres in size, a city of gold amid amber fields of wheat. Formerly, it seemed that by 1200 B.C. Troy was a shabby place, well past its prime, but now we know that in 1200 the city was in its heyday.

Meanwhile, independent confirmation proves that Troy was a byword in the ancient Near East. This outside evidence comes not from Homer or any Greek source but from Hittite texts. In these documents, the city that Homer calls Troy or Ilion is referred to as Taruisa or Wilusa and in the early form of the Greek language, "Ilion" was rendered as "Wilion."

A generation ago scholars thought that the Trojans were Greeks, like the men who attacked them. But new evidence suggests otherwise. The recently discovered urban plan of Troy looks less like that of a Greek than of an Anatolian city. Troy's combination of citadel and lower town, its house and wall architecture, and its religious and burial practices are all typically Anatolian, as is the vast majority of its pottery. To be sure, Greek pottery and Greek speakers were also found at Troy, but neither predominated. New documents suggest that most Trojans spoke a language closely related to Hittite and that Troy was a Hittite ally. The enemy of Troy's ally was the Greeks.

The Greeks were the Vikings of the Bronze Age. They built some of history's first warships. Whether on large expeditions or smaller sorties, whether in the king's call-up or on freebooting forays, whether as formal soldiers and sailors or as traders who turned into raiders at a moment's notice, whether as mercenaries, ambassadors, or hereditary guest-friends, the Greeks fanned out across the Aegean and into the eastern and central Mediterranean, with one hand on the rudder and the other on the hilt of a sword. What the sight of a dragon's head on the stein post of a Viking ship was to an Anglo-Saxon, the sight of a bird's beak on the stem post of a Greek galley was to a Mediterranean islander or Anatolian mainlander. In the 1400s B.C., the Greeks conquered Crete, the southwestern Aegean islands, and the city of Miletus on the Aegean coast of Anatolia, before driving eastward into Lycia and across the sea to Cyprus. In the 1300s they stirred up rebels against the Hittite over-lords of western Anatolia. In the 1200s they began muscling their way into the islands of the northeastern Aegean, which presented a big threat to Troy. In the 1100s they joined the wave of marauders, known to us as the Sea Peoples, who descended first on Cyprus, then on the Levant and Egypt, and settled in what became the Philistine country. Scratch a philosopher and find a predator: those were the Bronze Age Greeks.

The Trojan War, which probably dates to around 1200 B.C., is just a piece in a larger puzzle. But if the resulting picture builds on Homer, it differs quite a bit from the impression most readers get from his poems. And "impression" is the right word, because much of the conventional wisdom about the war, from Achilles' heel to Cassandra's war flings, is not in Homer at all.

Consider what Homer does say: He tells the story in two long poems, the *Iliad* or Story of Ilion (that is, Troy) and the *Odyssey* or Story of Odysseus. According to Homer, the Trojan War lasted ten years. The conflict pitted the wealthy city of Troy and its allies against a coalition of all Greece. It was the greatest war in history, involving at least 100,000 men in each army as well as 1,184 Greek ships. It featured heroic champions on both sides. It was so important that the Olympian gods played an active role. Troy was a magnificent city and impregnable fortress. The cause of the war was the seduction, by Prince Paris of Troy, of the beautiful Helen, queen of Sparta, as well as the loss of the treasure that they ran off with. The Greeks landed at Troy and demanded the return of Helen and the treasure to her husband, Sparta's King Menelaus. But the Trojans refused. In the nine years of warfare that followed, the Greeks ravaged and looted the Trojan countryside and surrounding islands, but they made no progress against the city of Troy. Ironically, the *Iliad* focuses on pitched battle on the Trojan Plain, although most of the war was fought elsewhere and consisted of raids. And the *Iliad* concentrates on only two months in the ninth year of the long conflict.

In that ninth year the Greek army nearly fell apart. A murderous epidemic was followed by a mutiny on the part of Greece's greatest warrior, Achilles. The issue, once again, was a woman: this time, the beautiful Briseis, a prize of war unjustly grabbed from Achilles by the Greek commander in chief, Agamemnon. A furious Achilles withdrew himself and his men from fighting. Agamemnon led the rest of the army out to fight, and much of the *Iliad* is a gory, blow-by-blow account of four days on the battlefield. The Trojans, led by Prince Hector, took advantage of Achilles' absence and nearly drove the Greeks back into the sea. At the eleventh hour, Achilles let his lieutenant and close friend Patroclus lead his men back into battle to save the Greek camp. Patroclus succeeded but overreached himself; and Hector killed him on the Trojan Plain. In revenge, Achilles returned to battle, devastated the enemy, and killed Hector. Achilles was so angry that he abused Hector's corpse. King Priam of Troy begged Achilles to give back his son Hector's body for cremation and burial, and a sadder but wiser Achilles at last agreed. He knew that he too was destined to die soon in battle.

The *Iliad* ends with the funeral of Hector. The *Odyssey is* set after the war and mainly describes the hard road home of the Greek hero Odysseus. In a series of flashbacks, it explains how Odysseus led the Greeks to victory at Troy by thinking up the brilliant trick of smuggling Greek commandos into Troy in the Trojan Horse, an operation which he also led. Achilles did not play a part in the final victory; he was long since dead. The *Odyssey* also shows Helen back in Sparta with Menelaus. But Homer leaves out most of the rest of the war. One has to turn to other and generally lesser Greek and Roman poets for additional detail.

Aeneas is a minor character in the *Iliad,* but the hero of a much later epic poem in Latin, written by Vergil, the *Aeneid*. Vergil makes Aeneas the founder of Rome (or, to be precise, of the Italian town that later founded Rome). But in Homer, Aeneas is destined to become king of Troy after the Greeks depart and the Trojans rebuild.

Now, consider how new evidence revises the picture: Much of what we thought we knew about the Trojan War is wrong. In the old view, the war was decided on the plain of Troy by duels between champions; the besieged city never had a chance against the Greeks; and the Trojan Horse must have been a myth. But now we know that the Trojan War consisted mainly of low-intensity conflict and attacks on civilians; it was more like the war on terror than World War II. There was no siege of Troy. The Greeks were underdogs, and only a trick allowed them to take Troy: that trick may well have been the Trojan Horse.

The *Iliad* is a championship boxing match, fought in plain view at high noon and settled by a knockout punch. The Trojan War was a thousand separate wrestling matches, fought in the dark and won by tripping the opponent. The *Iliad* is the story of a hero, Achilles. The Trojan War is the story of a trickster, Odysseus, and a survivor, Aeneas.

The *Iliad* is to the Trojan War what *The Longest Day* is to World War II. The four days of battle in the *Iliad* no more sum up the Trojan War than the D-Day invasion of France sums up the Second World War. The *Iliad* is not the story of the whole Trojan War. Far from being typical, the events of the *Iliad* are extraordinary.

Homer nods, and he exaggerates and distorts too. But overly skeptical scholars have thrown out the baby with the bathwater. There are clear signs of later Greece in the epics; Homer lived perhaps around 700 B.C., about five hundred years after the Trojan War. Yet new discoveries vindicate the poet as a man who knew much more about the Bronze Age than had been thought.

And that is a key insight because Bronze-Age warfare is very well documented. In Greece, archaeologists showed long ago that the arms and armor described by Homer really were used in the Bronze Age; recent discoveries help to pinpoint them, to the era of the Trojan War. Like Homer, Linear B documents refer to a Greek army as a collection of warrior chiefs rather than as the impersonal institution of later Greek texts.

But the richest evidence of Bronze Age warfare comes from the ancient Near East. And in the 1300s and 1200s B.C., Bronze Age civilization was international. Trade and diplomacy, migration, dynastic marriage, and even *war* all led to cultural cross-fertilization. So the abundant evidence of Assyria, Canaan, Egypt, the Hittites, and Mesopotamia puts in perspective the events of the *Iliad* and *Odyssey*. Some things in Homer that may seem implausible are likely to be true because the same or similar customs existed in Bronze Age civilizations of the ancient Near East. For example, false deserters, surprise attacks at night, wars over livestock, iron arrowheads in the Bronze Age, battles between champions instead of armies, the mutilation of enemy corpses, shouting matches between kings in the assembly, battle cries as measures of prowess, weeping as a mark of manhood—these and many other details are not Homeric inventions but well—attested realities of Bronze Age life.

Besides recording Bronze Age customs, Homer reproduces Bronze Age literary style. Although he was Greek, Homer borrows from the religion, mythology, poetry, and history of the Near East. By composing *in* the manner of a chronicler of the pharaohs or the Hittites or Babylon's King Hammurabi, Homer lends an air of authenticity to his poem. For instance, Homer portrays champions on both sides carving paths of blood through the enemy as if they were supermen—or as if they were pharaohs, often described by Egyptian texts as superheroes in battle. Ironically, the more Homer exaggerates, the more authentic he is as a representative of the Bronze Age. And even the prominence of the gods in Homer, which drives most historians to distraction, is a Bronze Age touch, because writers of that era always put the gods at the heart of warfare. Belief in divine apparitions on the battlefield, conviction that victories depended *on* a goddess's patronage, and faith that epidemics were unleashed by offended deities are all well documented.

Could Homer have preserved the truth about a war that preceded him by five centuries? Not in all its details, of course, but he could have known the *outline* of the conflict. After all, a remarkably accurate list of Late Bronze Age Greek cities survived to Homer's day and appears in the *Iliad* as the so-called Catalog of Ships. And it survived even though writing disappeared from Greece between 1180 and 750 B.C.

As for Trojan memories, writing did not disappear from the Near *East,* and trade routes between Greece and the Near East survived after 1200. Around 1000 B.C., Greeks crossed the Aegean Sea again in force and established colonies on the coast of Anatolia. Tradition puts Homer in one of those colonies or on a nearby Aegean island. If so, the poet could have come into contact with records of the Trojan War—maybe even with a Trojan version of the *Iliad.*

In any case, writing is only part of the story. The *Iliad* and *Odyssey* are oral poetry, composed as they were sung, and based in large part on time-honored phrases and themes. When he composed the epics, Homer stood at the end of a long tradition in which poems were handed down for centuries by word of mouth from generation to generation of professional singers, who worked without benefit of writing. They were bards, men who entertained by singing about the great deeds of the heroic past. Often, what made a bard successful was the ability to rework old material in ways that were new—but not too new, because the audience craved the good old stories.

We can presume that the Trojan War indeed happened: that is, that a Greek coalition attacked and eventually sacked Troy. But if the Trojan War really happened, how was it fought? What caused it? To answer these questions we will start with Homer and then scrutinize all the details in light of what we know about the Late Bronze Age.

Take, for instance, the war's length. Homer says that the Trojan War lasted ten years; to be precise, he says that the Greeks at Troy fought and suffered for nine years and finally won in the tenth. But these numbers should not be taken literally. Among many other reasons, consider that in the ancient Near East, there was an expression "nine times and then a tenth," which means "over and over until finally." It was a figure of speech, much as in today's English the phrase "nine times out of ten" means "usually" rather than the literal numbers. In all likelihood, Homer uses a time-honored expression to mean that the Trojan War lasted a long time. We should not understand it literally. Either that, or the meaning of the phrase was garbled by the time it reached Homer.

So how long did the Trojan War really last? We don't know. All we can say is that it lasted a long time but probably considerably less than ten years. Since they had limited resources, Bronze Age kingdoms are unlikely to have mounted a ten-years' campaign. It was a protracted war. But then, Troy was a prize worth fighting for.

Troy's fortune lay *in* its location. "Windy Troy," as Homer calls it, was not merely gusty, it was a meteorological miracle. The city rose because it was located at the entrance to the Dardanelles, the water link between the Aegean and the Black Sea. In its prime, Troy covered seventy-five acres and held 5,000–7,500 people, which made it a big city in Bronze Age terms and a regional capital.

The Troad, the hinterland of Troy, was a blessed land. There was fresh water in abundance, the fields were rich with grain, the pastures were perfect for cattle, the woods were overrun with deer, and the seas were swarming with tuna and other fish. And there was the special gift of Boreas, the Greek god of the north wind: Boreas usually blows in the Dardanelles for thirty to sixty days during the summer sailing season, sometimes for weeks at a time. In antiquity, when boats lacked the technology to tack, that is, to zigzag against the wind, Boreas stopped shipping in the Dardanelles. For much of the sailing season, ship captains were forced to wait in Troy's harbor until the wind fell. As lords of the waterfront, Trojans got rich, and they owed it to Boreas.

The Trojans were among the world's great middlemen. Middlemen are rarely beloved, especially if they get rich on bad weather. With the possible exception of textiles the Trojans had only one good to sell, their famous horses. Horse dealers were the used-car salesmen of the ancient world. The fast-talking Trojans probably found ways to cheat other men that outdid anything thought up in Thebes or Mycenae.

Troy may not have been popular but with its natural advantages and business savvy, Troy was peaceful and prosperous—or it would have been, had it been wrapped in a bubble. Unfortunately, Troy stood exposed on the bloody fault line where two empires met. There was no more dangerous piece of real estate in the ancient world. To the east lay the Hittites, great charioteers who rode out of the central highlands and dominated Anatolia as well as much of the Near East. To the west lay the Greeks, a rising power, whose navy exerted pressure across the Aegean Sea. These two warlike peoples were cousins of a sort. Both spoke an Indo-European language, and both had arrived in the Mediterranean from further east around 2000 B.C. Although these two rivals never invaded each other's heartland, they took out their fury on the people stuck between them.

Western Anatolia was the Poland of the Late Bronze Age: wealthy, cultured, and caught between two empires. In a region of about forty thousand square miles (roughly the size of Kentucky or about four-fifths the size of England), an ever-shifting set of countries struggled for power—with the Hittites and the Greeks always ready to stir the pot. There was a never-ending series of wars among the dozens of kingdoms that came and went over the years, vying for power in a turbulent no-man's-land.

To the Greeks, who laid claim to the Aegean islands and who held a foothold in Anatolia, the Troad was a threat and a temptation, both a dagger pointed at the Greek heart and a bridge to the Hittites' heartland. It was also the richest source of booty on the horizon. A major regional hub, Troy was a way station for goods from Syria and Egypt and occasionally even from the Caucasus and Scandinavia. How could the predatory hearts of the Greeks not have yearned to plunder it? But it was not a fruit to be easily picked.

Troy was a sturdy fortress. The plain of Troy was broad but, otherwise, it was no place for a bloody brawl. It was soggy for much of the year, which was bad for chariots. It may have been malarial—the evidence is unclear. Add to these factors the Trojan army and Troy's wide network of alliances. But though the city was strong, Troy had weak spots. Twenty-eight towns lay in Troy's rich hinterland, not to mention more towns on the nearby islands, and none of them had fortifications to match the walls of the metropolis. These places overflowed with the material goods and the women whom the Greeks coveted.

Practiced and patient raiders, the Greeks were ready for the challenge of protracted conflict. Living in tents and shelters between the devil and the wine dark sea would be miserable, but no one becomes a "Viking" in order to be comfortable. The Trojans enjoyed all the rewards of wealth and sophistication. But the Greeks had three advantages of their own: they were less civilized, more patient, and they had strategic mobility because of their ships. In the end, those trumped Troy's cultural superiority. And so we come to the Trojan War.

The war probably took place sometime between 1230 and 1180 B.C., more likely between 1210 and 1180. At that latter date the city of Troy was destroyed by a raging fire. The presence of weapons (arrowheads, spearheads, and sling stones) as well as unburied human bones points to a sack—that is, a sudden and violent attack. The towns in the Troad, according to a recent survey by archaeologists, may have been abandoned around 1200, consistent with an invasion.

Yet some skeptics deny the veracity of the Trojan War because few weapons have been found in the ruins of Troy compared to other ancient cities that had been sacked. But we must remember that Troy is no undisturbed site. It was the premier tourist attraction of the ancient world; its soil was dug up in search of relics for such VIP tourists as Alexander the Great and the Emperor Augustus. And later "urban renewal" flattened the citadel for terraces for Greek and Roman temples, a process that destroyed layers of Bronze Age remains. The archaeological evidence fits the picture of a city that was sacked, burned, and then, in later centuries, picked through by eager tourists.

The date of the Trojan War sticks in some historians' craws. Around 1180 B.C. the great palaces of mainland Greece, from Mycenae to Pylos, and many places in between, were themselves destroyed. With their own ruin looming, could the Greeks have possibly attacked Troy between 1210 and 1180? Yes. History is full of sudden reversals. For example, most Japanese cities were rubble in 1945 yet only four years earlier, in 1941, Japan had attacked the United States. Besides, the Greek myths say that the Trojan War gave way to civil war and chaos within the Greek homeland, and that might just fit the archaeological evidence. Finally, unrest in Greece in the period 1210–1180 might have made the Trojan War *more,* not less, likely, because it might have tempted Greek politicians to export violence abroad.

History is made up not of stones or words but of people. Was there ever a queen named Helen and did her face launch a thousand ships? Was there a warrior named Achilles who in a rage killed thousands? Did Aeneas suffer through a bitter war only to have the last laugh as a king? What about Hector, *Odysseus,* Priam, Paris, Hecuba, Agamemnon, Menelaus, and Thersites? Did they exist or did a poet invent them?

We don't know, but names are some of the easiest things to pass down in an oral tradition, which increases the likelihood that they were real people. Besides, we can almost say that if Homer's heroes had not existed, we would have had to invent them. There may not have been an Achilles, but Greek warriors used his tactics of raiding cities and of fighting battles by attacking chariots on foot. Whether Helen's face launched a thousand ships or none, queens of the Bronze Age wielded great power and kings made war over marriage alliances. Priam may never have ruled Troy, but Kings Alaksandu and Walmu did, and Anatolian rulers lived much as Homer describes Priam, from his dealings with uppity nobles to his practice of polygamy. So this book will refer to Homer's characters as real-life individuals. The reader should keep in mind that their existence is plausible but unproven. Descriptions of them are based on Homer and, whenever possible, on details drawn from archaeology, epigraphy, art, etc.

And with that, let us meet our leading lady. She is a character who sums up the spirit of her age, and new evidence increases the chances that she really did exist. And that she ran away from home to go to the windy city, blown by Boreas, and the fatal waterway by which it sat, where soldiers stole cattle and hunted men.

Consider

1. **Was there ever a Trojan War?**
2. **Did Schliemann find Homer's Troy?**
3. **Do the evidence of Bronze Age archaeology and the Linear B tablets provide any support for the historicity of the *Iliad* or *Odyssey?***
4. **Is the social system consistent and identical within both epics?**
5. **When do Finley, Snodgrass, and Strauss date the world of Homer?**
6. **What evidence does each scholar use to support his conclusions?**
7. **To what extent are the views of each scholar compatible with one another? How are they irreconcilable?**
8. **Which of the three scholars do you find most convincing? Why?**

CHAPTER 2
HOPLITE WARFARE
IN ARCHAIC GREEK SOCIETY

ONE OF THE MORE CONTROVERSIAL TOPICS of Archaic Greek history concerns the emergence of the hoplite phalanx. The use of a massed formation several rows deep of citizen-soldiers heavily armed with large wooden shields, bronze helmets, breastplates, greaves, and spears to fight decisive battles between rival Greek *poleis* has raised many questions. When precisely did hoplite warfare originate? Was it a gradual process of development or an immediate change in tactics? Why did it quickly become the dominant form of battle for Greek warriors? Was the rise of hoplite warfare related to other social, economic, and political changes in Greek society? How exactly was a hoplite battle fought? The nature of the limited contemporary literary and iconographic evidence has led scholars to remarkably different answers to these questions. There is no doubt, however, that once it took its classic form the hoplite phalanx dominated Western military history for several centuries. It might be helpful first to review two of the basic theories regarding hoplite tactics.

The orthodox view of the phalanx concentrates on the large hoplite shield which came into use by the end of the eighth century. The shield appears practical only for massed formation because it leaves the warrior's right-hand side vulnerable to attack, while the left-hand portion of the shield extends well beyond that side of his body. Therefore, in close formation a fighter can provide cover for the man stationed on his left but must seek protection from the shield of the soldier to his right. The sheer weight of the armor (about 55 pounds) also limited a warrior's mobility and made it unlikely for a hoplite to fight in isolation. In fact, the orthodoxy contends that rival heavy infantry formations deployed their soldiers about three feet apart and (normally) eight ranks deep, and then charged together in a horrific collision. The ensuing battle resembled a ritualized contest (*agón*), in which each side attempted to push through and tear apart the line of the opposition. Such fighting minimized the use of cavalry and projectile missiles and emphasized the need to work in unison, in order to maintain the line against "the push" (*othismos*) of the enemy.

Recently scholars have vigorously challenged the traditional model of hoplite warfare by arguing for a looser phalanx organization, with more emphasis on individual combat and greater use of projectile weapons. They find the notion that each rank of warriors pushed against the backs of the fighters in front of it to break through the enemy's line unconvincing. The alternative model of archaic warfare more closely resembles the fighting found in Homer's *Iliad* than in the Greek phalanx of the classical period. It is interesting that scholars argue against the orthodox view employing the same literary and iconographic evidence used to support it. This chapter presents discussions from leading proponents of two very different schools of thought regarding the emergence of the hoplite phalanx and its significance for the rise of the Greek polis.

Ancient Sources

1. Homer, *Iliad*, 11.17–46, THE ARMING OF AGAMEMNON
2. Homer, *Iliad*, 13.125–168, MASSED FIGHTING IN HOMER
3. Homer, *Iliad*, 7.219–312, AJAX VS. HECTOR
4. Tyrtaeus (Fragments), THE SEVENTH CENTURY PHALANX?
5. Herodotus, *Histories*, 7.9, MARDONIUS APPRAISES GREEK FIGHTING METHODS
6. Thucydides 1.15, WARFARE IN ARCHAIC GREECE
7. Thucydides 5.69–73, THE BATTLE OF MANTINEA
8. Polybius 13.3.4, ANCIENT PRINCIPLES OF WARFARE

Opinions of Modern Scholars

1. From Victor Davis Hanson, *Western Way of War: Infantry Battle in Classical Greece*
2. From Hans van Wees, "The Development of the Hoplite Phalanx: Iconography and Reality in the Seventh Century"

ANCIENT SOURCES FOR HOPLITE WARFARE

1. THE ARMING OF AGAMEMNON

Homer's *Iliad* (c. 750–650 BC) provides the earliest surviving literary evidence for Greek warfare. It is reasonable to expect that the poet's descriptions of the warfare contain some artificial elements and exaggerations designed to entertain his audience. Many scholars, however, believe that in his narrative Homer must have drawn upon the experiences of actual fighting from his own time, in order to engage his listeners and to make his story intelligible. His descriptions of arms and battle tactics may help illuminate the transition in Greek warfare from the pre-polis era to the archaic period when the hoplite warrior emerged. The *Iliad* might be helpful not only in shedding light on heroic fighting techniques but also on Greek values and attitudes toward war just before, or roughly contemporary with, the introduction of hoplite equipment. The material from Homer contains several types of martial scenes, including descriptions of warriors arming for battle, duels between champions, *aristeiai* (displays of martial prowess) of individual heroes, and scenes of fighting in masses.

The most elaborate of four extended arming scenes in the *Iliad* is that of the great Mycenaean king Agamemnon. *Iliad*, 11.15–46

[15] The son of Atreus shouted aloud and bade the Argives gird themselves for battle while he put on his armor. First he girded his goodly greaves about his legs, making them fast with ankle clasps of silver; and about his chest he set the breastplate [20] which Kinyras had once given him as a guest-gift. It had been noised [*kleos*] abroad as far as Cyprus that the Achaeans were about to sail for Troy, and therefore he gave it to the king. It had ten circles of dark lapis, [25] twelve of gold, and ten of tin. There were serpents of lapis that reared themselves up towards the neck, three upon either side, like the rainbows which the son of Kronos has set in the sky as a sign to mortal men. About his shoulders he threw his sword, studded with bosses [30] of gold; and the scabbard was of silver with a chain of gold wherewith to hang it. He took moreover the richly-wrought shield that covered his body when he was in battle—fair to see, with

ten circles of bronze running all round it. On the body of the shield there were twenty bosses of white tin,

[35] with another of dark lapis in the middle: this last was made to show a Gorgon's head, fierce and grim, with Rout and Panic on either side. The band for the arm to go through was of silver, on which there was a writhing snake of lapis with three heads

[40] that sprang from a single neck, and went in and out among one another. On his head Agamemnon set a helmet, with a peak before and behind, and four plumes of horse-hair that nodded menacingly above it; then he grasped two terrifying bronze-shod spears, and the gleam of his armor shot from him as a flame into the firmament,

[45] while Hera and Athena thundered in honor of the king of rich Mycenae.

Questions

1. **What are the various elements that comprise the arms and armor of Agamemnon?**
2. **Compare the panoply of the hoplite warrior of the archaic period with that of Homeric warriors.**

---

2.   MASSED FIGHTING IN HOMER

Extended fighting narratives in the *Iliad* provide examples of massed fighting which anticipate the type of warfare that would become commonplace with the development of the hoplite phalanx. The primary difference is that Homeric battle lines lack the high level of organization and cohesion that characterize the tight formation of the classical phalanx. Moreover, the success of an army depends on the valor of certain heavily armed front-line warriors *(promachoi)* who take a leading role in the battle.

In *Iliad* Book XIII the god Poseidon, the earth-encircler, drives the Greeks into battle and some tightly packed infantry fighting ensues. *Iliad,* 13.125–168

[125] Thus did the earth-encircler address the Achaeans and urge them on. Thereon round the two Ajaxes there gathered strong bands of men, of whom not even Ares nor Athena, marshaled of hosts could make light if they went among them, for they were the picked [*krinein*] men of all those who were now awaiting the onset of Hector and the Trojans. They made a living fence,

[130] spear to spear, shield to shield, buckler to buckler, helmet to helmet, and man to man. The horse-hair crests on their gleaming helmets touched one another as they nodded forward, so closely aligned were they; the spears they brandished in their strong hands were interlaced,

[135] and their hearts were set on battle. The Trojans advanced in a dense body, with Hector at their head pressing right on as a rock that comes thundering down the side of some mountain from whose brow the winter torrents have torn it; the foundations of the dull thing have been loosened by floods of rain,

[140] and as it bounds headlong on its way it sets the whole forest in an uproar; it swerves neither to right nor left till it reaches level ground, but then for all its fury it can go no further—even so easily did Hector for a while seem as though he would career through the tents and ships of the Achaeans till he had reached the sea

[145] in his murderous course; but the closely serried battalions stayed him when he reached them, for the sons of the Achaeans thrust at him with swords and spears pointed at both ends, and drove him from them so that he staggered and gave ground; thereon he shouted to the Trojans,

[150] "Trojans, Lycians, and Dardanians, fighters in close combat, stand firm: the Achaeans have set themselves as a wall against me, but they will not check me for long; they will give ground before me if the mightiest of the gods, the thundering spouse of Hera, has indeed inspired my onset."

[155] With these words he put heart and soul into them all. Deiphobos son of Priam went about among them intent on deeds of daring with his round shield before him, under cover of which he

strode quickly forward. Meriones took aim at him with a spear,

[160] nor did he fail to hit the broad orb of ox-hide; but he was far from piercing it for the spear broke in two pieces long before he could do so; moreover Deiphobos had seen it coming and had held his shield well away from him. Meriones

[165] drew back under cover of his comrades, angry alike at having failed to vanquish Deiphobos, and having broken his spear. He turned therefore towards the ships and tents to fetch a spear that he had left behind in his tent. The others continued fighting, and the cry of battle rose up into the sky.

Questions

1. **How do the massed fighting techniques of Homeric warriors compare with those of the citizen soldiers of the hoplite phalanx?**
2. **Bring out the similarities and the differences between the two forms of warfare?**

---

3.   AJAX VS. HECTOR

The Homeric duels between champions distinguish the fighting of Dark Age aristocrats, if not Bronze Age warriors, from the hoplite encounters of middling farmers of the polis period. The contest in *Iliad* Book VII between the great Achaean warrior Ajax and the most brilliant Trojan fighter Hector provides an excellent example. *Iliad*, 7.219–282

[219] Ajax came up bearing his shield in front of him like a wall

[220] a shield of bronze with seven folds of oxhide—the work of Tykhios, who lived in Hyle and was by far the best worker in leather. He had made it with the hides of seven full-fed bulls, and over these he had set an eighth layer of bronze. Holding this shield before him,

[225] Ajax son of Telamon came close up to Hector, and menaced him saying, "Hector, you shall now learn, man to man, what kind of champions the Danaans have among them even besides lion-hearted Achilles cleaver of the ranks of men. He now abides at the ships

[230] in anger with Agamemnon shepherd of his people, but there are many of us who are well able to face you; therefore begin the fight." And Hector answered, "Noble Ajax, son of Telamon, chief of the host of warriors,

[235] treat me not as though I were some puny boy or woman that cannot fight. I have been long used to the blood and butcheries of battle. I am quick to turn my leather shield either to right or left, for this I deem the main thing in battle.

[240] I can charge among the chariots and horsemen, and in hand to hand fighting can delight the heart of Ares; howbeit I would not take such a man as you are off his guard—but I will smite you openly if I can." He poised his spear as he spoke, and hurled it from him.

[245] It struck the sevenfold shield in its outermost layer—the eighth, which was of bronze—and went through six of the layers but in the seventh hide it stayed. Then Ajax threw in his turn,

[250] and struck the round shield of the son of Priam. The terrible spear went through his gleaming shield, and pressed onward through his cuirass of cunning workmanship; it pierced the shirt against his side, but he swerved and thus saved his life.

[255] They then each of them drew out the spear from his shield, and fell on one another like savage lions or wild boars of great strength and endurance: the son of Priam struck the middle of Ajax's shield, but the bronze did not break, and the point of his dart was turned.

[260] Ajax then sprang forward and pierced the shield of Hector; the spear went through it and staggered him as he was springing forward to attack; it gashed his neck and the blood came pouring from the wound, but even so Hector did not cease fighting; he gave ground, and with his brawny hand seized a stone,

[265] rugged and huge, that was lying upon the plain; with this he struck the shield of Ajax on the boss that was in its middle, so that the bronze rang again. But Ajax in turn caught up a far larger stone, swung it aloft, and hurled it with prodigious force.

[270] This millstone of a rock broke Hector's shield inwards and threw him down on his back with the shield crushing him under it, but Apollo raised him at once. Thereon they would have hacked at one another in close combat with their swords, had not heralds, messengers of gods and men,

[275] come forward, one from the Trojans and the other from the Achaeans—Talthybios and Idaios both of them honorable men; these parted them with their staves, and the good herald Idaios said, "My sons, fight no longer,

[280] you are both of you valiant, and both are dear to Zeus; we know this; but night is now falling, and the requests of night may not be well ignored."

Questions

1. **How do the arms and close combat techniques of Hector and Ajax compare with those of hoplite warriors?**
2. **What values do the Homeric fighters especially prize?**

---

4. THE SEVENTH CENTURY PHALANX?

The elegiac poems of Tyrtaeus are said to have taught the Spartans courage and to have made them willing to die for their country.

I. The First Poem was Recorded by Lycurgus, *Against Leocrates.*

It is a fine thing for a brave man to die when he has fallen among the front ranks while fighting for his homeland, and it is the most painful thing of all to leave one's city and rich fields for a beggar's life, wandering about with his dear mother and aged father, with small children and wedded wife. For giving way to need and hateful poverty he will be treated with hostility by whomever he meets, he brings disgrace on his line, belies his splendid form, and every indignity and evil attend him. If then there is no regard or respect for a man who wanders thus, nor yet for his family after him, let us fight with spirit for this land and let us die for our children, no longer sparing our lives. Come, you young men, stand fast at one another's side and fight, and do not start shameful flight or panic, but make the spirit in your heart strong and valiant, and do not be in love of life when you are fighting men. Do not abandon and run away from elders, whose knees are no longer nimble, men revered. For this brings shame, when an older man lies fallen among the front ranks with the young behind him, his head already white and his beard grey, breathing out his valiant spirit in the dust, clutching in his hands his bloodied genitals—this is a shameful sight and brings indignation to behold—his body naked. But for the young everything is seemly, as long as he has the splendid prime of lovely youth; while alive, men marvel at the sight of him and women feel desire, and when he has fallen among the front ranks, he is fair. Come, let everyone stand fast, with legs set well apart and both feet fixed firmly on the ground, biting his lip with his teeth.

II. The Second Poem was Recorded by Stobaeus in his *Anthology.*

Come, take courage, for your stock is from unconquered Heracles—not yet does Zeus hold his neck aslant—and do not fear throngs of men or run in flight, but let a man hold his shield straight toward the front ranks, despising life and loving the black death-spirits no less than the rays of the sun. You know how destructive the deeds of woeful Ares are, you have learned well the nature of grim war, you have been with the pursuers and the pursued, you young men, and you have had more than your fill of both. Those who dare to stand fast at one another's side and to advance towards the front ranks in hand-to-hand conflict, they die in fewer numbers and they keep safe the troops behind them; but when men run away, all esteem is lost. No one could sum up in words each and every evil that befalls a man, if he suffers disgrace. For to pierce a man behind the shoulder blades as he flees in deadly combat is gruesome, and a corpse lying in the dust, with the point of a spear driven through his back from behind, is a shameful sight. Come, let everyone stand fast, with legs set well apart and both feet fixed firmly on the ground, biting his lip with his teeth, and covering thighs, shins below, chest, and shoulders with the belly of his broad shield; in his right hand let him brandish a mighty spear and let him shake the plumed crest above his head in a fearsome manner. By doing mighty deeds let him learn how to fight and let him not stand — he has a shield — outside the range of missiles, but coming to close quarters let him strike the enemy, hitting him with long spear or sword; and also, with foot placed alongside foot and shield pressed against shield, let everyone draw near crest to crest, helmet to helmet, and breast to breast, and fight against a man, seizing the hilt of his sword or his long spear. You light-armed men, as you crouch beneath a shield on either side, let fly with huge rocks and hurl your smooth javelins at them, standing close to those in full armour.

III. The Third Poem also Comes from the *Anthology* of Stobaeus.

I would not mention or take account of a man for his prowess in running or in wrestling, not even if he had the size and strength of the Cyclopes and out-stripped Thracian Boreas in the race, nor if he were more handsome than Tithonus in form and richer than Midas and Cinyras, nor if he were more kingly than Pelops, son of Tantalus, and had a tongue that spoke as winningly as Adrastus, nor if he had a reputation for everything save furious valour. For no man is good in war unless he can endure the sight of bloody slaughter and, standing close, can lunge at the enemy. This is excellence; this is the best human prize and the fairest for a young man to win. This is a common benefit for the state and all the people, whenever a man with firm stance among the front ranks never ceases to hold his ground, is utterly unmindful of shameful flight, risking his life and displaying a steadfast spirit, and standing by the man next to him speaks encouragingly. This man is good in war. He quickly rents the bristling ranks of the enemy and by his zeal stems the tide of battle. And if he falls among the front ranks, pierced many times through his breast and bossed shield and corselet from the front, he loses his own dear life but brings glory to his city, to his people, and to his father. Young and old alike mourn him, all the city is distressed by the painful loss, and his tomb and children are pointed out among the people, and his children's children and his line after them, never do his name and good fame perish, but even though he is beneath the earth he is immortal, whoever it is that furious Ares slays as he displays his prowess by standing fast and fighting for land and children. And if he escapes the doom of death that brings long sorrow and by his victory makes good his spear's splendid boast, he is honoured by all, young and old alike, many are the joys he experiences before he goes to Hades, and in his old age he stands out among the townsmen; no one seeks to deprive him of respect and his just rights, but all men at the benches yield their place to him, the young, those of his own age, and the elders. Let everyone strive now with all his heart to reach the pinnacle of this excellence, with no slackening in war.

Questions

1. **How do the values and fighting techniques encouraged by Tyrtaeus compare with those of the Homeric heroes?**
2. **For whom do the warriors in the poems of Tyrtaeus fight and for what do they strive? Compare with Homeric warriors.**

5. MARDONIUS APPRAISES GREEK FIGHTING METHODS

In this particular section of Herodotus' *Histories* the Persian Mardonius advises King Xerxes about the fighting methods of the Greeks. *Histories* 7.9Hdt.

Yet, from what I hear, the Greeks are pugnacious enough, and start fights on the spur of the moment without sense or judgement to justify them. When they declare war on each other, they go off together to the smoothest and levellest bit of ground they can find, and have their battle on it—with the result that even the victors never get off without heavy losses, and as for the losers—well, they're wiped out.

6. WARFARE IN ARCHAIC GREECE

Thucydides, the fifth–century BC Greek historian of the Peloponnesian War fought between Athens and Sparta, is generally recognized as the greatest historian of antiquity. He describes the type of warfare that dominated early Greece in his "Archaeology" (Thuc. 1.15).

Wars by land there were none, none at least by which power was acquired; we have the usual border contests, but of distant expeditions with conquest the object we hear nothing among the Hellenes. There was no union of subject cities round a great state, no spontaneous combination of equals for confederate expeditions; what fighting there was consisted merely of local warfare between rival neighbors.

> **Questions**
>
> 1. **How does the type of warfare described by Herodotus and Thucydides compare with battles described in the *Iliad*?**

7. THE BATTLE OF MANTINEA

The Athenians had elected Alcibiades general for the first time in 420 BC. A year earlier he had been humiliated when the Spartans decided to collaborate with his rival Nicias to negotiate the peace that ended the Archidamian War, the name scholars give to the first 10 years of the Peloponnesian War. The Spartans had ignored Alcibiades despite the care he had shown the Spartan prisoners the Athenians had captured at Sphacteria years earlier. To take his revenge, Alcibiades persuaded the Athenians to form an anti-Spartan alliance with Argos, Mantinea, and Elis. He convinced both sides to stake everything on a single battle at Mantinea. King Agis of Sparta won a victory so decisive that it was the turning point in the struggle between the two great powers. Thucydides' description of the Battle of Mantinea in 418 BC provides perhaps the fullest and most detailed surviving account of a hoplite battle.

5.69.1 THE ARMIES BEING NOW ON THE EVE OF ENGAGING, each contingent received some words of encouragement from its own commander. The Mantineans were reminded that they were going to fight for their country and to avoid returning to the experience of servitude after having tasted that of empire; the Argives, that they would contend for their ancient supremacy, to regain their once equal share of the Peloponnesus of which they had been so long deprived, and to punish an enemy and a neighbor for a thousand wrongs; the Athenians, of the glory of gaining the honors of the day with so many and brave allies in arms, and that a victory over the Spartans in the

Peloponnesus would cement and extend their empire, and would besides preserve Attica from all invasions in future. **[2]** These were the incitements addressed to the Argives and their allies. The Spartans meanwhile, man to man, and with their war songs in the ranks, exhorted each brave comrade to remember what he had learnt before; well aware that the long training of action was of more use for saving lives than any brief verbal exhortation, though ever so well delivered.

5.70 After this they joined battle, the Argives and their allies advancing with haste and fury, the Spartans slowly and to the music of many flute players—a standing institution in their army, that has nothing to do with religion, but is meant to make them advance evenly, stepping in time, without breaking their order, as large armies are apt to do in the moment of engaging.

5.71.1 Just before the battle joined, King Agis resolved upon the following maneuver. All armies are alike in this: on going into action they get forced out rather on their right wing, and one and the other overlap with this their adversary's left; because fear makes each man do his best to shelter his unarmed side with the shield of the man next him on the right, thinking that the closer the shields are locked together the better will he be protected. The man primarily responsible for this is the first upon the right wing, who is always striving to withdraw from the enemy his unarmed side; and the same apprehension makes the rest follow him. **[2]** On the present occasion the Mantineans reached with their wing far beyond the *Sciritae*, and the Spartans and Tegeans still farther beyond the Athenians, as their army was the largest. **[3]** Agis afraid of his left being surrounded, and thinking that the Mantineans outflanked it too far, ordered the sciritae and Brasideans to move out from their place in the ranks and make the line even with the Mantineans, and told the polemarchs Hipponoidas and Aristocles to fill up the gap thus formed, by throwing themselves into it with two companies taken from the right wing; thinking that his right would still be strong enough and to spare, and that the line fronting the Mantineans would gain in solidity.

5.72.1 However, as he gave these orders in the moment of the onset, and at short notice, Aristocles and Hipponoidas refused to move (for which offense they were afterwards found guilty of cow-

ardice and banished from Sparta); and although Agis, when he saw that the two companies did not move, ordered the sciritae to return to their place in line, they did not have time to fill up the breach in question before the enemy closed. **[2]** Now it was, however, that the Spartans, utterly worsted in respect of skill, showed themselves as superior in point of courage. **[3]** As soon as they came to close quarters with the enemy, the Mantinean right broke the sciritae and Brasideans, and bursting in with their allies and the thousand picked Argives into the unclosed breach in their line cut up and surrounded the Spartans, and drove them in full rout to the wagons, slaying some of the older men on guard there. **[4]** But if the Spartans got the worst of it in this part of the field, it was not so with the rest of their army, and especially the center, where the three hundred knights, as they are called, fought round King Agis, and fell on the older men of the Argives and the five companies so named, and on the Cleonaeans, the Orneans, and the Athenians next them, and instantly routed them; the greater number not even waiting to strike a blow, but giving way the moment that they came on, some even being trodden under foot, in their fear of being overtaken by their assailants.

5.73.1 The army of the Argives and their allies having given way in this quarter was now completely cut in two, and as the Spartan and Tegean right simultaneously closed round the Athenians with the troops that outflanked them, these last found themselves placed between two fires, being surrounded on one side and already defeated on the other. Indeed they would have suffered more severely than any other part of the army, but for the services of the cavalry which they had with them. **[2]** Agis also, on perceiving the distress of his left opposed to the Mantineans and the thousand Argives, ordered all the army to advance to the support of the defeated wing; **[3]** and while this took place, as the enemy moved past and slanted away from them, the Athenians escaped at their leisure, and with them the beaten Argive division. Meanwhile the Mantineans and their allies and the picked body of the Argives ceased to press the enemy and, seeing their friends defeated and the Spartans in full advance upon them, took to flight. **[4]** Many of the Mantineans perished; but the bulk of the picked body of the Argives made good their escape. The flight and retreat, however, were neither hurried nor long; the Spartans fighting long and stubbornly until the rout of their enemy, but that once accomplished, pursuing for a short time and not far.

5.74.1 Such was the battle, as nearly as possible as I have described it; the greatest that had occurred for a very long while among the Hellenes, and joined by the most considerable states. **[2]** The Spartans took up a position in front of the enemy's dead, and immediately set up a trophy and stripped the slain; they took up their own dead and carried them back to Tegea, where they buried them, and restored those of the enemy under truce. The Argives, Orneans, and Cleonaeans had seven hundred killed; the Mantineans two hundred, and the Athenians and Aeginetans also two hundred, with both their generals. On the side of the Spartans, the allies did not suffer any loss worth speaking of; as to the Spartans themselves it was difficult to learn the truth; it is said, however, that there were slain about three hundred of them.

Questions

1. **What are the various stages of the Battle of Mantinea from start to finish as Thucydides describes them?**
2. **How does the advance and fighting techniques of the Spartans compare with those of the Argives?**
3. **What role does the hoplite shield play in determining fighting tactics according to Thucydides?**

---

8.   ANCIENT PRINCIPLES OF WARFARE

The following passage is often cited as evidence that the Greeks preferred short, decisive, and shock hoplite battles over other methods of fighting. Polybius contrasts the practices of warfare in his day with those of the classical Greeks.

The ancients, as we know, were far removed from such malpractices. For so far were they from plotting mischief against their friends with the purpose of aggrandizing their own power, that they would not even consent to get the better of their enemies by fraud, regarding no success as brilliant or secure unless they crushed the spirit of their adversaries in open battle. For this reason they entered into a convention among themselves to use against each other neither secret missiles nor those discharged from a distance, and considered that it was only a hand-to-hand battle at close quarters which was truly decisive. Hence they preceded war by a declaration, and when they intended to do battle gave notice of the fact and of the spot to which they would proceed and array their army. But at the present they say it is a sign of poor generalship to do anything openly in war. Some slight traces, however, of the ancient principles of warfare survive among the Romans. For they make declaration of war, they very seldom use ambuscades, and they fight hand-to-hand at close quarters.

Questions

1. **How do the "rules" of combat described by Polybius compare with the style of fighting portrayed in the *Iliad*?**
2. **Did the Spartans and Argives in the Battle of Mantinea seem to recognize such a code of conduct? Why or why not?**

OPINIONS OF MODERN SCHOLARS

1. THE WESTERN WAY OF WAR

In his book *The Western Way of War,* Victor Davis Hanson, Martin and Ilie Anderson Senior Fellow in Classics and Military History, The Hoover Institution, Stanford University, reconstructs the battle experience of infantry soldiers during the Classical Age of Greece. The following excerpts feature some highlights from his account. The first selection describes the initial charge of the two enemy phalanxes to commence the battle.

FROM VICTOR DAVIS HANSON, *WESTERN WAY OF WAR: INFANTRY BATTLE IN CLASSICAL GREECE*

I. The Charge of the Phalanx

[As they advanced toward the enemy, the feet of the charging soldiers kicked up a huge and blinding cloud of dust. And the shouting of the men and the rubbing and jostling of breastplates, shields and spears created a deafening roar. In the onset of battle hoplites sought to create a gap in the enemy line, an initial hole for the troops to push through.]

AFTER THE TROOPS HAD LINED UP into formation and the phalanxes had squared off on the agreed site of battle, Greek warfare suddenly lost the rigid conformity of finely tailored columns. The point of departure from the clear order of the battle squares did not begin—as most assume—when the two sides met together, but often much earlier at the very moment the men began to lumber forward at a trot of some four to six miles per hour.

Very rarely could the discipline of command extend down the line of allied contingents—a phalanx which might stretch on for nearly a mile. Consequently, as the tide of hoplites first surged forward, there was rarely uniformity in the moment of their departure, the rate of their advance, or the direction of their course. Among most Greek armies, the attack resembled more the rush of an armed mob than the march of disciplined troops in careful formation, though it is true from both ancient and modern sources we receive a picture of an ordered, deliberate advance of the Spartans. With reference to the literary evidence, Pritchett, for example, remarks:

The sequence of events seems to have been as follows. The commander-in-chief, whether general or king, gave the command to advance by beginning the paian. The trumpeter sounded the call. The soldiers joined in the song whether the advance was at normal or faster pace. All the evidence is that the paian was a sort of hymn or chant, and the use of the word "paian" in other connections favors this belief...The song was begun when the armies were three or four stades apart. Once the battle was joined, the marching paian might be replaced by the war cry. (1.107)

Thucydides' famous description of the Spartan advance at the first battle of Mantineia (418) may be the clearest picture of how the Spartans usually made their move forward.

And after this battle was joined. The Argives and their allies for their part went forward eagerly and wildly, but the Spartans slowly and in time to the many flute-players who were at their side—not out of any religious custom, but rather so that they might march evenly and their order might not disintegrate—a thing which large armies are prone to do as they march forward to battle. (5.70)

This progression of events is said to have occurred in most battles in which the Spartans, the only true professional soldiers in Greece, took part; but in truth, it remains an idealized picture of even the Spartan army, which often did not follow such a textbook procedure. At the Pactolos River, for example, Agesilaos ordered the first ten age groups to charge the enemy on the run. And, as Thucydides himself notes, most other armies, the Argives in particular, tended to be much more disorganized.

* * *

There were problems not merely in the speed but also in the direction of the advance. Only the men in the first three ranks of the phalanx had a clear view of the enemy and thus of the general point at which they would soon collide. Of course, while there was little chance that two phalanxes could ever miss each other entirely, the evidence is, nevertheless, that each side rarely charged straight ahead but came at each other obliquely. That characteristic, along with the difficulty of the run and the uncertainty of the initial start, added yet another dimension to the overall confusion. Most hoplites in the front ranks would realize that the men directly opposite, on the other side of the battlefield, were probably not the hoplites with whom they would actually collide. In his rich description of the battle of Mantineia of 418, Thucydides recalls the peculiar habit of most armies on the move to drift rightward, sometimes radically so, each hoplite wishing to shelter his own vulnerable right side within the protection of his neighbor's shield. So at Mantineia each side found their left wing nearly enveloped by the enemy's right. Later, at the battle of the Nemea River in 394, Xenophon tells us clearly that both sides "veered to the right in their advance", so much so that the Spartan right wing caught only a portion of the Athenian phalanx. More than twenty years later, at Leuktra, the Spartans apparently had moderated, or rather mastered, this natural drift and transformed it into a deliberate plan of envelopment from the right.

Opposing battle lines were not necessarily the same length. An army that was inferior in numbers or that had chosen to shorten its line by massing in column might find itself facing an enemy that stretched beyond both its wings. In most such cases, hoplites were probably forced to move at an angle, whatever their right-ward urge, natural or deliberate, just to meet the enemy: those charging in superior numbers would have angled in on their outnumbered foe, while the outnumbered were forced to move in mass to the right to prevent being outflanked on both wings, or to drift outward at both flanks and thus risk leaving a gap in the middle.

* * *

Once the signal was given to advance, the Greek hoplite—if he could hear it—had to pay attention not to be left behind, to stick close to the men around. In closing the final distance across no-man's-land, the formation of the phalanx was often disrupted as each man ran at a slightly different speed. And there were roars of men, animals, and equipment on both sides, as well as a general impairment of vision caused by the rising dust, the crests and spears of the men ahead, and the mass of moving humanity in general. In many instances the outcome of a hoplite battle was decided right here during the first charge when some men simply caved in to the fright and ruined the unity of their columns before they even reached the enemy. As we shall see, the key to success in a battle between phalanxes was to create a lethal gap in the enemy ranks, an initial hole through which troops could push, destroying the cohesion of the entire enemy formation. Some armies were rent before they even reached the spears of the enemy, the battle ending before it had even begun. Indeed, it is surprising that such a collapse in mass was not more common when we consider just how demanding, how awful that final move into the enemy actually was.

II.   The Collision

[The charge ended when both phalanxes crashed together in no-man's-land. The collision made an awful noise as bronze spear points pierced wooden hoplite shields, shields struck against the bronze breastplates and helmets of the enemy. The goal of this terrible collision was to achieve an initial shock that knocked the troops of the enemy back and enabled your own forces to pour in through tears and seams in the enemy line. Hanson describes "the mixing together" that resulted from the initial confrontation of battle.]

THE SOUND OF ARMORED MEN in contact was not a fanciful image solely for the poets, but the reality of the battlefield. Nearly three hundred years after the Lyric poets, Xenophon, in his famous description of the battle of Koroneia in 394—a battle "like none other" in his lifetime—was clearly impressed by the initial meeting of the two armies: "There was not any yelling, but there was not silence either; instead that particular sound was present which both anger and battle tend to produce." That "particular sound," that "awful crash," as Xenophon knew, was not human, at least not entirely: "and then there was a great slaughter of men, and too, a great thud of all types of weapons and missiles, together with a great shout of men calling out for help among the rank, or urging each other onward, or praying to the gods."

The Greeks recognized that the peculiar noise of this initial crash came from a variety of sources. First, there was the dull thud of bronze against wood as either the metal spear point made its way through the wood core of a hoplite shield, or as soldiers struck their shields against the bronze breastplates and helmets of the enemy, or as wooden shield was bashed into shield. To Aristophanes that sound was a synonym for war. Together with this, there was the sharp clatter of metal driven against metal as spear and sword met breastplate, helmet, and greave. Even breastplate might be driven into breastplate, as men in the front row lost control and were literally pushed into the enemy ranks, jammed together "chest against chest" (Tyrtaios 8.33). And repeated sharp sounds indicated when ash spears snapped under the pressure of contact in what Sophocles called "the storm of spears."

The live sounds were more animal-like than human: the concerted groans of men exerting themselves, pushing forward in group effort with their bodies and shields against the immovable armor of the enemy—grunts such as one hears around men sweating at work in field or shop, for battle, after all, as Homeric man knew, was "work" of the worst kind. Finally, whatever Tyrtaios advised about the hoplite "biting his lip," there were all too often the noises of human misery. Here arose a tortured symphony of shrieks as a man went down with a wound to the groin, the steady sobbing of a soldier in extremis, a final gasp of fright as the spear thrust found its way home. Ugly, indeed, Tyrtaios wrote, is the corpse in the dust.

* * *

The visual aspect of the troops on the battlefield was now drastically altered. True, the neat columns of the prebattle formations were already somewhat rent in the general, uneven surge forward, but after the impact, both sides regained their density as the ranks to the rear piled up behind their leaders and bunched together laterally to seek protection in the line of shields. Then the two armies became forever intertwined and irrevocably mingled as man pressed into man at front, side, and rear. The sea of dust was

now stationary, and still more stifling as men were shuffling but not really moving, at least at first. Friend and foe were quickly becoming indistinguishable. Pockets of brave fighters must have soon made their way into the ranks of the enemy phalanx, either to be absorbed and killed, or to grow steadily into a fatal cancer as their colleagues in line to the rear sensed a reward to their efforts and pushed them even farther inside the depths of the enemy. Some idea of this confusion is reflected in Greek literature where we are repeatedly told that those in the front ranks of hoplite battle are not merely fighting "hand to hand" or "spear to spear," by touching "chest-to-chest" and "helmet-to-helmet" as well:

> Let him fight toe to toe and shield against
> shield hard driven, crest against crest and
> helmet on helmet, chest against chest; let
> him close hard and fight it out with his
> opposite foeman, holding tight to the hilt of
> his sword, or to his long spear. (Tyrtaios
> 11.31–34)

These images also suggest that the rear ranks had been pushing madly at the very instant the two sides collided, literally thrusting their friends ahead into the faces of the first ranks of the enemy. In both prose and poetry, ancient Greek battle was often in these first few seconds understood as a "mixing together," as any clear separation between the two sides was now lost forever.

III.   Tears and Gaps

[How would it be possible to collapse a Greek phalanx? The goals in the initial stages of battle were to destroy the enemy psychologically, by convincing him before the advance that his forces were inadequate, and physically, by creating holes in and ripping open his phalanx on impact. Hanson describes the collision of arms. The first clash of spears was followed by fighting with the secondary short sword within seconds after their spears were broken, and then bare hands and even teeth might be used. It was important for hoplites to maintain their line.]

THE MOST COMMON WAY to collapse a Greek phalanx on the field of battle was to cause a collective loss of nerve that would sweep through the enemy ranks and so result in a mad dash from the rear. The key to that objective was to find gaps or, better yet, to create breaches in the enemy line and to stop at all costs opposing men from "standing their ground and closing their ranks together." If a space could be opened between downed hoplites, men might pour in, attacking at the enemy's sides and backs as they came on. Then the entire enemy column would totter, in fear of a general collapse at the front.

* * *

In most Greek battles there were essentially two methods of sowing disorder, one psychological, the other physical. In the seconds before the advance, even as the enemy made its way across the battlefield, a sudden disintegration of unity could occur when men suddenly realized that they were outnumbered, exposed on the flank, or poorly deployed. Perhaps, too, they discovered that they were supported by untrustworthy allies or had suffered disheartening losses of prebattle skirmishers and horsemen, or that the enemy arrayed against them consisted of frightening professionals (i.e., the Spartans), or simply that they had already lost order in a haphazard, reckless march. In such cases, when the army not merely lost its formation but was transformed into a mob of individuals, gaps and rents in the phalanx opened immediately and randomly along the entire face of the column. Then everyone knew that a battle of the classic type was now impossible, and the engagement was over before the two sides had even met. Men simply turned and fled, in what the Greeks sometimes termed a "tearless battle."

Usually, however, Greek battles were not so easily won; here my concern is with the breaches in the enemy line that had to be made by hard fighting and occasional dying. This was now the work of the first, second, and third ranks of the phalanx—men whose spears had reached the enemy at the first collision and who had survived the crash—to create holes like those the Macedonians ripped open at Chaironeia in 338, when the entire Greek line that faced them was "constantly turned open and exposed" (Diod. 16.86.3–4), or like those later at Pydna in 168, when the Macedonians themselves were "ripped open and torn" by their Roman adversaries under Aemilius Paulus; Plutarch remarks that initially breaches in the phalanx originated because

of the differing success of the combatants: one segment presses ahead in success, while not far away others are forced to fall back. Chabrias' attack in 388 on Aigina caused a Spartan-led phalanx to collapse when the front line of the enemy, no longer resembling "any dense mass," quickly disintegrated. In other words, the front two or three rows of the Spartan phalanx allowed Chabrias' men either to create or exploit gaps in their line, and the unity of the entire formation was quickly destroyed. How, in these first few seconds of battle, was one side able thus to penetrate the enemy line, making or finding gaps between the shields of the enemy infantry?

As the hoplites on each side began their final run in the last two hundred yards, they lowered the spear and carried it at the side in an underhand grip; this is clear from the literary evidence as well as scenes on vase paintings and sculpture. Momentum and power could be maximized through such an underhand thrust while on the move, and, of course, it was easier this way to maintain both speed and balance. Perhaps, too, there was less chance of accidental wounding, as the spear tip was kept well below the shield and breastplate of the man ahead. The idea must have been to penetrate the enemy's groin or unprotected upper thighs which were exposed under the lower lip of his shield: the groin was the area which Homer called "beyond all places where death in battle comes painfully to pitiful mortals." That such blows were favored in the initial collision may be apparent from Tyrtaios' sad description of the old man who holds his groin bloody from a spear thrust; that unfortunate man, he reminds us, had been fighting admirably in the first ranks. The advantages of such thrusts were that they might force the front-line fighters immediately to drop the shield and spear to cover up such a painful wound, and thus to withdraw from the active fighting within a few seconds. That seems to be the circumstances portrayed by some vase paintings where hoplites in various encounters thrust their spears at the groin with an underhand grip, attempting to direct a blow under the edge of the shield.

Another alternative was to strike the legs above the greave where a deep wound could stop a hoplite just as quickly. Archidamos, who commanded the Spartan phalanx that invaded Arcadia in 365, as soon as his troops were attacked, fell wounded in the thigh among the first ranks, suggesting that he was such a casualty of the initial charge by the Arcadians. Elsewhere in Greek literature we hear of many who suffered wounds to the knee or thigh, which confirms that this unprotected area was a favored target for the initial underhand thrust. A vase from Syracuse pictures a hoplite collapsed in convulsions with a terrible, gaping wound down the entire side of his thigh; in fact, on several ceramic representations we see soldiers on the ground with large, fresh tears along their unarmored, exposed thighs, the blood gushing out, the victim with grimaces of pain on the face, or simply his eyes closed in a near comatose state. The advantage of striking beneath the shield was that this was the first—and the last—chance to drive home the spear thrust into an unarmored area with enough power to take the hoplite instantly and completely out of battle. Moreover, these initial spear attacks would not only cripple these front-rank fighters but, more important, sometimes drive them backward, propelling their stunned bodies right into the faces of those to the rear, and so temporarily keeping others at bay as well. Again from vase paintings, we see that a spear thrust toppled the victim backward, while blows from less effective missiles or swords at times left the hoplite tottering or even falling *forward*.

* * *

We must not forget that hoplite battle, even at this crucial desperate stage, was still a group struggle; those brawling in the hand-to-hand fighting had to give their constant attention to the men at their side. Remember, they not only had to find a way through the enemy line, but also had to keep the foe out as well. If a hoplite could not find protective cover within the shield of his neighbor, then he had to be sure to do his fighting right next to the man at his side, where the sheer density of their flesh might keep out the enemy as they pressed forth. That close attention to order saved the Phocian phalanx at Plataia: initially surrounded on all sides by their Persian captors, they stood firm in the face of the Persian advance, "drawing themselves close and packing their ranks as densely as possible" (Hdt. 9.18.2). The men to the rear had to be ready constantly to rush up a rank and block any penetration that threatened to tear the phalanx apart. This general tendency of hoplites to bunch together is a recurring theme in most battle descriptions, where we are told that the successful side somehow maintained close order all down the line, advancing with locked shields into the tears in the enemy column without leaving even a small gap in their own. To endure that onset at close quarters, Tyrtaios wrote, the warrior must "close the ranks together" and thereby "protect the army behind him." The need for men to maintain their assigned places in the face of attack explains Sophocles' reference to the man who must "stand firm in his place during the storm of spears."

Any reckless departure from the line by individuals in quest of personal success was of little value: the resulting penetration in the enemy line was hardly worth the gap left behind. Aristodemos apparently was the most courageous of the Greek hoplites at the battle of Plataia, yet after the victory the Spartans passed him over in awarding the prize for valor, since "in a frantic state he left the formation to show all his brave deeds." Indeed, such a departure from the formation to meet the enemy in a single display of martial prowess was the worst thing any soldier might do. Herodotus reminds us that the Persians suffered from such recklessness; at Plataia they sealed their own fate when they ran out to meet the Spartans "in groups of ten or so, sometimes more, sometimes less." (Hdt. 9.62.3) The ephebic oath, required of young Athenians, described the ideal battle conduct: each swore, "I will not leave my comrade wherever I'm stationed on the battlefield."

IV.   The Push and Collapse

[The initial collision gave way to "the push" (othismos). The successful phalanx would break the enemy's line. Once a phalanx collapsed the losers would turn to flight, and, unless the defeated rallied, the battle would end.]

IN MOST HOPLITE BATTLES, it is true, the initial collision of men and subsequent hand-to-hand fighting soon gave way to the *othismos*, the "push" of shields, as one side eventually achieved a breakthrough, allowing its troops to force their way on into and through the enemy's phalanx. On occasion we hear that neither side could open up the requisite tear, and thus both sides simply butchered each other right where they stood, the dead discovered after the battle with "all their wounds to the front" (Diod. 15.55.2). In these rare cases, the soldiers in the rear could not push their way to victory, but were forced to step up a rank over the fallen corpses and take their own turn in the stand-up killing. For example, at the battle at the Nemea River, when men of Pallene crashed headlong into the phalanx of the Thespians, both sides fought and perished in their ranks. That the push of shields in hoplite battle might not lead to a quick collapse soon after the crash is clear also from the second stage of fighting at Koroneia, where the Theban and Spartan phalanxes met head-on: "throwing up their shields against each other, they pushed, fought, killed, and died" (*Hell.* 4.3.19). Such battles were often longer, and certainly more brutal. The writers realized the anomaly in such fighting where two locked phalanxes simply ground away at each other in constant slaughter without the expected advance. Had something gone drastically wrong in Greek warfare? When one side did not disintegrate, there is a certain trace of awe as well as sadness in the telling. It can be seen in Xenophon's famous remark on the battle of Koroneia, that "it proved to be such as none of the battles of our time" (*Hell.* 4.3.16), and in his account of the Nemea River, where the Thespians and the men of Pallene "died in their places."

The men stationed behind in ranks four through eight of most standard phalanxes were not idle as their comrades ahead met the enemy; they were in no sense "rear-echelon" troops as conceived and despised by modern fighting men. Indeed, often the best troops were placed at the rear, where they kept watch on the very pulse of battle. If there was no initial advance after the collision, their role was to stand firm, maintain their station, and resist any wave of back pressure that might come from jittery hoplites in the middle who saw little chance for forward motion and now had ideas of escape.

* * *

The real importance of these men in the rear was simply to push those in front with their shields—in Asklepiodotos' words, "to exert pressure with their bodies." Of course, from the moment of impact they had been doing essentially just that, as they piled up behind their file leaders; increasingly, their pressure grew stronger or more desperate, since they were striving "to force back the entire enemy mass which was itself trying to press forward. It is surprising how many ancient authors

saw the crucial phases of hoplite battle as 'the push,' where each side sought desperately to create the greater momentum through the superior 'weight' or 'mass.' " In Aristophanes' *Wasps* the veterans are made to say, "after running out with the spear and shield, we fought them...each man stood up against each man...we *pushed* them with the gods until evening." At Koroneia, Xenophon wrote, the Spartans "crashed against the Thebans face to face, and throwing up their shields, they pushed, fought, killed, and died."

The ancients took it for granted that the deeper the column, the greater its thrusting power and momentum; what the optimum number of additional rows was, we do not know. Surely, phalanxes with more than sixteen ranks must have also had other considerations in mind—at times perhaps they may have wished to shorten their exposed front (selfishly) in an effort to force reluctant allies to accept greater exposure along the battle line. In any case, most phalanxes were generally described not as rows, or ranks, or spears, but rather as "shields" in depth, which may indicate that the main idea for the ranks in the middle and rear was to push ahead with their shields and bodies. On occasion hoplite battle could be summarized simply an *othismos aspidon*, "the push of shields" (Thuc. 4.96.2). The goal was to break the deadlock in those precious few minutes before exhaustion set in; the *perception* of success, of movement forward, must have been nearly as important as any actual progress ahead, since it kept men hopeful that their strenuous efforts were not wasted.

Of course, there was never uniform pressure all down the line of any phalanx. One wing, or even a small segment of an individual contingent, might sense a tremor of weakness in the specific group of enemy hoplites facing them and, so, a chance of forward motion into their ranks. Yet, as they began to redouble their efforts, they likewise had to be wary lest somewhere along their own line their fellow warriors were like their yielding foe, giving ground, being torn away from the phalanx, allowing the enemy in the process to press in on their own sides and rear. We hear two contrasting cries of exhortation in Greek battle that express these extremes: the shouts of exultation as men suddenly believed that they had found success and merely needed additional effort, a last concentrated push, to crack the tottering enemy wide open—"Grant me one step forward and we shall have victory"; or, alternatively, a call to the beleaguered to stand firm and not give in to the press of bodies, not to be pushed off the field of battle:

> No, no, let him take a wide stance and stand
> up strongly against them, digging both heels
> in the ground, biting his lip with his teeth.
> (Tyrtaios 11.21–22)

* * *

How exactly was this mass pushing accomplished? References to the great "weight" or "mass" of one phalanx must be to the physical energy that row upon row of men generated; the infantry in the column behind the third rank—that is, rows four through eight in most phalanxes—doubtless leaned with their own bodies into the men ahead in the initial moments after the two sides collided. In other words, each hoplite pressed with the center of his shield against the back of the man to his front, probably steadying his balance at times with his upright spear shaft as he leaned forward. The shaft in this way served as a staff of sorts—used to push off, it provided extra momentum as well as balance. Xenophon had this image in mind when, in his fictionalized account of battle, he noted that Egyptians were especially well suited for fighting in column since their peculiar body-shields allowed the infantryman to rest the shoulder while he pushed. From reconstructions of the hoplite shield, evidence of vase painting, and suggestions in Greek literature, we know that the lip of the top rim of the hollow Greek model was ideal for precisely that steady pushing; the hoplite supported the shield on his shoulder as he drove it against the backs of his friends ahead. That way the weight was distributed over the entire body rather than the left arm alone, while the shield's broad surface ensured that such pressure would be distributed evenly across the back of the man in front, neither tripping him nor forcing him off balance. Polybius simply declared that men push by "the weight of their bodies" (18.30.4); that same image of pushing is found again in many varieties of authors and can only confirm our belief that men in fact shoved everyone forward as they dug their bodies into the spacious dish of their own shield. The poet Theocritos describes how Castor urged Hercules "to put his shoulder behind his shield," and the technique carried over into later warfare: Livy said of the famous battle at Zama that the Romans pushed their own men ahead by thrusting at their backs with the centers of their shields.

* * *

At some point, on one side or the other, a portion of the phalanx could withstand the pressure no longer and began to be pushed back. At that point, the unity of the entire column was endangered and all men—both those who had advanced into gaps along the enemy line and those to the rear who were pushing ahead—began to think for the first time of their own individual survival. In other words, the final rout began. Sometimes there was a dramatic, sudden collapse at one particular point in the phalanx; the Greek word *pararrexis* and its cognates (the "breaking" of the line) best capture the meaning of such a disaster. While the progression of events that followed is easily imaginable, we are more interested in the peculiar *environment* within the phalanx at this, the last desperate stage of Greek hoplite battle.

First, there would have arisen on one side of the battle line the element of self-interest: each hoplite, in varying degrees depending on his position relative to the point of the collapse and on his own physical status, confronted the ever-growing danger posed by remaining in rank within the phalanx, fighting to the bitter end, and choosing to "stand his ground and fighting hard for his children and land" (Tyrtaios 12.33–34). In a matter of seconds, each soldier, sensing that the battle was lost and that rank after rank was falling away from the rear, would have to decide when, how, and if he could make good his escape. For some there was never any dilemma, only the choice made by the old war poets Kallinos and Tyrtaios, or of the Three Hundred at Thermopylai: to die in one's tracks as the enemy poured in now from the side and rear, and to avoid at any cost the disgrace of flight.

* * *

After the localized breakthrough there followed the wide-scale collapse (*trope*). Despite the admonitions of Homer and the Lyric poets, for many men retreat seemed preferable to glorious annihilation; it was simply a question of finding a suitable avenue of escape. The choice depended on various factors: the desperation of the situation, the availability of routes to safety, the degree to which panic and fear had overcome reason, the shame and personal disgrace felt by the more self-possessed. If the phalanx had retained any cohesion, an improvised fighting withdrawal was still possible, if difficult.

* * *

Battle quickly exhausted those in the phalanx, both physically and psychologically—perhaps in little less than an hour's time. The killing was face-to-face; each blow required a maximum physical effort to drive the weapon through the bronze of his opponent, all this to be performed while the hoplite carried armor and was pushed constantly by the ranks to the rear. Since there was no real distance between the men who gave and received such blows, a sea of blood was everywhere. Hoplites were soon covered by the gore of those whom they met, struck, and were pressed on into. References to the blood of battle in literature are meant to be taken literally as firsthand, eyewitness descriptions from men who knew what the killing at close quarters was really like. For example, Tyrtaios says that only the true warrior can "endure to look upon the bloody slaughter." Mimnermos had that same image in mind when he wrote of a great anonymous warrior of the past who made his way through the clash of the "bloody battle." So, too, after the conclusion of the battle of Pydna in 168, Scipio was said to have come off the field "covered with the blood" of his enemies, "carried away by the pleasure"; here, it seems the Roman commander had nearly become "blood drunk" from the killing.

2. THE DEVELOPMENT OF THE HOPLITE PHALANX

Professor Hans van Wees of University College London challenges the accepted notion that the fighting style of the classical phalanx with its tightly packed ranks of heavy infantry was adopted soon after the invention of the hoplite shield in the late eighth or early seventh century BC. He reinterprets the contemporary iconographic and literary evidence to propose that the phalanx evolved gradually, perhaps over several centuries. His model for archaic warfare emphasizes individual combat and fighting in small groups and integrates light-armed and heavy-armed warriors. Battles display the fluid and open-order fighting represented by Homer in the *Iliad*.

FROM HANS VAN WEES, "THE DEVELOPMENT OF THE HOPLITE PHALANX: ICONOGRAPHY AND REALITY IN THE SEVENTH CENTURY"

EVER SINCE WOLFGANG HELBIG put the question on the academic map almost a century ago (1909, 1911), scholars have been asking when the Greeks first adopted their characteristic style of fighting, the close-range and close-order combat of the classical hoplite phalanx. Two camps have established themselves. One side argues that the introduction of hoplite armour, between 725 and 700 BC, must mean that something much like the classical hoplite formation was already in existence, or emerged almost immediately afterwards. The other side says that the introduction of hoplite armour was merely one stage in a longer process of development which did not reach completion until about 650 or 640 BC, when the classical phalanx was first represented in Greek art. I shall try to establish a third position here, and argue that even the later of these two dates is too early: the phalanx continued to develop throughout the seventh century, and quite possibly throughout the archaic age.

Much of the argument will turn on iconographic evidence, which has long played a curious part in the debate. By common consent, three or four vase-paintings of the mid-seventh century realistically represent the phalanx and allow us to date its emergence to 640 BC at the latest. Yet these images have hardly any successors, and the vast majority of battle scenes in later art show what is generally dismissed as a "heroic" form of combat which bears no relation to contemporary warfare. It is odd that a society in which participation in war was widespread and frequent should have produced only a few more-or-less realistic images of combat, and otherwise have confined itself to a repertoire of legendary images entirely divorced from reality. In fact, as we shall see, it did not. For the seventh century at any rate, our distinction between realistic and fantastic images is quite false: both types of pictures are highly stylized, each in its own way, but both are drawn from the experience.

I. Hoplite Armour: What It Does and Does Not Mean

Those who favour an early date for the emergence of the hoplite phalanx rely on one argument above all: the new type of shield adopted in the late eighth century, unlike its predecessors, could be used effectively only in an extremely close and rigid formation. This position, however, is based on assumptions about the hoplite's handling of his shield which are disproved by the iconographical evidence.

The crucial innovation of the hoplite shield was that it had a double grip instead of the single central handle of earlier types: the handle was set at the rim, while in the centre was fixed a bronze arm-band through which one passed one's arm up to the elbow. The weight of the shield was thereby transferred from the hand to the entire lower arm. Its concave shape allowed the shield to be rested on the shoulder, further lightening the burden. As a result, it became possible to carry larger, thicker shields for longer periods of time. But the new shield, it is said, also had serious drawbacks: it offered much reduced cover for the right flank, and, in retreat, no cover at all for the back. Hoplites supposedly could only find the protection which their shields failed to provide by taking refuge in the tightest possible formation.

It is true that the hoplite shield could not be slung across one's back in retreat, as had been possible with earlier types. Its double grip, its diameter of about 3 feet (90 cm), and its weight of some 15 lb (7 kg) made this almost impossible, and accordingly it is never shown equipped with the strap by which its predecessors were suspended. But we need not infer that the hoplite was forced by the nature of his shield to stand his ground at all times—unlike the Dark Age warrior who had been able to turn round and retreat from the mêlée. His back may no longer have been protected by his shield, but the hoplite amply compensated for this by wearing a cuirass. The bronze, "bell"-shaped cuirass which was introduced a decade or two before the shield provided at least as much cover for a soldier's back as the light shield of the Dark Age warrior, who otherwise had no armour except a helmet and a metal belt. The hoplite would thus have been no more and no less at risk than his predecessors when he turned his back towards the enemy. One might object that the greater weight of the shield would hamper his mobility and this, too, is no doubt true. Yet it is well known that classical hoplites were mobile enough to charge at a run over some 200 yards, and numerous vase paintings of running hoplites from 650 BC onwards show that this had always been so. The shield thus at most tended to slow down movement on the battlefield: it did not in itself impose a static form of combat.

As for lateral cover, the hoplite's right flank was certainly vulnerable. The sources speak of this flank *as* "unprotected" and regard a position on the right wing of an army as most dangerous and most honorific. In the classical phalanx, as Thucydides famously said, each hoplite "brings his unprotected side as near as possible to the shield of the man drawn up on his right and believes that density of formation is the best protection" (5.71.1). The question, however, is not whether the hoplite's right flank was vulnerable, but whether the new shield made it significantly more vulnerable than the right flank of the bearer of a single-grip shield had been. If it did not, there is no reason to think that the introduction of the hoplite shield in itself dictated or presupposed a denser formation.

There are two issues here: the manoeuvrability of the shield and the extent of the cover which it provided in its normal, frontal position. The hoplite shield is somewhat less manoeuvrable than some other kinds of shield, but its limitations should not be exaggerated. A shield with a single handle, grasped at its centre, could in principle be swung to the right rather further than a shield with a double grip, grasped at the rim. But in practice there would be very little, difference in how far to the right any shield could be brought without badly impeding the use of weapons. If there was a marginal loss of range in the new shield, this was again amply compensated for by the extra cover of the new cuirass. In this respect, then, the hoplite shield made very little difference.

When held in its normal, frontal position, the bearer of the shield, it is commonly said, was unable to use its full cover; The double grip supposedly meant that the hoplite in effect stood behind the right half of his shield, leaving his right-hand side relatively vulnerable to attack even from the front, and leaving the left half of his shield useless. Useless, that is, unless soldiers stood so close together that they could take cover behind the redundant left halves of their neighbours' shields (see Figure 2.1). Double-grip shields thus presupposed or imposed an extremely dense formation. The tacit assumption

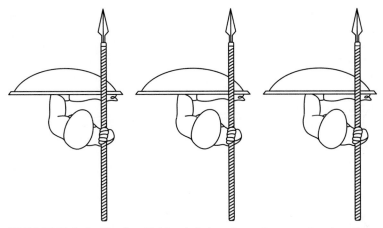

FIGURE 2.1   Hoplite shield and phalanx formation, assuming three-foot intervals and a frontal stance.

is that hoplites stood frontally opposed to their enemies, like wrestlers, rather than sideways-on, like fencers, holding their shields parallel to their bodies. But artistic representations show that this is *not* how hoplites fought.

The standard hoplite in Greek art strikes a "striding" pose with the left leg forward. Head and legs are shown in profile, but the torso is shown frontally or from the rear, as if twisted sideways. His shield, too, is most often shown frontally, from inside or outside, as if it were held by the side of his body (Figure 2.2).

This, of course, is a senseless way to carry a shield in battle, and it is obviously a conventional simplification of the more realistic and not uncommon scheme in which the shield is shown in profile, held in front of the bearer. When artists do take the trouble to draw the shield in profile, they always show it carried at a slope, tilted back against the left shoulder (Figure 2.3, top).

FIGURE 2.2   Conventional representation of position of the shield: the outside or inside is facing the viewer, as if the shield is held beside the body. Drawing after a black-figure amphora, showing Diomedes and Hektor fighting over "Skythes," late sixth century BC.

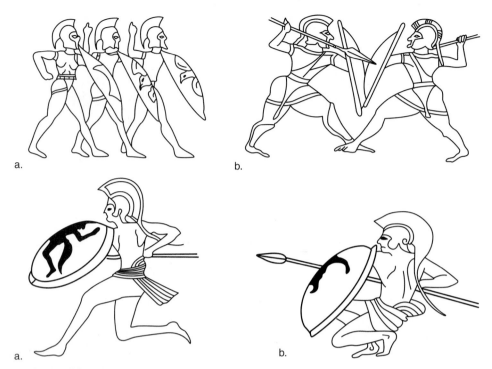

FIGURE 2.3 (top) Realistic representations of position of shield: shown in profile, held out in front of the body. Drawing (a) after Berlin aryballos, (b) after a Siana cup by the Heidelberg Painter, c. 560 BC.

(bottom) Realistic representations of position of the hoplite's body: left shoulder turned forwards, torso almost at a right angle to the shield. Drawing (a) after a terracotta plaque, c. 520–510 BC, from Athens; (b) after an Attic red-figure cup, c. 520–510 BC, from Chiusi.

The more simplified images are presumably also meant to represent this way of holding shields. What archaic art thus portrays with varying degrees of stylization would seem to be a sideways-on stance, with the upper body at almost right angles to the shield and to the enemy. More naturalistic images from the late archaic period remove all doubt. Standing, squatting, and even running hoplites are shown with torsos twisted sideways, their left shoulders pointing forward and supporting the shield (Figure 2.3, bottom).

Surely this was how hoplites in reality, too, stood in combat and handled their shields. Not only is it hard to see where else painters might have found the model for this standard pose, but it features in "realistic" and "heroic" images alike. Above all, common sense suggests that one would indeed naturally adopt a sideways-on stance when wielding a spear for thrusting or throwing, since it provides better balance and greater leverage on the weapon.

Now, a man standing sideways-on and holding his shield at right angles to his body places himself behind its *centre,* rather than to one side of it, even if it has a double grip (Figure 2.4). Hence the story of Epizelos, a veteran of the battle of Marathon, who claimed to have had a vision of a giant hoplite "whose beard overshadowed his entire shield" (Hdt. 6.117): the hoplite's beard evidently projected over its centre rather than its right half; in other words, the double-grip shield was normally carried in such a way that it did not fall short on the right and did not extend too far to the left. The bearer himself exploited its full cover on both sides. There was neither need nor room for the next man in line to seek direct cover behind it.

The hoplite shield, in short, did not require a closer formation than its predecessors had done, and the density of the classical phalanx must have been due to factors other than the use of the shield as such.

The only significant difference made by the hoplite shield was thus a straightforward, massive increase in frontal protection, at the cost of making

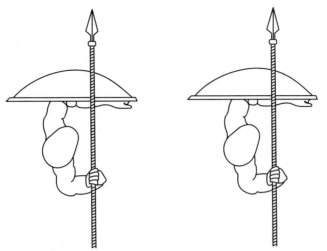

FIGURE 2.4 Hoplite shield and phalanx formation assuming six-foot intervals and a sideways-on stance.

its bearer rather less mobile. If this change to the shield did not necessarily entail a change in formation, it does suggest that in the late eighth century BC the trend in warfare was towards more frequent or prolonged hand-to-hand fighting, where improved protection was vital since blows landed with more force and were less easily dodged than in missile exchanges. The adoption of quite comprehensive body armour at the same time also makes perfect sense as a response to increasing exposure to the greater dangers of hand-to-hand combat. Arm- and thigh-guards were introduced in the sixth century, suggesting perhaps that the trend towards close combat continued to intensify; but such additional armour was apparently not widely used, and the limbs and lower body were evidently protected well enough by the shield alone.

Hand-to-hand fighting, classical sources tell us, involved "the pushing of shields." Modern scholars usually take this to mean that a front-rank soldier held his shield vertically before him and pushed the centre of its convex surface against the shield of his opponent, at times throwing his full bodily weight behind it. Since we have seen that the hoplite shield was actually carried diagonally, this cannot be right. Tilted back against the shoulder, the shield's bottom rim stuck out a couple of feet in front of its bearer, so that in very close combat the lower edges of opponents' shields were liable to touch (Figures 2.3 and 2.4). "Pushing" would thus consist of shoving the protruding lower part of one's shield against the corresponding part of the enemy's shield—with the

aim, no doubt, of driving him back, disturbing his balance, or at least breaking his cover. In this kind of action, one could only use the force of one's left arm and shoulder, rather than one's whole body, but, as Xenophon pointed out, this was far more than one was capable of doing with shields "supported by hands only." The hoplite shield thus not only offered *better* protection but was also a *more* effective offensive weapon than the single-grip shield. In this respect, too, its adoption can be understood as a response to the demands of close combat.

The sources regularly speak of the decisive moment of battle as "the push" (*öthismos*), and scholars often take this literally, as a collective, concerted effort of bodily pushing against the enemy front rank, with the rear ranks adding to the pressure by forcing their shields into the backs of those ahead of them. The uniqueness and extreme physical difficulty of such a manoeuvre have rightly been noted, and the iconography of the hoplite shield adds a further obstacle to this interpretation: how could any man possibly hold out his shield tilted in front of him when pushing against several ranks of opponents and being pushed by several ranks of his comrades? A decisive piece of literary evidence confirms that physical pushing was indeed confined to the front rank. Xenophon tells us that the ideal formation should be only two ranks deep since no one stationed further back could actively take part in the action. In his historical novel, *The Education of Cyrus*, he accordingly shows us a two-deep phalanx of Persians successfully resisting the shield-against-shield pushing of a hundred-deep

A realistic representation of the hoplite's sideways-on stance and his position behind the centre of his shield (here, a Bocotian shield).

phalanx of Egyptians. If a man of great military experience and acumen such as Xenophon felt that this was even theoretically possible, the rear ranks clearly cannot have physically contributed to the shoving. The decisive collective "push," we must conclude, was metaphor to describe the effort of driving the enemy back by means of intensive fighting. The expression is still common in modern military parlance.

If the rear ranks did not push or fight, they must have served to replace men who fell in the front-line or retired from the action, to help carry away the wounded and the dead, and to intimidate the enemy and boost the morale of their comrades by their very presence.

* * *

By the end of the eighth century, the type of soldier known in classical Greece as "hoplite," after his panoply of armour (*hopla*), had emerged, and his rise suggests a significant shift in tactics towards close combat. Nothing forces us to assume, however, that this shift was rapid or complete, let alone that it entailed the development of the classical phalanx formation. It is likely that the use of the hoplite shield spread gradually, and that there were initially only small numbers of fully armoured hoplites. Judging by the iconographical evidence and the increasing numbers of surviving pieces of armour, it may indeed have taken until the middle of the seventh century for the hoplite shield and panoply to become the norm, as has been argued by those who see the phalanx as a "piecemeal" creation.

But this is not the end of the story: there is no evidence that the shift towards close-range and close-order combat was complete by the mid-seventh century.

II. Battle Scenes: What They Do and Do Not Show

A frieze of warriors on the so-called Chigi vase, a Corinthian jug of *c.* 640 BC, has been hailed as "the earliest known wholly successful representation of the phalanx" (Cartledge, 1977, 19) and is generally regarded as definitive proof that a formation of the classical type had emerged. At first glance, one may be inclined to agree. The vase appears to show two rigidly and closely dressed ranks of uniformly equipped hoplites about to engage in hand-to-hand combat, while on each side a second rank follows close behind. What is more, among the ranks of the army on the left, we find a piper who, it may be supposed, is playing a marching rhythm to ensure that the formation keeps in step. Yet this picture is not what it seems.

First of all, as Anthony Snodgrass has pointed out, most of these hoplites carry two spears, rather than

Battle Frieze from the Chigi Vase. Middle Protocorinthian olpe, attributed to the Chigi/Macmillan Painter, c. 640 BC, from Veii (Villa Guilia 22679).

one, as their classical successors did. The men in the front ranks each hold a spear raised high in their right hands; their left hands grasp not only the shield-handle, but also a second, larger spear, carried upright. A scene of arming at the far left of the frieze shows not only that these hoplites do indeed carry two spears of unequal size, but also that each spear-shaft is fitted with a looped string. Such a string is shown elsewhere wound around the hoplite's index and middle fingers and is clearly designed to give the spear added spin and impetus when *thrown*. Oddly, then, we have two ranks of hoplites apparently about to engage in hand-to-hand combat with pairs of throwing-spears. It has been said that the painter must have misunderstood the purpose of these weapons, but it is unlikely that an artist so *au fait* with the practice of warfare that he could create this "wholly successful" picture—as well as the two next best-known images of hoplite warfare (see below)—should have made such an elementary mistake. Much more plausible is the suggestion that the two sides are meant to be standing at some distance from one another: "Obviously the two contingents have been brought so close together only to avoid leaving a blank space in the middle of the picture." Whether we have here a picture of close combat with the wrong weapons, or of missile warfare at the wrong distance, we do not have a picture that matches the classical phalanx.

Secondly, although one's first impression is that the two front lines consist of a single, closely-dressed rank each, there are two details which suggest otherwise. In the front line on the left we see four helmets, four shields, and four upright spears, but *ten*

legs. Given the meticulous draftsmanship of all the Chigi Painter's vases, this extra pair of legs is surely no careless mistake: we are given to understand that there are other men behind the four visible hoplites. Similarly, in the other army, we find an apparently redundant spear: since the last two hoplites in this front line each clearly raise one spear in their right hand while holding upright a second, taller spear in their left, the third, shorter, upright spear which protrudes behind them must belong to some other unseen hoplite. In other words, these rows of overlapping figures are not realistic images of single ranks, but schematic representations of larger groups of hoplites—whether in regular formations or bunched together in dense crowds, we cannot tell.

Thirdly, the supposed second ranks, which are almost unique in Greek vase-painting and the main reason for the "success" of this picture, are no such thing. For a start, whereas the ranks in a classical phalanx formation, of course, are of the same length, the Chigi Painter clearly imagines that there are notably more men in the second "rank" than in the first. On the left, nine men are visible in the rear against four in front; on the right, they are seven against five. Even more decisively, whereas the front lines are standing still, or, conceivably, moving at walking pace, the lines behind them are unmistakably *running*—at quite a pace, too, judging by the lift of their feet. Obviously, then, the artist could not have envisaged the second groups as following immediately behind the first.

That the running groups are meant to be at a considerable distance from the enemy is further indicated by the position of their spears. This is

FIGURE 2.5 Battle frieze from the Chigi Vase

clearest on the far left, where *all* spears are still carried upright. Literary and iconographical evidence agree that the (first) spear would initially, be carried in this position, but lowered and levelled forward during the run into battle, until finally the hoplite changed grip and raised his spear to the overarm position in which it appears among the front ranks on the vase. It has been attractively suggested that the curious position of the levelled spears of the second rank on the right of the Chigi vase, neither quite lowered nor fully raised, suggests that these hoplites are in the process of changing grip. If so, the Chigi Painter imagines that the running group on the right is getting close to the enemy and making ready to raise their spears for a throw (or thrust), while the running group on the left is so far away that they have not even got to the point where they would lower their spears.

First impressions have proved deceptive: the Chigi jug does not feature multiple ranks marching in step, and almost certainly no hand-to-hand combat. So what *does* it represent? The most cautious conclusion would be that the artist juxtaposed groups of hoplites at various stages of preparation for battle: arming, starting to run, raising their spears, and attacking. But I would argue that the Chigi Painter created a narrative as precise as his detailing of arms and armour. In the centre, two groups of hoplites are about to join battle and throw javelins at one another. The army on the right is about to be reinforced by a larger group of hoplites who have come running up and are just raising their spears to join the fray. In danger of being overwhelmed, the troops on the left call for help in turn, but their reinforcements, the largest group of all, still have some way to run, and indeed some are only just getting armed. The role of the piper in this scenario is not to set a marching rhythm, but to sound a call to arms, as trumpeters do elsewhere: this explains why he is evidently blowing at the top of his lungs, and why we see no piper on the other side, which has the temporary advantage.

This is not the story of a classical hoplite battle, but the kind of narrative one finds repeatedly in the *Iliad*. A close parallel is the sequence in which Idomeneus and Meriones re-enter battle to rally the Greeks, while the Trojans, "calling across the crowd," in turn flock together to face them. The initial result matches the central scene of the Chigi frieze: both sides move forward "all together,"

"bristling with spears"; a blinding light reflects from their bronze helmets, cuirasses, and shields, and they join a battle in which more spears are thrown than thrust at the enemy. Worried at the strength of the opposition, Idomeneus eventually calls out for help, and his comrades come to the rescue: "they all took a stand close by him, leaning their shields against their shoulders." In turn, the leader of the Trojans on this wing calls on his fellow commanders for help, and they come to his aid with "the crowd of their men." The parallel with the groups of hoplites running up from the rear in the Chigi frieze is obvious. A parallel for the troops (re-)arming on the far left occurs a little earlier in the narrative, when a group of Greeks who had returned to camp to rest and revive their spirits return to battle and make a stand beside their beleaguered comrades. The only thing missing in the *Iliad* is the signalling piper: Homer's heroes simply shout for help.

The Chigi Painter's two earlier warrior friezes, painted in miniature on perfume bottles dated to *c.* 650 BC, show less and are therefore more open to interpretation. They might represent battles in the classical manner, but they might equally well be battles in the epic style.

* * *

III. Missiles and Mobility: The Phalanx in the Seventh Century

So far the argument has been largely negative and has established only that neither the introduction of the hoplite shield nor the appearance of panoramic battle scenes in art implies the existence of the fully developed phalanx. This conclusion, however, allows us to re-evaluate the scrappy but precious evidence provided by the surviving fragments of seventh-century lyric poetry, with which we can start building a new picture of the realities of archaic warfare.

* * *

The persistence of the occasional throwing spear… suggests that the development of the phalanx was not complete, and this is even more evident from the fragments of the martial elegies of Tyrtaeus, composed for the Spartans waging the Second Messenian War (*c.* 640–600 BC). These poems have sometimes been cited as proof of the existence of the classical phalanx; more often they are described as "confused." They are neither.

Some of the main themes of Tyrtaeus' surviving work may indeed at first glance deceptively suggest phalanx tactics. One is the importance of fighting hand-to-hand:

> Go near, strike with a long spear or a sword
> at close range, and kill a man. Set foot against
> foot, press shield against shield, fling crest
> against crest, helmet against helmet, and chest
> against chest, and fight a man, gripping the
> hilt of a sword or a long spear.

A second key note is cohesion. "Fight while staying together, young men, he says: 'those who [fight] while staying together die in smaller numbers and save the men behind them'; 'speak encouraging words to the next man when you stand beside him.' The third and most prominent topic is the shame of, and danger in, running away—and its corollary, the importance of standing one's ground adopting the very pose which is standard for hoplites in Greek art: 'leg well apart, both feet planted firmly on the ground, biting your lip, covering thighs and shins below and chest and shoulders with the belly of the broad shield, shaking a mighty spear in your right hand.' All three themes would have been highly relevant to soldier in a classical phalanx, and indeed this is why the main fragments survive they were deemed suitable by the Athenian orator Lycurgus to illustrate the nature of courage and by Stobaeus to serve in his anthology as samples of poetry on 'war' and 'praise a valour.' But there are other elements, both in these pre-selected passages and more prominently in fragments which survive by chance on papyrus, which show that our poet did *not* have the classical phalanx in mind.

Tyrtaeus assumes a situation in which the soldier not only needs to be encouraged to hold his position in the line, but exhorted to make his way to the front-line in the first place. The full version of a passage just quoted reads "those who *dare go into close range and towards the front-line fighters (promachoi)*, while staying together, die in smaller numbers." The passage telling soldiers to fight "chest against chest" adds: "and do not stand with your shield *beyond the range of missiles*," a contrast which recurs in a papyrus fragment. By implication, the soldier has a choice; he can hang back or charge forwards. This gives added point to the comment that it is "a common asset to the city and all the people" when a man "remains among the front-line fighters *without pause*"—that is, when he does not drop back from time to time, as he might do.

Tyrtaeus' Spartans, in other words, have the space and freedom to move around the battlefield. They are still able to behave just like the warriors of the *Iliad,* who wander around their battlefields quite freely, individually and in small groups, moving "towards the front-line fighters" or dropping back "beyond the range of missiles," leaving and entering battle as they see fit. Just like Homer's heroes, the Spartans must be fighting in an *open and fluid order.*

What, then, of Tyrtaeus' exhortations to go in close, stay at the front, and stick together? It would seem that these appeals were so urgent precisely because they were addressed to soldiers who did not have a fixed place in an organized formation, but had the option of keeping their distance, falling back, and scattering. The warriors of the *Iliad* in fact receive precisely the same kind of encouragement as the Spartans, for precisely the same reasons:

Why do you stand off, skulking, waiting for others?
You ought to be making a stand in the front-line.
  (4.340–1)
Follow me! We must no longer fight the Greeks
  from a distance. (*15.55–7*)
You Greeks must no longer stand far away from the
  Trojans.
Let man go against man, intent on fighting.
  (20.354–5)

They are also constantly called upon to come to the rescue of their comrades and reminded of the advantages in "staying together": even a great warrior will give ground "when he [sees] two men staying together" (5.571–2; cf. 17.720–1), for "even the most worthless men can show *joint* bravery" (13.237). Tyrtaeus' claim that the casualty rate is lower among men who stay together is illustrated by the episode in the *Iliad,* already cited, where "far fewer of the Greeks were killed, since…they always remembered to protect one another" (17.364–5). Lastly, although Homeric heroes regularly retreat, they agonize about the shame of it, and, just as Tyrtaeus proclaims that standing firm at all times and at all costs is "the peak of excellence," indeed the *only* worthwhile form of excellence, Odysseus tells himself that "he who would excel in battle truly must stand his ground forcefully, and hit or be hit."

In Homer, as we have seen, the result of such exhortations is an improvised and temporary massing together of soldiers and intensification of battle, in the context of a normally open and fluid formation. What Tyrtaeus tells us about contemporary Spartan warfare implies that his martial elegies were nor designed or expected to inspire much more than that.

Unlike Callinus, Tyrtaeus does not tell the hoplites to *throw* their spears. This might simply be because the main passages only survive thanks to their emphasis on close combat, but more probably it does indeed reflect the same change in tactics implied by the steep decline of the number of throwing-spears in the hands of Greek hoplites in contemporary art.

The role of missiles in the hands of "the light-armed" (*gymnetes*), however, is prominent. Whereas in the classical period light-armed troops fought *outside* the phalanx and were virtually ignored by classical sources as a mere side-show, in Tyrtaeus they and the heavy-armed are part of a single, undifferentiated formation. One exhortation to fight hand-to-hand ends by turning to the light-armed and telling them to throw their missiles:

And you, light-armed, squatting under a shield here
   and there, must throw great rocks and hurl
   smooth javelins while you stand close by the
   heavy-armed. (F 11.35–8)

The light-armed here are clearly not a separate body of troops, but scattered "here and there" among the hoplites, and "squatting" for cover behind the latters' shields. The same mode of operation is described in the *Iliad*, where archers are protected by other men's shields, and only briefly break cover to shoot their arrows.

The phrase "here and there," and the fact that only a single brief exhortation of the light-armed survives, may seem to imply that javelin- and stone-throwers were few and far between, but other passages in Tyrtaeus indicate that they were present in large numbers. In a papyrus fragment, "light-armed fighters" are "running forward," immediately after a very fragmentary reference to "savage missiles" and "many men hurling sharp javelins" (F 23a. 10–14). More importantly, since the hoplites are repeatedly told not to stand "beyond the range of the missiles," and another papyrus fragment mentions the "rocks"

which clatter against soldiers' helmets during a clash of shields (F 19.19–20; cf. 19.2), the poet must have tacitly assumed the presence of many men launching these missiles. The same is true of the *Iliad,* in which few individual archers appear but many "arrows flying from bowstrings" are a constant presence in the background. At the end of the seventh century, Alcaeus, another poet with much combat experience, still spoke of greaves as "a defence against the forceful missile," as if hoplites were more at risk from arrows, stones, and javelins than from thrusting-spears.

* * *

What appears to have happened is that, as the hoplite emerged and gradually combat grew closer and formations denser, the archer was reduced from playing a prominent and independent part in battle to being an adjunct of the hoplite, dependent on the heavy-armed for cover and regarded as of secondary importance. Homeric epic retains traces of the archer's earlier status, but by and large reflects his seventh-century role and status. The decline of the archer, however, did not go so far as to exclude him from the formation: Tyrtaeus and the lead figurines show that light- and heavy-armed continue to mingle in the late seventh century.

Thus, the last third of the seventh century probably saw a general decrease in the hoplite use of javelins, but the mobility of the hoplites implied by Tyrtaeus' exhortations and the presence of numerous light-armed within the ranks show quite clearly that the slow movement towards close-range and close-order combat was as yet far from complete. In their degree of functional specialization, late seventh-century armies went beyond what we find in epic poetry; but in the openness and fluidity of their formations they remained very much like the armies described in the *Iliad* and a long way removed from the classical phalanx.

IV. Conclusion: The Slow Transformation of Greek Warfare

In the Dark Ages, Greek warriors wore little or no armour and carried a light shield; they used a sword for close combat, and either a pair of throwing spears or bow and arrows for fighting at long range. Archers and javelin-throwers fought independently from, and on a par with, one another, in what was evidently a wide open formation. The last quarter of the eighth century witnessed the creation of the hoplite, who, with his heavy armour and his heavy shield, was capable of engaging at closer range. As a result, spears began to be used for thrusting as well as throwing, formations became rather more dense, and archers were reduced to the status of auxiliaries, moving among the ranks while keeping cover behind the hoplites' shields. Not until the last third of the seventh century did the majority of hoplites stop carrying throwing-spears and begin to rely on the single thrusting-spear and sword only. Even then, as Tyrtaeus shows, formations remained relatively open and fluid: hoplites and light-armed intermingled and soldiers continued to enjoy considerable freedom of movement on the battlefield.

* * *

If not by 700, or 650, or even 600 BC when *did* the phalanx take its classical form? This is not a question easily answered, and all I can do here is point out that it is not clear whether the development was complete even by the time of the Persian Wars.

Consider

1. **Describe the various stages of hoplite battle that Hanson relates. How closely does Hanson's description match that found in the ancient sources, especially Thucydides' account of the Battle of Mantinea?**
2. **Does the orthodox model of hoplite warfare, developed mainly from sources of the classical period, fit the evidence of the archaic poets such as Tyrtaeus?**
3. **How about the images found on the Chigi vase?**
4. **Compare van Wees' reconstruction to the traditional account of hoplite battle, especially the role played by the hoplite shield. Consider how both Hanson and van Wees use both the literary and iconographical evidence?**
5. **Why might archaic warriors have integrated light- and heavy-armed troops in a manner contrary to later practice?**
6. **How would the presence of archers in the archaic phalanx affect the orthodox view? Why or why not is each scholar's model for hoplite battle realistic?**

CHAPTER 3
THE SPARTAN REVOLUTION

❦

THE GOVERNMENT AND WAY OF LIFE that characterized ancient Sparta has fascinated historians, philosophers, and political theorists since antiquity. Plato and Aristotle, for example, preferred the "mixed" constitution of the Spartans over the democracy of classical Athens. The Jewish historian Josephus, writing in Greek in the first century AD, remarked that "all hymn the praises of Sparta." Succeeding thinkers ranging from Machiavelli to Rousseau often viewed Sparta as a model for the constitution of liberty. Even the development of liberal democracy in the eighteenth century and the tendency of scholars since the 1930s to consider Sparta the forerunner of the totalitarian state have not destroyed the Spartan mirage. Modern readers continue to admire the institutions idealized by the ancient sources. This chapter sets forth the constitution and social structure of ancient Sparta and asks how and why such a polis came into existence and sustained itself for centuries.

In the ninth and eighth centuries BC, many Greek poleis witnessed a dramatic rise in population. Despite remarkable developments in agriculture, farmers were unable to meet the growing demand for food. As a result, many Greek states, such as Corinth and Eretria, sent out colonies in the eighth and seventh centuries to deal with the problem of land hunger. The Spartans, on the other hand, acquired fertile land by becoming the masters of all Laconia in the mid-eighth century. Then, between the late eighth and seventh centuries the Spartans fought the First and Second Messenian Wars. These long struggles culminated in Sparta's appropriation of the land of Messenia and the subjugation of the Messenians to the serf-like condition known as helotry. The helots, by working the land for their Spartan masters and paying a rent in kind, made it possible and necessary for the Spartans to devote themselves full time to matters of state, especially military training. By the mid-sixth century Sparta had become the most powerful state in Greece and had established a reputation for invincibility in hoplite warfare.

The Spartan constitution and social institutions fostered the development of a military state. The government, a mixture of monarchy, oligarchy, and democracy, was renowned for its stability. A severe state education (*agoge*) that regulated a citizen's upbringing from age 7 until age 18 defined Spartan society. Full citizens, known as Spartiates or equals (*homoioi*), had to submit to government control over nearly every aspect of their public and private lives. The banishment of all superfluous wealth, moreover, helped instill in the Spartiates a degree of loyalty and obedience to the state unparalleled in ancient Greece. But it was the Spartans' need to dominate the helots for sustenance that played an important role in the evolution of their unique social, political, and economic system. Scholars have traditionally argued that the constant threat of a rebellion by Laconian and Messenian helots, who vastly outnumbered the Spartiates, drove the Spartans to create their way of life. Recently this view has been challenged by scholars who believe that the helot threat did not determine Spartan policy to such a great extent.

Ancient Sources

1. Herodotus, *Histories,* 1.65–66, THE LEGEND OF LYCURGUS
2. Plutarch, *Life of Lycurgus,* 5–10; 13–18; 24–29, THE SPARTAN CONSTITUTION
3. Tyrtaeus (Fragments), EARLY SPARTAN HISTORY
4. Xenophon, *Constitution of the Lacedaemonians* (abridged), THE SPARTAN SYSTEM
5. Aristotle, *Politics,* 1269a–1271b, CRITIQUE OF THE SPARTAN CONSTITUTION
6. Thucydides 4.80, THE HELOT THREAT
7. Thucydides 5.23.3, THE ALLIANCE OF SPARTA AND ATHENS IN 421
8. Xenophon, *Hellenica,* THE REBELLION OF CINADON

Opinions of Modern Scholars

1. From Paul Cartledge, "Rebels and Sambos in Classical Greece: A Comparative View"
2. From Richard Talbert, "The Role of the Helots in the Class Struggle at Sparta"

ANCIENT SOURCES FOR THE SPARTAN REVOLUTION

The Spartan state, its constitution and the mode of life of its citizens, has exercised a fascination on the ancient Greeks as well as on modern students of the Greek world. Ancient tradition ascribed Sparta's peculiar constitution to a single law-giver, Lycurgus, who is said to have reformed the state and set forth a new way of life at a single stroke as early as the eighth or even the ninth century BC. Many modern scholars reject the idea of a single reform by a single lawgiver and some even deny that "Lycurgus" ever existed. Most scholars, in any case, agree on a more gradual change but one so fundamental that it deserves the name "revolution." However, they do not agree on the date of the change or, more important, its causes. The following selections contain most of the important ancient evidences.

1. THE LEGEND OF LYCURGUS

Herodotus gives the earliest account of "Lycurgus" and his reform of the Spartan constitution.

65 At an earlier date [the Spartans] had been the worst governed people in Greece, both in their internal and external relations—for they would have no dealings of any kind with strangers. How the change to good government came about I will now relate. Lycurgus, a distinguished Spartan, visited the Delphic oracle, and no sooner had he entered the shrine than he was greeted with these words:

Hither to my rich temple have you come, Lycurgus,
Dear to Zeus and to all gods that dwell in
   Olympus.

I know not whether to declare you human or
   divine—
Yet I incline to believe, Lycurgus, that you are a god.

There is a story that the Priestess also revealed to him the system of government which obtains at Sparta today, but the Lacedaemonians themselves say that Lycurgus brought it from Crete after he became guardian of his nephew Leobotas, king of Sparta, and acted as his regent; for it is a fact that as soon as he received this appointment he made fundamental changes in the laws and took good care that the new ones should not be broken. Later he reorganized the army, introducing the system of messes and the new tactical divisions of squadrons and companies, in addition to the new civil offices of Ephor and Elder.

[66] By these changes Spartan government was put upon a sound basis, and when Lycurgus died, a temple was built in his honour, and he is still regarded with profound reverence.

2. THE SPARTAN CONSTITUTION

Plutarch, the Greek biographer of the first and second century AD, discusses the radical transformation of the Spartan constitution in his *Life of Lycurgus*. Although writing biography many centuries after the events he describes, Plutarch is an important source for ancient historians, not least because he had access to many contemporary sources now lost (e.g., the Aristotelian *Laconian Constitution*). His intention was primarily moral and he did not intend to provide a detailed historical account, but his library was superb and he has preserved much material that would otherwise have been lost. Plutarch's sources included the works of the comic poets, historians, political theorists, and documentary inscriptions. In the beginning of his *Lycurgus*, Plutarch notes the uncertainty that surrounds the date, work, and very existence of the legendary lawgiver of Sparta. He settles on the ancient equivalent of a ninth-century date and mentions that Lycurgus consulted the oracle of Apollo at Delphi to determine what changes were necessary to remedy the ills of the state at that time.

5. First and most significant among Lycurgus' numerous innovations was the institution of the Elders. According to Plato, its combination with the kings' arrogant rule and the right to an equal vote on the most important matters, produced security and at the same time sound sense. For the state was unstable, at one moment inclining towards the kings and virtual tyranny, at another towards the people and democracy. But now by placing the office of the Elders in the middle as a kind of ballast, and thus striking a balance, it found the safest arrangement and organization, with the twenty-eight Elders always siding with the kings when it was a matter of resisting democracy, yet in turn reinforcing the people against the development of tyranny... In my view the main reason for fixing upon this number of Elders was so that the total should be thirty when the two kings were added to the twenty-eight.

6. Lycurgus was so enthusiastic about this council that he brought an oracle about it from Delphi which they call a *rhetra*. It goes as follows: after dedicating a temple to Zeus Scyllania and Athena Scyllania, forming *phylai* and creating *obai*, and instituting a Gerousia of thirty including the founder-leaders, then from season to season *apellaze* between *Babyca* and Cnacion so as to propose and withdraw. But to the people should be the right to respond as well as power. In this the phrases "forming *phylai*" and "creating *obai*" refer to the division and distribution of the people into groups, the former of which he termed *phylai*, the latter *obai*. The "founder-leaders" means the kings, while "to *apellaze*" means to summon the assembly, because Lycurgus related the origin and source of his constitution to Pythian Apollo... When the populace was assembled, Lycurgus permitted no one else except the Elders and kings to make a proposal, although the authority to decide upon what the latter put forward did belong to the people. Later, however, when the people distorted proposals and mauled them by their deletions and additions, the kings Polydorus and Theopompus supplemented the *rhetra* as follows: "If the people should make a crooked choice, the Elder and the founder-leaders are to set it aside"—that is, not to confirm it, but to withdraw it completely and to dismiss the people because they are altering and reformulating the proposal contrary to what was best. Moreover these kings persuaded the city that the god had ordered this supplement—as Tyrtaeus seems to be recalling in the following lines:

Having listened to Phoebus they brought home
    from Pytho
The oracles of the god and his words which were to
    be fulfilled:
To rule in council is for the kings (who are esteemed
    by the gods
And whose care is the lovely city of Sparta),
And for the aged Elders; but then it is for the
    common people
To respond in turn with straight *rhetras*.

7. [...] It was apparently about 130 [years?] after Lycurgus' time that the first ephors were appointed, headed by Elatus, during the reign of Theopompus...By its renunciation of excessive authority and the related resentment, the Spartan kingship escaped the danger of suffering the fate which the Messenians and Argives inflicted upon their kings, who refused to concede anything or yield any of their authority to the popular element...

8. Lycurgus' second, and most revolutionary, reform was his redistribution of the land. For there was dreadful inequality; many destitute people without means were congregating in the city, while wealth had poured completely into just a few hands. In order to expel arrogance, envy, crime, luxury and those yet older and more serious political afflictions, wealth and poverty, Lycurgus persuaded the citizens to pool all the land and then redistribute it afresh. Then they would all live on equal terms with one another, with the same amount of property to support each, and they would seek to be first only in merit. There would be no distinction or inequality between individuals except for what censure of bad conduct and praise of good would determine.

Acting upon his word, Lycurgus distributed the rest of Laconia to the *perioeci* in 30,000 lots and divided the part subject to the city of Sparta into 9,000. This was the number of lots for Spartiates....Each person's lot was sufficient to provide a rent of 70 *medimni* of barley for a man, and 12 for his wife, along with proportionate quantities of fresh produce...

9. He attempted to divide up their movable property too, in order to remove inequalities and contrasts altogether. But when he saw their adverse reaction to outright expropriation, he went about this in a different way and devised constitutional measures against their greed. First he declared that all gold and silver coinage was now invalid, and decreed that only iron should be used as currency; and then he assigned a low value to even a great weight and mass of this, so that a sum of ten *minas* demanded substantial storage space in a house and a waggon to shift it. Once this was made the legal tender, many types of crime disappeared from Sparta...

After this he effected an expulsion of useless and superfluous alien crafts...Thus gradually cut off from the things that animate and feed it, luxury atrophied of its own accord...

10. With the aim of stepping up the attack on luxury and removing the passion for wealth, he introduced his third and finest reform, the establishment of common messes. The intention was that they should assemble together and eat the same specified meat-sauces and cereals. This prevented them from spending the time at home, lying at table on expensive couches, being waited upon by confectioners and chefs, fattened up in the dark like gluttonous animals, and ruining themselves physically as well as morally, and by giving free rein to every craving and excess which demanded lengthy slumbers, warm baths, plenty of rest, and, in a sense, daily nursing...

* * *

13. Lycurgus did not put his laws in writing: in fact one of the so-called *rhetras* is a prohibition to this effect. Instead he reckoned that the guiding principles of most importance for the happiness and excellence of a state would remain securely fixed if they were embedded in the citizens' character and training...

Thus, as has been explained, one of the *rhetras* prohibited the use of written laws. Another in turn was directed against extravagance, to the effect that in every house the ceiling should be made with an axe, and the doors only with a saw, not with any other tools...It was such conditioning which (according to the story) prompted the elder Leotychidas, when he was dining at Corinth and viewed the lavish, coffered design of the ceiling of the room, to ask his host if timber there grew square...

Ordinances such as these, then, Lycurgus called *rhetras*, because they were considered to come from the god and to be oracles.

14. Since he regarded the upbringing of children as the greatest and noblest responsibility of the legislator, at an early stage he took his start from that by first showing concern for matters relating to marriages and births...Lycurgus...showed all possible concern for [women] too. First he toughened them physically by making them run and wrestle and throw the discus and javelin. Thereby their children in embryo would make a strong start in strong bodies and would develop better, while the women themselves would also bear their pregnancies with vigour and would meet the challenge of childbirth in a successful, relaxed way. He did away with prudery, sheltered upbringing and effeminacy of any kind. He made young girls no less than young men grow, used to walking nude in processions, as well as to dancing and singing at certain festivals with the young men present and looking on. On some occasions the girls would make fun of each of the young men, helpfully criticizing their mistakes. On other occasions they would rehearse in song the praises which they had composed about those meriting them, so that they filled the youngsters with a great sense of ambition and rivalry. For the one who was praised for his manliness and became a celebrated figure to the girls went off priding himself on their compliments; whereas the jibes of their playful humour were no less cutting than warnings of a serious type, especially as the kings and the Elders attended the spectacle along with the rest of the citizens.

There was nothing disreputable about the girls' nudity. It was altogether modest, and there was no hint of immorality. Instead it encouraged simple habits and an enthusiasm for physical fitness, as well as giving the female sex a taste of masculine gallantry, since it too was granted equal participation in both excellence and ambition. As a result the women came to talk as well as to think in the way that Leonidas' wife Gorgo is said to have done. For when some woman, evidently a foreigner, said to her: "You Laconian women are the only ones who can rule men," she replied: "That is because we are the only ones who give birth to men."

15. There were then also these inducements to marry. I mean the processions of girls, and the nudity and the competitions which the young men watched, attracted by a compulsion not of an intellectual type, but (as Plato says) a sexual one. In addition Lycurgus placed a certain civil disability on those who did not marry, for they were excluded from the spectacle of the Gymnopaediae. In winter the magistrates would order them to parade naked in a circle around the *agora* and as they paraded they sang a special song composed about themselves, which said that their punishment was fair because they were flouting the laws. In addition they were deprived of the respect which young men habitually showed their elders. Thus nobody objected to what was said to Dercyllidas, even though he was a distinguished general. When he approached, one of the younger men did not give up his seat to him, but said: "You have produced no son who will give his seat to me."

The custom was to capture women for marriage — not when they were slight or immature, but when they were in their prime and ripe for it. The so-called "bridesmaid" took charge of the captured girl. She first shaved her head to the scalp, then dressed her in a man's cloak and sandals, and laid her down alone on a mattress in dark. The bridegroom — who was not drunk and thus not impotent, but was sober as always — first had dinner in the messes, then would slip in, undo her belt, lift her and carry her to the bed. After spending only a short time with her he would depart discreetly so as to sleep wherever he usually did along with the other young men. And this continued to be his practice thereafter: while spending the days with his contemporaries, and going to sleep with them, he would warily visit his bride in secret, ashamed and apprehensive in case someone in the house might notice him. His bride at the same time devised schemes and helped to plan how they might meet each other unobserved at suitable moments. It was not just for a short period that young men would do this, but for long enough that some might even have children before they saw their own wives in daylight. Such intercourse was not only an exercise in self-control and moderation, but also meant that partners were fertile physically, always fresh for love, and ready for intercourse rather than being sated and pale from unrestricted sexual activity. Moreover some lingering glow of desire and affection was always left in both.

After making marriage as modest and orderly as this, Lycurgus showed equal concern for removing absurd, unmanly jealousy. While excluding from marriage any kind of outrageous and disorderly behaviour, he made it honourable for worthy men to share children and their production, and derided people who hold that there can be no combination or sharing of such things, and who avenge any by assassinations and wars. Thus if an older man with a young wife should take a liking to one of the well-bred young men and approve of him he might well introduce him to her so as to fill her with noble sperm and then adopt the child as his own. Conversely a respectable man who admired someone else's wife noted for her lovely children and her good sense, might gain the husband's permission to sleep with her—thereby planting in fruitful soil, so to speak, and producing fine children who would be linked to fine ancestors by blood and family.

First and foremost Lycurgus considered children to belong not privately to their fathers, but jointly to the city, so that he wanted citizens produced not from random partners, but from the best...What was thus practised in the interests of breeding and of the state was at that time so far removed from the laxity for which the women later became notorious, that there was absolutely no notion of adultery among them. There is a story recorded about Geradas, a Spartiate of really ancient times, who when asked by a foreigner what their punishment for adulterers was, said: "There is no adulterer among us, stranger." When the latter replied: "But what if there should be one?" Geradas' answer was: "His fine would be a great bull which bends over Mount Taygetus to drink from the Eurotas." The foreigner was amazed at this and said: "But how could there be a bull of such size?" At which Geradas laughed and said: "But how could there be an adulterer at Sparta?" This, then, concludes my investigation of their marriages.

16. The father of a newborn child was not entitled to make his own decision about whether to rear it, but brought it in his arms to a particular spot termed a *lesche* where the eldest men of his tribe sat. If after examination the baby proved well built and sturdy they instructed the father to bring it up, and assigned it one of the 9,000 lots of land. But if it was puny and deformed, they dispatched it to what was called "the place of rejection" ('Apothetae'), a precipitous spot by Mount Taygetus, considering it better both for itself and the state that the child should die if right from its birth it was poorly endowed for health or strength...

Neither was it permissible for each father to bring up and educate his son in the way he chose. Instead, as soon as boys reached the age of seven, Lycurgus took care of them all himself and distributed them into Troops: here he accustomed them to live together and be brought up together, playing and learning as a group. The captain of [the troop] was conferred upon the boy who displayed the soundest

judgement and the best fighting spirit. The others kept their eyes on him, responded to his instructions, and endured their punishments from him, so that as a practice in learning ready obedience. Moreover as they exercised boys were constantly watched by their elders, who were always spurring them on to fight and contend with one another: in this their chief object was to get to know each boy's character, in particular how bold he was, and how far he was likely to stand his ground in combat.

The boys learned to read and write no more than was necessary. Otherwise their whole education was aimed at developing smart obedience, perseverance under stress, and victory in battle. So as they grew older they intensified their physical training, and got into the habit of cropping their hair, going barefoot, and exercising naked. From the age of twelve they never wore a tunic, and were given only one cloak a year. Their bodies were rough, and knew nothing of baths or oiling: only on a few days in the year did they experience such delights. They slept together by Squadron and Troop on mattresses which they made up for themselves from the tips of reeds growing along the River Eurotas, broken off by hand without the help of any iron blade. During winter they added the so-called thistledown and mixed it into the mattresses, since it was a substance thought to give out warmth.

17. By this age the boys came to be courted by lovers from among the respectable young men. The older men, too, showed even more interest, visiting the gymnasia frequently and being present when the boys fought and joked with one another. This was not just idle interest: instead there was a sense in which everyone regarded himself as father, tutor and commander of each boy. As a result everywhere, on all occasions, there would be somebody to reprimand and punished the boy who slipped up. In addition a Trainer-in-Chief was appointed from among the men with outstanding qualities; they in turn chose as leader for each Troop the one out of the so-called Eirens who had the most discretion and fighting spirit. Those who have proceeded two years beyond the boys' class are termed Eirens, and the oldest boys Melleirens ("prospective Eirens").

So such an Eiren, twenty years of age, commands those under him in his Troop's fights, while in his quarters he has them serve him his meals like servants. The burlier boys he instructs to bring wood, the slighter ones to collect vegetables. They steal what they fetch, some of them entering gardens, others slipping into the men's messes with a fine mixture of cunning and caution. If a boy is caught, he receives many lashes of the whip for proving to be a clumsy, unskilled thief. The boys also eat whatever provisions they can, thereby learning how to pounce skilfully upon those who are asleep or keeping guard carelessly. A boy is beaten and goes hungry if he is caught. The aim of providing them with only sparse fare is that they should be driven to make up its deficiencies by resort to daring and villainy...

18. The care which the boys take over their stealing is illustrated by the story of the one who had stolen a fox cub and had it concealed inside his cloak: in order to escape detection he was prepared to have his insides clawed and bitten out by the animal, and even to die. This tale is certainly not incredible, judging from Spartan ephebes today. I have witnessed many of them dying under the lashes they received at the altar of Artemis Orthia.

* * *

24. Spartiates' training extended into adulthood, for no one was permitted to live as he pleased. Instead, just as in a camp, so in the city, they followed a prescribed lifestyle and devoted themselves to communal concerns. They viewed themselves absolutely as part of their country, rather than as individuals, and so unless assigned a particular job they would always be observing boys and giving them some useful piece of instruction, or learning themselves from their elders. Abundant leisure was unquestionably among the wonderful benefits which Lycurgus had conferred upon his fellow citizens. While he totally banned their involvement in any mutual craft, there was equally no need for them to amass wealth (with all the work and concentration which that entails), since riches were emphatically neither envied nor esteemed. The helots worked the land for them and paid over the amount mentioned earlier. There was a Spartiate who happened to be in Athens when the courts were sitting, and he learned that a man who had incurred some penalty for refusal to work was going home depressed, escorted by some sympathetic friends who shared his mood. The Spartiate requested those who were there with him to point out this man who had been penalized for his freedom. This illustrates how they thought of a preoccupation with working at a craft and with moneymaking as only fit for slaves! As might be expected, legal disputes disappeared along with

coinage, since there was no longer greed or want among them, but instead equal enjoyment of plenty and the sense of ease which comes from simple living. Except when they went on campaign, all their time was taken up by choral dances, festivals, feasts, hunting expeditions, physical exercise and conversation....

25. Altogether he accustomed citizens to have no desire for a private life, nor knowledge of one, but rather to be like bees, always attached to the community, swarming together around their leader, and almost ecstatic with fervent ambition to devote themselves entirely to their country...

26. As already mentioned, Lycurgus himself appointed Elders initially from among those who had been associated with his plan. But later be arranged that whenever an Elder died his place should be taken over by the man over sixty whose merits were regarded as most outstanding. And this contest seemed to be the greatest in the world and the one most worth competing for. In it a man was to be chosen not as the swiftest of swift men nor the strongest of strong ones, but as the best and wisest of the good and wise, who as a lifelong reward for his merits would have in effect sweeping authority in the state, with control over death and loss of citizen rights and the most important matters generally...

27. Consequently [Lycurgus] did not grant Spartiates permission to be away from the city and to travel freely, acquiring foreign habits and copying lifestyles based upon no training as well as types of government different from that of Sparta. In fact he even expelled those people who were pouring into the city and congregating there for no useful purpose. He was not afraid (as Thucydides claims) that they might imitate the form of government or might gain some knowledge to enhance their personal qualities: his fear was rather that they might develop into teachers of evil practices. By definition foreigners must bring in foreign ideas with them, and novel ideas lead to novel attitudes. Hence inevitably many emotions and preferences emerge which—if the existing government be likened to a piece of music—are out of tune with it. Thus it was the need to protect the city from being invaded by harmful practices which concerned him more than any physical infection by unhealthy immigrants.

28. In all this there is no trace of the inequity or arrogance with which Lycurgus' laws are charged by some people; in their view the laws are well designed to develop valour, but fail to foster the practice of justice. It may be that Plato was likewise led to this opinion of Lycurgus and his constitution because of the Spartiates' so-called *krypteia* assuming this really was one of Lycurgus' institutions, as Aristotle has maintained. Its character was as follows.

Periodically the overseers of the young men would dispatch into the countryside in different directions the ones who appeared to be particularly intelligent; they were equipped with daggers and basic rations, but nothing else. By day they would disperse to obscure spots in order to hide and rest. At night they made their way to roads and murdered any helot whom they caught. Frequently, too, they made their way through the fields, killing the helots who stood out for their physique and strength. Similarly in his *History of the Peloponnesian War* Thucydides tells how those helots who had been singled out by the Spartiates for their bravery were first crowned as if they had been granted their freedom, and made a round of the sanctuaries of the gods; but then a little later they all vanished—over 2,000 of them—and nobody either at the time itself or later was able to explain how they had been eliminated. Aristotle makes the further notable point that immediately upon taking up office the ephors would declare war on the helots, so that they could be killed without pollution.

In other ways too, Spartiates' treatment of helots was callous and brutal. They would force them, for instance, to drink quantities of unmixed wine and then they would bring them into messes to show the young men what drunkenness was like. They would also order them to perform songs and dances which were vulgar and ridiculous, while excluding them from the ones fit for free men. So later, according to reports, when Theban forces penetrated Laconia and told the helots they captured to sing the works of Terpander and Alcman and Spendon the Spartan, the latter declined to, claiming that their masters did not approve. The class distinction is reflected fully in the statement that there is nothing to match either the freedom of the free man at Sparta or the slavery of the slave. In my view such ill-treatment on the part of the Spartiates only developed later—especially after the Great Earthquake, when the helots are said to have taken the offensive with the Messenians, to have done the country tremendous damage and to have posed a dire threat to the city. Personally I would not attribute such a foul exercise as the Krypteia to Lycurgus; in my estimation his disposition was otherwise mild and fair, a view which the god showed that he shared too.

29. Once he saw that his most vital measures had gained firm acceptance, and the form of government fostered by him was acquiring enough strength to support and protect itself unaided, then, like the god in Plato's description who was delighted at his universe coming into being and making its first movement, Lycurgus was deeply moved and well pleased by the beauty and extent of his legislation now that it was in action and proceeding on its way. In so far as human foresight could achieve this, he longed to leave it immortal and immutable in the future. So he summoned everyone to an assembly and declared that while what had already been established was sufficient and appropriate to secure the happiness and excellence of the state, there remained the greatest, most essential measure, which would not be disclosed to them before he had consulted the oracle. Consequently they must abide by the laws laid down without dropping or changing any until he should return in person from Delphi. On his return he would do whatever the god recommended. When they unanimously agreed to this and urged him to proceed, Lycurgus made first the kings and Elders, and then the other citizens, swear that they would abide by the established constitution, and continue to use it until he should return. Then he set out for Delphi.

Once he had reached the oracle and sacrificed to the god, he inquired if the laws which he had laid down were of sufficient quality to secure the happiness and excellence of the state. The god replied that the quality of the laws was high and that by adhering to Lycurgus' constitution the city would enjoy the most brilliant reputation. Lycurgus had this oracle written down and sent it to Sparta. He then made a second personal sacrifice to the god, embraced his friends and his son, and determined never to release the citizens from their oath, but to commit voluntary suicide on the spot. He had reached an age when choice of whether or not to go on living, and when those close to him seemed comfortably enough settled. So he starved himself to death. In his opinion it was wrong for a statesman's death to be of no benefit to his city or for the ending of his life to be valueless; instead there should be an element of distinction and effectiveness about it. In his own case, after his wonderful achievements, his end really would serve to crown his good fortune. As to the citizens, he would leave them his death as guarantor of the excellent benefits which he had provided for them during his lifetime, since they had sworn to observe his constitution until he should return. And he was not mistaken in his reckoning, since Sparta occupied the front for some 500 years thanks to her use of the laws of Lycurgus, which were not altered by any of the fourteen kings after him down to Agis the son of Archidamus. For the institution of ephors served to reinforce the constitution rather than weaken it, and even though it appeared to be to the people's advantage, in fact it strengthened the aristocracy.

Questions

1. **What new laws and constitutional changes did Lycurgus bring about in Sparta according to Plutarch?**
2. **In what ways are those laws and changes revolutionary? In what ways are they not?**
3. **Later political thinkers, such as Plato, claimed that Sparta enjoyed a "mixed" constitution. Does Plutarch's account support this view? Why or why not?**
4. **How do you think Plutarch's *Life of Lycurgus* has contributed to the development of the Spartan "mirage"?**

3.   EARLY SPARTAN HISTORY

The fragments of Tyrtaeus' poems which survive are a major source of our knowledge of the early history of Sparta. The following selections from Pausanias and the Scholiast on Plato and Strabo are reprinted from *Greek Elegy and Iambus*, Vol. I, Loeb Classical Library, translation by J. M. Edmunds.

Pausanias *Description of Greece* [the Second Messenian War]: The man who brought the war to an end was this Theopompus, as is testified by the Elegiac lines of Tyrtaeus, which *say* "to our King" etc. (II. 1–2).

Scholiast on Plato: On Tyrtaeus' arrival in Lacedaemon he became inspired, and urged the Spartans to end the war against the Messenians by every means in his power, among others by the famous line "Messene *is* good," etc.

Strabo *Geography*: Messene was taken after a war of nineteen years; compare Tyrtaeus: (11.4–8).

...to our king, the friend of the Gods, Theopompus, through whom we took spacious Messene, Messene so good to plough and so good to plant, for which there fought ever unceasingly nineteen years, keeping an unfaltering heart, the spearmen fathers of our fathers, and in the twentieth year the foeman left his rich lands and fled from the great uplands of Ithome.

Pausanias *Description of Greece*: The vengeance the Spartans took on the Messenians is referred to in these lines of Tyrtaeus:

...galled with great burdens like asses, bringing to their lords under grievous necessity a half of all the fruit of the soil.

And that they were obliged to join in their lamentations he shows in the following couplet:

making lamentation for their lords both themselves and their wives, whenever one was overtaken with the dolorous fate of Death.

Strabo *Geography*: They fought more than once because of rebellion on the part of the Messenians. The first conquest, according to the poems of Tyrtaeus, took place two generations before his time, and the second, when they rebelled in alliance with the Argives, Arcadians, and Pisatans, the Arcadians making Aristocrates king of Orchomenus their general and the Pisatans Pantaleon son of Omphalion; in the latter war he declares that he led the Lacedaemonians himself.

Questions

1. **What do these fragments of Tyrtaeus state or imply about the relationship between the Spartans and Messenians?**
2. **How might the poems of Tyrtaeus help scholars reconstruct early Spartan history?**

---

4. THE SPARTAN SYSTEM

Xenophon (c. 430–354 BC) was an Athenian who was exiled and lived much of his life in the Peloponnesus. He fought in the Spartan army as a mercenary under King Agesilaus whose friend and admirer he was. In his *Constitution of the Spartans*, Xenophon intends to show that "the laws of Lycurgus" were responsible for the greatness and fame of the Lacedaemonians more than to write a constitutional treatise.

1. It occurred to me one day that Sparta, though among the most thinly populated of states, was evidently the most powerful and most celebrated city in Greece; and I fell to wondering how this could have happened. But when I considered the institutions of the Spartans, I wondered no longer.

Lycurgus, who gave them the laws that they obey, and to which they owe their prosperity, I do regard with wonder; and I think that he reached the utmost limit of wisdom. For it was not by imitating other states, but by devising a system utterly different from that of most others, that he made his country preeminently prosperous.

First, to begin at the beginning, I will take the begetting of children. In other states the girls who are destined to become mothers and are brought up in the approved fashion live on the very plainest fare, with a most meagre allowance of delicacies. Wine is either withheld altogether, or, if allowed them, is diluted with water. The rest of the Greeks expect their girls to imitate the sedentary life that is typical of handicraftsmen—to keep quiet and do wool-work. How, then, is it to be expected that women so brought up will bear fine children?

But Lycurgus thought the labour of slave women sufficient to supply clothing. He believed motherhood to be the most important function of freeborn woman. Therefore, in the first place, he insisted on physical training for the female no less than for the male sex: moreover, he instituted races and trials of strength for women competitors as for men, believing that if both parents are strong they produce more vigorous offspring.

He noticed, too, that, during the time immediately succeeding marriage, it was usual elsewhere for the husband to have unlimited intercourse with his wife. The rule that he adopted was the opposite of this: for he laid it down that the husband should be ashamed to be seen entering his wife's room or leaving it. With this restriction on intercourse the desire of the one for the other must necessarily be increased, and their offspring was bound to be more vigorous than if they were surfeited with one another. In addition to this, he withdrew from men the right to take a wife whenever they chose, and insisted on their marrying in the prime of their manhood, believing that this too promoted the production of fine children. It might happen, however, that an old man had a young wife; and he observed that old men keep a very jealous watch over their young wives. To meet these cases he instituted an entirely different system by requiring the elderly husband to introduce into his house some man whose physical and moral qualities he admired, in order to beget children. On the other hand, in case a man did not want to cohabit with his wife and nevertheless desired children of whom he could be proud, he made it lawful for him to choose a woman who was the mother of a fine family and of high birth, and if he obtained her husband's consent, to make her the mother of his children…

Thus his regulations with regard to the begetting of children were in sharp contrast with those of other states. Whether he succeeded in populating Sparta with a race of men remarkable for their size and strength anyone who chooses may judge for himself.

2. Having dealt with the subject of birth, I wish next to explain the educational system of Lycurgus, and how it differs from other systems.

In the other Greek states parents who profess to give their sons the best education place their boys under the care and control of a moral tutor as soon as they can understand what is said to them, and send them to a school to learn letters, music and the exercises of the wrestling-ground. Moreover, they soften the children's feet by giving them sandals, and pamper their bodies with changes of clothing; and it is customary to allow them as much food as they can eat.

Lycurgus, on the contrary, instead of leaving each father to appoint a slave to act as tutor, gave the duty of controlling the boys to a member of the class from which the highest offices are filled, in fact to the "Warden" as he is called. He gave this person authority to gather the boys together, to take charge of them and to punish them severely in case of misconduct. He also assigned to him a staff of youths provided with whips to chastise them when necessary; and the result is that modesty and obedience are inseparable companions at Sparta. Instead of softening the boys' feet with sandals he required them to harden their feet by going without shoes. He believed that if this habit were cultivated it would enable them to climb hills more easily and descend steep inclines with less danger, and that a youth who had accustomed himself to go barefoot would leap and jump and run more nimbly than a boy in sandals. And instead of letting them be pampered in the matter of clothing, he introduced the custom of wearing one garment throughout the year, believing that they would thus be better prepared to face changes of heat and cold. As to the food, he required the prefect to bring with him such a moderate amount of it that the boys would never suffer from repletion, and would know what it was to go with their hunger unsatisfied; for he believed that those who underwent this training would be better able to continue working on an empty stomach, if necessary, and would be capable of carrying on longer without extra food, if the word of command were given to do so they would want fewer delicacies and would accommodate themselves more readily to anything put before them, and at the same time would enjoy better health. He also thought that a diet which made their bodies slim would do more to increase their height than one that consisted of flesh-forming food.

On the other hand, lest they should feel too much the pinch of hunger, while not giving them the opportunity of taking what they wanted without trouble he allowed them to alleviate their hunger by stealing something. It was not on account of a difficulty in providing for them that he encouraged them to get their food by their own cunning. No one, I suppose, can fail to see that. Obviously a man who intends to take to thieving must spend sleepless nights and play the deceiver and lie in ambush by day, and moreover, if he means to make a capture, he must have spies ready. There can be no doubt then, that all this education was planned by him in order to make the boys more resourceful in getting supplies, and better fighting men.

Someone may ask: But why, if he believed stealing to be a fine thing, did he have the boy who was caught beaten with many stripes? I reply: Because in all cases men punish a learner for not carrying out properly whatever he is taught to do. So the Spartans chastise those who get caught for stealing badly. He made it a point of honour to steal as many cheeses as possible [from the altar of Artemis Orthia], but appointed others to scourge the thieves, meaning to show thereby that by enduring pain for a short time one may win lasting fame and felicity. It is shown herein that where there is need of swiftness, the slothful, as usual, gets little profit and many troubles. …

I have now dealt with the Spartan system of education, and that of the other Greek states. Which system turns out men more obedient, more respectful, and more strictly temperate, anyone who chooses may once more judge for himself.

3. When a boy ceases to be a child, and begins to be a lad, others release him from his moral tutor and his schoolmaster: he is then no longer under a ruler and is allowed to go his own way. Here again Lycurgus introduced a wholly different system. For he observed that at this time of life self-will makes strong root in a boy's mind, a tendency to insolence manifests itself, and a keen appetite for pleasure in different forms takes possession of him. At this stage, therefore, he imposed on him a ceaseless round of work, and contrived a constant round of occupation. The penalty for shirking the duties was exclusion from all future honours. He thus caused not only the public authorities, but their relations also to take pains that the lads did not incur the contempt of their fellow citizens by flinching from their tasks.

Moreover, wishing modesty to be firmly rooted in them, he required them to keep their hands under their cloaks, to walk in silence, not to look about them, but to fix their eyes on the ground. The effect of this rule has been to prove that even in the matter of decorum the male is stronger than the female sex... Such was the care that he bestowed on the growing lads.

4. For those who had reached the prime of life he showed by far the deepest solicitude. For he believed that if these were of the right stamp they must exercise a powerful influence for good on the state. He saw that where the spirit of rivalry is strongest among the people, there the choruses are most worth hearing and the athletic contests afford the finest spectacle. He believed, therefore, that if he could match the young men together in a strife of valour, they too would reach a high level of manly excellence. I will proceed to explain, therefore, how he instituted matches between the young men.

The Ephors, then, pick out three of the very best among them. These three are called Commanders of the Guard. Each of them enrols a hundred others, stating his reasons for preferring one and rejecting another. The result is that those who fail to win the honour are at war both with those who sent them away and with their successful rivals; and they are on the watch for any lapse from the code of honour.

Here then you find that kind of strife that is dearest to the gods, and in the highest sense political—the strife that sets the standard of a brave man's conduct; and in which either party exerts itself to the end that it may never fall below its best, and that, when the time comes, every member of it may support the state with all his might. And they are bound, too, to keep themselves fit, for one effect of the strife is that they spar whenever they meet; but anyone present has a right to part the combatants. If anyone refuses to obey the mediator the Warden takes him to the Ephors; and they fine him heavily, in order to make him realize that he must never yield to a sudden impulse to disobey the laws.

To come to those who have passed the time of youth, and are now eligible to hold the great offices of state. While absolving these from the duty of bestowing further attention on their bodily strength, the other Greeks require them to continue serving in the army. But Lycurgus established the principle that for citizens of that age, hunting was the noblest occupation, except when some public duty prevented, in order that they might be able to stand the fatigues of soldiering as well as the younger men.

5. I have given a fairly complete account of the institutions of Lycurgus so far as they apply to the successive stages of life. I will now try to describe the system that he established for all alike. Lycurgus found the Spartans boarding at home like the other Greeks, and came to the conclusion that the custom was responsible for a great deal of misconduct. He therefore established the public messes outside in the open, thinking that this would reduce disregard of orders to a minimum. The amount of food he allowed was just enough to prevent them from getting either too much or too little to eat. But many extras are supplied from the spoils of the chase; and for these rich men sometimes substitute wheaten bread. Consequently the board is never bare until the company breaks up, and never extravagantly furnished. Another of his reforms was the abolition of compulsory drinking, which is the undoing alike of body of mind. But he allowed everyone to drink when he was thirsty, believing that drink is then most harmless and most welcome...

6. In the following respects, again, his institutions differ from the ordinary type. In most states every man has control of his own children, servants and goods. Lycurgus wanted to secure that the citizens should get some advantage from one another without doing any harm. He therefore gave every father authority over other men's children as well as over his own. When a man knows that fathers have this power, he is bound to rule the children over whom he exercises authority as he would wish his own to be ruled. If a boy tells his own father when he has been whipped by another father, it is a disgrace if the parent does not give his son another whipping. So completely do they trust one another not to give any improper orders to the children...

7. Nor does this exhaust the list of the customs established by Lycurgus at Sparta that are contrary to those of the other Greeks. In other states, I suppose, all men make as much money as they can. One is a farmer, another a ship-owner, another a merchant, and others live by different handicrafts. But at Sparta Lycurgus forbade freeborn citizens to have anything to do with business affairs. He insisted on their regarding as their own concern only those activities that make for civic freedom. Indeed, how should wealth be a serious object there, when he insisted on equal contributions to the food supply and on the same standard of living for all, and thus cut off the attraction of money for indulgence sake? Why, there is not even any need of money to spend on cloaks: for their adornment is due not to the price of their clothes, but to the excellent condition of their bodies. Nor yet is there any reason for amassing money in order to spend it on one's mess-mates; for he made it more respectable to help one's fellows by toiling with the body than by spending money, pointing out that toil is an employment of the soul, spending an employment of wealth.

By other enactments he rendered it impossible to make money in unfair ways. In the first place the system of coinage that he established was of such a kind that even a sum of ten minae could not be brought into a house without the master and the servants being aware of it: the money would fill a large space and need a wagon to draw it. Moreover, there is a right of search for gold and silver, and, in the event of discovery, the possessor is fined. Why, then, should money-making be a preoccupation in a state where the pains of its possession are more than the pleasures of its enjoyment?

8. To continue: we all know that obedience to the magistrates and the laws is found in the highest degree in Sparta. For my part, however, I think that Lycurgus did not so much as attempt to introduce this habit of discipline until he had secured agreement among the most important men in the state. I base my inference on the following facts. In other states the most powerful citizens do not even wish it to be thought that they fear the magistrates: they believe such fear to be a badge of slavery. But at Sparta the most important men show the utmost deference to the magistrates: they pride themselves on their humility, on running instead of walking to answer any call, in the belief that, if they lead, the rest will follow along the path of eager obedience. And so it has proved...

Among many excellent plans contrived by Lycurgus for encouraging willing obedience to the laws among the citizens, I think one of the most excellent was this: before delivering his laws to the people he paid a visit to Delphi, accompanied by the most important citizens, and inquired of the god whether it was desirable and better for Sparta that she should obey the laws that he himself had framed. Only when the god answered that it was better in every way did he deliver them, after enacting that to refuse obedience to laws given by the Pythian god was not only unlawful, but wicked.

9. The following achievement of Lycurgus, again, deserves admiration. He caused his people to choose an honourable death in preference to a disgraceful life. And, in fact, one would find on consideration that they actually lose a smaller proportion of their men than those who prefer to retire from the danger zone. To tell the truth, escape from premature death more generally goes with valour than with cowardice: for valour is actually easier and pleasanter and more resourceful and mightier. And obviously glory adheres to the side of valour, for all men want to ally themselves somehow with the brave.

However, it is proper not to pass over the means by which he contrived to bring about this result. Clearly, what he did was to ensure that the brave should have happiness, and the coward misery. For in other states when a man proves a coward, the only consequence is that he is called a coward. He goes to the same market as the brave man, sits beside him, attends the same gymnasium, if he chooses. But in Lacedaemon everyone would be ashamed to have a coward with him at the mess or to be matched with him in a wrestling bout. Often when sides are picked for a game of ball he is the odd man left out: in the chorus he is banished to the ignominious place; in the streets he is bound to make way; when he occupies a seat he must needs give it up, even to a junior; he must support his spinster relatives at home and must explain to them why they are old maids: he must make the best of a fireside without a wife, and yet pay forfeit for that: he may not stroll about with a cheerful countenance, nor behave as though he were a man of unsullied fame, or else he must submit to be beaten by his betters. Small wonder, I think, that where such a load of dishonour is laid on the coward, death seems preferable to a life so dishonoured, so ignominious.

10. The law by which Lycurgus encouraged the practice of virtue up to old age is another excellent measure in my opinion. By requiring men to face the ordeal of election to the Council of Elders near the end of life, he prevented neglect of high principles even in old age…

Again, the following surely entitles the work of Lycurgus to high admiration. He observed that where the cult of virtue is left to voluntary effort, the virtuous are not strong enough to increase the fame of their fatherland. So he compelled all men at Sparta to practise all the virtues in public life. And therefore, just as private individuals differ from one another in virtue according as they practise or neglect it, so Sparta, as a matter of course, surpasses all other states in virtue, because she alone makes a public duty of gentlemanly conduct. For was not this too a noble rule of his, that whereas other states punish only for wrong done to one's neighbour, he inflicted penalties no less severe on any who openly neglected to live as good a life as possible? For he believed, it seems, that enslavement, fraud, robbery, are crimes that injure only the victims of them; but the wicked man and the coward are traitors to the whole body politic. And so he had good reason, I think, for visiting their offences with the heaviest penalties.

And he laid on the people the duty of practising the whole virtue of a citizen as a necessity irresistible. For to all who satisfied the requirements of his code he gave equal rights of citizenship, without regard to bodily infirmity or want of money. But the coward who shrank from the task of observing the rules of his code he caused to be no more reckoned among the peers.

Now that these laws are of high antiquity there can be no doubt: for Lycurgus is said to have lived in the days of the Heracleidae. Nevertheless, in spite of their antiquity, they are wholly strange to others even at this day. Indeed, it is most astonishing that all men praise such institutions, but no state chooses to imitate them.

Questions

1. Compare Xenophon's account of the constitution of Lycurgus with that of Plutarch. In what ways are the versions of the two authors similar and how are they different?
2. Which factors might explain the similarities and differences between the two writers?

---

5.   CRITIQUE OF THE SPARTAN CONSTITUTION

Aristotle lived in the fourth century BC and his criticisms of Sparta's constitution in the *Politics* are influenced by the events of his time. Sparta had been in decline for a generation before Aristotle wrote his *Politics*. At the Battle of Leuctra in 371 the Spartans had suffered a devastating and humiliating defeat at the hands of the Thebans. The brilliant Theban general Epaminondas then led the first invasion of the Spartan homeland and a crusade to free Messenia from Spartan control. The Spartans lost the hegemony they had enjoyed over Greece since the end of the Peloponnesian War and never recovered. Yet it is the institutions themselves rather than their corruption that are judges and so the criticisms remain significant for the entirety of the Spartan experience.

1269a [1] On the subject of the constitution of Sparta and that of Crete, and virtually in regard to the other forms of constitution also, the questions that arise for consideration are two, one whether their legal structure has any feature that is admirable or the reverse in comparison with the best system, another whether it contains any provision that is really opposed to the fundamental principle and character of the constitution that the founders had in view.

[2] Now it is a thing admitted that a state that is to be well governed must be provided with leisure from menial occupations; but how this is to be provided it is not easy to ascertain. The serf class in Thessaly repeatedly rose against its masters, and so did the Helots at Sparta, where they are like an enemy constantly sitting in wait for the disasters of the Spartiates. **[3]** Nothing of the kind has hitherto occurred in Crete,

1269b the reason perhaps being that the neighbouring cities, even when at war with one another, in no instance ally themselves with the rebels, because as they themselves also possess a serf class this would not be for their interest; whereas the Laconians were entirely surrounded by hostile neighbours, Argives, Messenians and Arcadians. For with the Thessalians too the serf risings originally began because they were still at war with their neighbours, the Achaeans, Perrhaebi and Magnesians. **[4]** Also, apart from other drawbacks, the mere necessity of policing their serf class is a troublesome matter—the problem of how intercourse with them is to be carried on: if allowed freedom they grow insolent and claim to be as good as their masters, and if made to live a hard life they plot against them and hate them. It is clear therefore that those whose helot-system works out in this way do not discover the best mode of treating the problem. **[5]** Again, the freedom in regard to women is detrimental both in regard to the purpose of the constitution and in regard to the happiness of the state. For just as man and wife are part of a household, it is clear that the state also is divided nearly in half into its male and female population, so that in all constitutions in which the position of the women is badly regulated one-half of the state must be deemed to have been neglected in framing the law. And this has taken place in the state under consideration, for the lawgiver wishing the whole community to be hardy displays his intention clearly in relation to the men, but in the case of the women has entirely neglected the matter; for they live dissolutely in respect of every sort of dissoluteness, and luxuriously. **[6]** So

that the inevitable result is that in a state thus constituted wealth is held in honour, especially if it is the case that the people are under the sway of their women, as most of the military and warlike races are, except the Celts and such other races as have openly held in honour attachments between males. For it appears that the original teller of the legend had good reason for uniting Ares with Aphrodite, for all men of martial spirit appear to be attracted to the companionship either of male associates or of women. **[7]** Hence this characteristic existed among the Spartans, and in the time of their empire many things were controlled by the women; yet what difference does it make whether the women rule or the rulers are ruled by the women? The result is the same. And although bravery is of service for none of the regular duties of life, but if at all, in war, even in this respect the Spartans' women were most harmful; and they showed this at the time of the Theban invasion, for they rendered no useful service, like the women in other states, while they caused more confusion than the enemy. **[8]** It is true therefore that at the outset the freedom allowed to women at Sparta seems to have come about with good reason,

1270a for the Spartans used to be away in exile abroad for long periods on account of their military expeditions, both when fighting the war against the Argives and again during the war against the Arcadians and Messenians, and when they had turned to peaceful pursuits, they handed over themselves to the lawgiver already prepared for obedience by military life (for this has many elements of virtue), but as for the women, though it is said Lycurgus did attempt to bring them under the laws, yet since they resisted he gave it up. **[9]** So the Spartan women are, it is true, to blame for what took place then and therefore manifestly for the present defect; although for our own part we are not considering who deserves excuse or does not, but what is right or wrong in the constitution as it is. But, as was also said before, errors as regards the status of women seem not only to cause a certain unseemliness in the actual conduct of the state but to contribute in some degree to undue love of money. **[10]** For next to the things just spoken of one might censure the Spartan institutions with respect to the unequal distribution of wealth. It has come about that some of the Spartans own too much property and some extremely little; owing to which the land has fallen into few hands, and this has also been badly regulated by the laws; for the lawgiver made it dishonourable to sell a family's existing estate, and did so rightly, but he granted liberty to alienate land at will by gift or bequest; yet the result that has happened was bound to follow in the one case as well as in the other. **[11]** And also nearly two-fifths of the whole area of the country is owned by women, because of the number of women who inherit estates and the practice of giving large dowries; yet it would have been better if dowries had been prohibited by law or limited to a small or moderate amount; whereas in fact he is allowed to give an heiress in marriage to whomever he likes, and if he dies without having made directions as to this by will, whoever he leaves as his executor bestows her upon whom he chooses. As a result of this the country is capable of supporting fifteen hundred cavalry and thirty thousand heavy-armed troopers, they numbered not even a thousand. **[12]** And the defective nature of their system of land-tenure has been proved by the actual facts of history: the state did not succeed in enduring a single blow, but perished owing to the smallness of its population. They have a tradition that in the earlier reigns they used to admit foreigners to their citizenship, with the result that dearth of population did not occur in those days, although they were at war for a long period; and it is stated that at one time the Spartiates numbered as many as ten thousand. However, whether this is true or not, it is better for a state's male population to be kept up by measures to equalize property. **[13]** The law in relation to parentage is also somewhat adverse to the correction of this evil.

1270b For the lawgiver desiring to make the Spartiates as numerous as possible holds out inducements to the citizens to have as many children as possible: for they have a law releasing the man who has been father of three sons from military service, and exempting the father of four from all taxes. Yet it is clear that if a number of sons are born and the land is correspondingly divided there will inevitably come to be many poor men. **[14]** Moreover the regulations for the Ephorate are also bad. For this office has absolute control over their most important affairs, but the Ephors are appointed from the entire people, so that quite poor men often happen to get into the office, who owing to their poverty used to be easily bought. This was often manifested in earlier times, and also lately in the affair at Andros; for certain Ephors were corrupted with money and so far as lay in their power ruined the whole state. And because the office was too powerful, and equal to a tyranny,

the kings also were compelled to cultivate popular favour, so that in this way too the constitution was jointly injured, for out of an aristocracy came to be evolved a democracy. **[15]** Thus this office does, it is true, hold together the constitution—for the common people keep quiet because they have a share in the highest office of state, so that owing to the lawgiver's foresight, or else to accident, the Ephorate is advantageous for the conduct of affairs; for if a constitution is to be preserved, all the sections of the state must wish it to exist and to continue on the same lines; so the kings are in this frame of mind owing to their own honourable rank, the nobility owing to the office of the Elders, which is a prize of virtue, and the common people because of the Ephorate, **[16]** which is appointed from the whole population—but yet the Ephorate, though rightly open to all the citizens, ought not to be elected as it is now, for the method is too childish. And further the Ephors have jurisdiction in lawsuits of high importance, although they are any chance people, so that it would be better if they did not decide cases on their own judgement but by written rules and according to the laws. Also the mode of life of the Ephors is not in conformity with the aim of the state, for it is itself too luxurious, whereas in the case of the other citizens the prescribed life goes too far in the direction of harshness, so that they are unable to endure it, and secretly desert the law and enjoy the pleasures of the body. **[17]** Also their regulations for the office of the Elders are not good; it is true that if these were persons of a high class who had been adequately trained in manly valour, one might perhaps say that the institution was advantageous to the state, although their life-tenure of the judgeship in important trials is indeed a questionable feature (for there is old age of mind as well as of body);

1271a but as their education has been on such lines that even the lawgiver himself cannot trust in them as men of virtue, it is a dangerous institution. **[18]** And it is known that those who have been admitted to this office take bribes and betray many of the public interests by favouritism; so that it would be better if they were not exempt from having to render an account of their office, but at present they are. And it might be held that the magistracy of the Ephors serves to hold all the offices to account; but this gives altogether too much to the Ephorate, and it is not the way in which, as we maintain, officials ought to be called to account. Again, the procedure in the election of the Elders as a mode of selection is not only childish, but it is wrong that one who is to be the holder of this honourable office should canvass for it, for the man worthy of the office ought to hold it whether he wants to or not. [19] But as it is the lawgiver clearly does the same here as in the rest of the constitution: he makes the citizens ambitious and has used this for the election of the Elders, for nobody would ask for office if he were not ambitious; yet surely ambition and love of money are the motives that bring about almost the greatest part of the voluntary wrongdoing that takes place among mankind. [20] As to monarchy, the question whether it is not or is an advantageous institution for states to possess may be left to another discussion; but at all events it would be advantageous that kings should not be appointed as they are now, but chosen in each case with regard to their own life and conduct. But it is clear that even the lawgiver himself does not suppose that he can make the kings men of high character: at all events he distrusts them as not being persons of sufficient worth; owing to which the Spartans used to send their enemies with them as colleagues on embassies, and thought that the safety of the state depended on division between the kings. [21] Also the regulations for the public mess-tables called Phiditia have been badly laid down by their originator. The revenue for these ought to come rather from public funds, as in Crete; but among the Spartans everybody has to contribute, although some of them are very poor and unable to find money for this charge, so that the result is the opposite of what the lawgiver purposed. For he intends the organization of the common tables to be democratic, but when regulated by the law in this manner it works out as by no means democratic; for it is not easy for the very poor to participate, yet their established regulation for citizenship is that it is not to belong to one who is unable to pay this tax. [22] The law about the Admirals has been criticized by some other writers also, and rightly criticized; for it acts as a cause of sedition, since in addition to the kings who are military commanders the office of Admiral stands almost as another kingship.

1271b Another criticism that may be made against the fundamental principle of the lawgiver is one that Plato has made in the *Laws*. The entire system of the laws is directed towards one part of virtue only, military valour, because this is serviceable for conquest. Owing to this they remained secure while at war, but began to decline when they had won an empire, because they did not know how to live a peaceful life, and had been trained in no other form of training more important than the art of war. [23] And another error no less serious than that one is this: they think that the coveted prizes of life are won by valour more than by cowardice, and in this they are right, yet they imagine wrongly that these prizes are worth more than the valour that wins them. The public finance of Sparta is also badly regulated: when compelled to carry on wars on a large scale she has nothing in the state treasury, and the Spartiates pay war taxes badly because, as most of the land is owned by them, they do not scrutinize each other's contributions. And the lawgiver has achieved the opposite result to what is advantageous—he has made the state poor and the individual citizen covetous. So much for a discussion of the constitution of Sparta: for these are the main points in it for criticism.

Questions

1. **Which aspects of the Spartan state does Aristotle find fault with and why?**
2. **Do the criticisms of Aristotle seem valid? Why or why not?**

THE HELOT PROBLEM

Ancient historians agree that the need to control the helots of both Laconia and Messenia helped shape Sparta's policy and way of life. Recent scholarship, however, has debated the extent to which fear of a helot rebellion dominated Spartan thinking. The following selections from Thucydides and Xenophon play a key role in that discussion.

6. THE HELOT THREAT

In Book IV of *History* (4.80), Thucydides states that fear of the helots influenced Spartan policy and discusses a revealing incident. The book was translated by Richard Crawley.

4.80.1 The fact that at the time Sparta was doing so badly made it easier for them to get this army from the Peloponnese. For now that the Athenians were making their attacks on the Peloponnese, and particularly on the actual territory of Sparta, the Spartans thought that the best way of diverting these attacks would be to give Athens, too, the same kind of trouble by sending an army to her allies, particularly as these allies were prepared to supply the army and were asking for it in order to be able to revolt. **[2]** The Spartans were also glad to have a good excuse for sending some of their helots out of the country, since in the present state of affairs, with Pylos in enemy hands, they feared a revolution. **[3]** In fact they were so frightened of their unyielding character and of their numbers that they had had recourse to the

following plan. (Spartan policy with regard to the helots had always been based almost entirely on the idea of security.) They made a proclamation to the effect that the helots should choose out of their own number those who claimed to have done the best service to Sparta on the battlefield, implying that they would be given their freedom. This was, however, a test conducted in the belief that the ones who showed most spirit and came forward first to claim their freedom would be the ones most likely to turn against Sparta. **[4]** So about 2,000 were selected, who put garlands on their heads and went round the temples under the impression that they were being made free men. Soon afterwards, however, the Spartans did away with them, and no one ever knew exactly how each one of them was killed.

7.   THE ALLIANCE OF SPARTA AND ATHENS IN 421

Thucydides in Book V records the terms of the treaty of alliance between Athens and Sparta in 421 BC following the end of the Archidamian War. One clause (5.23.3) listed below has particular relevance to the helot question:

5.23.3 Should the slave population rise, the Athenians shall help the Spartans with all their might, according to their power.

8.   THE REBELLION OF CINADON

Xenophon's *Hellenica*, a history of Greek affairs from 411 to 362 BC, relates the attempted rebellion of Cinadon in about 398 BC. In the fourth century, the Lycurgan organization, which carefully distinguished between Spartiates, *perioikoi*, and helots, was starting to break down. A number of Spartiates had lost their citizenship because of economic hardship and were now ranked as "inferiors." The situation became critical when the inferior Cinadon sought to enlist the helots in order to overthrow the Spartan state. Xenophon's account shows the underlying tension that had long been present in Spartan society between the Spartiates and their underclasses, especially the helots. The following passage picks up the narrative after the Spartans choose Agesilaus king.

3.3.4 In the first year of his reign, while he was making one of the official sacrifices on behalf of the state, the prophet said that the gods were revealing that there was some very terrible conspiracy afoot. He sacrificed again, and the prophet said that the signs were worse still. Then, when he had sacrificed

for the third time, he said: "Agesilaus, the signs that I read here are just as they would be if we were surrounded by enemies." After this they made sacrifices to the powers who turn evil aside and to the powers who preserve us from evil, and it was some time before they obtained favourable omens and stopped sacrificing. Within five days of these sacrifices some-one brought information to the ephors not only of the existence of a conspiracy but also of the name of the leader of the whole affair.

3.3.5 This leader was a young man called Cinadon, strong, healthy and with plenty of courage, but not one of the regular officer class. In reply to the ephors' question of how Cinadon proposed to carry his plan into effect, the informer told them that Cinadon had taken him to the edge of the market place and then told him to count how many Spartans of the officer class were there. "And I," said the informer, "counted up the king and the ephors and the members of the Council and about forty others," and then asked him "What was the point, Cinadon, in asking me to make this count?" Then he said, "I want you to consider these men as your enemies and all the others in the market place, who are more than 4,000, as your allies." Then too, the informer said, Cinadon would comment on the people they met in the streets, pointing out sometimes one, sometimes two as "enemies," all the rest being "allies." And in looking over the people who happened to be on the country estates belonging to the officer class, he would point out one more, namely, the owner, as an "enemy," but would find on each estate a great many "allies."

3.3.6 The ephors then asked how many people, according to Cinadon, were in the plot with him and the informer told them that on that point Cinadon had said that those actually in the plot with himself and the leaders were not very many, though they were trustworthy; it was rather the case, the leaders claimed, that they were in the plot with everyone else—helots, freedmen, lower-grade Spartans and Perioeci—since all these people showed clearly enough, if there was ever any mention of the Spartan officer class, that they would be glad to eat them up even raw.

Questions

1. **Do the accounts Thucydides and Xenophon give of the helot danger seem believable?**
2. **What in the material you have read in the ancient sources makes you trust or suspect the words of these two historians?**

OPINIONS OF MODERN SCHOLARS

1. Paul Cartledge, Professor of Greek History, the A. G. Leventis Professor of Greek Culture and a Fellow of Clare College, Cambridge, holds the traditional view that the need to control the helots and deter rebellion played a dominant role in shaping Spartan society. But his analysis emphasizes the importance of an actual class-struggle between helots and Spartiates.

FROM PAUL CARTLEDGE, "REBELS AND SAMBOS IN CLASSICAL GREECE: A COMPARATIVE VIEW"

THIS CHAPTER IS DIVIDED INTO TWO PARTS. In the first and longer part I attempt to apply systematically to Classical Greece those of the criteria for successful servile revolt elaborated by [Eugene] Genovese that I deem relevantly applicable. Here I am attempting to account for a null case, the *non*-occurrence of servile revolt as opposed to servile *resistance*, which is to be assumed and can be documented. In the second part of the chapter I apply those same criteria of Genovese's to the Helots of Sparta, both those of Lakonia and those of Messenia. As was notorious in antiquity and is still a matter for rightful preoccupation today, this servile group—or rather groups—did actually manage to revolt, more than once, and indeed not merely to revolt but, with a lot of help from their friends (or at any rate their Spartan masters' enemies), actually revolt into full civic freedom (for the adult males of the new *polis* of Messene) as well as personal liberty.

An important part of what is at stake for modern scholars who wish to explain as well as understand this near-unique historical phenomenon is the general question of how important the Helots were to the entire Spartan political and social and cultural regime, and especially how much of a threat they posed to that regime on a regular, everyday basis—as opposed to the searingly manifest moments of concerted and open revolt. Much hangs, in this debate, on one's reading of Thucydides 4.80.2, which is irritatingly not unambiguous. Either Thucydides is saying that as a general principle of governance "Spartan policy had *always* been determined by the necessity of taking precautions against the Helots," or he is making a more restricted claim and saying something like "in the Spartans" relations with the Helots the central issue had *always* been to keep them under surveillance (my emphasis—the Greek word *aiei* appears first in its sentence). Whichever of those readings is correct, it is in this same passage that Thucydides goes on to relate an instance of extreme Spartan surveillance involving the calculatedly duplicitous slaughter of 2000 Helots that the historian believed to be and presented as an illustration of a general rule—"always," as—e.g.—in this particular instance. Those modern scholars who wish to play down the importance of the Helot "danger" to Sparta or the determining influence of that perceived danger on the whole Spartan regime tend to favour the second, more minimal translation of Thuc. 4.80.2 given above and are even willing—some of them—to deny the factual veracity of that reported massacre. So not only is the nature of the Spartan regime at scholarly stake here but so also are Thucydides' reputation and standing.

Now, the testimony of Thucydides is no longer read today as it once was as the equivalent of holy writ, and more and more attention has been devoted to unmasking the powerful passions, even prejudices, by which he was moved both to write history and in the writing of his history. That is in my view quite proper and fair. It is therefore perfectly correct and legitimate to ask, first, what Thucydides' source for this story might have been (as usual, he doesn't tell us explicitly), and, second, whether there might have been any ideological or other motive that might have led him to abandon in this case what seem to have been his usual high standards of verification and authentication and so to believe a contrived and malicious fiction. As for the first issue,

that of Thucydides' sources, I note that it is in connection with a centrally important aspect of Sparta's behaviour, their performance at the battle of Mantineia in 418, and with a matter involving knowledge of numbers that Thucydides declares (5.68.2)—very honestly but still somewhat surprisingly, since such confessions of ignorance are very rare indeed—that he could not estimate the Spartans' casualties in 418 with any accuracy on account of "the secrecy of their *politeia*"—the last word is ambiguous: it could mean either the Spartan state authorities specifically in 418 or the Spartans' whole way of life in general. I infer that he did not feel such qualms in the case of the Helot massacre, even though that had been accomplished in total secrecy ("no one ever knew how each of them perished"—4.80.4). From what, to him, reliable witness could he have received such a report? What could have been his reason(s) for believing, or wanting to believe, the report?

Since Spartan or Perioikic deserters or defectors were probably thin on the ground or non-existent and in any case deeply untrustworthy on principle, the likeliest potential Lakonian source is a fugitive Helot, though presumably not one of the 2000 supposedly being liberated for services to Sparta only to discover that by volunteering for freedom they had volunteered for their own death-sentence. Such fugitive Helots had two possible main routes of escape from Sparta's own home territory: *via* the position occupied by the Athenians at Pylos in Messenia since 425 (it was the capture of this that provoked the Spartans to extreme fear of Helot *skaiotês*, "obstinacy," and Helot numbers in 424, according to Thuc. 4.80.3) or *via* the "sort of isthmus" in the Malea peninsula in Lakonia opposite the island of Kythera that the Athenians occupied and fortified in 413, precisely as a place "to which the Helots might desert" (Thuc. 7.26.2). There are other possibilities too. In both those occupations of Spartan territory the key Athenian commander had been Demosthenes, who had established special relations with the ex-Helot Messenians settled by the Athenians in *c.* 460 at Naupaktos and used them profitably both during and after the Pylos success. Thucydides' source might therefore have been a Naupaktos Messenian as well as a Lakonian or Messenian Helot deserter. Or indeed Demosthenes himself.

Why then, finally, did Thucydides choose to believe the story? Why did he find the witness or witnesses reliable and believable? Was his favourable reception of the story dictated by some more or less hidden agenda? Pro-Athenian patriotic prejudice on big issues such as war-guilt has been alleged against Thucydides, but not in my view sustainably. It is, moreover, implausible in the highest degree that as a non-democratic exile from democratic Athens he shared such fellow-feeling for slaves and Helots (who not only were unfree but Greek) as Athenian ideological democrats may—perhaps—have held. His general under-emphasis in his work on the importance of Helot dissidence and revolt is at any rate in line with an under-emphasis by all major Greek historians on the role of slaves and the unfree in Greek warfare.

The most economical explanation would therefore seem to me to be that the reported massacre of some 2000 Helots some time before 424 fitted into a pattern already in the eyes of Thucydides firmly established and rigorously tested, a pattern of Spartan precaution to the point of paranoia towards the Helots that might entail exemplary punishments of outstanding brutality. Thucydides does not mention the Spartan Krypteia, though it undoubtedly existed in his day, nor does he cite the annual declaration of war on the Helots by the Ephors, which also has a good chance of being in force in the late fifth century. But if he knew of them, as he surely did, they will have been part and parcel of this reassuringly consistent picture. (He does cite a number of telling instances of Spartan murder of free Greeks: 2.67.3, the Spartans' murder of neutrals as well as Athenian and allied traders at the outset of the war; 3.68.2, their massacre of at least 200 Plataians in 427; and 5.83, their killing of all available freemen of Hysiai in 419. An *a fortiori* inference so far as Spartan treatment of Helots was concerned would therefore seem justifiable.)

One last, historiographical argument: Thucydides' overall method of presentation was paradigmatic. The chilling description of the massacre of 2000 Helots in 4.80 should therefore be read in my view as his paradigm case of the Spartans' regular treatment of the Helots. I see no reason in conclusion not to believe the authenticity of the report and every reason to regard it as powerful evidence of at least the Spartans' all too vivid perception of a Helot "danger."

* * *

In case any reader should still be tempted to hold fast to the notion that it is easy to draw up an order of priority for any given servile population, let alone for all servile populations at all times and in every place, let me consider briefly and in outline the one servile population in Classical Greece that did revolt more than once, and the majority of which eventually revolted successfully into full political as well as purely personal freedom: the Helots of Lakonia and Messenia. Their unique experience may further illuminate the problem of why the other servile populations of Greece...did not apparently revolt either regularly or successfully. Again, I shall take Genovese's list of favouring factors (where relevant) as a series of working hypotheses, only in this case to see whether they are verified rather than falsified, bearing in mind throughout that the evidence, though more abundant than for any other Greek servile group, is presented to us by largely hostile sources and never by the Helots themselves.

(1) The Master–Slave Relationship

First, on a point of definition, the Helots were in Greek parlance *douloi* (the commonest term for the unfree), no less than were the chattel slaves of, say, Athens. To take two telling illustrations: the collective noun *douleia*, "servile population" or "slave class," appears in the terms of the treaty of defensive alliance between Sparta and Athens in 421, and the pro-Spartan Athenian oligarch Kritias, writing for a non-Spartan public, went so far as to describe the Helots as being *douloi* to a greater extent or degree than any other *douloi* in Greece. If we have regard solely to the Helots' economic function as involuntary and exploited producers of the Spartans' surplus, their designation as *douloi* is indeed perfectly correct. But legally, socially, even politically, they differed markedly from chattel slaves. They were not foreigners bought and sold on the market, outsiders wrenched from native ties of kin and religion. Nor were they wholly owned by and totally at the disposal of individual Spartan masters. Rather, they were Greeks, enslaved collectively upon and tied to the land their ancestors had once tilled as free men, and they were held in subjection by explicit and repeated acts of the Spartan political community, the *polis* of the Spartans. They had, moreover, some kind of family life, which is part of the reason they were able to reproduce themselves as a servile population over many generations. Finally, in the case at least of the more numerous Messenian Helots, they had a sense of common identity that may fairly be called political. Legally, that is to say, they were a kind of state-serfs. Socially and politically, they were a people, almost a nation.

Turning from definition to practice, we find absenteeism, depersonalization and cultural estrangement all relevantly present in the master–slave relationship. Precisely how production was organized on a Helot-run estate (*klaros*, literally "allotment") we shall never know. But the Spartan *klaros*-owners were for most of the year necessarily absentee landlords, at least until they were exempted from active military service at the age of sixty. The *klaroi* in Lakonia, however, were far more accessible than those in ultramontane Messenia, and it was doubtless in Lakonia that rich Spartans kept ready their supplies of horses, dogs and provisions with a view to indulging in their favourite pursuit of hunting boar and other wild game. It is possible that organization of labour and distribution of its products were left immediately in the hands of the Helot equivalent of an overseer (*epitropos*; cf. the Spartan dialect word *monomoitos* glossed as "leader of Helots" in the lexicon of Hesychios); but it is doubtful whether there were Helot equivalents of slave-drivers, and if there was any Helot-breaking to be done, that could be arranged by the notorious Spartan "Secret Service" (Krypteia).

Depersonalization and cultural estrangement are harder factors to assess. In this, as indeed in all respects except the strictly legal and economic, it makes sense to distinguish more or less sharply between the Helots of Messenia and those of Lakonia. The Messenians lived further away from their collective master, on the far side of a formidable (2407 m) mountain barrier. This physical separation will have done nothing to attenuate the psychological alienation they felt and expressed in the shared consciousness of having once been "the Messenians," members of their own independent *polis* of Messene (reconstituted as such after 369). It was immaterial to the efficacy of this "nationalist" myth that their ancestors had not in fact travelled far, if at all, along the road to *polis*—status before the Spartan conquest and annexation began in the latter part of the eighth century. Thus it was no doubt more particularly against the Messenian

Helots that the Spartans' remarkable, and to my knowledge unparalleled, annual declaration of war on the Helots was directed.

The Lakonian Helots, on the other hand, though they too were Greeks, seem to have been subjugated earlier and were more immediately within the reach of the long arm of Spartan physical and psychological repression. They were therefore perhaps more likely to have had their kinship and community solidarity undermined in any case, but a further contributory factor towards this end seems to have been that their ancestors had been enslaved before any shoot of "national" or *polis* consciousness had had time to grow. By the fifth century, anyhow, if not long before they had seemingly lost any notion of an anterior political independence. When the Theban Epameinondas led the first-ever invasion of Sparta's territory (370/69), we are told that he found Lakonian Helots so successfully indoctrinated that they refused to sing verses by various poets since these had been declared taboo by their masters. Yet at that very moment the Helots of Messenia were in revolt *en masse* and about to achieve permanent liberation.

However, even this apparently telling example should not be taken to mean that all Lakonian Helots were at all times entirely passive and submissive. Following the massive earthquake of *c.* 464 which directly affected Sparta town, some of them certainly joined in the revolt that ensued. Indeed, I would venture to suggest that it may well have been they who began the revolt, in apparent contradiction of their normal passivity. For exactly this contradiction between "Sambos" and rebels has been observed in the Old South, notably in the person of Nat Turner who led a slave rebellion in 1831. Paternalism in Genovese's sense, however heavy-handed, can cut in more than one way.

Undoubtedly, though, the great revolt of *c.* 464, which lasted several years, was essentially a Messenian affair. Like the successful revolt of 370/69, it perfectly exemplifies the observation of Aristotle that the Helots were "like an enemy constantly sitting in wait for the disasters of the Spartans." These revolts should, moreover, be classified as slave revolts (using "slave" loosely), notwithstanding the fact that in servile revolts the participants typically aim at purely individual liberation rather than social transformation. For the essence of slave revolts, before the thoroughly "modern" one led by Toussaint L'Ouverture in the wake of the French Revolution, was that they were "restorationist." In the sense that the Messenians were aiming to restore themselves to what they took to be their anterior political and social condition, their revolts were precisely that; and if their aim was a collective rather than individual transformation, this was because they were collective, not individual, *douloi* of Spartans.

(2) The Occurrence of Economic Distress and Famine

Only two famines are attested in all Spartan history; neither of them in the Classical era; and Sparta, even when stripped of Messenia, was (probably significantly) not among the states in Greece to receive grain from Cyrene during the shortage of the early 320s. A Spartan public regulation imposed a religious curse upon any *klaros*-holder who exacted more than the maximum stipulated rent (or tribute) payable by the Helots working his land; but this regulation may not antedate the reform of Kings Agis IV and Kleomenes III in the 240s and 230s. It is therefore possible that some Helots found themselves squeezed economically, whether by more powerful Helots or by their Spartan masters, especially perhaps in the late fifth and early fourth centuries, when some rich Spartans were displaying a countercultural propensity to self-differentiation that included consumption at a higher level than the officially recognized norm. Specific evidence is lacking, however, and this was probably not a major factor influencing Helots to revolt.

(3) Size of Slaveholding Units

We know nothing precise about the numbers of Helots working on any one *klaros*, but an important passage of Xenophon recounting an abortive conspiracy among the lower orders of Spartan society led by one Kinadon (a lapsed Spartan) virtually proves that there were more than one Helot family on each—and probably many more than one on the holdings of the richest Spartans (women as well as men). Again, though, this will have been by itself a relatively insignificant revolt-producing factor, especially if the Helots lived dispersed in their individual families among the several *klaroi* rather than grouped into hamlets or villages....

(4) Frequent Splits within the Ruling Class

According to the Spartan "mirage," the myth of Sparta promoted initially by the Spartans themselves but given wide currency and sustained by pro-Spartan oligarchs and philosophers in other states, one of the distinguishing features of developed Spartan society was the harmony and unanimity (*homonoia* or same-mindedness) that prevailed among the full Spartan citizens, who styled themselves *Homoioi* or "Peers." In reality, disharmony on occasion reached such a pitch that Aristotle felt justified in treating two outbreaks at the turn of the fifth and fourth centuries, including Kinadon's abortive conspiracy, as cases of potential *stasis* or open civil strife. To these may be added the Pausanias affair of the later 470s or early 460s, in which Regent Pausanias was accused—no doubt falsely in fact—of promising not just to free Helots but actually to make them into Spartan citizens. A causal connection may be postulated between this affair and the great Helot revolt of *c*. 464, as between the succession crisis of *c*. 400 and Kinadon's conspiracy.

As for splits between slaveholding states, Aristotle attributed the absence of servile revolt on Crete to deliberate abstention by the Cretan states from mutually inciting each other's servile underclasses (here called *perioikoi*). The contrast he had in mind particularly was with the attitude of Sparta's enemies to the Helots, which became blatant in the early fourth century. The liberation of the Messenian Helots and the reconstitution of the *polis* of Messene could not have been accomplished without outside, especially Theban, material aid. And not just material but also moral aid. There are no Classical Greek abolitionists on record, it is true, but the Sophist Alkidamas need not have been alone in justifying the liberation of the Messenian Helots on the (strictly non-Aristotelian) ground that "God has left all men free; nature has made no man a slave."

(5) Proportion of Slave to Free and of (6) Imported to Home-Bred Slaves

Factor (6) does not apply as such, since the Spartans owned few if any chattel slaves, and the Helots were self-reproducing. But unlike slaves in the Old South, they also reproduced themselves as members of a homogeneous ethnic group who spoke the same ancestral language as their masters. Plato and Aristotle rightly linked these shared characteristics with the Helots' propensity to revolt. Factor (5), on the other hand, could hardly be more relevant and significant.

Whatever the precise numbers may have been on either side, there is no doubt that the Helots collectively grossly outnumbered the Spartans, and that this gross and indeed growing numerical disparity was a vital factor governing relations between the two antagonistic classes. The Peloponnesian War (431–404) seems to have marked a turning-point in this regard. The felt disparity encouraged the Spartans, on the one hand, to create privileged ex-Helot statuses, thereby furthering the traditional ruling class aim of dividing and ruling their subjects, and, on the other, to conduct a savage exemplary massacre of those Helots thought most likely to prove rebellious.

(7) Emergence of an Autonomous Black Leadership

Given the technologically undeveloped, agrarian character of the Spartan economy, potential rebel leaders cannot be sought among an urban and privileged artisan section of Helots. Indeed, it is hard to see where such leaders could emerge from within the Helot population itself, unless it be from a postulated "kulak" stratum of richer Helots—the kind who were eventually in a position to pay the not inconsiderable cash sum of five *minai* required by Kleomenes III to buy their freedom in 223 or 222 BC. The only rebel leader known to us by name, the Messenian Aristomenes, has been transmitted to posterity under a halo of legend and propaganda assiduously polished in the aftermath of the 370/69 liberation. Even his date is uncertain, though more likely to be mid-seventh century than early-fifth. Otherwise, it is revealing that leaders are offered, or put themselves forward, from within the ranks of the master class—a Pausanias, a Kinadon. The Helots were in a sense insiders as well as deliberately excluded outsiders in this peculiar society.

(8) Colonies of Runaways

For a slave revolt to be sustained for any length of time a "maroon dimension," so it has been argued from the comparative Brazilian and Caribbean evidence, is indispensable: the establishment, that is, of a more or less autonomous and self-sufficient colony of runaways. Naupaktos was in a sense such a colony after *c.* 460, but the parallel is not close, not least because the Naupaktian Messenians were too distant from the homeland to offer continuous succour to their enslaved brethren in revolt.

However, during the revolt following the great earthquake of *c.* 464 some considerable number of Messenian Helots was able to subsist and withstand siege on Mount Ithome for an appreciable period in the 460s and perhaps into the 450s, which argues the establishment of semi-permanent communal institutions. Resort to Ithome was facilitated by the great distance separating it from Sparta, not to mention the 2407 m Taygetos massif running between the two sites. It was probably not just at times of generalized revolt that the sanctuary of the mountain was sought, although it was apparently only at Poseidon's shrine at Tainaron in southern Lakonia that Helots might legitimately seek asylum.

* * *

To conclude: the underlying cause of the revolts of the Helots, as of servile revolts everywhere, was the simple fact that they wanted to be free. But the Helots were only *able* to revolt outright because their ethnic and political solidarity provided the Messenians with the appropriate ideological inspiration and organizational cohesion, and because their numerical, geographical and international situation gave them (and Sparta's enemies) the requisite room for manoeuvre and ultimately justified hope of success.

These conditions did not obtain for the chattel slaves of Classical Greece. That they did not to our knowledge revolt is not therefore a sign that they were mostly happy with their unsought lot but rather a mark of the success with which their owners conducted a conscious and unremitting class struggle against them. That struggle was not a simple phenomenon: by employing a comparative approach, I hope to have been able to demonstrate that the factors potentially relevant to explaining servile revolt are many and complex and that the absence of slave revolts in Classical Greece cannot be fully explained in terms of just one of them.

2. Richard Talbert, W. R. Kenan, Jr., Professor of History and Classics at the University of North Carolina at Chapel Hill, challenges Paul Cartledge's position that a class struggle existed between helots and Spartiates. Instead, in his article "The Role of the Helots in the Class Struggle at Sparta" Talbert argues that in general the helots understood and accepted their lowly place in Spartan society.

FROM RICHARD TALBERT, "THE ROLE OF THE HELOTS IN THE CLASS STRUGGLE AT SPARTA"

"THE HISTORY OF SPARTA, it is not too much to say, is fundamentally the history of the class struggle between the Spartans and the Helots," claims Paul Cartledge in his substantial study *Agesilaos and the Crisis of Sparta*. For Cartledge, Sparta was a society "the very existence of which was constantly menaced by the Helots," who "were always apt to take advantage of their masters' misfortunes." Sparta's stability was "shot through with aggressive competitiveness and constant, sometimes unbearable tensions at all levels." He confirms his earlier view "that the dominant and decisive contradiction or tension of Spartan society can fruitfully be analysed in terms of a class struggle between the Spartiates and the Helots." All modern writers on the helots have seen such "contradiction or tension" to a greater or lesser degree, and Cartledge in effect now presses the accepted view to an extreme. The aim of this article is to swing towards the opposite extreme with the arguments that the tension was limited, and that the class struggle at Sparta requires fresh definition as a result.

The obscurity surrounding almost every aspect of helots' status and lives is not to be underestimated. Their status is not conveyed satisfactorily by any modern term: "state-serf" possibly comes nearest. At any rate it is agreed that they did not belong to the individual Spartiate landlords to whom they were somehow assigned and to whom they paid a rent in kind; rather, all helots remained the property of the Spartan state. It alone could free them, though for a long period it never even considered doing so. In practice helots were recognized to have certain property and marriage rights, and also presumably some kind of community life. However, it is hardly possible to do much more than speculate about these matters. For the whole period to the third century the surviving contemporary historical writers are all non-Spartans, and while they do have a consuming interest in Spartan society, this hardly extends to helots, about whom they make few general statements. No helot community can be securely identified either by name or location; for this reason among others, none has yet been excavated.

Two features about helots do at once stand out clearly, however. First, they certainly did not experience the alarming and irreversible drop in numbers which the Spartiate class suffered for various reasons during the century and more following the Persian Wars—from perhaps about 8,000 adult males in 480 B.C. down to 1,100 or so at most after 371. No figures survive for total numbers of helots. Thucydides says that there were more in Messenia than Laconia. Otherwise we may note that an observer in the agora at Sparta one day at the beginning of the fourth century counted about eighty Spartiates present and over 4,000 other people (of other classes undifferentiated). Similarly, for what they are worth, the modern estimates that the helot population comprised between 170,000 and 224,000 at least have the merit of underlining the scale of disparity which must have developed with the Spartiate class.

Second, it is clear that substantial numbers of helots served in the Spartan army in various capacities as a matter of routine. According to later tradition, Sparta had enlisted helots as far back as the time of her campaigns in Messenia. But the earliest date for which we have reliable information is the beginning of the fifth century. Helots are known to have accompanied King Cleomenes' army on the campaign against Argos in 494, and they were at the battle of Thermopylae against the Persian invaders in 480. After it, spectators of the carnage could not distinguish their bodies from those of their masters. At Plataea in 479, according to Herodotus, there were as many as seven light-armed helots to every Spartiate hoplite—thus a total of 35,000 helot troops. For the period between the Persian and Peloponnesian Wars our evidence is altogether thin, and precise information on Spartan forces is lacking. But thereafter Thucydides states that the 420 hoplites trapped on Sphacteria by the Athenians in 425 B.C. were accompanied by helots. Later he mentions that during the siege many other helots (even from beyond the immediate vicinity) were attracted by offers of silver and freedom to bring up their boats and run the Athenian blockade with supplies. Even more significant is his account of the panic measures taken by the authorities following the Athenians' capture of the forces on Sphacteria and their occupation of Pylos and Cythera: "They announced that the helots should choose out of their own number those who claimed to have done the best service to Sparta on campaign, implying that they would be given their freedom. This was, however, a test conducted in the belief that the ones who showed most spirit and came forward first to claim their freedom would be the ones most likely to turn against Sparta. So about 2,000 were selected, who put on garlands and went round the temples under the impression that they were being freed. Soon afterwards, however, the Spartans did away with them, and no one ever knew exactly how each one of them was killed."

Assuming that the story is to be credited at all, Thucydides thus indicates that in the mid-420s there existed a body of well over 2,000 helots who could claim to have done distinguished military service—presumably for the most part on Sparta's campaigns in the first years of the Peloponnesian War, though this is never made clear. The alleged liquidation of the 2,000 judged by their fellows to be the most outstanding is much more a reflection of Spartan fears of revolution than of any overt threat posed by the helots themselves in this regard. Around the very same time 700 helots were recruited as hoplites to campaign under Brasidas in Thrace, alongside mercenaries from elsewhere in the Peloponnese. Thucydides implies understandably that it was a relief to the Spartans to have these helot hoplites serve so far from home. But in fact any feelings of alarm were unfounded and the men remained loyal. When the survivors returned to Sparta in summer 421, the state freed them and conferred on them the privilege of living where they pleased. Shortly afterwards they were offered land at Lepreum, and the natural inference from Thucydides' account is that most accepted it—even though they had been away for three years and had seen much of other areas of Greece. At any rate these "Brasideioi," as they evidently came to be termed, could still be mustered as a distinct unit three years later, when they formed part of the Spartan forces at the battle of Mantinea.

Since Lepreum, in northwest Laconia, was a frontier area long disputed between Sparta and Elis,

the offer of land there represented a dubious gift: sooner or later the settlers might have to fight for their holdings. When the Brasideioi accepted the offer, they could at least be encouraged by the knowledge that they were joining another group loyal to Sparta settled in the same area, the *neodamodeis* or literally "new men of the people," whose status and privileges will be discussed further below. The first mention of these freed helots enlisted to serve as hoplites is no more than an incidental one in connection with the settlement of the Brasideioi. It seems a fair guess that the creation of such a new class was one of the measures taken to strengthen the state after the disasters of the mid 420s. We lack information on the numbers of *neodamodeis* either at this date or at the battle of Mantinea in 418, when they are mentioned next as fighting alongside the Brasideioi. Only helots are heard of forming part of the full Spartan levies sent to attack Argos in 419 and to relieve Tegea the following year. By contrast the expedition despatched to Sicily in 413 included 600 men specially selected from both the helots and the *neodamodeis* to serve as hoplites under a Spartiate commander.

Thereafter only *neodamodeis*, rather than helots, are mentioned as serving in the Spartan army, and their numbers increase so dramatically that during the 390s there were as many as 3,000 in the field at one time. The expeditionary force sent out to Asia Minor under the Spartiate commander Thibron in 400 comprised in the first instance 1,000 *neodamodeis* and 4,000 troops from elsewhere in the Peloponnese. King Agesilaus followed in 396 with a force made up at his own request of 30 Spartiates, 2,000 of the *neodamodeis* (the implication being that there were more available) and 6,000 allied troops. These *neodamodeis* were later among the troops who returned to Greece with him and fought under his command at the battle of Coronea in 394.

* * *

After 404 B.C. mercenaries could readily have been recruited rather than helots, but this was seldom done on a large scale, even though helots, unlike any group of mercenaries, needed to be withdrawn from the agrarian labour force, trained at Sparta's expense and presumably armed likewise too. Instead, as already noted, in 396 Agesilaus actually requested a substantial force comprising just neodamodeis and allied troops, under a handful of Spartiate officers. While the disasters of the mid 420s did prompt changes, it is important to appreciate that they were modest in scope and actually served to increase reliance upon troops drawn from the helot class, even if brigades of them were always kept separate from Spartiates and perioeci.

As it happened, the expedient of recruiting helots to serve as hoplites whenever required was not maintained, and instead the new permanent group of freed helots (*neodamodeis*) was formed for the purpose. This development was initiated even before the experiment of employing helots as hoplites abroad under Brasidas had been success-fully completed. Moreover the *neodamodeis* were originally stationed in Laconia, rather than sent abroad for greater security. Their privileges were slight. The land grants made in the first instance effectively carried with them an obligation to defend disputed territory; whether any land grants at all were made later is not known. To be sure, all *neodamodeis* were freed, but there was no move to take the further step of conferring citizenship upon them. Some such outstanding reward was considered justified elsewhere in Greece, where the enlistment of slaves for military service was normally seen as unnatural except in an extreme crisis. But, of course, helots were not slaves. To them, and equally to their masters, the notion of a helot being admitted to the closed group of Spartiates without the requisite birth or upbringing was unthinkable. Only the disturbed regent Pausanias, in contemplating a desperate bid for power after the Persian Wars, had allegedly dared *to* hold out such a prospect to helots in secret, and he was duly reported to the authorities by some of them.

* * *

It would be patently absurd to claim that all helots showed consistent loyalty to the Spartan state throughout the fifth and early fourth centuries. No Spartiate's opinion on the issue has survived at first-hand, but it is clear that other Greeks were left with an impression of disloyalty and tension. Thucydides commented that "most Spartan institutions have always been designed with a view to security against the helots," and Aristotle compared the helots to "an enemy constantly sitting in wait for the disasters of the Spartans," who were "often in revolt." Moreover we know that a great earthquake of the mid 460s

was followed by a major helot uprising, in which even two perioecic communities (both in Messenia) joined the rebel cause.

However the significance of this revolt ought not to be over-rated. While it was very serious, we should not necessarily assume that it was universal, let alone "nationalist" in its inspiration. "Nationalism" was hardly a concept known to the ancient world, and it is most unlikely that many helots of all people could be inspired by loyalty to a region as amorphous as Messenia, rather than just to their own local centre or neighbourhood. Thucydides' account of the scandalous dismissal of the Athenian reinforcement contingent from the siege of the rebel stronghold on Mount Ithome could suggest that any well-formulated revolutionary aims were precisely what the helot side lacked. The Spartans' sudden fear was that their energetic, freethinking Athenian allies would actually sympathize with the rebel cause and contribute vital revolutionary inspiration to it. Moreover, with one dubious exception (a revolt in 490 which is probably fictional), this rising was unique in the period, triggered by the altogether extraordinary catastrophe which had overwhelmed the Spartiates and no doubt thousands of their sub-jects too. To many helots it must have seemed as if society had broken down. There may also have been a special sense of outrage among them at an incident which, according to Thucydides, the Spartans in his time continued to regard as the cause of the great earthquake: at some unspecified earlier date Spartans had infringed certain helots' right of asylum in the temple of Poseidon at Taenarum and had removed and killed them. On the other hand the Spartiates were sufficiently confident of stability at home to be on the point of sending an expedition to aid the Thasian revolt against Athens just before the earthquake struck. This suggests that no helot rising was anticipated.

After the suppression of the revolt the helots' leaders must mostly have been dead or in exile. The exiles, installed by the Athenians at Naupactus on the northern shore of the Corinthian Gulf, at least now gained the advantage of a base from which to resume their cause. As it turned out, however, not for nearly a century was there another major revolt. Of course it is always possible that local risings did occur and were successfully suppressed without ever becoming known to outsiders, thanks to the geo-graphical isolation of the state and the secretiveness of the authorities, which Thucydides comments upon. But the absence of any underlying Spartiate fear of rebellion (treated further below) does argue strongly against this hypothesis.

After the 460s there was no catastrophe comparable to the earthquake, and no further known revolt, until the Thebans under Epaminondas had shattered Spartan power at the battle of Leuctra in 371. This was the case even though during the Peloponnesian War Athens maintained a foothold on the Messenian coast at Pylos for as much as fifteen years off and on, with the special assistance of Messenian exiles. Other enemy occupations occurred too. The Athenians held a spot on the Laconian mainland north of Cythera from 413, for example, and Pharnabazus and Conon held the island of Cythera itself in 393. But Cartledge's claim that these occupations "encouraged many Helots to desert" is only an assumption. Naturally, as Thucydides and Diodorus both say, the Athenians hoped that helots might desert to their bases during the Peloponnesian War, but from this it will not automatically follow that they did so in significant numbers. Thucydides never suggests that any of the Athenian bases in Spartan territory caused harm comparable to that inflicted by the Spartan occupation of Decelea in Attica from 413: by his estimate over 20,000 slaves deserted there.

Though some helots did go over to the Athenians, there was never any mass defection, and this is perhaps hardly surprising. Helots' more natural inclination would surely be to rally to the defence of their homeland rather than to throw themselves on the mercies of its attackers, of whom they could know next to nothing beyond what their masters told them. Those who did gain accurate information about the Athenians must soon have realized that Athens would remain concerned for the helots' condition only so long as it suited her war aims. Thus after the great earthquake she had duly fulfilled her treaty obligations to aid the suppression of rebellious helots, and later agreed to the same clause in the treaty of 421.

* * *

Of course not all helots necessarily lived a pitiful existence in any case. Most notably, as Cartledge suggests, some must have been deputed to supervise others as bailiffs or *chefs d' enterprise*. These men's opportunities for exploitation or personal gain are obvious, and may even have extended over successive generations where a helot family and a Spartiate family remained linked to one another. Life must have been good for some helots. We know that they were all permitted to profit from their labour and that the prospect of acquiring precious metals could appeal to them. Above all, however, the widespread willingness to undertake loyal military service demonstrates that by the fifth century the overwhelming majority had accommodated themselves to the demands of their masters.

* * *

Only among a limited group of Messenians is it possible to discern any independent vision or any devotion to resistance. Full credibility can hardly attach to claims by Pausanias in the second century A.D.—strongly influenced by post-liberation literature—that the Messenians had kept their Doric dialect and native customs uncontaminated throughout the centuries of Spartan domination and even into his own day. But it is certain that some very ancient cults were maintained and that under Spartan rule there were individuals who conceived of an autonomous state of Messene. How their ideas were formed, and to what extent (if any) they were developed are insoluble puzzles, but the first unequivocal sign of them is the renaming of Zankle in north-east Sicily as Messene (Doric Messana) sometime after 490. Naturally this was done by exiles. It was also exiles, the undefeated rebels finally permitted to leave Ithome under safe conduct about 460 (thus marking the end of the revolt after the great earthquake), who maintained their struggle against Sparta from Naupactus. They inspired their descendants to do the same from Cephallenia, until these were expelled by Sparta around 400 and fled to Sicily and North Africa. The Athenians in their capture and occupation of Sphacteria and Pylos during the Peloponnesian War depended not just upon the local knowledge of these exiles, but also upon their wish to rouse the helots against Sparta.

However all the signs are that such ideas of resistance and independence made only a limited impact inside Messenia, and even less in Laconia. Helots as a class displayed no impatience for change, even though so many of the essentials for forging it lay at their disposal. For they, unlike slaves, all lived side by side in their own homelands and knew the surroundings intimately.

They were Greeks like their masters, and shared a common language with them. They were even equipped with tools and weapons which they were trained to use. Thus although the launching of any revolt would of course still be a formidable challenge, at the outset helots had a far better prospect of success than slaves. On the other hand helots, unlike slaves, seldom came into contact with people who enjoyed genuine freedom (Spartiates certainly did not), and so were perhaps less likely to desire it for themselves.

It follows that the acquiescence of the helots is of far greater significance than their occasional rebelliousness. Even so, there is nothing inherently peculiar or surprising about it. To look no further than elsewhere in ancient Greece, the shadowy *penestai* of Thessaly could be represented as rebellious, yet were willing to serve their masters in war by land and sea. As seems to be the case in many slave societies, helots are likely to have been much more pre-occupied by relations with their fellows than with their masters. Moreover the maintenance of their numbers can be seen as a pointer to their well-being: comparative studies of slavery in the Americas have underlined that the extent to which a subject class reproduces itself is one useful measure of its welfare. The extreme argument that the helots suffered from some kind of group neurosis which distorted their vision of reality is quite unwarranted.

I mean these impressions to apply to the whole helot class. There was no "ideological warfare" on the part of Spartiates, nor a systematic policy of dividing the helots among themselves. It is fantastic to imagine that once the new class of *neodamodeis* was created, thousands agreed to serve as hoplites in return for improved status, all of whom turned miraculously and consistently loyal to Sparta. The fact that after a time they were usually employed on campaigns far from home hardly accounts for their inertia as dissidents. On their return they remained a distinctive group and as such could still have planned action; as men liable to call-up at any time, they may even have retained their weapons. Meantime their fellows who would not, or could not, acquire such privileges and strength supposedly continued to seethe for the day of revolution, yet made no open move towards it.

We may fairly ask why not, however. After all, the implied split between unbroken loyalty among some helots and restrained frustration among the rest is extraordinary. If this is what the Spartan authorities really planned to create among a subject group whom they characterized as generally hostile, then our conclusion can hardly be that they were subtle manipulators, but rather that they were mad fools, prepared to play ever more recklessly with fire. The risk that their gamble would not pay off, and that their divided subjects might reunite against them, would have been an increasingly frightful one.

* * *

Geography and demography support the claim that the Spartiates were in fact for the most part confident of their helots' loyalty. By contemporary Greek standards the state's territory was unusually extensive—about 8,500 sq. km, much of it difficult country broken by mountains. On the other hand, the number of Spartiates was small and shrinking from the mid fifth century; moreover all had to reside at Sparta itself unless abroad on official business. In such circumstances the helots could not have been controlled without a considerable measure of acquiescence on their own part. This is not to suggest that the Spartiates were ever totally complacent about their helots' loyalty. Naturally all of them had some awareness of why the Spartiate upbringing and lifestyle took the form they did, and appreciated the need to regulate the helots with a firm hand...

It was equally useful that the *krypteia* (whereby young men in training were sent out into the countryside with no more than daggers and basic rations, under instructions to kill helots by day or night) should still be continued, especially as the purpose of the exercise looks likely to have been much more to "blood" young Spartiates than to keep down the helots. We are not told how often it occurred, or on what scale, but it is hard to conceive that it was continued with much frequency, or over extensive areas, from around the mid fifth century. By then the numbers of Spartiate youth were in steep decline, and the increasing degree of trust placed in helots would make widespread provocation of the class seem senseless.

Despite Spartiates' customary confidence and rational precautions, inevitably at times their nerves were shaken. The mid-420s are the obvious instance (for reasons already noted), although we should recognize that masters' fear of a rising by their subjects in no sense constitutes proof of impending revolt. Hardly less shocking for Spartiates was the discovery of Cinadon's plot in the first year of Agesilaus' reign. While we are fortunate in having a full account of this from Xenophon, it is still important to clarify the main causes of alarm. Cinadon himself was almost certainly a *hypomeion*, or degraded Spartiate, who had no special concern for the welfare of Sparta's subordinate classes, but schemed to mobilize them all in an attempt to secure his own reinstatement by force: "The ephors asked how many people, according to Cinadon, were in the plot with him and the informer told them that on that point Cinadon had said that those actually in the plot with himself and the leaders were not very many, though they were trustworthy; it was rather the case, the leaders claimed, that they were in the plot with everyone else—helots, neodamodeis, hypomeiones and perioeci—since all these people showed clearly enough, if there was ever any mention of Spartiates, that they would be glad to eat them up even raw."

Although Cartledge is ready to allow for "a good deal of agit-prop exaggeration" in this last claim, he still accepts it as a valid reflection of the attitudes which these four groups are supposed to have shown towards the Spartiates. In fact, while Sparta's lower classes may often have expressed the most uncomplimentary sentiments about their arrogant rulers, there is no sign that the majority seriously meant to translate these into organized rebellion. So far as is known, perioeci had never rebelled (expect for the mere two communities which joined the rising after the great earthquake), and they never did rebel until after Leuctra, even though their communities were repeatedly faced with Spartan demands for troops, as well as having to bear the brunt of enemy seaborne raids. The prevailing attitudes among helots and neodamodeis have already been reviewed: these, too, were not to change until after Leuctra.

The two really alarming features about the discovery of the plot were different. The first was the depth of bitterness felt by a degraded Spartiate concerning his demotion, which highlights the growing tension within the master class documented by other evidence. The second was the turmoil which might be caused by such a degraded Spartiate who (like the regent Pausanias eighty years or so earlier) tried to stir up discontent among the subject classes and offer them leadership, merely in order to settle a grievance borne against his fellow Spartiates. But the authorities never sought to reduce this risk by tackling the problem of the increasing number of demotions from the Spartiate class. It should follow that they had no underlying fear of a rebellion by the subject classes. As mentioned earlier, they had mobilized 1,000 *neodamodeis* the year before the discovery of the plot, and they fulfilled King Agesilaus' request for 2,000 more three years afterwards.

We may be sure that outwardly the normal attitude of Spartiates towards helots remained the same aristocratic haughtiness which the class typically exhibited towards all underlings and outsiders. In the case of helots, brutality too could be added to the regular contempt and disdain. However, this was of course behaviour which Spartiates had been conditioned by their upbringing to display even towards each other, not just towards inferiors. Fighting between young Spartiates was continual and serious, while the clumsier ones assigned to the *krypteia* were all too liable to be killed or badly beaten up, especially during the daytime when (we are told) they were supposed to tackle helots outstanding for their physique and strength. It was easy for masters not even to think of their helots as individuals, since technically the whole class belonged to the state and Spartiates held property in common. Although the details may be fanciful, there is every reason to believe that another fragment of Myron does reflect accurately the general Spartiate attitude towards helots: "They impose on the helots every kind of insulting work which leads to total degradation. For they made it a requirement that each should wear a dogskin cap and be dressed in leather as well as receive a fixed number of lashes annually—without reference to any offence—so that they should never forget to behave like slaves. Moreover, if the physical well-being of any surpassed the usual appearance of slaves, they prescribed a death sentence and also a penalty for owners who failed to curb those putting on weight."

Plutarch in his discussion of Spartiate brutality towards helots reports likewise that "they would force them to drink quantities of unmixed wine and then they would bring them into *messes* to show the young men what drunkenness was like." Yet the helot class submitted to such brutality, not without complaint perhaps, but without resort to any revolt between the mid fifth century and the aftermath of Leuctra. It has often been urged that there were crucial differences between Laconian and Messenian helots: while the former were well treated and loyal, the reverse was true of the latter. Such differences are hard to substantiate, however.

* * *

Once the rebellion of the 460s was over, it was only further external shocks in swift succession—comparable to the great earthquake, though naturally very different in character—which triggered another rising. These shocks began with the crushing defeat at Leuctra in 371 and Epaminondas' acceptance of an invitation from the Arcadians, Argos and Elis to invade Laconia the following year. Only the fact that very few perioeci joined the helots in raising revolt during the 460s betrays divided opinions among the subject classes in that instance. We can affirm with much more confidence, however, that there was similar division of opinion in 370. In Laconia, according to many perioeci defected prior to the Theban advance, and all the helots too. The latter claim must be an exaggeration, however. Plutarch mentions Laconian helots who, when captured by Thebans and told to sing the works of Terpander, Alcman and Spendon the Spartan, declined to do so on the excuse that their masters did not approve. Even if this incident occurred in one of the subsequent Theban invasions rather than in 370 itself, it was undoubtedly during this year that neodamodeis were employed for the last time known, and a frantic promise of freedom made to any helot who agreed to enlist. Xenophon says that over 6,000 did so. Not surprisingly, on the immediate enlistment of such a horde Spartan nerves were shaken for a time, just as they had been during the crises of the 420s; we do also hear that some perioeci and helots deserted during the fighting. However, the striking feature is the number of Laconian helots willing to fight loyally for Sparta even in these desperate straits.

* * *

By the fifth century, generations of subjugation had eventually conditioned most helots in both Laconia and Messenia to accept their inferior condition—in all likelihood by gradual stages which can no longer be distinguished. As has been shown, helots when called upon were even willing to undertake military or naval service, and were content with such modest rewards for this as the state began to offer from the late fifth century. Once enlisted they followed unswervingly wherever they were led, without ever attempting to question the justification for any campaign; in the same way, after their obedient return from abroad they caused no trouble. Consciously or otherwise they assimilated many traditional "Spartiate" qualities—conservatism, obedience, self-denial, and pride in military service alongside Spartiates and under their leadership. It does not seem to have been the case with helots, as it clearly was with many Spartiates, that service abroad had an adverse, unsettling effect on their behaviour and opinions. It is true that ideas of an independent Messenia were somehow formed and maintained, and that helots did revolt after the shock of the great earthquake. But once this rising had been suppressed, most of them quickly returned to their old loyalties and stuck to them until after Leuctra. Even then only the Messenians broke free, and the initiatives taken thereafter to keep them free were all external: in its first years the new state was restricted in area, weak, and in no sense prepared for independence. Not unsurprisingly Sparta for her part long continued keen to maintain her claim to Messenia.

The evidence suggests that helots smarted under Spartiate haughtiness and brutality, but endured them passively. To be sure, the self-confidence of the master class was shaken from time to time, and certain precautions were taken to reduce the potential danger of a rising. But not until Athens made devastating gains in Messenia during the 420s did the Spartiates fully realize just how much the nature of their relationship with the helots had become transformed to their own great advantage. This new perception was hardly imparted to other Greeks. But as a result of it the Spartiates could increasingly exploit the helots without making them any significant sacrifices or concessions. From the mid fifth century fear of the helots was seldom, if ever, an over-riding concern in the determination of state policy. By about 400 the number of *neodamodeis* available for call-up even exceeded that of the Spartiates themselves. The latter could normally apply themselves to the wider affairs of Greece and beyond, or seek to satisfy their private cravings for wealth and luxury, without fear of a helot onslaught.

The state's real problems, and the causes of its downfall, lay elsewhere. Most serious of all were the tensions and inequalities within the Spartiate group and the pursuit of overambitious foreign policies. By this date the helots were an insignificant element in the Spartan class struggle. Indeed their unquestioning service on the land and on campaign played a major role in supporting the state's foreign ambitions long after the Spartiate class had lost the capacity to pursue them by itself. Paradoxically those military disasters of the mid 420s which produced extreme fear of helot revolt among the Spartiates in all probability also galvanized them into creating neodamodeis. However the supreme irony was that the thousands of helots who served as loyal troops during the late fifth and early fourth centuries faithfully upheld the old Spartiate ideals at just the same time as these were lapsing beyond recovery among their masters. Only the cataclysm of Leuctra and its aftermath offered the right opportunity to rouse helots from their subservience, and in Laconia even these shocks were not enough.

Consider

1. How does the Thucydides passage 4.80 figure into Cartledge's argument about the threat helot rebellion posed to Sparta?
2. What questions does Cartledge raise about Thucydides as a historian?
3. How might Thucydides have come upon the story of the helot massacre and why did he believe it?
4. Why does Cartledge think Thucydides included the story about the massacre?
5. How does Cartledge define the term "helot" and how do helots compare with chattel slaves?
6. How does he distinguish between Laconian and Messenian helots?
7. What factors might have led to the helot rebellions in 464 and 370 BC according to Cartledge?
8. How does Talbert explain these two great helot risings?
9. What factors does each scholar downplay?
10. How might civil strife (*stasis*) have contributed to the risk of a helot uprising?
11. What factors does Cartledge think are essential for a slave revolt to succeed?
12. Analyze Talbert's ideas about the political awareness and class consciousness of the helots in light of the opinion of Cartledge. Why does Talbert discuss the service of helots and freed helots (*neodamodeis*) in the Spartan army?
13. Compare Talbert's ideas concerning the attempted rebellion of Cinadon with those of Cartledge.

CHAPTER 4
SOLON'S CONSTITUTION

SOLON HAS BEEN KNOWN since antiquity as one of the Seven Wise Men of Greece and as the great lawgiver of Athens. He first achieved fame in the late seventh or early sixth century BC by playing a critical role in Athens' victory over its bitter rival Megara. In 594 Solon's countrymen appointed him sole archon (i.e., chief magistrate) for one year to settle the economic and political crisis of Attica. At that time many Athenian citizens had fallen into debt bondage and many more (*hektemoroi*) were on the verge of servitude. The resulting conflict between the large land–owning aristocrats and the smallholders threatened to erupt into civil war. Infighting among the aristocrats themselves aggravated the situation. Furthermore, the hostility felt by the new class of well-to-do Athenians, who were barred from high office because of the birth requirement, added to the political tension. The threat that a tyrant might rise to power in Athens forced the aristocrats to turn to one of their peers to resolve their problems. In an attempt to stave off a tyranny, Solon took office and enacted the laws and established the constitution that makes up the subject for this chapter.

The phenomenon of tyranny in the Greek world forms the context within which Solon's rise to power and his reforms took place. In the seventh century, figures known as tyrants seized power in a number of poleis, such as Argos, Corinth, and Megara. The words "tyrant" and "tyranny" are of non-Greek origin and refer to the nature of a tyrant's rule without the negative connotations the terms later acquired in the Greek and modern world. A tyrant was almost certainly an aristocrat, but neither his peers nor the people elected him to office according to the laws nor did he inherit his power. The tyrants invariably used violence to secure their positions and to rule with absolute power once in office. The illegitimate and irresponsible nature of their rule caused the eventual overthrow of a Greek tyrant or family of tyrants. This was despite the fact that the tyrant was often a popular leader who benefited his city. For example, in about 655 BC, Cypselus of Corinth overthrew the ruling clan of the Bacchiads and made himself tyrant with the support of the people. He set up a dynasty which lasted for over 70 years. The Cypselids promoted trade, undertook a public building program, and made Corinth the most prosperous state in Greece. Like Solon, Periander, the son and successor of Cypselus, was included among the Seven Wise Men. However, the tradition was hostile toward him and the rule of the Cypselids ended after his brutal reign. It was typical for a tyranny to become harsh in the second generation, and no tyranny could maintain its power past the third as the people would grow tired of a tyrant's absolute power, and the aristocrats, no doubt, would abhor the figure that was responsible for destroying their power if not their lives.

In 632 the Olympic victor Cylon made an abortive attempt to seize the acropolis and establish himself as tyrant of Athens. Unlike the situation in many Greek poleis in the seventh century, there was insufficient support in Athens from the emerging hoplite class for Cylon to overthrow the ruling aristocrats. Several years later, in 621, the Athenians entrusted Draco to draw up the city's first written law code to put an end to the aristocrats' (i.e., the Eupatrids') monopoly on knowledge of the laws. But Draco's "constitution," infamous for its severity, failed to resolve the growing economic, social, and political problems of Attica. When Solon took office in 594 BC, he abolished enslavement for debt through a measure known as the *seisachtheia* or "shaking off of burdens." Henceforth it was illegal to use one's body to secure a loan. Next, he set up four census classes (*pentakosiomedimnoi, hippeis, zeugitai,* and *thetai*) which substituted wealth for birth as the criterion for holding political office. Solon's laws also made it possible for any citizen to appeal the decision of a magistrate and to institute a public action (i.e., the *graphe*) on behalf of any wronged citizen or in the public interest. A spirit of compromise and moderation marked the legislation and political reforms of Solon. For example, in defiance of the hopes of the poor, he did not cancel all debts or redistribute the land; at the same time, contrary to the wishes of the aristocrats, Solon refused to maintain the status quo. His ideal for Athens was *eunomia*, the reign of good law. This meant that wealthy landowners should control the government but recognize the legitimate and essential function of the lower classes in the polis.

The reforms of Solon had great significance for the rise of Athenian democracy under Cleisthenes and Pericles. On the other hand, although the fourth-century Athenians asserted that Solon was the founder of their democracy, the word *demokratia* was not coined until the fifth century. In any case, Solon would have opposed placing dominant political power in the hands of the lower classes. But the fact that later Greek writers, especially Aristotle and Plutarch, attributed certain concepts and institutions of the fifth and fourth centuries to Solon raises problems of interpretation for modern scholars. The tradition that Solon established a Council of Four Hundred with 100 members from each of the four Ionian tribes is of particular interest. Plutarch states that under Solon the council prepared the agenda for the assembly. Many scholars, such as Charles Hignett, dispute that claim and believe that the original Boule was the Council of Five Hundred of Cleisthenes. For Hignett, Solon was an agent of the aristocrats who hoped to open up the archonship to non-Eupatrids while maintaining the status quo. However, G.E.M. de Ste. Croix sees in the Council of Four Hundred the revolutionary character of Solon's reform.

Ancient Sources

1. Solon (Selections), THE ATHENIAN CRISIS
2. Aristotle, *Constitution of the Athenians*, 5–12, REFORM OF SOLON
3. Aristotle, *Politics,* 1273b35–1274a22; 1296a1–22, SOLON'S MODERATION
4. Plutarch, *Life of Solon*, 13–18, THE CONSTITUTION OF SOLON

Opinions of Modern Scholars

1. From Charles Hignett, *A History of the Athenian Constitution to the End of the Fifth Century B.C.*
2. From G. E. M. de Ste. Croix, *Athenian Democratic Origins: and Other Essays*

ANCIENT SOURCES FOR SOLON'S CONSTITUTION

1.   THE ATHENIAN CRISIS

The surviving fragments come from a variety of sources and shed light on how Solon viewed the nature and significance of his political actions.

THE SUDA

Solon, son of Execestides, was an Athenian philosopher, lawgiver, and leader of the people. He flourished in the 47th Olympiad (592/89), according to others in the 56th (556/3). When the tyrant Pisistratus plotted against him, he spent time abroad in Cilicia and founded a city which he called Soloi after himself. Others say that also Soloi in Cyprus was named after him and that he died in Cyprus. He wrote laws for the Athenians which were given the name *axones* because they were written on wooden axles in Athens. He wrote an elegiac poem entitled *Salamis*, elegiac exhortations, and others. He is also one of the Seven Sages, as they are called. The maxims "Nothing in excess" and "Know yourself" are said to be his.

FROM DEMOSTHENES, *ON THE EMBASSY*

Please take and read these elegiac verses of Solon, so that you (the jury) may know that Solon too hated such men (as the defendant)...Now read:

> Our state will never perish through the dispensation of Zeus or the intentions of the blessed immortal gods; for such a stout-hearted guardian, Pallas Athena, born of a mighty father, holds her hands over it. But it is the citizens themselves who by their acts of foolishness and subservience to money are willing to destroy a great city, and the mind of the people's leaders is unjust; they are certain to suffer much pain as a result of their great arrogance. For they do not know how to restrain excess or to conduct in an orderly and peaceful manner the festivities of the banquet that are at hand...they grow wealthy, yielding to unjust deeds...sparing neither sacred nor private property, they steal with rapaciousness, one from one source, one from another, and they have no regard for the august foundations of Justice, who bears silent witness to the present and the past and who in time assuredly comes to exact retribution. This is now coming upon the whole city as an inescapable wound and the city has quickly approached wretched slavery, which arouses civil strife and slumbering war, the loss for many of their lovely youth. For at the hands of its enemies the much-loved city is being swiftly worn down amid conspiracies dear to the unjust. These are the evils that are rife among the people, and many of the poor are going to a foreign land, sold and bound in shameful fetters...And so the public evil comes home to each man and the courtyard gates no longer have the will to hold it back, but it leaps over the high barrier and assuredly finds him out, even if he takes refuge in an innermost corner of his room. This is what my heart bids me teach the Athenians, that Lawlessness brings the city countless ills, but Lawfulness reveals all that is orderly and fitting, and often places fetters round the unjust. She makes the rough smooth, puts a stop to excess, weakens insolence, dries up the blooming flowers of ruin, straightens out crooked judgements, tames deeds of pride, and puts an end to acts of sedition and to the anger of grievous strife. Under her all things among men are fitting and rational.

You hear, men of Athens, what Solon has to say about such men and about the gods who, he says, keep our city safe...And again showing how the masses should be treated:

> And in this way the masses would best follow their leaders, if they are neither given too much freedom nor subjected to too much restraint. For excess breeds insolence, whenever great prosperity comes to men who are not sound of mind.

FROM DIODORUS SICULUS, *WORLD HISTORY*

Solon is said to have foretold the Athenians of the coming tyranny (i.e., Pisistratus) in elegiac verses:

> From a cloud comes the force of snow and
> hail, thunder from a flash of lightning,

from powerful men a city's destruction, and through ignorance the masses fall enslaved to a tyrant. If they raise a man too high, it's not easy to restrain him afterwards; it is now that one should consider everything.

FROM DIODORUS SICULUS

And afterwards, when Pisistratus was tyrant, he said:

> If you have suffered grief because of your
> wrong action, do not lay the blame for
> this on the gods. You yourselves increased
> the power of these men by providing a

bodyguard and that is why you have foul slavery. Each one of you follows the fox's tracks, and collectively you are empty-headed. You look to the tongue and words of a crafty man, but not to what he does.

FROM STOBAEUS

Resplendent daughters of Memory and Olympian Zeus, Pierian Muses, hearken to my prayer. Grant that I have prosperity from the blessed gods and a good reputation always from all men; grant that in these circumstances I be sweet to my friends and bitter to my enemies, viewed with respect by the former and with dread by the latter. I long to have money, but I am unwilling to possess it unjustly, for retribution assuredly comes afterwards. Wealth which the gods give remains with a man, secure from the lowest foundation to the top, whereas wealth which men honour with violence comes in disorder, an unwilling attendant persuaded by unjust actions, and it is quickly mixed with ruin. Ruin has a small beginning, like that of fire, insignificant at first but grievous in the end, for mortals' deeds of violence do not live long. Zeus oversees every outcome, and suddenly, just as the clouds are quickly scattered by a spring wind which stirs up the bottom of the swelling and undraining [?] sea, ravages the lovely fields over the wheat-bearing land, reaches the gods' high seat in heaven, and again brings a clear sky to view; the strong sun shines in beauty over the fertile land and no longer can even a single cloud be seen—such is the vengeance of Zeus. He is not, like a mortal man, quick to anger at every incident, but anyone who has a sinful heart never ever escapes his notice and in the end he is assuredly revealed. But one man pays the penalty at once, another later, and if they themselves escape the penalty and the pursuing destiny of the gods does not overtake them, it assuredly comes at another time; the innocent pay the penalty, either their children or a later progeny. And thus we mortals, whatever our estate, think that the expectation which each one has is progressing well [?], until he suffers some mishap, and then afterwards he wails. But until then we take eager delight in empty hopes. Whoever is oppressed by grievous sickness thinks that he will be healthy; another man of low estate considers that it's high and that he's handsome, though his form is without beauty. If someone is lacking means and is constrained by the effects of poverty, he thinks that he will assuredly acquire much money. Everyone has a different pursuit. One roams over the fish-filled sea in ships, longing to bring home profit; tossed by cruel winds, he has no regard for life. Another, whose concern is the curved plough, cleaves the thickly wooded land and slaves away for a year. Another who has learned the works of Athena and Hephaestus, the god of many crafts, gathers in his livelihood with his hands; another, taught the gifts that come from the Olympian Muses and knowing the rules of the lovely art of poetry, makes his living. Another has been made a seer by lord Apollo who works from afar and, if the gods are with him, he sees a distant calamity coming upon a man; but assuredly neither augury nor sacrifice will ward off what is destined. Others, engaged in the work of Paeon, rich in drugs, are physicians; for them too there is no guarantee. Often agony results from a slight pain and no one can provide relief by giving soothing drugs, whereas another, in the throes of a terrible and grievous disease, he quickly restores to health with the touch of his hands. Fate brings good and ill to mortals and the gifts of the immortal gods are inescapable. In all actions there is risk and no one knows, when something starts, how it is going to turn out. The man who tries to act rightly falls unawares into great and harsh calamity, while to the one who acts badly the god gives success in all things, an escape from his folly. But of wealth no limit lies revealed to men, since those of us who now have the greatest livelihood show twice as much zeal. What could satisfy everyone? In truth the immortals give men profit, but from it [them?] there is revealed ruin, which now one, now another has, whenever Zeus sends it to punish them.

Questions

1. **What were Solon's views on justice and tyranny?**
2. **How does the concept of moderation figure into the thought of Solon?**

---

2.   REFORM OF SOLON

Aristotle's *Athenian Constitution* is one of the main sources for Solon's archonship. The account of the philosopher draws heavily on the poetry of Solon.

5. Such being the system in the constitution, and the many being enslaved to the few, the people rose against the notables. The party struggle being violent and the parties remaining arrayed in opposition to one another for a long time, they jointly chose Solon as arbitrator and Archon, and entrusted the government to him, after he had composed the elegy that begins:

I mark, and sorrow fills my breast to see,
Ionia's oldest land being done to death,

in which he does battle on behalf of each party against the other and acts as mediator, and after this exhorts them jointly to stop the quarrel that prevailed between them. Solon was by birth and reputation of the first rank, but by wealth and position belonged to the middle class, as is admitted on the part of the other authorities, and as he himself testifies in these poems, exhorting the wealthy not to be covetous:

Refrain ye in your hearts those stubborn moods,
Plunged in a surfeit of abundant goods,

And moderate your pride! We'll not submit,
Nor even you yourselves will this befit.

And he always attaches the blame for the civil strife wholly to the rich; owing to which at the beginning of the elegy he says that he fears

Both love of money and overweening pride—
implying that these were the causes of the enmity
    that prevailed.

6. Solon having become master of affairs made the people free both at the time and for the future by prohibiting loans secured on the person, and he laid down laws, and enacted cancellations of debts both private and public, the measures that are known as "the Shaking-off of Burdens," meaning that the people shook off their load. In these matters some people try to misrepresent him; for it happened that when Solon was intending to enact the Shaking-off of Burdens, he informed some of the notables beforehand, and afterwards, as those of popular sympathies say, he was out-manoeuvred by his friends, but according to those who want to malign him he himself also took a share. For these persons borrowed money and bought up a quantity of land, and when not long afterwards the cancellation of debts took place they were rich men; and this is said to be the origin of the families subsequently reputed to be ancestrally wealthy. Nevertheless, the account of those of popular sympathies is more credible; for considering that he was so moderate and public-spirited in the rest of his conduct that, when he had the opportunity to reduce one of the two parties to subjection and so to be tyrant of the city, he incurred the enmity of both, and valued honour and the safety of the state more than his own aggrandizement, it is not probable that he besmirched himself in such worthless trifles. And that he got this opportunity is testified by the disordered state of affairs, and also he himself alludes to it in many places in his poems, and everybody else agrees with him. We are bound therefore to consider this charge to be false.

7. And he established a constitution and made other laws, and they ceased to observe the ordinances of Draco, except those relating to homicide. They wrote up the laws on the Boards and set them in the Royal Colonnade, and all swore to observe them; and the Nine Archons used to make affirmation on oath at the Stone that if they transgressed any one of the laws they would dedicate a gold statue of a man; owing to which they are even now still sworn in with this oath. And he fixed the laws to stay unaltered for a hundred years. And he arranged the constitution in the following way: he divided the people by assessment into four classes, as they had been divided before, Five-hundred-measure man, Horseman, Teamster and Labourer, and he distributed the other offices to be held from among the Five-hundred-measure men, Horsemen and Teamsters—the Nine Archons, the Treasurers, the Vendors of Contracts, the Eleven and the Paymasters, assigning each office to the several classes in proportion to the amount of their assessment; while those who were rated in the Labourer class he admitted to the membership of the assembly and law-courts alone. Any man had to be rated as a Five-hundred-measure man the produce from whose estate was five hundred dry and liquid measures jointly, and at the cavalry-rate those who made three hundred,—or as some say, those who were able to keep a horse, and they adduce as a proof the name of the rating as being derived from the fact, and also the votive offerings of

the ancients; for there stands dedicated in the Acropolis a statue of Diphilus on which are inscribed these lines:

Anthemion Diphilus's son dedicated this statue to
  the gods
having exchanged the Labourer rating for the
  Cavalry

and a horse stands beside him, in evidence that "cavalry" meant the class able to keep a horse. Nevertheless it is more probable that the cavalry were distinguished by their amounts of produce as the Five-hundred-measure men were. And men had to be rated in the Teamster class who made two hundred measures, wet and dry together; while the rest were rated in the Labourer class, being admitted to no office: hence even now when the presiding official asks a man who is about to draw lots for some office what rate he pays, no one whatever would say that he was rated as a Labourer.

8.1 For the offices of state he instituted election by lot from candidates selected by the tribes several by a preliminary vote. For the Nine Archons each tribe made a preliminary selection of ten, and the election was made from among these by lot; hence there still survives with the tribes the system that each elects ten by lot and then they choose from among these by ballot. And a proof that he made the offices elective by lot according to assessments is the law in regard to the Treasurers that remains in force even at the present day; for it orders the Treasurers to be elected by lot from the Five-hundred-measure men. **[2]** Solon, therefore, legislated thus about the Nine Archons; for in ancient times the Council on the Areopagus used to issue a summons and select independently the person suitable for each of the offices, and commission him to hold office for a year. **[3]** And there were four Tribes, as before, and four Tribal Kings. And from each Tribe there had been assigned three Thirds and twelve Ship-boards to each, and over the Ship-boards there was established the office of Ship-commissioners, appointed for the levies and the expenditures that were made; because of which in the laws of Solon, which are no longer in force, the clauses frequently occur, "the Ship-commissioner to levy" and "to spend out of the Ship-commission Fund." And he made a Council of four hundred members, a hundred from each tribe, but appointed the Council of the Areopagus to the duty of guarding the laws, just as it had existed even before as overseer of the constitution, and it was this Council that kept watch over the greatest number and the most important of the affairs of state, in particular correcting offenders with sovereign powers both to fine and punish, and making returns of its expenditure to the Acropolis without adding a statement of the reason for the outlay, and trying persons that conspired to put down the democracy, Solon having laid down a law of impeachment in regard to them. [4] And as he saw that the state was often in a condition of party strife, while some of the citizens through slackness were content to let things slide, he laid down a special law to deal with them, enacting that whoever when civil strife prevailed did not join forces with either party was to be disfranchised and not to be a member of the state.

9.1 This then was the nature of his reforms in regard to the offices of state. And the three most democratic features in Solon's constitution seem to be these first and most important the prohibition of loans secured upon the person, secondly the liberty allowed to anybody who wished to exact redress on behalf of injured persons, and third, what is said to have been the chief basis of the powers of the multitude, the right of appeal to the jury-court—for the people, having the power of the vote, becomes sovereign in the government. [2] And also, since the laws are not drafted simply nor clearly, but like the law about inheritances and heiresses, it inevitably results that many disputes take place and that the jury-court is the umpire in all business both public and private. Therefore some people think that Solon purposely made his laws obscure, in order that the people might be sovereign over the verdict. But this is unlikely—probably it was due to his not being able to define the ideal in general terms; for it is not fair to study his intention in the light of what happens at the present day, but to judge it from the rest of his constitution.

10.1 Solon therefore seems to have laid down these enactments of a popular nature in his laws; while before his legislation his democratic reform was his cancellation of debts, and afterwards his raising the standard of the measures and weights and of the coinage. [2] For it was in his time that the measures were made larger than those of Pheidon, and that the mina, which previously had a weight of seventy drachmae, was increased to the full hundred. The ancient coin-type was the two-drachma piece.

Solon also instituted weights corresponding to the currency, the talent weighing sixty-three minae, and a fraction proportionate to the additional three minae was added to the stater and the other weights.

11.1 When Solon had organized the constitution in the manner stated, people kept coming to him and worrying him about his laws, criticizing some points and asking questions about others; so as he did not wish either to alter these provisions or to stay and incur enmity, he went abroad on a journey to Egypt, for the purpose both of trading and of seeing the country, saying that he would not come back for ten years, as he did not think it fair for him to stay and explain his laws, but for everybody to carry out their provisions for himself. [2] At the same time it befell him that many of the notables had become at variance with him because of the cancellations of debts, and also that both the factions changed their attitude to him because the settlement had disappointed them. For the people had thought that he would institute universal communism of property, whereas the notables had thought that he would either restore the system in the same form as it was before or with slight alteration; but Solon went against them both, and when he might have been tyrant if he had taken sides with whichever of the two factions he wished, he chose to incur the enmity of both by saving the country and introducing the legislation that was best.

12.1 That this is how it happened is the unanimous account of everybody, and in particular Solon himself in his poetry recalls the matter in these words:

For to the people gave I grace enough,
Nor from their honour took, nor proffered more
While those possessing power and graced with
    wealth,
These too I made to suffer nought unseemly;
I stood protecting both with a strong shield,
And suffered neither to prevail unjustly.

[2] And again, when declaring about how the multitude ought to be treated:

Thus would the people with the chiefs best follow,
With neither too much freedom nor compulsion;
Satiety breeds insolence when riches
Attend the men whose mind is not prepared.

[3] And again in a different place he says about those who wish to divide up the land:

They that came on plunder bent were filled with
    over-lavish hope,
Each and all imagining that they would find abun-
    dant wealth,
And that I, though smoothly glozing, would display
    a purpose rough.
Vain and boastful then their fancies; now their bile
    against me is stirred,
And with eyes askance they view me, and all deem
    me as a foe—
Wrongly: for the things I promised, those by
    heaven's aid I did,
And much else, no idle exploits; nothing did it please
    my mind
By tyrannic force to compass, nor that in our father-
    land
Base and noble should have equal portion in her
    fertile soil.

[4] And again about the cancellation of debts, and those who were in slavery before but were liberated by the Shaking-off of Burdens:

But what did I leave unachieved, of all
The ends for which I did unite the people?
Whereof before the judgement-seat of Time
The mighty mother of the Olympian gods,
Black Earth, would best bear witness, for twas I
Removed her many boundary-posts implanted:
Ere then she was a slave, but now is free.
And many sold away I did bring home

To god-built Athens, this one sold unjustly,
That other justly; others that had fled
From dire constraint of need, uttering no more
Their Attic tongue, so widely had they wandered,
And others suffering base slavery
Even here, trembling before their masters'
    humours,
I did set free. These deeds I made prevail,
Adjusting might and right to fit together.
And did accomplish even as I had promised.
And rules of law alike for base and noble,
Fitting straight justice unto each man's case,
I drafted. Had another than myself
Taken the goad, unwise and covetous,
He'd not have held the people! Had I willed
Now that pleased one of the opposing parties,
And then whatever the other party bade them,
The city had been bereft of many men.
Wherefore I stood at guard on every side,
A wolf at bay among a pack of hounds!

[5] And again in his taunting reply to the later queru-lous complaints of both the parties:

If openly I must reprove the people.
Ne'er in the dreams of sleep could they have seen
    the things that they have now
While all the greater and the mightier men
Might praise me and might deem me as a friend;
for had another, he says, won this office,
He had not checked the people nor refrained,
Ere he had churned and robbed the milk of cream;
But I as 'twere betwixt their armed hosts
A frontier-post did stand.

Questions

1. **What were the political and economic circumstances in Athens under which Solon came to power?**
2. **What steps did Solon take to remedy the ills of the state according to Aristotle?**
3. **How does Aristotle use Solon's poetry to support his interpretation of the reforms?**
4. **Is his explanation convincing? Why or why not?**

---

3. SOLON'S MODERATION

Certain excerpts from Aristotle's *Politics* tell us about his ideas on moderation and good government as well as his thoughts on Solon's constitution.

1273b [2] As for Solon, he is considered by some people to have been a good lawgiver, as having put an end to oligarchy when it was too unqualified and having liberated the people from slavery and established our traditional democracy with a skilful blending of the constitution: the Council on the Areopagus being an oligarchic element, the elective magistracies aristocratic and the law-courts democratic. And although really in regard to certain of these features, the Council and the election of magistrates, **1274a** Solon seems merely to have abstained from destroying institutions that existed already, he does appear to have founded the democracy by constituting the jury-courts from all the citizens. [3] For this he is actually blamed by some persons, as having dissolved the power of the other parts of the community by making the law-court, which was elected by lot, all-powerful. For as the law-court grew strong, men courted favour with the people as with a tyrant, and so brought the constitution to the present democracy; and Ephialtes and Pericles docked the power of the Council on the Areopagus, while Pericles instituted payment for serving in the law-courts, and in this manner finally the successive leaders of the people led them on by growing stages to the present democracy. [4] But this does not seem to have come about in accordance with the intention of Solon, but rather as a result of accident (for the common people having been the cause of naval victory at the time of the Persian invasion became proud and adopted bad men as popular leaders when the respectable classes opposed their policy); inasmuch as Solon for his part appears to bestow only the minimum of power upon the people, the function of electing the magistrates and of calling them to account (for if even this were not under the control of the populace it would be a mere slave and a foreign enemy), whereas he appointed all the offices from the notable and the wealthy, the Five-hundred-bushel class and the Teamsters and a third property-class called the Knighthood; while the fourth class, the Thetes, were admitted to no office.

* * *

1296a [9] That the middle form of constitution is the best is evident; for it alone is free from faction, since where the middle class is numerous, factions and party divisions among the citizens are least likely to occur. And the great states are more free from faction for the same reason, because the middle class is numerous, whereas in the small states it is easy to divide the whole people into two parties leaving nothing in between, and also almost everybody is needy or wealthy. Also democracies are more secure and more long-lived than oligarchies owing to the citizens of the middle class (for they are more numerous and have a larger share of the honours in democracies than in oligarchies), since when the poor are in a majority without the middle class, adversity sets in and they are soon ruined. [10] And it must be deemed a significant fact that the best lawgivers are from among the middle citizens; for Solon was of that class, as appears from his poetry, and so was Lycurgus (for he was not a king) and Charondas and almost the greatest number of the other lawgivers.

Questions

1. How does Aristotle believe Solon achieved a "mixed" constitution with his reforms?
2. Compare and contrast Aristotle's account of the reforms of Solon in the *Athenian Constitution* with that found in the *Politics*? Why might the two works differ from one another?

---

4. THE CONSTITUTION OF SOLON

The most extensive ancient source of Solon is Plutarch's *Life of Solon*. The extract below concentrates on the circumstances under which Solon became archon and also the changes the lawgiver made in the constitution of the Athenians.

13. However, once the disturbances concerning Cylon were past and those involved in the blood-guilt had been banished, as I have described, the Athenians relapsed into their perennial squabbles about the form their government should take. The city was divided into as many parties as there were geographical features in its territory. The party of the Hill supported an extreme democracy, the Plain an extreme oligarchy, while the Shore formed a third party, which wanted a mixed form of government somewhere in between, opposed the other two and prevented either of them from getting the upper hand. At this point, too, the inequalities between rich and poor had, as it were, conic to a head. The city stood on the brink of revolution, and it seemed as if the only way to put a stop to its perpetual disorders and achieve stability was to set up a tyranny. All the common people were weighed down with the debts they owed to a few rich men. They either cultivated their lands for them and paid them a sixth of the produce and were hence called Hektemoroi and Thetes, or else they pledged their own persons to raise money and could be seized by their creditors, some of them being enslaved at home, and others being sold to foreigners abroad. Many parents were even forced to sell their own children (for there was no law to prevent this), or to go into exile because of the harshness of their creditors. However, the majority, which included the men of most spirit, began to make common cause together and encourage one another not to resign themselves to these injustices, but to choose a man they could trust to lead them. Having done this, they proposed to set all enslaved debtors free, redistribute the land and make a complete reform of the constitution.

14. At this point the most level-headed of the Athenians began to look towards Solon. They saw that he, more than anyone else, stood apart from the injustices of the time and was involved neither in the extortions of the rich nor the privations of the poor, and so finally they appealed to him to come forward and settle their differences. Phanias of Lesbos, however, maintains that Solon of his own accord went behind the backs of both parties in order to save the city, and secretly promised the poor that he would redistribute the land, and the rich that he would guarantee the pledges which were their security. Solon's own version is that he only engaged in politics very unwillingly, because he was afraid of the grasping nature of the one party and the arrogance of the other. However, he was chosen archon in succession to Philombrotus to act both as arbitrator and as legislator, for the rich were ready to accept him as a man of wealth and the poor as a man of principle. It is also said that a remark of his to the effect that "equality breeds no strife" was widely repeated before his election and pleased property-owners and paupers alike; the first assumed that he meant an equality based on merit and achievement, and the second a quantitative equality based on the counting of heads. Consequently, both sides' hopes were raised and both sets of leaders repeatedly pressed upon Solon the idea of establishing a tyranny: they sought to persuade him that he could seize control of the city with all the greater confidence now that he had it in his power. There were many people, besides, who were not attached to either party and who saw that it would be a weary and laborious process to bring about any radical change by means of debate and legislation, and they were by no means unwilling to have a single man, the justest and wisest in the state, placed at the head of affairs. There are some who say that Solon received an oracle from Delphi, which ran as follows:

Seat yourself now amidships, for you are the pilot of
    Athens.
Grasp the helm fast in your hands; you have many
    allies in your city.

His intimate friends reproached him most of all for turning his back upon absolute power merely because he shrank from the name of tyrant, without allowing for the fact that the virtues of the man who assumed such authority could transform it at once into a lawful sovereignty. They quoted the earlier precedent of Tynnondas in Euboea and the contemporary one of Pittacus, whom the people of Mytilene had chosen to be their tyrant.

None of these arguments could shake Solon's resolution. His reply to his friends, we are told, was that tyranny is a fine place in itself but there is no way down from it, and in one of his poems he writes to Phocus:

And if I spared my country
Refrained from ruthless violence and tyranny
And chose to keep my name free from all taint
I fed no shame at this; instead, I believe
It will be my greatest glory?

From this it seems clear that he enjoyed a great reputation, even before he became the lawgiver of Athens. As for the taunts that were hurled at him for refusing the tyranny, he has written as follows:

Solon was no deep thinker, not even a man of sound
    judgement;
When the gods showered good fortune upon him, he
    only refused it.
When his nets swarmed with fish, he could not pull
    them in for amazement.
Give me the chance to be tyrant, with such power
    and infinite riches
I should not turn it down, though I ruled but a day
    over Athens;
Then I could bear to be flayed and my name cast
    into oblivion.

15. This is how he makes the unscrupulous elements and, indeed, the people in general speak of him. But in spite of his refusal to become a tyrant, he was by no means over-indulgent in his handling of affairs and there was nothing feeble about his legislation. It did not make concessions to the strong, nor did it humour the whims of the voters. Wherever he approved of the existing arrangement, he made no attempt to remedy or meddle with it, for he feared that if he turned everything upside down and thoroughly disorganized the state, he might not have power enough to restore order and reconstitute it for the best. He only introduced changes where he believed he could get his way by persuasion or enforce it by authority, and, in this fashion, as he puts it, he

Made force and justice work in harmony.

And so, when at a later date he was asked whether he had provided the best laws for the Athenians, his reply was, "The best that they would accept."

    Later writers point out that the Athenians were in the habit of disguising the unpleasant aspects of things by giving them endearing and charitable names and finding polite equivalents for them. Thus they refer to whores as *mistresses*, taxes as *contributions*, garrisons of cities as *guards*, and the common gaol as *the residence*. Solon, it appears, became a pioneer of this device, when he referred to his cancelling of all debts as a *discharge*. The first measure which he put into force decreed that

existing debts were wiped out and that in future nobody could accept the person of a debtor as security. Some writers, however, Androtion among them, maintain that Solon relieved the poor, not by wiping out their debts, but by reducing the interest on them, and that they were so delighted by this act of humanity, that they gave the name of "discharge" not only to that decree, but also to the enlargement of various Attic measures and the rise in the value of money which took place at the same time. Solon fixed the value of the mina at 100 drachmas, whereas it had previously consisted of seventy-three. In this way, although the actual amount of payment remained the same, its value was less, so that the debtors received a substantial benefit without their creditors being any the worse. However, most writers agree that the so-called "discharge" meant the abolition of pledges, and Solon's own poems support this interpretation, for in these he prides himself on having uprooted the mortgage stones that everywhere were planted and freed the fields that were enslaved before. He also speaks of bringing back from foreign countries some of the citizens whose persons had been seized for debt

Who speak no more their native tongue, So far their
    wanderings in distant lands;
And others who dwelt at home in shameful
    bondage...he says he set free.

This problem is said to have involved him in the greatest trouble of his whole life. When he had made up his mind to abolish the debts and was thinking over the best arguments to justify the measure and the best occasion for introducing it, he confided to his most intimate friends, Conon, Cleinias, and Hipponicus, that he did not intend to touch the land, but had decided to abolish debts. They promptly took advantage of this confidence and anticipated the decree by borrowing large sums from the rich and buying up big estates. Then, when the decree was published, they went on enjoying the use of their property but refused to pay their creditors. This affair gave rise to the most damning accusations against Solon and brought him into great discredit, for people could hardly believe that he was the victim of such a trick and concluded that he must have been a party to it. However, he was able to repudiate this charge at once by the well-known sacrifice he made of five talents; for it came to light that he had lent this amount and he was the first to comply with his own law by cancelling the debt. Some people, among them Polyzelus the Rhodian, say that the sum was fifteen talents. His friends, on the other hand, were for ever after known as *chreocopidae*, or swindlers.

16. At first, however, his policy did not please either party. The rich were angry at being deprived of their securities, and the poor even more so, because Solon did not carry out a redistribution of the land, as they had expected, or impose a strictly equal and uniform style of living upon everybody, as Lycurgus had done. But Lycurgus, it must be remembered, was the eleventh in direct descent from Heracles; he had reigned for many years in Sparta, enjoyed great prestige and possessed many friends and exceptional authority, all of which he knew how to employ in support of his policy. Lycurgus also relied on force rather than on persuasion, to such an extent indeed that he actually lost an eye, but he did enact the most important measure for ensuring the safety and unity of Sparta, by making it impossible for any citizen to be either poor or rich. Solon, on the other hand, because his own fortune was modest and he was a man chosen by the people, did not achieve anything so far-reaching in his constitution; and yet, considering that his position rested on the will of the voters and their confidence in him, he certainly made full use of the power that was placed in his hands. Still, we have his own word for it in the following verses that he offended the majority, who had expected different results:

the people once placed
Extravagant hopes in me, but now they are angry
And look askance, as if I were their enemy.

And yet if anyone else, he adds, had been granted the same power

He would not have forborne nor stopped where I did, till he had shaken up the laws of the state
And skimmed the cream for himself

However, it was not long before they saw the advantages of his policy, put aside their private complaints and offered a public sacrifice, which they called the *Seisachtheia* or discharge of burdens, and they went on to appoint Solon to reform the constitution and draw up a code of laws. No limit was set to his powers and every function of the state was committed to his charge, the magistracies, the public assemblies, the courts of law and the Councils. He had authority to decide the property qualifications, the numbers and the times of meeting of each of these bodies and also to preserve or dissolve all existing institutions as he thought fit.

17. First of all, then, he repealed all the Draconian laws because of their harshness and the excessively heavy penalties they carried; the only exceptions were the laws relating to homicide. Under the Draconian code almost any kind of offence was liable to the death penalty, so that even those convicted of idleness were executed, and those who stole fruit or vegetables suffered the same punishment as those who committed sacrilege or murder. This is the reason why, in later times, Denudes became famous for his remark that Draco's code was written not in ink but in blood. Draco himself, when he was once asked why he had decreed the death penalty for the great majority of offences, replied that he considered the minor ones deserved it, and so for the major ones no heavier punishment was left.

18. Secondly, Solon was anxious to leave all the offices of state as he found them, in the hands of the rich, but at the same time to give the masses a share in the other processes of government which they had never before possessed, and he therefore took a census of every citizen's property. Those who received an annual income of 500 measures or more of wet and dry produce, he placed in the first class and called *Pentacosiomedimni*. The second class consisted of men who could afford a horse, or possessed an income of 300 measures, and these, because they paid a "horse tax," were known as Knights. The third class were the *Zeugitai*, whose yearly income amounted to 200 measures wet and dry produce. The rest of the citizen body were known as *Thetes*; they were not entitled to hold office and their only political function consisted in sitting in the Assembly or on a jury. This latter privilege appeared at first to be worth very little, but later became extremely important, because the majority of disputes were finally settled before a jury. Even in those cases which Solon placed under the jurisdiction of the magistrates, he also allowed the right of appeal to the popular court. He is said also to have framed the laws in obscure and contradictory terms and to have done this deliberately so as to increase the power of the popular courts. In consequence, since the parties to a dispute were unable to settle it according to the letter of the law, they were constantly obliged to resort to the juries and lay every disagreement before them, so that in a sense the jurors became the arbiters of the laws. Solon himself claims the credit for this in the following verses:

To the mass of the people I gave the power they
    needed,
Neither degrading them, nor giving them too much
    rein:
For those who already possessed great power and
    wealth
I saw to it that their interests were not harmed.
I stood guard with a broad shield before both
    parties
And prevented either from triumphing unjustly.

Solon considered that the common people were still weak enough to need further protection, and so he gave every citizen the privilege of going to law on behalf of any one whose rights had been infringed. If a man was assaulted or suffered violence or injury, anybody who had the ability and the desire to do so was entitled to bring a suit and prosecute the offender. In this way the lawgiver wisely accustomed the citizens as members of one body to feel and sympathize with one another's wrongs. We are also told of a saying of Solon's which echoes the spirit of this law. He was apparently asked which city he considered the best governed of all, and his reply was "The city where those who have not been wronged show themselves just as ready to punish the offender as those who have been."

19. He established the Council of the Areopagus, which was composed of men who had held the annual office of archon, and as he had done so himself; he, too, became a member of this body. He then observed that the people were becoming restive and unruly because of their release from their debts, and he therefore formed a second chamber consisting of 400 men, 100 being drawn from each of the four tribes. Its functions were to deliberate public business in advance of the general assembly, and not to allow any matter to be brought before the people without its having been previously considered. He charged the upper chamber with the task of exercising a general supervision and acting as guardian of the laws. His object here was that the state with its two Councils should ride, as it were, at double anchor and should therefore be less exposed to the buffetings of party politics and better able to secure tranquillity for the people.

Now most writers agree that the Council of the Areopagus was constituted by Solon as I have explained above. This view seems to be strongly reinforced by the fact that Draco at no point makes any mention of the members of the Areopagus, but in all cases of homicide refers to the Ephetae. On the other hand Solon's thirteenth table contains his eighth law, which is set down in these very words:

> All citizens who were disfranchised before the archonship of Solon shall recover their rights, except for those who were convicted either by the Areopagus, or by the Ephetae, or by the king-archons in the Prytaneum on charges of murder or manslaughter or attempting to set up a tyranny, and except also for those who were in exile when this law was published.

This surely points to the conclusion that the Council of the Areopagus existed before Solon's archonship and so before his legislation. For how could anybody have been condemned in the Areopagus before Solon's time if he was the first to give that court its powers of criminal jurisdiction? It may be that there is some obscurity or omission in the phrasing of the law, and that its meaning is that citizens convicted on charges coming under the jurisdiction of those who were members of the Areopagus, or Prytanes, or Ephetae when the law was published shall remain disfranchised, while those convicted on other charges shall regain their rights. However, the reader must decide this question for himself.

Questions

1. Why did the Athenians elect Solon archon according to Plutarch?
2. What changes did Solon make to the constitution to remedy the problems facing his countrymen?
3. How does Plutarch's account of these changes compare with the explanations offered by Aristotle?
4. Why might the views of Plutarch differ from those of Aristotle?

OPINIONS OF MODERN SCHOLARS

1. Charles Hignett sees Solon as a conservative politician interested in maintaining the status quo. In his view, Solon did nothing revolutionary; he sought to address the social, economic, and political crisis of the early sixth century BC by defining and limiting the functions and powers of the political organs of the aristocratic state, which remained essentially unaltered. The innovations of Solon were aimed at breaking up the Eupatrids' monopoly on political power. According to Hignett, the later political developments that culminated in Athenian democracy had little to do with either the intentions or the reforms of Solon. Charles Hignett was a fellow of Hertford College, Oxford.

FROM CHARLES HIGNETT, *A HISTORY OF THE ATHENIAN CONSTITUTION TO THE END OF THE FIFTH CENTURY B.C.*

THE CAUSES OF THIS ECONOMIC CRISIS are not revealed by Solon, and the modern attempts at an explanation are far from satisfactory. It is tempting to connect it with the economic development elsewhere in Greece already mentioned, and to suggest as many have done that it was due to the introduction of money into a society unfamiliar with it as a medium of exchange. But it is very doubtful whether money was in common use in Attica before the middle of the sixth century. Probably the real causes of the distress which drove the farmers to borrow from their rich neighbours were simpler, such as plundering raids of Megarians and other enemies, and a succession of bad harvests.

Whatever may have been the causes, the consequence was the expropriation of a number of farmers and the acquisition of their farms by the rich. Hence the dispossessed demanded a redistribution of land both before and after the reforms of Solon. But it is improbable that all the farmers had lost their freeholds; the statement in the *Athenaion Politeia* that the whole land was in the hands of a few is bound up with a fundamentally false view of the situation which Solon had to face. There must have been many freeholders left whose determination to resist expropriation constrained the nobles to accept the appointment of Solon; these farmers formed the mass of Solon's supporters and benefited from his cancellation of debts.

Their agitation against the nobles was mainly economic, but though their primary object was the redress of their immediate grievances, they might be induced to see in the composition of the government the cause of their sufferings and to support a programme of political reform. It is generally agreed that Solon's supporters included not only the farmers but some of the rich and influential citizens as well. Naturally these people joined forces with the farmers on political, not on economic grounds; they saw in this agrarian agitation an excuse for wresting political power from its present holders. Solon claims that he "brought the people together," but the sequel indicates that in his organization of the people he was aided by powerful men whose motives were not disinterested. To what class did these men belong, and what were the sources of their power? These questions must be deferred until a detailed examination of the scope of Solon's reforms has made it possible to attempt an answer to them.

In the past the true significance of Solon's reforms has been obscured by the erroneous fourth-century view which made him the founder of Athenian democracy and resulted in the ascription to Solon of institutions and changes for which he was not responsible. Even Aristotle in the *Politics*, while reacting against the current account, hardly realized to what extent the truth had been distorted by a false historical tradition. Solon retained the political organs of the aristocratic state, and in the following discussion I shall try to prove that their functions and powers, though carefully defined and limited by Solon in his code, remained substantially the same as before.

The powers of the Areopagus were apparently defined by Solon and to that extent limited, but the author of the *Athenaion Politeia* seems to be justified in his assumption that they remained essentially unaltered. He gives a summary of them, but this is incomplete, and the ancient authorities who describe the transference in 462 of most of the old powers of the Areopagus to the Council of Five Hundred and the dikasteria fail to give a clear account of the change. As the Areopagus continued to hold an important position in the state until the revolution of 462 it is essential to reconstruct as far as possible the functions which it exercised in the sixth century.

(1) It retained its previous jurisdiction under the presidency of the basileus in trials for deliberate homicide. (2) In later times, trials for impiety were held in the dikasteria but were always presided over by the basileus. Before 462 the Areopagus had probably tried such cases, and all others connected with the state religion. After 462 they still tried those who were charged with the destruction of any of the sacred olive trees. (3) The Areopagus as the council of the basileus must have exercised a general supervision over the temporalities of the official cults. In the fourth century the basileus brought before the Council of Five Hundred the question of the leases of temple-lands; presumably the Areopagus had dealt with this before 462. (4) It is stated in the *Athenaion Politeia* that Solon allowed it to retain the right to hear complaints against wrongdoers and to punish those who were convicted; it could impose fines and was not bound to give reasons for its decision in such cases. Its power of arrest is implied in a story which is apparently unhistorical, but the Council of Five Hundred possessed this power later, and it is safe to assume that it was enjoyed by the Areopagus also before 462. (5) In the fourth century those who were accused of plotting to subvert the constitution were impeached before the people, and the law under which they were prosecuted was the nomos eisangeltikos. The author of the *Athenaion Politeia* ascribes to Solon the first law on this subject, and says that cases under it were tried by the Areopagus. He implies that this was an addition made by Solon to the previous powers of the Areopagus. His authority for the ascription of this law to Solon is unknown, and he does not explain its relation to the old law (which he quotes later) against those who attempted to set up a tyranny. Anyhow the amnesty-law suggests that the Areopagus had even before Solon been the court which tried conspirators against the constitution, and if Solon passed a law on this subject his purpose can only have been to give more precise

definition to the previous powers of the Areopagus in this sphere. (6) Magistrates accused of illegal conduct could be denounced to the council in the fourth century by private citizens. In the *Athenaion Politeia* the Areopagus is said to have had this power of hearing complaints in the time of Drakon, and it may be assumed that it continued to exercise this power until it was transferred by Ephialtes to the Council of Five Hundred. The right to ensure that the magistrates kept their oath to obey the laws presumably belonged to the Areopagus, and these powers, combined with its function of prosecuting conspirators against the constitution, may be held to constitute the "guardianship of the laws" ascribed to it by ancient writers.

Under the later democracy every magistrate had to pass a scrutiny (*dokimasia*) before entering an office. The Council of Five Hundred was responsible for the scrutiny of its successors; other officials were examined in a law-court. The nine archons alone had to submit to a double scrutiny, first before the council, then in a law-court. Some have maintained that the *dokimasia* of the magistrates was entrusted to the Areopagus by Solon, but it is more probable that it was first instituted by Kleisthenes and belonged from its inception to the Council of Five Hundred.

* * *

Our authorities throw no light on the relations between the Areopagus and the magistrates in the sixth century, and it is not known whether the archon was required by constitutional custom to consult the Areopagus before he submitted any important proposal to the people. It is reasonable to suppose that he safeguarded himself in this way when the Areopagus was still supreme, and that it acted at one time, like the Roman senate, as the *consilium* of the magistrates. But by the time of Solon its authority had been so undermined by the dissensions between its members that magistrates with a strong backing could probably defy it with impunity. The right to convene and preside over the popular assembly belonged to the archon, and he could now safely disregard the claim of the Areopagus to be consulted first.

A council which prepared the agenda for a popular assembly was described by the Greeks as probouleutic, but the description is inapplicable to the part played by the Areopagus in this respect.

And even if the archon always took its opinion on questions which he proposed to bring before the ekklesia, it must be remembered that apart from the annual assembly for the election of magistrates the ekklesia had no regular meetings in the pre-Solonian period; it was the policy of the aristocrats to restrict the number of its meetings and the extent of its competence to a minimum. The presence in a state of a probouleutic council implies the existence of an ekklesia with extensive and important powers. Hence the statement of Plutarch that Solon created a new probouleutic council of 400 members, if correct, would be a decisive proof that he intended the ekklesia to develop into the effective sovereign of the state. The crucial importance of this question to our understanding of Solon's constitutional reforms demands a detailed examination of the arguments which have been urged for and against the truth of Plutarch's account.

In the *Athenaion Politeia* there is only a curt reference to the creation of the new council: "Solon made a Council of Four Hundred, 100 from each tribe." Aristotle in the *Politics* ignores it altogether. Plutarch says that Solon, apprehensive of the revolutionary temper of the people, created the new council and ordained that no business could come before the assembly without the previous sanction of this council; he also implies that the original 400 were chosen by Solon himself.

The first reference to the existence in the sixth century of a Council of Four Hundred is found in the constitution promulgated by the oligarchs in 411, which ordains that there shall be a council of 400 members *kata ta patria*, and a council of 401 members appears in the so-called constitution of Drakon, which is a fabrication of oligarchic propaganda. It might be suggested that the oligarchs genuinely proposed to revive a Solonian institution, and that they chose the number 400 for their own council because Solon's had contained the same number. But it is far more probable that the number was one chosen by them to suit their own requirements, the minimum necessary to ensure the success of their experiment, and that they then proceeded to invent a precedent for it, fathering their invention on either Drakon or Solon. The invention was later accepted by the radicals, who found in it a Solonian anticipation of the Council of Five Hundred, the citadel of the developed democracy.

Though the Atthidographers accepted the Solonian Council of Four Hundred as historical, they had nothing more to record of it than the bare mention of its creation by Solon, repeated by the author of the *Athenaion Politeia*. The brevity of his reference to it is only intelligible on the assumption that his sources contained no details, and the fuller version in Plutarch looks like the conjecture of a later scholar who assumed that the functions of this council were the same as those of the later Council of Five Hundred. It has been suggested that Plutarch's comparison of the two councils (the new boule and the Areopagus) to two anchors steadying the ship of state was derived from an actual poem by Solon, but if this had been the case surely he would have quoted the original poem, and the comparison may easily have been due to Plutarch himself.

There is no certain evidence of the existence in Athens of a council other than the Areopagus in the period between the legislation of Solon and the introduction of Kleisthenes' reforms. We read in Herodotus that soon after the expulsion of the tyrants the Boule offered vigorous opposition to Kleomenes of Sparta when he tried to dissolve it. Herodotus seems to date this incident after the acceptance of Kleisthenes' reforms; thus the boule in question might be Kleisthenes' new Council of Five Hundred. It has been objected to this that Herodotus had telescoped the events, that according to the more precise account in the *Athenaion Politeia* the reforms had been introduced by Kleisthenes but not yet accepted by the people, that even if they had been accepted there had been no time to carry them into effect, and that therefore the council in question was not the Council of Five Hundred; the possibility that it may have been the Areopagus is brushed aside in a footnote, and so the required conclusion is obtained that it must have been another council, which can have been none other than the shadowy Solonian Council of Four Hundred.

Every link in this chain of proof is weak. Wade-Gery has shown that the order of events in the account of the *Athenaion Politeia* is really the same as in Herodotus, but that for convenience the author delays his description of Kleisthenes' reforms until he has finished his narrative of the party struggles in Athens which followed their introduction. It is true that the new council was to be based on an elaborate reorganization of Attica which could not be carried out in a moment, but Kleisthenes may have secured the appointment of a provisional Council of Five Hundred to hold office until the necessary preparations for his new constitution were completed. But though the boule which opposed Kleomenes may have been a new Council of Five Hundred, it is more probable that it was the Areopagus, which possessed the prestige and personnel required for vigorous and effective action in this crisis. Since the time of Solon it had been recruited from ex-archons, and during the years 546–510 the tyrants had secured the appointment of their relations and friends to the chief annual magistracies; thus the Areopagus in 507 would be mainly composed of the supporters of the tyrants, and the Athenian oligarchs headed by Isagoras, relying on the presence of their ally Kleomenes with a small Spartan force, would naturally attempt its dissolution.

The evidence of epigraphy has been called in to prove directly and indirectly the existence and probability of a Solonian Council of Four Hundred. Fragments of a stele found on the Acropolis contain a mutilated sixth-century inscription recording a decree of the people. When this inscription was first known, the last letters preserved on the stone were *i t e s b*; some scholars explained the last letter as the first of a proper name, that of the archon for the year, but others assumed that it was the first letter of the word *Boules* (in the form *b o l e s*). The latter view has received some additional support from the discovery of a new fragment, which joins the other and gives the reading *i t e s b . l e*. Yet a reference at the end of the inscription to the *Boule*, which is not mentioned in the preamble, raises difficulties, as is shown by the variety of the restorations proposed, and even now the restoration of an archon-name remains a possible solution.

At one time the inscription was dated before 560 and regarded as proof of the early existence of a probouleutic council which could only be the Council of Four Hundred attributed by tradition to Solon. Recent writers prefer to assign the inscription to a date soon after the adoption of Kleisthenes' reforms, so that even if *boles* is read in the last line it cannot prove the existence of a popular council before those reforms.

Another inscription, found in Chios and ascribed to a date about 600, refers to the existence in Chios of a *boule demosia*, apparently side by side with an aristocratic council. But the precision of the date suggested for this inscription seems illusory, and the argument that because Chios had two councils in 600 Athens must have been provided with a second council by Solon is manifestly inconclusive. In the early sixth century the Ionians of Asia Minor had far outstripped their Athenian kinsmen in all the arts of civilization, and were politically mature enough to experiment with constitutional novelties which would have been incongruous in a community just emerging from aristocratic control.

This incongruity provides the principal argument against the existence of a second council in Solonian Athens. Though we have refuted the attempts to find positive proofs of its existence in the ancient sources earlier than the propagandists of 411, it must be admitted that their silence is not decisive. But unless we can accept the fourth-century account of Solon as a statesman who with uncanny prescience foresaw and provided for all the requirements of radical democracy, we are entitled to ask what was the function contemplated by Solon for his second council. Even if Solon, like the author of the Spartan rhetra, made provision for regular monthly meetings of the ekklesia, the business of preparing the agenda for these meetings was surely not so exacting as to require the creation of a new council for the purpose. According to one modern explanation, which recalls that suggested by Plutarch, it was "needed to prevent hasty decisions in times of excitement." But if the second council existed for this purpose, what was it doing when Aristion was able to propose and the ekklesia to approve the grant of a bodyguard to Peisistratos, who was thereby assisted to make himself tyrant? If Solon created a new council, it must have been one of the most futile constitutional experiments recorded in history. As the evidence and the arguments for its existence are unconvincing, we can dismiss it as an invention and conclude that after Solon's reforms, as before, there was only one council at Athens, the Areopagus.

The powers and composition of the ekklesia were probably not much altered by Solon's legislation. Aristotle asserts that Solon gave to the people the bare minimum of political power, but this is apparently no more than an inference from Solon's own words: "to the demos I have given such a measure of privilege as is sufficient, neither robbing them of their former rights nor holding out the hope of greater." This passage implies that the political privileges possessed by the people were the same after Solon's reforms as before, but that its full exercise of them was now guaranteed by the reign of law which he had established. They included the election of the chief magistrates and presumably the final voice in the declaration of war and the conclusion of peace; these prerogatives may have belonged *de iure* to the assembly in the pre-Solonian state, but must often have been reduced *de facto* to an empty formality by aristocratic management. It may also be assumed that after Solon the assembly alone was competent to make or modify laws, though Solon's code was guaranteed against any alteration for a period of ten years, and it certainly had the right to confer on individuals privileges contrary to the laws.

Aristotle says that Solon empowered the demos to demand from the magistrates an account of their administration (*euthynein*). This statement is apparently an anticipation of the later functions of the popular courts, the Dikasteria, which are usually regarded by fourth-century writers as one of Solon's innovations. So the author of the *Athenaion Politeia* declares that Solon's most democratic reform was the institution of appeal from the magistrates to the Dikasterion. An archaic law, possibly Solonian, which is quoted by Lysias and Demosthenes, indicates that the popular court was called *Heliaia*. This court is authorized in the law to impose a punishment of five days in the stocks as an additional penalty in convictions for theft.

As Heliaia seems to be connected with a word for assembly found in inscriptions of some Peloponnesian states, it is reasonable to suppose that the Heliaia was the ekklesia sitting in a judicial capacity. Probably it was the only popular court established by Solon; the references to dikasteria in some ancient accounts of his reforms must be anachronistic. The most plausible explanation of the function assigned to the Heliaia by Solon is that of Wilamowitz. He conjectured that each of the Solonian laws regulating the competence of the magistrates defined the penalties which the magistrate could inflict on his own authority, and that if he wished to exceed them he had to secure the approval of a jury of citizens. With this view may be combined the suggestion put forward by Adcock, that the magistrates may have tried cases on market days and that their courts were attended by such

citizens as had the leisure. This innovation may be looked upon as the seed which was to develop into the popular courts of the Periklean Age, when the judicial powers of the magistrate had been limited to the preliminary investigation (*anakrisis*), but no such development can have been contemplated by its author, who apparently intended the Heliaia to act merely as a safeguard against the infliction of excessive penalties by magistrates.

Was the composition of the assembly altered by Solon? In the Atthis he is credited with the admission of the thetes to the ekklesia and to the popular court(s), and this evidence has usually been accepted as decisive. But it is impossible to regard all the statements of the Atthis about Solon as based on the text of his laws, and this one may well be no more than a plausible conjecture. Confirmation of it might be found in the rise of Peisistratos to power, as the ekklesia which voted him his bodyguard must have contained a large number of his supporters, and many of these were landless men who looked to him for the redistribution of land which they desired. Yet the admission of landless citizens to the ekklesia would have been a bold expedient which seems alien to the cautious conservative temperament of Solon and would have played straight into the hands of the revolutionaries. The true explanation may be that Solon made no alteration in the qualification for membership of the ekklesia, but that in the troubled years which followed his legislation there was a difference between *de iure* and *de facto* membership. Possibly the farmers who had once owned land and had lost it to their creditors continued to attend the assembly; it is even conceivable that, as the tide of popular agitation rose, poor citizens were present at its meetings without any justification, and that the authorities were either unable or unwilling to enforce their exclusion.

The powers previously possessed by the magistrates were limited, like those of the Areopagus, by the fact that they were carefully defined in Solon's code and that safeguards were provided against their arbitrary extension, but in substance they seem to have been the same as before. The chief archon continued to be the supreme executive in the state and to preside over the meetings of the ekklesia, perhaps even to convene them. He also presided over the sessions of the Areopagus with the exception of those for judicial and religious business in which the presidency was still reserved for the basileus. Election of the magistrates by the people had existed in form before Solon, and though the author of the *Athenaion Politeia* asserts that he changed the method of appointment, it is more probable that he allowed the ekklesia to retain its prerogative, which was henceforth made more effective by the disunion of the nobility and the competition of ambitious politicians for popular favour.

From the point now reached in this survey of Solon's reforms it might appear that with reference to the three principal organs of the state, the council, the assembly, and the magistracy, he had merely given legal confirmation to their existing functions. But though their functions remained the same,

their composition was transformed, that of the ekklesia apparently *de facto* only and in defiance of Solon's intention, whereas the innovations introduced by him into the composition of the magistracy and of the Areopagus represent a deliberate attempt to wrest the monopoly of effective political power from its former holders. The means adopted by Solon to this end were extremely simple. It is unnecessary to assume, as some scholars have done, that he drew up an elaborate written constitution; he merely inserted into those parts of his code which dealt with the magistrates and the Areopagus provisions on the conditions of eligibility which automatically ensured the achievement of his main political objective.

2. G. E. M. de Ste. Croix maintains that the reforms and constitution of Solon had great significance for the development of democracy in Athens. In one of a series of essays written in the 1960s but published posthumously he argues in favor of the historicity of Solon's Council of Four Hundred. Geoffrey de Ste. Croix was Fellow and Tutor in Ancient History, New College, Oxford

FROM G. E. M. DE STE. CROIX, *ATHENIAN DEMOCRATIC ORIGINS: AND OTHER ESSAYS*

The Introduction of Majority Voting at Athens

BY FAR THE MOST IMPORTANT single step in the development of democracy was the decision to settle major political questions by actually counting heads, or rather hands (or pebbles), and allowing the numerical majority to have its *way—making political decisions by majority vote*. When this began in Greece, it may have been the first time in human history that such a thing had regularly happened, at any rate in a civilised society. It is very strange indeed that all writers known to me, both ancient and modern, with the single exception of Larsen, have ignored this extraordinarily significant development. Other writers, while giving careful attention to the emergence of relatively minor features of democracy, such as the Council and its probouleusis, have strangely neglected the fundamental innovation, which is similarly overlooked by all ancient writers, even Aristotle.

It is often taken for granted that in societies such as those of "Dark Age" Greece, "sovereign power" is likely to have resided in the hands of the

"demos" in some form, whether as the assembled people at home, or as the collective body of warriors, on campaign and perhaps at home also. This, I believe, is likely to be true only in the sense that the rulers, whether kings or aristocrats, could not afford to go too far in opposition to the will of the great majority of their subjects, and might— although if they felt strong enough they might not— consult the common people, or at any rate the army, before they took some step which might not be effective without their co-operation. Legalistic thinking in the modern manner, which demands an explicit recognition of "sovereignty" in some organ of state, whether kings or nobles or assembly of the people or the warriors, should not be forced upon such societies, where power is likely to be exercised by whoever possesses it at a given moment, above all at periods when institutions are unstable and in process of change, as in the Greek "Dark Age." In Homer the demos decides nothing: it is the king who decides; the army or the people in assembly merely express their approval or disapproval by shouts or silence or—at a pinch—mutiny. Similarly, the most probable etymology of the Latin word for "vote," *suffragium*, suggests that the earliest assemblies at Rome made their will known by noisy demonstrations. Among the Israelites the people (not in any formal assembly) signified their approval by shouting: at the election of Saul as king, "all the people shouted and said, 'God save the king' "; and Nehemiah's *seisachtheia* was ratified when "all the congregation said 'Amen' and praised the Lord"—never do we hear of a vote being taken. In what has been described as the "primitive democracy" of some of the ancient Mesopotamian cities there is equally no clear sign of any voting, in the form of counting "those in favour" and "those against," nor is any such procedure visible in our records of other "pre-Classical" Near Eastern societies such as those of the Hittites or the Phoenicians. We do not know when or in which state or by what stages the demos as a whole first gained the constitutional power of decision in a Greek city. By the mid-seventh century the Spartan *damos* had it; but it exercised it then and thereafter "by shouting and not by vote," the presiding magistrate—an ephor, in the historical period—no doubt deciding which shout was the louder or loudest.

Athens, like other Greek states, was ruled first by a king. During the Dark Age, monarchy was succeeded by a form of aristocratic government. Where supreme power lay at this period, in theory or in practice, we cannot say: perhaps no firm constitutional principles had crystallised at this stage. Eventually—not later, surely, than Solon—sovereign power was held to reside in the Assembly, and was exercised by majority vote, by counting hands. As I have indicated, this development is of enormous interest and importance, as the indispensable *sine qua non* of political democracy. How and when did it take place? There must have been a particular occasion on which, for the first time, a political decision was taken by "the demos of the Athenians" after a counting of votes, in which each man's vote counted equally—a principle calculated to make an aristocrat shudder. When did this happen? Were such decisions taken *de facto* before being accepted as constitutionally proper? Was the practice copied from another Greek state? At any rate, if any single step taken by any Greek state, Athens included, in the whole field of social institutions is to be regarded as the most fruitful, it must surely be this.

I should like to leave open the possibility that formal recognition of the taking of political decisions by majority vote at Athens was first given, expressly or implicitly, by Solon's constitution. I do not think that a later date is possible, but of course this fundamental step towards democracy may have been taken at some time during the seventh century.

The Eupatrid Monopoly of the "State Machine"

I have already expressed the view that Solon's most important political reform was the destruction of the eupatrid monopoly (or virtual monopoly) of state office, and the basing of qualification for such office upon the four property classes. Now we ourselves are used to states which have an elaborate machinery of government, an apparatus which in many cases will continue to function irrespective of what individuals or groups hold the reins of power, and can often be taken over more or less intact even by a revolutionary regime. We too easily forget, therefore, that at the moment when the Solonian constitution began to operate, virtually the whole of such rudimentary "state machinery" as existed at Athens must have been entirely in the hands of the eupatrids, and that there was no *other* apparatus which could be used to coerce the eupatrids if—as would be only too natural—they refused to work the new constitution, or quietly sabotaged it. (There is an obvious analogy in the "Struggle of the Orders" at Rome, where the mere passing of *plebiscita* or *leges* was sometimes evidently insufficient to procure the observance of constitutional innovations disliked by the patricians.) The scorn and bitterness with which Greek aristocrats could regard wealthy upstarts who deprived them of their monopoly of political privilege, or merely married into noble families, is nicely illustrated by the poetry of Theognis, a citizen of Athens' nearest neighbour, Megara, not so long after Solon's day.

To my mind the appreciation of this fact is fundamental to an understanding of the course of events between Solon's archonship and the tyranny of Peisistratus. It was the eupatrids alone who, as a class, lost by Solon's constitutional reforms; and the most likely explanation of the *anarchiai* ["years during which there was no archon"] of (probably) 590/89 and 586/5 and the Damasias episode of c. 582–0 is surely that the eupatrids refused, when they could, to allow the election of non-eupatrid archons. I do not see how we can decide whether the arrangement described by Aristotle, *Ath. Pol.* 13.2 (five of ten archons from the Eupatridai, three from the Agroikoi and two from the Demiourgoi), represented an outright reaction, in which the eupatrids succeeded in claiming a half share in the archonship, or was a relative setback for them, a realistic compromise whereby the eupatrids, who had been having a monopoly of elected archons, were forced to draw back and claim only a half share, but at least received that recognition of their special position in the state which Solon had denied them. (I think the latter explanation is probably true, if only because a Damasias had been archon in 639/8, and it is not unlikely that the later Damasias was a relative of his—he could easily have been his grandson—and therefore a eupatrid. But all this is uncertain.) We may sympathise with Solon's detestation of tyranny and his refusal to assume the role of tyrant which the discontented demos would have thrust upon him. At the same time we must admit that Solon's great work might have been largely nullified had not Peisistratus, using violence to overcome aristocratic resistance, *enforced* Solon's constitution—for which there is a remarkable unanimity in the best sources that Peisistratus did preserve the laws of Solon, apart from keeping hold on the offices.

At the moment Solon's constitution came into effect the administration of the state seems to have been mainly in the hands of the nine archons, above all the *archon eponymus*. Doubtless the Areopagus played an important part, but unfortunately we are quite unable to define the manner in which the alleged *nomophylakia* "guardianship of the laws" was exercised by the Areopagus, or to identify any single action on its part at any time which might illustrate that guardianship. Aristotle believed that the Areopagus always consisted of ex-archons; and although this statement has been doubted for the pre-Solonian period, we must surely accept it as a fact from at least the time of Solon onwards. Once non-eupatrid archons began to be elected, the composition of the Areopagus would begin to change; but it must have remained predominantly eupatrid for many years. Apart from the archons and the Areopagus there were doubtless other officials, such as the tribe-kings (*phylobasileis*), who are said to have been eupatrids, and the *kolakretai*, whose very name

attests their antiquity; but there is no evidence what powers any of these magistrates enjoyed.

An appreciation of the eupatrid monopoly of the machinery of state in Solon's day is important not only for the understanding of the period between Solon and Peisistratus but also in connection with the problem of the Solonian Council of Four Hundred, to which I now turn.

The Solonian Council of Four Hundred

Many modern writers have expressed their opinions on the question whether Solon created a Council of Four Hundred, as stated by Aristotle (*Ath. Pol.* 8.4) in the terse phrase, *boule d' epoiese tetrakosious, hekaton ex hekastes phyles* ["and he set up a Council of Four Hundred, a hundred from each tribe"]. The only other important source to mention such a Solonian Council, namely Plutarch (*Sol.* 19.1–2), cannot be shown to possess any earlier authority than Aristotle, although of course he may be using an older Atthidographer, directly or indirectly. Aristotle gives no details about the composition or method of election or functions of this council, and some scholars, including De Sanctis and Beloch, have treated it as a fiction. Recently Hignett has described it as a fabrication of oligarchic propaganda in 411 B.C., and Jacoby, in the Addendum to his commentary on the Atthidographers, was "rather inclined to agree with him." On the other hand, there are plenty of historians who have not seriously doubted the existence of a Solonian Council. The reader of Wade-Gery's *Essays* would not even become aware, I fancy, that the existence of Solon's Council had been called in question but for the statement on p. 199 that "the Chian Boule is surely probouleutic and is good evidence for the reality of Solon's 400."

I have dealt elsewhere in this book with the general problem of the credibility of Aristotle's account of early Athenian history and with some particular parts of that account. In the light of the conclusions which emerge, I would maintain that we cannot tell for certain whether or not Aristotle had good authority for his statement. Some have found it suspicious that he does not explain the functions of the Solonian Council or how it was elected or from whom; but this is quite unjustified, for—not to mention other inexplicable omissions in the *Ath. Pol.*—Aristotle is equally silent about the Cleisthenic Council. Whether he had reliable authority or not, Aristotle may be reporting a correct tradition.

To my mind, some of the arguments which have been used in this controversy are worthless. For example, how can we decide whether the oligarchs in 411 first decided upon the number 400 because that was the size of the council they wanted, and then pretended there was ancestral precedent for it, or whether they chose the number 400 because there was already a tradition that this had been the number of Solon's Council? To me the second alternative seems much more likely, but that is probably because I believe in a Solonian Council on other grounds. Again, how can we possibly be sure whether the "two anchors" of Plutarch, *Sol.* 19.2, come from one of Solon's poems or not? I shall merely state those considerations which seem to me to have some real force:

1. The principal argument which leads me to accept the existence of a Solonian Council of Four Hundred is as follows:

   (a) As we have just seen, all such "state machinery" as existed at the moment when the Solonian constitution began to operate must have been entirely in the hands of eupatrids, the one class which had suffered politically by Solon's reforms; and of course it was all too likely that for at least some time to come a high proportion of archons—and therefore new Areopagites—would similarly be eupatrid. This could not be prevented. Solon must have known perfectly well that (as indeed, I think, events proved) the eupatrids would not voluntarily surrender power; and in the absence of any state machinery to compel them, the only possible way of giving the new constitution a real chance to work was by giving a measure of real power to the demos as a whole: that is to say, ultimately to the Assembly.

   (b) Solon cannot have wished, however, to give such power directly to the Assembly, a mass meeting of all citizens, the great majority of whom as yet lacked political maturity. In the bitter class strife which had led to his appointment as *diallaktes kai archon* ["mediator and archon"] he conceived his own role to be essentially that of an arbitrator, giving to each side exactly what it deserved: to the demos, he

says, he gave such privilege as was fitting, neither more nor less; and at the same time he provided that the rich and powerful should suffer nothing unseemly. He describes himself as standing with a strong shield before both sides, allowing neither to win an unjust victory. What he wanted was that the demos should "*follow its leaders best*, neither under too little restraint nor under compulsion." Yet of the "leaders" of the day he had spoken in stern rebuke in an elegiac poem apparently written before his archonship: they had an "unjust mind" and were arrogant and greedy, and they took no heed of "the dread foundations of Justice." What was more natural than that he should give to the demos a body which would guide and inform its deliberations, quite independently of the older organs of state, and at the same time act as a check upon spontaneous disorder *en synodois tois adikeousi philais* ["in conspiracies beloved of wrong-doers"], such as had occurred during the crisis preceding his archonship?

   (c) Unless a special Council were created to provide it, probouleusis would inevitably remain a prerogative of the Areopagus; and this would be unfortunate, both because of the eupatrid domination of the Areopagus and because of the prestige of that body—any proposals it might bring forward would have been invested with great authority, and the Assembly might well have tended to become a mere rubber-stamp. On the other hand, a new probouleutic Council elected from all three of the upper property classes, and consisting of as many as 400 men (large enough, especially if iteration were prohibited or restricted, to ensure the presence of a good number, surely an actual majority, of non-eupatrids), would have nothing like the prestige and authority of the Areopagus, and the Assembly might play its proper part.

   (d) And it was not only a probouleutic body which was required: an organ of state which could act in an administrative capacity, if only in routine matters, was also necessary, unless the still entirely or mainly eupatrid archons and Areopagus were to continue as the sole executive.

   (e) There is good reason to suppose that the Council was also given considerable judicial powers. According to Aristotle, *Ath. Pol.* 45.1, *he de boule proteron men en kyria kai chremasin zemiosai kai desai kai apokteinai* ["In former times the Council had the power to impose fines, imprisonment, and the death penalty"] (cf. 45.2–3; also 41.2: *kai gar ai tes boule kriseis eis ton demon eleluthasin* ["for the Council's jurisdiction has passed into the hands of the demos"]). The date at which the powers of the Council were restricted is disputed; but even if Aristotle is thinking here (as he probably is) of the Cleisthenic Council only, we may surely infer that Solon's Council is also likely to have had much greater authority in the judicial sphere than the Council which we know in the late fifth and fourth centuries. The Council described as the *bole he demosie* ["Council of the People"] at Chios in the second quarter of the sixth century, to which I shall refer presently, had important judicial functions.

In the circumstances with which Solon was confronted, therefore, a new Council, probouleutic and executive and probably possessing judicial powers, was certainly a wise innovation, and Solon might have reason to hope that it would prevent the new constitution from being wrecked by eupatrid hostility.

2. The second argument which I find attractive is that the Council which Cleomenes is said by Herodotus and Aristotle to have tried to dissolve, and to have led the resistance to him, must surely have been the Solonian Four Hundred. In the first place, it certainly cannot have been the Areopagus, as some scholars have supposed. Both Herodotus and (following him) Aristotle speak of *hé boulé* "the Council," not of *hé boulé he en Areio pago* ["the Council on the Areopagus"] or any similar phrase; and I do not see how *hé boulé tout court*, in such a context, can possibly mean the Areopagus. (Is there a parallel in the whole of the surviving sources?) Nor, one may think, is the Areopagus very likely to have been the main source of resistance to the ally of Isagoras. That *hé boulé* in question is the Five Hundred of Cleisthenes has been maintained by some historians. However, it seems to me (as, I think, to most people) very unlikely that the intervention of Cleomenes can have come as late as this, when the new constitution was

actually working—the Council could not have come into being until the membership of demes and trittyes and tribes had been settled (a lengthy process), and elections had taken place. That Cleisthenes "may have secured the appointment of a provisional Council of Five Hundred to hold office until the necessary preparations for his new constitution were completed" seems to me an unnecessary and exceedingly implausible conjecture, inspired by nothing but a determination to reject a Solonian Council. Herodotus, I conclude, was certainly thinking of the Four Hundred. There was, then, in his day a tradition of a pre-Cleisthenic Council, known to us in a context which has nothing to do with the constitutional activity of the Council, and therefore the less likely to have been invented for a propagandist purpose, such as attributing as many as possible of the institutions of the developed democracy to the great lawgiver.

3. A third argument which seems to have some weight is that the Cleisthenic constitution evidently worked quite remarkably well from the moment it was instituted; and it would be much easier to understand this if the Council, a vital part of the whole fabric, were not an entirely new and untried invention. No one nowadays will suppose that it was the tyrants who created the Council, and if we feel that it is likely to be older than Cleisthenes we have no reason to doubt a Solonian origin.

4. The Council described as the *bole he demosie* ["Council of the People"] which existed at Chios in the second quarter of the sixth century affords evidence that within a generation after Solon a Greek city could have an elected body of this nature. Perhaps, as Tod believed, "the epithet *demosie* twice added to bole suggests that another council continued to exist at Chios, just as at Athens the Areopagus lived on side by side with the Solonian, and later the Cleisthenic, *boule*."

5. Diog. Laert. I 49 uses the phrase *hé boulé, Peisistratidai ontes* ["the Council, who were Peisistratids"], in relation to the Council existing just before the time at which Peisistratus seized power. I am not sure this passage is worth anything at all; but, such as it is, it can only refer to the Council of Four Hundred and not to the Areopagus. Consequently, although I think it may perhaps be wrong to assert the

existence of a Solonian Council as a positive historical fact, the arguments for it seem to me very much stronger than any which can be brought against it: these amount to little more than that there could have been no need for such a Council in Solon's day, when the importance of the Assembly had scarcely begun to develop, and the fact that Aristotle may have had no details of its composition and so forth—arguments which I have dealt with already.

Consider

1. Who does Hignett think formed the mass of Solon's supporters and what were their grievances?
2. How might they have sought to benefit from Solon's reforms?
3. Why did later generations in Athens consider Solon the founder of their democracy?
4. What is the significance of that question for assessing Solon's legislation and constitution?
5. According to de Ste. Croix, why was Solon's constitution critical to the development of Athenian democracy?
6. Why does he place such great significance on Solon's destruction of the Eupatrid monopoly of state office?
7. What role did Peisistratus play in the survival of Solon's reforms?
8. How large a role did the Ekklesia play in pre-Solonian Athens?
9. How did Solon's reforms affect the powers and composition of the Ekklesia, the magistracies, and the Areopagus according to Hignett?
10. How did the Heliaia function?
11. Why is the question whether Solon created a Council of Four Hundred important for Hignett?
12. How does Hignett and de Ste Croix make use of Herodotus, Aristotle, Plutarch, and inscriptions to substantiate their cases about Solon's council?
13. What function and powers does de Ste Croix think the Council of Four Hundred might have had in Athens?
14. Contrast the arguments of de Ste. Croix's in favor of the council's existence with the contrary view of Hignett. Why do you think Solon may or may not have created the council?

CHAPTER 5
GREEK STRATEGY
IN THE PERSIAN WAR

❧

IN THE SUMMER OF 480 BC, Xerxes, Great King of Persia, led an enormous invading army into Europe. He was determined to take vengeance on the Athenians for defeating Darius 10 years earlier at the battle of Marathon and to conquer all of Greece. The Greeks who had formed the Hellenic League to resist the invasion met in 481 BC to organize a defense. Having abandoned an initial plan to make a stand at Tempe in Thessaly, they fell back to central Greece. The Greeks then took up a position with a small army under the Spartan king Leonidas in the narrow pass at Thermopylae and with a sizable navy off the coast of Artemisium. The heroic stand of Leonidas at Thermopylae and the devastating Greek naval victory at Salamis have attained fame for preserving Greek freedom and Western civilization. However, the details of the Greek strategy remain obscure due to the nature of our main source, the *Histories* of Herodotus. This chapter deals with how scholars have attempted to account for the Greek victory.

The Persian Empire began with Cyrus' defeat of Gyges, the king of Lydia and the ancestor of Croesus, in 550 BC and expanded rapidly under the Achaemenid dynasty. Persia first came into contact with Greeks when Cyrus conquered the Lydian kingdom of Croesus in 547 BC and took over his Greek subjects on the coast of Asia Minor. The further conquests of the Persian kings Cambyses and Darius in Egypt (525 BC) and in Thrace (513 BC) respectively made a confrontation between the Greeks and the vast Persian Empire inevitable. The Ionian Revolt against Persian rule in 499 BC gave Darius a pretext to intervene in the affairs of the mainland Greeks, as the Athenians and Eretrians had lent ships to the city of Miletus to aid in the rebellion and had taken part in the burning of the Persian city of Sardis. After the Athenian hoplite victory at Marathon in 490, Darius planned a massive campaign of revenge and conquest that fell to his son and successor Xerxes to complete. Meanwhile, the Athenian leader Themistocles convinced his countrymen in 483/2 to use a surplus of revenue from the silver mines at Laurium to build a fleet of 200 triremes. The brilliant statesman told the Athenians that they could use the triremes in their war against Aegina but was really looking ahead to the Persian menace. Scholars estimate that Xerxes reached Europe with about 200,000–300,000 fighting men and as many as 1,200 warships.

The strategy of the Great King required careful coordination between the army and navy to keep his troops supplied. It appears that the Greeks had hoped to prevent the Persian land and sea forces from communicating north of Attica. They placed Leonidas' contingent at the narrow pass of Thermopylae and stationed more than 250 triremes off the coast of Artemisium. But Leonidas and the Spartans were annihilated when the Peloponnesians failed to send the proper reinforcements up north. The defeat forced the Greek fleet to withdraw from Artemisium after inconclusive fighting at sea. According to Herodotus, a hasty evacuation of Attica was necessary because the Peloponnesians had failed to block the Persian route to Athens. Instead of taking up a position in Boeotia with their full army, the Peloponnesians had turned to fortifying the Isthmus. Only the last minute maneuvering by Themistocles and luck enabled the Greeks to crush the Persian fleet at Salamis. Scholars have long debated whether the campaign up north was in fact planned as a holding operation or whether the decisive sea battle at Salamis was the unexpected result of failing to stop the advance of Xerxes. The debate has often focused on an inscription known as the "Decree of Themistocles," which contradicts the picture drawn by Herodotus.

Ancient Sources

1. Herodotus, *Histories*, 7.138–45, 175, 182–4; 207, 213, 217–19; 222–25; 228; 8.4–15, 18, 21, 40–2; 49–52; 56–63; 71–76, 78–83, THE INVASION OF XERXES
2. The Themistocles Decree
3. Plutarch, *Life of Themistocles*, 9–10, DIVINE SALAMIS

Opinions of Modern Scholars

1. From Peter Green, *The Greco-Persian Wars*
2. From J. F. Lazenby, *The Defence of Greece 490–479 B.C.*

ANCIENT SOURCES FOR GREEK STRATEGY IN THE PERSIAN WAR

1. THE INVASION OF XERXES

Herodotus is our main source for the Persian Wars. But his narrative of the Greek battles against Persian forces at Thermopylae and Artemisium has led scholars to widely varying interpretations of Greek strategy. For one thing, it is unclear why the Spartans committed so few troops to guard the pass at Thermopylae and what the relationship was between the Thermopylae–Artemisium line of defense and the later sea battle fought at Salamis. Did the Greeks plan to send reinforcements to Leonidas in the hope of stopping the Persians for good at Thermopylae, or was their intention to force a sea battle at Artemisium? On the other hand, were both the army and fleet intended to fight only holding actions until the Athenians could evacuate their women and children out of Attica and prepare for the decisive naval contest at Salamis? Herodotus attributes the actions of the Greeks mostly to the fear they felt in the face of Xerxes' overwhelming force and to personal motives. The historian also states that the Spartans betrayed the Greek cause by abandoning the original plan to meet Xerxes in Boeotia in order to prevent his advance, if the Persians should break through the Thermopylae pass. The following selections from the *Histories* begin with the Greek response upon receiving word of Xerxes' approach sometime in 481.

Book Seven

7.138 The purpose of Xerxes' expedition, which was directed nominally against Athens, was in fact the conquest of the whole of Greece. The various Greek communities had long been aware of this, but they viewed the coming danger with very different eyes. Some had already made their submission, and were consequently in good spirits, because they were sure

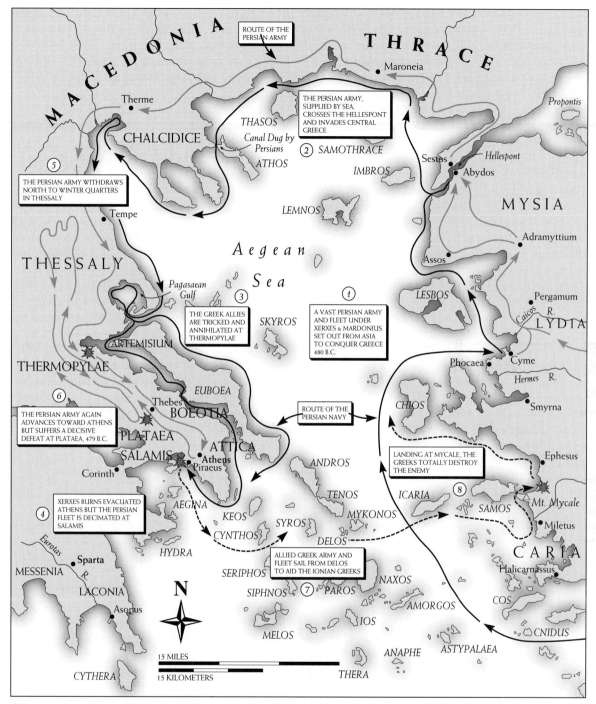

This map traces the route taken by the Persian king Xerxes in his invasion of Greece in 480 BC. The dotted arrows show movements of Xerxes' army, the dashed arrows show movements of his navy, and the solid arrows show movements of the Greek army and navy.

of getting off lightly at the invaders' hands; others, who had refused to submit, were thrown into panic partly because there were not enough ships in Greece to meet the Persians with any chance of success, and partly because most of the Greeks were unwilling to fight and all too ready to accept Persian dominion.

7.139 At this point I find myself compelled to express an opinion which I know most people will object to; nevertheless, as I believe it to be I will not suppress it. If the Athenians, through fear of the approaching danger, had abandoned their country, or if they had stayed there and submitted to Xerxes, there would have been no attempt to resist the Persians by sea; and, in the absence of a Greek fleet, it is easy to see what would have been the course of events on land. However many lines of fortification the Spartans had built across the Isthmus, they would have been deserted by their confederates; not that their allies would have willingly deserted them, but they could not have helped doing so, because one by one they would have fallen victims to the Persian naval power. Thus the Spartans would have been left alone to perform great deeds and to die nobly. Or, on the other hand, it is possible that before things came to the ultimate test, the sight of the rest of Greece submitting to Persia might have driven them to make terms with Xerxes. In either case the Persian conquest of Greece would have been assured; for I cannot myself see what possible use there could have been in fortifying the Isthmus, if the Persians had command of the sea. In view of this, therefore, one is surely right in saying that Greece was saved by the Athenians. It was the Athenians who held the balance: whichever side they joined was sure to prevail. It was the Athenians, too, who, having chosen that Greece should live and preserve her freedom, roused to battle the other Greek states which had not yet submitted. It was the Athenians who—after the gods—drove back the Persian king. Not even the terrifying warnings of the oracle at Delphi could persuade them to abandon Greece; they stood firm and had the courage to meet the invader.

7.140 The Athenians had sent their envoys to Delphi to consult the oracle, and as soon as the customary rites were performed and they had entered the shrine and taken their seats, the Priestess Aristonice uttered the following prophecy:

Why sit you, doomed ones? Fly to the world's end,
    leaving
Home and the heights your city circles like
    a wheel.
The head shall not remain in its place, nor
    the body,
Nor the feet beneath, nor the hands, nor the parts
    between;

But all is ruined, for fire and the headlong god war
Speeding in a Syrian chariot shall bring you low.
Many a tower shall he destroy, not yours alone,
And give to pitiless fire many shrines of gods,
Which even now stand swearing, with fear
    quivering,
While over the roof-tops black blood runs
    streaming
In prophecy of woe that needs must come. But rise,
Haste from the sanctuary and bow your hearts
    to grief

7.141 The Athenian envoys heard these words with dismay; indeed they were about to abandon themselves to despair at the dreadful fate which was prophesied, when Timon, the son of Androbulus and one of the most distinguished men in Delphi, suggested that they should take branches of olive in their hands and, in the guise of suppliants, approach the oracle a second time. The Athenians acted upon this suggestion. "Lord Apollo," they said, "can you not, in consideration of these olive boughs which we have brought you, give us some better prophecy about our country? Otherwise we will never leave the holy place but stay here till we die." Thereupon the Prophetess uttered a second prophecy, which ran as follows:

Not wholly can Pallas win the heart of Olympian
    Zeus,
Though she prays him with many prayers and all her
    subtlety;
Yet will I speak to you this other word, as firm as
    adamant:
Though all else shall be taken within the bound of
    Cecrops
And the fastness of the holy mountain of
    Cithaeron,
Yet Zeus the all-seeing grants to Athena's prayer
That the wooden wall only shall not fall, but help
    you and your children.
But await not the host of horse and foot coming
    from Asia,
Nor be still, but turn your back and withdraw from
    the foe.
Truly a day will come when you will meet him face
    to face.
Divine Salamis, you will bring death to
    women's sons
When the corn is scattered, or the harvest
    gathered in.

7.142 This second answer seemed to be, as indeed it was, less menacing than the first; so the envoys wrote it down and returned to Athens. When it was made public upon their arrival in the city, and the attempt to explain it began, amongst the various opinions which were expressed there were two mutually exclusive interpretations. Some of the older men supposed that the prophecy meant that the Acropolis would escape destruction, on the grounds that the Acropolis was fenced in the old days with a thorn-hedge, and that this was the "wooden wall" of the oracle but others thought that by this expression the god indicated the ships, and they urged in consequence that everything should be abandoned in favour of the immediate preparation of a fleet. There was, however, for those who believed "wooden wall" to mean ships, one disturbing thing—namely, the last two lines of the Priestess' prophecy:

Divine Salamis, you will bring death to
    women's sons
When the corn is scattered, or the harvest
    gathered in.

This was a very awkward statement and caused profound disturbance amongst all who took the wooden wall to signify ships; for the professional interpreters understood the lines to mean that they would be beaten at Salamis in a fight at sea.

7.143 There was, however, a man in Athens who had recently come into prominence—Themistocles called Neocles' son; he now came forward and declared that there was an important point in which the professional interpreters were mistaken. If, he maintained, the disaster referred to was to strike the Athenians, it would not have been expressed in such mild language. "Hateful Salamis" would surely have been a more likely phrase than "divine Salamis," if the inhabitants of the country were doomed to destruction there. On the contrary, the true interpretation was that the oracle referred not to the Athenians but to their enemies. The "wooden wail" did, indeed, mean the ships; so he advised his countrymen to prepare at once to meet the invader at sea.

The Athenians found Themistocles' explanation of the oracle preferable to that of the professional interpreters, who had not only tried to dissuade them from preparing to fight at sea but had been against offering opposition of any sort. The only thing to do was, according to them, to abandon Attica altogether and seek a home elsewhere.

7.144 Once on a previous occasion Themistocles had succeeded in getting his views accepted, to the great benefit of his country. The Athenians had amassed a large sum of money from the produce of the mines at Laurium, which they proposed to share out amongst themselves at the rate of ten drachmas a man; Themistocles, however, persuaded them to give up this idea and, instead of distributing the money, to spend it on the construction of two hundred warships for use in the war with Aegina. The outbreak of this war at that moment saved Greece by forcing Athens to become a maritime power. In point of fact the two hundred ships were not employed for the purpose for which they were built, but were available for Greece in her hour of need. The Athenians also found it necessary to expand this existing fleet by laying down new ships, and they determined in debate after the discussion on the oracle, to take the god's advice and meet the invader at sea with all the force they possessed, and with any other Greeks who were willing to join them.

7.145 At a conference of the Greek states who were loyal to the general cause guarantees were exchanged, and the decision was reached that the first thing to be done was to patch up their own quarrels and stop any fighting which happened to be going on amongst members of the confederacy. There were a number of such disputes at the time, the most serious being the quarrel between Athens and Aegina. Having learnt that Xerxes and his army had reached Sardis, they next resolved to send spies into Asia to get information about the Persian forces; at the same time, in the hope of uniting, if it were possible, the whole Greek world and of bringing all the various communities to undertake joint action in face of the common danger, they decided to send an embassy to Argos to conclude an alliance, another to Gelon, the son of Deinomenes, in Sicily, and others, again, to Corcyra and Crete. Gelon was said to be very powerful—far more powerful than anyone else of Greek nationality.

[After unsuccessful missions to secure aid from Argos, Syracuse, Corcyra, and Crete and after a quickly abandoned expedition to Tempe the Greeks met again at the Isthmus of Corinth.]

7.175 The Greeks on their return to the Isthmus then discussed, in consideration of the warning they had received from Alexander, where they should make a stand. The proposal which found most favour was to guard the pass of Thermopylae, on the grounds that it was narrower than the pass into Thessaly and at the same time nearer home. They knew nothing as yet about the mountain track by means of which the men who fell at Thermopylae were taken in the rear, and only learnt of its existence from the people of Trachis after their arrival.

The decision, then, was to hold the pass in order to prevent the Persians from entering Greece and at the same time to send the fleet to Artemisium on the coast of Histiaea; for these two places being close together, communication would be easy.

Questions

1. **What difficulties did the Greeks face once they decided to resist the Persian invasion?**
2. **Why does Herodotus think the Greeks prevailed?**
3. **What did each of the oracles from Delphi advise?**
4. **What role did Themistocles play in determining the Greek strategy?**
5. **How was the pass vulnerable to attack?**

---

* * *

[The Greeks choose to make their stand at the narrow pass at Thermopylae to prevent the Persians from using their cavalry or taking advantage of their far superior numbers. The oracle at Delphi advises the Greeks to "pray to the winds, for they will be good allies to Greece." Xerxes' fleet now left Therma and sent ten of his fastest ships south, which encountered and captured three look-out ships of the Greeks.]

7.182 Two of the three Greek vessels thus fell into Persian hands; the third, commanded by the Athenian Phormos, went ashore, while trying to escape, at the mouth of the Peneus. Here she was taken, though the men in her got away; for the instant the vessel grounded the Athenians aboard leapt out and made their way back to Athens through Thessaly.

7.183 News of what had happened was flashed to the Greeks at Artemisium by fire-signal from Sciathus. In the panic which ensued they left their station and moved to Chalcis, intending to guard the Euripus, and leaving look-outs on the high ground of Euboea. Three of the ten Persian ships ran aground on the Ant, a sunken reef between Sciathus and Magnesia; in consequence of this the Persians marked the reef with a stone beacon, after which, the danger being removed, the whole fleet set sail from Therma, eleven days after Xerxes had marched from the town with his army. The Ant lies right in the fairway; Pammon, a native of Scyros, took the Persians to it when they erected their beacon. A day's voyage brought the Persian fleet to Sepias in Magnesia and the strip of coast between Cape Sepias and the town of Casthanea.

7.184 The Persian fleet got as far as Sepias, and the army as far as Thermopylae, without loss...

[At this point Herodotus gives very large figures for the size of the Persian army and navy. A fierce storm, however, destroyed a vast number of the ships and encouraged the Greeks who waited at Artemisium opposite the Persian fleet. At the same time Xerxes marched his army to Thermopylae where he faced the Greeks under the Spartan king Leonidas.]

...The three hundred men whom he brought on this occasion to Thermopylae were chosen by himself, all fathers of living sons. He also took with him the Thebans I mentioned, under the command of Leontiades, the son of Eurymachus. The reason why he made a special point of taking troops from Thebes, and from Thebes only, was that the Thebans were strongly suspected of Persian sympathies, so he called upon them to play their part in the war in order to see if they would answer the call, or openly refuse to join the confederacy. They did send troops, but their sympathy was nevertheless with the enemy.

7.206 Leonidas and his three hundred were sent by Sparta in advance of the main army, in order that the sight of them might encourage the other confederates to fight and prevent them from going over to the enemy, as they were quite capable of doing if they knew that Sparta was hanging back; the intention was, when the Carneia was over (for it was that festival which prevented the Spartans from taking the field in the ordinary way), to leave a garrison in the city and march with all the troops at their disposal. The other allied states proposed to act similarly; for the Olympic festival happened to fall just at this same period. None of them ever expected the battle at Thermopylae to be decided so soon—which was the reason why they sent only advance parties there.

7.207 The Persian army was now close to the pass, and the Greeks, suddenly doubting their power to resist, held a conference to consider the advisability of retreat. It was proposed by the Peloponnesians generally that the army should fall back upon the Peloponnese and hold the Isthmus; but when the Phocians and Locrians expressed their indignation at this suggestion, Leonidas gave his vote for staying where they were and sending, at the same time, an appeal for reinforcements to the various states of the confederacy, as their numbers were inadequate to cope with the Persians.

* * *

[After a delay of some days the Persians attacked, but the Greeks withstood their assaults, inflicting heavy casualties and holding the pass for several days.]

7.213 How to deal with the situation Xerxes had no idea; but just then, a man from Malis, Ephialtes, the son of Eurydemus, came, in hope of a rich reward, to tell the king about the track which led over the hills to Thermopylae—and thus he was able to prove the death of the Greeks who held the pass...

7.217 This, then, was the mountain track which the Persians took, after crossing the Asopus. They marched throughout the night, with the mountains of Oeta on their right hand and those of Trachis on their left. By early dawn they were at the summit of the ridge, near the spot where the Phocians, as I mentioned before, stood on guard with a thousand men, to watch the track and protect their country. The Phocians had volunteered for this service to Leonidas, the lower road being held as already described.

7.218 The ascent of the Persians had been concealed by the oak-woods which cover all these hills, and it was only when they were up that the Phocians became aware of their approach; for there was no wind, and the marching feet made a loud swishing and rustling in the fallen leaves. Leaping to their feet, the Phocians were in the act of arming themselves when the enemy was upon them. The Persians were surprised at the sight of troops preparing to resist; they had expected no opposition—yet here was a body of men barring their way. Hydarnes asked Ephialtes who they were, for his first fearful thought was that they might be Spartans but on learning the truth he prepared to engage them. The Persian arrows flew thick and fast, and the Phocians, supposing themselves to be the main object of the attack, hurriedly withdrew to the highest point of the mountain, where they made ready to face destruction. But the Persians with Ephialtes and Hydarnes paid no further attention to them, but passed on along the descending track with all possible speed.

7.219 The Greeks at Thermopylae had their first warning of the death that was coming with the dawn from the seer Megistias, who read their doom in the victims of sacrifice; deserters, too, came in during the night with news of the Persian flank movement, and lastly, just as day was breaking, the look-out men came running from the hills. In council of war their opinions were divided, some urging that they must not abandon their post, others the opposite. The result was that the army split: some dispersed, contingents returning to their various cities, while others made ready to stand by Leonidas.

7.220 It is said that Leonidas himself dismissed them, to spare their lives, but thought it unbecoming for the Spartans under his command to desert the post which they had originally come to guard. I myself am inclined to think that he dismissed them when he realized that they had no heart for the fight and were unwilling to take their share of the danger, at the same time honour forbade that he himself should go. And indeed by remaining at his post he left great glory behind him, and Sparta did not lose her prosperity, as might otherwise have happened; for right at the outset of the war the Spartans had been told by the Delphic oracle that either their city must be laid waste by the foreigner or a Spartan king be killed. The prophecy was in hexameter verse and ran as follows:

Hear your fate, O dwellers in Sparta of the wide
　　spaces;
Either your famed, great town must be sacked
　　by Perseus' Sons,
Or, if that be not, the whole land of Lacedaemon
Shall mourn the death of a king of the house of
　　Heracles,
For not the strength of lions or of bulls shall hold him,
Strength against strength; for he has the power
　　of Zeus,
And will not be checked till one of these two he has
　　consumed.

I believe it was the thought of this oracle, combined with his wish to lay up for the Spartans a treasure of fame in which no other city should share, that made Leonidas dismiss those troops; I do not think that they deserted, or went off without orders, because of a difference of opinion.

* * *

7.222 Thus it was that the confederate troops, by Leonidas' orders, abandoned their posts and left the pass, all except the Thespians and the Thebans who remained with the Spartans. The Thebans were detained by Leonidas as hostages very much against their will; but the Thespians of their own accord refused to desert Leonidas and his men, and stayed, and died with them. They were under the command of Demophilus the son of Diadromes.

7.223 In the morning Xerxes poured a libation to the rising sun, and then waited until the time when the market-place is filled before he began to move forward. This was according to Ephialtes' instructions, for the way down from the ridge is much shorter and more direct than the long and circuitous ascent. As the Persian army advanced to the assault, the Greeks under Leonidas, knowing that they were going to their deaths, went out into the wider part of the pass much further than they had done before; in the previous days' fighting they had been holding the wall and making sorties from behind it into the narrow neck, but now they fought outside the narrows. Many of the barbarians fell; behind them the company commanders plied their whips indiscriminately, driving the men on. Many fell into the sea and were drowned, and still more were trampled to death by one another. No one could count the number of the dead. The Greeks, who knew that the enemy were on their way round by the mountain track and that death was inevitable, put **7.224** forth all their strength and fought with fury and desperation. By this time most of their spears were broken, and they were killing Persians with their swords. In the course of that fight Leonidas fell, having fought most gallantly, and many distinguished Spartans with him—their names I have learned, as those of men who deserve to be remembered; indeed, I have learned the names of all the three hundred. Amongst the Persian dead, too, were many men of high distinction, including two brothers of Xerxes, Habrocomes and Hyperanthes, sons of Darius by Artanes' daughter Phratagune. Artanes, the son of Hystaspes and grandson of Arsames, was Darius' brother; as Phratagune was his only child, his giving her to Darius was equivalent to giving him his entire estate.

7.225 There was a bitter struggle over the body of Leonidas; four times the Greeks drove the enemy off, and at last by their valour rescued it. So it went on, until the troops with Ephialtes were close at hand; and then, when the Greeks knew that they had come, the character of the fighting changed. They withdrew again into the narrow neck of the pass, behind the wall, and took up a position in a single compact body—all except the Thebans—on the little hill at the entrance to the pass, where the stone lion in memory of Leonidas stands today. Here they resisted to the last, with their swords, if they had them, and, if not, with their hands and teeth, until the Persians, coming on from the front over the ruins of the wall and closing in from behind, finally overwhelmed them with missile weapons.

* * *

7.228 The dead were buried where they fell, and with them the men who had been killed before those dismissed by Leonidas left the pass. Over them is this inscription, in honour of the whole force:

Four thousand here from Pelops' land
Against three million once did stand.

The Spartans have a special epitaph; it runs:

Go tell the Spartans, you who read:
We took their orders, and here lie dead.

For the seer Megistias there is the following:

Here Megistias lies, who died
When the Mede passed Spercheius' tide.
A prophet; yet he scorned to save
Himself, but shared the Spartans' grave.

The columns with the epitaphs inscribed on them were erected in honour of the dead by the Amphictyons—though the epitaph upon the seer Megistias was the work of Simonides, the son of Leoprepes, who put it there for friendship sake.

Questions

1. **Why did the Greek fleet withdraw from Artemisium to Chalcis?**
2. **Why did the Spartans send Leonidas to Thermopylae with only 300 men?**
3. **Describe each of Xerxes' three attacks on the pass. How did he ultimately succeed?**
4. **According to Herodotus, why did not Leonidas (or the Thebans or the Thespians) retreat when the situation became hopeless?**

Book Eight

8.1 The following is the roll of the Greek naval force: 127 ships from Athens—partly manned by the Plataeans, whose courage and patriotism led them to undertake this service in spite of their ignorance of nautical matters; 40 from Corinth, 20 from Megara, 20 more from Athens manned by crews from Chalcis, 18 from Aegina, 12 from Sicyon, 10 from Sparta, 8 from Epidaurus, 7 from Eretria, 5 from Troezen, 2 from Styra, and 2—together with two penteconters—from Ceos. Lastly, the Locrians of Opus joined with seven penteconters.

8.2 These, then, were the states which sent ships to Artemisium, and I have given the number which each contributed. The total strength of the fleet, excluding the penteconters, was thus 271 ships of war. The general officer in command, Eurybiades, the son of Eurycleides, was provided by Sparta; for the other members of the confederacy had stipulated for a Lacedaemonian commander, declaring that rather than serve under an Athenian they would break up the intended expedition altogether.

* * *

8.4 When the Greeks on their arrival at Artemisium found a large Persian fleet lying at Aphetae and all the neighbourhood full of troops, it was evident to them that things had gone very differently with the Persians from what they had expected. They were seized by panic, and began to consider abandoning Artemisium and, making their escape into the inner parts of Greece. This greatly alarmed the Euboeans, who no sooner realized what they had in mind than they begged Eurybiades to stay at any rate long enough to allow them to move their children and servants to a place of safety. Eurybiades refused, whereupon they went to Themistocles, the Athenian commander, and by a bribe of thirty talents induced him so to arrange matters that the Greek fleet should stay and fight on the coast of Euboea.

8.5 The method Themistocles adopted to attain this object was to pass on to Eurybiades, as if it were a personal present from himself, a sixth part of the sum he had received from the Euboeans. This was enough to secure Eurybiades' consent; of the other commanders, however, there was still one who hesitated—Adeimantus son of Ocytus, the Corinthian, who declared that he would withdraw his ships from Artemisium. To him, therefore, Themistocles now addressed himself. "Never," he cried with an oath, "shall you leave us in the lurch! I will give you more for staying with us than the Persian king would ever send you if you deserted us"; and without further delay he sent aboard Adeimantus' ship three talents of silver. So Adeimantus and Eurybiades yielded to bribery and the Euboeans' wishes were gratified; Themistocles, too, made something out of the transaction, for he kept the rest of the money himself. Nobody knew he had it, and the two men who had received their share imagined that it came from Athens especially for the purpose.

8.6 These were the circumstances which led to the Greeks engaging the Persians on the Euboean coast, and I will now describe the battle itself. The Persians reached Aphetae early in the afternoon, and saw for themselves what they had previously heard reported—namely that a small Greek force was concentrated at Artemisium. At once they were eager to engage, in the hope of capturing the Greek ships. It did not, however, seem advisable to advance, in the first instance, openly to the attack; for the Greeks, seeing them coming, might try to escape, and then, when darkness overtook them, they would be sure to get clear away. This would not do, as the Persians were determined that not even a fire-signaller (as they put it) must be allowed to escape alive.

8.7 Laying their plans accordingly, they detached a squadron of 200 ships with orders to sail outside Sciathus, in order to escape enemy observation, and then to turn southward round Euboea and into the Euripus by way of Caphareus and Geraestus; in this way they hoped to catch the Greeks in a trap, one squadron taking them in the rear and blocking their retreat, the rest of the fleet pressing upon them from in front. With this purpose in view the two hundred ships were dispatched, while the main body waited—for they did not intend to attack on that day, or until they knew by signal that the squadron coming up the Euripus had arrived.

8.8 Meanwhile a review of the main fleet was held at Aphetae, and while it was going on the following event occurred. Serving with the Persian force there was a man named Scyllias, a native of Scione and the most accomplished diver of his day, who after the wreck of the Persian ships at Pelion had saved a great deal of valuable property for his masters—besides getting a good deal for himself. This man had apparently been thinking for some time past of deserting to the Greeks, but no opportunity had occurred until then. I cannot say for certain how it was that he managed to reach the Greeks, and I am amazed if what is said is true; for, according to this, he dived underwater at Aphetae and did not come up until he reached Artemisium—a distance of about ten miles. There are other somewhat tall stories, besides this, told about Scyllias—and also a few true ones; as to the one I have just related, my personal opinion is that he came to Artemisium in a boat. In any case, come he did; and on his arrival he lost no time in giving an account to the Greek commanders of all the circumstances of the disaster to the Persian fleet in the storm, and also told them about the squadron which was on its way round Euboea.

8.9 The Greek commanders at once proceeded to discuss the situation which this piece of intelligence produced; and after a long debate it was decided to stay where they were until after midnight, and then put to sea to meet the Persians who were coming up the Euripus. However, as time went on and they met with no opposition, they waited till the evening of the following day and then attacked the main enemy fleet, with the intention of testing Persian seamanship and tactics.

8.10 When the officers and men of Xerxes' fleet saw the Greeks moving to the attack with such a small force, they thought they were mad and at once got under way themselves, in confident expectation of making an easy capture; nor, indeed, was the expectation unreasonable, in view of the disparity in numbers—the Greek ships being few, and their own many times as numerous, as well as faster. Thus assured of their superiority, they developed a movement to surround the enemy. Those of the Ionians who had been forced to serve with the Persian fleet in spite of their real sympathy with the Greek cause were much distressed at the sight of the gradual encirclement of the Greeks, and convinced, in view of their apparent weakness, that not a man amongst them would escape alive; those, on the other hand, who welcomed the situation, entered into competition with each other to be the first to win a reward from Xerxes for the capture of an Athenian ship—for throughout the Persian fleet it was the Athenians who were most talked of.

8.11 At the first signal for action the Greek squadron formed into a close circle—bows outward, stems to the centre; then, at the second signal, with little room to manoeuvre and lying, as they were, bows-on to the enemy, they set to work, and succeeded in capturing thirty Persian ships. Amongst the prisoners was Philaon, the son of Chersis and brother of Gorgus the king of Salamis, and a person of repute in the enemy force. The first Greek to take a prize was the Athenian Lycomedes son of Aeschraeus. He was decorated for valour after the battle. After this success, when darkness put an end to the fighting, the Greeks returned to Artemisium, and the Persians—who had had a considerable shock—to Aphetae. The only Greek in the Persian force to desert and join his countrymen during the action was Antidorus, the Lemnian; the Athenians afterwards showed their appreciation by giving him a grant of land in Salamis.

8.12 After dark—the season was midsummer—there was a very violent rainstorm, which lasted all night, accompanied by much thunder from the direction of Pelion. Dead bodies and bits of wreckage, drifting up to Aphetae, fell athwart the bows of the ships which lay there, and fouled the oar-blades of any that were under way; this, and the noise of the thunderstorm, caused a panic amongst the Persian troops, who began to think their last hour was come: they had, indeed, had much to put up with—for almost before they could draw breath again after the storm at Pelion, which wrecked so many of their ships, they were faced with a hard fight at sea, and now, on top of that, they were exposed to floods of rain, the rushing of swollen streams into the sea, and a tremendous thunderstorm.

8.13 For the Persians at Aphetae it was a bad enough night, but it was far worse for the squadron which had been ordered to sail round Euboea, for they were at sea when the storm taught them. Their fate was miserable: just as they were off the Hollows of Euboea the wind and rain began, and every ship, overpowered and forced to run blind before it, piled up on the rocks. God was indeed doing everything possible to reduce the superiority of the Persian fleet and bring it down to the size of the Greek. So much for the disaster off the Hollows.

8.14 The Persians at Aphetae were very glad to see the dawn next morning, and did not feel like taking any further risks; it was enough for them, badly shaken as they were, to let the ships lie and attempt nothing for the present. Meanwhile the Greeks received a reinforcement of fifty-three ships from Athens, the arrival of this fresh squadron, together with the news of the loss in the storm of the whole Persian force which was sailing round Euboea, was a great encouragement, and the Greeks, on the strength of it, waiting till, the same time as on the previous day, once again put to sea and attacked some Cilician vessels; these they destroyed and then, at the approach of darkness, they returned to Artemisium.

8.15 The Persian commanders were humiliated at receiving such rough treatment from so small a fleet; they were beginning, moreover, to be alarmed at the thought of what Xerxes might do to them; so on the third day they took the initiative, and, without waiting for the Greeks to move, made their preparations and put to sea round about midday. It so happened that these battles at sea took place on the same days as the battles at Thermopylae, and in each case the object was similar—to defend the passage into the heart of Greece: the fleet was fighting for the Euripus just as the army with Leonidas was fighting for the pass. So the Greek-cry was to stop the enemy from getting through, while the Persians aimed at destroying the defending forces in order to clear the passage. Xerxes' fleet now moved forward in good order to the attack, while the Greeks at Artemisium quietly awaited their approach. Then the Persians adopted a crescent formation and came on with the intention of surrounding their enemy, whereupon the Greeks advanced to meet them, and the fight began. In this engagement the two fleets were evenly matched—the Persian, by its mere size, proving its own greatest enemy, as constant confusion was caused by the ships fouling one another. None the less they made a brave fight of it, to avoid the disgrace of defeat by so small an enemy force. The Greek losses both in ships and men were heavy, those of the Persians much heavier. Finally the action was broken off.

* * *

8.18 Both sides were glad when they parted and made all speed back to their moorings. The Greeks, once they were clear of the fighting, did, indeed, manage to possess themselves of the floating bodies and to salvage the wreckage; nevertheless they had been so roughly handled—especially the Athenians, half of whose ships were damaged—that they determined to quit their station and withdraw further south.

* * *

8.21 While the Greeks were thus occupied, their observer arrived from Trachis. The Greeks had employed two, to keep communication between the fleet and the army: at Artemisium Polyas, a native of Anticyra, kept a boat ready to report to the army at Thermopylae any reverse which might be suffered by the fleet, while the Athenian Abronichus, the son of Lysicles, did similar duty with Leonidas, and had a thirty–oared galley always available to report to Artemisium, if the army got into any trouble. It was this Abronichus who now arrived with the news of the fate of Leonidas and his men. The effect was immediate; the Greeks put off their withdrawal not a minute longer, but got under way at once, one after another, the Corinthians leading, the Athenians bringing up the rear. The Persians next marched south toward Attica.

8.40 The Greek fleet, having sailed from Artemisium, brought up, at the Athenians' request, at Salamis. The Athenians' object in urging the commanders to take up this position was to give themselves an opportunity of getting their women and children out of Attica, and also of discussing their next move—as their present circumstances, and the frustration of their hopes, most evidently demanded. They had expected that the full strength of the Peloponnesian army would concentrate in Boeotia to hold up the Persian advance, but now they found nothing of the sort; on the contrary, they learned that the Peloponnesians were concerned only with their own safety and were fortifying the Isthmus in order to protect the Peloponnese, while the rest of Greece, so far as they cared, might take its chance. It was this news which led to the request to the fleet to put in at Salamis.

8.41 While, therefore, the rest of the fleet lay at Salamis, the Athenians returned to their own harbours, and at once issued a proclamation that everyone in the city and countryside should get his children and all the members of his household to safety as best he could. Most of them were sent to Troezen, but some to Aegina and some to Salamis. The removal of their families was pressed on with all possible speed, partly because they wished to heed the warning which had been given them by the oracle, but more especially for an even stronger reason. The Athenians say that the Acropolis is guarded by a great snake, which lives in the temple; indeed they believed so literally in its existence that they put out monthly offerings for it to eat in the form of a honey-cake. Now in the past the honey-cake used always to be consumed, but on this occasion it was untouched. The temple Priestess told them of this, and in consequence, believing that the goddess herself had abandoned the Acropolis, they were all the more ready to evacuate the town. As soon as everything was removed, they rejoined the fleet on its station.

8.42 There were some other Greek ships which had been ordered to assemble at Pogon, the harbour of Troezen, and these, when news came through that the fleet from Artemisium had put into Salamis, left Troezen and joined it. Thus the fleet was larger than it had been at the battle of Artemisium, and made up of ships from more towns. It was still under the same commander, Eurybiades, the son of Eurycleides—a Spartan but not of the royal blood; but the city which furnished by far the greatest number of ships, and the fastest, was Athens.

Questions

1. **How did Eurybiades and Themistocles prevent the Greek fleet from retreating?**
2. **Describe each of the engagements between the Greek and the Persian fleets, according to Herodotus. What was the motivation for each side to attack?**
3. **What were the strategy, tactics, objectives for, and reaction to each sea fight?**
4. **How did the Greek plan at Artemisium fit into the overall strategy against the Persians?**
5. **How did the Athenians (and the Peloponnesians) respond to the defeat up north? Why?**

* * *

[After giving a catalogue of the Greeks at Salamis, Herodotus describes the decision to fight.]

8.49 When the commanders of the various contingents I have mentioned met at Salamis, a council of war was held, and Eurybiades called for suggestions, from anyone who wished to speak, on the most suitable place for engaging the enemy fleet in the territory still under their control—Attica was excluded, as it had already been given up. The general feeling of the council was in favour of sailing to the Isthmus and fighting in defence of the Peloponnese, on the grounds that if they were beaten at Salamis they would find themselves blocked up in an island, where no help could reach them, whereas if disaster overtook them at the Isthmus, they could find refuge amongst their own people.

8.50 This was the view of the Peloponnesian officers. While the discussion was still going on, a man arrived from Athens with the news that the Persians had entered Attica and were firing the whole country. This was the work of the division of the army under Xerxes which had taken the route through Boeotia; they had burnt Thespia after the inhabitants had escaped to the Peloponnese and Plataea too, and then entered Attica, where they were causing wholesale devastation. The Thebans had told them that Thespia and Plataea had refused to submit to Persian domination: hence their destruction. The march of the Persian army from the Hellespont to Attica had taken three months—and the actual crossing of the strait an additional one; it reached Attica during the archonship of Calliades.

8.51 The Persians found Athens itself abandoned except for a few people in the temple of Athene Polias—temple stewards and needy folk, who had barricaded the Acropolis against the invaders with planks and timbers. It was partly their poverty which prevented them from seeking shelter in Salamis with the rest, and partly their belief that they had discovered the real meaning of the Priestess' oracle—that "the wooden wall would not be taken." The wooden wall, in their minds, was not the ships but the barricade, and that would save them.

8.52 The Persians occupied the hill which the Athenians call the Areopagus, opposite the Acropolis, and began the siege. The method they used was to shoot into the barricade arrows with burning tow attached to them. Their wooden wall had betrayed them, but still the Athenians, though in imminent and deadly peril, refused to give in or even to listen to the proposals which the Pisistratidae made to them for a truce. All their ingenuity was employed in the struggle to defend themselves; amongst other things, they rolled boulders down the slope upon the enemy as he tried to approach the gates, and for a long time Xerxes was baffled and unable to take them.

8.53 But in the end the Persians solved their problem: a way of access to the Acropolis was found—for it was prophesied that all Athenian territory upon the continent of Greece must be overrun by the Persians. There is a place in front of the Acropolis, behind the way up to the gates, where the ascent is so steep that no guard was set, because it was not thought possible that any man would be able to climb it; here, by the shrine of Cecrops' daughter Aglaurus, some soldiers managed to scramble up the precipitous face of the cliff. When the Athenians saw them on the summit, some leapt from the wall to their death, others sought sanctuary in the inner shrine of the temple; but the Persians who had got up first made straight for the gates, flung them open and slaughtered those in sanctuary. Having left not one of them alive, they stripped the temple of its treasures and burnt everything on the Acropolis.

* * *

8.56 Meanwhile at Salamis the effect of the news of what had happened to the Acropolis at Athens was so disturbing, that some of the naval commanders did not even wait for the subject under discussion to be decided, but hurried on board and began hoisting sail for immediate flight. Some, however, stayed; and by these a resolution was passed to fight in defence of the Isthmus.

8.57 During the night, when the various commanders had returned to their ships after the break-up of the conference, an Athenian named Mnesiphilus made his way to Themistocles' ship and asked him what plan it had been decided to adopt. On learning that they had resolved to sail to the Isthmus and to fight there in defence of the

Peloponnese, "No, no," he exclaimed; "once the fleet leaves Salamis, it will no longer be one country that you'll be fighting for. Everyone will go home, and neither Eurybiades nor anybody else will be able to prevent the total dissolution of our forces. The plan is absurd and will be the ruin of Greece. Now listen to me: try, if you possibly can, to upset the decision of the conference—it may be that you will be able to persuade Eurybiades to change his mind and remain at Salamis."

8.58 Themistocles highly approved of this suggestion, and without saying a word he went to the ship of the commander-in-chief and told him that he had something of public importance to discuss. Eurybiades invited him aboard and gave him permission to speak his mind, whereupon Themistocles, taking a seat beside him, repeated Mnesiphilus' arguments as if they were his own, with plenty of new ones added, until he convinced him, by the sheer urgency of his appeal, that the only thing to do was to go ashore and call the officers to another conference.

8.59 The conference met, and then, before Eurybiades even had time to announce its purpose, Themistocles, unable to restrain his eagerness, broke into a passionate speech. He was interrupted by Adeimantus, the son of Ocytus, commander of the Corinthian contingent. "Themistocles," he observed, "in the races, the man who starts before the signal is whipped." "Yes," was Themistocles' retort, "but those who start too late win no prizes."

8.60 It was a mild retort—for the moment. To Eurybiades he used none of his previous arguments about the danger of the force breaking up if they left Salamis; for it would have been unbecoming to accuse any of the confederates actually to their faces. The line he took this time was quite different. **[a]** "It is now in your power," he said, "to save Greece, if you take my advice and engage the enemy's fleet here in Salamis, instead of withdrawing to the Isthmus as these other people suggest. Let me put the two plans before you, and you can weigh them up and see which is the better. Take the Isthmus first: if you fight there, it will have to be in the open sea, and that will be greatly to our disadvantage with our smaller numbers and slower ships. Moreover, even if everything else goes well, you will lose Salamis, Megara, and Aegina. Again, if the enemy fleet comes south, the army will follow it; so

you will yourself be responsible for drawing it to the Peloponnese, thus putting the whole of Greece in peril. **[b]** Now for my plan: it will bring, if you adopt it, the following advantages: first, we shall be fighting in narrow waters, and there, with our inferior numbers, we shall win, provided things go as we may reasonably expect. Fighting in a confined space favours us but the open sea favours the enemy. Secondly, Salamis, where we have put our women and children, will be preserved; and thirdly—for you the most important point of all—you will be fighting in defence of the Peloponnese by remaining here just as much as by withdrawing to the Isthmus—nor, if you have the sense to follow my advice, will you draw the Persian army to the Peloponnese. **[c]** If we beat them at sea, as I expect we shall, they will not advance to attack you on the Isthmus, or come any further than Attica; they will retreat in disorder, and we shall gain by the preservation of Megara, Aegina, and Salamis—where an oracle has already foretold our victory. Let a man lay his plans with due regard to common sense, and he will usually succeed; otherwise he will find that God is unlikely to favour human designs."

8.61 During his speech Themistocles was again attacked by the Corinthian Adeimantus, who told him to hold his tongue because he was a man without a country, and tried to prevent Eurybiades from putting any question to the vote at the instance of a mere refugee. Let Themistocles, he cried, provide himself with a country before he offered his advice. The point of the jibe was, of course, the fact that Athens had fallen and was in Persian hands. This time Themistocles' retort was by no means mild; he heartily abused both Adeimantus and the Corinthians, and made it quite plain that so long as Athens had two hundred warships in commission, she had both a city and a country much stronger than theirs—for there was not a single Greek state capable of repelling them, should they choose to attack.

8.62 With this he turned to Eurybiades again, and, speaking more vehemently than ever, "As for you," he cried, "if you stay here and play the man— well and good; go, and you'll be the ruin of Greece. In this war everything depends upon the fleet. I beg you to take my advice; if you refuse, we will immediately put our families aboard and sail for Siris in Italy—it has long been ours, and the oracles have foretold that Athenians must live there someday. Where will you be without the Athenian fleet? When you have lost it you will remember my words."

8.63 That was enough to make Eurybiades change his mind; and I think that his chief motive was apprehension of losing Athenian support, if he withdrew to the Isthmus; for without the Athenian contingent his strength would not have been adequate to offer battle. So he took the decision to stay where they were and fight it out at Salamis.

[The following extract from Herodotus describes how Themistocles helped bring about the battle at Salamis. It suggests that the Greeks made their decisions in a state of panic and that they lacked the planning indicated by the Themistocles decree. Herodotus' account also shows the unwillingness of the Peloponnesians to fight north of the Isthmus.]

8.70 The Greeks were in a state of acute alarm, especially those from the Peloponnese: for there they were, waiting at Salamis to fight for Athenian territory, and certain, in the event of defeat, to be caught and blocked up in an island, while their own country was left without defence, **8.71** and the Persian army that very night was on the march for the Peloponnese.

Nevertheless everything that ingenuity could contrive had been done to prevent the Persian army from forcing the Isthmus. On the news of the destruction of Leonidas' force at Thermopylae, troops from all the states hurried to the Isthmus, where they took up their position under Cleombrotus, the son of Anaxandrides and brother of Leonidas. Their first act was to break up and block the Scironian Way; then, in accordance with a decision taken in council, they began work on a wall across the Isthmus. As there were many thousands there and every man turned to, the work went fast. Stones, bricks, timbers, sand-baskets—all were used in the building, and the labour went on continuously night and day.

8.72 The peoples which joined in this work in full force were the following: Sparta, all the Arcadians, Elis, Corinth, Sicyon, Epidaurus, Phlius, Troezen, and Hermione: all these, in their overriding

fear for the safety of Greece, helped in the work; but the other Peloponnesian communities (though the Olympic and Carneian festivals were now over) remained indifferent.

* * *

8.74 The Greeks at the Isthmus, convinced that all they possessed was now at stake and not expecting any notable success at sea, continued to grapple with their task of fortification. The news of how they were employed nevertheless caused great concern at Salamis; for it brought home to everyone there not so much his own peril as the imminent threat to the Peloponnese. At first there was whispered criticism of the incredible folly of Eurybiades; then the smothered feeling broke out into open resentment, and another meeting was held. All the old ground was gone over again, one side urging that it was useless to stay and fight for a country which was already in enemy hands, and that the fleet should sail and risk an action in defence of the Peloponnese, while the Athenians, Aeginetans, and Megarians still maintained that they should stay and fight at Salamis.

8.75 At this point Themistocles, feeling that he would be outvoted by the Peloponnesians, slipped quietly away from the meeting and sent a man over in a boat to the Persian fleet, with instructions upon what to say when he got there. The man—Sicinnus—was one of Themistocles' slaves and used to attend upon his sons; afterwards, when the Thespians were enrolling new citizens, Themistocles established him at Thespia and made him a rich man. Following his instructions, then, Sicinnus made his way to the Persian commanders and said: "I am the bearer of a secret communication from the Athenian commander, who is a well-wisher to your king and hopes for a Persian victory. He has told me to report to you that the Greeks are afraid and are planning to slip away. Only prevent them from slipping through your fingers, and you have at this moment an opportunity of unparalleled success. They are at daggers drawn with each other, and will offer no opposition—on the contrary, you will see the pro-Persians amongst them fighting the rest,"

8.76 His message delivered, Sicinnus lost no time in getting away. The Persians believed what he had told them, and proceeded to put ashore a large force on the islet of Psyttaleia, between Salamis and the coast; then, about midnight, they moved their western wing in an encircling movement upon Salamis, while at the same time the ships off Ceos and Cynosura also advanced and blocked the whole channel as far as Munychia. The object of these movements was—ironically—that the Greeks might be cut off in Salamis and there give the Persians their revenge for the battles of Artemisium. The troops were landed on Psyttaleia because it lay right in the path of the impending action, and once the fighting began, many men and damaged vessels would be carried on to it, and could be saved or destroyed according as they were friends or enemies. These tactical moves were carried out in silence, to prevent the enemy from being aware of what was going on; they occupied the whole night, so that none of the men had time for sleep.

* * *

8.78 The Greek commanders at Salamis were still at loggerheads. They did not yet know that the enemy ships had blocked their escape at both ends of the channel, but supposed them to occupy the same **8.79** position as they had seen them in during the day. However, while the dispute was still at its height, Aristides came over in a boat from Aegina. This man, an Athenian and the son of Lysimachus, had been ostracized by the Athenians, but the more I have learned of his character, the more I have come to believe that he was the best and most just man that Athens ever produced. Arrived at Salamis, Aristides went to where the conference was being held and, standing outside, called for Themistocles. Themistocles was no friend of his; indeed he was his most determined enemy; but Aristides was willing, in view of the magnitude of the danger which threatened them, to forget old quarrels in his desire to communicate with him. He was already aware of the anxiety of the Peloponnesian commanders to withdraw to the Isthmus; as soon, therefore, as Themistocles came out of the conference in answer to his call, he said: "At this moment, more than ever before, you and I should be rivals, to see which of us can do most good to our country. First, let me tell you that the Peloponnesians may talk as much or as little

as they please about withdrawing from Salamis it will make not the least difference. What I tell you, I have seen with my own eyes: they *cannot* now get out of here, however much the Corinthians or Eurybiades himself may wish to do so, because our fleet is surrounded. So go in and tell them that!"

8.80 "Good news and good advice," Themistocles answered; "what I most wanted has happened—and you bring me the evidence of your own eyes that it is true. It was I who was responsible for this move of the enemy; for as our men would not fight here of their own free will, it was necessary to make them, whether they wanted to do so or not. But take them the good news yourself; if I tell them, they will think I have invented it and will not believe me. Please, then, go in and make the report yourself. If they believe you, well and good; if they do not, it's all the same; for if we are surrounded, as you say we are, escape is no longer possible."

8.81 Aristides accordingly went in and made his report, saying he had come from Aegina and had been hard put to it to slip through the blockading enemy fleet, as the entire Greek force was surrounded. He advised them, therefore, to prepare at once to repel an attack. That said, he left the conference, whereupon another dispute broke out, because most of the commanders still refused to believe in the report.

8.82 But while they still doubted, a Tenian warship, commanded by Panaetius, the son of Sosimenes deserted from the Persians and came in with a full account. For this service the name of the Tenians was afterwards inscribed on the tripod at Delphi amongst the other states who helped to defeat the invader. With this ship which came over to them at Salamis, and the Lemnian one which previously joined them at Artemisium, the Greek fleet was brought up to the round number of 380. Up till then it had fallen short of that figure by two.

8.83 Persuaded by the Tenians' report, the Greeks now at last prepared for action. At dawn the fighting men were assembled and Themistocles gave the finest speech there. The whole burden of what he said was a comparison of all that was best and worst in human nature and fortune, and an exhortation to the men to choose the better. Then, having rounded off his speech, he ordered the men to embark onto the ships.

> **Questions**
>
> 1. **How did the Persians seize the Athenian Acropolis?**
> 2. **Which factors convinced the Greeks to fight the Persians at Salamis, according to Herodotus?**
> 3. **Discuss the role the following figures play in that decision: Mnesiphilus, Themistocles, Eurybiades, Adeimantus, Sicinnus, and Aristides. How did Themistocles force the Peloponnesians and Xerxes to fight at Salamis?**
> 4. **Does Herodotus' narrative seem consistent? Why or why not?**

2.   THE THEMISTOCLES DECREE

In 1932 or 1933 a Greek farmer, while digging a pit for a lemon tree near the site of ancient Troezen, found an inscription from the third century BC, which purports to be an Athenian decree passed in 480 before the Battle of Artemisium. Michael H. Jameson in 1959 identified and restored the inscription, which has become known as the "Themistocles Decree." The decree provides for the evacuation of Attica and, it appears, for a naval battle at Salamis before the Greeks could have known the result of the Battles of Thermopylae and Artemisium. This seems to contradict Herodotus, who explains the evacuation of Attica and the Battle of Salamis as last minute decisions the Greeks made after the Spartans failed to meet Xerxes in Boeotia. The authenticity of the decree is still in question, but if it reflects a reliable tradition it must influence our view of Greek strategy in important ways.

The Gods

Resolved by the Council and People

Themistocles, son of Neocles, of Phrearri, made the motion

To entrust the city to Athena the Mistress of Athens and to all the other Gods to guard and defend from the Barbarian for the sake of the land. The Athenians themselves and the foreigners who live in Athens are to send their children and women to safety in Troizen, their protector being Pittheus, the founding hero of the land. They are to send the old men and their movable possessions to safety on Salamis. The treasurers and priestesses are to remain on the acropolis guarding the property of the gods.

All the other Athenians and foreigners of military age are to embark on the 200 ships that are ready and defend against the Barbarian for the sake of their own freedom and that of the rest of the Greeks along with the Lacedaemonians, the Corinthians, the Aeginetans, and all others who wish to share the danger.

The generals are to appoint, starting tomorrow, 200 trierarchs [captains of triremes], from among those who have land and house in Athens and legitimate children and who are not older than fifty; to these men the ships are to be assigned by lot. They are to enlist marines, 10 to each ship, from men between the ages of twenty and thirty, and four archers. They are to distribute the servicemen [perhaps "petty officers" would be more accurate: see Morrison and Williams, *Greek Oared Ships*, p. 253 ff.] by lot at the same time as they assign the trierarchs to the ships by lot. The generals are to write up the sailors ship by ship on white boards, (taking) the Athenians from the lexiarchic registers (citizen-rolls), the foreigners from those registered with the polemarch [formerly Commander-in-Chief of the armed forces, now a senior magistrate]. They are to write them up assigning them by divisions, two hundred of about one hundred (men) each, and to write above each division the name of the trireme and the trierarch and the serviceman [petty officer], so that they may know on which trireme each division is to embark. When all the divisions have been composed and allotted to the triremes, the Council and the generals are to man all the two hundred ships, after sacrificing a placatory offering to Zeus the Almighty and Athena and Nike [Victory: perhaps we should read "Athena Nike" here] and Poseidon the Securer.

When the ships have been manned, with a hundred of them they are to meet the enemy at Artemisium in Euboea, and with the other hundred they are to lie off Salamis and the coast of Attica and keep guard over the land. In order that all Athenians may be united in their defence against the Barbarians, those who have been sent into exile for ten years are to go to Salamis and stay there until the people come to some decision about them, while[those who have been deprived of citizen rights are to have their rights restored...]

Questions

1. If authentic, what significance does the Decree of Themistocles have for the Greek strategy?
2. How do the contents of the decree compare with the narrative of Herodotus?

---

3. DIVINE SALAMIS

Plutarch gives the fullest account of the Persian Wars after Herodotus. His account is similar to that of the historian but he appears to have some knowledge of the Themistocles Decree. The extract below picks up after the defeat of Leonidas at Thermopylae. The section contains both the famous account of the alleged Spartan betrayal of the Greek cause in Boeotia and the apparent reference to the decree.

9. However, when the news of Thermopylae was brought to Artemisium and the Greeks learned that Leonidas had fallen and that Xerxes now commanded the passes, they withdrew southwards into Greece, with the Athenians guarding the rear because of the courage they had shown, and full of pride at their exploits in the battle. As Themistocles sailed along the coast, whenever he saw places where the enemy would have to land or put in for shelter or for supplies, he left messages conspicuously inscribed on the stones, some of which he found on the spot, while others he arranged to have set up by the likely anchorages and watering-places. In these inscriptions he appealed to the Ionians to come over, if they found the opportunity, to the side of the Athenians, who were their ancestors and who were risking everything for their liberty: if this was impossible, they should do their utmost to hinder the barbarians in battle and throw them into confusion. By these tactics he hoped he might either bring the Ionians over to his side, or else create chaos by making the barbarians suspect them.

Meanwhile, although Xerxes had marched up from Doris into Phocis and was burning and destroying the Phocian cities, the Greeks did not come to their rescue. The Athenians, it is true, pressed them to make a stand in Boeotia and protect Attica, just as they themselves had gone out by sea to fight in defence of the rest of Greece at Artemisium, but nobody would listen to them; instead, the remainder of the allies refused to budge from the Peloponnese. They were anxious to concentrate all their forces west of the Isthmus of Corinth and began to build a wall across it from sea to sea. The Athenians were furious at this betrayal, but at the same time felt thoroughly disheartened and dejected at being thus abandoned to their fate. They could not seriously think of engaging so vast an army by themselves, but the only choice which was now left to them—namely to give up their city and entrust their very existence to the fleet—seemed utterly repugnant. The majority felt that they did not want victory on these terms and that safety meant nothing to them if it required that they should abandon the temples of their gods and the tombs of their forefathers to the enemy.

10. At this point Themistocles, seeing no hope of winning over the people to his plans by any power of human reasoning, set to work to influence them with oracles and signs from heaven, just as a poet introduces a *deus ex machina* into his tragedy. He seized upon the episode of the snake, which is believed to have disappeared at this time from its sacred enclosure on the Acropolis, and treated it as a divine portent. When the priests discovered that the first fruits of sacrifice which were offered to it every day had been left untouched, they gave out to the people on Themistocles' instructions that the goddess Athena had abandoned her city and was showing them their way to the sea. In his efforts to sway the people he again invoked the famous oracle from Delphi, and insisted that the "wooden wall" could only refer to their ships and that Apollo had spoken of Salamis in his verses as divine, not as terrible or crude, for the very reason that its name would one day be associated with a great blessing for the Greeks. At last he got his way and thereupon proposed a decree that the city should be handed over to the keeping of its patron goddess, Athena, but that all men of military age should be embarked on the warships, after everyone had provided as best they could for the safety of their wives, children, and slaves. As soon as the decree was passed, most of the Athenians sent their wives and children to Troezen, where the citizens vied with one another in welcoming them. They even voted to maintain the refugees at the public expense; they gave each family two obols a day, allowed the children to pick the fruit wherever they pleased as soon as it was ripe, and went so far as to pay schoolmasters to teach them. These measures were proposed by a man named Nicagoras.

Questions

1. **Is the account of Plutarch consistent with either what Herodotus or the Decree of Themistocles says?**
2. **Discuss the similarities and differences among the three sources for the Greek strategy.**
3. **What source do you find gives the most convincing explanation for the Greek victory? Explain.**

OPINIONS OF MODERN SCHOLARS

THE THEMISTOCLES DECREE

1. In his book, *The Greco-Persian Wars*, Peter Green, the James R. Dougherty, Jr., Centennial Professor of Classics Emeritus at the University of Texas at Austin, provides a detailed reconstruction from the ancient sources of the Battles of

Thermopylae and Artemisium. He considers those campaigns "the corner-stone of freedom" for the Greeks. It is significant that Professor Green believes the Themistocles Decree comes very close to the famous motion Themistocles persuaded the Athenian assembly to ratify in 480. He describes Greek strategy as emphasizing the role of the fleet at Artemisium, with the army acting as a subservient holding force. For Green, the wording of the decree reflects the fact that both the invasion of Xerxes and the Greek resistance depended on careful coordination between land and sea forces.

FROM PETER GREEN, *THE GRECO-PERSIAN WARS*

WE KNOW, TODAY, THE GIST—if not the *ipsissima verba*—of that famous motion which Themistocles put forward, and the Assembly, to its eternal credit, ratified. In 1959 Professor Michael Jameson of Pennsylvania found a third-century BC copy of the draft decree at Troezen in the Argolid—a town which, as we shall see, befriended many Athenian evacuees during the Persian Wars. Over two centuries and more, intervening generations had edited and modernised the original text, much as we nowadays will modernise the spelling or diction of an early writer such as Chaucer or Piers Plowman. The decree also diverges somewhat in substance—though far less than is commonly supposed—from our soundest historical account of these events, that by Herodotus. Fierce scholarly debate still continues over the inscription's authenticity: many scholars regard it as a late forgery, perhaps intended to whip up patriotic feeling against Macedonia. Many others, however—including the present writer—believe that the fragmentary inscription does, in fact, give us something very close to Themistocles' actual proposals, though it may possibly run together several motions passed on different days. I quote it here (with one small textual change) in the revised version published by Professor Jameson:

[See Green's translation of the revised version above]

* * *

The stone breaks off at this point, but it is probable that we have the larger part of it. We are left with a brief, vivid glimpse of Athens preparing to meet her crisis—and of the practical, far-sighted statesman who brought her safely through the storm.

One cardinal fact should never be forgotten. This decree was a strictly *internal* measure, passed by and for Athenians alone. It had no direct connection with the League Congress, a fact which makes its dating of some importance. Herodotus [7.174] suggests that the Greek force under Themistocles and Euaenetus went straight from Tempe to the Isthmus, where it was voted, in full session, to defend the Thermopylae–Artemisium line. The natural deduction from this evidence—and so taken, to the best of my knowledge, by all scholars—is that the "Troezen Decree" was passed *after Themistocles returned from the Isthmus*. Jameson's version of events is typical: "The decision must have been reported by Themistocles and his colleagues to the Athenians, and put into effect by them in this decree." In that case what, one wonders, would have happened if the Athenian Assembly, in one of its more perversely whimsical moods, had thrown the motion out? Never in its chequered history—and now least of all—do we find that unpredictable body acting as a mere rubber stamp. Quite apart from this, Themistocles' previous experience could scarcely have led him to believe that so controversial a measure would win automatic approval, crisis or no crisis. He had failed before; he might well fail again.

One interesting point about the "Troezen Decree" is that it mentions Artemisium, but not Thermopylae. Themistocles, of course, knew very well from the beginning that only an amphibious defence-line, with close liaison between fleet and army, stood any real chance of success. Whether he could sell this basic strategy at the Isthmus, however, was by no means certain. He clearly intended that the fleet (to which Athens contributed by far the largest individual contingent) should play the dominant role in these combined operations, while the army merely acted as a subservient holding force. Such a concept of their respective functions was unlikely to prove popular with Spartan militarists. Indeed, when it came to the point, Nepos tells us, "many of the states did not approve of Themistocles' plan, but preferred to fight on land"—the old, stubborn chimaera created by Marathon. The obvious inference from this is that when the "Troezen Decree" was voted, no one actually knew whether Athens' unpredictable Peloponnesian allies would endorse it or not. In other words, it must be dated to a time *before* the League Congress met for its final decision on the defence of Greece.

One last but important point. Whatever policy Themistocles advanced at the Isthmus, he was, clearly, acting in his capacity as Athenian *proboulos*. Our evidence for the nature and functioning of the League is sadly sketchy; but I have always thought it odd that no modern study, not even the most exhaustive, has fully considered the matter of the League's executive authority. Could its decisions be carried out at once, without subsequent ratification by the governments of member-states? In other words, did the *probouloi* have plenipotentiary powers? The answer must, surely, be in the affirmative. The object of the League was to take fast collective action against Persia. Such action would be impossible—especially in Greece—if every vote was referred back to member-states for debate, with the chance of veto rather than ratification. The *probouloi* must have had full powers to act on behalf of the states they represented, and the League's majority decisions will have been binding on all members. Now if Themistocles, as *proboulos*, spoke for Athens, at least one point covered by the "Troezen Decree," mobilisation of the fleet, would not have required ratification at all; and the other two main clauses— the evacuation of Attica, the recall of political exiles—though domestic in application, stand or fall by this first one.

If, then, we date the decree *after* that final meeting at the Isthmus, its logical *raison d'être* is severely reduced—to the point, indeed, where *it* becomes virtually nonsensical. But if we place it *before* the League Congress, immediately after Themistocles' return from Tempe, it takes on a very different complexion. It is not only Themistocles' original mandate as Athenian *proboulos*, the policy for which he was obliged to win Assembly approval

(and without which approval, no doubt, Athens would have had a different representative at the Isthmus). It is also an emergency measure designed to cover Athens' betrayal or abandonment by the Peloponnesian League. The decision to fight for freedom "along with the Lacedaemonians, the Corinthians, the Aeginetans, and all others who wish to share the danger" is no more than a hopeful acknowledgement of the League's existence: it does not imply any preconcerted policy. No one could guess how the voting at the Isthmus would go. Sparta's isolationists might well carry the day; in which case Themistocles, and Athens, would find themselves out on a north Greek limb, while their allies busied themselves with the defence of the Peloponnese. That this was no idle fear became all too obvious after the defeat at Thermopylae, when the Peloponnesians, predictably, were found to be "fortifying the Isthmus, and letting all else go"; it took tough Athenian pressurising to bring them back north in time for Plataea.

The "Troezen Decree," then, was passed by the Athenian Assembly after the retreat from Tempe, but prior to the final meeting of League delegates at the Isthmus: in the archonship of Hypsichides, which means before the end of June. Xerxes was still little farther than Doriscus, and Athens had ample time to take full defensive measures against his coming. The League army's calamitous experience up north had demonstrated, beyond any shadow of doubt, that if Xerxes was to be stopped in central Greece, it would not be by land alone. Themistocles, we need not doubt, made the most of this point. The return of Athens' contingent meant that just about enough men were now available to man the fleet. Two hundred triremes (and these were only the front-line vessels) called for an ideal complement of 40,000 men. The decree—if Jameson's restoration here is correct—allots no more than a hundred citizens and resident aliens to each vessel: half the normal crew, in fact. The likeliest explanation is that this deficiency was made good by conscripting slaves, as Athens did at every crisis in her history from Marathon to Arginusae. The important point, however, is that there *was* a manpower shortage. The crews which fought at Artemisium were reinforced by Plataeans, while no less than twenty Athenian triremes had volunteer crews from Chalcis: at full strength this represented an addition of four thousand men. In other words, every Athenian, bond or free, who could bend an oar was now pressed into service with the fleet. From this two inevitable consequences followed. First, Athens could contribute no land-forces to the defence of the north, and in any case (as we have seen) was probably relying on naval strategy alone. All military action, then, would be Sparta's responsibility. Secondly, the evacuation of Attica now became inevitable, since mobilisation of Themistocles' new fleet would leave the frontiers totally undefended, except by boys and old men.

Here, of course, is where the "Troezen Decree" would seem to diverge most radically from Herodotus's version of events. In the latter, the abandonment of Athens is a last-minute, scrambling, *sauve qui peut* affair, carried out only after the collapse of the Thermopylae-Artemisium line, with a Persian breakthrough imminent. This is almost certainly untrue. To evacuate the whole of Attica in perhaps no more than forty-eight hours would be neither provident nor, indeed, physically possible. If we then ask how Herodotus came to believe the story as he tells it, the answer is, almost certainly, that his aristocratic informants were to blame. It was they who prejudiced him in so astonishing a fashion against Themistocles: it is not hard to see why. The great statesman had been largely responsible for ruining the careers of many highly distinguished noblemen, and their descendants were not liable to give any enquirer an unbiased picture of him. Themistocles' principal victims, moreover, had all been Alcmaeonidae; and to judge by the way Herodotus goes out of his way to give any Alcmaeonid the benefit of the doubt, this family had proved most cooperative when he sought their help in collecting material for the *Histories*. The inference is obvious. But that is not, I suspect, the whole story. Herodotus's friends in Athens were all old-fashioned conservatives, well-bred gentlemen who could not bear the shame of Athenians having actually *voted* to abandon hearths, temples and ancestral shrines without a fight—and in favour, what was worse, of that ultra-plebeian institution the fleet. An emergency evacuation was somewhat less of a blot, as they saw it, on the civic scutcheon. What made these diehards so angry in retrospect, however, was the underlying belief that this appalling sacrifice had been quite unnecessary. If heavy-armed Spartan and Athenian infantrymen could break a Persian army at Plataea, surely they could equally well have

done so before Salamis? The mild juggling of historical fact which the decree reveals in Herodotus's narrative does not affect any vital issue, and is all too understandable in terms of upper-class Athenian prejudice.

It is clear that this complex operation consisted, in fact, of two quite separate stages. First came the general transfer of civilians and movable property: a precautionary measure, carried out (in theory at least) immediately Themistocles' measures became law. At the same time the fleet was mobilised to defend Euboea, the coastline of Attica, and Salamis. This evacuation, however, was by no means total. A skeleton administrative staff had to remain in Athens. Shops, farms, and public services must have carried on. As usual on such occasions, many people simply ignored the decree, preferring to wait on events: quite enough to account for the chaotic last-minute flight so dramatically chronicled by Herodotus and Plutarch. Even then, so strong was the force of inertia or stubborn indifference, no less than five hundred prisoners were taken by the Persians during their advance through Attica. However, a very large proportion of the noncombatant population did remove to Troezen or Salamis during that July, taking their goods and chattels with them.

One can sympathise with their predicament. Even if the Peloponnesian states stood firm, any defence which rested on the fleet still left Attica itself fatally vulnerable. The decision to hold Thermopylae may have reassured some; but others, while welcoming it, doubtless saw the danger of this new defence line being turned, sooner or later, through central Greece. It has, indeed, been argued that Thermopylae–Artemisium was never planned as more than a long-term holding action—as Jameson says, "to give time for the building of the Isthmus wall and the rallying of naval units." Most Athenians, on this showing, must have believed that the final choice lay between a last-ditch campaign off Salamis, and mass emigration to Southern Italy. There may be something in this, but it ignores the possibility (which Themistocles surely at least considered) of snatching a quick naval victory at Artemisium while Xerxes was held up before the Hot Gates. Such an outside chance, however, could not be relied on, much less made the guarantee for innumerable Athenian lives. So the refugees sailed from Piraeus, like all Greek travellers, then or now, amid a great clutter of baskets, baggage, goats, hen-coops and babies, to receive a most hospitable welcome across the water. The citizens of Troezen even "voted to maintain the refugees at the public expense; they gave each family two obols a day, allowed the children to pick the fruit wherever they pleased as soon as it was ripe, and went so far as to pay schoolmasters to teach them"—an odd anticipation of Welfare State procedure.

2. J. F. Lazenby, Emeritus Professor of Ancient History at Newcastle University, takes a skeptical view of the Decree of Themistocles. He finds a number of the provisions of the inscription odd and in light of the more plausible narrative of Herodotus rejects the decree as a fourth-century fabrication.

FROM J. F. LAZENBY, *THE DEFENCE OF GREECE 490–479 B.C.*

THE PROBLEM OF THE "WOODEN WALL" ORACLE has been further complicated by the discovery of the "Themistokles Decree" at Trozen. This purports to contain the actual text of the decree that is implied by Herodotos' use of the technical term for a decision of the Athenian people—("*edoxe*," literally "it seemed good": 7.144.3)—in reporting the result of the debate on the oracle. Controversy about the authenticity of the decree has continued to rage since it was first published, and it is difficult to imagine how the question can ever finally be settled. However, it is now generally agreed that the inscription itself dates from the mid-3rd century, and few would argue that it is an accurate copy in every detail—for example, most commentators accept that some of the terminology of the preamble is anachronistic, and that the gods to whom the trierarchs are required to sacrifice are inappropriate for early-5th century Athens.

If genuine, the decree clearly antedates the Artemision campaign, since it provides for the sending there of 100 ships (lines 41–2), but by how long? It has been argued that some of the decree's provisions do indeed fit the situation in the autumn of 481, which is the implied date of Herodotos' decree, as we have seen. For example, the places to which the evacuees from Athens are to be taken do not include Aigina, and this might suggest that Athens was still at war with the island, whereas one of the outcomes of the first conference of the Greek resisters was the ending of this war (7.145.1); the provision that 100 ships are to be based "off Salamis and the rest of Attica and guard the land" (lines 42–4), might also indicate that Athens still feared Aiginetan attacks.

But is it really plausible to suppose that as soon as the Athenians decided to resist, they thought of sending part of their fleet to Artemision? This place was later chosen for the fleet's position because it tied in with the defence of Thermopylai, but that would require help from allies, and at this point *ex hypothesi*, the Athenians had none, since the first meeting of those determined to resist had not yet taken place. It is true that the decree assumes that the Spartans and others will "share the danger" (lines 16–8), though unfortunately the other names are not clear on the stone. But would the Athenians have assumed that the others would accept Athenian strategy? Indeed, would they publicly have named potential allies, before any alliance had been concluded?

Secondly, one wonders whether the Athenians would already have been planning the evacuation of Attica as early as the autumn of 481. It will be argued below that the decision to evacuate was taken long before Herodotos seems to imply—certainly before the Artemision campaign, and possibly before the abortive expedition to Tempe. But in the autumn of 481 the important thing, surely, was to unite all Athenians behind the decision to resist, and to resist at sea. This was no time for spelling out the possibly alarming consequences of such a decision, even if there were those prescient enough to appreciate what those consequences might be.

One even wonders, finally, whether this was an appropriate time for deciding in detail how to mobilize the fleet. Nobody, surely, expected the Persians to arrive before the following spring, and although there might have been something to be said for allocating trierarchs and crews to their ships as soon as possible, so that they could begin to train together, the fleet would presumably have had to be stood down during the winter. These provisions, like the allocation of half the fleet to Artemision, the assumption that Athens will have allies, and the planning of evacuation, really fit the context of the spring, or even early summer, of 480, much better than the autumn of 481. It is the general, but decisive, terms of Herodotos' decree which are right for the autumn of 481. Thus, even if the Trozen decree is an authentic copy of one passed at the time of Xerxes' invasion, it is very unlikely to be the one to which Herodotos refers.

Other apparent discrepancies with Herodotos need not detain us—for example, even those who believe in the authenticity of the decree are prepared to accept that it was "modified in execution," and that two hundred Athenian ships eventually fought at Artemision—twenty manned by "Chalkidians"—whereas the decree provides for only one hundred to go there, while the rest remained "off Salamis and the rest of Attica" (lines 41–4). But can we accept the detailed provisions for mobilization, and, in particular, the number of marines for each vessel? Obviously when the Athenians did mobilize their fleet in 481 or 480 they would have had to make detailed arrangements in something like the way the decree envisages, but one wonders whether the details would ever have been embodied in a full-blown decree of the assembly, and some do not ring true—for example, the apparent implication (lines 30–2) that the "foreigners" (*xenoi*), living in Athens, are to provide half the crews.

It is also odd that the ships are apparently to be assigned to their trierarchs by lot (lines 22–3). We do not, of course, know how such things were done in 481/0, but it was later practice for the state to assign hulls to trierarchs to equip, and there was great rivalry between them to do this on a lavish scale (cf. e.g., Thucydides 6.31). Herodotos tells us that at least one trierarch at Artemision, Kleinias, son of Alkibiades, served at his own expense and with his own ship (8.17), and this may be a loose way of describing the later system. For what it is worth the author of *The Constitution of the Athenians* (22.7) implies that the way Themistokles' new triremes had been built was that the state lent the richest men in Athens a talent each, on the understanding that they would use it to build ships, and although he differs from Herodotos on the

number of ships so built, the mechanism for building them makes sense (8). If so, men like Kleinias would surely have been extremely disgruntled if their ships and crews had then been allotted to someone else!

As for the manning of the ships, the decree says ten *epibatai*' (i.e., hoplites) between the ages of twenty and thirty, and four archers, are to be assigned to each (lines 23–5), and this too is odd. The numbers are consistent with what Herodotos appears to have thought was the normal complement of Greek warships at this time, but both he and the decree may be anachronistic here. As we have seen, in view of what he says about the number of marines on Chiot ships at Lade (6.15.2), and on those in Xerxes' fleet (7.184.1), it is likely that the Greek ships at Artemision and Salamis had more than the decree allows. One also wonders why the hoplites assigned to ships are to be under thirty years of age, and what those over thirty were to do. There were no Athenian hoplites at Thermopylai, so are we to imagine that those over thirty simply stayed in Attica when the fleet went north?

There are also problems with what the decree says about the rest of the crews. Thus the "*hyperesiai*" are to be allotted to ships at the same time as the trierarchs (lines 26–7), and not only is the use of the lot here as odd as it is in the case of the trierarchs, but it is not at all clear what is meant by "*hyperesiai*." Later the term usually refers to deck-crews apart from marines and archers, but if this is the meaning here, we are not told how the latter are to be assigned. Hence it has been conjectured that here the term either refers to marines and archers, or includes them. But this would be an unparalleled usage, and perhaps again betrays the hand of a later forger. There is also, finally, the problem of the number of men to be assigned to each crew, apart from marines, archers and "*hyperesiai*." On the face of it, the decree appears to assign 100 men to each crew (line 32), and this is too few, if these triremes were similar to later ones, and were to be fully manned.

All in all, then, it seems less and less likely that the decree can be a true copy of an actual decree of 480, and, if the truth were known, the survival of anything like an authentic text has always seemed too good to be true. It is more likely that what we have is basically a patriotic fabrication of the fourth century, put in its final form in the third, and, again, Herodotos' shorter, vaguer version (7.144.3) looks much more like what could have been remembered.

Consider

1. When was the stone containing the Decree of Themistocles inscribed?
2. How does Green suggest the document might have changed from the time it was ratified?
3. Why do some scholars, such as Lazenby, suspect that the decree is a forgery?
4. According to Green, who ratified the decree and how does his opinion compare with that of Herodotus and that of other scholars?
5. When does Lazenby date the Decree of Themistocles (Trozen Decree)?
6. What provisions of the decree does Lazenby consider useful in dating it?
7. How does Lazenby distinguish between the decree to which Herodotus refers and the Troezen inscription?
8. How might both the decree and Herodotus be anachronistic?
9. How does Green interpret the part played by Themistocles in Athenian politics and Greek strategy?
10. Why does Green date the decree to the time before the Hellenic League met to vote?
11. How does the decree depart most from the account of Herodotus?
12. Why does Green think Herodotus accepted the story he records about the events of 480 BC?
13. What were the two separate stages of Athenian strategy according to Green?

CHAPTER 6

WHAT WAS THE NATURE AND IMPORTANCE OF GREEK SLAVERY?

❧

LIKE ALL CIVILIZED ANCIENT PEOPLES, the Greeks practiced the institution of slavery. From the time of Homer through the time when Greeks were subjects of the Romans, we read of slaves of one kind or another playing a significant part in the lives of the Greeks. But what part? The available evidence has not permitted any answer that is generally accepted. How many slaves were there? Where did they come from? What work did they do? How were they treated? How did they interact with the nonslave population? How did the Greeks regard slavery? Did they simply accept the institution that seemed to be universal, or did any of them criticize or denounce it?

Few of these questions received much attention over the millennia that separate us from the Greeks until the second half of the twentieth century, but since then it has been the subject of keenest controversy. Moses I. Finley, whose essay appears below, explains much of the difficulty in dealing with the subject as the result of "two extraneous factors":

The first is the confusion of the historical study with moral judgments about slavery. We condemn slavery, and we are embarrassed for the Greeks, whom we admire so much; therefore we tend either to underestimate its role in their life, or we ignore it altogether, hoping that somehow it will quietly go away. The second factor is more political, and it goes back at least to 1848, when the Communist Manifesto declared that "The history of all hitherto existing society is the history of class struggles. Free man and slave, patrician and plebeian, lord and serf, guild-master and journeyman, in a word, oppressor and oppressed, stood in constant opposition to one another..." Ever since, ancient slavery has been a battleground between Marxists and non-Marxists, a political issue rather than a historical phenomenon.

In recent years still another external element has entered the debate, producing perhaps more heat than light. Arguments over the virtues and vices of Western civilization have produced attacks on and defenses of the society of its founders, the ancient Greeks, with slavery as a major battleground. This chapter contains a selection of the scattered evidence of ancient Greek slavery and a variety of opinions about its place in Greek society.

Ancient Sources

1. Xenophon, *Memorabilia*, 2.8.1–5, WORK AND SLAVERY
2. Xenophon, *Memorabilia*, 2.7.1–4, GENTLEFOLK AND SLAVES
3. Demosthenes, 27.9, THE ATHENIAN ECONOMY
4. Demosthenes 36.4–5, 11, PASION
5. Aeschines, *Against Timarchus*, 1.97, LEASING SKILLED SLAVES
6. Lysias, *For Callias* 5, A SLAVE SOCIETY?
7. Thucydides 7.27, HOW MANY SLAVES IN ATHENS?
8. Xenophon, *Ways and Means* (Poroi), 4.14, ATHENIAN SLAVE OWNERS

ANCIENT SOURCES ON THE FUNCTIONS OF SLAVES AND ATTITUDES TOWARD SLAVERY

1. WORK AND SLAVERY

These are presented by Xenophon as recollected conversations between Socrates and various people.

Again, on meeting an old comrade after long absence he said: "Where do you come from, Eutherus?" "I came home when the war ended, Socrates, and am now living here," he replied. "Since we have lost our foreign property, and my father left me nothing in Attica, I am forced to settle down here now and work for my living with my hands. I think it's better than begging, especially as I have no security to offer for a loan."

"And how long will you have the strength, do you think, to earn your living by your work?"

"Oh, not long, of course."

"But remember, when you get old you will have to spend money, and nobody will be willing to pay you for your labour."

"True."

"Then it would be better to take up some kind of work at once that will assure you a competence when you get old, and to go to somebody who is better off and wants an assistant, and get a return for your services by acting as his bailiff, helping to get in his crops and looking after his property."

"I shouldn't like to make myself a slave, Socrates."

"But surely those who control their cities and take charge of public affairs are thought more respectable, not more slavish on that account."

"Briefly, Socrates, I have no inclination to expose myself to any man's censure."

Questions

1. **Why is Eutherus unwilling to take a regular job?**
2. **What does this reveal about the Greek attitude toward different kinds of labor?**

2. GENTLEFOLK AND SLAVES

One day, noticing that Aristarchus looked glum, he said: "Aristarchus, you seem to have a burden on your mind. You should let your friends share it; possibly we may do something to ease you." "Ah yes, Socrates," replied Aristarchus, "I am in great distress. Since the revolution there has been an exodus to the Piraeus, and a crowd of my women-folk, being left behind, have come to me—sisters, nieces and cousins—so that we are fourteen in the house without counting the slaves. We get nothing from our land, because our enemies have seized it, and nothing from our house property, now there are so few residents in the city. Portable property finds no buyers, and it's quite impossible to borrow money anywhere: I really think a search in the street would have better result than an application for a loan. It's hard, Socrates, to let one's people die, but impossible to keep so many in times like these." When Socrates heard this, he asked: "How is it that with so many mouths to feed Ceramon not only contrives to provide for the needs of himself and his family, but actually saves enough to make him a rich man, whereas you, with so many mouths to feed, fear you will all be starved to death?" "The explanation, of course, is this: my dependants are gentlefolk, his are slaves."

Question

1. Why are "gentlefolk" harder to take care of than slaves?

3. THE ATHENIAN ECONOMY

This passage from a speech written by Demosthenes for a client contains evidence for some of the largest known holdings of slaves and how they were used.

From this evidence it is clear what the value of the property was. Three talents is the tax on an estate of fifteen, and this tax they saw fit to pay. But you will see this more clearly if you hear what the property was. My father, men of the jury, left two factories, both doing a large business. One was a sword-manufactory, employing thirty-two or thirty-three slaves, most of them worth five or six minae each and none worth less than three minae. From these my father received a clear income of thirty minae each year. The other was a sofa-manufactory, employing twenty slaves, given to my father as security for a debt of forty minae. These brought him in a clear income of twelve minae. In money he left as much as a talent, loaned at the rate of a drachma a month, the interest of which amounted to more than seven minae a year.

Question

1. What does this passage reveal about the place and function of slavery in the Athenian economy?

4. PASION

This passage tells of the career of Pasion, a slave who made so much money with his skills that he bought his freedom and became a very rich banker in Athens.

First the clerk shall read to you the articles of agreement, in accordance with which Pasion leased to the defendant the bank and the shield-factory. Take, please, the articles of agreement, the challenge, and these depositions.

These, men of Athens, are the articles of agreement in accordance with which Pasion leased the bank and the shield-factory to the defendant, after the latter had now become his own master.

But you must hear and understand how it was that Pasion came to owe the eleven talents to the bank.... He owed that amount, not because of poverty, but because of his thrift. For the real property of Pasion was about twenty talents, but in addition to this he had more than fifty talents in money of his own lent out at interest. Among these were eleven talents of the bank's deposits, profitably invested.

Question

1. What do we learn here about the sources of wealth available to this very unusual slave and then freedman?

5. LEASING SKILLED SLAVES

In this passage from a speech in court we learn of the profit that could be earned from the lease of skilled slaves.

His father left him a fortune which another man would have found sufficient for the service of the state also. But Timarchus was not able even to preserve it for himself. There was a house south of the Acropolis, a suburban estate at Sphettus, another piece of land at Alopeke, and besides there were nine or ten slaves who were skilled shoemakers, each of whom paid him a fee of two obols a day, and the superintendent of the shop three obols. Besides these there was a woman skilled in flax-working, who produced fine goods for the market, and there was a man skilled in embroidery. Certain men also owed him money, and there were house furnishings.

Question

1. How did the individual mentioned here profit from slavery?

6. A SLAVE SOCIETY?

This passage has been used as evidence for the widespread possession of slaves in Athenian society. Bottom of form

The trial, in my opinion, ought to be regarded, not as the personal affair of the accused, but as the common concern of everybody in the city; for these are not the only people who own servants; they are owned by everyone else, and looking at the fate of the accused will no longer ask themselves by what great service to their masters they might gain their freedom, but by what lying information about them...

Questions

1. How strong is the evidence of this passage for the widespread presence of slavery in Athens?
2. What questions can be raised about its reliability?

7. HOW MANY SLAVES IN ATHENS?

Thucydides tells of the great harm done to the Athenians when the Spartans established a permanent fort in Attica in the latter part of the Peloponnesian War. The large number of escaped slaves represented a major loss.

7.27.3 Indeed since Decelea had been first fortified by the whole Peloponnesian army during this summer, and then occupied for the annoyance of the country by the garrisons from the cities relieving each other at stated intervals, it had been doing great mischief to the Athenians; in fact this occupation, by the destruction of property and loss of men which resulted from it, was one of the principal causes of their ruin. **[4]** Previously the invasions were short, and did not prevent their enjoying their land during the rest of the time: the enemy was now permanently fixed in Attica; at one time it was an attack in force, at another it was the regular garrison overrunning the country and making forays for its subsistence, and the Lacedaemonian king, Agis, was in the field and diligently prosecuting the war; great mischief was therefore done to the Athenians. **[5]** They were deprived of their whole country: more than twenty thousand slaves had deserted, a great part of them artisans, and all their sheep and beasts of burden were lost; and as the cavalry rode out daily upon excursions to Decelea and to guard the country, their horses were either lamed by being constantly worked upon rocky ground, or wounded by the enemy.

Question

1. **What portion of the entire population of Attica was 20,000 slaves? What portion of its entire slave population did these escaped slaves represent?**

8.   ATHENIAN SLAVE OWNERS

In this work Xenophon proposes ideas for improving the financial condition of Athens. In the following passage we learn of the largest Greek slave holdings of which there is evidence.

But what may well excite surprise is that the state, being aware that many private individuals are making money out of her, does not imitate them. Those of us who have given thought to the matter have heard long ago, I imagine, that Nicias son of Niceratus, once owned a thousand men in the mines, and let them out to Socias the Thracian, on condition that Socias paid him an obol a day per man net and filled all vacancies as they occurred. Hipponicus, again, had six hundred slaves let out on the same terms and received a rent of a mina a day net. Philemonides had three hundred, and received half a mina. There were others too, owning numbers in proportion, I presume, to their capital.

Question

1. **What evidence does this passage provide for the number of slaves held by an average Athenian?**

9.   THE OLD OLIGARCH

The following passage by an anonymous writer living during the early years of the Peloponnesian War is part of a general critique of the Athenian democracy. Its description of the condition of slaves in Athens must be understood in the context of that purpose.

Another point is the extraordinary amount of license granted to slaves and resident aliens at Athens, where a blow is illegal, and a slave will not step aside to let you pass him in the street. I will explain the reason of this peculiar custom. Supposing it were legal for a slave to be beaten by a free citizen, or for a resident alien or freedman to be beaten by a citizen, it would frequently happen that an Athenian might be mistaken for a slave or an alien and receive a beating; since the Athenian People is not better clothed than the slave or alien, nor in personal appearance is there any superiority. Or if the fact itself that slaves in Athens are allowed to indulge in luxury, and indeed in some cases to live magnificently, be found astonishing, this too, it can be shown, is done of set purpose. Where you have a naval power dependent upon wealth we must perforce be slaves to our slaves, in order that we may get in our slave-rents, and let the real slave go free.

Where you have wealthy slaves it ceases to be advantageous that my slave should stand in awe of you. In Lacedaemon my slave stands in awe of you. But if your slave is in awe of me there will be a risk of his giving away his own moneys to avoid running a risk in his own person. It is for this reason then that we have established an equality between our slaves and free men; and again between our resident aliens and full citizens, because the city stands in need of her resident aliens to meet the requirements of such a multiplicity of arts and for the purposes of her navy. That is, I repeat, the justification of the equality conferred upon our resident aliens.

Questions

1. **What does this passage reveal about the treatment of slaves in Athens?**
2. **How does he explain it?**

10. SLAVERY AND DEMOCRACY

In this passage, depicting Socrates in dialogue with a young follower, Plato paints a similar picture of the excessive freedom of slaves in a democracy.

[562b] "How is that?" "The good that they proposed to themselves and that was the cause of the establishment of oligarchy—it was wealth, was it not?" "Yes." "Well, then, the insatiate lust for wealth and the neglect of everything else for the sake of money-making was the cause of its undoing." "True," he said. "And is not the avidity of democracy for that which is its definition and criterion of good the thing which dissolves it too?" "What do you say its criterion to be?" "Liberty," I replied; [562c] "for you may hear it said that this is best managed in a democratic city and for this reason that is the only city in which a man of free spirit will care to live." "Why, yes," he replied, "you hear that saying everywhere." "Then, as I was about to observe, is it not the excess and greed of this and the neglect of all other things that revolutionizes this constitution too and prepares the way for the necessity of a dictatorship?" "How?" he said. "Why, when a democratic city athirst for liberty gets bad [562d] cupbearers for its leaders and is intoxicated by drinking too deep of that unmixed wine, and then, if its so-called governors are not extremely mild and gentle with it and

do not dispense the liberty unstintedly, it chastises them and accuses them of being accursed oligarchs." "Yes, that is what they do," he replied. "But those who obey the rulers," I said, "it reviles as willing slaves and men of naught, but it commends and honors in public and private rulers who resemble subjects and subjects who are like rulers. [562e] Is it not inevitable that in such a state the spirit of liberty should go to all lengths?" "Of course." "And this anarchical temper," said I, "my friend, must penetrate into private homes and finally enter into the very animals." "Just what do we mean by that?" he said. "Why," I said, "the father habitually tries to resemble the child and is afraid of his sons, and the son likens himself to the father and feels no awe or fear of his parents, so that he may be forsooth a free man. [563a] And the resident alien feels himself equal to the citizen and the citizen to him, and the foreigner likewise." "Yes, these things do happen," he said. "They do," said I, "and such other trifles as these. The teacher in such case fears and fawns upon the pupils, and the pupils pay no heed to the teacher or to their overseers either. And in general the young ape their elders and vie with them in speech and action, **[563b]** while the old, accommodating themselves to the young, are full of pleasantry and graciousness, imitating the young for fear they may be thought disagreeable and authoritative." "By all means," he said. "And the climax of popular liberty, my friend," I said, "is attained in such a city when the purchased slaves, male and female, are no less free than the owners who paid for them. And I almost forgot to mention the spirit of freedom and equal rights in the relation of men to women and women to men."

Questions

1. **Can Plato's statement be taken as a factual account of the condition of Athenian slaves?**
2. **What would his contemporaries have thought of it?**
3. **What view of Athenian democracy does the above statement represent?**

---

11. THE GOOD LIFE

The fullest discussion on slavery we have from an ancient writer comes in the *Politics* of Aristotle. There he argues that slavery is a natural phenomenon and essential to the good life as lived in the polis.

1252b The female and the slave are by nature distinct (for nature makes nothing as the cutlers make the Delphic knife, in a niggardly way, but one thing for one purpose; for so each tool will be turned out in the finest perfection, if it serves not many uses but one). Yet among barbarians the female and the slave have the same rank; and the cause of this is that barbarians have no class of natural rulers, but with them the conjugal partnership is a partnership of female slave and male slave. Hence the saying of the poets—

Tis meet that Greeks should rule barbarians –

implying that barbarian and slave are the same in nature. From these two partnerships then is first composed the household, and Hesiod was right when he wrote,

First and foremost a house and a wife and an ox for
    the ploughing—
for the ox serves instead of a servant for the poor...

* * *

1253b [1] And now that it is clear what are the component parts of the state, we have first of all to discuss household management; for every state is composed of households. Household management falls into departments corresponding to the parts of which the household in its turn is composed; and the household in its perfect form consists of slaves and freemen. The investigation of everything should begin with its smallest parts, and the primary and smallest parts of the household are master and slave, husband and wife, father and children; we ought therefore to examine the proper constitution and character of each of these three relationships, **[2]** I mean that of mastership, that of marriage (there is no exact term denoting the relation uniting wife and husband), and thirdly the progenitive relationship (this too has not been designated by a special name). Let us then accept these three relationships that we have mentioned. There is also a department which some people consider the same as household management and others the most important part of it, and the true position of which we shall have to consider: I mean what is called the art of getting wealth.

Let us begin by discussing the relation of master and slave, in order to observe the facts that have a bearing on practical utility, and also in the hope that we may be able to obtain something better than the notions at present entertained, with a view to a theoretic knowledge of the subject. **[3]**

For some thinkers hold the function of the master to be a definite science, and moreover think that household management, mastership, statesmanship and monarchy are the same thing, as we said at the beginning of the treatise; others however maintain that for one man to be another man's master is contrary to nature, because it is only convention that makes the one a slave and the other a freeman and there is no difference between them by nature, and that therefore it is unjust, for it is based on force.

Since therefore property is a part of a household and the art of acquiring property a part of household management (for without the necessaries even life, as well as the good life, is impossible), **[4]** and since, just as for the particular arts it would be necessary for the proper tools to be forthcoming if their work is to be accomplished, so also the manager of a household must have his tools, and of tools some are lifeless and others living (for example, for a helmsman the rudder is a lifeless tool and the look-out man a live tool—for an assistant in the arts belongs to the class of tools), so also an article of property is a tool for the purpose of life, and property generally is a collection of tools, and a slave is a live article of property. **[5]** And every assistant is as it were a tool that serves for several tools; for if every tool could perform its own work when ordered, or by seeing what to do in advance, like the statues of Daedalus in the story, or the tripods of Hephaestus which the poet says "enter self-moved the company divine,"—if thus shuttles wove and quills played harps of themselves, master-craftsmen would have no need of assistants and masters no need of slaves.

* * *

1254a9 And the term "article of property" is used in the same way as the term "part": a thing that is a part is not only a part of another thing but absolutely belongs to another thing, and so also does an article of property. Hence whereas the master is merely the slave's master and does not belong to the slave, the slave is not merely the slave of the master but wholly belongs to the master. **[7]** These considerations therefore make clear the nature of the slave and his essential quality: one who is a human being belonging by nature not to himself but to another is by nature a slave, and a

person is a human being belonging to another if and if being a man he is an article of property, and an article of property is an instrument for action separable from its owner. But we must next consider whether or not anyone exists who is by nature of this character, and whether it is advantageous and just for anyone to be a slave, or whether on the contrary all slavery is against nature. **[8]** And it is not difficult either to discern the answer by theory or to learn it empirically. Authority and subordination are conditions not only inevitable but also expedient; in some cases things are marked out from the moment of birth to rule or to be ruled... It is in a living creature, as we say, that it is first possible to discern the rule both of master and of statesman the soul rules the body with the sway of a master, the intelligence rules the appetites with that of a statesman or a king and in these examples it is manifest that it is natural and expedient for the body to be governed by the soul and for the emotional part to be governed by the intellect, the part possessing reason, whereas for the two parties to be on an equal footing or in the contrary positions is harmful in all cases. **[12]** Again, the same holds good between man and the other animals: tame animals are superior in their nature to wild animals, yet for all the former it is advantageous to be ruled by man, since this gives them security. Again, as between the sexes, the male is by nature superior and the female inferior, the male ruler and the female subject. And the same must also necessarily apply in the case of mankind as a whole; **[13]** therefore all men that differ as widely as the soul does from the body and the human being from the lower animal (and this is the condition of those whose function is the use of the body and from whom this is the best that is forthcoming) these are by nature slaves, for whom to be governed by this kind of authority is advantageous, inasmuch as it is advantageous to the subject things already mentioned. For he is by nature a slave who is capable of belonging to another (and that is why he does so belong), and who participates in reason so far as to apprehend it but not to possess it; for the animals other than man are subservient not to reason, by apprehending it, but to feelings. **[14]** And also the usefulness of slaves diverges little from that of animals; bodily service for the necessities of life is forthcoming from both, from slaves and from domestic animals alike. The intention of nature therefore is to make the bodies also of freemen and of slaves different—the latter strong for necessary service, the former erect and unserviceable for such occupations, but serviceable for a life of citizenship (and that again divides into the employments of war and those of peace); but as a matter of fact often the very opposite comes about—some persons have the bodies of free men and others the souls; **[15]** since this is certainly clear, that if persons were born as distinguished only in body as are the statues of the gods, everyone would say that those who were inferior deserved to be these men's slaves. And if this is true in the case of the body, there is far juster reason for this rule being laid down in the case of the soul; but beauty of soul is not so easy to see as beauty of body. **1255a** It is manifest therefore that there are cases of people of whom some are freemen and the others slaves by nature, and for these slavery is an institution both expedient and just.

[16] But at the same time it is not difficult to see that those who assert the opposite are also right in a manner. The fact is that the terms "slavery" and "slave" are ambiguous; for there is also such a thing as a slave or a man that is in slavery by law, for the law is a sort of agreement under which the things conquered in war are said to belong to their conquerors. Now this conventional right is arraigned by many jurists just as a statesman is impeached for proposing an unconstitutional measure; they say that it is monstrous if the person powerful enough to use force, and superior in power, is to have the victim of his force as his slave and subject; and even among the learned some hold this view, though others hold the other. **[17]** But the reason of this dispute and what makes the theories overlap is the fact that in a certain manner virtue when it obtains resources has in fact very great power to use force, and the stronger party always possesses superiority in something that is good, so that it is thought that force cannot be devoid of goodness, but that the dispute is merely about the justice of the matter (for it is due to the one party holding that the justification of authority is good-will, while the other identifies justice with the mere rule of the stronger); because obviously if these theories be separated apart, the other theories have no force or plausibility at all, implying that the superior in goodness has no claim to rule and be master. **[18]** But some persons, simply clinging, as they think, to principle of justice (for the law is a principle of justice), assert that the enslavement of prisoners of

war is just; yet at the same time they deny the assertion, for there is the possibility that wars may be unjust in their origin and one would by no means admit that a man that does not deserve slavery can be really a slave—otherwise we shall have the result that persons reputed of the highest nobility are slaves and the descendants of slaves if they happen to be taken prisoners of war and sold. Therefore they do not mean to assert that Greeks themselves if taken prisoners are slaves, but that barbarians are. Yet when they say this, they are merely seeking for the principles of natural slavery of which we spoke at the outset; for they are compelled to say that there exist certain persons who are essentially slaves everywhere and certain others who are so nowhere. **[19]** And the same applies also about nobility: our nobles consider themselves noble not only in their own country but everywhere, but they think that barbarian noblemen are only noble in their own country—which implies that there are two kinds of nobility and of freedom, one absolute and the other relative, as Helen says in Theodectes:

But who would dare to call me menial,
The scion of a twofold stock divine?

1255b Yet in so speaking they make nothing but virtue and vice the distinction between slave and free, the noble and the base-born…

It is clear therefore that there is some reason for this dispute, and that in some instances it is not the case that one set are slaves and the other freemen by nature; **[20]** and also that in some instances such a distinction does exist, when slavery for the one and mastership for the other are advantageous and just, and it is proper for the one party to be governed and for the other to govern by the form of government for which they are by nature fitted, and therefore by the exercise of mastership, while to govern badly is to govern disadvantageously for both parties (for the same thing is advantageous for a part and for the whole body or the whole soul, and the slave is a part of the master—he is, as it were, a part of the body, alive but yet separated from it; **[21]** hence there is a certain community of interest and friendship between slave and master in cases when they have been qualified by nature for those positions, although when they do not hold them in that way but by law and by constraint of force the opposite is the case).

12.   NATURAL SLAVES?

After the Peloponnesian War, the great rhetorician Isocrates repeatedly called on the Greeks to launch an invasion of the Persian Empire to solve their economic and social problems. This selection reveals the common Greek belief that non-Greeks were unworthy of freedom and natural candidates for slavery.

And none of these things has happened by accident, but all of them have been due to natural causes; for it is not possible for people who are reared and governed as are the Persians, either to have a part in any other form of virtue or to set up on the field of battle trophies of victory over their foes. For how could either an able general or a good soldier be produced amid such ways of life as theirs? Most of their population is a mob without discipline or experience of dangers, which has lost all stamina for war and has been trained more effectively for servitude than are the slaves in our country. Those, on the other hand, who stand highest in repute among them have never governed their lives by dictates of equality or of common interest or of loyalty to the state; on the contrary, their whole existence consists of insolence toward some, and servility towards others—a manner of life than which nothing could be more demoralizing to human nature. Because they are rich, they pamper their bodies; but because they are subject to one man's power, they keep their souls in a state of abject and cringing fear, parading themselves at the door of the royal palace, prostrating themselves, and in every way schooling themselves to humility of spirit, falling on their knees before a mortal man, addressing him as a divinity, and thinking more lightly of the gods than of men. So it is that those of the Persians who come down to the sea, whom they term satraps, do not dishonor the training which they receive at home, but cling steadfastly to the same habits: they are faithless to their friends and cowardly to their foes; their lives are divided between servility on the one hand and arrogance on the other; they treat their allies with contempt and pay court to their enemies.

* * *

These things may well rouse our indignation and make us look to the means by which we shall take vengeance for the past and set the future right. For verily it is shameful for us, who in our private life think the barbarians are fit only to be used as household slaves, to permit by our public policy so many of our allies to be enslaved by them; and it is disgraceful for us, when our fathers who engaged in the Trojan expedition because of the rape of one woman, all shared so deeply in the indignation of the wronged that they did not stop waging war until they had laid in ruins the city of him who had dared to commit the crime, [182]—it is disgraceful for us, I say, now that all Hellas is being continually outraged, to take not a single step to wreak a common vengeance, although we have it in our power to accomplish deeds as lofty as our dreams. For this war is the only war which is better than peace; it will be more like a sacred mission than a military expedition; and it will profit equally both those who crave the quiet life and those who are eager for war; for it will enable the former to reap the fruits of their own possessions in security and the latter to win great wealth from the possessions of our foes.

Questions

1. **Why does Isocrates think the Persians are natural slaves?**
2. **What policy does he recommend as following from that opinion?**

OPINIONS OF MODERN SCHOLARS

1. By far the best documented record of ancient Greek slavery comes from Athens, especially in its democratic phase. A. H. M. Jones was a staunch defender of the Athenian democracy against its critics, ancient and modern. Though much influenced by Marxist thought, he argued that democracy did not depend on its empire or on the institution of slavery. A. H. M. Jones was Professor of Ancient History at Cambridge University.

FROM A. H. M. JONES, THE ECONOMIC BASIS OF THE ATHENIAN EMPIRE

TWO CHARGES HAVE BEEN BROUGHT against the Athenian democracy, one both by ancient and by modern critics, the other in recent times only. The first is that the pay, which was an essential part of the system, was provided by the tribute paid by Athens' allies in the Delian League, and that the democracy was therefore parasitic on the empire: the second, that Athenians only had the leisure to perform their political functions because they were supported by slaves—the democracy was in fact parasitic on slavery.

To the first charge there is a very simple answer, that the democracy continued to function in the fourth century when Athens had lost her empire; the Second Athenian League, which lasted effectively only from 377 to 357, was never a paying proposition, the contributions of the allies by no means covering the cost of military and naval operations. And not only did the democracy continue to function, but a new and important form of pay, that for attendance in the assembly, was introduced early in the century.

* * *

The second charge against the Athenian democracy, that it was parasitic on slavery, is more difficult to answer with any certainty. It will be as well to make plain the elements of the problem. The Athenians, like all Greek peoples, regarded themselves as a kinship group, and citizenship depended strictly on descent (always on the father's side and, by a law passed in 451 and re-enacted in 403, on the mother's side also) and not on residence, however long. The population of Attica therefore consisted not only of citizens but of free aliens, mainly immigrants who had settled permanently and often lived at Athens for generations, but also including freed slaves and persons of mixed descent; and of slaves, mainly imported but some home-bred. It is unhistorical to condemn the Athenian democracy because it did not give political rights to all residents of Attica; it was the democracy of the Athenian people. It is however relevant to enquire whether the Athenian people was a privileged group depending on the labour of others. Sparta might be called technically a democracy (though the hereditary kings and the council of elders balanced the power of the people) inasmuch as the whole body of Spartiates chose the ephors, in whose hands the government effectively lay, but the Spartiates were a body of rentiers supported by native serfs, the helots, who far outnumbered them. Was the Athenian democracy of this order? The resident aliens (metics) do not concern us here. They made a great contribution to Athenian prosperity, particularly in the fields of industry, commerce and banking—indeed they seem to have dominated the two latter. They were voluntary immigrants and could leave when they wished (except in time of war). That so many domiciled themselves permanently in Attica—a census taken at the end of the fourth century showed 10,000 metics as against 21,000 citizens—is a testimony to their liberal treatment. They enjoyed full civil (as opposed to political) rights, except that they could not own land—hence their concentration on industry and commerce—and were subject to all the duties of citizens, including military and naval service and taxation at a slightly higher scale. They were a contented class, and many demonstrated their loyalty to their adoptive city by generous gifts at times of crisis.

What of slaves? Here it will be as well to clear up another misconception. It is often stated, mainly on the authority of Plato and Aristotle, that "the Greeks" considered manual work degrading. Now it is true that gentlemen like Plato and Aristotle despised workers and justified their contempt by asserting that manual work deformed the body and the soul. But that this was the attitude of the average poor Greek there is no evidence. An anecdote recorded by Xenophon probably gives a better insight into his point of view. Eutherus, who has lost his overseas estates as a result of the war, has been reduced to earning his living by manual labour. Socrates asks what he will do when his bodily strength fails and suggests that he find a job as a rich man's bailiff. Eutherus is horrified at the suggestion—"I could not endure to be a slave . . . I absolutely refuse to be at any man's beck and call." What the Athenian thete objected to was not hard work—incidentally his main military duty in the fifth century was rowing in the galleys, a task in most later civilisations considered fit only for infidel slaves or convicts—but being another man's servant. He would work as an independent craftsman or at a pinch as a casual labourer, but he would not take even a black-coated job as a regular employee; we find that such highly responsible posts as the manager of a bank or the foreman overseer of a mine are filled by slaves or freedmen of the owner.

Is it true, as we are still too often told, that the average Athenian, in the intervals between listening to a play of Sophocles and serving as a magistrate, councillor or juror, lounged in the market place, discussing politics and philosophy, while slaves toiled to support him? Contemporary critics of the democracy did not think so. Plato's Socrates, analysing the people in a democracy, divides them into the drones, that is the active politicians and their cliques of supporters, and the mass of the people "who support themselves by their labour and do not care about politics, owning very little property; this is the largest and most powerful clement in a democracy when it is assembled." Xenophon's Socrates, rebuking Charmides for his shyness at addressing the assembly, asks if he is afraid "of the fullers among them or the shoemakers or the carpenters or the smiths or the peasants or the merchants or the shopkeepers: for the assembly is composed of all of them." Aristotle, analysing the people (that is the mass of poor citizens) in different cities, classifies them as craftsmen, shopkeepers, seamen of various kinds—fishermen, ferrymen, sailors on merchantmen or warships—and casual day labourers and those who have little property so that they can enjoy no leisure. Slaves were employed in many capacities—as domestic servants, as clerks and agents in commerce and banking, in agriculture, and in industry and mining. All well-to-do Athenian families had several servants, and no doubt wealthy men kept large households of a dozen or more—precise figures are lacking—but the domestic servant probably did not go very far down the social scale. A man for whom Lysias wrote a little speech does indeed roundly assert that everyone has slaves; but he is trying to convince the jury that it is contrary to public policy to encourage slaves to inform against their masters. In comedy domestic slaves appear when dramatically convenient, even in the poorest households, but this evidence is suspect: comedy was written after all by well-to-do authors, and slaves provided a variety of stock comic turns. It has been argued that because in the fifth century every hoplite took with him an attendant to carry his food and kit, and was allowed a drachma a day by the State on his account (in addition to his own drachma), every hoplite must have owned an able-bodied male slave. Those hoplites who owned suitable slaves certainly used them for this purpose, but there is no evidence that every hoplite's attendant was his own slave. The high rate of the State allowance, on the contrary, is only explicable on the assumption that many hoplites would have to hire a man for the purpose, and Thucydides' inclusion of the baggage carriers with the light-armed among the Athenian casualties at Delium implies that they were citizens. More significant than these uncertain inferences is a remark by Demosthenes, who, castigating the harshness with which Androtion and Timocrates collected the arrears of war tax, pictures them "removing doors and seizing blankets and distraining on a servant girl, if anyone employed one." Now the payers of war tax can be estimated to have numbered only about 6,000 out of a population of 21,000. If not all of them had a domestic servant, one may hazard that under a quarter of the population enjoyed that luxury. Commerce and banking need not detain us, as the numbers were small. In agriculture, too we hear little of slaves. The property of large landowners did not normally consist of a single great estate, but of several farms scattered over Attica. Some of these farms were let to free tenants, Athenian or metic; one at least—the home farm—would be worked by a minimum staff of slaves, supplemented by hired labour; for it was uneconomic in a seasonal trade like agriculture to maintain all the year round enough slaves to cope with peak demands. The hired labour was sometimes supplied by slave gangs, leased from a contractor to do a particular job, such as to get in the harvest or the vintage; but it often consisted of free persons—in one of his private speeches Demosthenes remarks that many citizen women were driven by poverty to work in the harvest. Shepherds seem normally to have been slaves, but the politician Phrynichus is alleged to have been one in his poverty-stricken youth. How far down the scale of wealth the use of agricultural slaves went it is difficult to say, but the greater part of Attica was probably occupied by peasant farmers too poor to afford them. Of the 6,000 citizens who paid war tax, a large number were, as Demosthenes puts it, "farmers who stinted themselves, but owing to the maintenance of their children and domestic expenses and other public demands fell into arrears with their war tax." These were the men who sometimes could not afford a single domestic servant, and certainly did not maintain a farm hand; they would fall into the class which Aristotle described as using the labour of their wives and children through lack of slaves. Below them were the remaining 3,000 of the hoplite class who did not qualify for war tax, and will have owned property to the value of between 25 and 20 minae. These were quite poor men; Demosthenes introducing a poor hoplite witness apologises to the jury—"he is poor, it is true, but not a rascal"—and the wealthy Mantitheus, when his deme mustered for a call-up, found that many of his fellow demesmen were embarrassed for journey money, and distributed 30 drachmae to each. A farm worth 20 minae would, on the basis of the single land price recorded, comprise about 5 acres, and would bring in if let only about 160 drachmae a year in rent, not enough to feed, let alone clothe, a single man; it can only have supported a family if worked by family labour.

In industry, and particularly mining, slaves were employed on a larger scale. The wealthy Nicias in the fifth century is said to have owned 1,000 slaves, whom he let out to a mining contractor at 1 obol a day, the contractor feeding and clothing them and replacing casualties; two rich contemporaries are said to have owned 600 and 300 respectively whom they exploited in a similar way. In the fourth century another mine concessionaire owned thirty slaves, which was probably a more usual number. Well-to-do Athenians also normally invested a small proportion of their wealth in slave craftsmen, who either worked together in a factory, or independently, paying their owner a fixed sum and keeping for themselves whatever they earned beyond it. The largest factory of which we hear, the shield factory of the brothers Lysias and Polemarchus, numbered nearly 120 men; but this is quite exceptional, and is due to the fact that the owners were metics, who could not invest in land, and that the thirty years of the Peloponnesian war had naturally led to a boom in armaments. In the fourth century Pasion the banker also ran a shield factory as a side-line; it brought in a net revenue of a talent a year, and must have contained over sixty men; Pasion again was a metic, until he was rewarded with the citizenship for his public services, and he was the richest man in Athens of the time—he had before he died acquired land to the value of 20 talents besides his bank and factory. Demosthenes' father was also exceptional in owning two factories, thirty-two knife makers and twenty bed makers, with a capital value of nearly 6 1/2 talents (4 talents in slaves and 2 1/2 talents in raw materials in stock) out of a total fortune of 14 talents, the rest of which was in cash and investments with the exception of his house and furniture. We hear of some others in the fifth century whose wealth was entirely invested in slaves; Isocrates' father rose to affluence from the profits of a group of flute-makers, and Xenophon makes Socrates cite five contemporaries, including a miller, a baker and cloak maker, who lived comfortably on the earnings of their slaves. More usually rich Athenians seem to have distributed their capital between land, house property, some cash investments and a dozen or so slave craftsmen. Socrates, asking a high-class prostitute where her money came from, suggests (ironically) land, house property or craftsmen as typical sources of income. Timarchus inherited, besides land and houses, nine or ten shoemakers, who paid him 2 obols a day each: Leocrates owned bronze smiths to the value of 35 minae (about a dozen, that is): Ciron, besides an estate worth a talent, and two houses, owned a few rent-paying slaves, valued with three domestic slaves and the furniture at 13 minae: Euctemon possessed a farm, a house, a baths, and a brothel and wine shop and some craftsmen.

These facts and figures concern the well-to-do families who could afford to pay a professional speech writer to compose a plea in their mutual litigation about their inheritances, and who normally belonged to the 1,200 richest families enrolled on the trierarchic register. How far humbler folk owned industrial slaves it is very difficult to say. Xenophon in one passage speaks of those who could buy slaves as fellow workers, which might suggest that a craftsman sometimes bought a man and trained him as an apprentice; and a poor cripple, pleading for his public assistance of 1 obol a day, complains that he is getting old and his children are too young to support him (a rather unlikely conjunction of pleas) and that he is too poor to buy a slave to carry on his work. This may suggest that a craftsman who bought a slave and trained him was looking forward to retiring on his earnings. But, as Aristophanes recognised, the greater part of the work in industry as in agriculture was done by poor citizens. Addressing them Poverty declared in the Plutus: "If wealth should gain his sight again and distribute himself equally, no one would practise a craft or skill. And when you have lost both of these, who will work as a smith or a shipwright or a tailor or a wheelwright or a shoemaker or a bricklayer or a launderer or a tanner or plough the land or harvest the crops, if you can live in idleness and neglect all this work?"

We have no reliable evidence for the total number of slaves in Attica at any time. For the late fourth century we have two figures, which, if we could rely on them, would be startling. The Byzantine lexicon of Suidas cites Hypereides (probably in connection with his proposal to free the slaves after the battle of Chaeronea in 338 B.C.) as speaking of "more than 150,000 from the silver mines and over the rest of the country." Athenaeus, who wrote at the end of the second century A.D., quotes Ctesicles, a chronicler of unknown date, as stating that at the census held by Demetrius of Phaleron (317–07) 400,000 slaves were registered. These are, as Beloch has convincingly demonstrated, quite impossible figures, and must have been corrupted in the course of their transmission to the late sources in which we read them. To

turn to more reliable if less explicit evidence, according to Thucydides more than 20,000 slaves, mainly skilled men, escaped during the ten years' occupation of Deceleia by the Spartans; these would probably be in the main miners and agricultural slaves, but would include many city workers, since the sixteen miles of city walls cannot have been so completely patrolled as to prevent escapes. Xenophon declares that the mines could provide employment for many more than 10,000, as those—if any—who remembered what the slave tax used to fetch before the Deceleian war could testify (he was writing sixty years later). But whatever their numbers their distribution is fairly clear. They were owned in the main by the 1,200 richest families and in decreasing numbers by the next 3,000 or so. It is unlikely that any slaves were owned by two-thirds to three-quarters of the citizen population. The great majority of the citizens earned their living by the work of their hands, as peasant farmers, craftsmen, shopkeepers, seamen and labourers; so contemporary witnesses state, and so the detailed evidence, so far as it goes, suggests. In only one occupation was slave labour predominant, in mining, and even here, contrary to common belief, some citizens worked. Xenophon, advocating that the State acquire a large body of slaves to be leased to the citizens for use in the mines, suggests that not only will existing contractors add to their manpower but that "there are many of those who are themselves in the mines who are growing old, and many others, both Athenians and aliens, who would not or could not work with their hands, but would gladly make their living by supervising." In one of the Demosthenic speeches we meet a man who boasts "In earlier times I made a lot of money from the silver mines, working and toiling myself with my own hands": he had struck lucky and was now one of the 300 richest men in Athens.

That the poorer citizens lived on State pay for political services is, even for the fourth century, when the system was most fully developed, demonstrably false. A man could only be a councillor two years in his life, and could hold none of the magistracies chosen by lot for more than one annual tenure. He could by attending the assembly—and getting there in time to qualify for pay—earn a drachma on thirty days and 1 1/2 drachmae on ten days in the year. On some festivals—the number varied according to the state of the exchequer—he could draw his theoric payment of 2 obols. On other days, if lucky enough to be successful in the annual ballot for the 6,000 jurors, he could queue in hopes of being empanelled on a jury and earning 3 obols, just enough to feed himself. At this rate a bachelor without dependants could barely with consistent good luck scrape a living; for a man with a family it was quite impossible.

The majority of the citizens were then workers who earned their own livings and whose political pay served only to compensate them in some measure for loss of working time. Agricultural and industrial slaves in the main merely added to the wealth of a relatively small rentier class, whose principal source of income was land; this same class employed most of the domestic slaves. It only remains to ask how far the Athenian State drew its revenue, directly or indirectly, from slaves. The State owned a certain number of slaves. Most famous are the 1,200 Scythian archers who policed the assembly and the law courts and enforced the orders of the magistrates. There were a number of others ranging from the workers in the mint to the city gaoler and the public slave par excellence who had custody of the public records and accounts. Athens thus ran her police force and her rudimentary civil service in part by slave labour — the clerks of the magistrates were mostly salaried citizens. There was apparently a tax on slaves, known only from the mention in Xenophon cited above, but it can hardly have been an important item in the revenue to receive so little notice. The mines, which were mainly exploited by slave labour, also brought in revenue to the State, but less than might have been expected seeing that concessionaires sometimes made large fortunes. The mines flourished in the fifth century, from their first serious exploitation in 483 till the Spartan occupation of Deceleia in 413. They then went through a prolonged bad period till the 330s, when they were again in full swing. We have no figures for the fifth century. In the fourth we have a full record of one year's concessions (367–6), when the sums paid totalled 3,690 drachmae, and a partial record of a later year — probably 342–1 — when the revenue came to about 3 talents. There was probably a royalty payment of one twenty-fourth in addition to the prices paid for concessions. It is somewhat mysterious where the 400 talents of Athenian revenue came from, but a negligible proportion of it arose even indirectly from slave labour.

The charge brought by fifth-century oligarchic critics (and thoughtlessly repeated by many modern writers), that the Athenian democracy depended for its political pay on the tribute of the subject allies, was brought to the test of fact when Athens lost her empire in 404 B.C., and was proved to be a calumny when the democracy continued to pay the citizens for their political functions out of domestic revenues. The modern charge that the Athenian democracy was dependent on slave labour was never brought to the test, since the Athenians never freed all their slaves. This is not surprising, for slavery was an established institution, which most people accepted without question as "according to nature," and to abolish it would have meant a wholesale disregard of the rights of property, which the Athenians throughout their history were careful to respect. It is more surprising that on some occasions of crisis motions for a partial or wholesale freeing of slaves were carried. In 406 all male slaves of military age were freed and granted the citizenship to man the ships which won the battle of Arginusae. After the expulsion of the Thirty in 403, Thrasybulus, the left-wing leader of the restored democracy, carried a measure, later quashed as illegal by the moderate leader Archinus, to free and enfranchise all slaves who had fought for the democracy. In 338, after the defeat of Chaeronea, the left-wing politician Hypereides proposed and carried a motion to free all (able-bodied male) slaves to resist the Macedonians; this motion was again quashed as illegal by a conservative politician.

These facts suggest that there was no bitterness between the mass of the citizens and the slaves, but rather a sense of fellow-feeling. This was a point which shocked contemporary Athenian oligarchs. The "Old Oligarch" speaks bitterly of the insolence of slaves at Athens, and complains that it is illegal to strike them — the reason, he explains, is that the people are indistinguishable in dress and general appearance from slaves, and it would be easy to strike a citizen by mistake. The moderate oligarch Theramenes is careful to assure his colleagues among the Thirty that he is not one of "those who think there would not be a good democracy until slaves and those who through poverty would sell the city for a drachma participate in it." Plato mocks at the excess of freedom in the democracy, in which "men and women who have been sold are no less free than their purchasers."

Though the Athenians treated their slaves with a humanity which was exceptional according to the standards of the time, they never abolished slavery, and the charge that Athenian democracy was dependent on their labour was never brought to the test of fact. But had Hypereides' motion been allowed to stand, and extended to slaves of all ages and both sexes, it would not seem, on the basis of the evidence cited earlier in this article, that its effects would have been catastrophic. All wealthy and well-to-do citizens (or rather their wives and unmarried daughters) would have been incommoded by having to do their own housework. A very small number of wealthy or comfortably off men who had invested all their money in mining and industrial slaves would have been reduced to penury, and a larger number, but still a small minority, would have lost the proportion of their income which derived from industrial slaves, and would have had to let their farms instead of cultivating them by slave labour. A number of craftsmen would have lost their apprentices and journeymen. But the great majority of Athenians who owned no slaves but cultivated their own little farms or worked on their own as craftsmen, shopkeepers or labourers would have been unaffected.

2. In this selection, Victor Hanson sets forth his understanding of how the polis arose in the late eighth century BC, that is, in concert with and as a consequence of a revolutionary agricultural change—the rise of the small, independent family farm. Part of that change was the increased use of slaves, not in great gangs on large plantations but as one or two farm hands on each of many family farms. This, in Hanson's view, was the characteristic style of farming until the Hellenistic Age brought new changes. He derives some of the evidence for his interpretation from a study of the farm worked by Laertes, father of Odysseus, described in Homer's *Odyssey*. In making his case he also supports the view of those who believed that agricultural slaves were an essential part of Greek society.

FROM VICTOR DAVIS HANSON, *THE OTHER GREEKS*

DURING THE SHIFT from Dark-Age pastoralism and cereal-based agriculture to intensive farming and the rise of the polis, slave labor—like homestead farmhouses and irrigation—became common in the Greek countryside. Unfree workers were known throughout the Mycenean period and no doubt during the later Dark Ages as well. Yet with the appearance of the polis, Greece began to import increasing numbers of servile adult male laborers. Understandably, Greek authors believed that commonplace chattel slavery was a phenomenon of recent history, one contemporaneous with the establishment of their own polis institutions. The preponderant agrarian nature of the Greek population, the need for extra labor under intensive farming practices, the absence of legal restraints to slave ownership, the rising social disdain among independent yeomanry for manual wage labor, the growing wealth of the Greek economy, the extension of the Greek presence overseas and to the north as well, and the absolute absence of moral stricture in owning other human beings—all explain why during the polis period slaves in growing numbers entered Greece. It was an area that must have had an appetite for workers quite out of proportion in the Eastern Mediterranean to its small size and scant natural resources. Sponge-like, Greece at the end of the Dark Ages began absorbing manpower for its farms from around the Mediterranean, drawing laborers apparently not in demand in their native (and often superior) agricultural environments. Plainly, the Greeks were farming in ways far different from their northern, eastern, and southern neighbors—and in ways that clearly required much more labor.

Not surprisingly, Homer shows us that Laertes closely supervises his own agricultural slaves, who live in a barracks right beside his own home. An elderly Sicilian slave woman, kept free from field work, apparently cooks and presides over the indoor tasks, while the aged Dolios and the other slaves under the direct orders of Laertes himself gather stones from the fields to build a retaining or terrace wall. As they work on the farm's terraces, Odysseus approaches and discovers his father, bent down and weeding around a tree. Laertes is clearly not portrayed as an absentee or even a large landowner, a country gentleman like Ischomachos, who appears in the philosopher-historian Xenophon's fourth-century treatise, the Oeconomicus, and who sees his servile help more as capital to be exploited for profit than as a means to ensure income and a way of life. Instead, old Laertes apparently is intimate with his slaves, living and working among them at similar tasks. At the end of the Odyssey, Laertes fights right at their side against the families of the suitors.

Dolios and his sons are not a temporary harvest gang, men needed in the crush of the season and then dismissed to avoid idling once the crops are picked. Nor do they appear as helot-like indentured serfs. At this particular place in the Odyssey, Laertes' servile help is not mentioned as engaged in harvesting, but rather in soil reclamation and food preparation, "the old man guiding them on their errand." Apparently Laertes needs slaves year-round for a variety of farm improvement and more mundane daily tasks; he can keep the men busy even outside the harvest periods. Steady employment allows the workers to obtain an expertise otherwise not possible through temporary wage labor; slave farmhands now have achieved a skill in all aspects of farm work.

Interestingly enough, the slaves' labor does not free Laertes from work for fulfillment of social or political obligations. Nor is it designed to. Not only does there seem to be a real need for Laertes to engage in manual activity himself, but the old man apparently enjoys his hard work — despite the supposed aristocratic dislike for stoop labor — and seems to feel that it is also somehow critical in ensuring the productivity of his own workers. In other words, Laertes leads by example.

These references to servile workers are striking in light of the traditional scholarly denial of the presence of slaves in ancient Greek agriculture. Only for the Marxist historian is it axiomatic that slaves were found at every level of Greek society: the slave mode of production offered up bodies to be exploited for their masters' pleasure, part and parcel of the brutal process of extracting the critical surplus in agricultural productivity and creating the free time that their owners' more "leisured" lifestyle required.

Others bristled at the notion that the Greeks should have had to rely on an institution so intrinsically brutish and "undemocratic" as agricultural slavery in order to find time to engage in the niceties of this new idea of "politics." Thus champions of Athenian democracy — and a great many other Greek historians — rejected the presence of farm slaves on any wide scale — at least, and especially, at Athens.

Most citizens of Attica were in some way connected to farming: if it was argued that only a few farmers used slaves, Athens became a city-state of "peasants," of truly free men who did not base their democratic institutions on the backs of an exploited class. In this view, Athenians practiced a low-input type of agriculture, extensive farming that not only did not require servile help, but also allowed the farmers themselves ample free time. As evidence, critics of agricultural slavery in the Greek polis maintain there is a lack of clear-cut, unambiguous literary evidence for agricultural slavery. They also cite the impracticality of keeping extra mouths to feed on small "subsistence" plots whose workers were constantly underemployed. They note the exorbitant expense involved for a small farmer in purchasing slaves, and point to mechanisms other than chattel slavery to explain why Greek citizenry of the polis did not engage in class struggle until Hellenistic and Roman times. Yet it is evident that Laertes owns a few slaves. He himself does not seem to have much leisure. Nor is he underemployed.

In truth, the references in literature to chattel slaves who work on Greek farms in the seventh through fourth centuries throughout the Greek-speaking world are unambiguous and they have been collated by a number of ancient historians. These passages occur in nearly every genre of Greek literature. Although there could in some cases be exaggeration, distortion, or confusion, the sheer diversity of authors, places, and contexts suggests that servile workers were commonplace in the Greek countryside throughout the polis period, essential to the success of intensive agriculture itself. The literary references further imply that not merely the wealthy few, but also the many middling farmers, like Laertes, employed slaves. They appear not as large gangs of unattended workers, but rather as close, intimate, fellow manual laborers.

Just because Greek farms were small need not suggest underemployment or the absence of either sustenance or work for a permanent servile laborer. Most farms, like Laertes', were diversified, with harvests occurring throughout the year. Many crops were planted or grown on reclaimed land. Like Laertes' plot, they needed constant attention to both terrace and fence upkeep. Also, trees and vines can require more labor than cereals and can produce dramatically higher yields when pruned, fertilized, cultivated, planted densely, and watered methodically.

The picking of olives from large trees, as anyone can attest who has attempted it, is a nightmarish task. It is the agronomic situation that the modern agricultural advisor implores the farmer to avoid: large trees, small, unevenly ripening fruit, no chance for mechanization—a process extending over not days, not weeks, but rather months on end. On Greek vases the olive harvest appears as a confused affair: pickers are simultaneously kneeling on the ground, perched on limbs of the tree, and standing beating the leaves with sticks. The introduction of vine stakes and trellises—typical in the polis period—although requiring far more labor and capital, could also enhance grape production and quality. Cereals, too, produce higher yields when fertilized, weeded, and cultivated.

The degree of labor required on any farm, ancient or modern, depends on the level of intensification, the frequency of true fallowing, and the particular crops farmed, not merely on the size of the plot in question. Ten acres of vines and trees could easily require more labor than a thirty-acre grain field. Xenophon remarked that land "unfarmed and not planted in trees and vines" (argos kai aphuteutos) became "many times more valuable" once an orchard or vineyard was propagated (Oec. 20.23–24). The Greeks of the polis were aware that intensive farming often could take a toll on trees and vines, that the efforts to force maximum production sometimes led to decreased life expectancy of vineyards and orchards—a realization that must suggest Greek farmers normally invested capital and labor in their land to produce as much as possible. Intensification and diversification also invite a whole host of related tasks in addition to the cultivation of the soil: time spent marketing and exchanging produce, additional equipment and infrastructure, and renewed worries over storage.

Anywhere diverse crops are grown intensively, fertilization, planting, cultivation, plowing, grafting, and harvesting allow for little slack time in the agricultural calendar. Xenophon knew well that on a diversified farm on any given day men were planting orchards and vineyards (*phuteuontes*), clearing new land (*neiopoiountes*), sowing grain (*speirontes*), or harvesting fruit (*karpon proskomizontes*). "Produce," advises the Aristotelian *Oeconomica*, "should be so used that we do not risk all our possessions at the same time." Although there are references to specialized harvest-time

wage laborers who could come in handy at peak demand in the agricultural year, their employment was less common and more often confined to cereal culture during harvests. Hired free and landless agricultural workers were always despised in Greece as engaging in "brutish" work. The impression we receive from Greek literature is that the successful middling farmer usually sought to acquire one or two slaves, and then often relied on the unfortunate poorer grower or the landless to augment his permanent help during the few weeks of cereal harvesting or fruit picking.

The need at the end of the eighth century to acquire permanent agricultural workers must have led to the development of skilled field laborers, since farmers, like Laertes, were able themselves to train slaves in particular tasks year-round on the farm. Thucydides much later during the Peloponnesian War refers to Attic slaves who fled their farms during the enemy invasions of 413–404 B.C. as *cheirotechnai* (skilled workers), a denotation that probably reflected their accumulated agricultural expertise. At any rate, despite occasional complaints in literature that the agricultural slave could become fat and lazy, workers of this sort seem a far cry from harvest-time gangs, who were known to be undependable and occasionally slackers.

Nor is there evidence that agricultural slaves were inordinately expensive. They were not beyond the reach of most Greek farmers. If bought on the open market, servile workers in general might cost between 150 and 200 drachmas at Athens by the end of the fifth century—about the price of a pair of oxen or the small farmer's own arms and armor. There is good evidence to suggest that most agricultural slaves were not purchased through traditional peacetime markets, but rather were cheap byproducts of war as booty and plunder, and thus often sold sporadically in mass auctions at depressed prices. A traditional tale attested that the sudden acquisition of slaves in mass at Locris disrupted the market for free labor in general. In a more precise agricultural context, the anonymous Oxyrhynchus Historian of the early fourth century says that the Thebans bought slaves from the countryside of Athens at a "cheap" price in the closing years of the Peloponnesian War. In explanation, he adds that the Athenians themselves habitually "brought into their own fields whatever they took from other Greeks when fighting." This passage suggests that the slaves on the farms of Attica were themselves originally acquired cheaply by the Athenians through conquest and wartime raiding, not merely in small numbers at private sales.

Most farmers in Greece were landed infantrymen, usually (as at Athens) drawn from the *zeugitai*, the census class usually associated exclusively until the latter fifth century with independent moderate property owners. As hoplite soldiers, Greek farmers were accompanied on campaign by a servile attendants, charged with carrying the hoplite's seventy pounds of armor and weaponry. In nearly every case, we hear that such helpers were not relatives nor hired hands, but rather slaves.

If hoplite soldiers owned land, and took their own servants into war, it makes sense to conclude that in peacetime the slaves were employed on the soldiers' farms. Though this direct relationship during the latter polis period between middling farmer and citizen militiaman was finally modified and even ended at various locales, it remains a valid generalization for the first three centuries of the city-state: the hoplite's armor carrier proved the existence of his servile agricultural laborer. Thus Greek agrarianism itself was predicated on chattel slavery, the unknown mass of now-forgotten men like—Manes, Syra, Thratta, Sosias, Sikon, and countless others—who dug vines, terraced hillsides, picked fruit, cooked food, carried armor, prepared rations, and helped the battle-weary *georgos* trudge back to his farm. They made possible both Greek farming and fighting throughout the lifetime of the city-state.

Slaves were critical to the success of a rising breed of new agriculturalists, men whose freedom was now defined as owning land and not living or working under constraint to another. The clear distinction between those who worked under compulsion and those who managed that labor clearly went hand in hand with the farmers' own middling but chauvinistic identity as a group neither aristocrat nor serf. From this point on, the ubiquitous presence of chattel slaves on the farms of the *georgoi* was—like the pairing of hoplite and hoplite attendant—a constant reminder of the farmers' own freedom, of the fact they were not indentured, but rather free men who employed slaves of unambiguously inferior social status. Even modern rural sociologists tell us that nothing undermines a rural community so quickly as a large body of farm wage-laborers, with a concurrent small group of independently employed farmers. In Greece, however, only a slave or two was attached to each farm, ensuring that neither wage nor servile laborers outnumbered the *georgoi* themselves.

Paradoxically, the unambiguously unfree status of Greek farmer-workers attached to the plots of the *georgoi* ensured that there would not be a shiftless population of wage earners disrupting local agrarian communities. Nor under such a system would there be a few despots on top to siphon off the work of thousands as was typical in the East.

3. In the given passage, Bruce Thornton examines the ways in which the Greeks thought about slaves and the institution of slavery. Bruce Thornton is Professor of Classics and Humanities at California State University at Fresno.

FROM BRUCE THORNTON, *GREEK WAYS*

EVERY PRE-MODERN SOCIETY known to history practiced slavery in some form or other. From China to India, Africa to the New World, the ownership of humans by other humans was a ubiquitous evil. Indeed, slavery still exists today: in March of 2000, the human rights group Christian Solidarity International purchased 4,968 children out of bondage in the Sudan. Yet in the West, slavery was eradicated by the beginning of the modern age, with the exception of the Spanish colonies and the American South; and Americans fought a long, bloody civil war partly because the continued existence of chattel slavery was considered an atavistic barbarism incompatible with both Christianity and the progress humanity had made. One of the remarkable stories of human history is how an institution once so commonly accepted as an inevitable fact of life is now practiced in only a few parts of the world—and even there is kept hidden, in recognition of its universal condemnation.

The story of emancipation begins among the Greeks, yet . . . many scholars today see slavery in ancient Greece as proof of hypocrisy. Such attitudes are not new. In 1935, R. W. Livingstone noted that "some people put the Greeks out of court at the outset because they owned slaves," a fact that presumably "deprives their life of significance for us." Livingstone went on to point out the flaws in such thinking, not the least being that judging a society so removed in time requires a superhuman wisdom and impartiality. And when the terms and assumptions underlying our criticism derive mostly from the Greeks—when it was Greek humanistic ideals of rational inquiry and freedom of dissent that started humanity down the long road of emancipation—it shows a peculiarly arrogant ingratitude and lack of historical perception to condemn the Greeks for owning slaves. As Moses Finley, the great historian of ancient slavery, put it, "Slavery is a great evil: there is no reason why a historian should not say that, but to say only that, no matter with how much factual backing, is a cheap way to score a point on a dead society to the advantage of our own."

Another impediment to understanding ancient slavery is the tendency of most people to think of bondage in terms of American slavery, an emotional topic in our public discourse, bound up as it is with contemporary issues of racial equality. Any attempt to address the complexities and ambiguities of slavery often invites the charge that one is apologizing for it or failing adequately to acknowledge its full horror. Yet slavery in Greece was very different from slavery in the American South, which was based on race and limited to an easily identified minority considered to be incapable of rational thought and hence less than human. Slavery was thought to be a condition justly suited to such a minority, and therefore a fate that would never be experienced by whites. The barrier of skin color separated the free and unfree, making it difficult for the former to sympathize with the latter's experience, or to acknowledge their common humanity.

In the ancient world, on the other hand, slavery was an evil that anyone potentially could suffer. Although theories of natural slavery such as those of Isocrates and Aristotle postulated that some peoples, especially non-Greeks, were by nature suited to slavery, and although many slaves in fifth-century Athens were not Greeks, throughout the historical period Greeks were enslaved not just by foreigners but by fellow Greeks as well (the latter practice one that Plato condemns in his Utopia). "Such a fate could befall anyone, no matter how exalted his status." In the *Odyssey*, Odysseus' swineherd Eumaeus was the son of a king who had been kidnapped by Phoenicians, who sold him to Odysseus' father. In addition to being kidnapped by slave-traders and

pirates, children sometimes were sold by their parents, and people were frequently enslaved for debt—both practices abolished in Athens by Solon as part of his reforms of 594. And if we can believe the Stoic Posidonius, some people even sold themselves into slavery, ensuring that at least their material wants would be taken care of.

War, of course, was the common catastrophe that enslaved many people, especially women and children after a city was sacked; as the philosopher Heracleitus said, "War has made some slaves, others free." Frequently in Greek literature the pitiful fate of enslaved women and children is sympathetically described. One of the most touching instances occurs in Book Six of the *Iliad*, when Hector, taking a brief respite from the fighting to speak with his wife, Andromache, foresees the doom of Troy and says, "But it is not so much the pain to come of the Trojans / that troubles me … / as troubles me the thought of you, when some bronze-armoured / Achaian leads you off, taking away your day of liberty." In the *Odyssey* too, a grieving Odysseus is compared to a woman weeping for her dead husband, "while the men behind her, / hitting her with their spear butts on the back and shoulders, / force her up and lead her away into slavery, to have / hard work and sorrow."

Nor was this disaster merely a literary one: the reality was experienced by many Greeks, at the hands not only of "barbarians" but of other Greeks. Thucydides describes several occasions during the Peloponnesian War when the Athenians punished their rebellious subjects by enslaving their women and children, including the Samians, the Skionians, the Mytileneans, and most notoriously the Melians. Contrary to American slavery, then, in the ancient world the possibility of ending up the property of somebody else was part of a larger tragic necessity that defined the human condition, not just the destiny of an alien race. In Greece, the gulf between master and slave was not so great as to close off any possibility of empathy.

Another important difference between American and ancient slavery is the higher level of education and training of some ancient slaves, who served as government clerks, skilled craftsmen and tutors, as well as domestics and laborers. For example, surviving records concerning the workmen on the Erechtheum, a building on the Acropolis, reveal that about a quarter were slaves who worked alongside citizens and free resident aliens for the same pay. A slave tutor, or paidagogos, was more than just an attendant; he also had responsibility for shaping his charge's character. Konnidas, the tutor of Theseus, legendary king of Athens, was honored along with his master at the Athenian festival dedicated to Theseus. Another famous slave tutor was Sicinnus, the teacher of Themistocles' sons. At the battle of Salamis, Themistocles entrusted Sicinnus with the false message to the Persians that tricked them into fighting the sea battle in the narrows, where the Greeks had an advantage. After the war Themistocles freed Sicinnus, enrolled him as a citizen of Thespiae, and made him a rich man. Such an event involving an American slave is unthinkable. The belief in the natural inferiority of African slaves necessarily meant that they could not be educated, let alone entrusted with shaping the character of their masters' sons. To do so would disprove the assumptions of intellectual inferiority by which slavery was justified. In ancient Greece, on the other hand, at least some slaves had a chance for education; a few even became philosophers, the most famous being the Stoic Epictetus.

In addition to being better educated, slaves in the ancient world had much greater opportunities for manumission than did slaves in the South. Sometimes military service would earn freedom—slaves who fought at Marathon in 490 were freed before the battle. Before the critical naval battle at Arginusae in 406, the Athenians enlisted slaves as rowers and then freed them after the victory. Indeed, in the *Frogs of Aristophanes*, this act of emancipation and enfranchisement is praised and recommended as a sound policy to follow in the future. To be sure, these were exceptional events made necessary by pressing circumstances, yet the contrast with the South is instructive: nothing frightened Southern slave-owners more than the thought of arming their slaves, something they never did, even during the darkest days of the Civil War.

More typically, ancient slaves had to buy themselves from their masters. They could save their own money, be "sold" to a god who became a sort of supervisory authority over the transaction until the price was repaid, or borrow money from associations (eranoi) that advanced to slaves the price of manumission. Sometimes several people would form a consortium and advance the money, as did the former lovers of Neaira.... Unwilling to see their former mistress under the control of a pimp, they advanced her part of the purchase price; the balance she provided herself from the gifts of other lovers.

Though freedmen in Greece did not suffer the permanent stigma of race that black freedmen in America did, they were still hemmed in by contractual obligations to their former masters, who remained their legal patrons. A contract surviving from Delphi from the first century A.D. states that the slave Onasiphoron will upon emancipation have to remain with her former master Sophrona until the latter dies. She will have to do whatever Sophrona says, and provide her with a child. For their part, former masters were obliged to intervene, on the pain of a fine, if anyone tried to re-enslave the freedman. All in all, though, a freedman's existence was more precarious than a citizen's, and his freedom was far from absolute. In Athens, freedman status was similar to that of a "metic" or resident alien: freedmen could not become citizens or own land, but they had to pay taxes and serve in the military. And always their status could be challenged, or they could be called to account for failure to fulfill their obligations to their former masters.

Yet despite these liabilities, the absence of physical differences between freedman and free meant that emancipated Greek slaves had greater opportunities for improving their status than did American ex-slaves. A certain Nicomachus, whose father was a slave, became an Athenian commissioner for recording the laws. Two slaves in Athens manumitted by their masters, Pasion and Phormion, even became citizens. And eventually the freedman's descendants at least could become indistinguishable from the free. The fourth-century B.C. comic poet Anaxandrides illustrated the role of providence in each man's life by saying, "There are many who are not free right now, but tomorrow they will be registered as citizens." The possibility, however remote, of free men becoming slaves and slaves, free men made it easier to acknowledge the slave's humanity and understand his lot than was the case with the race-based slavery of the South.

* * *

New attitudes evident in the comedy and tragedy of the late fifth century reflect developments in Greek philosophy that would someday lay the groundwork for a wholesale challenge to the institution of slavery. Plato and Aristotle, however, accepted without question the need for slavery, and assumed that slaves were more or less deficient in reasoning power. A speaker in Plato's Laws says that "there is no element in the soul of a slave that is healthy.

A sensible man should not entrust anything to their care." Slaves "will never be friends with their masters." In the philosopher's Utopias, laws concerning slaves are proposed that are much harsher than the actual laws or practices of his times. In the *Laws* he suggests that slaves ought to be punished as they deserve, and not admonished as if they were freemen, which will only make them conceited. The language used to a servant ought always to be that of a command, and we ought not to jest with them . . . This is a foolish way which many people have of setting up their slaves, and making the life of servitude more disagreeable both for them and for their masters. Plato's pupil Aristotle agreed that a deficiency in reasoning power made some people naturally fit to be slaves and submit to the greater rationality and authority of a superior:

> One who is a human being belonging by
> nature not to himself but to another is
> by nature a slave . . . For he is by nature
> a slave who is capable of belonging to
> another . . . and who participates in reason
> so far as to apprehend it but not to possess
> it . . . Hence there are by nature various
> classes of rulers and ruled. For the free rules
> the slave . . . for the slave has not got the
> deliberative part of the soul at all.

Slaves are also necessary for doing menial tasks, thus freeing citizens to pursue the good life for both themselves and the state. Hence as a thing apart from the master used for his benefit, the slave is a "kind of instrument," or as Aristotle puts it in the *Eudemian Ethics*, "a slave is as it were a member or tool of his master; a tool is a sort of inanimate slave." He concludes, "It is clear, then, that some men are by nature free, and others slaves, and that for these latter slavery is both expedient and right." As Peter Garnsey summarizes Aristotle's position, "The net result of his analysis is that there is very little humanity in his natural slave."

Yet in the *Politics* we find evidence of a different point of view, and some ambivalence in Aristotle's position. His remarks in the *Politics* are in part a response to a very different position apparently significant enough for him to answer: "There are others, however, who regard the control of slaves by a master as contrary to nature. In their view the distinction of master and slave is due to law or convention; there is no natural difference between them: the relation of master and slave is based on force, and being so based has no warrant in justice." Later, just following his endorsement of "natural" slavery, Aristotle agrees that war captives who become slaves are not necessarily natural slaves, and so should not be enslaved, for "no one would ever say that he is a slave who is unworthy to be a slave." The problem then becomes determining the criteria by which natural slaves could be distinguished from those unjustly enslaved. Aristotle's solution is to designate barbarians as natural slaves, an idea that flattered Greek xenophobia. As Euripides' Iphigenia says, accepting her sacrifice to further the Greek expedition against the barbarian Trojans, "It is / a right thing that Greeks rule barbarians . . . They are bondsmen and slaves, and we, / Mother, are Greeks and free." Yet the existence of numerous Greek slaves made Aristotle's theoretical discussion an implicit indictment of slavery, at least as it was actually practiced by Greeks, for many slaves were Greeks who had perforce been enslaved unjustly. At any rate, we see in Aristotle the consequences of making slavery an object of rational analysis. Once that happened, it could become an object of criticism as well.

The "others" Aristotle mentions give further evidence that slavery was not completely taken for granted as natural and just among Greek thinkers. They very likely were the Sophists, those philosophers of the late fifth century who inquired critically into traditional beliefs and received wisdom, often advancing a relativism that saw human institutions and customs as reflecting force or chance or other arbitrary causes rather than innate right or justice. Perhaps the influence of the Sophists can best be seen in the tragedies of Euripides. The idea that slaves are inferior by nature and thus deserving of their status is contradicted by a passage from the *Ion*, a play about a noble temple slave; the line is spoken by an old, faithful slave: "A slave bears only this / Disgrace: the name. In every other way / An honest slave is equal to the free." So too in the Helen, Menelaus' slave says, "I, though I wear the name of lackey [bondsman], yet aspire / to be counted in the number of the generous [noble] slaves, for I do not have the name of liberty / but have the heart [mind]." Merely modifying the noun "slave" with the adjective "noble" in itself was a striking challenge to conventional views.

Fragments from lost plays suggest sentiments like those found in extant tragedies. One fragment goes so far as to discount entirely the equation of innate value with free status: "The name of slave does not exclude quality. Many slaves are worth more than free men." Judging from the surviving fragments, it appears that Euripides' lost play the *Alexander* (ca. 415), about the Trojan prince's upbringing at the hands of slave shepherds after being exposed by his mother, Hecuba, centered on debates about the justice of slavery. After Paris bests his noble brothers at the games, a debate ensues on the issues of nobility and natural slavery. His brother Deiphobus indulges the common stereotypes about slaves as appetite-driven and reason-impaired (slaves "only think about their bellies, and have no thought for the consequences of their actions"). Paris retorts by invoking the Sophists' argument that contingencies are responsible for slave or free status, whereas true nobility and freedom derive from an individual's character: "vile people like you have become slaves in all but name, for Fortune [chance] has made you so." The chorus of shepherds endorses Paris's view: "Nature's creation is equally base and noble; / it is Custom, and Time, which make people proud of their rank. / True nobility lies in good sense and judgment, / and God alone, not wealth, bestows it."

A fragment from a play by Sophocles, the *Tereus*, makes the same argument, suggesting that these ideas were widely discussed in Athens:

> Mankind is one tribe; one day in the life of
> father and mother brought to birth all of us;
> none was born superior to any other. But
> some are nurtured by a fate of misfortune,
> others of us by prosperity, and others are
> held down by the yoke of compulsion that
> enslaves us.

Servile status, rather than reflecting innate inferiority, is an accident of chance, just as nobility is, and all humans are united by their common subjection to fortune. For Sophocles, a slave with a noble character is a possibility, one that undermines the kind of rationalization for slavery that would be articulated by Aristotle.

These scattered references tell us that in Athens of the late fifth century, ideas were circulating that challenged the prevailing justifications for slavery. As we see in the passages from Euripides, the idea that the quality of one's character and mind, rather than the status of one's body, makes one genuinely free was widespread enough by this time to appear in the public forum of Athenian tragedy. This focus on character changes the meaning of "natural slave": the free man can be a slave if he submits his reason to appetites and passions, and the slave a free man if he displays the right sorts of rational virtues. He will be, as a fragment of Sophocles puts it, "Servile in body, but the mind is free." Two hundred years later, Bion would write, "Good slaves are free, but bad free men are slaves of many passions."

This view of slavery as a condition of the soul rather than the body, implicit in the imagery used by Plato and Aristotle to describe the soul of the man dominated by appetite, became widespread in Stoicism. According to this Greco-Roman philosophy, the world is an orderly structure reflecting a divine, providential intention, a rational structure in which all humans—who by virtue of being human hold a spark of divine reason within them—have a duty to play whatever role providence has given them in order to further the good of the whole. True freedom is the choice of the wise man to do his moral duty. As Diogenes Laertius paraphrases Stoic doctrine, "Only he [the wise man] is free, but the bad are slaves. For freedom is the power of autonomous action, but slavery is the lack of autonomous action." Moreover, everybody is rational and capable of virtue. "All men have natural tendencies to virtue," said Cleanthes (c. 260), and so potentially can learn to make the right choices and hence be free.

Even if such ideas tended indirectly to legitimize slavery as something beyond our control, and irrelevant anyway to our souls in their submission to whatever sphere providence has assigned us, they repudiated the notion of natural slavery. As the late-fourth-century comic poet Philemon put it, "No one by nature ever becomes a slave, but chance enslaves his body." Stoic doctrine broke down the absolute distinctions between slave and free assumed in the theory of natural slavery, stressing instead their similarities in the common human condition—something more difficult to do in the race-based slavery of the American South.

The most important development in the nascent critique of slavery was the Stoic idea of the "brotherhood of man." The Stoics recognized a shared human nature transcending the accidental differences of environment, language, ethnicity or civic status, based on the common possession of reason and leading to affinity for other humans. "The mere fact of their common humanity requires that one human should feel another man to be akin to him," the Roman Stoic Cicero put it.

This idea of human kinship has antecedents in earlier Greek thought. The late-fifth-century Sophist Antiphon said,

> For by nature we are all in every way made in the same fashion to be either barbarians or Greeks. That is what is shown by the things which are by nature necessary to all men. All men, in similar fashion, have the possibility of enjoying them and in all this no man is marked out as a barbarian or a Greek. We all breathe the air through our mouths and nostrils, and we all eat with our hands.

A few decades later the orator Isocrates, in his *Panegyricus* (380), defined Greekness not as a matter of common blood but as one of common culture: "the name 'Hellenes' suggests no longer a race but an intelligence, and . . . the title 'Hellenes' is applied rather to those who share our culture than to those who share a common blood." Human identity rests on universal natural needs and abilities, together with a peculiar kind of culture that anyone can learn and embrace. Just as Greekness is not inborn, neither is slavery a reflection of innate racial or ethnic inferiority, but rather an accident of chance. And freedom, as the Sophist Alcidamas says, . . . is a natural possession of every human being.

In the Stoic brotherhood of man, the common possession of divine reason binds all men together. Of course, some people have more reason than others, and humans can be hierarchically divided between the superior few who develop their reason to its maximum potential, and the foolish many who let their divine potentiality slumber unused. Still, if Plutarch can be believed, Zeno, the fourth-century founder of Stoicism, wrote that "our life should not be based on cities or peoples each with its own view of right and wrong, but we should regard all men as our fellow-countrymen and fellow-citizens, and that there should be one life and one order, like that of a single flock on a common pasture feeding together under a common law." If Zeno did not actually intend the "world state" idea that Plutarch perhaps reads back into his work, certainly later Stoics, living in the more unified, cosmopolitan world created by Alexander and later the Romans, envisioned a human community not defined by artificial distinctions of ethnicity or status. The slave Epictetus, in the late first century A.D., best articulated this idea when he advised that we identify ourselves not as citizens of Athens or Corinth or some other state but as "citizens of the world," since our true human identity as rational beings comes not from our families or local communities but from God, and so the one true community is that of rational humans and God.

These philosophical ideas carried with them obvious implications for how slaves should be treated, even if they did not frontally challenge the institution itself. Epictetus asked slave-owners, "Don't you remember what you are, and over whom you rule, that they are kinsmen, that they are brothers by nature, that they are the offspring of Zeus?" A generation before Epictetus, the Roman Stoic Seneca, in one of his literary letters, criticized the dehumanizing abuse of slaves ("We abuse them as one does pack animals, not even as one abuses men") and invoked their common humanity: "Remember, if you please, that the man you call slave sprang from the same seed, enjoys the same daylight, breathes like you, lives like you, dies like you. You can easily conceive him a free man as he can conceive you a slave." Since a larger order beyond the individual's deserts determines whether one is slave or free, Seneca advised his correspondent to "treat your slave with compassion, even with courtesy; admit him to your conversation, your planning, your society." Though neither Seneca, himself a slave-owner, nor anybody else in the Greco-Roman world called for the abolition of slavery, nonetheless these sentiments would in time help build the critical mass necessary to end human bondage.

Nowhere else in the ancient world—in the Near East, Asia, or northern Europe—can one find slaves and slavery discussed in this critical way. Works like the dialogue *Slavery and Freedom*, by the first-century philosopher Dio Chrysostom, in which a slave vigorously, intelligently, and passionately challenges the received wisdom of his free interlocutor, are unheard of outside Greece. There the debate began, and once the Greeks made slavery an object of free thought, analysis and discussion, the possibility of challenging the institution itself opened up. We should no more chastise the Greeks for not taking the next step, the abolition of slavery, than fault them for knowing the earth is round but not sailing to America. M. I. Finley economically summarizes the significance of Greek thinking about slavery: "Shot through with ambiguity, and not rarely with tension," the Greeks' attitudes were articulated in an "academic conflict," to be sure, "but no society can carry such a conflict within it, around so important a set of beliefs and institutions, without the stresses erupting in some fashion, no matter how remote and extended the lines and connections may be from the original stimulus." Much had to happen historically—the rise of Christianity is important here—before the seeds sown by the Greeks bore fruit. Yet rather than criticize the Greeks for a practice universally accepted in the ancient world, we should instead acknowledge them as the first to question it, thus pointing humanity down the road of emancipation.

Consider

1. What does Jones think was the Athenian attitude, or attitudes, toward work?
2. What evidence and arguments does he use to reduce the number of slaves in Athens?
3. What does he think of the role of slaves in agriculture? In commerce?
4. Where does he think slave labor was most concentrated?
5. Who does he think benefited chiefly from slavery?
6. What does he think were the differences in feelings between the slaves and the free?
7. What does he think would have been the effect of the absence of slaves on the Athenian society? Did it depend on slavery?
8. When did the Greeks think chattel slavery became common among them?
9. How does Hanson account for the phenomenon?
10. Hanson uses Laertes' farm described in Homer's *Odyssey* as a model for real farms toward the end of the eighth century BC and later. Is this appropriate?
11. What arguments does he mention against the reality of widespread use of slaves in agriculture?
12. What arguments does he use in favor of his own view?
13. What does he think were the consequences of this new way of farming for Greek freedom?
14. What differences does Thornton find between ancient Greek slavery and slavery in the American South?
15. How does he indicate the complexity of Greek ideas about slaves and slavery?
16. How are slaves depicted in comedy and tragedy?
17. Who were critics of slavery?
18. How did Stoic thinkers compare with Aristotle on the subject of slavery?

CHAPTER 7
THE STATUS OF WOMEN IN ANCIENT GREECE

SCHOLARS AND STUDENTS OF ANTIQUITY often criticize the Greeks for having excluded women from many of the rights enjoyed by male full citizens; for even the Athenians during the height of their democracy denied women citizens the right to participate in the assembly and to hold political office. In general, the Greeks confined their women to the household (*oikos*) and to domestic duties such as weaving cloth and producing and rearing children. Many infer that Greek males dominated and oppressed women, who, in turn, were forced to accept a subordinate role in society, despite their feelings of frustration and resentment.

Some feminists have argued that the Greeks hated women and organized their society to exploit them systematically to serve the needs of the state. In fact, much of the surviving literature supports the idea that the Greeks were misogynists. Hesiod, for example, explains that the gods created Pandora, the first woman, to punish mankind for Prometheus' theft of fire. Aristotle, perhaps the greatest Greek philosopher, argued that women were by nature inferior to men and were meant to be ruled by them.

On the other hand, the literary sources are far from clear regarding the standing of women in ancient Greek society. Women like Penelope and Nausicaa, for instance, have an essential and honored place in the epics of Homer. The powerful heroines of Greek tragedy such as Antigone and Medea contradict the image of the subservient female in classical Greece. In the *Republic* of Plato, perhaps the most influential work on political philosophy in the Western tradition, women may not only become soldiers but also philosopher kings and rule the state. Recent scholarship, moreover, has emphasized the importance of the domestic sphere to the preservation of the oikos and the prominent role of women in important religious festivals, such as the Panathenaia. This research places less stress on the antagonism between men and women than on how their roles complemented one another. It has also become obvious that not all women held the same status in relation to men and different classes of women served different functions in society. But scholars are far from a consensus on the position of women. This chapter raises several questions. What was the legal, political, social, and cultural status of women in ancient Greece? What was the character of their relations to men? How might one reconcile the contradictory nature of the literary sources with the actual role of women in ancient Greek society?

Ancient Sources

1. Hesiod, *Theogony* 560–615; *Works and Days,* 44–105, PANDORA
2. Semonides, "PEDIGREE OF WOMEN"
3. Sophocles, *Antigone,* 445–525, ANTIGONE
4. Euripides, *Medea,* 230–250, MEDEA
5. Thucydides 2.45.2, THE FUNERAL SPEECH
6. Plato, *Menexenus,* 234a–249e, ASPASIA

Greek houses had no running water. This scene painted c. 520 BC shows five women carrying water home from a fountain.

7. Lysias I, *On the Murder of Eratosthenes,* 6–27, WOMEN IN THE HOME
8. Xenophon, *Oeconomicus,* 3.10–15; 7.22–31, THE NATURE OF WOMEN
9. Plato, *Republic,* WOMEN AS GUARDIANS
10. Aristotle, *Politics,* THE INFERIOR SEX?

Opinions of Modern Scholars

1. A. W. Gomme, "The Position of Women in Athens in the Fifth and Fourth Centuries B.C."
2. John Gould, "Law, Custom and Myth: Aspects of the Social Position of Women in Classical Athens"
3. Joan Breton Connelly, *Portrait of a Priestess: Women and Ritual in Ancient Greece*

ANCIENT SOURCES FOR WOMEN'S STATUS IN ANCIENT GREECE

It should be pointed out that nearly all the surviving ancient literary sources were written by elite males for mostly a male audience. However, the literature does not present anything resembling a homogeneous viewpoint.

1. PANDORA

Hesiod was a poet who lived in Boeotia and composed two epic poems, the *Theogony* and the *Works and Days*, at around 700 BC. The *Theogony* tells about the origins of the universe (cosmos) and the creation of the gods. In the section below,

Hesiod, infamous for his misogyny, describes how the Titan Prometheus outwitted Zeus, the father of the Olympian deities. In retaliation Zeus ordered Hephaestus, the divine smith of the gods, to fashion the first woman, Pandora, as an evil gift for humans.

Then cloud-compelling Zeus addressed him, greatly displeased: "Son of Iapetos, skilled in wise plans beyond all, **[560]** you do not, good sir, yet forget subtle craft." Thus spoke in his wrath Zeus knowing imperishable counsels: from that time forward, ever mindful of the fraud, he did not give the strength of untiring fire to wretched mortal men, who dwell upon the earth. **[565]** But the good son of Iapetos cheated him, and stole the far-seen splendor of untiring fire in a hollow fennel-stalk; but it stung High-thundering Zeus to his heart's core, and incensed his spirit, when he saw the radiance of fire conspicuous among men.

[570] Forthwith then he fashioned evil for men in requital for the fire bestowed. For from the earth the famous Hephaistos, halting in both feet, fashioned the image of a modest maiden, through the counsels of the son of Kronos. And the goddess glancing-eyed Athena girded and arrayed her in silver-white raiment; **[575]** and from her head she held with her hands a curiously embroidered veil, a marvel to look upon: and Pallas Athena placed around her about her head lovely garlands fresh-budding with meadow-flowers, and around her head she set a golden coronet, which renowned Hephaistos lame with both feet had made himself, **[580]** having wrought it carefully by hand, out of compliment to Zeus his father. On it had been wrought many curious monsters, a marvel to view, as many as in great abundance the continent and the sea maintain. Many of these he introduced, and much elegance beamed from it, of wondrous beauty, like to living animals gifted with sounds. **[585]** But when he had wrought a beauteous evil instead of good, he led her forth even where were the rest of gods and men, exulting as she was in the adornment of the gleaming-eyed daughter-of-a-strong-father: and wonder seized immortal gods as well as mortal men, when they beheld a deep snare, against which man's craftiness is in vain.

[590] From her is the race of tender women. For from her is a pernicious race. Tribes of women, a great source of hurt, dwell with mortal men, helpmates not in consuming poverty, but in surfeit. And as when in close-roofed hives bees **[595]** feed drones, sharers in bad works, the former through the whole day till sunset are busy day by day, and make white combs, while the latter, remaining within in the close-roofed hives, reap the labors of others for their own stomachs. **[600]** Just as to mortal men high-thundering Zeus gave women as an evil, accomplices of painful toils: another evil too did he provide instead of good; to wit whosoever shunning marriage and the ills that women work, declines to marry, and has come to old age pernicious, **[605]** through want of one to tend his final days; he lives not, it is true, in lack of subsistence, but, when he is dead, distant kindred divide his possessions; while to whomsoever, on the other hand, the lot of marriage shall have fallen, and he has had a good wife congenial to his heart, to him then forever ill contends with good to be with him: **[610]** but whoso finds a baneful breed, lives with an incessant care to spirit and heart within his breast, and it is an irremediable woe. Thus it is not possible to deceive or overreach the mind of Zeus, for neither did Prometheus, helpful son of Iapetos, **[615]** escape from beneath his severe wrath; but a great chain, by necessity, constrains him, very knowing though he is.

In his second poem, the *Works and Days*, Hesiod relates another version of the Pandora myth. Its view of the role women play in making men miserable is striking for a modern audience.

WORKS AND DAYS 44–105, TRANSLATED BY GREGORY NAGY

The gods had hidden away the true means of livelihood for humankind, and they still keep it that way.
    If it were otherwise, it would be easy for you to do in just one day all the work you need to do,
      and have enough to last you a year, idle though you would be.

45 Right away, you could store your steering-oar over the fireplace,
    and what you had plowed with your oxen or hard-working mules could go to waste.
    But Zeus hid it [the true means of livelihood for humankind], angry in his thoughts,

because Prometheus, with crooked plans,
   deceived him.
For that reason he [Zeus] devised plans that
   were to be baneful for humankind.
50   And he [Zeus] hid fire. But [deceiving Zeus
   again] the good son of Iapetos [Prometheus]
stole it for humankind from Zeus the Planner
inside a hollow fennel-stalk, escaping the notice
   of Zeus the Thunderer.
Angered at him, Zeus, the cloud-gatherer, spoke:
"Son of Iapetos, knowing more schemes than
   anyone else,
55   you rejoice over stealing the fire and over
   deceiving my thinking.
But a great pain awaits both you and future
   mankind.
To make up for the fire, I will give them an evil
   thing, in which they may all
take their delight in their hearts, embracing this
   evil thing of their own making."
Thus spoke the father of men and gods, and he
   laughed out loud.
60   Then he ordered Hephaistos, renowned all
   over, to shape
some wet clay as soon as possible, and to put
   into it a human voice
and strength, and to make it look like the
   immortal goddesses,
with the beautiful and lovely appearance of a
   virgin. And he ordered Athena
to teach her own craft to her, weaving a very
   intricate web.
65   And he ordered Aphrodite to shed golden
   charm over her head;
also harsh longing, and anxieties that eat away
   at the limbs.
And he ordered Hermes, the messenger and
   Argos-killer,
to put inside her an intent that is doglike and a
   temperament that is stealthy.
Zeus spoke, and the gods obeyed the Lord Son
   of Kronos.
70   Right away the famed Lame One shaped out of
   the clay of the Earth
something that looked like a comely virgin—all
   on account of the will of Zeus, son of Kronos.
Athena dressed her and tied her girdle,
   adorning her.
And the goddesses who are named *Kharites*
   [Graces], as well as the Lady Peithō
   [Persuasion],

placed golden necklaces on its skin, and the
   Hōrai,
75   with their beautiful hair, plaited springtime
   garlands around her head.
Pallas Athena placed on her skin every manner
   of ornament [*kosmos*].
And within her breast the messenger and
   Argos-killer fashioned
falsehoods [*pseudea*], crafty words, and a
   stealthy disposition,
according to the plans of Zeus the loud-
   thunderer. And the messenger of the gods
80   put inside her a voice, and he called this woman
Pandōrā, because all the gods who abide in
   Olympus
gave her as a gift [*dōron*], a pain for grain-
   eating men.
But when the gods completed this deception
   of sheer doom, against which there is no
   remedy,
Father Zeus sent the famed Argos-killer to
   Epimetheus,
85   the swift messenger of the gods, bringing the
   gift [*dōron*]. Nor did Epimetheus
take notice [verb *phrazesthai*] how
   Prometheus had told him never to accept
   a gift [*dōron*]
from Zeus the Olympian, but to send it
right back, lest an evil thing happen to mortals.
But he [Epimetheus] accepted it, and only then
   did he take note in his *noos* that he had an
   evil thing on his hands.
90   Before this, the various kinds of humanity lived
   on earth
without evils and without harsh labor,
92   without wretched diseases that give disasters
   to men.
94   But the woman took the great lid off the jar
95   and scattered what was inside. She devised
   baneful anxieties for humankind.
The only thing that stayed within the unbreakable
   contours of the jar was *Elpis* [Hope].
It did not fly out.
Before it could, she put back the lid on top
   of the jar,
according to the plans of aegis-bearing Zeus,
   the cloud-gatherer.
100   But as for the other things, countless baneful
   things, they are randomly scattered all
   over humankind.
Full is the earth of evils, full is the sea.

Diseases for humans are a day-to-day thing. Every night,
  they wander about at random, bringing evils upon mortals

silently—for Zeus had taken away
  their voice.
105 So it is that there is no way to elude the intent [*noos*] of Zeus.

Hesiod gives a more balanced view of women when he discusses marriage in the *Works and Days*:

695 Make sure that you are the right age [seasonal, having the right *hōra*] when you bring home a wife to your house,
  when you are not much less than thirty years old nor much more than that. This is a seasonal marriage.
  The wife should have four years after puberty, and then she can marry in the fifth year.
  Marry a virgin, so that you may teach her the ways of affection.
700 Try your hardest to marry someone who lives near you.

And take a good look all around you, so that you will not marry someone who will become the occasion for jokes by your neighbors.
  There is no better possession for a man than a wife
  who is good. And there is nothing worse than a bad one,
  one who sneaks away the dinner for herself. The man, no matter how strong he may be,
705 is burned out by the fire of such a woman. No need for a torch! And she brings him to a raw old age.

2. "PEDIGREE OF WOMEN"

The Greek iambic poet Semonides (not to be confused with the fifth-century poet Simonides) composed in the mid-seventh century. The longest surviving fragment from his work proposes that different types of women were created from different animals and share their qualities.

[1] In the beginning God made woman's mind apart from man's.

One made her of a bristly Sow; all that is in her house lies disorderly, defiled with dirt, and rolling upon the floor, and she groweth fat a-sitting among the middens in garments [5] as unwashed as herself.

Another did God make of a knavish Vixen, a woman knowing in all things, who taketh note of all, be it bad or good; [10] for the bad often calleth she good and the good bad; and she hath now this mood and now that.

Another of a Bitch, a busybody like her mother, one that would fain hear all, know all, and peering and prying everywhere barketh e'en [15] though she see nothing; a man cannot check her with threats, no, not if in anger he dash her teeth out with a stone, nor yet though he speak gently with her, even though she be sitting among strangers—[20] she must needs keep up her idle baying.

Another the Olympians fashioned of Earth, and gave to her husband all wanting in wits; such a woman knoweth neither evil nor good; her only art is to eat; [25] and never though God give a bad winter draweth she her stool nigher the fire for the cold.

Another of the Sea, whose thoughts are in two minds; one day she laughs and is gay—a stranger seeing her within will praise her, saying [30] "There's no better wife in all the world, nay, nor comelier"; the next she is intolerable to behold or draw nigh to, for then she rageth unapproachably, like a bitch with young; implacable and nasty is she to all, alike foe and friend. [35] Even as the sea in summertime often will stand calm and harmless, to the great joy of the mariners, [40] yet often will rage and toss with roaring waves, most like unto it is such a woman in disposition, nor hath the ocean a nature of other sort than hers.

Another's made of a stubborn and belaboured She-Ass; [45] everything she doeth is hardly done, of necessity and after threats, and then 'tis left unfinished; meanwhile eateth she day in day out, in bower and in hall, and all men alike are welcome to her bed.

[50] Another of a Cat, a woeful and miserable sort; for in her there's nought of fair or lovely or pleasant or desirable; she is wooed for a love-mate, and yet when she hath him turneth his stomach; [55] she doeth her neighbours much harm underhand, and often eateth up unaccepted offerings.

Another is the child of a dainty long-maned Mare; she refuseth menial tasks and toil; she'll neither set hand to mill nor take up sieve, [60] nor cast forth the muck, nor, for that she shunneth the soot, will she sit beside the oven. She taketh a mate only of necessity. Every day will she wash herself twice, or even thrice, and anointeth her with unguents. [65] She ever weareth her hair deep-combed and wreathed with flowers. Such a wife may be a fair sight for other men, but she's an ill to her husband if he be not a despot or a king, [70] such as take pride in adornments like to her.

Another cometh of an Ape; she is the greatest ill of all Zeus giveth man. Foul of face, such a woman maketh laughter for all men as she goeth through the town; [75] short in neck, she moveth hardly, hip-less, lean-shanked—alas for the wretched man that claspeth such a mischief! Like an ape she knoweth all arts and wiles, nor recketh of men's laughter. [80] Neither will she do a man any kindness; all her care, all her considering, is how she shall do the greatest ill she may.

Another of a Bee; and happy he that getteth her. On her alone alighteth there no blame, [85] and life doth flourish and increase because of her; loving and loved groweth she old with her husband, the mother of a fair and name-honoured progeny; she is preeminent among all the women, and a divine grace pervadeth her; [90] neither taketh she delight in sitting among women where they tell tales of venery. Such wives are the best and wisest that Zeus bestoweth upon men; these other kinds, thanks unto Him, both are [95] and will ever be a mischief in the world.

For this is the greatest ill that Zeus hath made, women. Even though they may seem to advantage us, a wife is more than all else a mischief to him that possesseth her; [100] for whoso dwelleth with a woman, he never passeth a whole day glad, nor quickly shall he thrust out of doors Hunger the hated housefellow and hostile deity. But when a man thinketh within doors to be gladdest at heart by grace of God or favour of man, [105] then of all times will she find cause for blame and gird herself for battle. For where a woman is they e'en cannot receive a stranger heartily. And she that most seemeth to be discreet, she is all the time doing the greatest harm; [110] her husband is all agape for her, but the neighbours rejoice that yet another is deceived. And no man but will praise his own wife when he speaketh of her, and blame another's, yet we cannot see that we be all alike. [115] Aye, this is the greatest ill that Zeus hath made, this hath he put about us as the bondage of a fetter irrefragable, ever since Death received them that went a-warring for a woman.

Questions

1. What is the attitude of Hesiod and Semonides toward women?
2. How does the portrayal of women in *Theogony* compare with that in the *Works and Days* and that in Semonides' poem?

3. ANTIGONE

Sophocles of Athens (497/6–406 BC) produced *Antigone*, one of his greatest tragedies, for the festival of Dionysus in 441 BC. In the scene below, the heroine Antigone has defied the decree of the Theban king Creon by burying her brother Polynices who had attacked the city. The play expresses brilliantly the tension in fifth-century Athens between the conflicting demands of the polis and the oikos, public authority and individual conscience, and male and female.

Creon [441] You, you with your face bent to the ground, do you admit, or deny that you did this?

Antigone I declare it and make no denial.

Creon [To the Guard] You can take yourself wherever you please, [445] free and clear of a heavy charge. Exit Guard. [To Antigone] You, however, tell me—not at length, but briefly—did you know that an edict had forbidden this?

Antigone I knew it. How could I not? It was public.

Creon And even so you dared overstep that law?

Antigone [450] Yes, since it was not Zeus that published me that edict, and since not of that kind are the laws which Justice who dwells with the gods below established among men. Nor did I think that your decrees were of such force, that a mortal could override the unwritten **[455]** and unfailing statutes given us by the gods. For their life is not of today or yesterday, but for all time, and no man knows when they were first put forth. Not for fear of any man's pride was I about to owe a penalty to the gods for breaking these. **[460]** Die I must, that I knew well (how could I not?). That is true even without your edicts. But if I am to die before my time, I count that a gain. When anyone lives as I do, surrounded by evils, how can he not carry off gain by dying? **[465]** So for me to meet this doom is a grief of no account. But if I had endured that my mother's son should in death lie an unburied corpse, that would have grieved me. Yet for this, I am not grieved. And if my present actions are foolish in your sight, **[470]** it may be that it is a fool who accuses me of folly.

Chorus She shows herself the wild offspring of a wild father, and does not know how to bend before troubles.

Creon Yet remember that over-hard spirits most often collapse. It is the stiffest iron, baked to **[475]** utter hardness in the fire, that you most often see snapped and shivered. And I have witnessed horses with great spirit disciplined by a small bit. For there is no place for pride, when one is his neighbors' slave. **[480]** This girl was already practiced in outrage when she overstepped the published laws. And, that done, this now is a second outrage, that she glories in it and exults in her deed. In truth, then, I am no man, but she is, **[485]** if this victory rests with her and brings no penalty. No! Whether she is my sister's child, or nearer to me in blood than any of my kin that worship Zeus at the altar of our house, she and her sister will not escape a doom most harsh. For in truth **[490]** I charge that other with an equal share in the plotting of this burial. Call her out! I saw her inside just now, raving, and not in control of her wits. Before the deed, the mind frequently is convicted of stealthy crimes when conspirators are plotting depravity in the dark. **[495]** But, truly, I detest it, too, when one who has been caught in treachery then seeks to make the crime a glory.

Antigone What more do you want than to capture and kill me?

Creon I want nothing else. Having that, I have everything.

Antigone Why then do you wait? In none of your maxims **[500]** is there anything that pleases me — and may there never be! Similarly to you as well my views must be displeasing. And yet, how could I have won a nobler glory than by giving burial to my own brother? All here would admit that they approve, **[505]** if fear did not grip their tongues. But tyranny, blest with so much else, has the power to do and say whatever it pleases.

Creon You alone out of all these Thebans see it that way.

Antigone They do, too, but for you they hold their tongues.

Creon [510] Are you not ashamed that your beliefs differ from theirs?

Antigone No, there is nothing shameful in respecting your own flesh and blood.

Creon Was not he your brother too, who died in the opposite cause?

Antigone A brother by the same mother and the same father.

Creon Why, then, do you pay a service that is disrespectful to him?

Antigone [515] The dead man will not support you in that.

Creon Yes, he will, if you honor him equally with the wicked one.

Antigone It was his brother, not his slave, who died.

Creon But he died ravaging this land, while he fell in its defense.

Antigone Hades craves these rites, nevertheless.

Creon [520] But the good man craves a portion not equal to the evil's.

Antigone Who knows but that these actions are pure to those below?

Creon You do not love someone you have hated, not even after death.

Antigone It is not my nature to join in hate, but in love.

Creon Then, go down to hell and love them **[525]** if you must. But while I live, a woman shall not rule.

Questions

1. **Are the arguments of Creon or those of Antigone more convincing? Explain why.**
2. **Does the gender of Antigone affect your opinion and understanding of the issues at stake? Why or why not?**

4. MEDEA

In 431 BC, the tragic playwright Euripides (c. 485–406 BC) produced his *Medea* at the festival of Dionysus in Athens. The heroine Medea describes the condition of women in the following speech. Euripides shows remarkable sympathy with his female character in what appears to be an accurate depiction of a woman's life in fifth-century Athens.

[230] Of all creatures that have breath and sensation, we women are the most unfortunate. First at an exorbitant price we must buy a husband and master of our bodies. [This misfortune is more painful than misfortune.] [235] And the outcome of our life's striving hangs on this, whether we take a bad or a good husband. For divorce is discreditable for women and it is not possible to refuse wedlock. And when a woman comes into the new customs and practices of her husband's house, she must somehow divine, since she has not learned it at home, [240] how she shall best deal with her husband.

If after we have spent great efforts on these tasks our husbands live with us without resenting the marriage-yoke, our life is enviable. Otherwise, death is preferable. A man, whenever he is annoyed with the company of those in the house, [245] goes elsewhere and thus rids his soul of its boredom [turning to some male friend or age-mate]. But we must fix our gaze on one person only. Men say that we live a life free from danger at home while *they* fight with the spear. [250] How wrong they are! I would rather stand three times with a shield in battle than give birth once.

Questions

1. **What response do you think Euripides expected Medea's speech to elicit from his presumably all male audience? Why?**
2. **Is it significant if the actors playing both Medea and Antigone were male? Explain your answer.**

5. THE FUNERAL SPEECH

At the conclusion of the first year of the Peloponnesian War, Pericles was chosen to deliver the funeral speech for the Athenians who were killed. Toward the end of his speech reported by Thucydides, Pericles gives advice to the women in the audience.

2.45.2 If I must say anything on the subject of female excellence to those of you who will now be in widowhood, it will be all comprised in this brief exhortation.

Great will be your glory in not falling short of your natural character; and greatest will be hers who is least talked of among the men whether for good or for bad.

Questions

1. **What do you think Pericles means by his admonition to the women of Athens?**
2. **How do his words compare with what a contemporary politician might say on such an occasion?**

6. ASPASIA

The Socratic dialogue *Menexenus* of Plato (427–347 BC) purports to give a funeral speech composed by Aspasia and reported by Socrates. Aspasia was a prostitute by trade and the lover of Pericles. She also had a reputation for great intellectual prowess and is even said to have been the driving force behind the policies of Pericles. The two pieces of dialogue before and after the funeral speech indicate the standing of Aspasia.

Socrates is discussing with his friend Menexenus whom the Athenians will choose for the honor of delivering the funeral oration over the city's men who died in the war.

[235e] Menexenus And do you think that you yourself would be able to make the speech, if required and if the Council were to select you?

Socrates That I should be able to make the speech would be nothing wonderful, Menexenus; for she who is my instructor is by no means weak in the art of rhetoric; on the contrary, she has turned out many fine orators, and amongst them one who surpassed all other Greeks, Pericles, the son of Xanthippus.

Menexenus Who is she? But you mean Aspasia, no doubt.

* * *

Menexenus What, then, would you have to say, if you were required to speak?

Socrates Nothing, perhaps, myself of my own invention; **[236b]** but I was listening only yesterday to Aspasia going through a funeral speech for these very people. For she had heard the report you mention, that the Athenians are going to select the speaker; and thereupon she rehearsed to me the speech in the form it should take, extemporizing in part, while other parts of it she had previously prepared, as I imagine, at the time when she was composing the funeral oration which Pericles delivered; and from this she patched together sundry fragments.

Menexenus Could you repeat from memory that speech of Aspasia?

Socrates Yes, if I am not mistaken; for I learnt it, to be sure, from her as she went along, **[236c]** and I nearly got a flogging whenever I forgot.

Menexenus Why don't you repeat it then?

Socrates But possibly my teacher will be vexed with me if I publish abroad her speech.

Menexenus Never fear, Socrates; only tell it and you will gratify me exceedingly, whether it is Aspasia's that you wish to deliver or anyone else's; only say on.

Socrates But you will probably laugh me to scorn if I, at my age, seem to you to be playing like a child.

Menexenus Not at all, Socrates; but by all means say on.

Socrates Nay, then, I must surely gratify; you for indeed I would almost gratify you **[236d]** if you were to bid me strip and dance, now that we two are alone. Listen then. In her speech, I believe, she began by making mention of the dead men themselves in this wise: [Socrates delivers Aspasia's Funeral Speech.] There, Menexenus, you have the oration of Aspasia, **[249d]** the Milesian.

Menexenus And by Zeus, Socrates, Aspasia, by your account, deserves to be congratulated if she is really capable of composing a speech like that, woman though she is.

Socrates Nay, then, if you are incredulous, come along with me and listen to a speech from her own lips.

Menexenus I have met with Aspasia many a time, Socrates, and I know well what she is like.

Socrates Well, then, don't you admire her, and are you not grateful to her now for her oration?

Menexenus Yes, I am exceedingly grateful, Socrates, for the oration **[249e]** to her or to him—whoever it was that repeated it to you; and what is more, I owe many other debts of gratitude to him that repeated it.

Socrates That will be fine! Only be careful not to give me away, so that I may report to you later on many other fine political speeches of hers.

Menexenus Have no fear: I won't give you away; only do you report them.

Socrates Well, it shall be done.

Questions

1. **Does Plato's dialogue imply a different attitude toward women than the other selections you have read in this chapter?**
2. **Is the figure of Aspasia unique in Greek treatments of women? Support your answers with examples from the sources.**

---

7.   WOMEN IN THE HOME

Lysias was an Attic orator (459/8–c. 380 BC) who wrote speeches for litigants of the courts in Athens. In the following speech a husband, Euphiletus, who had murdered the seducer of his wife gives his defense. His account provides a vivid picture of his relationship with his wife and their living arrangements.

[6] When I, Athenians, decided to marry, and brought a wife into my house, for some time I was disposed neither to vex her nor to leave her too free to do just as she pleased; I kept a watch on her as far as possible, with such observation of her as was reasonable. But when a child was born to me, thence-forward I began to trust her, and placed all my affairs in her hands, presuming that we were now in perfect intimacy.

[7] It is true that in the early days, Athenians, she was the most excellent of wives; she was a clever, frugal housekeeper, and kept everything in the nicest order. But as soon as I lost my mother, her death became the cause of all my troubles.

[8] For it was in attending her funeral that my wife was seen by this man, who in time corrupted her. He looked out for the servant-girl who went to market, and so paid addresses to her mistress by which he wrought her ruin.

[9] Now in the first place I must tell you, sirs (for I am obliged to give you these particulars), my dwelling is on two floors, the upper being equal in space to the lower, with the women's quarters above and the men's below. When the child was born to us, its mother suckled it; and in order that, each time that it had to be washed, she might avoid the risk of descending by the stairs, I used to live above, and the women below.

[10] By this time it had become such an habitual thing that my wife would often leave me and go down to sleep with the child, so as to be able to give it the breast and stop its crying. Things went on in this way for a long time, and I never suspected, but was simple-minded enough to suppose that my own was the chastest wife in the city.

[11] Time went on, sirs; I came home unexpectedly from the country, and after dinner the child started crying in a peevish way, as the servant-girl was annoying it on purpose to make it so behave; for the man was in the house—

[12] I learnt it all later. So I bade my wife go and give the child her breast, to stop its howling. At first she refused, as though delighted to see me home again after so long; but when I began to be angry and bade her go—"Yes, so that you," she said, "may have a try here at the little maid. Once before, too, when you were drunk, you pulled her about."

[13] At that I laughed, while she got up, went out of the room, and closed the door, feigning to make fun, and she took the key away with her. I, without giving a thought to the matter, or having any suspicion, went to sleep in all content after my return from the country.

[14] Towards daytime she came and opened the door. I asked why the doors made a noise in the night; she told me that the child's lamp had gone out,

and she had lit it again at our neighbor's. I was silent and believed it was so. But it struck me, sirs, that she had powdered her face, though her brother had died not thirty days before; even so, however, I made no remark on the fact, but left the house in silence.

[15] After this, sirs, an interval occurred in which I was left quite unaware of my own injuries; I was then accosted by a certain old female, who was secretly sent by a woman with whom that man was having an intrigue, as I heard later. This woman was angry with him and felt herself wronged, because he no longer visited her so regularly, and she was keeping a watch on him until she should discover what was the cause.

[16] So the old creature accosted me where she was on the look-out, near my house, and said— "Euphiletus, do not think it is from any meddlesomeness that I have approached you; for the man who is working both your and your wife's dishonor happens to be our enemy. If, therefore, you take the servant-girl who goes to market and waits on you, and torture her, you will learn all. It is," she said, "Eratosthenes of Oe who is doing this; he has debauched not only your wife, but many others besides; he makes an art of it."

[17] With these words, sirs, she took herself off; I was at once perturbed; all that had happened came into my mind, and I was filled with suspicion,— reflecting first how I was shut up in my chamber, and then remembering how on that night the inner and outer doors made a noise, which had never occurred before, and how it struck me that my wife had put on powder. All these things came into my mind, and I was filled with suspicion.

[18] Returning home, I bade the servant-girl follow me to the market, and taking her to the house of an intimate friend, I told her I was fully informed of what was going on in my house: "So it is open to you," I said, "to choose as you please between two things—either to be whipped and thrown into a mill, and to be irrevocably immersed in that sort of misery, or else to speak out the whole truth and, instead of suffering any harm, obtain my pardon for your transgressions. Tell no lies, but speak the whole truth."

[19] The girl at first denied it, and bade me do what I pleased, for she knew nothing; but when I mentioned Eratosthenes to her, and said that he was the man who visited my wife, she was dismayed, supposing that I had exact knowledge of everything. At once she threw herself down at my knees, and having got my pledge that she should suffer no harm,

[20] she accused him, first, of approaching her after the funeral, and then told how at last she became his messenger; how my wife in time was persuaded, and by what means she procured his entrances, and how at the Thesmophoria, while I was in the country, she went off to the temple with his mother. And the girl gave an exact account of everything else that had occurred.

[21] When her tale was all told, I said: "Well now, see that nobody in the world gets knowledge of this; otherwise, nothing in your arrangement with me will hold good. And I require that you show me their guilt in the very act; I want no words, but manifestation of the fact, if it really is so." She agreed to do this.

[22] Then came an interval of four or five days…as I shall bring strong evidence to show. But first I wish to relate what took place on the last day. I had an intimate friend named Sostratus. After sunset I met him coming from the country. As I knew that, arriving at that hour, he would find none of his circle at home, I invited him to dine with me; we came to my house, mounted to the upper room, and had dinner.

[23] When he had made a good meal, he left me and departed; then I went to bed. Eratosthenes, sirs, entered, and the maid-servant roused me at once, and told me that he was in the house. Bidding her look after the door, I descended and went out in silence; I called on one friend and another, and found some of them at home, while others were out of town.

[24] I took with me as many as I could among those who were there, and so came along. Then we got torches from the nearest shop, and went in; the door was open, as the girl had it in readiness. We pushed open the door of the bedroom, and the first of us to enter were in time to see him lying down by my wife; those who followed saw him standing naked on the bed.

[25] I gave him a blow, sirs, which knocked him down, and pulling round his two hands behind his back, and tying them, I asked him why he had the insolence to enter my house. He admitted his guilt; then he besought and implored me not to kill him, but to exact a sum of money.

[26] To this I replied, "It is not I who am going to kill you, but our city's law, which you have transgressed and regarded as of less account than your pleasures, choosing rather to commit this foul offence against my wife and my children than to obey the laws like a decent person."

[27] Thus it was, sirs, that this man incurred the fate that the laws ordain for those who do such things;

he had not been dragged in there from the street, nor had he taken refuge at my hearth, as these people say. For how could it be so, when it was in the bedroom that he was struck and fell down then and there, and I pinioned his arms, and so many persons were in the house that he could not make his escape, as he had neither steel nor wood nor anything else with which he might have beaten off those who had entered?

Questions

1. **What can you infer about the role of women in Greece from this passage of Lysias?**
2. **How does the speech's depiction of the couple compare with contemporary views and expectations of marriage?**

---

8. THE NATURE OF WOMEN

The *Oeconomicus* is Xenophon's work on estate management. In the following passage from Book VII, Ischomachus explains to Socrates that nature has assigned women to work in the home.

[22] And since both the indoor and the outdoor tasks demand labour and attention, God from the first adapted the woman's nature, I think, to the indoor and man's to the outdoor tasks and cares.

[23] For he made the man's body and mind more capable of enduring cold and heat, and journeys and campaigns; and therefore imposed on him the outdoor tasks. To the woman, since he has made her body less capable of such endurance, I take it that God has assigned the indoor tasks. [24] And knowing that he had created in the woman and had imposed on her the nourishment of the infants, he meted out to her a larger portion of affection for new-born babes than to the man. [25] And since he imposed on the woman the protection of the stores also, knowing that for protection a fearful disposition is no disadvantage, God meted out a larger share of fear to the woman than to the man; and knowing that he who deals with the outdoor tasks will have to be their defender against any wrong-doer, he meted out to him again a larger share of courage. [26] But because both must give and take, he granted to both impartially memory and attention; and so you could not distinguish whether the male or the female sex has the larger share of these. [27] And God also gave to both impartially the power to practise due self-control, and gave authority to whichever is the better—whether it be the man or the woman—to win a larger portion of the good that comes from it. [28] And just because both have not the same aptitudes, they have the more need of each other, and each member of the pair is the more useful to the other, the one being competent where the other is deficient.

[29] Now since we know, dear, what duties have been assigned to each of us by God, we must endeavour, each of us, to do the duties allotted to us as well as possible. [30] The law, moreover, approves of them, for it joins together man and woman. And as God has made them partners in their children, so the law appoints them partners in the home. And besides, the law declares those tasks to be honourable for each of them wherein God has made the one to excel the other. Thus, to be woman it is more honourable to stay indoors than to abide in the fields, but to the man it is unseemly rather to stay indoors than to attend to the work outside. [31] If a man acts contrary to the nature God has given him, possibly his defiance is detected by the gods and he is punished for neglecting his own work, or meddling with his wife's.

9. WOMEN AS GUARDIANS

In Plato's greatest dialogue, the *Republic*, the figure of Socrates argues for the equality of female guardians with male guardians. He points out the importance of identical education in training both sexes.

[452d] Do we expect the females of watch-dogs to join in guarding what the males guard and to hunt with them and share all their pursuits or do we expect the females to stay indoors as being incapacitated by the bearing and the breeding of the whelps while the males toil and have all the care of the flock?" "They have all things in common," [451e] he replied, "except that we treat the females as weaker and the males as stronger." "Is it possible, then," said I, "to employ any creature for the same ends as another if you do not assign it the same nurture and education?" "It is not possible." "If, then, we are to use the women for the same things as the men, [452a] we must also teach them the same things." "Yes." "Now music together with gymnastic was the training we gave the men." "Yes." "Then we must assign these two arts to the women also and the offices of war and employ them in the same way." "It would seem likely from what you say," he replied. "Perhaps, then," said I, "the contrast with present custom would make much in our proposals look ridiculous if our words are to be realized in fact." "Yes, indeed," he said. "What then," said I, "is the funniest thing you note in them? Is it not obviously the women exercising unclad in the palestra [452b] together with the men, not only the young, but even the older, like old men in gymnasiums, when, though wrinkled and unpleasant to look at, they still persist in exercising?" "Yes, on my word," he replied, "it would seem ridiculous under present conditions." "Then," said I, "since we have set out to speak our minds, we must not fear all the jibes with which the wits would greet so great a revolution, and the sort of things they would say about gymnastics [452c] and culture, and most of all about the bearing of arms and the bestriding of horses." "You're right," he said. "But since we have begun we must go forward to the rough part of our law, after begging these fellows not to mind their own business but to be serious, and reminding them that it is not long since the Greeks thought it disgraceful and ridiculous, as most of the barbarians do now, for men to be seen

naked. And when the practice of athletics began, first with the Cretans [452d] and then with the Lacedaemonians, it was open to the wits of that time to make fun of these practices, don't you think so?" "I do." "But when, I take it, experience showed that it is better to strip than to veil all things of this sort, then the laughter of the eyes faded away before that which reason revealed to be best, and this made it plain that he talks idly who deems anything else ridiculous but evil, and who tries to raise a laugh by looking to any other pattern of absurdity than [452e] that of folly and wrong or sets up any other standard of the beautiful as a mark for his seriousness than the good." "Most assuredly," said he. "Then is not the first thing that we have to agree upon with regard to these proposals whether they are possible or not? And we must throw open the debate to anyone who wishes either in jest or earnest to raise the question [453a] whether female human nature is capable of sharing with the male all tasks or none at all, or some but not others, and under which of these heads this business of war falls. Would not this be that best beginning which would naturally and proverbially lead to the best end?" "Far the best," he said. "Shall we then conduct the debate with ourselves in behalf of those others so that the case of the other side may not be taken defenceless and go by default?" [453b] "Nothing hinders," he said. "Shall we say then in their behalf: 'There is no need, Socrates and Glaucon, of others disputing against you, for you yourselves at the beginning of the foundation of your city agreed that each one ought to mind as his own business the one thing for which he was fitted by nature?' 'We did so agree, I think; certainly!' 'Can it be denied then that there is by nature a great difference between men and women?' 'Surely there is.' 'Is it not fitting, then, that a different function should be appointed [453c] for each corresponding to this difference of nature?' 'Certainly.' 'How, then, can you deny that you are mistaken and in contradiction with yourselves when you turn around and affirm that the men and the women ought to do the same thing, though their natures are so far apart?' Can you surprise me with an answer to that question?" "Not easily on this sudden challenge," he replied: "but I will and do beg you to lend your voice to the plea in our behalf, whatever it may be." "These and many similar difficulties, Glaucon," said I, [453d] "I foresaw and feared, and so shrank from touching on the law concerning the getting and breeding of women and children." "It does not seem an easy thing, by heaven," he said, "no, by heaven." "No, it is not," said I; "but the fact is that whether one tumbles into a little diving-pool or plump into the great sea he swims all the same." "By all means." "Then we, too, must swim and try to escape out of the sea of argument in the hope that either some dolphin will take us on its back or some other desperate rescue." [453e] "So it seems," he said. "Come then, consider," said I, "if we can find a way out. We did agree that different natures should have differing pursuits and that the nature of men and women differ. And yet now we affirm that these differing natures should have the same pursuits. That is the indictment." "It is." "What a grand thing, Glaucon," said I, [454a] "is the power of the art of contradiction!" "Why so?" "Because," said I, "many appear to me to fall into it even against their wills, and to suppose that they are not wrangling but arguing, owing to their inability to apply the proper divisions and distinctions to the subject under consideration. They pursue purely verbal oppositions, practising eristic, not dialectic on one another." "Yes, this does happen to many," he said; "but does this observation apply to us too at present?" [454b] "Absolutely," said I; "at any rate I am afraid that we are unawares slipping into contentiousness." "In what way?" "The principle that natures not the same ought not to share in the same pursuits we are following up most manfully and eristically in the literal and verbal sense but we did not delay to consider at all what particular kind of diversity and identity of nature we had in mind and with reference to what we were trying to define it when we assigned different pursuits to different natures and the same to the same." "No, we didn't consider that," he said. [454c] "Wherefore, by the same token," I said, "we might ask ourselves whether the natures of bald and long-haired men are the same and not, rather, contrary. And, after agreeing that they were opposed, we might, if the bald cobbled, forbid the long-haired to do so, or vice versa." "That would be ridiculous," he said. "Would it be so," said

I, "for any other reason than that we did not then posit likeness and difference of nature in any and every sense, but were paying heed solely to the kind of diversity [454d] and homogeneity that was pertinent to the pursuits themselves?" "We meant, for example, that a man and a woman who have a physician's mind have the same nature. Don't you think so?" "I do." "But that a man physician and a man carpenter have different natures?" "Certainly, I suppose." "Similarly, then," said I, "if it appears that the male and the female sex have distinct qualifications for any arts or pursuits, we shall affirm that they ought to be assigned respectively to each. But if it appears that they differ only in just this respect that the female bears [454e] and the male begets, we shall say that no proof has yet been produced that the woman differs from the man for our purposes, but we shall continue to think that our guardians and their wives ought to follow the same pursuits." "And rightly," said he. "Then, is it not the next thing to bid our opponent tell us [455a] precisely for what art or pursuit concerned with the conduct of a state the woman's nature differs from the man's?" "That would be at any rate fair." "Perhaps, then, someone else, too, might say what you were saying a while ago, that it is not easy to find a satisfactory answer on a sudden, but that with time for reflection there is no difficulty." "He might say that." "Shall we, then, beg the raiser of such objections to follow us, [455b] if we may perhaps prove able to make it plain to him that there is no pursuit connected with the administration of a state that is peculiar to woman?" "By all means." "Come then, we shall say to him, answer our question. Was this the basis of your distinction between the man naturally gifted for anything and the one not so gifted—that the one learned easily, the other with difficulty; that the one with slight instruction could discover much for himself in the matter studied, but the other, after much instruction and drill, could not even remember what he had learned; and that the bodily faculties of the one adequately served his mind, [455c] while, for the other, the body was a hindrance? Were there any other points than these by which you distinguish the well endowed man in every subject and the poorly endowed?" "No one," said he, "will be able to name any others." "Do you know, then, of anything practised by mankind in which the masculine sex does not surpass the female on all these points? Must we make a long story of it by alleging weaving and the watching of pancakes **[455d]** and the boiling pot, whereon the sex plumes itself and wherein its defeat will expose it to most laughter?" "You are right," he said, "that the one sex is far surpassed by the other in everything, one may say. Many women, it is true, are better than many men in many things, but broadly speaking, it is as you say." "Then there is no pursuit of the administrators of a state that belongs to a woman because she is a woman or to a man because he is a man. But the natural capacities are distributed alike among both creatures, and women naturally share in all pursuits and men in all—**[455e]** yet for all the woman is weaker than the man." "Assuredly." "Shall we, then, assign them all to men and nothing to women?" "How could we?" "We shall rather, I take it, say that one woman has the nature of a physician and another not, and one is by nature musical, and another unmusical?" "Surely." "Can we, then, deny that one woman is naturally athletic **[456a]** and warlike and another unwarlike and averse to gymnastics?" "I think not." "And again, one a lover, another a hater, of wisdom? And one high-spirited, and the other lacking spirit?" "That also is true." "Then it is likewise true that one woman has the qualities of a guardian and another not. Were not these the natural qualities of the men also whom we selected for guardians?" "They were." "The women and the men, then, have the same nature in respect to the guardianship of the state, save in so far as the one is weaker, the other stronger." "Apparently." **[456b]** "Women of this kind, then, must be selected to cohabit with men of this kind and to serve with them as guardians since they are capable of it and akin by nature." "By all means." "And to the same natures must we not assign the same pursuits?" "The same." "We come round, then, to our previous statement, and agree that it does not run counter to nature to assign music and gymnastics to the wives of the guardians." **[456c]** "By all means." "Our legislation, then, was not impracticable or utopian, since the law we proposed accorded with nature. Rather, the other way of doing things, prevalent today, proves, as it seems, unnatural." "Apparently." "The object of our inquiry was the possibility and the desirability of what we were proposing." "It was." "That it is possible has been admitted." "Yes." "The next point to be agreed upon is that it is the best way." "Obviously." "For the production of a guardian, then, education will not be one thing for our men and another for our women, especially since **[456d]** the nature which we hand over to it is the same." "There will be no difference." "How are you minded, now, in this matter?" "In what?" "In the matter of supposing some men to be better and some worse, or do you think them all alike?" "By no means." "In the city, then, that we are founding, which do you think will prove the better men, the guardians receiving the education which we have described or the cobblers educated by the art of cobbling?" "An absurd question," he said. **[456e]** "I understand," said I; "and are not these the best of all the citizens?" "By far." "And will not these women be the best of all the women?" "They, too, by far." "Is there anything better for a state than the generation in it of the best possible women and men?" "There is not." "And this, music and gymnastics **[457a]** applied as we described will effect." "Surely." "Then the institution we proposed is not only possible but the best for the state." "That is so." "The women of the guardians, then, must strip, since they will be clothed with virtue as a garment, and must take their part with the men in war and the other duties of civic guardianship and have no other occupation. But in these very duties lighter tasks must be assigned to the women than to the men **[457b]** because of their weakness as a class. But the man who ridicules unclad women, exercising because it is best that they should, 'plucks the unripe fruit' of laughter and does not know, it appears, the end of his laughter nor what he would be at. For the fairest thing that is said or ever will be said is this, that the helpful is fair and the harmful foul." "Assuredly."

Questions

1. **How does Plato's conception of the nature of men and women compare with that of Xenophon?**
2. **What factors might account for their different views of the two genders?**

10.   THE INFERIOR SEX?

Aristotle, in response to Plato's ideas on sexual equality, argues that women are by nature subordinate to men. His views are striking and even offensive to modern readers.

1259a [1] And since, as we saw, the science of household management has three divisions, one the relation of master to slave, of which we have spoken before, one the paternal relation, and the third the conjugal—for it is a part of the household science to rule over wife and children (over both as over freemen, yet not with the same mode of government, but over the wife to exercise republican government and over the children monarchical); **1259b [2]** for the male is by nature better fitted to command than the female (except in some cases where their union has been formed contrary to nature) and the older and fully developed person than the younger and immature. It is true that in most cases of republican government the ruler and the ruled interchange in turn (for they tend to be on in equal level in their nature and to have no difference at all), although nevertheless during the period when one is ruler and the other ruled they seek to have a distinction by means of insignia and titles and honors, just as Amasis made his speech about the foot-bath; but the male stands in this relationship to the female continuously. The rule of the father over the children on the other hand is that of a king; for the male parent is the ruler in virtue both of affection and of seniority, which is characteristic of royal government (and therefore Homer finely designated Zeus by the words father of men and gods, as the king of them all). For though in nature the king must be superior, in race he should be the same as his subjects, and this is the position of the elder in relation to the younger and of the father in relation to the child. **[3]** It is clear then that household management takes more interest in the human members of the household than in its inanimate property, and in the excellence of these than in that of its property, which we style riches, and more in that of its free members than in that of slaves. First of all then as to slaves the difficulty might be raised, does a slave possess any other excellence, besides his merits as a tool and a servant, more valuable than these, for instance temperance, have the courage, justice and any of the other moral virtues, or has he no excellence beside his bodily service? For either way

there is difficulty; if slaves do possess moral virtue, wherein will they differ from freemen? Or if they do not, this is strange, as they are human beings and participate in reason. **[4]** And nearly the same is the question also raised about the woman and the child: have they too virtues, and ought a woman to be temperate, brave and just, and can a child be intemperate or temperate, or not? This point therefore requires general consideration in relation to natural ruler and subject: is virtue the same for ruler and ruled, or different? If it is proper for both to partake in nobility of character, how could it be proper for the one to rule and the other to be ruled unconditionally? We cannot say that the difference is to be one of degree, for ruling and being ruled differ in kind, and difference of degree is not a difference in kind at all. **[5]** Whereas if on the contrary it is proper for the one to have moral nobility but not for the other, this is surprising. For if the ruler is not temperate and just, how will he rule well? And if the ruled, how will he obey well? **1260a** If intemperate and cowardly he will not perform any of the duties of his position. It is evident therefore that both must possess virtue, but that there are differences in their virtue (as also there are differences between those who are by nature ruled). And of this we straightway find an indication in connection with the soul; for the soul by nature contains a part that rules and a part that is ruled, to which we assign different virtues, that is, the virtue of the rational and that of the irrational. **[6]** It is clear then that the case is the same also with the other instances of ruler and ruled. Hence there are by nature various classes of rulers and ruled. For the free rules the slave, the male the female, and the man the child in a different way. And all possess the various parts of the soul, but possess them in different ways; for the slave has not got the deliberative part at all, and the female has it, but without full authority, while the child has it, but in an undeveloped form. **[7]** Hence the ruler must possess intellectual virtue in completeness (for any work, taken absolutely, belongs to the master-craftsman, and rational principle is a master-craftsman); while each of the other parties must have that share of this virtue which is appropriate to them. We must suppose therefore that the same necessarily holds good of the moral virtues: all must partake of them, but not in the same way, but in such measure as is proper to each in relation to his own function. **[8]** Hence it is manifest that all the persons mentioned have a moral virtue of their own, and that the temperance of a woman and that of a man are not the same, nor their courage and justice, as Socrates thought, but the one is the courage of command, and the other that of subordination, and the case is similar with the other virtues. And this is also clear when we examine the matter more in detail, for it is misleading to give a general definition of virtue, as some do, who say that virtue is being in good condition as regards the soul or acting uprightly or the like; those who enumerate the virtues of different persons separately, as Gorgias does, are much more correct than those who define virtue in that way. Hence we must hold that all of these persons have their appropriate virtues, as the poet said of woman:

Silence gives grace to woman (Sophocles, *Ajax* 293)

though that is not the case likewise with a man. **[9]** Also the child is not completely developed, so that manifestly his virtue also is not personal to himself, but relative to the fully developed being, that is, the person in authority over him. And simi-

larly the slave's virtue also is in relation to the master.

* * *

1260b But on these subjects let us conclude our decisions in this manner; while the question of the virtue severally belonging to man and woman and children and father, and of the right and wrong mode of conducting their mutual intercourse and the proper way of pursuing the good mode and avoiding the bad one, are matters that it will be necessary to follow up in the part of our treatise dealing with the various forms of constitution. **[12]** For since every household is part of a state, and these relationships are part of the household, and the excellence of the part must have regard to that of the whole, it is necessary that the education both of the children and of the women should be carried on with a regard to the form of the constitution, if it makes any difference as regards the goodness of the state for the children and the women to be good. And it must necessarily make a difference; for the women are a half of the free population, and the children **[20]** grow up to be the partners in the government of the state. So that as these questions have been decided, and those that remain must be discussed elsewhere, let us relinquish the present subjects as completed, and make a fresh start in our discourse, and first let us consider those thinkers who have advanced views about the ideal State.

Questions

1. **Compare Aristotle's conception of the nature of men and women with that of Plato.**
2. **What implications does each of their views have for how an ideal state is governed?**
3. **Which thinker seems more contemporary and why?**

OPINIONS OF MODERN SCHOLARS

1.   THE STATUS OF WOMEN IN ATHENS

In this article, Gomme challenges the prevailing view that women in classical Athens occupied a low place in society. A. W. Gomme was Professor of Greek at the University of Glasgow.

FROM A. W. GOMME, "THE POSITION OF WOMEN IN ATHENS IN THE FIFTH AND FOURTH CENTURIES B.C."

IT IS A COMMONPLACE THAT, whereas in the Aegean age and in Homer the position of women was a noble one, in Athens of the classical period it was ignoble. For example:

> The best woman, according to the Athenian definition, is she of whom "least is said for either good or harm."...In this respect the Athenians were far less liberal than Sparta and other Grecian states. [Tucker, *Life in Ancient Athens*, p.51]
>
> "women, whom we nourish at home," a passage expressive of the contempt felt by the cultured Greeks for their wives [Starkie on Aristophanes' *Wasps*, 313]
>
> The position of Athenian women [in the time of Aristophanes] precluded the possibility of comedy in the highest sense.
>
> In Menander's hands the individualizing of female character and the freeing of the female will have gone but a little way: women were emerging from a state hardly above slavery, and his women are mentally without distinction.
>
> Women of the respectable class were condemned to comparative seclusion. They enjoyed far less freedom in fourth-century Athens than in the Homeric age.

And so forth. It will be admitted that these passages fairly give the prevailing view on the position of women in Athens; that this view is almost universally held...; and that it is expressed confidently, as on a matter which admits of no doubt, about which there is no conflict of evidence and which is well known to everyone. This paper is not an attempt to prove that this view is untrue; but that there is a conflict of evidence; that much that is relevant is ignored and other evidence misunderstood and misapplied; that is, that the confidence in the prevailing view is quite unjustified.

This view, then, is that legally, socially, and in general estimation women occupied a low place in Athens in the fifth and fourth centuries, lower than in most other Greek—especially Dorian—cities of the time, lower than in Homeric and in Aegean society and than in Rome, and of course much lower than in our own enlightened age. It will be agreed that these three aspects—the legal, the social, and that of general estimation—must be kept distinct. The women of France, for instance, in the matter of property and of political rights, are in an inferior position to those of England, but no one would suggest that they are socially less free or held in less honour. A resident alien in Athens and other Greek states had few rights, but he was free and had honour where honour was due. Slaves had no rights at all; but socially there was a nearer approach to equality between them and their masters than between rich and poor in England today, as can be seen from Aristophanes and Menander. Further, the *Arabian Nights* gives us a picture of a society where women have (practically) no legal rights and are socially confined, yet are the equals of men; for there love, and especially the comic side of being in love, is almost the only thing that matters, and (as in no other book that I know) men and women are equal, and very much alike, in this important part of life. And in fact the prevailing, and surely correct, view about the women of Homer is based not on the external details of their life, for after all Penelope weaves, Nausicaa washes clothes, and even glorious Helen works at her loom, but, rightly, on the part they play in the story, the way their characters are studied, the interest shown in them. But in Athens, we are told, women were powerless in law, scarcely stirred from the rooms in which they were locked, and were systematically treated with contempt.

Now there is a certain inconsistency in the expressions of the prevailing view, which is worth examining, as it at once suggests that our confidence should be modified. It has often been observed how great an interest is shown by the Athenian vase-painters of the late Fine Period in family life; but this period is that between 470 and 430 B.C., the period of Kimon and Perikles when women are generally thought to have been of least account, the period that closes with the Funeral Speech; and these vases were made chiefly for the Athenian market. To Van Leeuwen, as to many, Euripides is the rebel, and the herald of a new age; but of what age? Presumably of the fourth century; but others, such as Neil and Walker, assert the seclusion of women then; and I know of no general evidence pointing to any difference between the fourth and fifth centuries in this respect; we do not find—as we surely should—writers pointing out, whether for praise or blame, that women who in our fathers' time were slaves now are free. Aristophanes, of course, laughs at Euripides for making women talkative; but also for doing the same disservice to their husbands, making them different from Marathon men; so that does not help us.

Further: "Euripides gave the first place on his stage to women." True, but surely not more than Sophocles and Aeschylus had done? "It was no longer thought, as in their fathers' time, that to be silent was the first duty of women; nor that to say nothing about them was the highest merit of a work of art." Do, then, Clytemnestra and Antigone say nothing? Are their creators silent about them? In a fine passage on Euripides' women, Van Leeuwen writes:

> In brief, [Euripides] presented real women on stage, not some puppets making false claims to the female gender; there he appropriated for women the place which nature allotted to them in life itself, but men often denied them; thus he portrayed them as men—not true men primarily—but as men others had drawn before him. And this very thing Aristophanes rejected in his art; Aristophanes would have thought nothing of it, if a tragic poet had sometimes spoken contemptuously about women, while ignoring them in his work at other times.

But who were the others who had depicted men as Euripides did women? Who were the poets admired by Aristophanes who occasionally expressed contempt for women, and were otherwise silent about them? Certainly neither of the two great Athenians. I am not denying that Euripides may have raised questions then new to tragedy. But I am speaking of the general attitude of the three poets; and if the attitude of Euripides is significant in a discussion of the position of women at Athens, that of Aeschylus and Sophocles is not less so. There is, in fact, no literature, no art of any country, in which women are more prominent, more important, more carefully studied and with more interest, than in the tragedy, sculpture, and painting of fifth-century Athens.

* * *

When we make statements about the position of women in the Homeric age or in Minoan Crete as confident as those we make about Athens, we are relying, rightly, on the imaginative literature of the period in one case, on the art in the other. We have evidence of both kinds for Athens of the fifth century, and in far greater quantity. We have three poets—of very different temperaments—instead of one; we have sculpture, and hundreds, nay thousands, of painted vases. Yet this evidence is regularly ignored. Homer's Andromache, like Hektor, is proof of epic feeling; but for Athens only Jason and Kreon, not Antigone and Medea, are evidence. We may trust the paintings and the statuettes of Crete, but the Dresden Athena and the Sosandra of Kalamis mean nothing—that statue which Lucian so much admired for the grace of its pose, the comely arrangement and order of the drapery, the modest courtesy of its expression, the noble, scarcely visible smile, the foot just made for the dance, the pretty ankle....But even if we regard Attic tragedy and temple sculpture as remote from Attic life, as I think we cannot do, but if we do, we still have the innumerable vases and the sculptured tombs, which, if anything, give us a picture of contemporary Athens. They tell the same tale as tragedy. We can observe in them as in life, as indeed we might expect, that there are two sexes, and neither creates more interest, is more prominent, than the other. Imagine a student, especially favoured of Heaven, to come to the study of Homer, say, Sappho, Alkman, Simonides, and the three tragedians, and of Attic vases and sculpture, without having read anything that scholars have written about ancient life; would he suppose that there was anything remarkable about the position of women in Athens, except perhaps the special honour paid to them? Could he imagine that they were kept locked up and despised? "Ah," will be the answer, "that only shows the dangers of half-knowledge; wait till he comes to Thucydides and Aristotle." But at least there is a conflict of evidence, something that challenges thought and demands explanation? There is a puzzle?

* * *

I now come to evidence of another kind, which is generally supposed to establish, not merely to support, the prevalent view, and which I consider to be generally misapplied. There are numerous passages, numerously quoted, in Attic tragedies and comedies, expressive of the general sentiment, "a woman's sphere is the home" or "a good wife obeys her husband" (not a sentiment, by the way, very foreign to our own or any other time); others again of the type, "a wife is a necessary evil...." But what is the value of passages thus divorced from their context, dead fragments torn from the living organism of which they were once a part?

* * *

It is not difficult to recognize dramatic character in passages from books of our own time, when the whole books are known, just as we can guard ourselves against taking language too literally, and do not conclude from the existence of a women's corner in the newspaper that it necessarily follows that their interests are confined to subjects treated there, nor from the "Ladies' Enclosure" at Lord's that at the headquarters of cricket women are admitted indeed to the *agones* but excluded from the sight of men; it is difficult to be on our guard in dealing with ancient writings and fragments from them. But we have no right to suppose sententiousness in the place of dramatic propriety; to think that Euripides and Menander, any more than Jane Austen or Mr. Galsworthy, were not building up characters, but only felt inspired to add their quota to man's proud store of knowledge as to the proper conduct and destiny of women. I shall not be believed, I know; I shall be told I am reading into the Greek a meaning which the author never intended; but that seems to me at least more intelligent than to suppose that such lines had no meaning at all. If you glance at the chapters of Stobaios in which he has collected excerpts on marriage (that it is good to marry, that it is not good to marry, and that it is sometimes good and sometimes bad—such is his simple philosophy), if you look through these passages you will find that two, from Euripides, are as follows:

I envy the unmarried and childless of mortals;
For they have a single soul, and to feel its pain is
   only a moderate burden
and I shall say that marriage never causes delight
   more than grief

But these passages, though of much the same character, are never quoted by us, as the rest are, to prove the Athenian contempt for marriage. And no wonder, for we have their context. They come from the *Alcestis*.

It will be argued: "Well, there may be some truth in what you say; but what of those passages in which men most certainly spoke their real opinions? What, for example, of Perikles and Aristotle?"

[In his famous Funeral Oration] Perikles says:

If I must speak of women's special virtue,
I will put the whole matter in a nutshell:
great is their glory who can live up to
the nature that Providence has given to
women, and hers especially who is least
talked of amongst men either for good
or for evil.

I do not say that this means nothing; on the contrary, it is of great historical and psychological interest—note how Perikles speaks with the confidence which all men assume when talking on this subject; note also the contradiction involved in saying that her fame is great who is quite unknown. But what is its significance compared with the fact that Antigone, Alkestis, Hekabe, are heroines of the Attic stage? That you cannot read an Attic tragedy without finding women who are far from being unknown among men? What does it matter that Xenophon thought that girls up to the age of fifteen should be trained to see and hear as little as possible and ask as few questions as possible (and then be married and at once put into a position of great responsibility at the head of a large household)—on which we base our view that Athenian women had no intellectual education when we gather from the *Thesmophoriazusae* that they at least knew all about Euripides, from the *Lysistrata* that they were well up in politics, and from the *Ecclesiazusae* that they had the usual popular knowledge of the latest social theories? Women were at least educated enough to be corrupted by sophists and poets, just like men....

If Perikles said that women's only virtue was to be least spoken of among men either for good or for evil, that is, if this sentiment is rightly attributed to him (as I believe—he had a taste for paradox) and is not Thucydides' own, remember that these words were spoken by the man who was living with and was devotedly attached to the woman who was most talked about in Athens both for good and for evil—Aspasia, the Hera to his Zeus, the Deianira to his Herakles, the mistress of his household, and the hostess to that circle of men and women who were the acquaintance of Perikles....

We [next] come to Aristotle. That philosopher was a consistent believer in the inferiority of the female sex; it is a view which enters into his physiology and biology, his political and ethical, and his aesthetic theories. He does not say that women ought to be and in fact are confined to their homes, that they ought not and do not ever mix in society, that they are negligible beings, to be ignored or despised; only that they are, intellectually and morally, inferior to men. In this, as far as I can see, he is not peculiarly Greek, still less peculiarly Attic; in all ages, I suppose, we should find, if we were as honest and as outspoken as the Greeks, that the majority of men believed in their own superiority. Now Aristotle's expression of this view is interesting. In the *Politics* he is at great pains to distinguish between the rule of a master over his servants (the rule of superior over inferior), that of a parent over his children, and "citizen rule," *politiche arche*, the rule over persons free and equal, and to place the rule of husband over wife in the last category. There is indeed an important distinction; for whereas among citizens a man rules and is ruled in turn, the rule of husband over wife is permanent. But it is at least worthy of notice that Aristotle should, in any sense, put women in the class of the "free and equal." But he is even more interesting in the *Poetics;* as we should expect, both on general grounds and because he is dealing with Attic tragedy. He is speaking of Character in tragedy, in which

> there are four points to aim at. First and foremost, that they shall be good...Each type of personage has his own goodness; for a woman has hers, and a slave his, though the former's is perhaps less than a man's, and the latter's is wholly inferior. The second point is to make them appropriate. The Character before us may be, say, manly; but it is not appropriate in a female character to be manly, or clever. The third is to make them like the reality, which is not the same thing as their being good and appropriate, in our sense of the term...We have an instance...of the incongruous and unbefitting...in the speech of Melanippe...The right thing, however, is in the Characters just as in the

> incidents of the play to endeavour always after the necessary or the probable.
> [Aristotle, *Poetics*, 1454a16 ff.]

But if Aristotle in the words "perhaps less than a man's" is, as all now suppose, simply expressing the typical Greek "view" (as opposed, that is to say, to the Roman or the modern view), and if, moreover, he was living in a society where this view was put most vigorously into practice, where women had in fact no chance of showing character of *any* kind save in domestic wrangling, why does he only notice the incongruity of Melanippe's speech? Why not the far greater incongruity, unfemininity, unlikeness to life, of all the women of Attic tragedy—all but a few, Chrysothemis, Ismene, Andromache, and, if you will, Alkestis? Melanippe's speech is objected to apparently because it was a good politician's or lawyer's speech, and women were not public speakers. But Antigone—not one speech, but everything she does and says? "The right thing is always to endeavour after the necessary and the probable." How was Antigone a probable character in such an Athens as we suppose Aristotle to have known? We expect at least that he would have explained that this kind of improbability was inevitable, without it there would be no tragedy, though we could have wished it *exo tou dramatos.* ["outside the drama"] Indeed, there is no sense in which we can say that the "goodness" of Antigone is inferior to the "goodness" of Oedipus. Great observer as he was, Aristotle, as we know, was ever inclined to make his facts fit into his theories of the universe; and this instance is no exception. But here his cautious "perhaps"—a caution rare with him in general and not found in his other declarations of the inferiority of females—may be a sign that he was half-conscious of being up against facts that he could neither explain nor get rid of.

But we can go farther. The male, says Aristotle, is by nature superior, and the female inferior; and the former rules, and the latter is ruled; this principle, of necessity, extends to all mankind. But we have something else equally, if not more significant. We, when we wish to contrast our own practice with that of other peoples, speak—I do not profess to say with what justice—of an oriental treatment of women; we say, for instance, that Athenians treated their wives with a truly oriental contempt. It is surprising, but Aristotle uses much the same language: it is characteristic of barbarians, he says, that women are there treated as slaves. (I say surprising, because this passage is not quoted in our treatises on the subject, though it is from no remote book, but from the opening pages of the *Politics*). Plato says the same, so does Plutarch. I am not saying that Plato and Aristotle are correct in thus contrasting Greek and barbarian; but only that when they come across this phenomenon their feelings about it and their language are similar to our own.

* * *

Every country has its own conventions and customs, and Athens had hers: one gathers from the first speech of Lysias and elsewhere, for example, that it was a common thing for a man to invite a friend to dinner, at which his wife would not be present; there are no women in the glimpses of social life at Athens which Plato gives us; it would be difficult to imagine a modern comedy in the subject of the *Clouds* or the *Wasps,* in which the wives of Strepsiades and Philokleon did not play a prominent part (they are both mentioned, remember, but do not appear). One might recall other similar instances. But it has not been my intention to examine, however briefly, all the evidence. Let me repeat that all that I have tried to do is to prove that the matter is doubtful, that there is a problem to be solved. I do indeed believe that it is certainly wrong to speak of "Attic contempt" for women; and also

that there is no reason to suppose that in the matter of the social consequence and freedom of women Athens was different from other Greek cities, or the classical from the Homeric age—ancient writers seem to be unconscious of any such difference except in the special matter of the athletic training which girls received at Sparta. But, for the rest, I consider it very doubtful if Greek theory and practice differed fundamentally from the average, say, prevailing in mediaeval and modern Europe. When Theognis said, "I hate a woman who gads about and neglects her home," I think he expressed a sentiment common to most people of all ages; and at least there were gadabouts for him to disapprove of. After all, a great deal of Greek literature deals with the relations between the sexes in one form or another; and it would have died long ago if Greek sentiments had been radically opposed to ours. And, if the view which now obtains is correct, I would emphasize certain paradoxes: first and foremost, that in that case Attic tragedy and art are in one most important respect remote from Attic life—a phenomenon surely unique in history; that it was the lover of Aspasia who is thought particularly to have despised women; that it is when you come to the inner shrine, the intimate secrets of the platonic philosophy, that you meet Diotima; and that it was this unromantic people of Greece who created and preserved the story of Helen.

2. LAW, CUSTOM, AND MYTH: ASPECTS OF THE SOCIAL POSITION OF WOMEN IN CLASSICAL ATHENS

John Gould does not think that the imaginative literature of classical Athens can shed light on the role of women in that society. To avoid what he considers oversimplification of the issues, Gould examines the question from three points of view, that of law, custom, and myth. The selection from his article below considers law and custom. John Gould was HO Wills Professor of Greek at the University of Bristol.

FROM JOHN GOULD, *"LAW, CUSTOM AND MYTH: ASPECTS OF THE SOCIAL POSITION OF WOMEN IN CLASSICAL ATHENS"*

DISCUSSION OF THE SOCIAL POSITION of women in antiquity has been characterised by over—simplification of the issues, by concentration on the part of different investigators on mutually exclusive sets of data, and by a tendency (I think it is fair to say more marked here than elsewhere) to false statement which the actual evidence is enough

to rebut. If we ask why, as we must, the answer is surely clear. It is that we are dealing with a question which involves powerful and deep-seated emotional drives and in which, therefore, rationalisation plays a correspondingly large role. Part of the pleasure in reading Gomme's essay (and part of the danger in believing him) comes from our sense of the extent to which he is engaged emotionally in the quest for a satisfactory answer to the question as he puts it. But we have to be aware that the answer is going to have to satisfy emotional as well as rational requirements; and here is a second, and by far the most important ground for vigilance, for the tendency to rationalise can lead to strange conclusions. When Gomme sums up his position by saying that to the unprejudiced reader of Homer, Sappho, Alcman, Simonides and the three tragedians there is nothing "remarkable about the position of women in Athens, except perhaps the special honour paid to them" I can only gasp: that seems to me a simplistic fantasy.

* * *

When we speak of the social position of women, and mean by that more than just the social milieu in which they move, we are being dangerously vague in the terms we use, for it will make a very great difference whether we are speaking of women as daughters, as sisters, or as wives, and whether as wives or mothers; and it may make an equal difference whether we are speaking of the women of the rich or of the poor. We shall have to bear this vagueness in mind as we proceed: for the moment I only draw attention to it.

The juridical status of women in Athens is beautifully indicated by the single entry under "women" in the index to Harrison's *Law of Athens* i: it reads simply "women, disabilities." A woman, whatever her status as daughter, sister, wife or mother, and whatever her age or social class, is in law a perpetual minor: that is, like a male minor, but throughout her life she was in the legal control of a male *kyrios* who represented her in law. If unmarried she was in the *kyrieia* of her father, her brother(s) by the same father, or her paternal grandfather. Upon marriage a kind of divided *kyrieia* arose: the evidence seems to suggest that a father could dissolve his daughter's marriage, even against her wishes, whereas in other respects the husband acts as *kyrios*. On her husband's death she either passes to the *kyrieia* of her son(s) (if any) or reverts to that of her father if still alive: if her sons are minors she falls under the *kyrieia* of their *kyrios*. If she is pregnant on her husband's death she may (and perhaps must) remain in the *kyrieia* of whatever male affine will become her future child's guardian, that is to say, in the *oikos* of her deceased husband.

In relation to marriage the most instructive case of female disability at law is, of course, the situation of the *epikleros*. If a man dies leaving only a daughter or daughters, none of whom is married to one whom the father had already adopted as his son, such daughters become *epidiktoi*, "assignable," and are "assigned" by the archon eponymos to the nearest male kinsman in a fixed order of precedence....

The position of the *epikleros* is an extreme instance of the general rule that a woman has in law no standing in any question relating to her marriage, just as she has no legal right to own or dispose of property (I am using "just as" here in its strongest sense: the two disabilities are parallel and connected): in other cases it is her *kyrios* who, in law, determines whom a woman shall marry, and included in this right of the *kyrios* is a husband's right to dispose of his widow-to-be in prospect of his death. The connection with property is maintained in the rules governing dowries: any dowry that went with the woman in marriage is controlled by her husband *qua kyrios* but cannot be disposed of by him; on the husband's prior death or on dissolution of the marriage the dowry passes with her to her new *kyrios;* on the death of the wife without children born to her, the dowry reverts to her original *kyrios*. The maintenance of these rules, like those which govern the care and protection of wives, *epikleroi* and wards, are the concern of society in its formal, legal aspect and were probably the responsibility of the archon—again just as the oversight of "empty *oikoi*." In all this what is most striking is the strict parallelism between the formal rules controlling the treatment of women and those that govern the transmission and inheritance of property and of the right or obligation to avenge. Two further points will serve to bring this parallelism into sharper focus. The first act of the archon on entering office was to proclaim "all that any man possessed before he entered upon his office, that he should possess and control until the end of that office." It is hard not to see the archon's responsibility for preventing the ill treatment of women who are potential transmitters of property as stemming from this primary duty of protecting the rights of property. And the association of women and property is beautifully realised in the dual use of the word *engue*: Harrison rightly draws attention to H. J. Wolff's observation that "in origin the word *engue* (marriage), like *engue* (surety), implied transference with a reserved right to the transferor." The common element of a retained right in what is transferred derives, in the case of marriage, as Wolff points out, from the fact that the role of the woman in the transmission of property is a dual one: she may be required to produce the son necessary to ensure continuity of the *oikos* in the descent line of her father as well as (or instead of) in that of husband: hence, of course, the institution of the *epikleros*.

It is thus in their role as transmitters of property that the community displays concern for and extends protection to its women, and expresses such concern and protection within its formal, legal rules and institutions. The way in which it does so defines the woman as incapable of a self-determined act, as almost in law an un—person, outside the limits of those who constitute society's responsible and representative agents; and yet, at the same time, as precious and essential to the maintenance of a continuing social order and in particular to the continuity of property.

This contradictoriness of status becomes even more marked in the anomalous situation which we find when we try to define formally the sense in which a woman is a member of the community. In one sense, as we have already noticed, she clearly stands outside: she is not registered on the deme register and she is not a member of a phratry. It is significant that the pattern of naming and referring to women in public contexts reflects this: here we have a clear instance of "muting" in Ardener's sense. On Attic tombstones of women, even of the Hellenistic period, when a demotic (indicating membership of the community) occurs it agrees invariably with the name of the dead woman's father or husband, not with her own name: this contrasts with the case of non-Athenians, where the ethnic normally agrees with the name of the woman. The situation in legal contexts is even more striking. In the private speeches of Demosthenes twenty—seven women are actually named, in eight speeches: fourteen of these occur in one speech, Apollodorus' speech *against Neaira,* and significantly ten of these are alleged to be *hetairai:* the remaining four are slaves. There are for comparison five hundred and nine male names spread over thirty-three speeches. Demosthenes' own mother and sister, though he refers to them repeatedly in the five speeches devoted to the tangled issues of his inheritance, are never named. Neither is the unfaithful wife at the centre of Lysias' first speech, though the story of the marriage is told

in considerable detail. This is not accidental: David Schaps has recently shown how systematic is the avoidance of women's names throughout the speeches of the Attic orators. The only exceptions are women of low status or none (prostitutes, slaves); women connected with one's opponent (a clear extension of the first category); and the dead. Thus the names of women who have a respected place in the community are suppressed and they are referred to by complex periphrases which stress their status— dependence upon male kinsmen. Respect requires that they be treated, almost, as part of the property of father or husband. We may compare these facts both with our own system of surname changing by women upon marriage and with modern Greek usage, whereby a woman's surname is that of her father, then of her husband, in the possessive: "so and so's Miss or Mrs". Maniote custom is even more extreme: to address a married woman by the possessive use of her husband's Christian name, and never utter the woman's first name at all....

Thus in these contexts it is as though the woman has no personality and exists only as an extension of her male *kyrios*. On the other hand, after Pericles' citizenship law of 451/50 and its re-enactment in 403/2 the citizenship of a male Athenian and hence his legal personality depend upon his being the son of a mother who was, in Plutarch's formulation, "Athenian"; the word regularly used is *aste*. But status as an *aste* is not easy to define. It is noticeable that Aristotle offers no definition in the *Politics*. As we have seen, it is characteristically through her relationship to males or by her participation in deme or other rituals and by evidence of her marriage that a woman's status is upheld in courts of law: in other words, where it is not derived from kinship with males, a woman's status tends to be defined in terms of ritual functions.

In terms of law we are left then with a situation which appears internally contradictory and with definitions that seem inherently circular: women stand "outside" society, yet are essential to it (and in particular to its continued, ordered existence); their status derives from males but theirs, in turn, from the women who are their mothers.

* * *

Now in approaching the question of custom as it concerns the social position of women at Athens it is important, once again, to make ourselves aware of and be on our guard against the dangers of rationalisation and a *priori* argument. Those who, like Gomme, have sought to deny that anything that might be termed "seclusion" was characteristic of the customary treatment of women have evidently been largely motivated by their sense that if Athenian women were "secluded" it must follow that they were regarded and treated by men with "contempt"; that in some way, occupying the same space as men or moving in space with the same freedom is a necessary condition of equality of regard, or even of any degree of "respect" felt and shown by men to women. Gomme and his followers seemed to feel that if it is accepted that there were physical boundaries separating men from women in Athenian society, then in the eyes of men women are disregarded and despised and no account taken of their feelings in decisions that we should see as involving both. But of course it does not follow and the evidence is enough, I think, to show that it was not so.

On the one hand evidence for the existence of separate spheres of activity and within the house for separate areas of customary life is so strong and widespread that only a very powerful rationalising need could account for its being denied or ignored. I have already mentioned cases where this customary separation impinges on the social order of Greek tragedy; the orators provide us with more than enough to satisfy the most sceptical that such separation of male and female areas of life was normal.

* * *

The speaker of Lysias 1, Euphiletos, is charged with murder: it is therefore vital for him to show that there was no premeditation, and he provides a highly circumstantial account of all that led up to the killing of his wife's lover. He lays stress on the (apparent) normality of relations between himself and his wife: whether he is telling the truth or not is irrelevant to us. All we need bear in mind is that Euphiletos' domestic life is intended to sound normal. He describes the lay-out of his house, with its separate quarters for men and women, and how his wife, who was feeding their baby, frequently slept in the women's quarters so that she could feed and wash it in the night. The picture that emerges is, as it is intended to be, simple and convincing: a wife who leads a private, sheltered life, who goes out little (the affair with Eratosthenes begins, as so often in Menander, with a first sight of her at a public religious ritual, in this case a funeral); whose shopping is done by a slave woman; who, once her child is born, is no longer under her husband's surveillance, but who is not expected to be present when Euphiletos brings home a male friend for an evening meal. This last is of course a well-known feature of relationships within marriage in classical Athens: evidence of eating and drinking together with males who are not kinsmen is frequently presented in Athenian law courts as by itself establishing that a woman is a *pallake* or *hetaira* but not a wife.

This overall picture is not one that we have any *a priori* right, or evidence on which, to challenge. It can be reinforced in two ways. The first is from the evidence of house plans and vase paintings, as well as the comparative evidence of other cultures. Greek houses seem almost always to have one external door only: there is no "back door" at or through which women may come into contact with other outsiders than those who enter the house through the "front door." The men's quarters are commonly near to this street door or across the courtyard from the sole entrance. In two—storey houses it is a fair inference from the evidence of Lysias i that the women's quarters were normally on the upper floor: hence, it seems likely, the association between the women's quarters and the *mychos,* "recesses," of the house. On Attic vases women are characteristically seen indoors and in the company of other women. Outside the house they are shown fetching water and taking part in religious rituals, or in the doorway saying farewell to men leaving the house. In ancient Greece, as in modern, the woman's orientation is domestic: "of the house" as against "of the road." Moreover, the spatial distinction has its analogue in the temporal definition of a woman's role. It is of the essence of women's tasks that they be time—consuming; the provision of food, combing and spinning wool, weaving. The significance of this has recently been brought out by Hirschon in her study of female sexuality in a Peiraeus neighbourhood: just as spatial seclusion protects the woman from contact with males not of her own kin, so time-consuming tasks keep her out of mischief (the symbolism of Penelope's weaving is certainly relevant here, as is the night—milling slave woman of Od. xx)....

However, as I have suggested, it does not follow from this state of things that "contempt" is the appropriate term to describe male attitudes to, or behaviour towards, women. The evidence indeed contradicts any such assumption. But in examining it we have to make three preliminary distinctions: the first between private and public worlds, between "inside" and "outside" and the behaviour appropriate to each; the second between relationships which associate women with male kinsmen and the absence of any such relationships with unrelated males; and the third between relationships with men in general and those with other women, in particular the network of gossip relationships with neighbouring women. There is a nice example of the last in the water—rights case against Kallikles, Dem. lv. The speaker is arguing that any flood damage caused on Kallikles' estate by his father's having built a wall along the road separating the two estates, was minimal, and he produces the hearsay evidence of a conversation between his mother and Kallikles' mother which took place during a visit made by the former (by implication a normal occurrence). The impression left by this speech is of two parallel networks of relationship between unrelated neighbours, one involving the men, the other the women. What we do not find is any sort of relationship pattern between neighbours of opposite sex, and that is what we should expect from the evidence already produced.

On the other hand, relationships between women and their male kinsmen can be very close, can display a very high degree of warmth, tenderness and concern; of mutual understanding and tolerance; and of male acceptance, not only of the right of women to be consulted, but also of the initiative of women in the affairs of the family. On the other hand, of course, we can find in the evidence examples of an equally striking absence of these qualities. These facts will surprise only those who have accepted Gomme's tacit assumption and infer from the evidence for "seclusion" that such human feelings cannot have existed between men and women or, conversely (like Gomme himself) feel certain of the latter, and find themselves therefore impelled to deny the former.

The world "outside," the public world, is the world of men. In that world it is true that silence is the only ornament a woman has—with one striking exception. In the sacred and ritual activities of the community the active presence of women in the public world is not merely tolerated but required. As priestesses in many of the major cults of the *polis* (priestesses of gods as well as of goddesses), as *kanephoroi* and *hydrophoroi* in the great religious processions, as the *arrhephoroi* of Athena Polias, the "bears" of Artemis Brauronia, as raisers of the ritual scream, the *ololyge* at the blood sacrifice, in mourning and at funerals, in the rituals of marriage, the participation of women is indispensable to the sacral continuity, the ordering of society. The magnificent Panathenaic procession of the Parthenon frieze displays the ritual splendour and solemnity of the woman's role. And alongside the great civic rituals in which women stand with men as equal participants are those other rituals, just as much part of the sacred action of the community, which are either the exclusive domain of women or in which women play the leading role—rituals such as the Arrhephoria, the Skira, the Thesmophoria, the Lenaia, the Adonia. In these too the community expresses its sense of the necessary participation of women in its continuing life. Walter Burkert has recently shown that the eight-month long ritual tasks of the two young girls called *arrhephoroi*, chosen by the archon basileus from the great families of Athens, constitute a rite of initiation and incorporation into the community; and how the sacred objects round which the ritual revolves—the peplos of Athena Polias and the snake or phallos, the *arreta* ("secret [unspoken] things") contained in the covered basket that the girls carried in their night descent to the cave and well under the north cliff of the Akropolis—celebrate and symbolise the dual function of women in the community: spinning and weaving, the making of clothes, the *epya yvaikon* ("tasks of women"); and sex and marriage, the conception of the child, the continued existence of the community itself.

* * *

I have tried in this paper to show something of the true complexity of what we men summarize, brashly and arrogantly, as the social position of women, and to display the "complementarity" of law, custom and myth as they can contribute to a fuller grasp of that complexity.

I would like to end by going back to Gomme. It was the stimulation of qualified disagreement with him that first set me thinking about this subject: I hope it will be clear how much I owe to him. He was right, of course, to make such full use of the evidence of myth and imaginative literature; but surely wrong to insist that everything there is perfectly familiar to us and unsurprising. He refers, among other things, to the significance of "love" in the literature of Athens. When it is a matter of the "happy ever after" endings of Menander's comic universe, we are on familiar ground, indeed, but Gomme also quotes *Antigone*: "Eros, undefeated in battle, *eros*..." and there I want to say that *Eros* is not "love," and that Gomme might have gone on to quote the rest of the chorus. The *Eros* of that chorus is an implacable antagonist in an all—out war; *Eros*

"falls on property" (as a destroyer); he who "has *eros*" is out of his mind; *eros* warps the minds of the just (*dikaioi*) to injustice (*adika*) and destruction: above all, *eros* produces "quarrels between men who are tied by blood." It seems to me that any contemporary of Sophocles would have understood very well the bafflement of the Fingo elders when confronted with the impact of "love" on things as they understood them. They were trying, in 1883, to explain to the Cape Government Commissioners the sudden increase in illegitimate births and runaway marriages in their community, and they said: "the trouble arises through a thing called love. We do not comprehend this at all...This thing called love has been introduced."

3.   WOMEN AND RITUAL IN ANCIENT GREECE

In her 2007 book Joan Breton Connelly, Professor of Art History, Classics, at New York University, challenges the traditional belief among scholars that women did not play a prominent role in the public life of ancient Greece.

FROM JOAN BRETON CONNELLY, *PORTRAIT OF A PRIESTESS: WOMEN AND RITUAL IN ANCIENT GREECE*

AT THE END OF THE SECOND CENTURY B.C., Athenian worshippers set out in procession, marching from Athens to the sanctuary of Apollo at Delphi to celebrate the Pythais festival. The pageant was held in a grand manner "worthy of the god and his particular excellence." One individual stood out among the participants: Chrysis, priestess of Athena Polias. For her role in making the occasion one that befitted both Athens and Delphi, the people of Delphi bestowed upon Chrysis the crown of Apollo. The city also voted to grant her, as well as all her descendants, an impressive series of rights and privileges: status as a special representative of Athens to Delphi (*proxenos*), the right to consult the oracle, priority of trial, inviolability (*asylia*), freedom from taxes, a front seat at all competitions held by the city, the right to own land and houses, and all other honors customary for *proxenoi* and benefactors of the city. Back in Athens, Chrysis's cousins, Dionysios, Niketes, and Philylla, set up a statue of their famous

relative on the Acropolis. They themselves were prominent Athenians from a family distinguished by its numerous cult officials. Chrysis had a great-great-grandfather who was a sacred supervisor (*epimeletes*) of the Eleusinian Mysteries and a grandfather who was a priest of Asklepios. The decree set up by the people of Delphi and the statue base from the Athenian Acropolis provide a tantalizing glimpse into the life of an exceptional woman. While scores of inscriptions survive to honor men in this way, Chrysis stands out as one of the few women who received special privileges by decree. Her public record brought substantial rights for her and all her descendants, She further enjoyed the honor of having her statue set up on the Athenian Acropolis, ensuring that she would be remembered always in her priestly status.

Despite wide contemporary interest in the role of women in world religions, the story of the Greek priestess remains elusive. Scattered references, fragmentary records, and ambiguous representations confound attempts to form a coherent view of women who held sacred offices in ancient Greece. Yet the scope of surviving evidence is vast and takes us through every stage on the path through priesthood. It informs us about eligibility and acquisition of office, costume and attributes, representations, responsibilities, ritual actions, compensation for service, authority and privileges, and the commemoration of priestesses at death. Only by gathering far-flung evidence from the epigraphic, literary, and archaeological records can we recognize larger patterns that reveal the realities of the women who held office. This evidence provides firm, securely dated documentation from which we can bring to life the vibrant story of the Greek priestess.

This narrative is particularly important because religious office presented the one arena in which Greek women assumed roles equal and comparable to those of men. Central to this phenomenon is the fact that the Greek pantheon includes both gods and goddesses and that, with some notable exceptions, the cults of male divinities were overseen by male officials and those of female divinities by female officials. The demand for close identification between divinity and cult attendant made for a class of female sacred servants directly comparable to that of men overseeing the cults of gods. Indeed, it was this demand that eventually led to a central argument over the Christian priesthood, exclusively granted to male priests in the image of a male god. As Simon Price has stressed, the equality of men and women as priests and priestesses in ancient Greece was nothing short of remarkable. In a world in which only men could hold civic office and enjoy full political rights, it would have been easy enough for cities to organize their priesthoods on the model of magistracies. But the power of gender in the analogy between sacred servant and deity was so strong that it warranted a category of female cult agents who functioned virtually as public-office holders. Price has challenged us to consider the deeper question of why the Greeks so emphasized both genders for their gods. . . .

Evidence for priestesses can be found in nearly all categories of Greek texts, from Linear B tablets to epic and lyric poetry, histories, tragedies, comedies, political speeches, legal documents, public decrees, and antiquarian commentaries. Inscribed dedications attest to the generosity of priestesses in making benefactions to cities and sanctuaries, their pride in setting up images of themselves, and their authority in upholding sanctuary laws. Inscriptions also provide evidence that these women were publicly honored with gold crowns, portrait statues, and reserved theater seats. Priestesses are represented in nearly every category of visual culture, including architectural sculpture, votive statues and reliefs, funerary monuments, vases, painted shields, wooden plaques, and bronze and ivory implements. In the face of this abundant evidence it is hard to understand how the prominent role of the Greek priestess has, until recently, been ignored by modern commentators or, worse yet, denied.

* * *

Two important developments in scholarly thinking have made conditions ripe for a seasoned and comprehensive review of the evidence for Greek priestesses. One is a reassessment of the alleged seclusion of women in classical Athens and the implications of this for our understanding of their public roles, The other is a new questioning of the validity of the category of regulations called "sacred laws;" long viewed as distinct and separate from the larger body of legislation within the Greek polis. This opens the way for understanding female cult agents as public- office holders with a much broader civic engagement than was previously recognized. These two paradigm shifts make for a fresh and forward-looking environment in which we can evaluate the evidence, one that allows for a new understanding of the ancient realities of priestly women.

First, let us track developments on the question of the "invisibility" of women. Over the past thirty years, it has become a broadly accepted commonplace that Athenian women held wholly second-class status as silent and submissive figures restricted to the confines of the household where they obediently tended to domestic chores and child rearing. This has largely been based on the reading of certain well-known and privileged texts, including those from Xenophon, Plato, and Thucydides, and from certain images of women portrayed in Greek drama. The consensus posture of this view has, to a certain extent, been shaped by the project of feminism and its work in recovering the history of gender oppression.

* * *

"Presentist" Assumptions

The Greek priestess presents something of a dilemma, one that is often misunderstood by those who look to ancient models to find support for contemporary views. Any leap from Greek female priesthood to contemporary claims regarding ancient matriarchy or "Goddess cult" is off the mark and not founded upon hard evidence. Other misconceptions are more subtle and, understandably, emerge from the often-contradictory evidence. It is profoundly true that priesthood offered women a unique opportunity for public life, one in which they played leadership roles equal to those of their male counterparts. But this opportunity is too often described as a vehicle for a temporary "escape" from the private sphere of the household. "To choose to become a priestess meant a choice for becoming extraordinary," writes one scholar, though how much choice a woman had in the acquisition of priesthood remains doubtful. Her family's social status and financial resources were the determining factors in qualifying her for sacred office. She is more likely to have followed a family tradition of priestly service rather than to have schemed for an escape from household life. The equation of priesthood with independence suffers from the distorting effects of modern feminist hindsight.

This "escape" is regularly and wrongly described as one into a marginal position, that of the religious sphere, a place peripheral to the political and economic center of the polis. One common view holds that the dominant patriarchal ideology manipulated a supposed female aptitude for making contact with things dirty, dark, and polluted by assigning to women ritual presidency over transitional experiences, such as mourning and death. This is, by extension, seen as a justification for women's marginalized position within society at large. To be sure, women did oversee the tending of corpses and funerary rites. But while corpses were certainly considered polluting, women themselves were not at all regarded as dirty. The Greek attitude stands in contrast to how women were viewed within some Jewish and Christian traditions. A second common theme is one in which priesthood is understood as part of a strategy by which women, disenfranchised from the social and political life of their communities, could "establish indirect claims to status and attention." We are told that ritual enabled women to vent their aggression and frustration and to negotiate imbalances inherent in their subordinate positions. Ritual confirmed the constraints on women's lives and at the same time provided a release from them, a place where they could "develop a position of dissidence." The tone of these arguments seems to be colored by late twentieth-century political sensibilities. A third approach sees ritual as a respite for the drudgery of women's daily routine, a reward for good behavior in the home. Religious service has been described as one of the few "forms of entertainment open" to women. While there may be some truth in each of these positions, when taken together they leave us with a rather depressing, and not wholly accurate, view of the prospects for female cult agency. They seem to result from a theory of gender oppression that leaves little room for balancing or mitigating factors. The cumulative force of these arguments strips feminine sacred service of a measure of its dignity and discounts the potency of female agency within the totality of Greek cult and culture.

Religious festivals provided women and girls with important opportunities for public exposure and interaction, including the chance to see and be seen by potential candidates for marriage. A position of power in the organization of festivals allowed for increased opportunities to advance family interests. While festival participation has been viewed as an opportunity to satisfy the "male gaze;" and surely there was some of this at work, we can recognize a far more complex reality than this. Advancing family interests benefited women as well as men, and the priestesses presented in this study had a real stake in making the system work. One can, of course, take the position that priestly women were simply manipulated by a system that subjected them to the requirements of a male-dominated society. But one can also consider the force of the material evidence brought forward in this book and recognize a world in which women realized genuine accomplishment through their agency within the system. Greek priesthood was a religious, social, political, and economic business and women were indispensable in making this business a success.

* * *

As with so many aspects of the interpretative process, individual readings are greatly influenced by one's inclination to embrace the evidence with a "glass is half full" or a "glass is half empty" point of view, The pessimist will see limitations in the same place that the optimist will recognize opportunities. When it comes to ancient women, there has been a long-standing tendency to view the evidence through the "half empty" lens. Fascinatingly, the same position has been reached through very different paths, starting from very different places. Nineteenth century classicists, projecting the gender ideology of the Victorian elite onto the Greek household, ended up in roughly the same place as twentieth-century feminists who employed a "subordination theory" construct for managing the material. The result is the widely accepted commonplace of silent, submissive, "invisible" women, confined to the privacy of their households and wholly dominated by their men.

The cumulative effect of this long-standing tendency toward pessimism is that women's most visible roles in ancient Greek society have remained veiled, regularly relegated to footnotes advising us: "except in the case of priestesses." But we have seen evidence, fragmentary as it is, that priestesses spoke before Assemblies; fixed their seals on official documents; and, at least by Hellenistic times and maybe earlier, took their honored places in the front rows of theaters, Instead of highlighting the women who led public processions, made dedications in sanctuaries, and stepped forward on festival days to perform rituals and initiate sacrifices, the focus has rested on women locked indoors.

* * *

Modern interpreters have tended to read ancient evidence through a political lens rather than through a religious one. In doing so, they mostly see the limitations placed on Athenian women, excluded from the political and military life of the city. We must remember that the right to vote and to join the military were open to women in our own country just in the past century, roughly twenty-five hundred years after the Athenian women in question. The expectation that ancient women would have needed these same twentieth-century rights in order to lead meaningful and satisfying lives seems off the mark. Also, we can no longer say that women were excluded from the political life of the city, as we have redefined *political* to include the religious dimension, so deeply embedded within it. Athenian women did not, of course,

have the right to vote. But, as Josine Blok has pointed out, the Assembly met only 145 days a year, in contrast with the 170 annual festival days in the Athenian religious calendar. By a rough estimate, women participated in some 85 percent of all religious activities at Athens. They were in charge of more than forty major cults in the city, not to mention many minor ones. Modern skepticism toward things religious, and the marginalization of the importance of religious offices, have clearly contributed to the "muting" of ancient Greek women and the perception of their powers within the polis.

Even when women are recognized as central players within the religious sphere, we can detect a subtle whittling away of their status and position. Inscribed advertisements for the sale of priesthoods preserve the prices at which sacred offices were sold. It has been stressed that female priesthoods sold for less money than male priesthoods did and, by extension, that female offices were nor valued as highly.... [P]rices for priesthoods were directly commensurate with the privileges and dispensations that they brought. Male priesthoods could carry extraordinarily valuable dispensations from military service and garrison duties, burdens with no comparable hardship on the female side. This allowed them to be sold at a much higher rate than that of female offices, but in no way diminished the value that Greek society placed on women's sacred service. Similarly, perquisites paid to priestesses have been interpreted as reimbursements or taxes rather than as compensation for work. While the evidence may be inconclusive, we should be open to the possibility that, at least in some cases, women could keep their pay.

Benefactions from women donors have often been interpreted as gifts from husbands, who are perceived to have been the actual source of the finances. But many dedicatory inscriptions give women's proper names without mention of a husband or father. Indeed, roughly half of the 160 women named in dedicatory inscriptions from Hellenized Asia Minor are listed without any mention of male kin. Some dedications explicitly state that the financing came from the woman's own means. Yet there remains a predisposition to transfer the philanthropy to a husband or male relative. To be sure, most women functioned under the legal and financial guardianship of male relatives. But evidence shows that women had little trouble getting access to funds and directing them as they wished. Scores of female cult agents turned the resources of their *oikoi* toward sanctuaries that held very personal meaning for them.

Perhaps the most extreme example of modern denial of female cult agency is found in the discussion of women and blood sacrifice. The view that women were excluded from sacrifice because, like animal victims, they bleed, is a contemporary construct fabricated on cultural assumptions not shared in Greek antiquity.... [E]pigraphic evidence directly attests to women preparing, distributing, and eating sacrificial meat. Women's status within the hierarchy of cult service, in turn, has been qualified by those who view the butcher as the agent with highest rank. This notion is a product of Christianizing assumptions that see the priest as the singular representative of Christ in the reenactment of the sacrifice of Christ's body and blood. The primacy of the priest is a wholly alien concept in Greek worship, where anyone with a knife and victim could offer sacrifice. Women did not usually slit the throats of sacrificial victims because within the gender roles codified in the Greek household, the task of butchery usually fell to men. But this in no *way* suggests that a priestess's cult responsibilities were regarded as less than those of male priests.

Even the primacy of the most famous of all Greek priestesses, the Pythia at Delphi, has been questioned. As Maurizio has stressed, not one ancient source suggests that anyone other than the Pythia issued oracular responses. Still, modern interpreters persist in denying her the commanding role, shifting the authority for Delphic pronouncements to knowledgeable male priests. When we view the demotion of the Pythia within the broader context of widespread dismissal of female priestly prestige, we see a pattern through which sources are discounted in favor of what makes sense from a modern perspective.

Subtle biases can also be observed in the reading of images. [W]e considered the so-called eunuch priest from Ephesos, long regarded as a male rather than female figure, under the influence of tantalizing references to Megabyzos in Xenophon and Pliny. The inclination to view the Archaic *korai* from the Athenian Acropolis as goddesses may reflect a lingering disbelief that real maidens could merit such impressive images of their own. Even the statue of Nikeso, whose inscribed dedication

identifies her as the priestess of Demeter and Kore, has sometimes been viewed as an image of the goddess instead. When we do have a certain case in which an inscribed base holds a statue of a priestess, as that of Lysimache on the Athenian Acropolis, some interpreters try to reconstruct the lost portrait using a totally unrelated copy of a haggard, old woman. It is highly unlikely that a classical Greek priestess would have her life service on Acropolis represented through anything but a dignified, idealized image.

On the literary side, we see a hesitancy to recognize as "real" a number of women named as key players. Diotima, the wise prophetess of Mantineia whom Sokrates consults on the meaning of love, is regularly dismissed as a product of fiction (Plato *Symposium* 173–209). Yet interpreters are willing to accept any number of male characters in Plato's *Symposium* as reflections of historical men, including Sokrates, Aristophanes, Alkibiades, and Agathon. It is widely accepted that Aristophanes poked fun at the men of his day, Perikles, Alkibiades, Kleon, Sokrates, Euripides, and Kinesias among them. But with the exception of the forward-looking David Lewis, few have understood the profound implications of Aristophanes' choice in putting the historical priestesses Lysimache and Myrrhine on stage.

This brings us to the issue of the naming of Athenian women. From the 1970s, it has generally been agreed that the names of respectable women were not spoken aloud in classical Athens. This avoidance has been seen as part of the general "muting" of women in Athenian society, as reflected in the writings of Thucydides, Xenophon, Demosthenes, and Isaios, among others, and in Greek comedy. Again, we see the privileging of certain texts that support this view. But... the practice of sacred and civic eponymy ensured that priestly women, and their names, would never be forgotten. We have seen scores of female personal names inscribed on votive offerings, statue bases, and grave monuments and on dedications in streets, temples, and marketplaces.

In view of the evidence gathered here, it may be time to reconsider this consensus position. Certainly, there were contexts, including legal cases and the speeches of orators, in which women were identified, not by their personal names, but in relationship to their husbands, fathers, or other male relatives. But this could be out of respect or in order to identify them through the *oikoi* that offered them protection. Even today, we can speak of Mrs. Astor and Madonna in a single breath, but this does not mean that Mrs. Astor is being "muted"; or that she is without power in the society that identifies her in this way. Nonetheless, the prevailing view has been expressed as follows: " 'a woman' was not somebody to respect, but somebody's mother—or sister, or wife, or daughter—that was another matter." I imagine that some of the priestesses profiled in this book would be amazed by this statement. Indeed, we have seen women who were accorded enormous respect in their own rights by the cities and citizens that honored them.

* * *

At the end of Euripides' play, Praxithea stands alone on the Acropolis, having lost her husband as well as all her daughters in the saving of the city. Athena instructs her to build tombs and sacred precincts in honor of her family and to celebrate their memory with annual sacrifices and festivals. Then, Athena grants Praxithea the high honor of her priesthood and the extraordinary right to make burned sacrifice on the great altar. As queen, wife, mother, baker, builder, defender of the city's laws, initiator of fire sacrifice, and guardian of ritual, Praxithea stands as the prototype par excellence for Greek female priesthood. Hers is an ennobling model, one that embraces the selfless altruism that rests at the very heart of the democratic system that made Athens unique in the ancient world.

For at least seven centuries, Athenian women proudly took up the sacred office that was modeled on the ideal of Praxithea's service to goddess and city. Priestesses of Athena Polias, and priestly women like them across the Mediterranean world, assumed responsibilities, performed rites, made benefactions, instructed in traditions, and received substantial honors in return. As we have seen, these tributes included statues, crowns, theater seats, grave monuments, and the collective esteem of their communities. The body of evidence examined in this study has survived by chance across the great distances of time and space that separate us from Greek antiquity. There was surely even more that has been lost to us, at least for now, Yet it is brilliantly clear that priestesses loved their communities, served them well, and were long remembered by them. We can be certain that the contributions of these exceptional women deeply enriched, not just their cities, but also the ancient lives lived in them.

Consider

1. What difficulties do Gomme and Gould see with the prevailing view regarding the social position of women in classical Greece?
2. Discuss Gomme's understanding of Plato's and Pericles' view of women. Is the experience of Aspasia relevant and indicative of the status of classical Greek women?
3. How does Gomme handle the misogyny of Aristotle?
4. What is the connection between the legal and social status of women for Gould when considering marriage, inheritance, and dowries?
5. Use examples to show how Gould's position differs from that of Gomme regarding the Greek custom of separating the spheres of activity of men from those of women?
6. Why is examining religious office important in determining the position of women in Greek society according to Connelly?
7. How does ancient Greek religion compare with modern Christianity?
8. Contrast modern Western Christian notions of priesthood with those of the ancient Greeks.
9. What were the functions of priests and priestesses in ancient Greece?

10. Explain the modern misconceptions about Greek female priesthood and the sources of these errors according to Connelly?
11. Discuss several factors she thinks have stood in the way of a proper assessment of the role of women.
12. What might be the result of recognizing Connelly's alternative model of the status of women in classical Greece?

CHAPTER 8
PERICLEAN ATHENS: WAS IT A DEMOCRACY?

ﻬ

ATHENS IN THE TIME OF PERICLES is often regarded as the perfect model of a direct democracy. With its popular assembly, its law courts, and its magistrates popularly elected or chosen by lot, Athens might seem beyond dispute the most democratic of states. Yet, to a shrewd contemporary observer, Thucydides the historian, it was a "democracy in name but the rule of the first citizen in fact."

The problem is compounded by the absence of any systematic statement of democratic theory written by a Greek democrat. Our understanding of Greek democracy, therefore must be achieved by putting together scattered references in speeches by democratic statesmen—the funeral oration of Pericles, for instance, with the accounts of such enemies of democracy as Plato and the "Old Oligarch." Even less tendentious accounts such as those of Aristotle, Thucydides, and Plutarch are tinged with antidemocratic bias.

We should remember that by the time of Pericles' acme (c. 443–429 BC) democracy was over a half-century old in Athens. Cleisthenes had introduced what we may properly call a democratic regime in the last decade of the sixth century BC. Although the highest offices in the state were reserved for the upper classes, all male adult Athenians could vote and serve on the Council of Five Hundred and on the juries. The reforms of Themistocles in the years between Marathon (490 BC) and the great Persian War (480–479 BC) opened all offices to the people and, in increasing the importance of the navy, gave increased political power to the lower classes, who rowed the ships. Ephialtes' successful attack on the Areopagus (462 BC), the great bastion of aristocratic influence, cleared the way for even greater popular power.

Pericles continued the trend toward democracy by introducing pay for public service. It was possible, nevertheless, for ancient and modern writers to speak of Periclean Athens as undemocratic and even monarchical. To be sure, after the ostracism of Thucydides, son of Melesias, in 443 BC, Pericles was never again faced with a serious political rival. It is also true that he seemed to guide Athenian policy without much hindrance. Yet none of this need be inconsistent with democratic government properly understood, as Malcolm McGregor argues.

Modern scholars have taken up the debate and added several dimensions to it by arguing that a society that ruled an empire, employed slaves, consigned women to a subordinate position, and had significantly illiberal characteristics can hardly be called a democracy. Paul Rahe argues that Periclean Athens was significantly different from modern liberal democracies.

Ancient Sources

1. Thucydides, 2.35–46, PERICLES ON DEMOCRACY
2. Aristotle, *Constitution of the Athenians*, 26–28, ARISTOTLE ON PERICLES AND ATHENIAN DEMOCRACY

Pericles (c. 495–429 BC) was the leading statesman of Athens for much of the fifth century. This is a Roman copy in marble of the Greek bronze bust that was probably cast in the last decade of Pericles' life. *Source:* Library of Congress.

3. Pseudo-Xenophon, *Constitution of the Athenians*, 1–3, THE OLD OLIGARCH
4. Plato, *Gorgias*, 515–517, CRITIQUE OF PERICLEAN DEMOCRACY
5. Plutarch, *Pericles*, 9, 11–12, 14–16, 31–35, 37, THE AGE OF PERICLES

Opinions of Modern Scholars

1. From Georg Busolt, *Griechische Geschichte*
2. From Malcolm McGregor, "The Politics of the Historian Thucydides"
3. From Paul A. Rahe, *Republics Ancient and Modern*

ANCIENT SOURCES FOR PERICLEAN ATHENS

1. PERICLES ON DEMOCRACY

In the winter following the first campaigns of the Peloponnesian War, Pericles was chosen to pronounce the customary eulogy over the fallen warriors. He turned it instead into an occasion to praise the Athenian state, its constitution, and its way of life. Thucydides, who was almost surely present, reported the speech in full.

2.35.1 Most of my predecessors in this have commended him who made this speech part of the law, telling us that it is well that it should be delivered at the burial of those who fall in battle. For myself, I should have thought that the worth which had displayed itself in deeds would be sufficiently rewarded by honours also shown by deeds; such as you now see in this funeral prepared at the people's cost. And I could have wished that the reputations of many brave men were not to be imperiled in the mouth of a single individual, to stand or fall according as he spoke well or ill. **[2]** For it is hard to speak properly upon a subject where it is even difficult to convince your hearers that you are speaking the truth. On the one hand, the friend who is familiar with every fact of the story may think that some point has not been set forth with that fullness which he wishes and knows it to deserve; on the other, he who is a stranger to the matter may be led by envy to suspect exaggeration if he hears anything above his own nature. For men can endure to hear others praised only so long as they can severally persuade themselves of their own ability to equal the actions recounted: when this point is passed, envy comes in and with it incredulity. **[3]** However, since our ancestors have stamped this custom with their approval, it becomes my duty to obey the law and to try to satisfy your several wishes and opinions as best I may.

2.36.1 I shall begin with our ancestors: it is both just and proper that they should have the honour of the first mention to an occasion like the present. They dwelt in the country without break in the succession from generation to generation, and handed it down free to the present time by their valour. **[2]** And if our more remote ancestors deserve praise, much more do our own fathers, who added to their inheritance the empire which we now possess, and spared no pains to be able to leave their acquisitions to us of the present generation. **[3]** Lastly, there are few parts of our dominions that have not been augmented by those of us here, who are still more or less in the vigour of life; while the mother country has been furnished by us with everything that can enable her to depend on her own resources whether for war or for peace. **[4]** That part of our history which tells of the military achievements which gave us our several possessions, or of the ready valour with which either we or our fathers stemmed the tide of Hellenic or foreign aggression, is a theme too familiar to my hearers for me to dilate on, and I shall therefore pass it by. But what was the road by which we reached our position, what the form of government under which our greatness grew, what the national habits out of which it sprang; these are questions which I may try to solve before I proceed to my panegyric upon these men; since I think this to be a subject upon which on the present occasion a speaker may properly dwell, and to which the whole assemblage, whether citizens or foreigners, may listen with advantage.

2.37.1 Our constitution does not copy the laws of neighbouring states; we are rather a pattern to others than imitators ourselves. Its administration favours the many instead of the few; this is why it is called a democracy. If we look to the laws, they afford equal justice to all in their private differences; if to social standing, advancement in public life falls to reputation for capacity, class considerations not being allowed to interfere with merit; nor again does poverty bar the way, if a man is able to serve the state, he is not hindered by the obscurity of his condition. **[2]** The freedom which we enjoy in our government extends also to our ordinary life. There, far from exercising a jealous surveillance over each other, we do not feel called upon to be angry with our neighbour for doing what he likes, or even to indulge in those injurious looks which cannot fail to be offensive, although they inflict no positive penalty. **[3]** But all this ease in our private relations does not make us lawless as citizens. Against this fear is our chief safeguard, teaching us to obey the magistrates and the laws, particularly such as regard the protection of the injured, whether they are actually on the statute book, or belong to that code which, although unwritten, yet cannot be broken without acknowledged disgrace.

2.38.1 Further, we provide plenty of means for the mind to refresh itself from business. We celebrate games and sacrifices all the year round, and the elegance of our private establishments forms a daily source of pleasure and helps to banish the spleen; **[2]** while the magnitude of our city draws the produce of the world into our harbour, so that to the Athenian the fruits of other countries are as familiar a luxury as those of his own.

2.39.1 If we turn to our military policy, there also we differ from our antagonists. We throw open our city to the world, and never by alien acts exclude foreigners from any opportunity of learning or observing, although the eyes of an enemy may occasionally profit by our liberality; trusting less in system and policy than to the native spirit of our citizens; while in education, where our rivals from their very cradles by a painful discipline seek after manliness, at Athens we live exactly as we please, and yet are just as ready to encounter every legitimate danger. **[2]** In proof of this it may be noticed that the Lacedaemonians do not invade our country alone, but bring with them all their confederates; while we Athenians advance unsupported into the territory of a neighbour, and fighting upon a foreign soil usually vanquish with ease men who are defending their homes. **[3]** Our united force was never yet encountered by any enemy, because we have at once to attend to our marine and to despatch our citizens by land upon a hundred different services; so that, wherever they engage with some such fraction of our strength, a success against a detachment is magnified into a victory over the nation, and a defeat into a reverse suffered at the hands of our entire people. **[4]** And yet if with habits not of labour but of ease, and courage not of art but of nature, we are still willing to encounter danger, we have the double advantage of escaping the experience of hardships in anticipation and of facing them in the hour of need as fearlessly as those who are never free from them.

2.40.1 Nor are these the only points in which our city is worthy of admiration. We cultivate refinement without extravagance and knowledge without effeminacy; wealth we employ more for use than for show, and place the real disgrace of poverty not in

owning to the fact but in declining the struggle against it. **[2]** Our public men have, besides politics, their private affairs to attend to, and our ordinary citizens, though occupied with the pursuits of industry, are still fair judges of public matters; for, unlike any other nation, regarding him who takes no part in these duties not as unambitious but as useless, we Athenians are able to judge at all events if we cannot originate, and instead of looking on discussion as a stumbling-block in the way of action, we think it an indispensable preliminary to any wise action at all. **[3]** Again, in our enterprises we present the singular spectacle of daring and deliberation, each carried to its highest point, and both united in the same persons; although usually decision is the fruit of ignorance, hesitation of reflexion. But the palm of courage will surely be adjudged most justly to those who best know the difference between hardship and pleasure and yet are never tempted to shrink from danger. **[4]** In generosity we are equally singular, acquiring our friends by conferring not by receiving favours. Yet, of course, the doer of the favour is the firmer friend of the two, in order by continued kindness to keep the recipient in his debt; while the debtor feels less keenly from the very consciousness that the return he makes will be a payment, not a free gift. **[5]** And it is only the Athenians who, fearless of consequences, confer their benefits not from calculations of expediency, but in the confidence of liberality.

2.41.1 In short, I say that as a city we are the school of Hellas; while I doubt if the world can produce a man, who where he has only himself to depend upon, is equal to so many emergencies, and graced by so happy a versatility as the Athenian. **[2]** And that this is no mere boast thrown out for the occasion, but plain matter of fact, the power of the state acquired by these habits proves. **[3]** For Athens alone of her contemporaries is found when tested to be greater than her reputation, and alone gives no occasion to her assailants to blush at the antagonist by whom they have been worsted, or to her subjects to question her title by merit to rule. **[4]** Rather, the admiration of the present and succeeding ages will be ours, since we have not left our power without witness, but have shown it by mighty proofs; and far from needing a Homer for our panegyrist, or other of his craft whose verses might charm for the moment only for the impression which they gave to melt at the touch of fact, we have forced every sea and land to be the highway of our daring, and everywhere, whether for evil or for good, have left imperishable monuments behind us. **[5]** Such is the Athens for which these men, in the assertion of their resolve not to lose her, nobly fought and died; and well may every one of their survivors be ready to suffer in her cause.

2.42.1 Indeed if I have dwelt at some length upon the character of our country, it has been to show that our stake in the struggle is not the same as theirs who have no such blessings to lose, and also that the panegyric of the men over whom I am now speaking might be by definite proofs established. **[2]** That panegyric is now in a great measure complete; for the Athens that I have celebrated is only what the heroism of these and their like have made her, men whose fame, unlike that of most Hellenes, will be found to be only commensurate with their desserts. And if a test of worth be wanted, it is to be found in their closing scene, and this not only in the cases in which it set the final seal upon their merit, but also in those in which it gave the first intimation of their having any. **[3]** For there is justice in the claim that steadfastness in his country's battles should be as a cloak to cover a man's other imperfections; since the good action has blotted out the bad, and his merit as a citizen more than outweighed his demerits as an individual. **[4]** But none of these allowed either wealth with its prospect of future enjoyment to unnerve his spirit, or poverty with its hope of a day of freedom and riches to tempt him to shrink from danger. No, holding that vengeance upon their enemies was more to be desired than any personal blessings, and reckoning this to be the most glorious of hazards, they joyfully determined to accept the risk, to make sure of their vengeance and to let their wishes wait; and while committing to hope the uncertainty of final success, in the business before them they thought fit to act boldly and trust in themselves. Thus choosing to die resisting, rather than to live submitting, they fled only from dishonour, but met danger face to face, and after one brief moment, while at the summit of their fortune, escaped, not from their fear, but from their glory.

2.43.1 So died these men as became Athenians. You, their survivors, must determine to have as unaltering a resolution in the field, though you may pray that it may have a happier issue. And not contented with ideas derived only from words of the advantages which are bound up with the defence of your country, though these would furnish a valuable text to a speaker even before an audience so

alive to them as the present, you must yourselves realise the power of Athens, and feed your eyes upon her from day to day, till love of her fills your hearts; and then when all her greatness shall break upon you, you must reflect that it was by courage, sense of duty, and a keen feeling of honour in action that men were enabled to win all this, and that no personal failure in an enterprise could make them consent to deprive their country of their valour, but they laid it at her feet as the most glorious contribution that they could offer. **[2]** For this offering of their lives made in common by them all they each of them individually received that renown which never grows old, and for a sepulchre, not so much that in which their bones have been deposited, but that noblest of shrines wherein their glory is laid up to be eternally remembered upon every occasion on which deed or story shall fall for its commemoration. **[3]** For heroes have the whole earth for their tomb; and in lands far from their own, where the column with its epitaph declares it, there is enshrined in every breast a record unwritten with no tablet to preserve it, except that of the heart. **[4]** These take as your model, and judging happiness to be the fruit of freedom and freedom of valour, never decline the dangers of war. **[5]** For it is not the miserable that would most justly be unsparing of their lives; these have nothing to hope for: it is rather they to whom continued life may bring reverses as yet unknown, and to whom a fall, if it came, would be most tremendous in its consequences. **[6]** And surely, to a man of spirit, the degradation of cowardice must be immeasurably more grievous than the unfelt death which strikes him in the midst of his strength and patriotism!

2.44.1 Comfort, therefore, not condolence, is what I have to offer to the parents of the dead who may be here. Numberless are the chances to which, as they know, the life of man is subject; but fortunate indeed are they who draw for their lot a death so glorious as that which has caused your mourning, and to whom life has been so exactly measured as to terminate in the happiness in which it has been passed. **[2]** Still I know that this is a hard saying, especially when those are in question of whom you will constantly be reminded by seeing in the homes of others blessings of which once you also boasted: for grief is felt not so much for the want of what we have never known, as for the loss of that to which we have been long accustomed. **[3]** Yet you who are still of an age to beget children must bear up in the hope of having others in their stead; not only will they help you to forget those whom you have lost, but will be to the state at once a reinforcement and a security; for never can a fair or just policy be expected of the citizen who does not, like his fellows, bring to the decision the interests and apprehensions of a father. **[4]** While those of you who have passed your prime must congratulate yourselves with the thought that the best part of your life was fortunate, and that the brief span that remains will be cheered by the fame of the departed. For it is only the love of honour that never grows old; and honour it is, not gain, as some would have it, that rejoices the heart of age and helplessness.

2.45.1 Turning to the sons or brothers of the dead I see an arduous struggle before you. When a man is gone, all are wont to praise him, and should your merit lie ever so transcendent, you will still find it difficult not merely to overtake, but even to approach their renown. The living have envy to contend with, while those who are no longer in our path are honoured with a goodwill into which rivalry does not enter. **[2]** On the other hand, if I must say anything on the subject of female excellence to those of you who will now be in widowhood, it will be all comprised in this brief exhortation. Great will be your glory in not falling short of your natural character; and greatest will be hers who is least talked of among the men whether for good or for bad.

2.46.1 My task is now finished. I have performed it to the best of my ability, and in words, at least, the requirements of the law are now satisfied. If deeds be in question, those who are here interred have received part of their honours already, and for the rest, their children will be brought up till manhood at the public expense: the state thus offers a valuable prize, as the garland of victory in this race of valour, for the reward both of those who have fallen and their survivors. And where the rewards for merit are greatest, there are found the best citizens. **[2]** And now that you have brought to a close your lamentations for your relatives, you may depart.

Questions

1. **What qualities does Pericles claim for the city of Athens and its people?**
2. **With whom does he compare these qualities?**
3. **What reasons does he give the Athenians for fighting the war to a victorious conclusion?**

---

2. ARISTOTLE ON PERICLES AND ATHENIAN DEMOCRACY

Here is the Aristotelian view of Pericles and the Athenian democracy of his time.

26.1 [After the reduction in the powers of the Aeropagus] there came about an increased relaxation of the constitution, due to the eagerness of those who were the leaders of the People. For it so happened that during these periods the better classes had no leader at all but the chief person among them, Cimon son of Miltiades, was a rather young man who had only lately entered public life; and in addition, that the multitude had suffered seriously in war, for in those days the expeditionary force was raised from a muster roll, and was commanded by generals with no experience of war but promoted on account of their family reputations, so that it was always happening that the troops on an expedition suffered as many as two or three thousand casualties, making a drain on the numbers of the respectable members both of the people and of the wealthy. **[2]** Thus in general all the administration was conducted without the same attention to the laws as had been given before, although no innovation was made in the election of the Nine Archons, except that five years after the death of Ephialtes they decided to extend to the zeugitai class eligibility to the preliminary roll from which the Nine Archons were to be selected by lot; and the first of the zeugitai class to hold the archonship was Mnesitheides. All the Archons hitherto had been from the hippeis and pentakosiomedimnoi, while the zeugitai held the ordinary offices, unless some provision of the laws was ignored. **[3]** Four years afterwards, in the archonship of Lysicrates, the thirty judges called the Local Justice were instituted again; and two years after Lysicrates, in the year of Antidotus owing to the large number of the citizens an enactment was passed on the proposal of Pericles confining citizenship to persons of citizen birth on both sides.

27.1 After this, when Pericles advanced to the leadership of the people, having first distinguished himself when, while still a young man, he challenged the audits of Cimon who was a general, it came about that the constitution became still more democratic. For he took away some of the functions of the Areopagus, and he urged the state very strongly in the direction of naval power which resulted in emboldening the multitude, who brought all the government more into their own hands. **[2]** Forty-eight years after the naval battle of Salamis, in the archonship of Pythodorus, the war against the Peloponnesians broke out during which the people being locked up in the city, and becoming accustomed to earning pay on their military campaigns, came partly of their own will and partly against their will to the decision to administer the government themselves. Also Pericles first made service in the jury-courts a paid office, as a popular counter-measure against Cimon's wealth. **[3]** For as Cimon had an estate large enough for a tyrant, in the first place he discharged the general public service in a brilliant manner, and moreover he supplied maintenance to a number of the members of his deme; nor anyone of the Laciadae who liked could come to his house every day and have a moderate supply, and also all his farms were unfenced, to enable anyone who liked to avail himself of the harvest. **[4]** So as Pericles' means were insufficient for this lavishness, he took the advice of Damonides of Oea (who was believed to suggest to Pericles most of his measures, owing to which they afterwards ostracized him), since he was getting the worst of it with his private resources, to give the multitude what was their own, and he instituted payment for the jury-courts; the result of which according to some critics was their deterioration, because ordinary persons always took more care than the respectable to cast lots for the duty. **[5]** Also it was after this that the organized bribery of juries began, Anytus having first shown the way to it after his command at Pylos; for when he was brought to trial by certain persons for having lost Pylos he bribed the court and got off.

28.1 So long, then, as Pericles held the headship of the People, the affairs of the state went better, but when Pericles was dead they became much worse. For the People now for the first time adopted a head who was not in good repute with the respectable classes, whereas in former periods those always continued to lead the People.

Questions

1. How would you characterize Aristotle's judgment of Periclean Athens?

2. What does he praise and with what does he find fault?

---

3. THE OLD OLIGARCH

The following selection is from a pamphlet on the Athenian constitution that has come down to us among the works of Xenophon. The anonymous author is usually called the "Old Oligarch." Internal evidence places the date of the treatise toward the beginning of the Peloponnesian War (c. 425 BC). The author was thus, like Thucydides the historian, a contemporary of Pericles. His views, though different from those of Thucydides, are not to be dismissed.

1.1 Now, as for the constitution of the Athenians, and the type or manner of constitution which they have chosen, I praise it not, in so far as the very choice involves the welfare of the baser folk as opposed to that of the better class. I repeat, I withhold my praise so far; but, given the fact that this is the type agreed upon, I propose to show that they set about its preservation in the right way; and that those other transactions in connection with it, which are looked upon as blunders by the rest of the Hellenic world, are the reverse.

1.2 In the first place, I maintain, it is only just that the poorer classes and the common people of Athens should be better off than the men of birth and wealth, seeing that it is the people who man the fleet, and have brought the city her power. The steersman, the boatswain, the lieutenant, the look-out man at the prow, the shipwright—these are the people who supply the city with power far rather than her heavy infantry and men of birth and quality. This being the case, it seems only just that offices of state should be thrown open to everyone both in the ballot and the show of hands, and that the right of speech should belong to any one who likes, without restriction.

1.3 For, observe, there are many of these offices which, according as they are in good or in bad hands, are a source of safety or of danger to the People, and in these the People prudently abstains from sharing; as, for instance, it does not think it incumbent on itself to share in the functions of the general or of the commander of cavalry. The commons recognises the fact that in forgoing the personal exercise of these offices, and leaving them to the control of the more powerful citizens, it secures the balance of advantage to itself. It is only those departments of government which bring pay and assist the private estate that the People cares to keep in its own hands.

1.4 In the next place, in regard to what some people are puzzled to explain—the fact that everywhere greater consideration is shown to the base, to poor people and to common folk, than to persons of good quality—so far from being a matter of surprise, this, as can be shown, is the keystone of the preservation of the democracy. It is these poor people, this common folk, this worse element, whose prosperity, combined with the growth of their numbers, enhances the democracy. Whereas, a shifting of fortune to the advantage of the wealthy and the better classes implies the establishment on the part of the commons of a strong power in opposition to itself. **1.5** In fact, all the world over, the cream of society is in opposition to the democracy. Naturally, since the smallest amount of intemperance and injustice, together with the highest scrupulousness in the pursuit of excellence, is

to be found in the ranks of the better class, while within the ranks of the People will be found the greatest amount of ignorance, disorderliness, rascality—poverty acting as a stronger incentive to base conduct, not to speak of lack of education and ignorance, traceable to the lack of means which afflicts the average of mankind.

1.6 The objection may be raised that it was a mistake to allow the universal right of speech and a seat in council. These should have been reserved for the cleverest, the flower of the community. But here, again, it will be found that they are acting with wise deliberation in granting to even the baser sort the right of speech, for supposing only the better people might speak, or sit in council, blessings would fall to the lot of those like themselves, but to the commons the reverse of blessings. Whereas now, anyone who likes, any base fellow, may get up and discover something to the advantage of himself and his equals. **1.7** It may be retorted, "And what sort of advantage either for himself or for the People can such a fellow be expected to hit upon?" The answer to which is, that in their judgment the ignorance and the baseness of this fellow, together with his goodwill, are worth a great deal more to them than your superior person's virtue and wisdom, coupled with animosity. **1.8** What it comes to, therefore, is that a state founded upon such institutions will not be the best state; but, given a democracy, these are the right means to secure its preservation. The People, it must be borne in mind, does not demand that the city should be well governed and itself a slave. It desires to be free and to be master. As to bad legislation it does not concern itself about that. In fact, what you believe to be bad legislation is the very source of the People's strength and freedom. **1.9** But if you seek for good legislation, in the first place you will see the cleverest members of the community laying down the laws for the rest. And in the next place, the better class will curb and chastise the lower orders; the better class will deliberate in behalf of the state, and not suffer crack-brained fellows to sit in council, or to speak or vote in the assemblies. No doubt; but under the weight of such blessings the People will in a very short time be reduced to slavery.

1.10 Another point is the extraordinary amount of license granted to slaves and resident aliens at Athens, where a blow is illegal, and a slave will not step aside to let you pass him in the street. I will explain the reason of this peculiar custom. Supposing it were legal for a slave to be beaten by a free citizen, or for a resident alien or freedman to be beaten by a citizen, it would frequently happen that an Athenian might be mistaken for a slave or an alien and receive a beating; since the Athenian People is not better clothed than the slave or alien, nor in personal appearance is there any superiority. **1.11** Or if the fact itself that slaves in Athens are allowed to indulge in luxury, and indeed in some cases to live magnificently, be found astonishing, this too, it can be shown, is done of set purpose. Where you have a naval power dependent upon wealth we must perforce be slaves to our slaves, in order that we may get in our slave-rents, and let the real slave go free. Where you have wealthy slaves it ceases to be advantageous that my slave should stand in awe of you. In Lacedaemon my slave stands in awe of you. But if your slave is in awe of me there will be a risk of his giving away his own moneys to avoid running a risk in his own person. **1.12** It is for this reason then that we have established an equality between our slaves and free men; and again between our resident aliens and full citizens, because the city stands in need of her resident aliens to meet the requirements of such a multiplicity of arts and for the purposes of her navy. That is, I repeat, the justification of the equality conferred upon our resident aliens.

1.13 The common people put a stop to citizens devoting their time to athletics and to the cultivation of music, disbelieving in the beauty of such training, and recognising the fact that these are things the cultivation of which is beyond its power. On the same principle, in the case of the choregia, the management of athletics, and the command of ships, the fact is recognised that it is the rich man who trains the chorus, and the People from whom the chorus is trained; it is the rich man who is naval commander or superintendent of athletics, and the People that profits by their labours. In fact, what the People looks upon as its right is to pocket the money. To sing and run and dance and man the vessels is well enough, but only in order that the People may be the gainer, while the rich are made poorer. And so in the courts of justice, justice is not more an object of concern to the jurymen than what touches personal advantage.

1.14 To speak next of the allies, and in reference to the point that emissaries from Athens come out, and, according to common opinion, calumniate and vent their hatred upon the better sort of people, this is done on the principle that the ruler cannot help being hated by those whom he rules; but that if wealth and respectability are to wield power in the subject cities the empire of the Athenian People has but a short lease of existence. This explains why the better people are punished with infamy, robbed of their money, driven from their homes, and put to death, while the baser sort are promoted to honour. On the other hand, the better Athenians protect the better class in the allied cities. And why? Because they recognise that it is to the interest of their own class at all times to protect the best element in the cities. **1.15** It may be urged that if it comes to strength and power the real strength of Athens lies in the capacity of her allies to contribute their money quota. But to the democratic mind it appears a higher advantage still for the individual Athenian to get hold of the wealth of the allies, leaving them only enough to live upon and to cultivate their estates, but powerless to harbour treacherous designs.

* * *

3.1 I repeat that my position concerning the constitution of the Athenians is this: the type of constitution is not to my taste, but given that a democratic form of government has been agreed upon, they do seem to me to go the right way to preserve the democracy by the adoption of the particular type which I have set forth.

Questions

1. **What does the author criticize in the Athenian democracy?**
2. **How does his description compare with that of Pericles in the funeral oration?**

4.   CRITIQUE OF PERICLEAN DEMOCRACY

In the Gorgias dialogue, Plato makes his view of Pericles' contribution to the Athenian constitution perfectly clear. Plato was little more than a generation removed from the time of Pericles and undoubtedly had good second-hand evidence of its character. It is possible, however, that his opinion was influenced by his own experience of the Athenian democracy of the fourth century, which he cordially disliked. The dialogue was written c. 385 BC; Socrates and Callicles are the speakers.

[515a] Soc. And now, my friend, as you are already beginning to be a public character, and are admonishing and reproaching me for not being one, suppose that we ask a few questions of one another. Tell me, then, Callicles, how about making any of the citizens better? Was there ever a man who was once vicious, or unjust, or intemperate, or foolish, and became by the help of Callicles good and noble? Was there ever such a man, whether citizen or stranger, slave or freeman? **[515b]** Tell me, Callicles, if a person were to ask these questions of you, what would you answer? Whom would you say that you had improved by your conversation? There may have been good deeds of this sort which were done by you as a private person, before you came forward in public. Why will you not answer?

Cal. You are contentious, Socrates.

Soc. Nay, I ask you, not from a love of contention, but because I really want to know in what way you think that affairs should be administered among us—whether, when you come to the administration of them, **[515c]** you have any other aim but the improvement of the citizens? Have we not already admitted many times over that such is the duty of a public man? Nay, we have surely said so; for if you will not answer for yourself I must answer for you. But this is what the good man ought to effect for the benefit of his own state; allow me to recall to you the names of those whom you were just now mentioning, **[515d]** Pericles, and Cimon, and Miltiades, and Themistocles, and as whether you still think that they were good citizens.

Cal. I do.

Soc. But if they were good, then clearly each of them must have made the citizens better instead of worse?

Cal. Yes.

Soc. And, therefore, when Pericles first began to speak in the assembly, the Athenians were not so good as when he spoke last?

Cal. Very likely.

Soc. Nay, my friend, "likely" is not the word; **[515e]** for if he was a good citizen, the inference is certain.

Cal. And what difference does that make?

Soc. None; only I should like further to know whether the Athenians are supposed to have been made better by Pericles, or, on the contrary, to have been corrupted by him; for I hear that he was the first who gave the people pay, and made them idle and cowardly, and encouraged them in the love of talk and of money.

Cal. You heard that, Socrates, from the Laconising set who bruise their ears [philo-Spartans].

Soc. But what I am going to tell you now is not mere hearsay, but well known both to you and me: that at first, Pericles was glorious and his character unimpeached by any verdict of the Athenians—this was during the time when they were not so good—yet afterwards, when they had been made good and gentle by him, **[516a]** at the very end of his life they convicted him of theft, and almost put him to death, clearly under the notion that he was malefactor.

Cal. Well; but how does that prove Pericles' badness?

Soc. Why, surely you would say that he was a bad manager of asses or horse or oxen, who had received them originally neither kicking nor butting nor biting him, and implanted in them all these savage tricks? Would he not be bad manager **[516b]** of any animals who received them gentle, and made them fiercer than they were when he received them? What do you say?

Cal. I will do you the favour of saying "yes."

Soc. And will you also do me the favour of saying whether man is an animal?

Cal Certainly he is.

Soc. And was not Pericles a shepherd of men?

Cal. Yes.

Soc. And if he was a good political shepherd, ought not the animals **[516c]** who were his subjects, as we were just now acknowledging, to have become more just, and not more unjust?

CAL. Quite true.

Soc. And are not just men gentle, as Homer says?—or are you of another mind?

CAL. I agree.

Soc. And yet he really did make them more savage than he received them, and their savageness was shown towards himself; which he must have been very far from desiring.

CAL. Do you want me to agree with you?

Soc. Yes, if I seem to you to speak the truth.

516d CAL. Granted then.

Soc. And if they were more savage, must they not have been more unjust and inferior?

CAL. Granted again.

Soc. Then upon this view, Pericles was not a good statesman?

CAL. That is, upon your view.

Soc. Nay, the view is yours, after what you have admitted. Take the case of Cimon again. Did not the very persons whom he was serving ostracize him, in order that they might not hear his voice for ten years? and they did just the same to Themistocles, adding the penalty of exile; and they voted that **[516e]** Miltiades, the hero of Marathon, should be thrown into the pit of death, and he was only saved by the Prytanis. And yet, if they had been really good men, as you say, these things would never have happened to them. For the good charioteers are not those who at first keep their place, and then, when they have broken-in their horses, and themselves become better charioteers, are thrown out—that is not the way either in charioteering or in any profession—What do you think?

CAL. I should think not.

Soc. Well, but if so, the truth is as I have said already, **[517a]** that in the Athenian State no one has ever shown himself to be a good statesman—you admitted that this was true of our present statesmen, but not true of former ones, and you preferred them to the others; yet they have turned out to be no better than our present ones; and therefore, if they were rhetoricians, they did not use the true art of rhetoric or of flattery, or they would not have fallen out of favour.

CAL. But surely, Socrates, **[517b]** no living man ever came near any of them in his performances.

Soc. O, my dear friend, I say nothing against them regarded as the servingmen of the State; and I do think that they were certainly more serviceable than those who are living now, and better able to gratify the wishes of the State but as to transforming those desires and not allowing them to have their way, and using the powers which they had, whether of persuasion or of force, in the improvement of their fellow-citizens, which is the prime object of the truly good citizen, **[517c]** I do not see that in these respects they were a whit superior to our present statesmen, although I do admit that they were more clever at providing ships and walls and clocks, and all that.

Questions

1. **What is Socrates' criterion for judging Pericles and the other democratic leaders? Is it appropriate and adequate?**

5.   THE AGE OF PERICLES

Plutarch's *Life of Pericles* uses Thucydides but compares his views with those of other historians who may have employed reliable information not used by Thucydides. This selection, which describes Pericles' rise to power and his early career, was written c. AD 150.

9. Thucydides characterizes Pericles' administration as having been distinctly aristocratic— "democracy in name, but in practice government by the first citizen." But many other writers maintain that it was he who first led on the people into passing such measures as the allotment: to Athenians of

lands belonging to subject peoples, or the granting of allowances for the public festivals and fees for various public services, and that because of his policy they fell into bad habits and became extravagant and undisciplined instead of frugal and self-sufficient as they had once been. Let us consider in the light of the facts what may account for this change in his policy.

At the beginning of his career, as we have seen, Pericles had to measure himself against Cimon's reputation, and he therefore set out to win the favour of the people. He could not compete with the wealth or the property by means of which Cimon captured the affections of the poor; for the latter supplied a free dinner every day to any Athenian who needed it, provided clothes for the old, and took down the fences on his estates so that anyone who wished could pick the fruit. So finding himself outmatched in this kind of popular appeal, Pericles turned his attention to the distribution of the public wealth. He did this on the advice of Damonides of the deme of Oa, as Aristotle tells us; and before long, what with the allowances for public festivals, fees for jury service, and other grants and gratuities, he succeeded in bribing the masses wholesale and enlisting their support in his attack on the Council of the Areopagus. Pericles was not himself a member of this body, since he had never been appointed by lot to the post either of chief archon or archon thesmothete or king archon or polemarch. These positions had traditionally been filled by lot, and it was only through them that men who had acquitted themselves well in office could rise to membership of the Areopagus. Because he had thus been excluded, Pericles, once he had gathered popular support, exerted himself all the more to lead his party in a campaign against the Areopagus, and he succeeded so well that not only was it deprived of most of its judicial powers through a bill brought forward by Ephialtes, but Cimon himself was ostracized on the charge of being a friend of Sparta and an enemy of the people's interests. Yet this was a man who was second to none in Athens in birth or in wealth, who had won the most brilliant victories over the Persians and filled the city with money and treasure, as has been recorded in his life. Such was the strength of Pericles' hold over the people.... Cimon's death took place later during his campaign in Cyprus.

* * *

11. The aristocratic party had already recognized for some time that Pericles was now the most important man in Athens and that he wielded far more power than any other citizen. But they were anxious that there should be someone in the city capable of standing up to him so as to blunt the edge of his authority and prevent it from becoming an outright monarchy. They therefore put forward Thucydides, of Alopece, a man of good sense and a relative of Cimon, to lead the opposition. He was less of a soldier than Cimon, but better versed in forensic business and an abler politician, and by watching his opportunities at home and engaging Pericles in debate, he soon succeeded in creating a balance of power in Athenian affairs. He did not allow the aristocrats, the so-called party of the good and true, to become dispersed among the mass of the people in the Assembly, as they had done in the past, with the result that their influence had been swamped by sheer numbers. Instead, by separating and grouping them in a single body, he was able to concentrate their strength and make it an effective counterweight in the scale. Below the surface of affairs in Athens, there had existed from the very beginning a kind of flaw or seam, such as one finds in a piece of iron, which gave a hint of the rift that divided the aims of the popular and the aristocratic parties but now these two men's rival ambitions and their struggle for power sharply widened this cleavage and caused the one side to be named the party of the many and the other of the few. Pericles therefore chose this moment to hand over the reins of power to the people to a greater extent than ever before and deliberately shaped his policy to please them. He constantly provided public pageants, banquets, and processions in the city, entertaining the people like children with elegant pleasures; and he sent out sixty triremes to cruise every year, in which many of the citizens served with pay for eight months and learned and practised seamanship at the same time. Besides this, he dispatched 1,000 settlers to the Chersonese, 500 to Naxos, 250 to Andros, 1,000 to Thrace to make their homes with the Bisaltae, and others to the new colony named Thurii, which was founded in Italy near the site of Sybaris. In this way he relieved the city of a large number of idlers and agitators, raised the standards of the poorest classes, and, by installing garrisons among the allies, implanted at the same time a healthy fear of rebellion.

12. But there was one measure above all which at once gave the greatest pleasure to the Athenians, adorned their city and created amazement among the rest of mankind, and which is today the sole testimony that the tales of the ancient power and glory of Greece are no mere fables. By this I mean his construction of temples and public buildings; and yet it was this, more than any other action of his, which his enemies slandered and misrepresented. They cried out in the Assembly that Athens had lost her good name and disgraced herself by transferring from Delos into her own keeping the funds that had been contributed by the rest of Greece, and that now the most plausible excuse for this action, namely, that the money had been removed for fear of the barbarians and was being guarded in a safe place, had been demolished by Pericles himself. "The Greeks must be outraged," they cried. "They must consider this an act of bare-faced tyranny, when they see that with their own contributions, extorted from them by force for the war against the Persians, we are gilding and beautifying our city, as if it were some vain woman decking herself out with costly stones and statues and temples worth millions of money."

Pericles' answer to the people was that the Athenians were not obliged to give the allies any account of how their money was spent, provided that they carried on the war for them and kept the Persians away. "They do not give us a single horse, or a soldier, or a ship. All they supply is money," he told the Athenians, "and this belongs not to the people who give it, but to those who receive it, so long as they provide the services they are paid for. It is no more than fair that after Athens has been equipped with all she needs to carry on the war, she should apply the surplus to public works, which, once completed, will bring her glory for all time, and while they are being built will convert that surplus to immediate use. In this way all kinds of enterprises and demands will be created which will provide inspiration for every art, find employment for every hand, and transform the whole people into wage-earners, so that the city will decorate and maintain herself at the same time from her own resources."

Certainly it was true that those who were of military age and physically in their prime could always earn their pay from the public funds by serving on Pericles' various campaigns. But he was also anxious that the unskilled masses, who had no military training, should not be debarred from benefiting from the national income, and yet should not be paid for sitting about and doing nothing. So he boldly laid before the people proposals for immense public works and plans for buildings, which would involve many different arts and industries and require long periods to complete, his object being that those who stayed at home, no less than those serving in the fleet or the army or on garrison duty, should be enabled to enjoy a share of the national wealth.

14. Thucydides [not the historian] and the other members of his party were constantly denouncing Pericles for squandering public money and letting the national revenue run to waste, and so Pericles appealed to the people in the Assembly to declare whether in their opinion he had spent too much. "Far too much," was their reply, whereupon Pericles retorted, "Very well then, do not let it be charged to the public account but to my own, and I will dedicate all the public buildings in my name." It may have been that the people admired such a gesture in the grand manner, or else that they were just as ambitious as Pericles to have a share in the glory of his works. At any rate they raised an uproar and told him to draw freely on the public funds and spare no expense in his outlay. Finally, Pericles ventured to put matters to the test of an ostracism, and the result was that he secured his rival's banishment and the dissolution of the party which had been organized against him.

15. From this point political opposition was at an end, the parties had merged themselves into one, and the city presented a single and unbroken front. Pericles now proceeded to bring under his own control not only home Lairs, but all issues in which the authority of Athens was involved: these included matters of tribute, the army, the navy, the islands, maritime Lairs, the great resources which Athens derived both from the Greek states and from the barbarians, and the leadership she exercised which was buttressed by subject states, friendships with kings and alliances with dynasties. But at the same time Pericles' own conduct took on quite a different character. He was no longer so docile towards the people, nor so ready to give way to their caprices, which were as shifting and changeable as the winds. He abandoned the somewhat nerveless and indulgent leadership he had shown on occasion, which might be compared to a soft and flowery melody, and struck instead the firm, high note of an aristocratic, even regal statesmanship. And since he used his authority honestly and unswervingly in the interests of the city, he was usually able to carry the people with him by rational argument and persuasion. Still there were times when they bitterly resented his policy, and then he tightened the reins and forced them to do what was to their advantage, much as a wise physician treats a prolonged and complicated disease, allowing the patient at some moments pleasures which can do him no harm, and at others giving him caustics and bitter drugs which cure him. There were, as might be expected, all kinds of disorders to be found among a mass of citizens who possessed an empire as great as that of Athens, and Pericles was the only man capable of keeping each of these under control. He achieved this most often by using the people's hopes and fears as if they were rudders, curbing them when they were arrogant and raising their hopes or comforting them when they were disheartened. In this way he proved that rhetoric, in Plato's phrase, is the art of working upon the souls of men by means of words, and that its chief business is the knowledge of men's characters and passions which are, so to speak, the strings and stops of the soul and require a most skilful and delicate touch. The secret of Pericles' power depended, so Thucydides tells us, not merely upon his oratory, but upon the reputation which his whole course of life had earned him and upon the confidence he enjoyed as a man who had proved himself completely indifferent to bribes. Great as Athens had been when he became her leader, he made her the greatest and richest of all dries, and he came to hold more power in his hands than many a king and tyrant. And in the end he did not increase the fortune his father left him by so much as a single drachma from the public funds, a source of wealth which some men even managed to pass on to their children.

16. But despite his unselfishness, there can be no doubt as to his power, which Thucydides describes to us dearly, while even the comic poets testify to it unwittingly in some of their malicious jokes. For example, they nickname him and his associates "the new Pisistratids," and call upon him to take the oath that he will never set himself up as tyrant, as if his supremacy were too oppressive and out of all proportion in a democracy. Telecleides says that the Athenians had handed over to him

The cities' tribute, even the cities themselves
To hold or to set free as he thinks fit,
And the cities' walls to build or to pull down,
Their treaties and their armies, their power, their peace,
Their wealth, and all the gifts good fortune brings.

And all this was by no means a sudden harvest, the climax of popularity of an administration which flourished only for a brief season. The fact is that for forty years Pericles held the first place among men such as Ephialtes, Myronides, Cimon, Tolmides, and Thucydides, and after the fall of Thucydides and his ostracism, he exercised for no less than fifteen years a continuous, unbroken authority through his annual tenure of the office of general. During the whole of this period he proved himself completely incorruptible by bribery, although he was not altogether averse to making money.

31. *[During years just prior to the Peloponnesian War, Pericles' political control was threatened by attacks on his friends and collaborators, among them the sculptor Phidias.]* So Pheidias was cast into prison and there he fell sick and died. According to some accounts he was poisoned by his enemies in an attempt to blacken Pericles' name still further. As for the informer, Menon, a proposal was passed, on Glycon's motion, to make hint exempt from all taxes and public burdens and the generals were ordered to provide for his safety.

32. About the same time Aspasia was put on trial for impiety. She was prosecuted by Hermippus the comic poet, who also accused her of procuring free-born Athenian women for Pericles and receiving them into her house. A decree was also introduced by Diopeithes, the diviner, to the effect that anybody who did not believe in the gods or taught theories about celestial phenomena should be liable to prosecution, and this was aimed to cast suspicion on Pericles through Anaxagoras. The people took up these slanders only too readily, and while they were in this mood a bill was passed on Dracontides' initiative directing that the accounts of the public funds that Pericles had spent should be deposited with the prytanes, and that the jurors should pronounce their verdict on his case with ballots which had lain on the altar of the goddess on the Acropolis. However, this clause of the decree was amended by Hagnon, who moved that the case should be tried in the usual way, but before a body of 1,500 jurors, no matter whether it was to be termed a prosecution for embezzlement or bribery or malversation.

Pericles contrived to beg off Aspasia by bursting into floods of tears during her trial, so Aeschines tells us, and making a personal appeal to the jurors, but he was so alarmed for Anaxagoras's safety that he smuggled him out of the city. Pericles had already fallen foul of the people on the occasion of Pheidias's trial and he dreaded the jury's verdict on his own case, and so now that the war was threatening and smouldering, we are told that he deliberately fanned it into flame. He hoped in this way to dispel the charges against him and make the people forget their jealousy, since he knew that as soon as any great enterprise or danger was in prospect, the city would put herself in his hands alone because of his great authority and prestige. These are the motives which are alleged for his refusal to allow the people to give way to the demands of Sparta, but the true history of these events is hidden from us.

33. The Spartans, for their part, recognized that if Pericles could be removed from power, they would find the Athenians much easier to deal with, and so they demanded that Athens should rid herself of the blood-guilt of Cylon, in which Pericles' family on his mother's side had been involved, as Thucydides explains. But this manoeuvre produced exactly the opposite effect to what was intended; instead of being slandered and treated with suspicion, Pericles now found himself more trusted and honoured by the Athenians than ever before, because they saw that the enemy feared and hated him more than any other single man. For this reason, before king Archidamus led the Peloponnesians into Attica, Pericles announced in public to the Athenians that if the king should ravage other estates but spare his own, either on account of the personal friendship between them or else to give his enemies cause to slander him, he would, present all his lands and the buildings on them to the state.

The Spartans and their allies then proceeded to invade Attica with an immense army commanded by Archidamus. They advanced, devastating the land as they went, as far as Acharnae, which is very close to Athens, and there they pitched camp, for

they imagined that the Athenians would never tolerate this, but would march out and fight them from sheer pride and anger. Pericles, however, judged that it would be a terrible risk to engage 60,000 Peloponnesian and Boeotian hoplites (for the first invading army was at least as strong as this), and stake Athens' very existence on the issue, so he tried to pacify those who were longing to fight and were becoming restive at the damage the enemy were doing. He pointed out that trees, even if they are lopped or cut down, can quickly grow again, but that you cannot easily replace the men who fall in battle. He would not summon the Assembly for fear that he might be forced to act against his better judgement. Instead, he behaved like the helmsman of a ship who, when a storm sweeps down upon it in the open sea, makes everything fast, takes in sail and relies on his own skill and takes no notice of the tears and entreaties of the sea-sick and terrified passengers. In the same way Pericles closed the gates of Athens, posted guards at all the necessary points for security and trusted to his own judgement shutting his ears to the complaints and outcries of the discontented. At the same time many of his friends continually pressed him to take the offensive, while his enemies threatened and denounced his policy, and the comic poets in their choruses taunted him with mocking songs and abused his leadership for its cowardice and for abandoning everything to the enemy. Cleon, too, was already attacking him, and exploiting the general resentment against Pericles to advance his own prospects as a popular leader, as we see from this poem in anapaests by Hermippus:

Come now, king of the satyrs, stop waging the war
With your speeches, and try a real weapon!
Though I do not believe, under all your fine talk
You have even the guts of a Teles.
For if somebody gets out a whetstone and tries
Just to sharpen so much as a pen-knife,
You start grinding your teeth and fly into a rage
As if Cleon had come up and stung you.

34. Pericles, however, remained immovable and calmly endured all the ignominy and the hatred which were heaped upon him without making any reply. He sent a fleet of 100 ships to the Peloponnese, but did not accompany it himself.

Instead, he remained behind to watch affairs at home and keep the city under his control until the Peloponnesians withdrew. Then he set himself to placate the people, who were suffering severely from the war even after the departure of the Peloponnesians, and he won back some of his popularity by giving them various subsidies and proposing grants of conquered territories: he expelled, for example, the whole population of Aegina and divided up the island among the Athenians by lot. The people could find some consolation, too, in the damage which was being inflicted on the enemy. The fleet, as it sailed round the Peloponnese, ravaged a very large area and sacked a number of villages and small towns, while Pericles himself led an expedition into the Megarid and devastated the whole territory. It was clear from this that although the enemy did the Athenians a great deal of harm by land, they themselves were also suffering severely from the sea. In fact, they would never have carried on the war so long, but would soon have called off hostilities had not an act of heaven intervened to upset human calculations.

For now the plague fell upon the Athenians and devoured the flower of their manhood and their strength. It afflicted them not only in body but also in spirit, so that they raved against Pericles and tried to ruin him, just as a man in a fit of delirium will attack his physician or his father. They were urged on by his personal enemies, who convinced them that the plague was caused by the herding together of the country folk into the city. Here, in the summer months, many of them lived huddled in shacks and stifling tents and were forced to lead an inactive indoor life, instead of being in the pure open air of the country, as they were accustomed. The man responsible for all this, they said, was Pericles: because of the war he had compelled the country people to crowd inside the walls, and he had then given them no employment, but left them penned up like cattle to infect each other, without providing them with any relief or change of quarters.

35. In the hope of relieving these troubles and at the same time doing some damage to the enemy, Pericles manned 150 warships, embarked a large number of the best hoplites and horsemen, and was all ready to put to sea. The Athenians had high hopes of what such a powerful expedition might achieve and the enemy was equally alarmed by it.

But at the very moment when the ships were fully manned and Pericles had gone on board his own trireme, an eclipse of the sun took place, darkness descended and everyone was seized with panic, since they regarded this as a tremendous portent. When Pericles saw that his helmsman was frightened and quite at a loss what to do, he held up his cloak in front of the man's eyes and asked him whether he found this alarming or thought it a terrible omen. When he replied that he did not, Pericles asked, "What is the difference, then, between this and the eclipse, except that the eclipse has been caused by something bigger than my cloak?" This is the story, at any rate, which is told in the schools of philosophy.

After this Pericles put to sea, but he seems to have achieved nothing worthy of such an important expedition. He besieged the sacred town of Epidaurus and raised hopes of capturing it, but he was frustrated by the plague which attacked and destroyed not only his own men but all who came into contact with them. He tried to console and to encourage the Athenians, who had now turned against him because of this reverse. But he could not appease their anger or win them over quickly enough, before they had snatched up their ballots and made themselves masters of his fate, and they proceeded to strip him of his command and punish him with a fine. This amounted to fifteen talents according to the lowest account, while the highest places it at fifty. Idomeneus says that the public prosecutor referred to in the records of the case was Cleon, although according to Theophrastus it was Simmias, and Heracleides of Pontus mentions Lacratides.

* * *

37. The people tried other generals and politicians in turn to carry on the war, but they found that none of these possessed a stature or an authority that was equal to the task of leadership. So the city came to long for Pericles and summoned him back to the Assembly and the War Department. Because of his grief he was lying at home in dejected spirits, but he was persuaded by Alcibiades and his other friends to appear again in public. After the people had made amends for their ungrateful treatment of him, he once more took over the direction of affairs and was elected general.

Questions

1. **How does Plutarch's judgment of Pericles' position in Athens compare with that of Thucydides and Plato?**
2. **How does Plutarch's last paragraph cited above shed light on the character of the Periclean democracy?**

OPINIONS OF MODERN SCHOLARS

1. Late in the nineteenth century this distinguished German historian adopted Thucydides' skeptical view that Periclean Athens was not a truly democratic state, an opinion that was vigorously reasserted in the latter part of the next century. Georg Busolt was Professor of Ancient History at the University of Kiel and then at the University of Göttingen.

FROM GEORG BUSOLT, *GRIECHISCHE GESCHICHTE*

The extensive and glittering outfitting of the Panathenaic festival, the construction of a splendid new temple of Athena; the whole building activity in general were features of the Periclean leadership which it shared with the regime of the Peisistratids, a democratic monarchy to which, according to the judgment of Thucydides, it was really related. Both regimes were concerned with the relief of the lower classes, the attempt to give them employment, to provide a livelihood for them, and also with the acquisition of overseas possessions and the provision of landed property for many citizens. Pericles' colonization of the Chersonnese and his restoration of circuit judges join directly with the tradition of the time of the Peisistratids [who introduced similar popular measures].

* * *

[Busolt describes the ostracism of Thucydides son of Melesias (not the historian, but the leader of the faction oppose to Pericles)]

The oligarchic party lost, with its organizer, its firm coherence and its capacity for robust opposition. Pericles was thus without a rival, and therefore, in the eyes of the people, he became something other than what he had been before. If he had earlier felt himself compelled to be at the people's disposal and to yield to the wishes of the masses, he now began to behave independently and to take the bridle into his hand. By using the weight of his personality he ruled the state—on the one hand by means of the official authority given to him, on the other hand by means of his decisive influence on the decisions of the popular assembly. For fifteen years he would be elected to the generalship each year. In difficult times of war he received the supreme command, and at the beginning of the Peloponnesian War he also obtained extraordinarily full powers. Although he did not usually have greater official power than the other generals, he nevertheless held the authoritative position in the college of the generals and thereby collected into his own hand its conduct of the military, maritime, financial, and administrative affairs that were in its competence. The unbroken continuity of office, in fact, released him still further from the principle of accountability and gave him an exceptional position, which would nevertheless be held within bounds by the fact that the people, by means of the epicheirotonia that took place each prytany, could suspend him from office and place him before a court. In addition to the most important ordinary annual offices, Pericles quite regularly held the extraordinary office of Epistates (supervisor) of a public building...

But, as the official power of Pericles was dependent on popular election and the mood of the people, he could only steer the entire ship of state in the direction he set if he could hold the leadership of the popular assembly in his hand. He succeeded by dint of his firmly based authority, his proven political insight, the integrity of his character, the dignity of his bearing, and the power of his speech. As he did not first need to acquire influence by improper means and was not accustomed to speak in order to please but, on the contrary, by virtue of the esteem in which he was already held, he could, under certain circumstances, even sharply oppose the people. He thus would not be led by the people, but instead he led them. As a result there developed a regime that was a popular government in name but one ruled by the first citizen in fact, a monarchical leadership on a democratic base, which frequently resumed the traditions of the democratic monarchy of the Peisistratids.

2. Malcolm McGregor presents a direct challenge to the interpretation of Thucydides and, indirectly to that of Busolt. What is more, he attempts to explain why Thucydides made such a claim. Malcolm McGregor was Professor of Classics at the University of British Columbia.

FROM MALCOLM MCGREGOR, "THE POLITICS OF THE HISTORIAN THUCYDIDES"

WHAT WE SEEK, IDEALLY, is reconciliation of those comments by Thucydides on government that seem to conflict. Our investigation commences with Perikles. From the ostracism of Kimon in 461 to his own death in 429 he was not out of office for more than a year or two; for the last fifteen years consecutively he was elected strategos, often, probably, strategos autokrator. Long tenure of office, as we know, becomes in itself a ground for criticism and Perikles did not escape. The Olympian figure in Aristophanes surely reflects a phase of contemporary gossip. Today students are often told that Athens was not really a democracy at all; rather, it was a dictatorship. In more fashionable circles, we read of the principate of Perikles, a term which immediately summons Augustus Caesar from the shades. It must be granted that for this view there is weighty authority, Thucydides himself: "What was in theory democracy," he writes, "became in fact rule by the first citizen." The sentence has since been adopted by many as a fundamental text.

Perhaps the most quoted of Thucydides' opinions, it withstands analysis least; a cynic might remark that it is seldom subjected to analysis. Throughout Perikles' tenure of office the ekklesia met at least forty times a year. Each spring it elected the generals for the following year. Each year their fellow-citizens examined the qualifications of the generals before they took office, ten times during the year the ekklesia heard reports from the generals. As they left office each year a jury of their fellow-citizens audited their records. One may employ other terms: during Perikles' political life the constitution functioned without interruption and Perikles had to retain the confidence of the sovereign and sensitive demos in order to remain in office. Not only was it possible for him to talk of re-election, as indeed he did in 444 B.C.; he might be removed from office, as indeed he was in 430 B.C. In the autumn of that year a disgruntled citizenry deposed and fined Perikles; more than that, they actually despatched a peace-mission to Sparta, while he remained in office, in direct contravention of his established policy. Now if democracy means and is government by the citizens, if the ekklesia decided policy by vote, if free elections persisted at their constitutional intervals, if Perikles was at all times responsible to the sovereign demos, and if an unoppressed political opposition survived, as it surely did—if all this is so, then Athens was as democratic, not only in theory but in day-to-day practice, as government can conceivably be. How such a system can be related to a dictatorship or to a principate is beyond my comprehension. The term principate is particularly unfortunate; for how does Augustus, the prototype, fit the conditions set out in this paragraph, which are not in dispute?

The principle of responsibility was paramount in the Athenian conception of democracy. The mere length of a responsible magistrate's tenure of office should not, by rational judges, be adopted at any time as a criterion of dictatorship. Within our own memories, however, a prolonged term has evoked the same indefensible protest in democratic countries, which should help us to understand, from our own experience, Perikles' position amidst his critics (and admirers) at the beginning of the Peloponnesian War. And nowhere in the modern world is the citizen's control over his representatives more direct and more constant than was the Athenian's. The truth is that Perikles had so won the confidence of his fellow-citizens that they elected him year after year and (wisely, I should say) allowed him, as their elder statesman, to guide them and shape their policies. But that they never surrendered, or diminished, their control of their own destinies is proved no more convincingly by Perikles' failure at the polis in 444 and his deposition in 430 than by his rapid re-election by a repentant demos a few months later. Athens remained a full and direct democracy.

* * *

We may find it simpler to understand Thucydides if we recognise that the democratic party at Athens itself developed two wings, one radical and one conservative. Perikles ended his life as a member of the latter. He had had his fling with the radical, aggressively imperialistic type of popular leadership and, by 446/5 B.C., had failed. His failure was remarkable in that he confessed it; he at once abandoned the aggressive policy by land and turned to the consolidation of the naval empire. He was thus able to guide Athens—and so most of the Aegean states—through what was probably the longest period of continuous prosperity and peace that Hellenes could remember. His thorough-going reversal I deem the surest evidence of his superior statecraft. This was the man who commanded the allegiance of Thucydides.

With the death of Perikles the restraining voice was gone and the way cleared for the imperialistic radicals, who followed to an avid demos a policy that was to prove as disastrous as Perikles had predicted. This transition allows Thucydides to give vent to his natural antipathy to democracy. His indictment of popular government, implied before the death of Perikles, is explicit in his treatment of Kleon, reaches a climax in the shameful words of the Athenian in the Melian Dialogue, and passes inexorably to the final collapse, which Thucydides, who lived to see it, attributes to the folly of the democracy. The state under Perikles, which we, unlike Thucydides, call democracy, Thucydides could endorse with enthusiasm; but Kleon and his

kind, in a state in which the machinery and the system had undergone not the slightest change, the oligarchic Thucydides could not stomach. To him Kleon was democracy; we know that Perikles was too. Worse was to come. Alkibiades, that brilliant renegade, borrowed the foreign policies of Kleon; having greater ability and less sense of responsibility, he wrought greater harm.

Yet there were those upon whom the mantle of Perikles fell. Of these Nikias was most prominent. Sometimes considered an oligarch, he was in truth, with his loyalty to Periklean tradition and policy, a conservative, or Periklean, democrat. Of him Thucydides, not surprisingly, writes with a nice appreciation, and in the increasingly grim pages one can detect a real sympathy for Nikias, so honest, so loyal, and at the last, so ineffective.

The situation after Perikles has been neatly described by John Finley: "Pericles...had four characteristics: he could see and expound what was necessary, he was patriotic and above money. Athens' misfortune and the essential cause of her ruin was that none of his successors combined all these traits. Nicias, who was honest but inactive, had the last two; Alcibiades, who was able but utterly self-interested, had the first two...."

This was Athens' tragedy, that she produced no successor who combined all the qualities of Perikles. I have heard it argued that Perikles was culpable for not having left a political heir, that is, that he did not brook rivalry. This, to be sure, is the charge that is commonly levelled at the great man. Apart from the fact that this assumes a principate that never existed and that Nikias was his heir, though not his intellectual peer, it is a formidable undertaking to show how one man could suppress others of comparable talent within his own party in a system in which an office-holder was ever subject to discipline and in which a popular assembly provided the ideal arena for the potential statesman to acquire education, training, and reputation. When we bewail the quality of those who received the reins from Perikles, we perhaps fail sufficiently to emphasize the surpassing genius of one who so excelled his contemporaries. "Perikles," Thucydides points out, "influential because of his reputation and intelligence and obvious integrity, was able freely to restrain the people; he led them rather than was led by them....His successors were more evenly matched with one another, striving, each one of them, to be first."

Perikles commanded the respect and the loyalty of men of various political persuasions. Thucydides was one of those to whom the man was more significant than their own partly inherited political convictions. It is a truism that the inspired leader draws support from the state as a whole, irrespective of party-lines. To Thucydides the events that followed the death of Perikles must have come as a bitter, if not entirely unexpected, disappointment: not unexpected, because he had no real faith in democracy and the death of Perikles removed the source of his self-deception. Steadily, as he saw it, the Periklean state was being destroyed. When Theramenes' moderate oligarchy of Five Thousand, with its unrestricted citizenship but restricted privilege, emerged from the revolution of 411/0, Thucydides, reverting easily to his tradition, could follow the dictates of his intellect and pronounce this the best government enjoyed by the Athenians in his time. It is his only categorical judgment on government; it is the key to his political convictions.

One might draw a parallel between Thucydides and the Old Oligarch. The Old Oligarch, it will be recalled, is so named for the nature of his anti-democratic essay written about 425 B.C. He writes, in effect, "I do not approve of democracy, but, if you must have it, I admit that the Athenians make a fine job of it." Thucydides, the oligarch born, might have said, "I do not approve of democracy, I see no strength or wisdom in the rabble; but I do admire and will support the Periklean state, which of course is not democracy at all."

We are ready to summarise. Thucydides was reared in the conservative anti-democratic tradition. His orderly and impartial mind was impressed by the genius of Perikles, and so he became a Periklean, though not a democrat; nor could he admit that by so doing he was, in essence, approving of democracy. Later, the oligarchic tradition of his family that had never been abandoned, reasserted itself, as he saw Periklean ideals forgotten, Periklean warnings ignored. He witnessed, with a brutally piercing eye, what seemed to him the evils of a democracy run to seed, its moral fibre weakening. He ended his life as he had begun it, a confirmed oligarch who had never renounced the creed of his fathers.

3. Paul Rahe, Professor of History at Hillsdale College, does not question the democratic character of Pericles' Athens, but he argues that it lacked the liberal characteristics that are generally associated with modern democracy. Indeed he speaks of the Athens of Pericles as "Athens' Illiberal Democracy." In the process he produces some of the chief complaints made by recent critics of the Athenian regime.

FROM PAUL A. RAHE, *REPUBLICS ANCIENT AND MODERN*

IT WOULD BE EASY to suppose that the city of Athena had somehow become an open society, with an ethos similar in character to that of James Madison's increasingly litigious liberal republic, and it is not at all surprising that, in the wake of the French Revolution, Athens was romanticized and came to represent in the eyes of many the modern, liberal democrat ideal. In our own day, especially among students of the classics, this vision retains considerable force. Athens has even been represented as the primitive, pre-modern prototype of a working-class democracy.

And yet nothing could be further from the truth. The ancient democracies were, as Tocqueville remarked, "aristocracies of masters," and Athens no exception. One could easily query the figures which Tocqueville gives; for the number of slaves and of freemen in Attica: that he greatly exaggerates the former and underestimates the latter there can be no doubt. But objections of this sort are beside the point. For on the main issue Tocqueville was surely right. The "universal suffrage" which Athens extended to adult, male citizens did not decisively set her apart from the less democrat regimes. The difference was simply a matter of degree. In the end, Athens's acceptance of slavery and its prevalence there made of that ancient city "an aristocratic republic"—albeit one "in which all the nobles had an equal right to the government." Despite the growth of the market economy and the concentration of population in the town of Athens and in the port community that grew up at the Peiraeus, the ordinary Athenian remained a peasant smallholder caught up in village life and intent on achieving a measure self-sufficiency; and partly as a consequence of the campaigns against Persia, the incessant wars elsewhere, and the plentiful supply and low price of slaves, he seems to have been at least as well situated to become a slaveowner as his counterpart the dirt farmer of the American South. Whether slavery dominated the productive sector of the economy or not is and will remain an open question. But, in the end, the answer is of no great importance, for there is no reason to suppose that the mode of production is the only or even the most important force shaping the ethos of a society. What matters in this case is that, like their counterparts among the free white population in the American South, ordinary Athenians could and did take their own measure by comparing themselves favorably with the multitude of slaves in their midst.

Democracy stood, in antiquity, for a limited extension of the circle of loyalty, not for a principled abandonment of the aristocratic sense of inborn superiority. The Athenians not only owned barbarian slaves in considerable numbers and excluded them from all participation in self-determination; they did so without any indication that they doubted the justice of their subjection. Furthermore, by the second half of the fifth century, they had transformed into a great empire of their own a league originally founded to defend the Greeks against Persia's appetite for dominion. The citizens of Athens ruled—and even boasted that they ruled—over an extraordinary number of their fellow Hellenes. As they were more than willing to acknowledge, this, too, involved a form of mastery and servitude. No Athenian would have denied the accuracy of James Madison's claim that "the money with which Pericles decorated Athens was raised by Aristides on the confederates of Athens for common defence, and on pretext of danger at Delos which was the common depository, removed to Athens, where it was soon regarded as the tribute of inferiors instead of the common property of associates, and applied by Pericles accordingly." Few seem to have worried that their dominion was unjust. The very fact that their allies tolerated this appropriation of the league monies was proof positive that these confederates were, indeed, inferiors and deserving of subjection. In short, the exercise of imperial dominion had much the same effect on Athenian morals and manners as slavery itself. "Dependent Colonies are to the superior State," Madison noted, "not in the relation

of Children and parent according to the common language, but in that of slave and Master; and have the same effect with slavery on the character of the Superior." Like slaveholders, the citizens of an imperial community like Athens "cherish pride, luxury, and vanity. They make the labor of one part tributary to the enjoyment of another."

There were, to be sure, other, more egalitarian influences on the ethos of Athens. Some Athenians did owe their livelihood to the despised professions of trade and industry. But, for the most part, these bourgeois pursuits were left in the hands of metics—and like the Jews of medieval Europe, these immigrants were kept on the periphery of the community: they were denied participation in politics, were refused the privilege of owning landed property, and were subjected to a resident alien's tax as a reminder of their low status. Circumstances and the atmosphere created by democracy rendered the city of Athena somewhat more cosmopolitan than the other cities of Greece. At Athens, in the classical period, as at Sparta, even the rich were plainly dressed. On the streets, we are told, one could hardly distinguish a citizen from a metic or slave, and the Athenians tolerated in both a freedom of speech purportedly unknown even to citizens in other communities. But Athens's openness to the outsider should not be exaggerated: it was the radical democracy of the elder Pericles that tightened the requirements for citizenship, reacting to the permanent presence of immigrants in large numbers by insisting on the exclusion of their offspring from the political community and by reasserting with redoubled fervor the traditional emphasis on purity of blood...

In the enforcement of morals, Athens was, at least when compared with other Greek poleis, quite notably lax. But the spirit that animated her regime was identical to that found elsewhere. Manliness and courage, public-spiritedness and piety—these were the standards by which the citizens as such were ultimately judged. James Madison summed up the difference between Sparta and Athens much as Plutarch had done: by juxtaposing not the goals but the approach taken by those who had framed laws for the two cities. "Lycurgus," he remarked, was "more true to his object," and he therefore placed himself "under the necessity of mixing a portion of violence with the authority of superstition; and of securing his final success, by a voluntary renunciation, first of his country, and then of his life." In contrast, "Solon...seems to have indulged a more temporising policy," for he "confessed that he had not given to his countrymen the government best suited to their happiness, but most tolerable to their prejudices."

To Athenian temporizing, there were limits — and for obvious reasons: at no time in the classical period did the ethos of the citizen-warrior cease to be predominant. Thus, even at Athens, a man would forfeit his political rights as a citizen for throwing away his shield in battle or for compromising his manhood by allowing another to use him as a woman for pay. Moreover, in that city, although the marketplace was left relatively unfettered by law, the force of custom and the ethos of civic friendship tended to prevent the interplay of supply and demand from dictating the price of services and goods. Citizen morality also imposed other limits on behavior which may to us seem utterly strange. There is, for example, no reason to suppose that, in Athens, estates were ever inalienable, and there is no clear-cut evidence that there was any legal limit to the acreage that any individual could own. But there was no real estate market and, in the democratic period, no public registry of property and contracts, for land seems only rarely to have changed hands.

Like other cities, Athens possessed sumptuary laws to prevent conspicuous consumption from inspiring jealousy. There, under the democracy, custom came to dictate simplicity in dress and demeanor, and this development was perfectly consonant with the public policy of the democracy: for, in the aftermath of the Persian Wars, when the Athenians commissioned the Milesian architect Hippodamus to develop a plan for their new port city the Peiraeus, they were quite self-consciously choosing to build private homes equal in size and virtually identical in plan. Moreover, in this period, as one would expect, the pressures on the wealthy to contribute to the public welfare through liturgies were not to be resisted.

Like other cities, Athens gave women short shrift, relegating them almost entirely to the domestic sphere and, where economically feasible, confining them indoors. In recording a universally acknowledged matter of fact, one client of Demosthenes told a jury, "For the sake of pleasure, we have courtesans; for the body's daily care, we have concubines; and for bearing legitimate children and faithfully guarding what lies within our homes, we have wives." There was even a law at Athens disallowing wills made by those

mentally incapacitated by insanity, old age, drugs, illness, or the influence of a woman.

Similarly, despite her much-touted love of novelty and her notorious openness to foreign cults, customs, and ways, Athens was by our standards quite conservative. Prior to the scientific revolution, what was fresh and new was but rarely thought improved: in Attic Greek, the word neos, when applied to an event, actually connotes that which is unexpected, strange, untoward, and evil. As one would then expect, Athens was intolerant of religious infractions: this was the polis that sentenced the popular general Alcibiades to death for parodying the Eleusinian Mysteries in a private home; this was the community that condemned the commanders victorious at Arginusae for failing to bury the citizen dead; and this was the city that executed Socrates for not believing in the city's gods and for corrupting the youth by teaching them the same doctrine.

It does not matter one whit that these particular prosecutions were politically motivated, as they all were. Nor does it matter that the contest for public offices and honors generally accounted for charges being brought against those, such as Demosthenes' ally Timarchus, who had continued to exercise their rights as citizens after purportedly allowing themselves to be used as women by other men. What counts above all else is that the rivals of Alcibiades, the opponents of the Arginusae generals, the enemies of Socrates, and the prosecutor of Timarchus had the religious and moral weapons ready to hand. No one — not even Socrates — ever dared to suggest that a man's religious beliefs and behavior were of no concern to the body politic, and no one argued that the city should concede full sexual freedom to all consenting adults. Not even in an emanation from its penumbra can one discern in the constitution of Athens a fundamental right to privacy. In that city, there were no effective institutional constraints on the exercise of popular will against those whose private demeanor had inspired public distrust; and to the best of our knowledge, none were ever even contemplated. Nor can one argue that these trials were isolated incidents. Though we are very poorly informed concerning day-to-day affairs in late fifth-century Athens, we do know that Diagoras of Melos was prosecuted for impiety, and there is evidence (some of it confused, but most of it quite plausible) that other philosophers and freethinkers suffered a similar fate. Prosecutions for impiety were by no means unknown in the fourth century.

As citizens, the Athenians exercised collective sovereignty, but they were not endowed with guarantees of civil liberty. Indeed, the body politic possessed in ostracism an instrument specifically designed to provide for the decade-long banishment of men guilty of no crime but the arousal of popular envy, fear, and distaste. And when ostracism fell into abeyance, the popular courts remained fully capable of rigorously enforcing the citizen morality dictated by public opinion. The orator Hyperides summed up the situation nicely in a speech prepared for one of his clients. "Do not form your judgment of me on the basis of the slanders made by the prosecutor," Hyperides' client urged the jury. "Do so, instead, on the basis of my entire life, examining the manner in which I have lived it. For no one in our city—neither the scoundrel nor the decent man—escapes the notice of the multitude, and the passage of time is the most precise witness for each man's way of conducting his affairs."

It should not be surprising that Athenian defendants and plaintiffs displayed an almost obsessive penchant for introducing into their forensic orations matter extraneous to the issue in dispute but pertinent to the defense of their conduct in general. It made perfect sense for them to recount in detail the services that they had performed on the community's behalf. Under Athenian law, any citizen could lay charges, and political disputes often played themselves out as contests in court. Moreover, by the late fifth century, malicious prosecution was quite common and rich men, because they were envied and because many were suspected of harboring a sympathy for oligarchical rule, were easy marks. Given the fact that orators were vulnerable to prosecution for accepting bribes and for making unlawful proposals and that the generals and the lesser magistrates were subject to an audit and judicial reckoning (euthyna) at the end of their term of office, prudence dictated that the wealthy think hard before entering the political arena. In anticipation of the day when a sycophant could not be bought off, the prosperous were well advised to perform liturgies and other services designed to curry popular favor. For, given the great size of the juries, to go on trial before a court was, in effect, to be judged as a citizen by the city itself.

Benjamin Constant's analysis of the Athenian regime deserves heed. Athens did fail in practice to complete "the subjection of individual existence to the collective body"; she provided her citizens with much "greater individual liberty than Rome and Sparta"; and this phenomenon was intimately linked with the important role played by "commerce" and trade in her development. But by the same token, other aspects of Athenian life—the size of the polity, the laws and customs she inherited, the central importance accorded piety, the prevalence of slavery, the subjection of women, and the possession of an empire—served to make her illiberal not just in principle, but quite often in practice as well. As Constant put it: "We discover there vestiges of the liberty proper to the ancients. The people make the laws, examine the conduct of the magistrates, summon Pericles to render his accounts, condemn to death all the generals who had commanded at the battle of Arginusae: At the same time, ostracism, an arbitrary law much vaunted by all the legislators of the age, ostracism, which seems to us and should seem a revolting iniquity, proves that the individual was still very much subject to the supremacy of the social body at Athens—which he is not, in our religious community reduced by circumstances and by conscious decisions to an advanced state of disarray and decay.

* * *

The illiberal character of the vision which Pericles projected cannot be gainsaid, but one must wonder whether Athens ever actually achieved that at which her greatest statesman evidently aimed. It is characteristic of human affairs that deeds nearly always fall short of the aspirations advertised in speech. If the women of that city were little noticed in public, the position of prominence they occupied within the comparatively invisible world of the household should generally have given them an emotional leverage enabling them to counter in some measure the Athenian fascination with public affairs, and it may have conferred on them a certain indirect, covert influence over the political behavior of their fathers, brothers, husbands, and sons. And yet, the natural allure of the domestic sphere seems to have counted for little when in competition with the erotic politics preached by Pericles—for if the ancient writers had been able to compare the polities of antiquity with those of our own time, there is one point on which they would have been agreed: the development of Athens's empire, the simultaneous and parallel elaboration of her democratic institutions, and the concomitant decay of the traditional ethos of reverence and shame really did unleash a mad and uncontrollable passion for dominion, for power, and for glory, one not just wholly foreign to the bourgeois temper of modern liberal democracy but, in fact, excessive even by the standards of ancient Greece.

Consider

1. **What is the evidence in favor of the theory that Periclean Athens was not a democracy but a monarchy, or at least "the rule of the first citizen"?**

2. **Busolt speaks of a "democratic monarchy." In what sense does he think it was democratic? In what sense was it monarchical?**

3. **How does McGregor's description of the Athenian constitution affect the debate?**

4. **How does he view Athenian politics and their effect on the position of Pericles?**

5. **How does he think Pericles attained and maintained such a dominant position if Athens was truly democratic?**

6. **Is such a dominant position sometimes possible in modern democracies?**

7. **Do Thucydides' own political preferences help shape his picture of Periclean Athens?**

8. **What are the aspects of Athenian society that Rahe considers "illiberal"?**

9. **How does his description of Athens differ from that of McGregor? Are they talking about the same things?**

10. **Can a state be democratic without being liberal?**

CHAPTER 9
THE UNPOPULARITY
OF THE ATHENIAN EMPIRE

ༀ

IN THE MID-NINETEENTH CENTURY George Grote wrote that the subjects of Athens' empire felt toward her "neither attachment nor hatred, but simple indifference and acquiescence in her supremacy." The opinion of Grote challenged the judgment of Thucydides and that of most of his readers since antiquity; for the historian says that the Greeks before the outbreak of the Peloponnesian War viewed Athens as a tyrant city which had "enslaved" its allies and wanted to enslave other states. For example, in Book II of the *History*, Pericles describes the hatred Athens had incurred in its rule. He points out that it may have been wrong for the Athenians to have seized an empire but warns them of the danger of giving it up. In Book III, Cleon states that the empire Athens holds is a "tyranny" exercised over unwilling subjects who hate and plot against it. He asserts that leading the "allies" depends on superior strength, not good will, and he advises the assembly not to feel pity or compassion for rebellious allies but to punish them with death. Scholars have for the most part accepted the verdict of Thucydides that the allies of Athens despised the empire and welcomed any opportunity to rebel against it. On the other hand, there has been at least one remarkable attempt to develop Grote's position. This chapter reviews the modern debate on whether or not the Athenian empire was popular among its subjects.

In Book I of his *History*, Thucydides explains how during the period from 478/7 BC to the outbreak of the war in 431 BC Athens transformed its hegemony of the Delian League's autonomous allies into an empire of oppressed subjects. The early campaigns in the war against Persia were led by the great Athenian admiral Cimon. The league fleet first captured the Persian fortress of Eion on the Strymon River in 476/5 BC. In the same year the fleet sailed against Scyros, east of Euboea, and enslaved the Dolopian pirates who inhabited the island. Next, the pro-Persian Greek state of Carystus in southwest Euboea was forced to join the league. In 470 BC the island of Naxos revolted against the league and had to be suppressed. Besides not being allowed to secede, Naxos was made a subject state contrary to the league guarantee of autonomy to its members. Thucydides uses the experience of Naxos to highlight a progression in Athens' aims for the Delian League as follows. Originally the hegemon used the league fleet to take the fight to the Persians and to clear the sea of pirates. But soon Cimon led expeditions against Greeks to force neutral states to join the league and to suppress members trying either to secede or to shirk their obligations of paying tribute or of supplying ships for the league fleet. Thucydides blames the reluctance of the allies to face military service abroad for the growth of Athenian power. As states chose to pay a corresponding sum of money to the league instead of producing ships, the Athenian navy grew strong at their expense. For instance, by 454 BC only 17 allies provided ships and by the 440s only Samos, Lesbos, and Chios still had navies. The result was that when cities revolted they lacked the resources and experience to resist and Athens became more powerful and more capable of enforcing its will.

In 467 BC Cimon scored a crushing victory over the Persians in the battle of Eurymedon in southern Asia Minor. He not only defeated and destroyed the 200 Persian ships preparing for an offensive against the coast, but Cimon also landed troops and annihilated the Persian army. This great success, by virtually removing the threat of Persian intervention in the Aegean, called into question the need to continue the Delian League. However, instead of curtailing league campaigns, Cimon in 465 BC attacked the island of Thasos, which had revolted, in order to acquire for Athens the markets and the mine the Thasians controlled in Thrace. After a two-year siege of their island the Thasians in 463/2 BC surrendered, destroyed their walls, forfeited their ships, paid a war indemnity, and became a tribute-paying subject of Athens. A few years later, the allies took up arms against the Greek state of Aegina in a quarrel that existed solely between that state and Athens. In 454/3 BC the league treasury was transferred from Delos to Athens, now the "capitol" city of the league. Another crucial turning point in the evolution of the Delian League into the Athenian empire came in 449 BC with the Peace of Callias. The treaty with the Great King formally ended the war between the Greek states and the Persian Empire, the

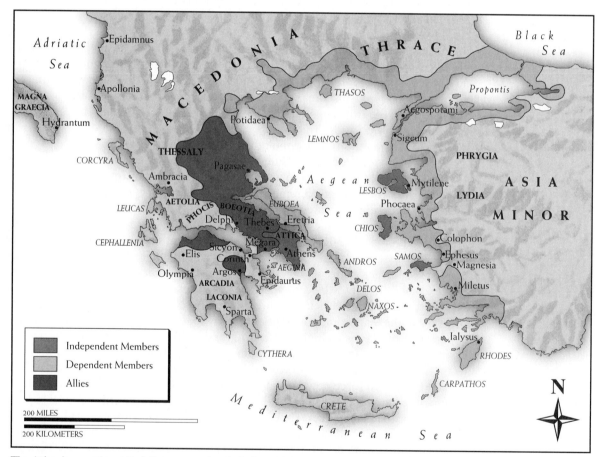

The Athenian empire at its fullest extent shortly before 450 BC. We see Athens and the independent states that provided manned ships for the imperial fleet but paid no tribute; dependent states that paid tribute; and states allied to, but not actually in, the empire.

reason for which the allies had paid tribute (*phoros*). But Athens continued to exploit league funds to finance its own navy, its democracy, and its grand building schemes in the manner of an openly imperial city.

Was the empire of the Athenians universally unpopular with its allies? On the one hand, some scholars suggest that the amount of tribute the allies paid was a small price for the protection and stability, in addition to the economic and legal benefits Athens provided for its subjects. De Ste. Croix, for instance, emphasizes that the *demos* in the allied cities should be distinguished from the oligarchs. The oligarchs bore the expense of imperialism, whereas the *demos* mostly reaped rewards from their alliance with Athens. In Thucydides' *History*, he mentions the rejoinder of Diodotus to Cleon that the common people in the cities are well disposed to and the refuge of Athens. However, many scholars contest any positive reading of Athenian imperialism. They stress the importance of freedom and autonomy to the Greeks in general and they cite the readiness of the allies to revolt at Samos, Mytilene, in Thrace and in Ionia, and so on. Moreover, they point out that the speeches of Thucydides often reveal the great disdain "the allies" felt for Athens.

Ancient Sources

1. Thucydides 1.88–101; 112–117, THE BIRTH AND GROWTH OF THE ATHENIAN EMPIRE
2. Thucydides 3.10, THUCYDIDES: FROM LEAGUE TO EMPIRE
3. Thucydides 6.82, ATHENIAN IMPERIALISM
4. Thucydides 1.75–76, FEAR, HONOR AND INTEREST
5. Thucydides 2.63, THE TYRANT CITY
6. Diodorus 11.70, DIODORUS: FROM LEAGUE TO EMPIRE
7. Pseudo-Xenophon, *The Constitution of the Athenians*, 1, 3, THE CLASS STRUGGLE IN THE ATHENIAN EMPIRE
8. Thucydides 3.26–28; 35–50, THE REVOLT AT MY TILENE
9. Thucydides 8.1–2, THE CONSEQUENCE OF THE SICILIAN DISASTER
10. Thucydides 8.68, PHRYNICHUS' VIEW OF OLIGARCHY, DEMOCRACY, AND EMPIRE
11. Thucydides 1.22.1, THUCYDIDES' SPEECHES
12. Thucydides 8.97.2, THE POLITICAL VIEWPOINT OF THUCYDIDES

Opinions of Modern Scholars

1. From G. E. M. de Ste. Croix, "The Character of the Athenian Empire"
2. From Donald W. Bradeen, "The Popularity of the Athenian Empire"

ANCIENT SOURCES FOR THE ATHENIAN EMPIRE

1.   THE BIRTH AND GROWTH OF THE ATHENIAN EMPIRE

Thucydides, I. 89–117 is the chief source for the growth of the Athenian empire. In this passage, the historian describes how the Athenians transformed the Delian League into their empire.

1.89.1 How the Athenians attained the position in which they rose to greatness I will now proceed to describe. **[2]** When the Persians, defeated both by sea and land, had retreated from Europe, and the remnant of the fleet, which had escaped to Mycale, had there perished, Leotychides, the

Lacedaemonian king, who had commanded the Hellenes in the battle, returned home with the allies from Peloponnesus. But the Athenians and their allies from Ionia and the Hellespont, who had recently revolted from the king, persevered and besieged Sestos, at that time still in the hands of the Persians. Remaining there through the winter they took the place, which the barbarians deserted. The allies then sailed back from the Hellespont to their respective homes. **[3]** Meanwhile the Athenian people, now quit of the barbarians, fetched their wives, their children, and the remains of their property from the places in which they had been deposited, and set to work, rebuilding the city and the walls. Of the old line of wall but a small part was left standing. Most of the houses were in ruins, a few only remaining in which the chief men of the Persians had lodged.

1.90.1 The Lacedaemonians knew what would happen and sent an embassy to Athens. They would rather themselves have seen neither the Athenians nor anyone else protected by a wall; but their main motive was the importunity of their allies, who dreaded not only the Athenian navy, which had until lately been quite small, but also the spirit which had animated them in the Persian War. **[2]** So the Lacedaemonians requested them not to restore their walls, but on the contrary to join with them in razing the fortifications of other towns outside the Peloponnesus which had them standing. They did not reveal their real wishes or the suspicion which they entertained of the Athenians, but argued that the barbarian, if he again attacked them, would then have no strong place which he could make his headquarters as he had lately made Thebes. Peloponnesus would be a sufficient retreat for all Hellas and a good base of operations. **[3]** To this the Athenians, by the advice of Themistocles, replied, that they would send an embassy of their own to discuss the matter, and so got rid of the Spartan envoys. He then proposed that he should himself start at once for Sparta, and that they should give him colleagues who were not to go immediately, but were to wait until the wall reached the lowest height which could possibly be defended. The whole people, men, women, and children, should join in the work, and they must spare no building, private or public, which could be of use, but demolish them all. **[4]** Having given these instructions and intimated that he would manage affairs at Sparta, he departed. **[5]** On his arrival he did not at once present himself officially to the magistrates, but delayed and made excuses; and when any of them asked him why he did not appear before the assembly, he said that he was waiting for his colleagues, who had been detained by some engagement; he was daily expecting them, and wondered that they had not appeared.

1.91.1 The friendship of the Lacedaemonian magistrates for Themistocles induced them to believe him; but when everybody who came from Athens declared positively that the wall was building and had already reached a considerable height, they knew not what to think. **[2]** He, aware of their suspicions, desired them not to be misled by reports, but to send to Athens men whom they could trust out of their own number who would see for themselves and bring back word. **[3]** They agreed; and he at the same time privately instructed the Athenians to detain the envoys as quietly as they could, and not let them go until he and his colleagues had got safely home. For by this time Habronichus the son of Lysicles, and Aristides the son of Lysimachus, who were joined with him in the embassy, had arrived, bringing the news that the wall was of sufficient height; and he was afraid that the Lacedaemonians, when they heard the truth, might not allow them to return. **[4]** So the Athenians detained the envoys, and Themistocles, coming before the Lacedaemonians, at length declared in so many words that Athens was now provided with walls and could protect her citizens; henceforward, if the Lacedaemonians or their allies wished at any time to negotiate, they must deal with the Athenians as with men who knew quite well what was for their own and the common good. **[5]** When they boldly resolved to leave their city and go on board ship, they did not first ask the advice of the Lacedaemonians, and, when the two states met in council, their own judgment had been as good as that of any one. **[6]** And now they had arrived at an independent opinion that it was better far, and would be more advantageous both for themselves and for the whole body of the allies, that their city should have a wall; **[7]** when any member of a confederacy had not equal military advantages, his counsel could not be of equal weight or worth. Either all the allies should pull down their walls, or they should acknowledge that the Athenians were in the right.

1.92.1 On hearing these words the Lacedaemonians did not openly quarrel with the Athenians;

for they professed that the embassy had been designed, not to interfere with them, but to offer a suggestion for the public good; besides at that time the patriotism which the Athenians had displayed in the Persian War had created a warm feeling of friendliness between the two cities. They were annoyed at the failure of their purpose, but they did not show it. And the envoys on either side returned home without any formal complaint.

1.93.1 In such hurried fashion did the Athenians rebuild the walls of their city. **[2]** To this day the structure shows evidence of haste. The foundations are made up of all sorts of stones, in some places unwrought, and laid just as each worker brought them; there were many columns too, taken from sepulchers, and many old stones already cut, inserted in the work. The circuit of the city was extended in every direction, and the citizens, in their ardour to complete the design, spared nothing. **[3]** Themistocles also persuaded the Athenians to finish the Piraeus, of which he had made a beginning in his year of office as Archon. The situation of the place, which had three natural havens, was excellent; and now that the Athenians had become sailors, he thought that a good harbour would greatly contribute to the extension of their power. **[4]** For he first dared to say that they must make the sea their domain, and he lost no time in laying the foundations of their empire. **[5]** By his advice, they built the wall of such a width that two wagons carrying the stones could meet and pass on the top; this width may still be traced at the Piraeus; inside there was no rubble or mortar, but the whole wall was made up of large stones hewn square, which were clamped on the outer face with iron and lead. The height was not more than half what he had originally intended; **[6]** he had hoped by the very dimensions of the wall to paralyse the designs of an enemy, and he thought that a handful of the least efficient citizens would suffice for its defence, while the rest might man the fleet. **[7]** His mind was turned in this direction, as I conceive, from observing that the Persians had met with fewer obstacles by sea than by land. The Piraeus appeared to him to be of more real consequence than the upper city. He was fond of telling the Athenians that if they were hard pressed they should go down to the Piraeus and fight the world at sea. Thus the Athenians built their walls and restored their city immediately after the retreat of the Persians.

1.94.1 Pausanias the son of Cleombrotus was now sent from Peloponnesus with twenty ships in command of the Hellenic forces; thirty Athenian ships and a number of the allies with him. **[2]** They first made an expedition against Cyprus, of which they subdued the greater part; and afterwards against Byzantium, which was in the hands of the Persians, and was taken while he was still in command.

1.95.1 He had already begun to be oppressive, and the allies were offended with him, especially the Ionians and others who had been recently emancipated from the king. So they had recourse to their kinsmen the Athenians and begged them to be their leaders, and to protect them against Pausanias, if he attempted to oppress them. **[2]** The Athenians took the matter up and prepared to interfere, being fully resolved to manage the confederacy in their own way. **[3]** In the meantime the Lacedaemonians summoned Pausanias to Sparta, intending to investigate certain reports which had reached them; for he was accused of numerous crimes by Hellenes returning from the Hellespont, and appeared to exercise his command more after the fashion of a tyrant than of a general. **[4]** His recall occurred at the very time when the hatred which he inspired had induced the allies, with the exception of the Peloponnesians, to transfer themselves to the Athenians. **[5]** On arriving at Lacedaemon he was punished for the wrongs which he had done to particular persons, but he had been also accused of conspiring with the Persians, and of this, which was the principal charge and was generally believed to be proven, he was acquitted. **[6]** The government however did not continue him in his command, but sent in his place Dorcis and certain others with a small force. To these the allies refused allegiance, and Dorcis, seeing the state of affairs, returned home. **[7]** Henceforth the Lacedaemonians sent out no more commanders, for they were afraid that those whom they appointed would be corrupted, as they had found to be the case with Pausanias; they had had enough of the Persian War; and they thought that the Athenians were fully able to lead, and at that time believed them to be their friends.

1.96.1 Thus the Athenians by the good-will of the allies, who detested Pausanias, obtained the leadership. They immediately fixed which of the cities should supply money and which of them ships for the war against the barbarians, the avowed object being to compensate themselves and the allies for their losses by devastating the King's country. **[2]** Then was first instituted at Athens the office of Hellenic treasurers, who received the tribute, for so the impost was termed. The amount was originally fixed at 460 talents. The island of Delos was the treasury, and the meetings of the allies were held in the temple.

1.97.1 At first the allies were independent and deliberated in common assemblies [*koinon xynodôn*] under the leadership of Athens. But in the interval between the Persian and The Peloponnesian Wars, by their military success in dealing with the barbarian, with their own rebellious allies and with the Peloponnesians who came across their path from time to time, the Athenians made immense strides in power. **[2]** I have gone out of my way to speak of this period because the writers who have preceded me treat rather of Hellenic affairs previous to the Persian invasion or of that invasion itself; the intervening portion of history has been omitted by all of them, with the exception of Hellanicus; and he, where he has touched upon it in his Attic history, is very brief, and inaccurate in his chronology. The narrative will also serve to explain how the Athenian empire grew up.

1.98.1 First of all under the leadership of Cimon, the son of Miltiades, the Athenians besieged and took from the Persians Eion upon the Strymon, and sold the inhabitants into slavery.

[2] The same fate befell Scyros, an island in the Aegean inhabited by Dolopes; this they colonised themselves. **[3]** They also carried on a war with the Carystians of Euboea, who, after a time, capitulated; the other Euboeans took no part in the war. **[4]** Then the Naxians revolted, and the Athenians made war against them and reduced them by blockade. This was the first of the allied cities which was enslaved contrary to Hellenic law; the turn of the others came later.

1.99.1 The causes which led to the defections of the allies were of different kinds, the principal being their neglect to pay the tribute or to furnish ships, and, in some cases, failure of military service. For the Athenians were exacting and oppressive, using coercive measures towards men who were neither willing nor accustomed to work hard. **[2]** And for various reasons they soon began to prove less agreeable leaders than at first. They no longer fought upon an equality with the rest of the confederates, and they had no difficulty in reducing them when they revolted. Now the allies brought all this upon themselves; **[3]** for the majority of them disliked military service and absence from home, and so they agreed to contribute a regular sum of money instead of ships. Whereby the Athenian navy was proportionally increased, while they themselves were always untrained and unprepared for war when they revolted.

Questions

1. **Discuss the key events that promoted the growth of the Athenian empire. When did the league become an empire?**
2. **Was Athenian imperialism an inevitable development? Why or why not?**

1.100.1 Next we come to the actions by land and by sea at the river Eurymedon in Pamphylia, between the Athenians with their allies, and the Medes, when the Athenians won both battles on the same day under the conduct of Cimon, son of Miltiades, and captured and destroyed the whole Phoenician fleet, consisting of two hundred vessels. **[2]** Some time afterwards occurred the defection of the Thasians, caused by disagreements about the marts on the opposite coast of Thrace, and about the mine in their possession. Sailing with a fleet to Thasos, the Athenians defeated them at sea and effected a landing on the island. **[3]** About the same time they sent ten thousand settlers of their own citizens and the allies to settle the place then called Ennea Hodoi or Nine Ways, now Amphipolis. They succeeded in gaining possession of Ennea Hodoi from the Edonians, but on advancing into the interior of Thrace were cut off in Drabescus, a town of the Edonians, by the assembled Thracians, who regarded the settlement of the place Ennea Hodoi as an act of hostility.

1.101.1 Meanwhile the Thasians being defeated in the field and suffering siege, appealed to Lacedaemon, and desired her to assist them by an invasion of Attica. **[2]** Without informing Athens she promised and intended to do so, but was prevented by the occurrence of the earthquake, accompanied by the secession of the Helots and the Thuriats and Aethaeans of the Perioeci to Ithome. Most of the Helots were the descendants of the old Messenians that were enslaved in the famous war; and so all of them came to be called Messenians. **[3]** So the Lacedaemonians being engaged in a war with the rebels in Ithome, the Thasians in the third year of the siege obtained terms from the Athenians by razing their walls, delivering up their ships, and arranging to pay the monies demanded at once, and tribute in future; giving up their possessions on the continent together with the mine.

* * *

[Thucydides next gives a summary of the First Peloponnesian War (459–445 BC).]

1.112.1 Three years afterwards a truce was made between the Peloponnesians and Athenians for five years. **[2]** Released from Hellenic war, the Athenians made an expedition to Cyprus with two hundred vessels of their own and their allies, under the command of Cimon. **[3]** Sixty of these were detached to Egypt at the instance of Amyrtaeus, the king in the marshes; the rest laid siege to Kitium, from which, however, **[4]** they were compelled to retire by the death of Cimon and by scarcity of provisions. Sailing off Salamis in Cyprus, they fought with the Phoenicians, Cyprians, and Cilicians by land and sea, and being victorious on both elements departed home, and with them the returned squadron from Egypt. **[5]** After this the Lacedaemonians marched out on a sacred war, and becoming masters of the temple at Delphi, placed it in the hands of the Delphians. Immediately after their retreat, the Athenians marched out, became masters of the temple, and placed it in the hands of the Phocians.

1.113.1 Sometime after this, Orchomenus, Chaeronea, and some other places in Boeotia, being in the hands of the Boeotian exiles, the Athenians marched against the above-mentioned hostile places with a thousand Athenian heavy infantry and the allied contingents, under the command of Tolmides, son of Tolmaeus. They took Chaeronea, and made slaves of the inhabitants, and leaving a garrison,

commenced their return. **[2]** On their road they were attacked at Coronaea, by the Boeotian exiles from Orchomenus, with some Locrians and Euboean exiles, and others who were of the same way of thinking, were defeated in battle, and some killed, others taken captive. **[3]** The Athenians evacuated all Boeotia by a treaty providing for the recovery of the men; **[4]** and the exiled Boeotians returned, and with all the rest regained their independence.

1.114.1 This was soon afterwards followed by the revolt of Euboea from Athens. Pericles had already crossed over with an army of Athenians to the island, when news was brought to him that Megara had revolted, that the Peloponnesians were on the point of invading Attica, and that the Athenian garrison had been cut off by the Megarians, with the exception of a few who had taken refuge in Nisaea. The Megarians had introduced the Corinthians, Sicyonians, and Epidaurians into the town before they revolted. Meanwhile Pericles brought his army back in all haste from Euboea. **[2]** After this the Peloponnesians marched into Attica as far as Eleusis and Thrius, ravaging the country under the conduct of King Pleistoanax, the son of Pausanias, and without advancing further returned home. **[3]** The Athenians then crossed over again to Euboea under the command of Pericles, and subdued the whole of the island: all but Histiaea was settled by convention; the Histiaeans they expelled from their homes, and occupied their territory themselves.

1.115.1 Not long after their return from Euboea, they made a truce with the Lacedaemonians and their allies for thirty years, giving up the posts which they occupied in Peloponnese, Nisaea Pegae, Troezen, and Achaia. **[2]** In the sixth year of the truce, war broke out between the Samians and Milesians about Priene. Worsted in the war, the Milesians came to Athens with loud complaints against the Samians. In this they were joined by certain private persons from Samos itself, who wished to revolutionize the government. **[3]** Accordingly the Athenians sailed to Samos with forty ships and set up a democracy; took hostages from the Samians, fifty boys and as many men, lodged them in Lemnos, and after leaving a garrison in the island returned home. **[4]** But some of the Samians had not remained in the island, but had fled to the continent. Making an agreement with the most powerful of those in the city, and an alliance with Pissuthnes, son of Hystaspes, the then satrap of Sardis, they got together a force of seven hundred mercenaries, and under cover of night crossed over to Samos. [5] Their first step was to rise on the commons, most of whom they secured, their next to steal their hostages from Lemnos; after which they revolted, gave up the Athenian garrison left with them and its commanders to Pissuthnes, and instantly prepared for an expedition against Miletus. The Byzantines also revolted with them.

1.116.1 As soon as the Athenians heard the news, they sailed with sixty ships against Samos. Sixteen of these went to Caria to look out for the Phoenician fleet, and to Chios and Lesbos carrying round orders for reinforcements, and so never engaged; but forty-four ships under the command of Pericles with nine colleagues gave battle, off the island of Tragia, to seventy Samian vessels, of which twenty were transports, as they were sailing from Miletus. Victory remained with the Athenians. [2] Reinforced afterwards by forty ships from Athens, and twenty-five Chian and Lesbian vessels, the Athenians landed, and having the superiority by land invested the city with three walls; it was also invested from the sea. [3] Meanwhile Pericles took

sixty ships from the blockading squadron, and departed in haste for Caunus and Caria, intelligence having been brought in of the approach of the Phoenician fleet to the aid of the Samians; indeed Stesagoras and others had left the island with five ships to bring them.

1.117.1 But in the meantime the Samians made a sudden sally, and fell on the camp, which they found unfortified. Destroying the look-out vessels, and engaging and defeating such as were being launched to meet them, they remained masters of their own seas for fourteen days, and carried in and carried out what they pleased. [2] But on the arrival of Pericles, they were once more shut up. Fresh reinforcements afterwards arrived — forty ships from Athens with Thucydides, Hagnon, and Phormio; twenty with Tlepolemus and Anticles, and thirty vessels from Chios and Lesbos. [3] After a brief attempt at fighting, the Samians, unable to hold out, were reduced after a nine months' siege, and surrendered on conditions; they razed their walls, gave hostages, delivered up their ships, and arranged to pay the expenses of the war by instalments. The Byzantines also agreed to be subject as before.

Questions

1. **How did the following events contribute to the evolution of the Athenian empire: the Battle of Eurymedon, the revolts of Naxos and Thasos, the helot rebellion of the 460s, and the Athenian campaign against Egypt?**
2. **How did Athens treat the various allies when they revolted?**
3. **How did the treatment of rebellions change over time?**

2. THUCYDIDES: FROM LEAGUE TO EMPIRE

The following passage presents a speech given in 428 during the Peloponnesian War by a spokesman for Mytilene, a Spartan ally, at a meeting of the Spartan alliance. The spokesman describes how Athens transformed the Delian League into an empire.

3.10.1. Justice and honesty will be the first topics of our speech, especially as we are asking for alliance; because we know that there can never be any solid friendship between individuals, or union between communities that is worth the name, unless the parties be persuaded of each other's honesty, and be generally congenial the one to the other; since from difference in feeling springs also difference in conduct. [2] Between ourselves and the Athenians

alliance began, when you withdrew from the Median war and they remained to finish the business. [3] But we did not become allies of the Athenians for the subjugation of the Hellenes, but allies of the Hellenes for their liberation from the Mede; [4] and as long as the Athenians led us fairly we followed them loyally; but when we saw them relax their hostility to the Mede, to try to compass the subjection of the allies, then our apprehensions began.

[5] Unable, however, to unite and defend themselves, on account of the number of confederates that had votes, all the allies were enslaved, except ourselves and the Chians, **[6]** who continued to send our contingents as independent and nominally free. Trust in Athens as a leader, however, we could no longer feel, judging by the examples already given; it being unlikely that she would reduce our fellow-confederates, and not do the same by us who were left, if ever she had the power.

3.   ATHENIAN IMPERIALISM

In this passage Thucydides presents an Athenian speech made in 415 to an audience of Sicilian Greeks. It concedes that the Delian League has become an empire and attempts to justify that development.

6.82.1. "Although we came here only to renew the former alliance, the attack of the Syracusans compels us to speak of our empire and of the good right we have to it. **[2]** The best proof of this the speaker himself furnished, when he called the Ionians eternal enemies of the Dorians. It is the fact; and the Peloponnesian Dorians being our superiors in numbers and next neighbours, we Ionians looked out for the best means of escaping their domination. **[3]** After the Median war we had a fleet, and so got rid of the empire and supremacy of the Lacedaemonians, who had no right to give orders to us more than we to them, except that of being the strongest at that moment; and being appointed leaders of the king's former subjects, we continue to be so, thinking that we are least likely to fall under the dominion of the Peloponnesians, if we have a force to defend ourselves with, and in strict truth having done nothing unfair in reducing to subjection the Ionians and islanders, the kinsfolk whom the Syracusans say we have enslaved. **[4]** They, our kinsfolk, came against their mother country, that is to say against us, together with the Mede, and instead of having the courage to revolt and sacrifice their property as we did when we abandoned our city, chose to be slaves themselves, and to try to make us so.

Questions
1. **Was the development of Athenian imperialism justified? Why or why not?**
2. **How might the allies have prevented Athens from imposing her will on the allies?**

4.   FEAR, HONOR AND INTEREST

In a speech at Sparta in 432 an Athenian spokesman explains why Athens entered the league and why it became an empire.

1.75.1 Surely, Lacedaemonians, neither by the patriotism that we displayed at that crisis, nor by the wisdom of our counsels, do we merit our extreme unpopularity with the Hellenes, not at least unpopularity for our empire. **[2]** That empire we acquired by no violent means, but because you were unwilling to prosecute to its conclusion the war against the barbarian, and because the allies attached themselves to us and spontaneously asked us to assume the command. **[3]** And the nature of the case first compelled us to advance our empire to its present height; fear being our principal motive, though honor and interest afterwards came in. **[4]** And at last, when almost all hated us, when some had already revolted and had been subdued, when you had ceased to be the friends that you once were, and had become objects of suspicion and dislike, it appeared no longer safe to give up our empire; especially as all who left us would fall to you. **[5]** And no one can quarrel with a people for making, in matters of tremendous risk, the best provision that it can for its interest.

1.76.1 You, at all events, Lacedaemonians, have used your supremacy to settle the states in Peloponnese as is agreeable to you. And if at the period of which we were speaking you had persevered to the end of the matter, and had incurred hatred in your command, we are sure that you would have made yourselves just as galling to the allies, and would have been forced to choose between a strong government and danger to yourselves. **[2]** It follows that it was not a very wonderful action, or contrary to the common practice of mankind, if we did accept an empire that was offered to us, and refused to give it up under the pressure of three of the strongest motives, fear, honor, and interest. And it was not we who set the example, for it has always been the law that the weaker should be subject to the stronger. Besides, we believed ourselves to be worthy of our position, and so you thought us till now, when calculations of interest have made you take up the cry of justice—a consideration which no one ever yet brought forward to hinder his ambition when he had a chance of gaining anything by might. **[3]** And praise is due to all who, if not so superior to human nature as to refuse dominion, yet respect justice more than their position compels them to do. **[4]** We imagine that our moderation would be best demonstrated by the conduct of others who should be placed in our position; but even our equity has very unreasonably subjected us to condemnation instead of approval.

5. THE TYRANT CITY

In 430 BC, the second year of the Peloponnesian War, Pericles urged his fellow Athenians to continue fighting even in the face of terrible suffering and sacrifice. In the process he frankly describes the Delian League in a new way.

2.63.1 Again, your country has a right to your services in sustaining the glories of her position. These are a common source of pride to you all, and you cannot decline the burdens of empire and still expect to share its honors. You should remember also that what you are fighting against is not merely slavery as an exchange for independence, but also loss of empire and danger from the animosities incurred in its exercise. **[2]** Besides, to recede is no longer possible, if indeed any of you in the alarm of the moment has become enamored of the honesty of such an unambitious part. For what you hold is, to speak somewhat plainly, a tyranny; to take it perhaps was wrong, but to let it go is unsafe. **[3]** And men of these retiring views, making converts of others, would quickly ruin a state; indeed the result would be the same if they could live independent by themselves; for the retiring and unambitious are never secure without vigorous protectors at their side; in fine, such qualities are useless to an imperial city, though they may help a dependency to an unmolested servitude.

6. DIODORUS: FROM LEAGUE TO EMPIRE

In this passage Diodorus describes and explains the transition of the Delian League to the Athenian empire.

WHEN ARCHEDEMIDES WAS ARCHON IN ATHENS, the Romans elected as consuls Aulus Verginius and Titus Minucius, and the Seventy-ninth Olympiad was celebrated, that in which Xenophon of Corinth won the "stadion." In this year [465] the Thasians revolted from the Athenians because of a quarrel over mines; but they were forced to capitulate by the Athenians and compelled to subject themselves again to their rule. Similarly also, when the Aeginetans revolted, the Athenians, intending to reduce them to subjection, undertook the siege of Aegina; for this state, being often successful in its engagements at sea, was puffed up with pride and was also well provided with both money and triremes, and, in a word, was constantly at odds with the Athenians.

Consequently they sent an army against it and laid waste its territory, and then, laying siege to Aegina, they bent every effort on taking it by storm. For, speaking generally, the Athenians, now that they were making great advances in power, no longer treated their allies fairly, as they had formerly done, but were ruling them harshly and arrogantly. Consequently most of the allies, unable longer to endure their severity, were discussing rebellion with each other, and some of them, scorning the authority of the General Congress, were acting as independent states.

Questions

1. **Compare the explanations of Thucydides and Diodorus about how the Athenians transformed the Delian League into an empire. What are the similarities and differences between the accounts of the two authors?**

---

7. THE CLASS STRUGGLE IN THE ATHENIAN EMPIRE

[1.14] In regard to the allies: the Athenians sail out and lay information, as they are said to do; they hate the aristocrats inasmuch as they realize that the ruler is necessarily hated by the ruled and that if the rich and aristocratic men in the cities are strong, the rule of the people at Athens will last for a very short time. This is why they disfranchise the aristocrats, take away their money, expel and kill them, whereas they promote the interests of the lower class. The Athenian aristocrats protect their opposite numbers in the allied cities, since they realize that it will be to their advantage always to protect the finer people in the cities. **[1.15]** Someone might say that the Athenians' strength consists in the allies' ability to pay tribute-money; but the rabble thinks it more advantageous for each one of the Athenians to possess the resources of the allies and for the allies themselves to possess only enough for survival and to work without being able to plot defection.

[1.16] Also in another point the Athenian people are thought to act ill-advisedly: they force the allies to sail to Athens for judicial proceedings. But they reason in reply that the Athenian people benefit from this. First, from the deposits at law they receive their dicastic pay through the year. Then, sitting at home without going out in ships, they manage the affairs of the allied cities; in the courts they protect the democrats and ruin their opponents. If the allies were each to hold trials locally, they would, in view of their annoyance with the Athenians, ruin those of their citizens who were the leading friends of the Athenian people.

[1.17] In addition, the people at Athens profit in the following ways when trials involving allies are held in Athens: first, the one percent tax in the Peiraeus brings in more for the city; secondly, if anyone has lodgings to rent, he does better, and so does anyone who lets out on hire a team of animals or a slave; further, the heralds of the assembly do better when the allies are in town.

[1.18] In addition, were the allies not to go away for judicial proceedings, they would honour only those of the Athenians who sail out from the city, namely generals, trierarchs, and ambassadors. As it is now, each one of the allies is compelled to flatter the Athenian populace from the realization that judicial action for anyone who comes to Athens is in the hands of none other than the populace (this indeed is the law at Athens); in the courts he is obliged to entreat whoever comes in and to grasp him by the hand. In this way the allies have become instead the slaves of the Athenian people.

[1.19] Furthermore, as a result of their possessions abroad and the tenure of magistracies which take them abroad, both they and their associates have imperceptibly learned to row; for of necessity a man who is often at sea takes up an oar, as does his slave, and they learn naval terminology. **[1.20]** Both through experience of voyages and through practice they become fine steersmen. Some are trained by service as steersmen on an ordinary vessel, others on a freighter, others—after such experience—on triremes. Many are able to row as soon as they board their ships, since they have been practising beforehand throughout their whole lives.

* * *

[3.10] Also in the following point the Athenians seem to me to act ill-advisedly: in cities embroiled in civil strife they take the side of the lower class. This they do deliberately; for if they preferred the upper class, they would prefer those who are contrary-minded to themselves. In no city is the superior element well disposed to the populace, but in each city it is the worst part which is well disposed to the populace. For like is well disposed to like. Accordingly the Athenians prefer those sympathetic to themselves.

[3.11] Whenever they have undertaken to prefer the upper class, it has not turned out well for them; within a short time the people in Boeotia were enslaved; similarly when they preferred the Milesian upper class, within a short time that class had revolted and cut down the people; similarly when they preferred the Spartans to the Messenians, within a short time the Spartans had overthrown the Messenians and were making war on the Athenians.

Questions

1. **What is the tone of the Old Oligarch in this passage?**
2. **To what does he attribute the success of the Athenian democracy?**
3. **How does he characterize the attitude of the aristocrats and the demos in the cities of the Athenian empire?**
4. **Is his analysis convincing? Why or why not?**

8. THE REVOLT AT MYTILENE

In 428 BC the chief city of Lesbos, Mytilene, revolted against Athens. The causes of this rebellion and the Athenian treatment of the rebels have been the center of much of the debate on the nature of the Athenian empire. Cleon and Diodotus debate not only the proper treatment of allies who rebel but also whether the death penalty acts as a deterrent to crime.

3.26.1. The next summer the Peloponnesians sent off the forty-two ships for Mytilene, under Alcidas, their high admiral, and themselves and their allies invaded Attica, their object being to distract the Athenians by a double movement, and thus to make it less easy for them to act against the fleet sailing to Mytilene. **[2]** The commander in this invasion was Cleomenes, in the place of King Pausanias, son of Pleistoanax, his nephew, who was still a minor. **[3]** Not content with laying waste whatever had shot up in the parts which they had before devastated, the invaders now extended their ravages to lands passed over in their previous incursions; so that this invasion was more severely felt by the Athenians than any except the second; **[4]** the enemy staying on and on until they had overrun most of the country, in the expectation of hearing from Lesbos of something having been achieved by their fleet, which they thought must now have got over. However, as they did not obtain any of the results expected, and their provisions began to run short, they retreated and dispersed to their different cities.

3.27.1. In the meantime the Mytilenians, finding their provisions failing, while the fleet from Peloponnese was loitering on the way instead of appearing at Mytilene, were compelled to come to terms with the Athenians in the following manner. **[2]** Salaethus having himself ceased to expect the fleet to arrive, now armed the commons with heavy armour, which they had not before possessed, with the intention of making a sortie against the Athenians. **[3]** The commons, however, no sooner found themselves possessed of arms than they refused any longer to obey their officers; and forming in knots together, told the authorities to bring out in public the provisions and divide them amongst them all, or they would themselves come to terms with the Athenians and deliver up the city.

3.28.1. The government, aware of their inability to prevent this, and of the danger they would be in, if left out of the capitulation, publicly agreed with Paches and the army to surrender Mytilene at discretion and to admit the troops into the town upon the understanding that the Mytilenians should be allowed to send an embassy to Athens to plead their cause, and that Paches should not imprison, make slaves of, or put to death any of the citizens until its return. **[2]** Such were the terms of the capitulation; in spite of which the chief authors of the negotiation with Lacedaemon were so completely overcome by terror when the army entered, that they went and seated themselves by the altars, from which they were raised up by Paches under promise that he would do them no wrong, and lodged by him in Tenedos, until he should learn the pleasure of the Athenians concerning them. **[3]** Paches also sent some triremes and seized Antissa, and took such other military measures as he thought advisable.

* * *

3.35.1. Arrived at Mytilene, Paches reduced Pyrrha and Eresus; and finding the Lacedaemonian, Salaethus, in hiding in the town, sent him off to Athens, together with the Mytilenians that he had placed in Tenedos, and any other persons that he thought concerned in the revolt. **[2]** He also sent back the greater part of his forces, remaining with the rest to settle Mytilene and the rest of Lesbos as he thought best.

3.36.1. Upon the arrival of the prisoners with Salaethus, the Athenians at once put the latter to death, although he offered, among other things, to procure the withdrawal of the Peloponnesians from Plataea, which was still under siege; **[2]** and after deliberating as to what they should do with the former, in the fury of the moment determined to put to death not only the prisoners at Athens, but the whole adult male population of Mytilene, and to make slaves of the women and children. It was remarked that Mytilene had revolted without being, like the rest, subjected to the empire; and what above all swelled the wrath of the Athenians was the fact of the Peloponnesian fleet having ventured over to Ionia to her support, a fact which was held to argue a long-meditated rebellion. **[3]** They accordingly sent a trireme to communicate the decree to Paches, commanding him to lose no time in despatching the Mytilenians. **[4]** The morrow brought repentance with it and reflection on the horrid cruelty of a decree, which condemned a whole city to the fate merited only by the guilty. **[5]** This was no sooner perceived by the Mytilenian ambassadors at Athens and their Athenian supporters, than they moved the

authorities to put the question again to the vote; which they the more easily consented to do, as they themselves plainly saw that most of the citizens wished some one to give them an opportunity for reconsidering the matter. **[6]** An assembly was therefore at once called, and after much expression of opinion upon both sides, Cleon, son of Cleaenetus, the same who had carried the former motion of putting the Mytilenians to death, the most violent man at Athens, and at that time by far the most powerful with the commons, came forward again and spoke as follows:

3.37.1. "I have often before now been convinced that a democracy is incapable of empire, and never more so than by your present change of mind in the matter of Mytilene. **[2]** Fears or plots being unknown to you in your daily relations with each other, you feel just the same with regard to your allies, and never reflect that the mistakes into which you may be led by listening to their appeals, or by giving way to your own compassion, are full of danger to yourselves, and bring you no thanks for your weakness from your allies; entirely forgetting that your empire is a despotism and your subjects disaffected conspirators, whose obedience is insured not by your suicidal concessions, but by the superiority given you by your own strength and not their loyalty. **[3]** The most alarming feature in the case is the constant change of measures with which we appear to be threatened, and our seeming ignorance of the fact that bad laws which are never changed are better for a city than good ones that have no authority; that unlearned loyalty is more serviceable than quick-witted insubordination; and that ordinary men usually manage public affairs better than their more gifted fellows. **[4]** The latter are always wanting to appear wiser than the laws, and to overrule every proposition brought forward, thinking that they cannot show their wit in more important matters, and by such behavior too often ruin their country; while those who mistrust their own cleverness are content to be less learned than the laws, and less able to pick holes in the speech of a good speaker; and being fair judges rather than rival athletes, generally conduct affairs successfully. **[5]** These we ought to imitate, instead of being led on by cleverness and intellectual rivalry to advise your people against our real opinions.

3.38.1. For myself, I adhere to my former opinion, and wonder at those who have proposed to reopen the case of the Mytilenians, and who are thus causing a delay which is all in favour of the guilty, by making the sufferer proceed against the offender with the edge of his anger blunted; although where vengeance follows most closely upon the wrong, it best equals it and most amply requites it. I wonder also who will be the man who will maintain the contrary, and will pretend to show that the crimes of the Mytilenians are of service to us, and our misfortunes injurious to the allies. [2] Such a man must plainly either have such confidence in his rhetoric as to adventure to prove that what has been once for all decided is still undetermined, or be bribed to try to delude us by elaborate sophisms. [3] In such contests the state gives the rewards to others, and takes the dangers for herself. [4] The persons to blame are you who are so foolish as to institute these contests; who go to see an oration as you would to see a sight, take your facts on hearsay, judge of the practicability of a project by the wit of its advocates, and trust for the truth as to past events not to the fact which you saw more than to the clever strictures which you heard; [5] the easy victims of newfangled arguments, unwilling to follow received conclusions; slaves to every new paradox, despisers of the commonplace; [6] the first wish of every man being that he could speak himself, the next to rival those who can speak by seeming to be quite up with their ideas by applauding every hit almost before it is made, and by being as quick in catching an argument as you are slow in foreseeing its consequences; [7] asking, if I may so say, for something different from the conditions under which we live, and yet comprehending inadequately those very conditions; very slaves to the pleasure of the ear, and more like the audience of a rhetorician than the council of a city.

3.39.1. In order to keep you from this, I proceed to show that no one state has ever injured you as much as Mytilene. [2] I can make allowance for those who revolt because they cannot bear our empire, or who have been forced to do so by the enemy. But for those who possessed an island with fortifications; who could fear our enemies only by sea, and there had their own force of triremes to protect them; who were independent and held in the highest honor by you—to act as these have done, this is not revolt—revolt implies oppression; it is deliberate and wanton aggression; an attempt to ruin us by siding with our bitterest enemies; a worse offence than a war undertaken on their own account in the acquisition of power. [3] The fate of those of their neighbors who had already rebelled

and had been subdued was no lesson to them; their own prosperity could not dissuade them from affronting danger; but blindly confident in the future, and full of hopes beyond their power though not beyond their ambition, they declared war and made their decision to prefer might to right, their attack being determined not by provocation but by the moment which seemed propitious. [4] The truth is that great good fortune coming suddenly and unexpectedly tends to make a people insolent: in most cases it is safer for mankind to have success in reason than out of reason; and it is easier for them, one may say, to stave off adversity than to preserve prosperity. [5] Our mistake has been to distinguish the Mytilenians as we have done: had they been long ago treated like the rest, they never would have so far forgotten themselves, human nature being as surely made arrogant by consideration, as it is awed by firmness. [6] Let them now therefore be punished as their crime requires, and do not, while you condemn the aristocracy, absolve the people. This is certain, that all attacked you without distinction, although they might have come over to us, and been now again in possession of their city. But no, they thought it safer to throw in their lot with the aristocracy and so joined their rebellion! [7] Consider therefore! if you subject to the same punishment the ally who is forced to rebel by the enemy, and him who does so by his own free choice, which of them, think you, is there that will not rebel upon the slightest pretext; when the reward of success is freedom, and the penalty of failure nothing so very terrible? [8] We meanwhile shall have to risk our money and our lives against one state after another; and if successful, shall receive a ruined town from which we can no longer draw the revenue upon which our strength depends; while if unsuccessful, we shall have an enemy the more upon our hands, and shall spend the time that might be employed in combating our existing foes in warring with our own allies.

3.40.1. No hope, therefore, that rhetoric may instil or money purchase, of the mercy due to human infirmity must be held out to the Mytilenians. Their offence was not involuntary, but of malice and deliberate; and mercy is only for unwilling offenders. [2] I therefore now as before persist against your reversing your first decision, or giving way to the three failings most fatal to empire—pity, sentiment, and indulgence. [3] Compassion is due to those who can reciprocate the feeling, not to those who will never pity us in return, but are our natural and necessary foes: the orators who charm us with sentiment may find other less important arenas for their talents, in the place of one where the city pays a heavy penalty for a momentary pleasure, themselves receiving fine acknowledgments for their fine phrases; while indulgence should be shown towards those who will be our friends in future, instead of towards men who will remain just what they were, and as much our enemies as before. **[4]** To sum up shortly, I say that if you follow my advice you will do what is just towards the Mytilenians, and at the same time expedient; while by a different decision you will not oblige them so much as pass sentence upon yourselves. For if they were right in rebelling, you must be wrong in ruling. However, if, right or wrong, you determine to rule, you must carry out your principle and punish the Mytilenians as your interest requires; or else you must give up your empire and cultivate honesty without danger. **[5]** Make up your minds, therefore, to give them like for like; and do not let the victims who escaped the plot be more insensible than the conspirators who hatched it; but reflect what they would have done if victorious over you, especially as they were the aggressors. **[6]** It is they who wrong their neighbor without a cause, that pursue their victim to the death, on account of the danger which they foresee in letting their enemy survive; since the object of a wanton wrong is more dangerous, if he escape, than an enemy who has not this to complain of. **[7]** Do not, therefore, be traitors to yourselves, but recall as nearly as possible the moment of suffering and the supreme importance which you then attached to their reduction; and now pay them back in their turn, without yielding to present weakness or forgetting the peril that once hung over you. Punish them as they deserve, and teach your other allies by a striking example that the penalty of rebellion is death. Let them once understand this and you will not have so often to neglect your enemies while you are fighting with your own confederates."

3.41.1. Such were the words of Cleon. After him Diodotus, son of Eucrates, who had also in the previous assembly spoken most strongly against putting the Mytilenians to death, came forward and spoke as follows:

3.42.1. "I do not blame the persons who have reopened the case of the Mytilenians, nor do I approve the protests which we have heard against important questions being frequently debated.

I think the two things most opposed to good counsel are haste and passion; haste usually goes hand in hand with folly, passion with coarseness and narrowness of mind. **[2]** As for the argument that speech ought not to be the exponent of action, the man who uses it must be either senseless or interested: senseless if he believes it possible to treat of the uncertain future through any other medium; interested if wishing to carry a disgraceful measure and doubting his ability to speak well in a bad cause, he thinks to frighten opponents and hearers by well-aimed calumny. **[3]** What is still more intolerable is to accuse a speaker of making a display in order to be paid for it. If ignorance only were imputed, an unsuccessful speaker might retire with a reputation for honesty, if not for wisdom; while the charge of dishonesty makes him suspected, if successful, and thought, if defeated, not only a fool but a rogue. **[4]** The city is no gainer by such a system, since fear deprives it of its advisers; although in truth, if our speakers are to make such assertions, it would be better for the country if they could not speak at all, as we should then make fewer blunders. **[5]** The good citizen ought to triumph not by frightening his opponents but by beating them fairly in argument; and a wise city without over-distinguishing its best advisers will nevertheless not deprive them of their due, and far from punishing an unlucky counsellor will not even regard him as disgraced. **[6]** In this way successful orators would be least tempted to sacrifice their convictions for popularity, in the hope of still higher honors, and unsuccessful speakers to resort to the same popular arts in order to win over the multitude.

3.43.1. This is not our way; and, besides, the moment that a man is suspected of giving advice, however good, from corrupt motives, we feel such a grudge against him for the gain which after all we are not certain he will receive, that we deprive the city of its certain benefit. **[2]** Plain good advice has thus come to be no less suspected than bad; and the advocate of the most monstrous measures is not more obliged to use deceit to gain the people, than the best counsellor is to lie in order to be believed. **[3]** The city and the city only, owing to these refinements, can never be served openly and without disguise; he who does serve it openly being always suspected of serving himself in some secret way in return. **[4]** Still, considering the magnitude of the interests involved, and the position of affairs, we orators must make it our business to look a little further than you who judge offhand; especially as we, your advisers, are responsible, while you, our audience, are not so. **[5]** For if those who gave the advice, and those who took it, suffered equally, you would judge more calmly; as it is, you visit the disasters into which the whim of the moment may have led you, upon the single person of your adviser, not upon yourselves, his numerous companions in error.

3.44.1. However, I have not come forward either to oppose or to accuse in the matter of Mytilene; indeed, the question before us as sensible men is not their guilt, but our interests. **[2]** Though I prove them ever so guilty, I shall not, therefore, advise their death, unless it be expedient; nor though they should have claims to indulgence, shall I recommend it, unless it be clearly for the good of the country. **[3]** I consider that we are deliberating for the future more than for the present; and where Cleon is so positive as to the useful deterrent effects that will follow from making rebellion capital, I who consider the interests of the future quite as much as he, as positively maintain the contrary. **[4]** And I require you not to reject my useful considerations for his specious ones: his speech may have the attraction of seeming the more just in your present temper against Mytilene; but we are not in a court of justice, but in a political assembly; and the question is not justice, but how to make the Mytilenians useful to Athens.

3.45.1. Now of course communities have enacted the penalty of death for many offences far lighter than this: still hope leads men to venture; and no one ever yet put himself in peril without the inward conviction that he would succeed in his design. **[2]** Again, was there ever city rebelling that did not believe that it possessed either in itself or in its alliances resources adequate to the enterprise? **[3]** All, states and individuals, are alike prone to err, and there is no law that will prevent them; or why should men have exhausted the list of punishments in search of enactments to protect them from evildoers? It is probable that in early times the penalties for the greatest offences were less severe, and that, as these were disregarded, the penalty of death has been by degrees in most cases arrived at, which is itself disregarded in like manner. **[4]** Either then some means of terror more terrible than this must be discovered, or it must be owned that this restraint is useless; and that as long as poverty gives men the courage of necessity, or plenty fills them with the

ambition which belongs to insolence and pride, and the other conditions of life remain each under the thraldom of some fatal and master passion, so long will the impulse never be wanting to drive men into danger. **[5]** Hope also and cupidity, the one leading and the other following, the one conceiving the attempt, the other suggesting the facility of succeeding, cause the widest ruin, and, although invisible agents, are far stronger than the dangers that are seen. **[6]** Fortune, too, powerfully helps the delusion, and by the unexpected aid that she sometimes lends, tempts men to venture with inferior means; and this is especially the case with communities, because the stakes played for are the highest, freedom or empire, and, when all are acting together, each man irrationally magnifies his own capacity. **[7]** In fine, it is impossible to prevent, and only great simplicity can hope to prevent, human nature doing what it has once set its mind upon, by force of law or by any other deterrent force whatsoever.

3.46.1. We must not, therefore, commit ourselves to a false policy through a belief in the efficacy of the punishment of death, or exclude rebels from the hope of repentance and an early atonement of their error. **[2]** Consider a moment! At present, if a city that has already revolted perceives that it cannot succeed, it will come to terms while it is still able to refund expenses, and pay tribute afterwards. In the other case, what city think you would not prepare better than is now done, and hold out to the last against its besiegers, if it is all one whether it surrender late or soon? **[3]** And how can it be otherwise than hurtful to us to be put to the expense of a siege, because surrender is out of the question; and if we take the city, to receive a ruined town from which we can no longer draw the revenue which forms our real strength against the enemy? **[4]** We must not, therefore, sit as strict judges of the offenders to our own prejudice, but rather see how by moderate chastisements we may be enabled to benefit in future by the revenue-producing powers of our dependencies; and we must make up our minds to look for our protection not to legal terrors but to careful administration. **[5]** At present we do exactly the opposite. When a free community, held in subjection by force, rises, as is only natural, and asserts its independence, it is no sooner reduced than we fancy ourselves obliged to punish it severely; **[6]** although the right course with freemen is not to chastise them rigorously when they do rise, but rigorously to watch them before they rise, and to prevent their ever entertaining the idea, and, the insurrection suppressed, to make as few responsible for it as possible.

3.47.1. Only consider what a blunder you would commit in doing as Cleon recommends. **[2]** As things are at present, in all the cities the people is your friend, and either does not revolt with the oligarchy, or, if forced to do so, becomes at once the enemy of the insurgents; so that in the war with the hostile city you have the masses on your side. **[3]** But if you butcher the people of Mytilene, who had nothing to do with the revolt, and who, as soon as they got arms, of their own motion surrendered the town, first you will commit the crime of killing your benefactors; and next you will play directly into the hands of the higher classes, who when they induce their cities to rise, will immediately have the people on their side, through your having announced in advance the same punishment for those who are guilty and for those who are not. **[4]** On the contrary, even if they were guilty, you ought to seem not to notice it, in order to avoid alienating the only class still friendly to us. **[5]** In short, I consider it far more useful for the preservation of our empire voluntarily to put up with injustice, than to put to death, however justly, those whom it is our interest to keep alive. As for Cleon's idea that in punishment the claims of justice and expediency can both be satisfied, facts do not confirm the possibility of such a combination.

3.48.1. Confess, therefore, that this is the wisest course, and without conceding too much either to pity or to indulgence, by neither of which motives do I any more than Cleon wish you to be influenced, upon the plain merits of the case before you, be persuaded by me to try calmly those of the Mytilenians whom Paches sent off as guilty, and to leave the rest undisturbed. **[2]** This is at once best for the future, and most terrible to your enemies at the present moment; inasmuch as good policy against an adversary is superior to the blind attacks of brute force."

3.49.1. Such were the words of Diodotus. The two opinions thus expressed were the ones that most directly contradicted each other; and the Athenians, notwithstanding their change of feeling, now proceeded to a division, in which the show of hands was almost equal, although the motion of Diodotus carried the day. **[2]** Another trireme was at once sent off in haste, for fear that the first might reach Lesbos in the interval, and the city be found destroyed; the first ship having about a day and a night's start. **[3]** Wine and barley-cakes were provided for the vessel by the Mytilenian ambassadors, and great promises made if they arrived in time; which caused the men to use such diligence upon the voyage that they took their meals of barley-cakes kneaded with oil and wine as they rowed, and only slept by turns while the others were at the oar. **[4]** Luckily they met with no contrary wind, and the first ship making no haste upon so horrid an errand, while the second pressed on in the manner described, the first arrived so little before them, that Paches had only just had time to read the decree, and to prepare to execute the sentence, when the second put into port and prevented the massacre. The danger of Mytilene had indeed been great.

3.50.1. The other party whom Paches had sent off as the prime movers in the rebellion were upon Cleon's motion put to death by the Athenians, the number being rather more than a thousand. The Athenians also demolished the walls of the Mytilenians, and took possession of their ships. **[2]** Afterwards tribute was not imposed upon the Lesbians; but all their land, except that of the Methymnians, was divided into three thousand allotments, three hundred of which were reserved as sacred for the gods, and the rest assigned by lot to Athenian shareholders, who were sent out to the island. With these the Lesbians agreed to pay a rent of two minae a year for each allotment, and cultivated the land themselves. **[3]** The Athenians also took possession of the towns on the continent belonging to the Mytilenians, which thus became for the future subject to Athens. Such were the events that took place at Lesbos.

Questions

1. **What arguments does Cleon advance in favor of executing all the adult males of Mytilene?**
2. **What case does Diodotus make against the proposal of Cleon?**
3. **In light of what you know about the political situation in Athens at the time, who was more convincing? Why?**

9. THE CONSEQUENCE OF THE SICILIAN DISASTER

The failure of the Athenian attempt to conquer Sicily and the terrible loss of men and ships which it entailed had a great effect on the attitude of the subject states to Athens. Thucydides (8.1–2) describes their response to the great defeat of 413.

8.1.1. Such were the events in Sicily. When the news was brought to Athens, for a long while they disbelieved even the most respectable of the soldiers who had themselves escaped from the scene of action and clearly reported the matter, a destruction so complete not being thought credible. When the conviction was forced upon them, they were angry with the orators who had joined in promoting the expedition, just as if they had not themselves voted it, and were enraged also with the reciters of oracles and soothsayers, and all other omen mongers of the time who had encouraged them to hope that they should conquer Sicily. **[2]** Already distressed at all points and in all quarters, after what had now happened, they were seized by a fear and consternation quite without example. It was grievous enough for the state and for every man in his proper person to lose so many heavy infantry, cavalry, and able-bodied troops, and to see none left to replace them; but when they saw, also, that they had not sufficient ships in their docks, or money in the treasury, or crews for the ships, they began to despair of salvation. They thought that their enemies in Sicily would immediately sail with their fleet against Piraeus, inflamed by so signal a victory; while their adversaries at home, redoubling all their preparations, would vigorously attack them by sea and land at once, aided by their own revolted confederates. **[3]** Nevertheless, with such means as they had, it was determined to resist to the last, and to provide timber and money, and to equip a fleet as they best could, to take steps to secure their confederates and above all Euboea, to reform things in the city upon a more economical footing, and to elect a board of elders to advise upon the state of affairs as occasion should arise. **[4]** In short, as is the way of a democracy, in the panic of the moment they were ready to be as prudent as possible.

These resolves were at once carried into effect. **8.2.1.** Summer was now over. The winter ensuing saw all Hellas stirring under the impression of the great Athenian disaster in Sicily. Neutrals now felt that even if uninvited they ought no longer to stand aloof from the war, but should volunteer to march against the Athenians, who, as they severally reflected, would probably have come against them if the Sicilian campaign had succeeded. Besides, they considered that the war would now be short, and that it would be creditable for them to take part in it. Meanwhile the allies of the Lacedaemonians felt all more anxious than ever to see a speedy end to their heavy labours. **[2]** But above all, the subjects of the Athenians showed a readiness to revolt even beyond their ability, judging the circumstances with passion, and refusing even to hear of the Athenians being able to last out the coming summer. **[3]** Beyond all this, Lacedaemon was encouraged by the near prospect of being joined in great force in the spring by her allies in Sicily, lately forced by events to acquire their navy. **[4]** With these reasons for confidence in every quarter, the Lacedaemonians now resolved to throw themselves without reserve into the war considering that, once it was happily terminated, they would be finally delivered from such dangers as that which would have threatened them from Athens, if she had become mistress of Sicily, and that the overthrow of the Athenians would leave them in quiet enjoyment of the supremacy over all Hellas.

10. PHRYNICHUS' VIEW OF OLIGARCHY, DEMOCRACY, AND EMPIRE

In 411 BC the Athenians were hard-pressed. Some of their subjects had rebelled; others were on the point of rebellion. Sparta was in league with Persia and able to match Athenian sea power. Alcibiades, the brilliant but treacherous Athenian politician, had been exiled by the democracy and was intriguing at the court of the Persian satrap Tissaphernes. He promised the Athenians that if they overthrew the democracy and established an oligarchy, Persia would break their Spartan alliance and come over to the Athenians.

8.48.1. The design was first mooted in the camp, and afterwards from thence reached the city. Some persons crossed over from Samos and had an interview with Alcibiades, who immediately offered to make first Tissaphernes, and afterwards the king, their friend, if they would give up the democracy, and make it possible for the king to trust them. The higher class, who also suffered most severely from the war, now conceived great hopes of getting the government into their own hands, and of triumphing over the enemy. **[2]** Upon their return to Samos the emissaries formed their partisans into a club, and openly told the mass of the armament that the king would be their friend, and would provide them with money, if Alcibiades were restored, and the democracy abolished. **[3]** The multitude, if at first irritated by these intrigues, were nevertheless kept quiet by the advantageous prospect of the pay from the king; and the oligarchical conspirators, after making this communication to the people, now re-examined the proposals of Alcibiades among themselves, with most of their associates. **[4]** Unlike the rest, who thought them advantageous and trustworthy, Phrynichus, who was still general, by no means approved of the proposals. Alcibiades, he rightly thought, cared no more for an oligarchy than for a democracy, and only sought to change the institutions of his country in order to get himself recalled by his associates; while for

themselves their one object should be to avoid civil discord. It was not the king's interest, when the Peloponnesians were now their equals at sea, and in possession of some of the chief cities in his empire, to go out of his way to side with the Athenians whom he did not trust, when he might make friends of the Peloponnesians who had never injured him. **[5]** And as for the allied states to whom oligarchy was now offered, because the democracy was to be put down at Athens, he well knew that this would not make the rebels come in any the sooner, or confirm the loyal in their allegiance; as the allies would never prefer servitude with an oligarchy or democracy to freedom with the constitution which they actually enjoyed, to whichever type it belonged. **[6]** Besides, the cities thought that the so-called better classes would prove just as oppressive as the commons, as being those who originated, proposed, and for the most part benefited from the acts of the commons injurious to the confederates. Indeed, if it depended on the better classes, the confederates would be put to death without trial and with violence; while the commons were their refuge and the chastiser of these men. **[7]** This he positively knew that the cities had learned by experience, and that such was their opinion. The propositions of Alcibiades, and the intrigues now in progress, could therefore never meet with his approval.

Questions

1. What do passages 9 and 10 suggest about the popularity of the Athenian empire among its subjects?
2. Do you think the attitude of the allies changed during the war or remained consistent from the beginning? Explain.

---

11. THUCYDIDES' SPEECHES

There has been a great deal of debate for centuries over the authenticity of the speeches Thucydides reports in his *History*. And scholars are still not close to agreeing on how accurately the speeches reflect what the speakers actually said. Readers must first consider what Thucydides claims for his speeches in his much discussed programmatic statement in Book I (1.22.1). Unfortunately the Greek text is not much less ambiguous than the best English translations:

1.22.1. With reference to the speeches in this history, some were delivered before the war began, others while it was going on; some I heard myself, others

I got from various quarters; it was in all cases difficult to carry them word for word in one's memory, so my habit has been to make the speakers say what was in my opinion demanded of them (*ta deonta*) by the various occasions, of course adhering as closely as possible to the general sense of what they really said. Some scholars stress the subjectivity of Thucydides in making the speakers say "what was in my [his] opinion demanded of them (*ta deonta*) by the various occasions." On the other hand, scholars such as Donald Bradeen insist on Thucydides' truthfulness in "adhering as closely as possible to the general sense of what they really said."

Questions

1. **What do you think Thucydides meant by *ta deonta*?**
2. **How might your view on the speeches affect the way you read and interpret the text of Thucydides?**

---

12. THE POLITICAL VIEWPOINT OF THUCYDIDES

Not long after the defeat of the Athenians in Sicily, for a brief time in 411/10 BC oligarchs managed to suppress the democracy. First the assembly elected a body of 400 persons to serve as a council, which ruled despotically until deposed by the Athenian four month later. The assembly then voted to turn the government over to the 5,000. In discussing this oligarchy, which lasted for nine months, Thucydides makes one of the few direct comments that reveal his political views.

8.97.2. It was during the first period of this constitution that the Athenians appear to have enjoyed the best government that they ever did, at least in my time. For the fusion (*metria xunkrasis*) of the high and the low was effected with judgment, and this was what first enabled the state to raise up her head after her manifold disasters.

Questions

1. **How might the political views of Thucydides influence his understanding and interpretation of the war?**
2. **Is it important for a historian to make moral judgments? Why or why not?**

OPINIONS OF MODERN SCHOLARS

1. G. E. M. de Ste. Croix offers a bold new reading of Thucydides in his famous article on the character of the Athenian empire. His approach is unique in that he claims to use the evidence of Thucydides himself to disprove the belief of the historian that the empire was a tyranny universally hated by its subjects.

FROM G. E. M. DE STE. CROIX, "THE CHARACTER OF THE ATHENIAN EMPIRE"

WAS THE ATHENIAN EMPIRE a selfish despotism, detested by the subjects whom it oppressed and exploited? The ancient sources, and modern scholars, are almost unanimous that it was, and the few voices (such as those of Grote, Freeman, Greenidge, and Marsh) raised in opposition to this harsh verdict—which will here be called "the traditional view"—have not succeeded in modifying or even explaining its dominance. Characteristic of the attitude of many historians is the severe judgment of Last, who, contrasting Athens as the "tyrant city" with Rome as *communis nostra patria*," can see nothing more significant in Athenian imperial government than that "warning which gives some slight value to even the worst of failures."

The real basis of the traditional view, with which that view must stand or fall, is the belief that the Athenian empire was hated by its subjects—a belief for which there is explicit and weighty support in the sources (above all Thucydides), but which nevertheless is demonstrably false. The first section of this paper will therefore be devoted to showing that whether or not the Athenian empire was politically oppressive or economically predatory, the general mass of the population of the allied (or subject) states, far from being hostile to Athens, actually welcomed her dominance and wished to remain within the empire, even—and perhaps more particularly—during the last thirty years of the fifth century, when the *hybris* of Athens, which bulks so large in the traditional view, is supposed to have been at its height.

The Alleged Unpopularity of the Empire

By far the most important witness for the prosecution, in any arraignment of Athenian imperialism, is of course Thucydides; but it is precisely Thucydides who, under cross-examination, can be made to yield the most valuable pieces of detailed evidence of the falsity of his own generalisations. Before we examine his evidence, it will be well to make clear the conception of his speeches upon which some of the interpretations given here are based. Whatever Thucydides may have meant by the much discussed expression *ta deonta*, whatever purpose he may originally have intended the speeches to serve, there can surely be no doubt that some of the speeches in fact represent what the speakers would have said if they had expressed *with perfect frankness* the sentiments which the historian himself attributed to them, and hence may sometimes depart very far from what was actually said, above all because political and diplomatic speeches are seldom entirely candid.

Now Thucydides harps constantly on the unpopularity of imperial Athens, at least during the Peloponnesian War. He makes no less than eight of his speakers accuse the Athenians of "enslaving" their allies or of wishing to "enslave" other states, and he also uses the same expression in his own person. His Corinthian envoys at Sparta, summarising the historian's own view in a couple of words, call Athens the "tyrant city." Thucydides even represents the Athenians themselves as fully conscious that their rule was a tyranny: he makes not only Cleon but also Pericles admit that the empire had this character. It must be allowed that in such political contexts both "enslavement" and "tyranny"—*douleia* and *tyrannis*, and their cognates—are often used in a highly technical sense: any infringement of the *eleutheria* of a city, however slight, might be described as "enslavement"; and terms such as *tyrannos polis* do not necessarily imply (as the corresponding English expressions would) that Athens was an oppressive or unpopular ruler. However, it will hardly be denied that Thucydides regarded the dominance of Athens over her allies as indeed oppressive and unpopular. The speech he puts into the mouths of the Athenians at Sparta in 432 admits that their rule is "much detested by the Hellenes" and that Athens has become "hateful to most people." At the outbreak of the war, says Thucydides, "people in general were strongly in favour of Sparta, especially as she professed herself the liberator of Hellas. Every individual and every city was eager to help her by word and deed, to the extent of feeling that personal participation was necessary if her cause were not to suffer. So general was the indignation felt against Athens, some desiring to be liberated from her rule, others dreading to pass under it." In the winter of 413–12, when the news of the Athenian disaster in Sicily had become known, Thucydides would have us believe that all Hellas was astir, neutrals feeling that they ought to attack Athens spontaneously, and the subjects of Athens showing themselves ready to revolt "even beyond their capacity to do so," feeling passionately on the subject and refusing even to hear of the Athenians' being able to last out the summer.

This is what Thucydides wanted his readers to believe. It is undoubtedly the conception he himself honestly held. Nevertheless, his own detailed narrative proves that it is certainly false. Thucydides was such a remarkably objective historian that he himself has provided sufficient material for his own refutation. The news columns in Thucydides, so to speak, contradict the editorial Thucydides, and the editor himself does not always speak with the same voice.

In the "Mytilenean Debate" at Athens in 427, Thucydides makes Diodotus tell the assembled Athenians that in all the cities the demos is their friend, and either does not join the Few, the *oligoi*, when they revolt, or, if constrained to do so, at once turns on the rebels so that in fighting the refractory state the Athenians have the mass of the citizens (*to plethos*) on their side. (The precise meaning of these expressions—demos, plethos, oligoi and the like—will be considered in the third section of this paper.) It is impossible to explain away the whole passage on the ground that Diodotus is just saying the kind of thing that might be expected to appeal to an Athenian audience. Not only do we have Thucydides' general statement that throughout the Greek world, after the Corcyraean revolution of 427, the leaders of the popular parties tried to in the Athenians, as *hoi oligoi* the Spartans; there is a great deal of evidence relating to individual cities, which we must now consider. Of course, the mere fact that a city did not revolt from Athens does not of itself necessarily imply fidelity: considerations of expediency, short-term or long-term, may often have been decisive—the fear of immediate Athenian counter-action, or the belief that Athens would ultimately become supreme. But that does not alter the fact that in almost every case in which we do have detailed information about the attitude of an allied city, we find only the Few hostile; scarcely ever is there reason to think that the demos was not mainly loyal. The evidence falls into two groups: for the 450s and 440s B.C. it is largely epigraphic, for the period of the Peloponnesian War it is mainly literary. We shall begin with the later period, for which the evidence is much more abundant.

The revolt of Lesbos in 428–7, in which Mytilene was the ringleader, is particularly interesting, because it is only at the very end of Thucydides' account that we gain any inkling of the real situation. At first, Thucydides implies that the Mytileneans were wholehearted and that only a few factious citizens, who were *proxenoi* of Athens, cared to inform the Athenians of the preparations for revolt. We hear much of the determined resistance of the Mytileneans and of their appeal to Sparta, and we may well be astonished when we suddenly discover from Thucydides that "the Mytileneans" who had organised and conducted the revolt were not the main body of the Mytileneans at all, but only the governing oligarchy, for no sooner had the Spartan commander Salaethus distributed hoplite equipment to the formerly light-armed demos, with the intention of making a *sortie en masse* against the besieging Athenian force, than the demos immediately mutinied and the government had to surrender to Athens.

In describing the activities of Brasidas in the "Thraceward region" in 424–3, Thucydides occasionally gives us a glimpse of the internal situation in the cities. First, it is worth mentioning that in recording the northward march of Brasidas through Thessaly, Thucydides says that the mass of the population there had always been friendly to Athens, and that Brasidas would never have been allowed to pass if *isonomia* instead of the traditional *dynasteia* had existed in Thessaly. When Brasidas arrived in the "Thraceward district," probably in September 424, there seem to have been few if any Athenian garrisons there, for Thucydides mentions none, except that at Amphipolis, and represents the Athenians as sending out garrisons at the end of that year, "as far as they could at such short notice and in winter." Brasidas made his first attempt on Acanthus. The inhabitants were divided, the common people being faithful to Athens; but eventually the citizens gave way and opened their gates, influenced not only by an able speech from Brasidas, a judicious blend of threats and promises, but also by "fear for their fruit," for it was just before vintage, and Brasidas had threatened to ravage. When the Spartan invited the surrender of Amphipolis, he at first found little support within that town. However, the combined effect of his military success in occupying the surrounding country, the advantageous terms he offered, and the efforts of his partisans within, was sufficient to procure the surrender of the city.

Thucydides declares now categorically that there was general enthusiasm for revolt among the Athenian subject cities of the district, which sent secret messages to Brasidas, begging him to come to them, each wishing to lead the way in revolting. They had the additional inducement, as Thucydides points out, of the recent Athenian defeat at Delium. On the face of it, Thucydides' account is plausible enough. There is good reason to suppose, however, that when he speaks of the "cities" that were subject to Athens, he is thinking merely of the propertied classes. When Brasidas marched into the peninsula of Acte, most of the towns (which were insignificant) naturally surrendered at once, but Sane and Dium, small as they were, and surrounded by cities now in alliance with Brasidas, held out, even when their lands were ravaged. Turning his attention to the Sithonian peninsula, Brasidas captured Torone, though it was held by an Athenian garrison (probably just arrived); but this was done only through the treachery of a few, to the dismay of the majority, some of whom joined the Athenian garrison when it shut itself up in the fort of Lecythus, only to be driven out to Pallene. A Spartan commander was subsequently put in charge of the town. In 423, after Scione had revolted spontaneously, its neighbour Mende was betrayed to Brasidas by a few. Later, when the Athenian army arrived, there were disturbances at Mende, and soon the common people fell upon the mixed Scionean and Peloponnesian garrison of seven hundred. After plundering the town, which had not made terms of surrender, the Athenians wisely told the Mendeans that they could keep their civic rights and themselves deal with their own traitors. In the case of Acanthus, Sane, Dium, Torone and Mende, then, we have positive evidence that the bulk of the citizens were loyal to Athens, in circumstances which were anything but propitious. In Aristophanes' *Peace*, produced in 421, it is hoi *pacheis kai plousioi* whom the Athenians are said to have pursued with charges of favouring Brasidas. It would be simple-minded to suppose that this happened just because the riches citizens were the most worth despoiling. It may be that some of the other town went over to Brasidas with the free consent of the demos, but only in regard to Scione, and possibly Argilus (whose citizens apparently hoped to gain control over Amphipolis by backing Brasidas) does the narrative of Thucydides provide any grounds for this assumption; and even at Scione, which did not revolt until 423, some at first "disapproved of what was being done."

* * *

We can now go back to the 450s and 440s B.C., a period for which, as mentioned above, the evidence on the questions under discussion is predominantly epigraphic. The revolt of Erythrae, from 454 or earlier to 452, was almost certainly due to the seizure of power by a Persian-backed tyranny. Miletus was also in revolt from at least 454 until 452/1; but during this period she was apparently under the control of a close oligarchy or tyranny, which seems to have driven out an important section of the citizen body (perhaps with Persian support), and was sentenced in its turn to perpetual and hereditary outlawry about

452, when the exiles returned and the city was brought back into the Athenian empire. The probable absence of Colophon from the tribute quota-lists of the second assessment period (450/49 to 447/6), and the Athenian decree relating to that city of (probably) 446, certainly point to a revolt about 450; but the known Persian associations of this inland city, the fact that was handed over to the Persian Itamenes in 430 by one of two parties in a stasis (presumably of the usual character—oligarchs against democrats), and the Colophonian oath to preserve democracy—perhaps newly introduced, or at any rate restored—in the treaty made with Athens in 446 or thereabouts, strongly suggest that the revolt was the work of oligarchs receiving Persian support. The revolt of Euboea in 446 may well have been mainly the work of the Hippobotae, the aristocrats of Chalcis, for the Athenians drove them out on the reduction of the island and probably gave their lands to cleruchs, but inflicted no punishment beyond the taking of hostages, as far as we know, on the other Euboeans, except that they expelled the Hestiaeans (who had massacred the crew of an Athenian ship) and settled an Athenian colony on their lands. The revolt of Samos in 440/39, after certain Samians who "wished to revolutionise the constitution" had induced the Athenians to set up a democracy, was certainly brought about by exiled oligarchs, who allied themselves with the Persian satrap Pissuthnes, employed a force of seven hundred mercenaries, and worked in conjunction with the remaining in the city. Here there is no evidence of general hostility to Athens among the Samians, although once the oligarchs had got a firm grip on the city, and had captured and expelled the democratic leaders, they put up a stout resistance to Athens and were no doubt able to enforce the adherence of a considerable number of common folk.

It is significant that in this early period, whenever we do have information about the circumstances of a revolt, we find good reason for attributing it to oligarchs or tyrants, who could evidently rely on Persian assistance wherever the situation of the city permitted. This is precisely the state of affairs we have already seen to exist later, during the Peloponnesian War. In some cases, both early and late, the bare fact of a revolt is recorded, without detail. Some of these revolts may have been wholehearted, but we certainly cannot assume so just because we have no evidence. Surely the reverse is true: surely we may assume that the situation we find in virtually all the towns for which we do have sufficient information existed in most of the remainder. The mere fact of the coming to power of an oligarchy in an allied city immediately upon a revolt from Athens, as evidently at Eretria in 411, tends to confirm that the democratic party in that city was pro-Athenian.

It is not difficult to find other examples of loyalty to Athens on the part of her allies, or pro-Athenian movements inside cities in revolt. When the Athenian armament in Sicily was at its last gasp, the division under Demosthenes being on the very point of surrender, the Syracusans made a proclamation offering freedom to any of the islanders (the Athenian allies) who were willing to come over to them. Further resistance was now quite hopeless, and nothing could have restrained the allies from deserting except the strongest sense of loyalty. Yet Thucydides tells us that "not many cities went over." The majority remained, to undergo a fate which they must have well known could only be death or enslavement. In 428 Methymna refused to follow the rest of the Lesbian cities in their revolt. In 430 there was a *stasis* at Colophon; one faction called in the Persians and expelled the other, which removed to Notium but itself split into two factions, one of which gained control of the new settlement by employing mercenaries and allied itself with the medising [pro-Persian] citizens remaining in Colophon. In 427 the defeated party, no doubt democratic in character, called in the Athenians, who founded a new colony at Notium for the exiled Colophonians. The capture of Selymbria and Byzantium by the Athenians in 408–7 was brought about in each case by the treachery of a faction inside the city.

In the light of all the evidence which has been cited above, we can understand and accept Plato's explanation of the long life of the Athenian empire: the Athenians, he says, kept their *arché* for seventy years "because they had friends in each of the cities."

* * *

An overwhelming body of evidence has now been produced to show that the mass of the citizens in the allied or subject states were loyal to Athens throughout the whole period of the empire, until the final collapse in the Ionian War, and could on occasion give proof of a deep devotion to the imperial city, which can only be compared with the similar devotion of contemporary oligarchs to Sparta. This judgment holds, whatever the character of Athenian imperialism may have been and whatever verdict we ourselves may wish to pass upon it. The evidence is all the more impressive in that it comes mainly from Thucydides, who, whenever he is generalising, or interpreting the facts rather than stating them, depicts the subjects of Athens as groaning under her tyrannous rule. A subsidiary conclusion of no small importance which has emerged from this survey is that Thucydides, generally (and rightly) considered the most trustworthy of all ancient historians, is guilty of serious misrepresentation in his judgments on the Athenian empire. He was quite entitled to disapprove of the later empire, and to express this disapproval. What we may reasonably object to is his representing that the majority of its subjects detested it. At the same time, it must be laid to Thucydides' credit that we are able to convict of this distortion precisely because he himself is scrupulously accurate in presenting the detailed evidence. The partiality of Thucydides could scarcely have been exposed but for the honesty of Thucydides.

The Political Outlook of Thucydides

Our subject is the Athenian empire and not its great historian; but as certain criticisms have been made of Thucydides in the first and second sections of this article, it is only right that an explanation should be offered of the reasons for the defects in his *History* which have been pointed out above. Why did Thucydides, who was an exceptionally truthful man and anything but a superficial observer, so deceive himself about the attitude of the Greeks towards the Athenian empire? There can only be one answer: political and social influences, at the end of the fifth century exceptionally powerful, drove the historian to look at the whole Greek world in terms of that relatively small section of the Athenian citizen body to which he himself belonged, so that when he wrote of the detestation of Athens, or the longing for revolt, felt by *hoi polloi*, or *hoi Hellenes pantes*, or *hai poleis hypekooi*, or *hoi xummachoi*, or *pas kai idiotes kai polis*, he was thinking only of the upper classes, of that comparatively small body of what is sometimes called "educated opinion." This point of view he quite honestly conceived as that of the Greeks in general. It is a perfectly natural and very common failing, and it is entirely characteristic of the Greek and Roman historians, most of whom, if they did not actually belong to the governing class of their day, had thoroughly acquired its outlook. When we are studying Thucydides, then, we must never forget that we are studying a member—if an exceptionally intelligent and gifted member—of Athenian propertied class.

* * *

What was Thucydides' attitude to the Athenian empire? This is a question to which almost everyone gives a different answer. The principal reason for this is that the historian's attitude to the empire was thoroughly ambivalent, that he could habitually entertain quite different feelings towards it at one and the same time, now one and now another coming uppermost. On the one hand he was much impressed by the greatness and brilliance of imperial Athens, in which, as a patriotic Athenian, he must have felt a deep pride. In inter-state politics he was a realist, calmly accepting the fact that in the relations between Greek cities force and not justice was in practice the supreme arbiter. He was not shocked by the calculated and restrained exercise of state power, which I regarded as an inevitable and in some ways a desirable feature of the contemporary scene. On the other hand, sharing as he did the outlook of the allied *oligoi*, he felt that Athens had abused her power—not as much as imperial city in her position might easily have been tempted to abuse it, but enough to provoke general hatred and a longing to be quit of her rule. In the Melian Dialogue, with enigmatic impartiality, he gives the Athenians an unanswerable case, according to the prevailing practice of inter-state relations based ultimately on the appeal to force, in the name of expediency; but he has chosen for this highly generalised debate a setting which could not fail to arouse in his readers, knowing of the massacre that was to come, the strongest prejudice against the Athenian speakers.

One thing Thucydides does not say, explicitly or implicitly, although the statement is often attributed to him: he does not say that the Athenian radical democrats believed that "Might is Right." When the Athenian envoys at Sparta say, *aiei kathestotos ton hesso hypo tou dynatoterou kateirgesthai*, they simply saying, "It has always been the rule for the weaker to be subject to the stronger." They are merely recognising a natural tendency, a "law of human nature," not trying to adduce a moral justification. The theory that the interest of the stronger is *to dikaion*, that Might is Right, does not seem to make its appearance in surviving literature until the time of Plato, who puts it into the mouths of Callicles, not an historical character, and Thrasymachus, a sophist of whom there is not the slightest reason to connect with the radical democrats. Did any fifth century Greek seriously maintain that Might is Right, or is this merely a clever distortion of the realist position actually held by the Athenian radicals. It is easy to imagine how this distortion could come about. The oligarchs had been accustomed to maintain that under the old regime, where they had been masters, Right rather than Might had prevailed. When the democrats exposed this pretence, the obvious counter-attack was to twist the democratic admission that force did govern into the claim that force ought to govern.

Why the Many Were Friendly to Athens

It is part of the traditional view of the Athenian empire that the common people of Athens, under the influence of the "demagogues," drove the allies hard, while the "best people" did what they could to protect them. Of course oligarchs like Thucydides the son of Melesias, and perhaps Antiphon, would pose as defenders of the allies, by way of showing their opposition to the whole policy of the democrats. But the traditional view cannot be allowed to stand here either. Apart from the other evidence, there is a very striking and important passage in the last book of Thucydides, which seldom receives the attention it deserves. The whole passage (which would presumably have been worked up into a set speech if the *History* had ever been finished) describes the point of view of Phrynichus, the Athenian oligarch, in 411. Phrynichus realised, says Thucydides, that the setting up of an oligarchy at Athens would not have the effect of making the allies, many of whom were then in revolt, any better disposed towards Athens. He admitted "that the allies expected the upper classes (of Athens) to prove just as troublesome to themselves as the demos, as being those who devised the acts injurious to the allies, proposed them to the demos, and gained most of the benefit from them; and that as far as the upper classes were concerned, they (the allies) might come to a violent end without trial, whereas the demos was their refuge and the chastiser of these men." This is a very remarkable statement, all the more valuable in that it is put by Thucydides (without contradiction) into the mouth of an oligarch, who could have no possible reason for making an admission so damaging to his own party if it were not true. It gives us two pieces of information: that most of the perquisites of empire went to the Athenian upper classes; and that the Athenian demos was more just and merciful towards the allies than were its "betters."

Humble folk in the allied cities who were oppressed by their own *oligoi* would have had no hesitation in trying to obtain redress from Athens, either in the form of assistance for a *coup d'*état or by recourse to recognised judicial procedure. The power to transfer certain cases to Athens, especially serious criminal cases, was one of the most important features of the government of the empire. The Old Oligarch shows how the process operated to the advantage of the common people both at Athens and in the allied states. He says outright that the Athenians persecute the *chrestoi, . . . tous de ponerous auxousin* and again that in the law courts *tous men tou demou sozousin, tous d' enantious apolluousin.* He explains that by compelling the allies to sail to Athens for judicial decisions the Athenians not only derive financial benefit (which he probably exaggerates); they can govern the allied states, supporting the popular side and making short work of their opponents, without having to go overseas; and thus the allies are obliged not merely to pay respect to visiting generals, trierarchs and ambassadors (who would at least be gentlemen) but also to curry favour with the Athenian demos itself and lick its boots, thus becoming "slaves of the Athenian demos." He adds the information that if the allies were allowed to try their cases at home, they in their turn, detesting Athens as they do, would make short work of the pro-Athenian parties in their midst—by which he means democratic agitators and suchlike. If you want real eunomia, he says, you must have the laws made for the demos by the *dexiotatoi* and then the *chrestoi* will chastise the *poneroi* and not allow *mainomenous anthropous* any voice at all. The Old Oligarch reflects with satisfaction that in such a desirable state of affairs the demos would rapidly fall into *douleia.* [slavery] These passages give us an interesting glimpse of the attitude of many influential members of the propertied classes in the fifth century against whose interests the Athenians were working when they claimed overriding powers in respect of certain judicial cases. We are able for a moment to foresee what would happen when Athenian control was removed—what actually did happen after the "liberation" of the allies by Sparta, when (as at Athens itself under the "Thirty") there were "many massacres," and "the slaughter of countless numbers of the popular party."

We need not be surprised, then, that the masses in the cities of the Athenian empire welcomed political subordination to Athens as the price of escape from the tyranny of their own oligarchs. This is not the place to consider whether they received other benefits from Athenian rule; protection against their own oligarchs is enough for our present purposes. Athens undoubtedly gave much support to the Many in the allied states against their own Few, who of course (with the sympathy of the Few at Athens, including Thucydides) regarded the resulting democratisation as the direct consequence of Athenian tyranny. Almost all our literary sources, imbued with oligarchical prejudice, present this point of view only. Active Athenian support of the Many must certainly have increased after 461, and may perhaps have become intensified again after the death of Pericles; but in the absence of confirmatory detailed evidence there is no reason to suppose that the Athenians became to any marked extent increasingly "oppressive," except in the peculiar oligarchical sense, during the second half of the fifth century.

We may accept the statement of Isocrates that the Athenians did not set up "opposition governments" unjustifiably in the allied states, and thus stir factional strife. On the contrary, it was the boast of the Athenian democrats that they had suppressed *stasis.* To borrow a phrase from a modern politician, Athens did not "export revolution," at any rate to states which were not already well supplied with that commodity. The way Isocrates puts it, in another speech, is that "our fathers tried to induce (*epeithon*) the allies to establish in their cities the same form of government as they themselves reserved with loving care." This may not be so very far from the truth. At any rate, it is a grave error to take the introduction of a democracy on the Athenian model as a necessary indication of Athenian "bullying." Would not the Many in an oligarchical state be only too delighted to copy, even in minute details, the famous constitution of democratic Athens? Might they not even be glad to have an Athenian garrison on hand while they were learning to work their new constitution? We know that the democrats at Corcyra. in c. 410, having reason to suspect that their *dynatatoi* were about to hand the city over to Sparta, obtained a garrison from the Athenians. And the Athenian garrison at Lesbian Methymna, as already mentioned, had probably been supplied at the request of the part in power. At Erythrae the well-known inscription shows the Athenians installing a garrison whose commander is given the task of supervising the selection by lot of the vital Council. But there not the slightest warrant for inferring from this that Erythrae required to be "held down" by an armed force; and as for what have been referred to as the "important political functions" of the garrison commander, these were limited (in the surviving portion of the decree) to supervising a choice by lot, and therefore amounted to no more than ensuring that there was *no* jiggery-pokery. Democracies cannot easily be created overnight; it may take a long time to learn how to work one. Clever oligarchs, skilled in the hereditary art of government, would know just how to take advantage of the inefficiency of a new democratic regime, and they could probably rely in most cases on getting power back into their own hands before very long, unless the popular government received assistance as well as advice from the parent democracy. If the city could not afford to pay its councillors and dicasts (and probably very few cities could), the Many would find it very difficult to prevent the Few from regaining domination of the Council and the courts, upon which so much

would depend. If it came to fighting, a small body of determined hoplites could be relied upon to deal with a much larger number of unpractised light-armed—and if the odds were too great, mercenaries could be hired. The Athenians, therefore, must have received many requests for assistance from the democratic parties in other states, and of course their intervention was regarded by the oligarchs—themselves quite prepared to call in the Spartans, if not Persians—as an intolerable infringement of *autonomia* and *eleutheria*. If the Athenian *hegemonia* changed by degrees into an arche, (arche) the responsibility would seem to lie partly with the Many in the allied states, who often welcomed and even invited intervention. It may well be embassies bearing appeals of this sort, demos to demos, which Aristophanes has in mind when he sneers in the Acharnians at allied ambassadors who come to Athens with fine, complimentary phrases, flattering the Athenians in order to gain their own ends; he adds an encomium of himself as *tous demous en tais polesin deixas, hos demokratountai.*

No attempt has been made here to present a complete defence of the Athenian empire, or to give a "balanced judgment" upon it. There is no doubt that the Athenians did derive considerable profits for themselves out of the empire, and to some extent exploit their allies. But if, as we have seen, the empire remained popular with the Many, then its benefits, from their point of view, must have outweighed the evils. The more abuses we find in Athenian imperialism (and of course abuses were not lacking), the more virtues, from the point of view of the Many, we must at the same time discover, or else we shall be further than ever from being able to account for the popularity of the empire.

2. Donald Bradeen takes issue with the attempt of de Ste. Croix to refute Thucydides. He finds unconvincing the thesis that the *demos* in the cities of the allies favored the Athenians in spite of the oligarchs. Donald Bradeen was Professor of Classics at Cincinnati University.

FROM DONALD W. BRADEEN, "THE POPULARITY OF THE ATHENIAN EMPIRE"

THE QUESTION OF THE POPULARITY of the Athenian Empire among its subjects is an important one, both for our understanding of the history of the fifth century and for our estimate of the reliability, judgment, and even the integrity of Thucydides. The historian clearly portrays the Empire as a tyranny,

hated by the majority of the subjects; he puts such sentiments into the mouths of the Athenian envoys to Sparta in 432 and attributes them to Perikles and Kleon when they are addressing the Athenian *demos.* He states much the same on his own in describing the feelings of the Greeks against Athens at the beginning of the war and their readiness to revolt after the failure of the Sicilian expedition. Although it has been noticed that these latter statements seem to be rather exaggerated generalizations in the light of what happened later, it has usually been assumed that Thucydides' judgment was the common one among the Athenians as well as the other Greeks and that the unpopularity of the Empire was a fact recognized during its existence.

Grote did question Thucydides' judgment to the extent that he claimed that the general feeling towards Athens among her subjects was one of "neither attachment nor hatred, but simple indifference and acquiescence in her supremacy." He thought that most of the trouble for Athens was stirred up by oligarchs playing upon "the general political instinct of the Greek mind—desire of separate autonomy;" he did not deny the existence of this feeling in all classes of the allies, yet he believed that it was often outweighed by the practical advantages of the Empire and thought that often the mass of the people in the allied cities were actively pro-Athenian. But Grote's position, in that he could not really bring himself to reject Thucydides' opinion completely, was basically inconsistent and won few followers; in general Thucydides' view of the unpopularity of the Empire has prevailed.

Recently, however, Grote's arguments have been revived and pushed to their logical extreme by A. H. M. Jones and G. E. M. de Ste. Croix. The latter's position, in sum, is that the Empire remained popular with "the mass of citizens in the allied or subject states," who "were loyal to Athens throughout the whole period of the empire, until the final collapse in the Ionian War;" a corollary to this is that Thucydides "is guilty of serious misrepresentation in his judgment on the Athenian Empire." The reason for this misrepresentation de Ste. Croix finds in Thucydides' oligarchic political outlook and his sympathy for the anti-Athenian Few among the allies. This is an intriguing thesis and the article is both interesting and impressive as it ranges far beyond this basic position by defending not only the Athenians and their Empire but also the demagogues and even the subjugation of Melos. In a way much of its appeal comes from the fact that de Ste. Croix sets out to prove his case against Thucydides primarily with evidence from Thucydides himself; as he puts it, "the news columns in Thucydides, so to speak, contradict the editorial Thucydides, and the editor himself does not always speak with the same

voice." Now the attraction here stems from the fact that most of us ancient historians have a sympathy for Athens and her Empire; no matter how impartial we try to be, our whole training as classicists, and possibly our political bent as well, incline us that way. We want to justify Athens' treatment of her subjects, but in the way of such a justification stands the judgment of Thucydides, for whose work we have a great respect. But now if we can prove from Thucydides himself that his judgment is wrong, then the obstacle is removed, and if it be true that the majority of the subjects approved of the Empire, then here is our justification. It is tempting to seize upon this and de Ste. Croix already has some converts. Perhaps most important of all is the fact that a recent textbook in its summary of the Empire presents de Ste. Croix' conclusions without qualification. This certainly calls for a re-examination of the evidence and de Ste. Croix' handling of it. I hope to show that his argument is based upon three general assumptions which are questionable, to say the least; that there are several serious omissions in the presentation of the case; and that what appears to be a mass of corroborative evidence consists for the most part of ambiguous situations interpreted from de Ste. Croix' point of view.

First we should discuss the basic assumptions underlying de Ste. Croix' case; the first two of these may best be analyzed together. One seems to be that Thucydides was a partisan oligarch who allowed his political convictions to distort his picture of the entire situation; the second is that the speeches in his history can be lumped with his expressed personal opinions as the "editorial" Thucydides. Objections may be raised to the former on two counts. The first objection, less important in that it is probably more semantic than real, is to calling Thucydides an oligarch. Undoubtedly he would have been one had he been involved in Athenian politics in 412, but so were many men who had been "democrats" twenty years before. The main question is whether their political thinking had changed in the meantime or had the nature of Athenian democracy. At any rate, the real basis of the belief that Thucydides was an oligarch is his judgment on the Constitution of the 5000, and de Ste. Croix himself has made such an inference suspect by his excellent analysis of that government as a true *metria xunkrasis*. Nevertheless there is no doubt that Thucydides was an aristocrat and that he disapproved of the "radical" democracy. But, arguments about names aside, the main objection to de Ste. Croix' assumption is rather this: Was Thucydides the kind of man who would allow political views to distort seriously his historical judgment? This may seem to be only a matter of opinion, but it certainly is difficult to see behind the history an author who was either of the two things implied in this assumption. For on this basis he must have been either a fool who, with many times the evidence we have now, could not see the "truth" which we can now discover, primarily from the evidence he gives us, or else a completely dishonest man who deliberately painted a false picture. De Ste. Croix obviously thinks of him as the former, for he calls him "an exceptionally truthful man and anything but a superficial observer" who deceived himself because "... political and social influences, at the end of the fifth century exceptionally powerful, drove the historian to look at the whole Greek world in terms of that relatively small section of the Athenian citizen body to which he himself belonged...." It may again be only a matter of opinion, but I cannot conceive that Thucydides, with the experience he must have had with the differences of opinion among the classes at Athens, was so blind as to think that the oligarchs' beliefs were those of "all the Greeks" or "every state and private citizen."

But be that as it may, if we consider this assumption in the light of the second, I think that the alternatives between which we must choose will be seen to be different. The second assumption is that the speeches are part of the "editorial" Thucydides, or, to put it bluntly, that they were completely his own and, so to speak, made from whole cloth. De Ste. Croix does not say this in so many words, but he does state that they "represent what the speakers would have said if they had expressed *with perfect frankness* the sentiments which the historian himself attributed to them." But if these speeches are "editorial," we must surely add that the sentiments which Thucydides attributes to the speakers are his own. So de Ste. Croix regards them, except when they happen to agree with his thesis. Now this raises the question of the much disputed passage in I, 22, 1, in which Thucydides discusses the composition of the speeches. Complete agreement will never be reached on this subject, but whatever is meant there by *ta deonta*, it can hardly indicate that the historian gave the speakers his own political views, since he states immediately thereafter

that he kept as closely as possible to the general meaning of what was actually said—an avowal which has been more or less ignored in much of the recent discussion of the passage but cannot be dismissed. This was Thucydides' announced intention, and it was certainly easier in some cases than in others to abide by it. The speeches easiest for him to report accurately were those delivered in Athens before his exile, and it is in two of these, by Perikles and Kleon, that the Empire is described as a tyranny which cannot be safely given up because of the hatred of the unwilling subjects. One cannot insist that Thucydides must have been present on these occasions, but it can hardly be denied that he must have known how the politicians spoke of the Empire before the *demos*. Granted this, the treatment of the Empire in these speeches can be explained in two ways. The first possibility is that the politicians did not recognize the unpopularity of the Empire but Thucydides deliberately misrepresented their attitude; this is very unlikely for an "exceptionally truthful man" who has announced that he would keep as closely as possible to what was actually said. The alternative is that the unpopularity of the Empire was recognized publicly by the orators and the *demos*, as we should expect from the tone of fifth century decrees which seem neither to mince words nor to make any pretense about the position of the allies. In this case we certainly should believe that this unpopularity existed, since these people were definitely not the type to present the views of oligarchs as those of all the subjects. Such are the alternatives with which we are left after analyzing the two assumptions together. I do not see how anyone can seriously doubt that the second represents the true situation; if one wishes to deny it, I should think that this would necessitate a frontal attack upon the integrity of Thucydides.

The third assumption which I wish to re-examine is that in almost every subject city the *demos*, in a political sense, represented the majority and was, more or less by definition, pro-Athenian. De Ste. Croix states that "it would be perverse in the extreme to pretend" otherwise, but I am not so sure, in these days of "People's Democracy." The one time when we have definite figures, the *demos* at Samos, in a political sense, seems to number 300 in 412/11. Of course this means very little, as the situation was complicated by the presence of Athenian troops and ships, but this is a condition which, in a lesser degree, we cannot ignore at any period of the Empire. We must certainly take into account the ever-present threat of the Athenian fleet and the amount of military and civil control which the Athenians exercised over her allies. This definitely was not negligible. Aristotle may well be exaggerating when he speaks of seven hundred Athenian officials abroad in the fifth century, but even back near the middle of the century we have epigraphic proof of the presence of *phrourarchoi*, *episkopoi*, and *archontes* in the allied cities. It would be naive to think that these would not use their influence wherever possible to encourage pro-Athenian democratic elements, whether these had the support of the majority of the citizens or not. It seems to me quite conceivable that in most cases the majority was not sympathetic with Athens or even with a democracy, at least in the sense of rule by an urban *demos*. In fact, many of the subject states could not have had an urban *demos* of the type which Athens had, and we surely must make a distinction here between agricultural towns and commercial cities. Certainly in the Chalkidike, for instance, most of the population was rural, with that traditional rural conservatism which would have been satisfied with the oligarchic constitution of their ancestors, whether they were under a democracy or not.

It is customary to think of a violent political antagonism between the rich (oligarchs) and the poor (democrats), but this was something which was brought on and fostered by the Peloponnesian War. Aristotle does, it is true, conceive of the basic difference between oligarchy and democracy as one of wealth, not numbers, but this was after the split caused by the war had been widened by the economic difficulties of the first half of the fourth century. Even then the poor were not always dissatisfied and ready to overthrow an oligarchy, since Aristotle states that they were quite willing to remain quiet as long as the government did them no violence, judicially or economically. Such, I think, must have been the normal situation in most of the subject states, although this certainly could have been changed later by the propaganda during the war. Even in cities where there were nominal democracies, it is unlikely that real control was in the hands of the poor, since this presupposes the ability of the state to pay salaries on a large scale.

There was little chance, then, in the smaller cities of the Empire, for a democracy of the Athenian type, but what of the larger commercial cities, like Chios,

Miletos, Mytilene, or Samos, which as centers of trade and usually possessing their own fleets, would have had a class equivalent to the *thetes* at Athens? Here, if anywhere, we should expect to find a pro-Athenian *demos*, eager for democracy. De Ste. Croix thinks that he can see one at Mytilene in Thucydides' account of the revolt of 428/7: towards the end, when that city was besieged by the Athenians and the Spartan commander gave shields and spears to the *demos* for a last-ditch sally, these men refused to obey and demanded that food should be brought out and shared equally or they would negotiate with the Athenians; this forced the government to surrender the city. Now this was the act of men driven by hunger and despair, not by any love for or loyalty to Athens. Diodotos presents it in this latter light when he has a case to plead, and so does de Ste. Croix, but this is not proving Thucydides' judgment wrong by the "news columns" in Thucydides, but by a distortion of them. I suggest that the important aspect of the situation at Mytilene is not the fact that the *demos* acted as it did in 428/7, but rather that the government was an oligarchy to the end and that the demos acquiesced in this, and in the revolt, so long. To me there can be only one reason for this—the people preferred autonomy under an oligarchy to the closer subjugation to Athens which a democracy would bring with it. For surely the setting up of a democracy would be possible only through the armed intervention of Athens, which would entail an Athenian garrison and probable loss of the fleet. It is true that de Ste. Croix denies the existence of an autonomous group of allies, either *de jure* or *de facto*. The question is debatable, but whether he be right or wrong, it is sufficient for our purposes here to note that the Mytileneans had, besides their oligarchic government, two things which would set them apart from most of the other allies—freedom from tribute and a fleet of their own; these could easily be equated with autonomy, at least in the popular mind. Now it is among the rowers in this fleet that one would expect to find the democratic Athenian sympathizers, but such was apparently not the case, since the Athenians threw into prison the crews of the ten Mytilenean ships at Athens when they suspected the revolt. And certainly long before this, if there had been any real desire for a democracy among the Mytilenean *demos*, the Athenian could have found a chance to support them against their oligarchs. Although the editors of *The Athenian Tribute Lists* have shown that the Athenians certainly did not impose democracy, one can hardly deny that they would have been sympathetic with a real "grass-roots" movement in any subject state. Therefore, it seems, the people of Mytilene did not have a desire for democracy and were so far from being pro-Athenian that they supported their own oligarchy; one of the main reasons for this must have been their preference for what at least seemed to them to be autonomy.

Much the same may be said of the *demos* in other large cities of the Empire, particularly Samos, Miletos, and Chios. As far as we know, the last of these was under an oligarchy during the whole fifth century, and it is worth noting that, had there been any strong feeling or support for a democracy, the Athenians had an excellent chance to take advantage of it when in 424 she forced Chios to tear down her new wall on suspicion of a revolt. The political history of Miletos is obscure; she seems definitely to have had an oligarchy after her revolt in the 450s, and although she may well have had a democracy at a later date, this is one of the few places in which de Ste. Croix can find no sign of pro-Athenian sympathies during the Ionian War. The Milesian readiness to revolt and their perseverance in revolting do not indicate the presence of any large pro-Athenian democratic element. As for Samos, it is instructive to analyze the political situation there during and after the revolt in 440/39. The Athenians, as a result of Samos' war with Miletos, set up a democracy at the instigation of an unspecified number of private citizens who wished to change the constitution. This government, however, did not last long, as the oligarchs' mercenaries and Persian help offset the Athenian garrison. The re-established oligarchy seems to have been able to trust its fleet during the siege, put up a stout resistance, but finally was forced by weight of numbers to surrender. It is often assumed that at this time Athens again set up a democracy but there is no certain evidence for this. It is not mentioned by Thucydides, who gives other terms of the settlement. Since Samos certainly had an oligarchy in 412, either the democracy was never restored, as seems likely, or possibly it was replaced peacefully; any real *stasis* would certainly have echoes in our sources. In either case, it is hard to see a pro-democratic, pro-Athenian *demos*, and the original Samian democrats in 440 must have been a rather unrepresentative group.

But now we come to another point. We have analyzed above in Mytilene the first and most impressive piece in what de Ste. Croix calls "an overwhelming body of evidence...that the mass of citizens in the allied or subject states were loyal to Athens." The rest of this evidence consists mainly of an analysis of the revolts of the "fifties" and "forties," of Brasidas' campaign in Thrace, and of the campaigns in Ionia after the defeat of the Sicilian expedition. But these are ambiguous situations and what de Ste. Croix offers is not evidence but a reinterpretation of what must have happened, granting always that his analysis of the political situation is right, Thucydides' wrong. But I submit that this is not legitimate evidence, since Thucydides' account is reasonable in itself and agrees in general with his conclusions. There is really no need to analyze in detail all of this "evidence"; one could write an expanded account of it on the basis that Thucydides was right which would not only be consistent but would also be likely to be far nearer the truth, since it would be backed by the main source for the period and also would take into account the military situation and the presence of Athenian garrisons. These were far more numerous than de Ste. Croix cares to admit, and one of the weaknesses of his case is that he continually ignores them. For instance, although it seems quite clear from Thucydides that the Athenian general Eukles and his garrison played a major role in the initial resistance to Brasidas at Amphipolis, de Ste. Croix does not even mention him in his account of this resistance and its collapse. The fact is that neither the Thracian nor Ionian campaigns, carried on during the course of the war, are really fair tests of Athens' popularity, for there were always extraordinary military pressures which distorted the situation. A garrison within a city, or the approach of a fleet, could insure in most cases the support of the majority, whose main interest was to be on the winning side, not necessarily of the war as a whole but of the local struggle at the moment. Furthermore, the propaganda during the war, as Thucydides points out in his analysis of the Corcyrean revolution, stressed Athens and democracy, Sparta and oligarchy, and this had certainly complicated matters, especially by 412. As for the evidence for the revolts of the earlier period, most of which is epigraphic and quite ambiguous, it seems to show that most of the uprisings were led by oligarchs, who were therefore obviously anti-Athenian, as we might expect, but it proves nothing as to whether the majority of the citizens supported the revolts or not. We have no way of telling whether the democrats who appear during or after the revolts are really representative of the majority or are only a few who took advantage of the situation to get in power as pro-Athenians; the latter seems definitely to have been the case in Samos in 440.

It has been stated above that the situation in the Chalkidike in 424 and that in Ionia in 412 were not fair tests of Athens' popularity because of the military action at the time. However, there are two occasions when we can see how the subject states acted when there was no actual war and the balance of military power definitely favored Athens. Neither of these, incidentally, is mentioned by de Ste. Croix. The first is the revolt of the Thracian Chalkidians in 433/2. Now it is true that this was instigated by Perdikkas and that the actual revolt did not take place until they were joined by the Potidaians, who had the backing of Korinth and the promise of a Peloponnesian invasion of Attika if Athens attacked them. But nevertheless these Chalkidians took a desperate chance in acting when they did. They were exposed to Athenian sea power, and that they fully realized this is made clear by their abandonment of their cities near the coast. They were certainly not coerced or frightened into the revolt, since Perdikkas was not a military threat, at least if they remained loyal to Athens. We can judge what was thought of his power from the fact that the Athenians sent against him 30 ships and only 1000 hoplites. The only motive which could have led the Chalkidians on was a desire for freedom, and I cannot see how their governments, whether they were democracies or oligarchies, could have taken this step against such great odds without the support of a large majority of their people.

An even clearer example of the attitude toward Athens of the people in an allied city, when acting as free agents, is that of Amphipolis after the Peace of Nikias. Although by the terms of that treaty this town was to be returned to the Athenians, the inhabitants opposed this stoutly. At first the Spartan commander, Klearidas, cooperated by refusing to act against the city's will, but later he was forced to withdraw his garrison along with all the Peloponnesian troops in Thrace. But even then the city refused to return to the Athenian alliance, in the face of Athens' might and with no hope of help from Sparta; it was resisting an attack of Athenians, Macedonians, and Thracians as late as 414.

It seems to me that these actions of the Chalkidians and the Amphipolitans, the situation being what it was in both cases, is the best evidence for the feelings towards Athens of the peoples in the subject and allied states, and for their desire for freedom above all else. It corroborates the opinion which Thucydides attributes to Phrynichos, who, while discussing the effects of a promise of oligarchy to the subject states in 412, says that the allies do not wish to be subject with either an oligarchy or a democracy but prefer to be free with whichever form of government they might get. De Ste. Croix does not discuss this passage, although he accepts as true without hesitation, and puts great stress upon, the next statement in the paragraph, which speaks of the allies' distrust of the Athenian oligarchs. But in this context these two statements are complementary and cannot be separated so arbitrarily, since the first, in a way, explains the second; that is, the oligarchs are not trusted because they are identified as the prime movers of the oppression of the cities and will infringe even more upon that freedom which these cities want above all.

This statement of Phrynichos, which agrees well with Thucydides' own views, would appear to sum up admirably the attitude of the subject and allied states. To most of these Greeks freedom was the most important of blessings, and this was the basis of the opposition to Athens. As Grote saw long ago, it was an emotional, not a rational, opposition. We may now think that the majority in the cities must have been far better off under a democracy, guided by Athenian overseers and protected by Athenian garrisons, that the imposition of Athenian coinage over the whole Empire was an economic blessing which they should have recognized, that Athenian juries must have acted more justly in trying allies than many of their own courts, and that the tribute was little to pay for the advantages which the Empire offered. We may even be right in this from a rational, historical point of view, but this is no reason to rewrite the history of Thucydides. For to the subject citizens, the carrying of the tribute and "first fruits" to Athens each spring, the forced appearances before a foreign court, the prohibition against coining their own silver, and the presence of Athenian garrisons and overseers were all signs of their loss of freedom and autonomy. When the chance came to try to win these back, they usually took it, whatever material advantages they threw away by so doing.

Consider

1. How does de Ste. Croix reconcile his criticism of what he calls "the traditional view" of the Athenian empire with the evidence of Thucydides?
2. Compare his interpretation of the speeches of Thucydides and his estimate of Thucydides as a historian with that of Bradeen.
3. Discuss how de Ste. Croix distinguishes the attitude of the Few from that of the *demos* in his reading of the revolts at Mytilene and in the Thraceward region. Why does Bradeen disagree with him?
4. How does de Ste. Croix use the epigraphic evidence for the revolts of the 450s and 440s to support his thesis?
5. For what reasons might the Many in the subject states have been well disposed toward Athens?
6. Discuss the three assumptions Bradeen analyzes that underlie de Ste. Croix's thesis.
7. What are the omissions de Ste. Croix makes in his discussion of the evidence that Bradeen points out?
8. How does Bradeen interpret the Mytilene revolt (and that of Chios, Miletus, and Samos) to make his case against de Ste. Croix?
9. What evidence supports Bradeen's argument that the majority in the allied states resented Athenian rule?
10. Compare Bradeen's interpretation of Phrynichus' view of empire with that of de Ste. Croix. 11. Do you believe that the Athenian empire was popular, why or why not?

CHAPTER 10
THE CAUSES OF THE
PELOPONNESIAN WAR

ॐ

THE PELOPONNESIAN WAR was the turning point in the history of the Greek city-states. Until its outbreak the city-states prospered and grew; agriculture, trade, and industry flourished. External threats had been repulsed and a golden age had descended upon the Hellenic world. The war was to end all that. It destroyed the economic prosperity of Greece, produced bitter class strife within the cities, opened the door to Persian control of Hellenic affairs, and set neighbor against neighbor in a long and bloody struggle. The causes of the war have been the subject of discussion since antiquity, and agreement has by no means been reached by modern scholars. Should one seek impersonal causes or villains and victims? Was one state to blame or did several share it? Were internal politics responsible? What was the role of economic factors or of power politics? Was the war inevitable or could it have been avoided? All these are questions which have been asked and which remain vital.

Ancient Sources

1. Thucydides 1.18–19; 23, THE CLASH OF EMPIRES
2. Thucydides 1.31–44, THE CORCYRAEAN ALLIANCE
3. Thucydides 1.66–67; 86–88, THE ASSEMBLY AT SPARTA
4. Plutarch, *Pericles*, 29–32, PLUTARCH ON THE ORIGINS OF THE WAR
5. Diodorus Siculus 12.38–40, DIODORUS ON THE ORIGINS OF THE WAR

Opinions of Modern Scholars

1. From Victor Davis Hanson, *A War Like No Other*
2. From G. E. M. de Ste. Croix, *The Origins of the Peloponnesian War*
3. From Donald Kagan, *The Outbreak of the Peloponnesian War*

ANCIENT SOURCES ON THE PELOPONNESIAN WAR

1.   THE CLASH OF EMPIRES

In the first book of his *History*, Thucydides describes the early history of Greece, concluding with an account of the growth of Spartan and Athenian power and the reasons for their clash.

1.18.1 But at last a time came when the tyrants of Athens and the far older tyrannies of the rest of Hellas were, with the exception of those in Sicily, once and for all put down by Lacedaemon; for this city, though after the settlement of the Dorians, its present inhabitants, it suffered from factions for an

263

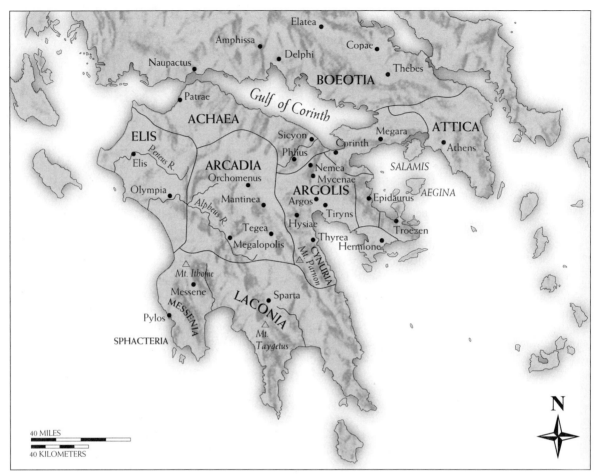

The Peloponnesus Sparta's region, Laconia, was in the Peloponnesus. Most nearby states were members of the Peloponnesian League under Sparta's leadership.

unparalleled length of time, still at a very early period obtained good laws, and enjoyed a freedom from tyrants which was unbroken; it has possessed the same form of government for more than four hundred years, reckoning to the end of the late war, and has thus been in a position to arrange the affairs of the other states. Not many years after the deposition of the tyrants, the battle of Marathon was fought between the Medes and the Athenians. **[2]** Ten years afterwards the barbarian returned with the armada for the subjugation of Hellas. In the face of this great danger the command of the confederate Hellenes was assumed by the Lacedaemonians in virtue of their superior power; and the Athenians having made up their minds to abandon their city, broke up their homes, threw themselves into their ships, and became a naval people. This coalition, after repulsing the barbarian, soon afterwards split into two sections, which included the Hellenes who had revolted from the king, as well as those who had aided him in the war. At the head of the one stood Athens, at the head of the other Lacedaemon, one the first naval, the other the first military power in Hellas. **[3]** For a short time the league held together, till the Lacedaemonians and Athenians quarrelled, and made war upon each other with their allies, a duel into which all the Hellenes sooner or later were drawn, though some might at first remain neutral. So that the whole period from the Median war to this, with some peaceful intervals, was spent by each power in war, either with its rival, or with its own revolted allies, and consequently afforded them constant practice in military matters, and that experience which is learnt in the school of danger.

1.19.1 The policy of Lacedaemon was not to exact tribute from her allies, but merely to secure their subservience to her interests by establishing oligarchies among them; Athens, on the contrary, had by degrees deprived hers of their ships, and imposed instead contributions in money on all except Chios and Lesbos. Both found their resources for this war separately to exceed the sum of their strength when the alliance flourished intact.

* * *

1.23.1 The Median war, the greatest achievement of past times, yet found a speedy decision in two actions by sea and two by land. The Peloponnesian war was prolonged to an immense length, and long as it was it was short without parallel for the misfortunes that it brought upon Hellas. **[2]** Never had so many cities been taken and laid desolate, here by the barbarians, here by the parties contending (the old inhabitants being sometimes removed to make room for others); never was there so much banishing and blood-shedding, now on the field of battle, now in the strife of action. **[3]** Old stories of occurrences handed down by tradition, but scantily confirmed by experience, suddenly ceased to be incredible; there were earthquakes of unparalleled extent and violence; eclipses of the sun occurred with a frequency unrecorded in previous history; there were great droughts in sundry places and consequent famines, and that most calamitous and awfully fatal visitation, the plague. **[4]** All this came upon them with the late war, which was begun by the Athenians and Peloponnesians by the dissolution of the thirty years' truce made after the conquest of Euboea. **[5]** To the question why they broke the treaty, I answer by placing first an account of their grounds of complaint and points of difference, that no one may ever have to ask the immediate cause which plunged the Hellenes into a war of such magnitude. **[6]** The real cause I consider to be the one which was formally most kept out of sight. The growth of the power of Athens, and the alarm which this inspired in Lacedaemon, made war inevitable. Still it is well to give the grounds alleged by either side, which led to the dissolution of the treaty and the breaking out of the war.

Questions

1. **When and how does Thucydides say the hostility between Sparta and Athens arose?**
2. **What does he believe was the true cause of the Peloponnesian War?**

2.   THE CORCYRAEAN ALLIANCE

One of the crucial turning points on the road to war was the Athenian decision in 433 to ally itself with Corcyra. Thucydides describes the arguments offered by both the Corcyraeans and the Corinthians to the Athenian assembly. In this way he dramatizes the issues confronting Athens; he then goes on to explain what considerations led to their decision. In 435 the Corcyraeans had defeated Corinth in a sea-battle. The debate in Athens took place two years later.

1.31.1 Corinth, exasperated by the war with the Corcyraeans, spent the whole of the year after the engagement and that succeeding it in building ships, and in straining every nerve to form an efficient fleet; rowers being drawn from Peloponnese and the rest of Hellas by the inducement of large bounties. **[2]** The Corcyraeans, alarmed at the news of their preparations, being without a single ally in Hellas (for they had not enrolled themselves either in the Athenian or in the Lacedaemonian confederacy), decided to repair to Athens in order to enter into alliance and to endeavour to procure support from her. **[3]** Corinth also, hearing of their intentions, sent an embassy to Athens to prevent the Corcyraean navy being joined by the Athenian, and her prospect of ordering the war according to her wishes being thus impeded. **[4]** An assembly was convoked, and the rival advocates appeared: the Corcyraeans spoke as follows:

1.32.1. "Athenians! When a people that have not rendered any important service or support to their neighbours in times past, for which they might claim to be repaid, appear before them as we now appear before you to solicit their assistance, they may fairly be required to satisfy certain preliminary conditions. They should show, first, that it is expedient or at least safe to grant their request; next, that they will retain a lasting sense of the kindness. But if they cannot clearly establish any of these points, they must not be annoyed if they meet with a rebuff. **[2]** Now the Corcyraeans believe that with their petition for assistance they can also give you a satisfactory answer on these points, and they have therefore dispatched us hither. **[3]** It has so happened that our policy as regards you with respect to this request, turns out to be inconsistent, and as regards our interests, to be at the present crisis inexpedient. **[4]** We say inconsistent, because a power which has never in the whole of her past history been willing to ally herself with any of her neighbours is now found asking them to ally themselves with her. And we say inexpedient, because in our present war with Corinth it has left us in a position of entire isolation, and what once seemed the wise precaution of refusing to involve ourselves in alliances with other powers, lest we should also involve ourselves in risks of their choosing, has now proved to be folly and weakness. **[5]** It is true that in the late naval engagement we drove back the Corinthians from our shores single-handed. But they have now got together a still larger armament from Peloponnese and the rest of Hellas; and we, seeing our utter inability to cope with them without foreign aid, and the magnitude of the danger which subjection to them implies, find it necessary to ask help from you and from every other power. And we hope to be excused if we forswear our old principle of complete political isolation, a principle which was not adopted with any sinister intention, but was rather the consequence of an error in judgment.

1.33.1 "Now there are many reasons why in the event of your compliance you will congratulate yourselves on this request having been made to you. First, because your assistance will be rendered to a power which, herself inoffensive, is a victim to the injustice of others. Secondly, because all that we most value is at stake in the present contest, and your welcome of us under these circumstances will be a proof of goodwill which will ever keep alive the gratitude you will lay up in our hearts. Thirdly, yourselves excepted, we are the greatest naval power in Hellas. **[2]** Moreover, can you conceive a stroke of good fortune more rare in itself, or more disheartening to your enemies, than that the power whose adhesion you would have valued above much material and moral strength should present herself self-invited, should deliver herself into your hands without danger and without expense, and should lastly put you in the way of gaining a high character in the eyes of the world, the gratitude of those whom you shall assist, and a great accession of strength for yourselves? You may search all history without finding many instances of a people gaining all these advantages at once, or many instances of a power that comes in quest of assistance being in a position to give to the people whose alliance she solicits as much safety and honour as she will receive. **[3]** But it will be urged that it is only in the case of a war that we shall be found useful. To this we answer that if any of you imagine that that war is far off, he is grievously mistaken, and is blind to the fact that Lacedaemon regards you with jealousy and desires war, and that Corinth is powerful there—the same, remember, that is your enemy, and is even now trying to subdue us as a preliminary to attacking you. And this she does to prevent our becoming united by a common enmity, and her having us both on her hands, and also to ensure getting the start of you in one of two ways, either by crippling our power or by making its strength her own. **[4]** Now it is our policy to be beforehand with her—that is, for Corcyra to make an offer of alliance and for you to accept it; in fact, we ought to form plans against her instead of waiting to defeat the plans she forms against us.

1.34.1 "If she asserts that for you to receive a colony of hers into alliance is not right, let her know that every colony that is well treated honours its parent state, but becomes estranged from it by injustice. For colonists are not sent forth on the understanding that they are to be the slaves of those that remain behind, but that they are to be their equals. **[2]** And that Corinth was injuring us is clear. Invited to refer the dispute about Epidamnus to arbitration, they chose to prosecute their complaints war rather than by a fair trial. **[3]** And let their conduct towards us who are their kindred be a warning to you not to be misled by their deceit, nor to yield to their direct requests; concessions to adversaries only end in self-reproach, and the more strictly they are avoided the greater will be the chance of security.

1.35.1 "If it be urged that your reception of us will be a breach of the treaty existing between you and Lacedaemon, the answer is that we are a neutral state, **[2]** and that one of the express provisions of that treaty is that it shall be competent for any Hellenic state that is neutral to join whichever side it pleases. **[3]** And it is intolerable for Corinth to be allowed to obtain men for her navy not only from her allies, but also from the rest of Hellas, no small number being furnished by your own subjects; while we are to be excluded both from the alliance left open to us by treaty, and from any assistance that we might get from other quarters, and you are to be accused of political immorality if you comply with our request. **[4]** On the other hand, we shall have much greater cause to complain of you, if you do not comply with it; if we, who are in peril and are no enemies of yours, meet with a repulse at your hands, while Corinth, who is the aggressor and your enemy, not only meets with no hindrance from you, but is even allowed to draw material for war from your dependencies. This ought not to be, but you should either forbid her enlisting men in your dominions, or you should lend us too what help you may think advisable. "But your real policy is to afford us avowed countenance and support. **[5]** The advantages of this course, as we premised in the beginning of our speech, are many. We mention one that is perhaps the chief. Could there be a clearer guarantee of our good faith than is offered by the fact that the power which is at enmity with you is also at enmity with us, and that that power is fully able to punish defection? And there is a wide difference between declining the alliance of an inland and of a maritime power. For your first endeavour should be to prevent, if possible, the existence of any naval power except your own; failing this, to secure the friendship of the strongest that does exist.

1.36.1 And if any of you believe that what we urge is expedient, but fear to act upon this belief, lest it should lead to a breach of the treaty, you must remember that on the one hand, whatever your fears, your strength will be formidable to your antagonists; on the other, whatever the confidence you derive from refusing to receive us, your weakness will have no terrors for a strong enemy. You must also remember that your decision is for

Athens no less than Corcyra, and that you are not making the best provision for her interests, if at a time when you are anxiously scanning the horizon that you may be in readiness for the breaking out of the war which is all but upon you, you hesitate to attach to your side a place whose adhesion or estrangement is alike pregnant with the most vital consequences. **[2]** For it lies conveniently for the coast-navigation in the direction of Italy and Sicily, being able to bar the passage of naval reinforcements from thence to Peloponnese, and from Peloponnese thither; and it is in other respects a most desirable station. **[3]** To sum up as shortly as possible, embracing both general and particular considerations, let this show you the folly of sacrificing us. Remember that there are but three considerable naval powers in Hellas—Athens, Corcyra, and Corinth—and that if you allow two of these three to become one, and Corinth to secure us for herself, you will have to hold the sea against the united fleets of Corcyra and Peloponnese. But if you receive us, you will have our ships to reinforce you in the struggle." **[4]** Such were the words of the Corcyraeans. After they had finished, the Corinthians spoke as follows:

1.37.1 "These Corcyraeans in the speech we have just heard do not confine themselves to the question of their reception into your alliance. They also talk of our being guilty of injustice, and their being the victims of an unjustifiable war. It becomes necessary for us to touch upon both these points before we proceed to the rest of what we have to say, that you may have a more correct idea of the grounds of our claim, and have good cause to reject their petition. **[2]** According to them, their old policy of refusing all offers of alliance was a policy of moderation. It was in fact adopted for bad ends, not for good; indeed their conduct is such as to make them by no means desirous of having allies present to witness it, or of having the shame of asking their concurrence. **[3]** Besides, their geographical situation makes them independent of others, and consequently the decision in cases where they injure any lies not with judges appointed by mutual agreement, but with themselves, because, while they seldom make voyages to their neighbours, they are constantly being visited by foreign vessels which are compelled to put in to Corcyra. **[4]** In short, the object that they propose to themselves, in their specious policy of complete isolation, is not to avoid sharing in the crimes of others, but to secure monopoly of crime to themselves—the licence of outrage wherever they can compel, of fraud wherever they can elude, and the enjoyment of their gains without shame. **[5]** And yet if they were the honest men they pretend to be, the less hold that others had upon them, the stronger would be the light in which they might have put their honesty by giving and taking what was just.

1.38.1 "But such has not been their conduct either towards others or towards us. The attitude of our colony towards us has always been one of estrangement and is now one of hostility; for, say they: 'We were not sent out to be ill-treated.' **[2]** We rejoin that we did not found the colony to be insulted by them, but to be their head and to be regarded with a proper respect. **[3]** At any rate our other colonies honour us, and we are much beloved by our colonists; **[4]** and clearly, if the majority are satisfied with us, these can have no good reason for a dissatisfaction in which they stand alone, and we are not acting improperly in making war against them, nor are we making war against them without having received signal provocation. **[5]** Besides, if we were in the wrong, it would be honourable in them to give way to our wishes, and disgraceful for us to trample on their moderation; **[6]** but in the pride and licence of wealth they have sinned again and again against us, and never more deeply than when Epidamnus, our dependency, which they took no steps to claim in its distress upon our coming to relieve it, was by them seized, and is now held by force of arms.

1.39.1 "As to their allegation that they wished the question to be first submitted to arbitration, it is obvious that a challenge coming from the party who is safe in a commanding position cannot gain the credit due only to him who, before appealing to arms, in deeds as well as words, places himself on a level with his adversary. **[2]** In their case, it was not before they laid siege to the place, but after they at length understood that we should not tamely suffer it, that they thought of the specious word arbitration. And not satisfied with their own misconduct there, they appear here now requiring you to join with them not in alliance but in crime, and to receive them in spite of their being at enmity with us. **[3]** But it was when they stood firmest that they should have made overtures to you, and not at a time when we have been wronged and they are in peril; nor yet at a time when you will be admitting to a share in your protection those who never admitted you to a share in their power, and will be incurring an equal amount of blame from us with those in whose offences you had no hand. No, they should have shared their power with you before they asked you to share your fortunes with them.

1.40.1 "So then the reality of the grievances we come to complain of, and the violence and rapacity of our opponents, have both been proved. But that you cannot equitably receive them, this you have still to learn. **[2]** It may be true that one of the provisions of the treaty is that it shall be competent for any state, whose name was not down on the list, to join whichever side it pleases. But this agreement is not meant for those whose object in joining is the injury of other powers, but for those whose need of support does not arise from the fact of defection, and whose adhesion will not bring to the power that is mad enough to receive them war instead of peace; which will be the case with you, if you refuse to listen to us. **[3]** For you cannot become their auxiliary and remain our friend; if you join in their attack, you must share the punishment which the defenders inflict on them. **[4]** And yet you have the best possible right to be neutral, or, failing this, you should on the contrary join us against them. Corinth is at least in treaty with you; with Corcyra you were never even in truce. But do not lay down the principle that defection is to be patronized. **[5]** Did we on the defection of the Samians record our vote against you, when the rest of the Peloponnesian powers were equally divided on the question whether they should assist them? No, we told them to their face that every power has a right to punish its own allies. **[6]** Why, if you make it your policy to receive and assist all offenders, you will find that just as many of your dependencies will come over to us, and the principle that you establish will press less heavily on us than on yourselves.

1.41.1 "This then is what Hellenic law entitles us to demand as a right. But we have also advice to offer and claims on your gratitude, which, since there is no danger of our injuring you, as we are not enemies, and since our friendship does not amount to very frequent intercourse, we say ought to be liquidated at the present juncture. **[2]** When you were in want of ships of war for the war against the Aeginetans, before the Persian invasion, Corinth supplied you with twenty vessels. That good turn, and the line we took on the Samian question, when we were the cause of the Peloponnesians refusing to assist them, enabled you to conquer Aegina and to punish Samos. And we acted thus at crises when, if ever, men are wont in their efforts against their enemies to forget everything for the sake of victory, **[3]** regarding him who assists them then as a friend, even if thus far he has been a foe, and him who opposes them then as a foe, even if he has thus far been a friend; indeed they allow their real interests to suffer from their absorbing preoccupation in the struggle.

1.42.1 "Weigh well these considerations, and let your youth learn what they are from their elders, and let them determine to do unto us as we have done unto you. And let them not acknowledge the justice of what we say, but dispute its wisdom in the contingency of war. **[2]** Not only is the straightest path generally speaking the wisest; but the coming of the war, which the Corcyraeans have used as a bugbear to persuade you to do wrong, is still uncertain, and it is not worthwhile to be carried away by it into gaining the instant and declared enmity of Corinth. It were, rather, wise to try and counteract the unfavourable impression which your conduct to Megara has created. **[3]** For kindness opportunely shown has a greater power of removing old grievances than the facts of the case may warrant. **[4]** And do not be seduced by the prospect of a great naval alliance. Abstinence from all injustice to other first-rate powers is a greater tower of strength than anything that can be gained by the sacrifice of permanent tranquillity for an apparent temporary advantage.

1.43.1 It is now our turn to benefit by the principle that we laid down at Lacedaemon, that every power has a right to punish her own allies. We now claim to receive the same from you, and protest against your rewarding us for benefiting you by our vote by injuring us by yours. **[2]** On the contrary, return us like for like, remembering that this is that very crisis in which he who lends aid is most a friend, and he who opposes is most a foe. **[3]** And

for these Corcyraeans—neither receive them into alliance in our despite, nor be their abettors in crime. **[4]** So do and you will act as we have a right to expect of you, and at the same time best consult your own interests."

1.44.1 Such were the words of the Corinthians. When the Athenians had heard both out, two assemblies were held. In the first there was a manifest disposition to listen to the representations of Corinth; in the second, public feeling had changed and an alliance with Corcyra was decided on, with certain reservations. It was to be a defensive, not an offensive alliance. It did not involve a breach of the treaty with Peloponnese: Athens could not be required to join Corcyra in any attack upon Corinth. But each of the contracting parties had a right to the other's assistance against invasion, whether of his own territory or that of an ally. **[2]** For it began now to be felt that the coming of the Peloponnesian war was only a question of time, and no one was willing to see a naval power of such magnitude as Corcyra sacrificed to Corinth; though if they could let them weaken each other by mutual conflict, it would be no bad preparation for the struggle which Athens might one day have to wage with Corinth and the other naval powers. **[3]** At the same time the island seemed to lie conveniently on the coasting passage to Italy and Sicily.

1.45.1 With these views, Athens received Corcyra into alliance and, on the departure of the Corinthians not long afterwards, sent ten ships to their assistance. **[2]** They were commanded by Lacedaemonius, the son of Cimon, Diotimus, the son of Strombichus, and Proteas, the son of Epicles. **[3]** Their instructions were to avoid collision with the Corinthian fleet except under certain circumstances. If it sailed to Corcyra and threatened a landing on her coast, or in any of her possessions, they were to do their utmost to prevent it. These instructions were prompted by an anxiety to avoid a breach of the treaty.

Questions

1. **What arguments did the Corcyraeans make to the Athenians in favor of an alliance?**
2. **What case did the Corinthians make against it?**
3. **What kind of alliance did the Athenians agree to? Why?**

3. THE ASSEMBLY AT SPARTA

The Athenian alliance with Corcyra soon led to open combat between Athens and Corinth at the battle of Sybota. In the Spring of 432 Potidaea, an ally of Athens but at the same time a colony of Corinth revolted against Athens. The town was besieged by the Athenians and defended by a Corinthian army. Doubly enraged, the Corinthians called for a meeting of the Peloponnesian League. Here is Thucydides' version of events:

1.66.1 The Athenians and Peloponnesians had these antecedent grounds of complaint against each other: the complaint of Corinth was that her colony of Potidaea, and Corinthian and Peloponnesian citizens within it, was being besieged; that of Athens against the Peloponnesians that they had incited one of the cities in their alliance and liable for tribute, to revolt, and that they had come and were openly fighting against her on the side of the Potidaeans. For all this, war had not yet broken out: there was still truce for a while; for this was a private enterprise on the part of Corinth.

1.67.1 But the siege of Potidaea put an end to her inaction; she had men inside it: besides, she feared for the place. Immediately summoning the allies to Sparta, she came and loudly accused Athens of breach of the treaty and aggression on the rights of the Peloponnesus. **[2]** With her, the Aeginetans, formally unrepresented from fear of Athens, in secret proved not the least urgent of the advocates for war, asserting that they had not the independence guaranteed to them by the treaty. **[3]** After extending the summons to any of their allies and others who might have complaints to make of Athenian aggression, the Spartans held their ordinary assembly, and invited them to speak. **[4]** There were many who came forward and made their several accusations; among them the Megarians, in a long list of grievances, called special attention to the fact of their exclusion from the ports of the Athenian empire and the market of Athens, in defiance of the treaty. **[5]** Last of all the Corinthians came forward, and having let those who preceded them inflame the Spartans, now followed with a speech to this effect:

[Thucydides reports speeches by the Corinthians and the Athenians who, he says, "happen to be there on other business." Then there is a speech by the Spartan King Archidamus who argues for a cautious policy of delay. He is answered by the ephor Sthenelaidas, who is chairman of the meeting:]

1.86.1 The long speech of the Athenians I do not pretend to understand. They said a good deal in praise of themselves, but nowhere denied that they are injuring our allies and the Peloponnesus. And yet if they behaved well against the Persians in the past, but ill toward us now, they deserve double punishment for having ceased to be good and for having become bad. **[2]** We meanwhile are the same then and now, and shall not, if we are wise, disregard the wrongs of our allies, or put off till tomorrow the duty of assisting those who must suffer today. **[3]** Others have much money and ships and horses, but we have good allies whom we must not give up to the Athenians, nor by lawsuits and words decide the matter, as it is anything but in word that we are harmed, but render instant and powerful help. **[4]** And let us not be told that it is fitting for us to deliberate under injustice; long deliberation is rather fitting for those who have injustice in contemplation. **[5]** Vote therefore, Spartans, for war, as the honor of Sparta demands, and neither allow the further aggrandizement of Athens, nor betray our allies to ruin, but with the gods let us advance against the aggressors.

1.87.1 With these words Sthenelaidas, as ephor, himself put the question to the assembly of the Spartans. **[2]** He said that he could not determine which was the loudest acclamation (their mode of decision is by acclamation, not by voting); the fact being that he wished to make them declare their opinion openly and thus to increase their ardor for war. Accordingly he said, "All Spartans who are of opinion that the treaty has been broken, and that Athens is guilty, leave your seats and go there," pointing out a certain place; "all who are of the opposite opinion, there." **[3]** They accordingly stood up and divided; and those who held that the treaty had been broken were in a decided majority. **[4]** Summoning the allies, they told them that their opinion was that Athens had been guilty of injustice, but that they wished to convoke all the allies and put it to the vote; in order that they might make war, if they decided to do so, on a common resolution. **[5]** Having thus gained their point, the delegates returned home at once; the Athenian envoys a little later, when they had dispatched the objects of their mission. **[6]** This decision of the assembly judging that the treaty had been broken was made in the fourteenth year of the Thirty Years' Peace, which was entered into after the affair of Euboea.

1.88.1 The Spartans voted that the treaty had been broken, and that war must be declared, not so much because they were persuaded by the arguments of the allies, as because they feared the growth of the power of the Athenians, seeing most of Hellas already subject to them.

Questions

1. **Who were the chief complainants against Athens and what were their complaints?**
2. **What reasons did Sthenelaidas give for the decision that Athens had broken the peace?**
3. **Why did he ask for a vote by division?**

4.   PLUTARCH ON THE ORIGINS OF THE WAR

Plutarch presents a more complicated account than does Thucydides, one that was probably more common among the Athenians and the Greeks.

29. A few years later [than the Samian rebellion], when the clouds were already gathering for the Peloponnesian war, Pericles persuaded the Athenians to send help to Corcyra in her war with Corinth and so bring over to their side an island with a powerful navy at a time when the Peloponnesians had all but declared war on them. And yet when the people had agreed to this measure, Pericles sent a squadron of no more than ten ships under Lacedaemonius, the son of Cimon, as if his object were to humiliate him because Cimon's family was on especially good terms with the Spartans. Pericles intended to make sure that if no particular success were achieved under Lacedaemonius's command, then the latter would be discredited for his pro-Spartan sympathies, and so he allowed him only a few ships and sent him out against his will. In general he made a point of thwarting all Cimon's sons, on the pretext that they were not true Athenians, but had something alien about them even in their names, since one of them was named Lacedaemonius, another Thessalus, and a third Eleius, and their mother was believed to be a woman of Arcadia.

In consequence, Pericles was sharply criticized for the paltry size of the force he had sent. It was felt that it was too small to help the Corcyraeans in their hour of need, but that at the same time it provided those enemies of Athens who were accusing her of interference with an invaluable pretext, and he therefore reinforced it later with a larger squadron which arrived after the battle.

This action enraged the Corinthians and they denounced the Athenians at Sparta. The Megarians also joined them to complain that they were being shut out and driven away from every market and every harbour which the Athenians controlled, contrary to the common rights of the Greeks and the articles of peace entered into upon oath. The people of Aegina also considered themselves oppressed and outraged and secretly bemoaned their grievances to the Spartans, as they did not dare to accuse the Athenians openly. At this point, too, Potidaea revolted, a city which, although a colony of Corinth, was subject to Athens, and the siege on which the Athenians then embarked further hastened the outbreak of the war.

In spite of all this a succession of embassies was sent to Athens, and Archidamus, the Spartan king, strove to placate his allies and bring about a peaceful settlement of most of their grievances. In fact, it seems likely that the Athenians might have avoided war on any of the other issues, if only they could have been persuaded to lift their embargo against the Megarians and come to terms with them. And since it was Pericles who opposed this solution more strongly than anyone else and urged the people to persist in their hostility towards the Megarians, it was he alone who was held responsible for the war.

30. It is said that a Spartan mission arrived in Athens to discuss this very subject and that Pericles took refuge in the pretext that there was a law which forbade the tablet on which the Megarian decree was inscribed to be taken down. "Very well, then," one of the envoys named Polyalces suggested, "there is no need to take it down. Just turn its face to the wall! Surely there is no law forbidding that!" This was neatly put, but it had no effect on Pericles, who seems to have harboured some private grudge against the Megarians. However, the charge which he brought against them in public was that they had appropriated for their own profane use the territory of Eleusis, which was consecrated to Demeter and Persephone, and he proposed that a herald should be sent first to them and should then proceed to Sparta to complain of their conduct. Pericles was certainly responsible for this decree, which sets out to justify his action in humane and reasonable terms. But then the herald who was sent, Anthemocritus, met his death at the hands of the Megarians, so it was believed, and thereupon Charinus proposed a decree against them. This laid it down that henceforth Athens should be the irreconcilable and implacable enemy of Megara, that any Megarian setting foot in Attica should be put to death, and that the generals, whenever they took the traditional oath of office, should swear besides this that they would invade the Megarid twice in each year, and that Anthemocritus should be buried with honours beside the Thriasian gates, which are now known as the Dipylon.

On their side the Megarians denied that they had murdered Anthemocritus, and threw the blame for the Athenians' actions upon Pericles and Aspasia, quoting those famous and hackneyed verses from Aristophanes' *Acharnians*:

Some young Athenians in a drunken frolic
Kidnapped Simaetha, the courtesan, from Megara.
The Megarians were furious, primed themselves
   with garlic
Just like their fighting-cocks, then came and stole
Two of Aspasia's girls to get their own back.

31. The real reasons which caused the decree to be passed are extremely hard to discover, but all writers agree in blaming Pericles for the fact that it was not revoked. Some of them, however, say that his firm stand on this point was based on the highest motives combined with a shrewd appreciation of where Athens' best interests lay, since he believed that the demand had been made to test his resistance, and that to have complied with it would have been regarded simply as an admission of weakness. But there are others who consider that he defied the Spartans out of an aggressive arrogance and a desire to demonstrate his own strength.

However, the most damning charge of all, and yet the one which finds most support, runs somewhat like this. Pheidias the sculptor had been entrusted, as I have mentioned, with the contract for producing the great statue of Athena. His friendship with Pericles, with whom he had great influence, earned him a number of enemies through sheer jealousy, while others made use of him to test the mood of the people and see what their temper would be in a case in which Pericles was involved. They therefore persuaded Menon, one of the artists working under Pheidias, to seat himself in the market-place as a suppliant and ask for the protection of the state in return for laying information against Pheidias. The people granted the man's plea and a motion for Pheidias's prosecution was laid before the Assembly. The charge of embezzlement was not proved, because from the very beginning, on Pericles' own advice, the gold used for the statue had been superimposed and laid around it in such a way that it could all be taken off and weighed, and this was what Pericles now ordered the prosecutors to do.

However, the fame of Pheidias's works still served to arouse jealousy against him, especially because in the relief of the battle of the Amazons, which is represented on the shield of the goddess, he carved a figure representing himself as a bald old man lifting up a stone with both hands, and also because he introduced a particularly fine likeness of Pericles fighting an Amazon. The position of the hand, which holds a spear in front of Pericles' face, seems to have been ingeniously contrived to conceal the resemblance, but it can still be seen quite plainly from either side.

So Pheidias was cast into prison and there he fell sick and died. According to some accounts he was poisoned by his enemies in an attempt to blacken Pericles' name still further. As for the informer,

Menon, a proposal was passed, on Glycon's motion, to make him exempt from all taxes and public burdens and the generals were ordered to provide for his safety.

32. About the same time Aspasia was put on trial for impiety. She was prosecuted by Hermippus the comic poet, who also accused her of procuring free-born Athenian women for Pericles and receiving them into her house. A decree was also introduced by Diopeithes, the diviner, to the effect that anybody who did not believe in the gods or taught theories about celestial phenomena should be liable to prosecution, and this was aimed to cast suspicion on Pericles through Anaxagoras. The people took up these slanders only too readily, and while they were in this mood a bill was passed on Dracontides' initiative directing that the accounts of the public funds that Pericles had spent should be deposited with the prytanes, and that the jurors should pronounce their verdict on his case with ballots which had lain on the altar of the goddess on the Acropolis. However, this clause of the decree was amended by Hagnon, who moved that the case should be tried in the usual way, but before a body of 1,500 jurors, no matter whether it was to be termed a prosecution for embezzlement or bribery or malversation.

Pericles contrived to beg off Aspasia by bursting into floods of tears during her trial, so Aeschines tells us, and making a personal appeal to the jurors, but he was so alarmed for Anaxagoras' safety that he smuggled him out of the city. Pericles had already fallen foul of the people on the occasion of Pheidias's trial and he dreaded the jury's verdict on his own case, and so now that the war was threatening and smouldering, we are told that he deliberately fanned it into flame. He hoped in this way to dispel the charges against him and make the people forget their jealousy, since he knew that as soon as any great enterprise or danger was in prospect, the city would put herself in his hands alone because of his great authority and prestige. These are the motives which are alleged for his refusal to allow the people to give way to the demands of Sparta, but the true history of these events is hidden from us.

Questions

1. **What complaints did Athenians make against the forces first sent to aid Corcyra?**
2. **How do you explain the decision to send just those forces?**
3. **What does Plutarch indicate was the importance of the Megarian Decree in bringing on the war?**
4. **How does this compare with Thucydides' estimate?**

5. DIODORUS ON THE ORIGINS OF THE WAR

Diodorus was a Sicilian Greek who lived in the time of Caesar and Augustus. Between 60 and 30 BC he wrote a world history in 40 volumes from the earliest times to Caesar' Gallic War (54 BC). His work is based on that of earlier writers and rarely on primary evidence. His chronology is often confused and his general reliability is debated. His greatest value is in preserving the works of historians now lost to us. In this passage he is probably following Ephorus of Cyme, a writer of the fourth century BC, as well as the comic poets.

12.38.1 In this year there began the Peloponnesian War, as it has been called, between the Athenians and the Peloponnesians, the longest of all the wars which history records; and it is necessary and appropriate to the plan of our history to set forth at the outset the causes of the war. **[2]** While the Athenians were still striving for the mastery of the sea, the funds which had been collected as a common undertaking and placed at Delos, amounting to some eight thousand talents, they had transferred to Athens and given over to Pericles to guard. This man stood far above his fellow citizens in birth, renown, and ability as an orator. But after some time he had spent a very considerable amount of this money for his own purposes, and when he was called upon for an accounting he fell ill, since he was unable to render the statement of the monies with which he had been entrusted. **[3]** While he was worried over the matter, Alcibiades, his nephew, who was an orphan and was being reared at the home of Pericles, though still a lad showed him a way out of making an explanation of the use of the money. Seeing how his uncle was troubled he asked him the cause of his worry. And when Pericles said, "I am asked for the explanation of the use of the money and I am seeking some means whereby I may be able to render an accounting of it to the citizens," Alcibiades replied, "You should be seeking some means not how to render but how not to render an accounting." **[4]** Consequently Pericles, accepting the reply of the boy, kept pondering in what way he could embroil the Athenians in a great war; for that would be the best way, he thought, because of the disturbance and distractions and fears which would beset the city, for him to escape giving an exact accounting of the money. Bearing upon this expedient an incident happened to him by mere chance for the following causes.

12.39.1. The statue of Athena was a work of Pheidias, and Pericles, the son of Xanthippus, had been appointed overseer of the undertaking. But some of the assistants of Pheidias, who had been prevailed upon by Pericles' enemies, took seats as suppliants at the altars of the gods; and when they were called upon to explain their surprising action, they claimed that they would show that Pheidias had possession of a large amount of the sacred funds, with the connivance and assistance of Pericles the overseer. **[2]** Consequently, when the Assembly convened to consider the affair, the enemies of Pericles persuaded the people to arrest Pheidias and lodged a charge against Pericles himself of stealing sacred property. Furthermore, they falsely accused the sophist Anaxagoras, who was Pericles' teacher, of impiety against the gods; and they involved Pericles in their accusations and malicious charges, since jealousy made them eager to discredit the eminence as well as the fame of the man.

[3] But Pericles, knowing that during the operations of war the populace has respect for noble men because of their urgent need of them, whereas in times of peace they keep bringing false accusations against the very same men because they have

nothing to do and are envious, came to the conclusion that it would be to his own advantage to embroil the state in a great war, in order that the city, in its need of the ability and skill in generalship of Pericles, should pay no attention to the accusations being lodged against him and would have neither leisure nor time to scrutinize carefully the accounting he would render of the funds.

[4] Now when the Athenians voted to exclude the Megarians from both their market and harbours, the Megarians turned to the Spartans for aid. And the Lacedaemonians, being won over by the Megarians, in the most open manner dispatched ambassadors in accordance with the decision of the Council of the League, ordering the Athenians to rescind the action against the Megarians and threatening, if they did not accede, to wage war upon them together with the forces of their allies. **[5]** When the Assembly convened to consider the matter, Pericles, who far excelled all his fellow citizens in skill of oratory, persuaded the Athenians not to rescind the action, saying that for them to accede to the demands of the Lacedaemonians, contrary to their own interests, would be the first step toward slavery. Accordingly he advised that they bring their possessions from the countryside into the city and fight it out with the Spartans by means of their command of the sea.

* * *

12.40.4. In addition to Athens' financial resources Pericles pointed out that, omitting the allies and garrisons, the city had available twelve thousand hoplites, the garrisons and metics amounted to more than seventeen thousand, and the triremes available to three hundred. **[5]** He also pointed out that the Lacedaemonians were both lacking in money and far behind the Athenians in naval armaments. After he had recounted these facts and incited the citizens to war, he persuaded the people to pay no attention to the Lacedaemonians. This he accomplished readily by reason of his great ability as an orator, which is the reason he has been called "The Olympian." **[6]** Mention has been made of this even by Aristophanes, the poet of the Old Comedy, who lived in the period of Pericles, in the following tetrameters:

O ye farmers, wretched creatures,
listen now and understand,

If you fain would learn the reason
why it was Peace left the land.
Pheidias began the mischief,
having come to grief and shame,
Pericles was next in order,
fearing he might share the blame,
By his Megara-enactment
lighting first a little flame,
Such a bitter smoke ascended
while the flames of war he blew,
That from every eye in Hellas
everywhere the tears it drew.

And again in another place:

The Olympian Pericles
Thundered and lightened and confounded Hellas.
[Aristophanes, *Acharnians* 531–532]

And Eupolis the poet wrote:

One might say Persuasion rested
On his lips; such charm he'd bring,
And alone of all the speakers
In his list'ners left his sting.

Questions

1. **Whom does Diodorus blame for bringing on the war? For what reasons?**
2. **Do you prefer Diodorus' explanation for the outbreak of the war or that of Plutarch or of Thucydides? Why?**

OPINIONS OF MODERN SCHOLARS

1. Victor Davis Hanson is a classical scholar and a student of war through the ages. His history illuminates the Peloponnesian War by comparison with other times and places; his conclusions about the causes of the war, like those of most scholars, is very close to that of Thucydides.

FROM VICTOR DAVIS HANSON, *A WAR LIKE NO OTHER*

THUCYDIDES FELT STRONGLY that the Spartans had invaded the Athenian countryside in the spring of 431 because "they feared the Athenians lest they might grow still more powerful, seeing most of Greece was already subject to them." That assessment—hardly true, because in the strict sense Athens really did not control "most of Greece"—is nevertheless thematic in his history. The Spartans, in other words, started the actual fighting with a preemptive strike into Attica. They, not the Athenians, were unhappy with the fifth-century status quo. At another point Thucydides concedes that such apprehensions of being slowly overwhelmed in peace "forced the Spartans into war."

"Forced"? Of course, there always seemed other, more immediate pretexts for war that made the conflict perhaps unavoidable. There always are. But in the last analysis, Thucydides at least felt in hindsight that there were such great underlying differences between the two powers, albeit perhaps not always perceptible to contemporary Athenians and Spartans themselves, that the more pressing (and minor) disagreements must eventually lead to a catastrophic face-off.

Although both sides claimed that they were coerced into the conflict, in Thucydides' way of determinist thinking, if Sparta did not go to war over the pretexts of Corinthian and Megarian grievances against Athens, then the sheer dynamism of Pericles' imperial culture—majestic buildings, drama, intellectual fervor, an immense fleet, radical democratic government, an expanding population, and a growing overseas empire—would eventually spread throughout its area of influence in southern Greece.

The Spartans might have lived with the existence of Athenian imperialism. They had done just that for much of the earlier fifth century. But once Athens began to combine its lust for power with a radical ideology of support for democracy abroad, Sparta rightly concluded that the threat transcended mere armed rivalry and promised to infect the very hearts and minds of Greeks everywhere. Their worries were legitimate. Athenian democracy, in fact, was not merely proselytizing and expansionary but also remarkably cohesive and stable. Even the brief revolutions during and after the war in 411 and 403 were short-lived, suggesting a level of support for popular government among a wide variety of Athenians well beyond the landless poor.

Spartans had also seen Athenian-inspired democracy spread throughout the Aegean and Asia Minor in the 450s. They bridled at Athenian influence over the supposedly Panhellenic colony of Thurii, in southern Italy. Their leaders were also furious that sympathetic oligarchs on the island of Samos had been crushed in 440. Elites at Sparta seethed that recalcitrant subject states like Potidaea were not merely besieged but faced with perpetual radical democratic government imposed and maintained by Athenian triremes. How threatening these purported demonstrations of Athenian power really were did not matter; Sparta was convinced that they represented a systematic and dangerous new aggression. Innate ethnic and linguistic differences between Ionian Athenians and Doric Spartans might have been mitigated, but democratic imperialism on the move was again another challenge altogether.

This new Athenian global village would offer incentives to Sparta's friends that a parochial town of infantrymen could not hope to match. Similarly, the die-hard wealthier supporters of Sparta throughout the Aegean must have felt that they were losing influence in their own communities to an upstart underclass. The poor, who did not farm, ride horses, or frequent the gymnasia, liked the security offered by the Athenian fleet and did not mind the obligations of tribute, which fell mostly upon their own rich and landed aristocracy. Behind all the realist calculations, however, was the undeniable fact that Athens just kept growing—King Archidamus believed that at the war's outbreak it was the largest city in the Greek world—while Sparta was shrinking.

"Athenianism" was the Western world's first example of globalization. There was a special word of sorts for Athenian expansionism in the Greek language, *attikizo*, "to Atticize," or to become like or join the Athenians. Contemporaries accepted the reality that Athens sought to promote the common people abroad whenever it could. In contrast,

when Athens engaged instead in Realpolitik—such as attacking the similar consensual government of Syracuse—without the necessary revolutionary fervor of democracy, it often failed.

Spartans were oligarchic fundamentalists par excellence, hating "people power" and the danger it represented. Their warrior-citizens were quite wary of the appetites for the hustle and bustle of the good life that even among their own stern elite grew faster than they could be repressed. Although they had been the preeminent Greeks earlier in the sixth and fifth centuries, by the time of the Peloponnesian War the Spartans could sense their own influence waning, based as it was almost exclusively on hoplite infantry rather than the ships, population growth, and money of an ever grasping hyper-democratic rival—one that in Pericles' own words had ruled "over more Greeks than any other Greek state."

To avoid war with Sparta, Athens was asked to cease its imperialist overstretch and essentially disband the empire: stop besieging cities like Potidaea and let nearby states like Aegina and Megara decide their own affairs. In short, "let the Greeks be independent." To do all that, however, would mean that Athens could no longer be Periclean Athens; rather, it would revert back to its agrarian modesty of an earlier century, when it had no ships, no Long Walls, no tribute, no majestic temples, and no lavish dramatic festivals but was a benign commonwealth not much different from other large Greek city-states.

The Burdens of the Past

War was inevitable as its logic of violence and death overrode what individual Spartan and Athenian leaders might do or not do to manage crises? The very idea bothers us that Sparta's fault in breaking the peace of 431 was not so much that it or Athens was rationally culpable in any given context. Rather, out of fear, a lot of envy, and some hatred, Sparta was mercurial in its actions, prone to all the wild urges that make men do what is not always in either their own or the general interest.

In almost all the various debates that surrounded the outbreak of the conflict, the enemies of Athens cited fundamental grievances that acerbated political and ethnic fault lines—reckless Athenian character, the growth of an unstoppable empire, and innate Athenian arrogance—just as frequently as adducing

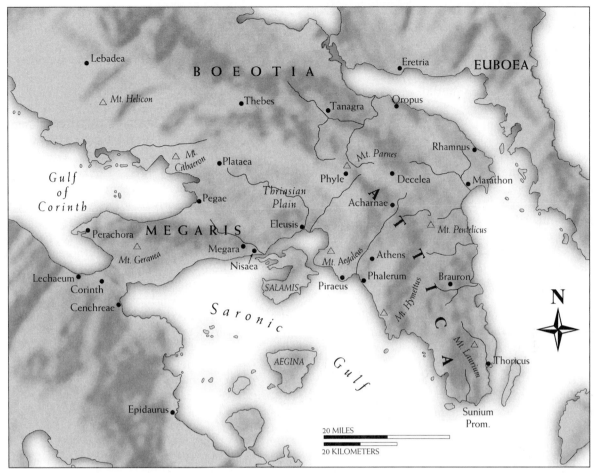

Attica and vicinity. Citizens of all towns in Attica were also citizens of Athens.

legitimate and more specific legal transgressions that demanded immediate redress. Perhaps there was something about Athens that sparked a certain hatred by rival city-states like Corinth, Thebes, and Sparta, a loathing that was deductive, anti-empirical, and hopelessly embedded with deep-seated feelings of antipathy.

Enemies hated Athens as much for what it was as for what it did. As early as 446 Athens had abandoned claims to almost everything sought in the First Peloponnesian War and was careful not to offer any concrete reason for war to the Spartans themselves. Perhaps that paradox is best summarized by Thucydides' fascinating description of the Spartan debate in late 432 over proposals to invade Attica the next spring. After Athenian envoys and the Spartan king Archidamus both offered sober and reasoned explanations of why war at that particular time with Athens was a bad idea, the dense ephor Sthenelaidas stepped forward in response. He shouted out a few slogans about Spartan pride and power. The Spartan military assembly then immediately voted for war. They seemed to be swayed (as were the Athenians who later voted to invade Sicily) by emotion rather than reason: "The long speeches of the Athenians I do not understand at all. Vote therefore, Lacedaemonians, for war as the honor of Sparta demands and do not allow Athens to become too powerful."

   2. Ste. Croix places the lion's share of the blame for the war with the Spartans, even as he claims to endorse the views of Thucydides. His most controversial claim is that the Megarian Decree of the Athenians had no political purpose and was purely religious in its concerns.

FROM G. E. M. DE STE. CROIX, *THE ORIGINS OF THE PELOPONNESIAN WAR*

THE PREDOMINANT VIEW among historians in recent years has been that Athens was the aggressor in the Peloponnesian war, and that she forced war on a reluctant Sparta. As I have made clear, I cannot accept that view at all: I think it has no basis in fact and is founded upon a series of misunderstandings, in particular of the Megarian decree and of the use of the expression anankasai by Thucydides 1.23.6. Many recent writers have simply taken for granted a whole series of assumptions about Athenian policy in the second half of the fifth century the truth of which has seemed to them self-evident. My disagreement with much modern scholarship in this field is often about the assumptions from which it proceeds, usually unformulated or mentioned only casually; and this makes it all the harder to disprove the theories I am attacking. My aim in these pages has been to make a completely fresh start, discarding the assumptions to which I have objected, and beginning from the best ancient evidence. I would claim that the picture I have drawn is thoroughly based upon the evidence of our most reliable sources, Thucydides above all, and that anyone who dislikes that picture had better begin by trying to discredit Thucydides, if he can.

In so far as anyone can be held immediately responsible for the outbreak of the war which did so much to eat away the great achievements of fifth-century Greece, I think it is the Spartans (and their allies, in particular the Corinthians) who must bear the blame. We know from Thucydides (vi, 18.2–3) that the Spartans themselves later realised they had been at fault in 432–1. It may well be that the Spartans and most of their allies conceived themselves as fighting to stop Athens from further aggrandissement, which might take place at their expense; but this, of course, does not excuse them from breaking the Thirty Years Peace and resorting to war.

It is a much more difficult task to allocate the ultimate responsibility for the war: as so often, our judgment is bound to be subjective, and it involves too many imponderables. All States, as Thucydides realised so well (see Chapter I, Part ii above), always do what they believe to be in their own best interests; and all we can do is to hope that those interests will be intelligently assessed, and that they will coincide as far as possible with those of the majority of mankind.

We might begin by pointing out that the dynamic, explosive, volatile factor in the situation was Athenian democracy, the imperialistic democracy which struck fear into the hearts of all Greek oligarchs, at Sparta and elsewhere. During the Pentecontaetia Athens pursued her own imperial policy, although for some time—until after the ostracism of Cimon early in 461—she was careful to avoid any direct conflict with the Peloponnesians. If Athens is to be given part of the blame for the eventual conflict of 432/1, it is above all those who controlled her policy between the years 461 and 446 who must presumably bear it. Precisely how the First Peloponnesian war broke out, c. 460, we do not know. At any rate, Athens and the Peloponnesians conducted very intermittent hostilities for some six years, c. 460 to c. 454, although very little happened after 457–6 […] There is nothing definite to connect Pericles with the policy of creating a "land empire" (by establishing control of the Megarid and of Boeotia and Phocis), which must have been a major bone of contention between Athens and Sparta. However that may be, the "land empire" was certainly lost forever in 446, although Athens did emerge from the First Peloponnesian war with one very important gain: Aegina, conquered in 457, and expressly listed on the Athenian side by the Thirty Years Peace. After the Peace, the power of Athens gradually grew again, and her financial reserves were built up anew; this aroused alarm among the Peloponnesians. While Sparta was ready, in 440 and again in 432, to break the oaths she had sworn, as were some of her allies (in 432 the majority), Athens kept strictly to the terms of the treaty. It was no part of the policy of Pericles and those who, with him, guided Athenian policy in the years between 446/5 and 432 to provoke a renewal of the war with Sparta and her allies—a war which Athens could have little or no hope of winning. It may be said that Athens was inflexible in her policy and would make no concessions to the Peloponnesians in 432/1; but it is difficult to see what concession she could have made without giving an impression of fear and weakness which Sparta would have been likely to exploit immediately. Athens did in fact offer to repeal the Megarian decree (on which Sparta laid special emphasis) if the Spartans on their side would make a reasonable concession in return.

Sparta was a strongly conservative power, interested primarily in keeping the Peloponnese under control, and not often, until the late fifth century and the early fourth, venturing far outside it. We might well ask why the Spartans needed to break the Peace and fight in 432/1; and we might then be tempted to reply that the one compelling reason was Sparta's uniquely dangerous position as mistress of the Messenian Helots: she was the one Greek State which held in a degrading servile status a very large number of fellow-Greeks. Sparta could not take the risks which an ordinary Greek State might afford: she could not allow another city to reach a position of power from which it could threaten either herself or even her allies. It is probable that by the summer of 432 something like a majority of Spartans had already

made up their minds to attack Athens, in spite of the powerful opposition of King Archidamus. And when in 432 Sparta's allies, led by Corinth, demanded action by Sparta against Athens, with a threat to secede if she did not act, the great majority of Spartans needed no further persuasion. Sparta had to fight to keep her League together, not only in order to keep open the one land exit from the Peloponnese, through the territories of Corinth and Megara, but even more because she needed to seal off the whole peninsula from the outside world. If a superior army ever invaded Laconia and Messenia (as in 370/69 and the years following), Sparta would lose control of Messenia and cease to be the strongest power in Greece. The Helot danger was the curse Sparta had brought upon herself, an admirable illustration of the maxim that a people which oppresses another cannot itself be free.

3. Kagan's interpretation challenges Thucydides' view that the war was caused by impersonal forces that made it inevitable and ranks the states involved in order of their responsibility. Donald Kagan is Sterling Professor of Classics and History at Yale University.

FROM DONALD KAGAN, *THE OUTBREAK OF THE PELOPONNESIAN WAR*

[The major assumptions that dominate many modern interpretations] are that the causes of the war must be sought chiefly, if not only, in Athens and Sparta, and that there was no way to avoid a final reckoning between these two great powers. But the Greek world of the years between the Persian War and the Peloponnesian War was not bipolar. By 435, Athens had come to dominate her allies to the degree that they were eliminated as independent factors in foreign affairs, but Sparta had not. Thebes and especially Corinth were free agents. To combat Athens with any hope of success, it is true, they must bring Sparta over to their cause. On the other hand—and this is decisive—Sparta could not prevent them from engaging in their own policies. This independent exercise of foreign policy was sometimes conducive to peace and sometimes to war; it was not, in any case, predictable. Its possibility is a serious argument against the inevitability of the war.

The un-persuasiveness of all theories of inevitability is best demonstrated by a resume of the events that led to the war. At each step it is clear that the decisions were not preordained,

although, of course, the options narrowed as time went on. Our analysis of the years between the wars shows that the theory that peace between Athens and Sparta could not last must be imposed on the facts from the outside; it does not arise from the evidence. The internal quarrel at Epidamnus had no relation to the outside world and need not have affected the international situation in any way. Corinth's decision to intervene was in no way the necessary consequence of previous conditions. Corinthian control of Epidamnus was not necessary for Corinth's economic well-being, her security, even her prestige. Corinth decided that the affair at Epidamnus would provide a splendid opportunity for revenge on its traditional enemies, die Corcyreans. The Corinthians could have chosen to refuse the Epidamnian appeal; had they done so there would have been no crisis and no war. To be sure, they knew in advance that intervention would probably mean war with Corcyra, and they did not flinch from the prospect, for they were confident that they could defeat Corcyra with the help of their Peloponnesian allies.

When some of their friends tried to dissuade them from their course out of fear that Corcyra would obtain the help of Athens and so bring on a larger war, the Corinthians ignored their counsel. They did not do so because they wanted a war with Athens, but because they expected that Athens would not fight. They were led to this belief by their interpretation of the informal detente between the Peloponnesians and the Athenians. Their interpretation was not correct, because Corcyra and its navy presented special problems not easily and obviously dealt with by the unspoken understanding that each side would be permitted freedom of action in its own sphere of influence. Sparta and Sicyon, at least, understood the danger, and the Corinthians should have too. They proceeded with their dangerous policy because they miscalculated the Athenian response. Their miscalculation arose not from a traditional hatred of Athens caused by a commercial rivalry, but rather from a combination of irrational hatred for the Corcyreans and wishful thinking, which led them to expect from Athens the response that they wanted. Had reason prevailed, the Corinthians would have accepted the Corcyrean offer of arbitration, which would have left them in a better position than when they first became involved at Epidamnus. The crisis would have ended before it ever involved either Athens or Sparta, and the war would have been averted.

By the time Athens became involved in 433, her freedom of action was somewhat limited. Corcyra was at war with Corinth. If Athens remained aloof, the Corinthians might win and attach the Corcyrean fleet to the Spartan alliance and challenge the unquestioned naval supremacy that was the basis of Athenian security. Once it became clear that Corinth would not retreat, the Athenians had no choice but to meet the challenge. It is clear, however, that the Athenians did not seek a confrontation with Corinth for commercial, imperial, or any other reasons; the conflict was forced on them. They first tried to limit their commitment in the hope that Corcyra would win with its own forces.

When the Battle of Sybota blocked this resolution, they did what they could to localize the conflict and avoid involving Sparta. The preparations they made for a likely conflict with Corinth were calculated to avoid giving the Corinthians a valid pretext for demanding Spartan assistance. Two of these measures, the ultimatum of Potidaea and the Megarian Decree, were errors in judgment by Pericles. In the case of Potidaea, he reacted too vigorously to the threat that Corinthian machinations might produce rebellion in the empire and gave the impression of Athenian tyranny and aggressiveness. In the case of Megara, again his reaction was greater than the situation required. He intended to punish Megara for helping the Corinthians in the Battle of Sybota and to issue a warning to them and to any other friends of Corinth to stay out of the affair and prevent its spread. The action was probably unnecessary, for Sparta seemed to be exercising a restraining hand on most of her allies; yet the decree had a very serious effect on the internal politics of Sparta. It appeared to be an attack on an ally of Sparta launched without sufficient provocation, and it reinforced the impression of Athens as a tyrant and an aggressor. Pericles misjudged the stability of the political situation at Sparta and unintentionally gave the war party a goad with which it could drive Sparta and its allies to war. If his judgment had been better and, perhaps, if the Athenian irritation with the Megarians had been less, he might have taken a gentler tone, avoided provocative actions, and allowed the friends of Athens and peace to keep their control of Spartan policy. If he had, there might not have been a majority of warlike ephors to promise help to Potidaea and to cooperate with the Corinthians in stirring up the war. Had the Athenians shown more restraint, there is a possibility that even after the Battle of Sybota a general war could have been prevented.

All this is not to say that there were no existing forces or conditions that helped bring on the war. The perfectly ordinary civil war in a remote and unimportant town on the fringes of the civilized world could hardly have led to a great war ex nihilo. Certainly there needed to be a solid core of suspicion and mutual distrust in Athens and Sparta. Another crucial factor originating long before the outbreak of the crisis was the deep and emotional hatred between Corinth and Corcyra. Still another was the organizational weakness of the Spartan alliance, which permitted a power of the second magnitude to drag the hegemonal power into a dangerous war for its own interests. Connected with that was the constitutional weakness of the Spartan executive, which divided the real responsibility for the formulation and conduct of foreign policy and permitted unpredictable shifts back and forth between policies in a rather short space of time. Such weaknesses made it difficult to restrain outbursts of passion and to follow a sober, cautious policy in times of crisis. After the death of Pericles, the Athenian constitution would show a similar weakness, but so long as he was alive Athens was free of this problem.

It is also true that the machinery of diplomacy was too rudimentary to preserve peace in time of crisis. The Thirty Years' Peace was open to varying interpretations, as are all diplomatic agreements, but it provided only one, rather clumsy, means for settling disagreements. It authorized the submission of all disputes to arbitration, but it made no provision for consultation before minor differences reached the level of disputes needing arbitration. By the time arbitration is required, disputants are often so hostile that they refuse to use it. When disputes reach the level of arbitration, they have become public issues and aroused powerful emotions not easily controlled.

All these may be considered as remote or underlying causes of the war. They may be seen as contributing to the situation that made war possible, but all of them together did not make war necessary. For that, a complicated chain of circumstances and decisions was needed. If any of its links had not been present, the war would not have come.

It is customary to apply the metaphor of the powder keg or tinder-box to international situations that are deemed the inevitable forerunners of war. The usual way of putting it is that the conflicting interests and passions of the contending parties provided the inflammatory material, and the final crisis was only a spark that had sooner or later to fall and cause the inevitable conflagration or explosion. If we were to apply this metaphor to the outbreak of the Second Peloponnesian War, we should put it this way: The growth of the Athenian Empire and Sparta's jealousy and fear of it provided the inflammable material that ignited into the First Peloponnesian War. The Thirty Years' Peace poured water on that flame and extinguished it. What was left of the flammable material was continually cooled and dampened by the mutual restraint of Athens and Sparta in the decade 445–435. To start the war, the spark of the Epidamnian trouble needed to land on one of the rare bits of flammable stuff that had not been thoroughly drenched. Thereafter it needed to be continually and vigorously fanned by the Corinthians, soon assisted by the Megarians, Potidaeans, Aeginetans, and the Spartan war party. Even then the spark might have been extinguished had not the Athenians provided some additional fuel at the crucial moment.

No one planned the Peloponnesian War, and no state wanted it, yet each of the three great states bears part of the blame for bringing it on. The Corinthians did not want war with Athens but a free hand against Corcyra. They were willing to risk such a war, however, because they hoped Athens would not really bring it on, because they counted on their proven ability to gain the help of Sparta in case of war, and because they were determined to have their way. Theirs is the greatest guilt, for they had the freest choice and sufficient warning of the consequences of their actions, yet they would not be deterred from their purpose.

The Spartans too deserve a share of the blame. They allowed their war party to frighten them with unfounded alarms of Athenian aggression and the Corinthians to blackmail them with empty threats of secession. They ignored the advice of Archidamus, which would have allowed them to avoid the war without any loss of power, honor, or influence. They rejected the opportunity to arbitrate specific disputes as specified in the treaty and were captured by the romantic vision of destroying the Athenian Empire, liberating Greece, and restoring Sparta to unchallenged primacy. They were quite right to go into the war burdened by a guilty conscience.

The Athenians, however, were not without guilt. To be sure, their security required that they accept the Corcyrean alliance and prepare for further conflict with Corinth. They need not, however, have behaved with such arrogance and harshness toward Potidaea and Megara. This frightened their rivals and lent plausibility to the charges of the Corinthians. In one sense, although probably not in the way they intended, the enemies of Pericles were right in fixing on the Megarian Decree as the cause of the war and on Pericles as its instigator. If he had not issued it, the Corinthians might not have been able to persuade the Spartans of the evil intentions of Athens and so to drive them to war. There is even some possibility that if he had been willing to rescind it at the request of the second Spartan embassy, the peace party might have returned to power and the war been avoided. By that time, however, Pericles' war strategy dominated his thinking. It demanded a policy of firmness, and the Spartan offer was rejected. The political situation at Sparta made arbitration impossible; the intransigence of Pericles prevented any other solution.

All the statesmen involved suffered from what might be called "a failure of imagination." Each allowed war to come and even helped bring it on because he thought he could gain something at a reasonable cost. Each evolved a strategy largely based on past wars and expected the next war to follow his own plan. None seems to have considered the consequences of miscalculation. None had prepared a reserve plan to fall back on in case his original estimation should prove wrong. All expected a short war; none was ready even for the ten years of the Archidamian War, much less the full twenty-seven years that it took to bring the conflict to a conclusion. They all failed to foresee the evil consequences that such a war would have for everyone, victors and vanquished alike, that it would bring economic ruin, class warfare, brutality, erosion of moral standards, and a permanent instability that left Greece vulnerable to foreign conquest. Had they done so they would scarcely have risked a war for the relatively minor disputes that brought it on. Had they done so, we should admit at once, they would have been far better men than most statesmen who have faced similar decisions in the millennia since then. The Peloponnesian War was not caused by impersonal forces, unless anger, fear, undue optimism, stubbornness, jealousy, bad judgment, and lack of foresight are impersonal forces. It was caused by men who made bad decisions in difficult circumstances. Neither the circumstances nor the decisions were inevitable.

Consider

1. How does Hanson's view of the importance of democracy in bringing on the war compare with that of Thucydides?
2. Is the weight he places on the roles of social class and political ideology in accord with Thucydides' account?
3. Which state, if any, does he blame most?
4. To what extent does he see the decisions for war as rational?
5. Why does Ste. Croix blame the Spartans for causing the war?
6. Why does he excuse the Athenians from any blame?
7. Is he right in each case?
8. In what way does Kagan think the international structure of the Greek world played a part in bringing on the war?
9. Why does he think the war was not inevitable?
10. What was the importance of the quarrel between Corinth and Corcyra over Epidamnus?
11. Why did the Athenians make the kind of alliance they did with Corcyra?
12. What was the importance of the ultimatum to Potidaea? Of the Megarian Decree?
13. In what ways was the machinery of international relations inadequate?
14. How does Kagan rank the states in regard to their responsibility for the war. How does he justify his ranking? Do you agree with it?
15. When does Kagan think the war became inevitable?
16. When does Thucydides? What point would you choose?

CHAPTER 11
WAS SOCRATES GUILTY?

✑

AT ATHENS IN 399 BC, the Athenian philosopher Socrates, at the age of 70, was brought to trial. The charge against him was impiety; more specifically he was accused of not believing in the gods worshipped by the city, of bringing other new divinities, and of corrupting the youth of Athens. The penalty proposed in the indictment was death. The jury of 500 found him guilty, probably by a vote of 280-220. When asked to suggest an alternate penalty, Socrates appears first to have proposed a lifetime support at the city's expense in the Prytaneum, a prize reserved to honor Olympic winners. Then he offered to pay an absurdly small fine, supplemented to respectability by some of his friends. The angered jurors then voted the death penalty by an even larger majority. Socrates was put to death, being made to drink a poisonous compound of hemlock.

Ever since, Socrates has been seen as a martyr—his trial and death as famous as that of Jesus. It has given rise to as many questions and produced, perhaps, as much debate. Socrates described himself as a gadfly who went about Athens all his life stinging his fellow Athenians, especially some of the prominent ones, with questions and dialectical interrogations about the most fundamental questions, including those about religion and politics.

The charges made against him seem to be religious, but religion and the state were integral in the ancient Greek world. Many scholars have concluded that we should consider the accusations, the trial, and the execution as fundamentally political in character. Others would give more weight to the religious issues.

Socrates seemed to many to be undermining the basic beliefs and institutions that made civil and social life possible. Although he raised serious questions about the faults of Athenian democracy and spoke positively of aspects of the Spartan state, he had fought bravely for his city during the Peloponnesian War and never left it in peacetime. Why did the Athenians wait so long to bring accusations against him? Why did they do so in 399? Why did they think him impious? How did they claim he corrupted the youth? Why did he defend himself as he did and not in some other way? Were the complaints against him religious, political, personal, or a combination of some of these? Was he innocent or guilty?

Ancient Sources

1. Aristophanes, *Clouds*, 86–153, THE CLOUDS
2. Plato, *Apology of Socrates* [abridged], APOLOGY OF SOCRATES
3. Xenophon, *Memorabilia*, 1.13; 1.2.1–2; 1.2.6–7; 1.29, 12–16; 1.2.24; 1.2.29–33; 4.7.6; 4.8.4–11, MEMORABILIA

Opinions of Modern Scholars

1. Mogens Herman Hansen, *The Trial of Sokrates—From the Athenian Point of View*
2. Paul Cartledge—*Democracy Reaffirmed*

ANCIENT SOURCES FOR SOCRATES' TRIAL

1.   THE CLOUDS

In Plato's *Apology* Socrates tells the jury that more than his immediate accusers he is afraid of those who caught hold of them years ago and said "There is a certain Socrates, a wise man, a ponderer over the things in the air and one who has investigated the things beneath the earth and who makes the weaker argument the stronger." He is referring chiefly to a comedy by Aristophanes called *Clouds*, first produced in 423 BC and later revised.

The play presents a character named Strepsiades who wishes to find a way not to pay debts run up by his horse-loving son Phidippides. He sends his son to study with Socrates at his "Thinking shop" and learn the rhetorical skills that will allow him to trick and escape his creditors. The following translations are slightly revised.

[86] Strep. If you really love me from your heart, my son, obey me.

Phid. In what then, pray, shall I obey you?

Strep. Reform your habits as quickly as possible, and go and learn what I advise.

Phid. Tell me now, what do you prescribe?

Strep. And will you obey me at all?

[90] Phid. By Dionysus, I will obey you.

Strep. Look this way then! Do you see this little door and little house?

Phid. I see it. What then, pray, is this, father?

Strep. This is a thinking-shop of wise spirits. There dwell men who in speaking of the heavens persuade people that it is an oven, and that it encompasses us, and that we are the embers. These men teach, if one give them money, to conquer in speaking, right or wrong.

Phid. Who are they?

[100] Strep. I do not know the name accurately. They are minute philosophers, noble and excellent.

Phid. Bah! They are rogues; I know them. You mean the quacks, the pale-faced wretches, the bare-footed fellows, of whose numbers are the miserable Socrates and Chaerephon.

Strep. Hold! Hold! Be silent! Do not say anything foolish. But, if you have any concern for your father's patrimony, become one of them, having given up your horsemanship.

Phid. I would not, by Dionysus, even if you were to give me the pheasants which Leogoras rears!

[110] Strep. Go, I entreat you, dearest of men, go and be taught.

Phid. Why, what shall I learn?

Strep. They say that among them are both the two causes—the better cause, whichever that is, and the worse: **[115]** they say that the one of these two causes, the worse, prevails, though it speaks on the unjust side. If, therefore you learn for me this unjust cause, I would not pay any one, not even an obolus of these debts, which I owe at present on your account. [Exit Phidippides]

* * *

[126] Strep. Though fallen, still I will not lie prostrate: but having prayed to the gods, I will go myself to the thinking-shop and get taught.

* * *

[181–183; Strepsiades arrives at the Thinking-shop.]

Strep. Open, open quickly the thinking-shop, and show to me Socrates as quickly as possible. For I desire to be a disciple. Come, open the door.

[The door of the thinking-shop opens and the pupils of Socrates are seen all with their heads fixed on the ground, while Socrates himself is seen suspended in the air in a basket.]

* * *

Strep. [Looking up and discovering Socrates.] Come, who is this man who is in the basket?

Dis. Himself.

Strep. Who's Himself?

Dis. Socrates.

[220] **Strep.** O Socrates! Come, you sir, call upon him loudly for me.

Dis. Nay, rather, call him yourself; for I have no leisure. [Exit Disciple.]

Strep. Socrates! My little Socrates!

Socrates. Why callest thou me, thou creature of a day?

Strep. First tell me, I beseech you, what are you doing.

[225] **Soc.** I am walking in the air, and speculating about the sun.

Strep. And so you look down upon the gods from your basket, and not from the earth?

Soc. For I should not have rightly discovered things celestial if I had not suspended the intellect, [230] and mixed the thought in a subtle form with its kindred air. But if, being on the ground, I speculated from below on things above, I should never have discovered them. For the earth forcibly attracts to itself the meditative moisture. Water-cresses also suffer the very same thing.

[235] **Strep.** What do you say? Does meditation attract the moisture to the water-cresses? Come then, my little Socrates, descend to me, that you may teach me those things, for the sake of which I have come.

[Socrates lowers himself and gets out of the basket.]

Soc. And for what did you come?

Strep. Wishing to learn to speak; for by reason of usury, and most ill-natured creditors, [240] I am pillaged and plundered, and have my goods seized for debt.

Soc. How did you get in debt without observing it?

Strep. A horse-disease consumed me—terrible at eating. But teach me the other one of your two causes, [245] that which pays nothing; and I will swear by the gods, I will pay down to you whatever reward you exact of me.

Soc. By what gods will you swear? For, in the first place, gods are not a current coin with us.

Strep. By what do you swear? By iron money, as in Byzantium?

[250] **Soc.** Do you wish to know clearly celestial matters, what they rightly are?

Strep. Yes, by Zeus, if it be possible!

Soc. And to hold converse with the Clouds, our divinities?

Strep. By all means.

Soc. [with great solemnity] Seat yourself, then, upon the sacred couch.

Strep. Well, I am seated!

[255] **Soc.** Take, then, this chaplet.

Strep. For what purpose a chaplet? Ah me! Socrates, see that you do not sacrifice me like Athamas!

Strep. No; we do all these to those who get initiated.

Strep. Then what shall I gain, pray?

[260] **Soc.** You shall become in oratory a tricky knave, a thorough rattle, a subtle speaker. But keep quiet.

Strep. By Zeus! You will not deceive me; for if I am besprinkled, I shall become fine flour.

Soc. It becomes the old man to speak words of good omen, and to hearken to my prayer. O sovereign King, immeasurable Air, who keepest the earth suspended, [265] and through bright Aether, and ye august goddesses, the Clouds, sending thunder and lightning, arise, appear in the air, O mistresses, to your deep thinker!

Strep. Not yet, not yet, till I wrap this around me lest I be wet through. To think of my having come from home without even a cap, unlucky man!

Soc. Come then, ye highly honoured Clouds, for a display to this man. [270] Whether ye are sitting upon the sacred snow-covered summits of Olympus, or in the gardens of Father Ocean form a sacred dance with the Nymphs, or draw in golden pitchers the streams of the waters of the Nile, or inhabit the Maeotic lake, or the snowy rock of Mimas, hearken to our prayer, and receive the sacrifice, and be propitious to the sacred rites.

[356–392 Socrates, having rejected the traditional gods, introduces Strepsiades to thè new gods, the Clouds.]

[356] **Strep.** Hail therefore, O mistresses! And now, if ever ye did to any other, to me also utter a voice reaching to heaven, O all-powerful queens.

Chorus Leader. Hail, O ancient veteran, hunter after learned speeches! And thou, O priest of most subtle trifles! Tell us what you require? **[360]** For we would not hearken to any other of the recent meteorological sophists, except to Prodicus; to him, on account of his wisdom and intelligence; and to you, because you walk proudly in the streets, and cast your eyes askance, and endure many hardships with bare feet, and in reliance upon us lookest supercilious.

Strep. O Earth, what a voice! How holy and dignified and wondrous!

[365] Soc. For, in fact, these alone are goddesses; and all the rest is nonsense.

Strep. But come, by the Earth, is not Zeus, the Olympian, a god?

Soc. What Zeus? Do not trifle. There is no Zeus.

Strep. What do you say? Who rains then? For first of all explain this to me.

Soc. These to be sure. I will teach you it by powerful evidence. **[370]** Come, where have you ever seen him raining at any time without Clouds? And yet he ought to rain in fine weather, and these be absent.

Strep. By Apollo, of a truth you have rightly confirmed this by your present argument. And yet, before this, I really thought that Zeus caused the rain. But tell me who is it that thunders. This makes me tremble.

Soc. These, as they roll, thunder.

[375] Strep. In what way? you all-daring man!

Soc. When they are full of much water, and are compelled to be borne along, being necessarily precipitated when full of rain, then they fall heavily upon each other and burst and clap.

Strep. Who is it that compels them to borne along? Is it not Zeus?

Soc. By no means, but ethereal Vortex.

[380] Strep. Vortex? It had escaped my notice that Zeus did not exist, and that Vortex now reigned in his stead. But you have taught me nothing as yet concerning the clap and the thunder.

Soc. Have you not heard me, that I said that the Clouds, when full of moisture, dash against each other and clap by reason of their density?

Strep. Come, how am I to believe this?

[385] Soc. I'll teach you from your own case. Were you ever, after being stuffed with broth at the Panathenaic festival, then disturbed in your belly, and did a tumult suddenly rumble through it?

Strep. Yes, by Apollo! And immediately the little broth plays the mischief with me, and is disturbed and rumbles like thunder, and grumbles dreadfully: **[390]** at first gently pappax, pappax; and then it adds papa-pappax; and finally, it thunders downright papapappax, as they do.

[1397–1511 Phidippides, having learned the necessary rhetorical tricks, argues that he is right to beat his father.]

[1397] Cho. It is thy business, thou author and upheaver of new words, to seek some means of persuasion, so that you shall seem to speak justly.

Phid. How pleasant it is to be acquainted with new and clever things, **[1400]** and to be able to despise the established laws! For I, when I applied my mind to horsemanship alone, used not to be able to utter three words before I made a mistake; but now, since he himself has made me cease from these pursuits, and I am acquainted with subtle thoughts, and arguments, and speculations, **[1405]** I think I shall demonstrate that it is just to chastise one's father.

Strep. Ride, then, by Zeus! Since it is better for me to keep a team of four horses than to be killed with a beating.

Phid. I will pass over to that part of my discourse where you interrupted me; and first I will ask you this. Did you beat me when I was a boy?

Strep. I did, through good-will and concern for you.

[1410] Phid. Pray tell me, is it not just that I also should be well inclined toward you in the same way, and beat you, since this is to be well inclined-to give a beating? For why ought your body to be exempt from blows and mine not? And yet I too was born free. **[1415]** The boys weep, and do you not think it is right that a father should weep? You will say that it is ordained by law that this should be the lot of boys. But I would reply, that old men are boys twice over, and that it is the more reasonable that the old should weep than the young, inasmuch as it is less just that they should err.

[1420] Strep. It is nowhere ordained by law that a father should suffer this.

Phid. Was it not then a man like you and me, who first proposed this law, and by speaking persuaded the ancients? Why then is it less lawful for me also in turn to propose henceforth a new law for the sons, that they should beat their fathers in turn? **[1425]** But as many blows as we received before the law was made, we remit: and we concede to them our having been thrashed without return. Observe the cocks and these other animals, how they punish their fathers; and yet, in what do they differ from us, except that they do not write decrees?

[1430] Strep. Why then, since you imitate the cocks in all things, do you not both eat dung and sleep on a perch?

Phid. It is not the same thing, my friend; nor would it appear so to Socrates.

Strep. Therefore do not beat me; otherwise you will one day blame yourself.

Phid. Why, how?

Strep. Since I am justly entitled to chastise you; and you to chastise your son, if you should have one.

[1435] Phid. But if I should not have one, I shall have wept for nothing, and you will die laughing at me.

Strep. To me, indeed, O comrades, he seems to speak justly; and I think we ought to concede to them what is fitting. For it is proper that we should weep, if we do not act justly.

Phid. Consider still another maxim.

[1440] Strep. No; for I shall perish if I do.

Phid. And yet perhaps you will not be vexed at suffering what you now suffer.

Strep. How, pray? For inform me what good you will do me by this.

Phid. I will beat my mother, just as I have you.

Strep. What do you say? What do you say? This other, again, is a greater wickedness.

[1445] Phid. But what if, having the worst Cause, I shall conquer you in arguing, proving that it is right to beat one's mother?

Strep. Most assuredly, if you do this, nothing will hinder you from casting yourself and your Worse Cause into the pit **[1450]** along with Socrates. These evils have I suffered through you, O Clouds! Having intrusted all my affairs to you.

Cho. Nay, rather, you are yourself the cause of these things, **[1455]** having turned yourself to wicked courses.

Strep. Why, pray, did you not tell me this, then, but excited with hopes a rustic and aged man?

Cho. We always do this to him whom we perceive to be a lover of wicked courses, **[1460]** until we precipitate him into misfortune, so that he may learn to fear the gods.

Strep. Ah me! it is severe, O Clouds! But it is just; for I ought not to have withheld the money which I borrowed. Now, therefore, come with me, my dearest son, **[1465]** that you may destroy the blackguard Chaerephon and Socrates, who deceived you and me.

Phid. I will not injure my teachers.

Strep. Yes, yes, reverence Paternal Zeus.

Phid. Paternal Zeus quoth'a! How antiquated you are! Why, is there any Zeus?

Strep. There is.

[1470] Phid. There is not, no; for Vortex reigns having expelled Zeus.

Strep. He has not expelled him; but I fancied this, on account of this Vortex here. Ah me, unhappy man! When I even took you who are of earthenware for a god.

[1475] Phid. Here rave and babble to yourself. [Exit Phidippides]

Strep. Ah me, what madness! How mad, then, I was when I ejected the gods on account of Socrates! But O dear Hermes, by no means be wroth with me, nor destroy me; **[1480]** but pardon me, since I have gone crazy through prating. And become my adviser, whether I shall bring an action and prosecute them, or whatever you think. You advise me rightly, not permitting me to get up a lawsuit, but as soon as possible to set fire to the house of the prating fellows. **[1485]** Come hither, come hither, Xanthias! Come forth with a ladder and with a mattock and then mount upon the thinking-shop and dig down the roof, if you love your master, until you tumble the house upon them. [Xanthias mounts upon the roof] **[1490]** But let someone bring me a lighted torch and I'll make some of them this day suffer punishment, even if they be ever so much impostors.

1st Dis. [from within] Hollo! Hollo!

Strep. It is your business, O torch, to send forth abundant flame.

[Mounts upon the roof]

1st Dis. What are you doing, fellow?

[1495] Strep. What am I doing? Why, what else, than chopping logic with the beams of your house? [Sets the house on fire]

2nd Dis. [from within] You will destroy us! You will destroy us!

[1500] Strep. For I also wish this very thing; unless my mattock deceive my hopes, or I should somehow fall first and break my neck.

Soc. [from within]. Hollo you! What are you doing, pray, you fellow on the roof?

Strep. I am walking on air, and speculating about the sun.

Soc. Ah me, unhappy! I shall be suffocated, wretched man!

[1505] Chaer. And I, miserable man, shall be burnt to death!

Strep. For what has come into your heads that you acted insolently toward the gods, and pried into the seat of the moon? Chase, pelt, smite them, for many reasons, but especially because you know that they offended against the gods!

[The thinking shop is burned down]

[1510] Cho. Lead the way out; for we have sufficiently acted as chorus for today.

[Exeunt omnes]

Questions

1. **What are the characteristics Aristophanes attributes to Socrates?**
2. **To which widely held prejudices does the picture painted of Socrates appeal? Which of them could be used to support the charges brought against him at his trial?**

---

2.   APOLOGY OF SOCRATES

This account of Socrates' defense before the jury was written by his most famous disciple, Plato, years after the event.

SOCRATES' DEFENSE

[17A] How you have felt, O men of Athens, at hearing the speeches of my accusers, I cannot tell; but I know that their persuasive words almost made me forget who I was—such was the effect of them; and yet they have hardly spoken a word of truth. But many as their falsehoods were, there was one of them which quite amazed me;—I mean when they told you to be upon your guard, and not to let yourselves be deceived by the force of my eloquence. They ought to have been ashamed of saying this, because they were sure to be detected as soon as I opened my lips and displayed my deficiency; **[17B]** they certainly did appear to be most shameless in saying this, unless by the force of eloquence they mean the force of truth; for then I do indeed admit that I am eloquent. But in how different a way from theirs!

* * *

[17C] I must beg of you to grant me one favor, which is this—If you hear me using the same words in my defence which I have been in the habit of using, and which most of you may have heard in the agora, and at the tables of the money-changers, or anywhere else, I would ask you not to be surprised at this, and not to interrupt me. **[17D]** For I am more than seventy years of age, and this is the first time that I have ever appeared in a court of law, and I am quite a stranger to the ways of the place; and therefore I would have you regard me as if I were really a stranger, whom you would excuse if he spoke in his native tongue, **[18A]** and after the fashion of his country;—that I think is not an unfair request. Never mind the manner, which may or may not be good; but think only of the justice of my cause, and give heed to that: let the judge decide justly and the speaker speak truly.

And first, I have to reply to the older charges and to my first accusers, and then I will go to the later ones. **[18B]** For I have had many accusers, who accused me of old, and their false charges have continued during many years; and I am more afraid of them than of Anytus and his associates, who are dangerous, too, in their own way. But far more dangerous are these, who began when you were children, and took possession of your minds with their falsehoods, telling of one Socrates, a wise man, who speculated about the heaven above, and searched into the earth beneath, and made the worse appear the better cause. **[18C]** These are the accusers whom I dread; for they are the circulators of this rumor, and their hearers are too apt to fancy that speculators of this sort do not believe in the gods. And they are many, and their charges against me are of ancient date, and they made them in days when you were impressible—in childhood, or perhaps in youth—and the cause when heard went by default, for there was none to answer. And, hardest of all, their names I do not know and cannot tell; **[18D]** unless in the chance of a comic poet. But the main body of these slanderers who from envy and malice have wrought upon you—and there are some of them who are convinced themselves, and impart their convictions to others—all these, I say, are most difficult to deal with; for I cannot have them up here, and examine them, and therefore I must simply fight with shadows in my own defence, and examine when there is no one who answers. I will ask you then to assume with me, as I was saying, that my opponents are of two kinds—**[18E]** one recent, the other ancient; and I hope that you will see the propriety of my answering the latter first, for these accusations you heard long before the others, and much oftener.

* * *

[19A] I will begin at the beginning, and ask what the accusation is which has given rise to this slander of me, and **[19B]** which has encouraged Meletus to proceed against me. What do the slanderers say? They shall be my prosecutors, and I will sum up their words in an affidavit. "Socrates is an evil-doer, and a curious person, who searches into things under the earth and in heaven, and he makes the worse appear the better cause; and he teaches the aforesaid doctrines to others." **[19C]** That is the nature of the accusation, and that is what you have seen yourselves in the comedy of Aristophanes; who has introduced a man whom he calls Socrates, going about and saying that he can walk in the air, and talking a deal of nonsense

concerning matters of which I do not pretend to know either much or little—not that I mean to say anything disparaging of anyone who is a student of natural philosophy.

* * *

[19D] As little foundation is there for the report that I am a teacher, and take money; **[19E]** that is no more true than the other. Although, if a man is able to teach, I honor him for being paid.... Had I the same [knowledge], I should have been very proud and conceited; but the truth is that I have no knowledge of the kind...

[20D] Men of Athens, this reputation of mine has come of a certain sort of wisdom which I possess. If you ask me what kind of wisdom, I reply, such wisdom as is attainable by man, for to that extent I am inclined to believe that I am wise; **[20E]** whereas the persons of whom I was speaking have a superhuman wisdom, which I may fail to describe, because I have it not myself; and he who says that I have, speaks falsely, and is taking away my character. And here, O men of Athens, I must beg you not to interrupt me, even if I seem to say something extravagant. For the word which I will speak is not mine. I will refer you to a witness who is worthy of credit, and will tell you about my wisdom—whether I have any, and of what sort—and that witness shall be the god of Delphi. You must have known Chaerephon; **[21A]** he was early a friend of mine, and also a friend of yours, for he shared in the exile of the people, and returned with you. Well, Chaerephon, as you know, was very impetuous in all his doings, and he went to Delphi and boldly asked the oracle to tell him whether—as I was saying, I must beg you not to interrupt—he asked the oracle to tell him whether there was anyone wiser than I was, and the Pythian prophetess answered that there was no man wiser. Chaerephon is dead himself, but his brother, who is in court, will confirm the truth of this story.

[21B] Why do I mention this? Because I am going to explain to you why I have such an evil name. When I heard the answer, I said to myself, what can the god mean? and what is the interpretation of this riddle? For I know that I have no wisdom, small or great. What can he mean when he says that I am the wisest of men? And yet he is a god and cannot lie; that would be against his nature. After a long consideration, I at last thought of a method of trying the question. I reflected that if I could only find a man wiser than myself, **[21C]** then I might go to the god with a refutation in my hand. I should say to him, "Here is a man who is wiser than I am; but you said that I was the wisest." Accordingly I went to one who had the reputation of wisdom, and observed to him — his name I need not mention; he was a politician whom I selected for examination — and the result was as follows: When I began to talk with him, I could not help thinking that he was not really wise, although he was thought wise by many, and wiser still by himself; and I went and tried to explain to him that he thought himself wise, but was not really wise; **[21D]** and the consequence was that he hated me, and his enmity was shared by several who were present and heard me. So I left him, saying to myself, as I went away: Well, although I do not suppose that either of us knows anything really beautiful and good, I am better off than he is — for he knows nothing, and thinks that he knows. I neither know nor think that I know. In this latter particular, then, I seem to have slightly the advantage of him. Then I went to another, **[21E]** who had still higher philosophical pretensions, and my conclusion was exactly the same. I made another enemy of him, and of many others besides him.

After this I went to one man after another, being not unconscious of the enmity which I provoked, and I lamented and feared this: but necessity was laid upon me — the word of God, I thought, ought to be considered first. And I said to myself, Go I must to all who appear to know, and find out the meaning of the oracle. And I swear to you, Athenians, by the dog I swear! — **[22A]** for I must tell you the truth — the result of my mission was just this: I found that the men most in repute were all but the most foolish; and that some inferior men were really wiser and better. I will tell you the tale of my wanderings and of the "Herculean" labors, as I may call them, which I endured only to find at last the oracle irrefutable. When I left the politicians, I went to the poets; tragic, dithyrambic, and all sorts. **[22B]** And there, I said to myself, you will be detected; now you will find out that you are more ignorant than they are. Accordingly, I took them some of the most elaborate passages in their own writings, and asked what was the meaning of them — thinking that they would teach me something. Will you believe me? I am almost ashamed to speak of this, but still I must say that there is hardly a person present who would not have talked better

about their poetry than they did themselves. That showed me in an instant **[22C]** that not by wisdom do poets write poetry, but by a sort of genius and inspiration; they are like diviners or soothsayers who also say many fine things, but do not understand the meaning of them. And the poets appeared to me to be much in the same case; and I further observed that upon the strength of their poetry they believed themselves to be the wisest of men in other things in which they were not wise. So I departed, conceiving myself to be superior to them for the same reason that I was superior to the politicians.

At last I went to the artisans, **[22D]** for I was conscious that I knew nothing at all, as I may say, and I was sure that they knew many fine things; and in this I was not mistaken, for they did know many things of which I was ignorant, and in this they certainly were wiser than I was. But I observed that even the good artisans fell into the same error as the poets; because they were good workmen they thought that they also knew all sorts of high matters, and this defect in them overshadowed their wisdom — therefore I asked myself on behalf of the oracle, **[22E]** whether I would like to be as I was, neither having their knowledge nor their ignorance, or like them in both; and I made answer to myself and the oracle that I was better off as I was.

[23A] This investigation has led to my having many enemies of the worst and most dangerous kind, and has given occasion also to many calumnies, and I am called wise, for my hearers always imagine that I myself possess the wisdom which I find wanting in others: but the truth is, O men of Athens, that God only is wise; and in this oracle he means to say that the wisdom of men is little or nothing; he is not speaking of Socrates, **[23B]** he is only using my name as an illustration, as if he said, He, O men, is the wisest, who, like Socrates, knows that his wisdom is in truth worth nothing. And so I go my way, obedient to the god, and make inquisition into the wisdom of anyone, whether citizen or stranger, who appears to be wise; and if he is not wise, then in vindication of the oracle I show him that he is not wise; and this occupation quite absorbs me, and I have no time to give either to any public matter of interest or to any concern of my own, **[23C]** but I am in utter poverty by reason of my devotion to the god.

There is another thing: — young men of the richer classes, who have not much to do, come about me of their own accord; they like to hear the pretenders examined, and they often imitate me, and examine others themselves; there are plenty of persons, as they soon enough discover, who think that they know something, but really know little or nothing: and then those who are examined by them instead of being angry with themselves are angry with me: This confounded Socrates, they say; **[23D]** this villainous misleader of youth!—and then if somebody asks them, Why, what evil does he practise or teach? they do not know, and cannot tell; but in order that they may not appear to be at a loss, they repeat the ready-made charges which are used against all philosophers about teaching things up in the clouds and under the earth, and having no gods, and making the worse appear the better cause; for they do not like to confess that their pretence of knowledge has been detected—which is the truth: **[23E]** and as they are numerous and ambitious and energetic, and are all in battle array and have persuasive tongues, they have filled your ears with their loud and inveterate calumnies. And this is the reason why my three accusers, Meletus and Anytus and Lycon, have set upon me; Meletus, who has a quarrel with me on behalf of the poets; Anytus, on behalf of the craftsmen; Lycon, on behalf of the rhetoricians: **[24A]** and as I said at the beginning, I cannot expect to get rid of this mass of calumny all in a moment.

* * *

[28A] I have said enough in answer to the charge of Meletus: any elaborate defence is unnecessary; but as I was saying before, I certainly have many enemies, and this is what will be my destruction if I am destroyed; of that I am certain;—not Meletus, nor yet Anytus, but the envy and detraction of the world, which has been the death of many good men, and will probably be the death of many more; **[28B]** there is no danger of my being the last of them....

[29C] And therefore if you let me go now, and reject the counsels of Anytus, who said that if I were not put to death I ought not to have been prosecuted, and that if I escape now, your sons will all be utterly ruined by listening to my words—if you say to me, Socrates, this time we will not mind Anytus, and will let you off, but upon one condition, that are to inquire and speculate in this way anymore, and that if you are caught doing this again you shall die; **[29D]**—if this was the condition on which you let

me go, I should reply: Men of Athens, I honor and love you; but I shall obey God rather than you, and while I have life and strength I shall never cease from the practice and teaching of philosophy, exhorting anyone whom I meet after my manner, and convincing him, saying: O my friend, why do you who are a citizen of the great and mighty and wise city of Athens, care so much about laying up the greatest amount of money and honor and reputation, **[29E]** and so little about wisdom and truth and the greatest improvement of the soul, which you never regard or heed at all? Are you not ashamed of this? And if the person with whom I am arguing says: Yes, but I do care; I do not depart or let him go at once; I interrogate and examine and cross-examine him, and if I think that he has no virtue, but only says that he has, **[30A]** I reproach him with undervaluing the greater, and overvaluing the less. And this I should say to everyone whom I meet, young and old, citizen and alien, but especially to the citizens, inasmuch as they are my brethren. For this is the command of God, as I would have you know; and I believe that to this day no greater good has ever happened in the state than my service to the God. For I do nothing but go about persuading you all, old and young alike, not to take thought for your persons and your properties, **[30B]** but first and chiefly to care about the greatest improvement of the soul. I tell you that virtue is not given by money, but that from virtue come money and every other good of man, public as well as private. This is my teaching, and if this is the doctrine which corrupts the youth, my influence is ruinous indeed. But if anyone says that this is not my teaching, he is speaking an untruth. Wherefore, O men of Athens, I say to you, do as Anytus bids or not as Anytus bids, and either acquit me or not; but whatever you do, know that I shall never alter my ways, **[30C]** not even if I have to die many times.

Men of Athens, do not interrupt, but hear me; there was an agreement between us that you should hear me out. And I think that what I am going to say will do you good: for I have something more to say, at which you may be inclined to cry out; but I beg that you will not do this. I would have you know that, if you kill such a one as I am, you will injure yourselves more than you will injure me. Meletus and Anytus will not injure me: they cannot; **[30D]** for it is not in the nature of things that a bad man should injure a better than himself. I do not deny that he may, perhaps, kill him, or drive him into exile, or deprive him of civil rights; and he may imagine, and others may imagine, that he is doing him a great injury: but in that I do not agree with him; for the evil of doing as Anytus is doing—of unjustly taking away another man's life—is greater far. And now, Athenians, I am not going to argue for my own sake, as you may think, but for yours, that you may not sin against the God, or lightly reject his boon by condemning me. **[30E]** For if you kill me you will not easily find another like me, who, if I may use such a ludicrous figure of speech, am a sort of gadfly, given to the state by the God; and the state is like a great and noble steed who is tardy in his motions owing to his very size, and requires to be stirred into life. I am that gadfly which God has given the state and all day long and in all places am always fastening upon you, arousing and **[31A]** persuading and reproaching you. And as you will not easily find another like me, I would advise you to spare me. I dare say that you may feel irritated at being suddenly awakened when you are caught napping; and you may think that if you were to strike me dead, as Anytus advises, which you easily might, then you would sleep on for the remainder of your lives, unless God in his care of you gives you another gadfly. And that I am given to you by God is proved by this:—**[31B]** that if I had been like other men, I should not have neglected all my own concerns, or patiently seen the neglect of them during all these years, and have been doing yours, coming to you individually, like a father or elder brother, exhorting you to regard virtue; this I say, would not be like human nature. And had I gained anything, or if my exhortations had been paid, there would have been some sense in that: but now, as you will perceive, **[31C]** not even the impudence of my accusers dares to say that I have ever exacted or sought pay of anyone; they have no witness of that. And I have a witness of the truth of what I say; my poverty is a sufficient witness.

Someone may wonder why I go about in private, giving advice and busying myself with the concerns of others, but do not venture to come forward in public and advise the state. I will tell you the reason of this. **[30D]** You have often heard me speak of an oracle or sign which comes to me, and is the divinity which Meletus ridicules in the indictment. This sign I have had ever since I was a child. The sign is a voice which comes to me and always forbids me to do something which I am going to do, but never commands me to do anything, and this is what stands in

the way of my being a politician. And rightly, as I think. For I am certain, O men of Athens, that if I had engaged in politics, I should have perished long ago and done no good either to you or to myself. **[30E]** And don't be offended at my telling you the truth: for the truth is that no man who goes to war with you or any other multitude, honestly struggling against the commission of unrighteousness and wrong in the state, will save his life; **[32A]** he who will really fight for the right, if he would live even for a little while, must have a private station and not a public one.

I can give you as proofs of this, not words only, but deeds, which you value more than words. Let me tell you a passage of my own life, which will prove to you that I should never have yielded to injustice from any fear of death, and that if I had not yielded I should have died at once. I will tell you a story—tasteless, perhaps, and commonplace, but nevertheless true. **[32B]** The only office of state which I ever held, O men of Athens, was that of senator; the tribe Antiochis, which is my tribe, had the presidency at the trial of the generals who had not taken up the bodies of the slain after the battle of Arginusae; and you proposed to try them all together, which was illegal, as you all thought afterwards; but at the time I was the only one of the Prytanes who was opposed to the illegality, and I gave my vote against you; and when the orators threatened to impeach and arrest me, and have me taken away, and you called and shouted, **[32C]** I made up my mind that I would run the risk, having law and justice with me, rather than take part in your injustice because I feared imprisonment and death.

This happened in the days of the democracy. But when the oligarchy of the Thirty was in power, they sent for me and four others into the rotunda, and bade us bring Leon the Salaminian from Salamis, as they wanted to execute him. This was a specimen of the sort of commands which they were always giving with the view of implicating as many as possible in their crimes; **[32D]** and then I showed, not in words only, but in deed, that, if I may be allowed to use such an expression, I cared not a straw for death, and that my only fear was the fear of doing an unrighteous or unholy thing. For the strong arm of that oppressive power did not frighten me into doing wrong; and when we came out of the rotunda the other four went to Salamis and fetched Leon, but I went quietly home. For which I might have lost my life, had not the power of the Thirty shortly afterwards come to an end. **[32E]** And to this many will witness.

Now do you really imagine that I could have survived all these years, if I had led a public life, supposing that like a good man I had always supported the right and had made justice, as I ought, the first thing? No, indeed, men of Athens, neither I nor any other. **[33A]** But I have been always the same in all my actions, public as well as private, and never have I yielded any base compliance to those who are slanderously termed my disciples or to any other. For the truth is that I have no regular disciples: but if anyone likes to come and hear me while I am pursuing my mission, whether he be young or old, he may freely come. **[33B]** Nor do I converse with those who pay only, and not with those who do not pay; but anyone, whether he be rich or poor, may ask and answer me and listen to my words; and whether he turns out to be a bad man or a good one, that cannot be justly laid to my charge, as I never taught him anything. And if anyone says that he has ever learned or heard anything from me in private which all the world has not heard, I should like you to know that he is speaking an untruth.

But I shall be asked, "Why do people delight in continually conversing with you?" **[33C]** I have told you already, Athenians, the whole truth about this: they like to hear the cross-examination of the pretenders to wisdom; there is amusement in this. And this is a duty which the God has imposed upon me, as I am assured by oracles, visions, and in every sort of way in which the will of divine power was ever signified to anyone. This is true, O Athenians; or, if not true, would be soon refuted. **[33D]** For if I am really corrupting the youth, and have corrupted some of them already, those of them who have grown up and have become sensible that I gave them bad advice in the days of their youth should come forward as accusers and take their revenge; and if they do not like to come themselves, some of their relatives, fathers, brothers, or other kinsmen, should say what evil their families suffered at my hands. Now is their time. Many of them I see in the court. **[33E]** There is Crito, who is of the same age and of the same deme with myself; and there is Critobulus his son, whom I also see. Then again there is Lysanias of Sphettus, who is the father of Aeschines—he is present; and also there is Antiphon of Cephisus, who is the father of Epignes; and there are the brothers of several who have associated with me. There is Nicostratus the son of

Theosdotides, and the brother of Theodotus (now Theodotus himself is dead, and therefore he, at any rate, will not seek to stop him); and there is Paralus the son of Demodocus, who had a brother Theages; **[34A]** and Adeimantus the son of Ariston, whose brother Plato is present; and Aeantodorus, who is the brother of Apollodorus, whom I also see. I might mention a great many others, any of whom Meletus should have produced as witnesses in the course of his speech; and let him still produce them, if he has forgotten—I will make way for him. And let him say, if he has any testimony of the sort which he can produce. Nay, Athenians, the very opposite is the truth. For all these are ready to witness on behalf of the corrupter, of the destroyer of their kindred, as Meletus and Anytus call me; **[34B]** not the corrupted youth only—there might have been a motive for that—but their uncorrupted elder relatives. Why should they too support me with their testimony? Why, indeed, except for the sake of truth and justice, and because they know that I am speaking the truth, and that Meletus is lying.

* * *

The jury finds Socrates guilty.

[35A] There are many reasons why I am not grieved, O men of Athens, at the vote of condemnation. I expected it, and am only surprised that the votes are so nearly equal; for I had thought that the majority against me would have been far larger; but now, had thirty votes gone over to the other side, I should have been acquitted. And I may say that I have escaped Meletus. And I may say more; for without the assistance of Anytus and Lycon, **[36B]** he would not have had a fifth part of the votes, as the law requires, in which case he would have incurred a fine of a thousand drachmae, as is evident.

And so he proposes death as the penalty. And what shall I propose on my part, O men of Athens? Clearly that which is my due. And what is that which I ought to pay or to receive? What shall be done to the man who has never had the wit to be idle during his whole life; but has been careless of what the many care about—wealth, and family interests, and military offices, and speaking in the assembly, and magistracies, and plots, and parties. **[36C]** Reflecting that I was really too honest a man to follow in this way and live, I did not go where I could do no good to you or to myself; but where I could do the greatest good privately to everyone of you, thither I went, and sought to persuade every man among you that he must look to himself, and seek virtue and wisdom before he looks to his private interests, and look to the state before he looks to the interests of the state; and that this should be the order which he observes in all his actions. What shall be done to such a one? **[36D]** Doubtless some good thing, O men of Athens, if he has his reward; and the good should be of a kind suitable to him. What would be a reward suitable to a poor man who is your benefactor, who desires leisure that he may instruct you? There can be no more fitting reward than maintenance in the Prytaneum, O men of Athens, a reward which he deserves far more than the citizen who has won the prize at Olympia in the horse or chariot race, whether the chariots were drawn by two horses or by many. **[36E]** For I am in want, and he has enough; and he only gives you the appearance of happiness, and I give you the reality. And if I am to estimate the penalty justly, **[37A]** I say that maintenance in the Prytaneum is the just return.

Perhaps you may think that I am braving you in saying this, as in what I said before about the tears and prayers. But that is not the case. I speak rather because I am convinced that I never intentionally wronged anyone, although I cannot convince you of that—for we have had a short conversation only; but if there were a law at Athens, such as there is in other cities, **[37B]** that a capital cause should not be decided in one day, then I believe that I should have convinced you; but now the time is too short. I cannot in a moment refute great slanders; and, as I am convinced that I never wronged another, I will assuredly not wrong myself. I will not say of myself that I deserve any evil, or propose any penalty. Why should I? Because I am afraid of the penalty of death which Meletus proposes? When I do not know whether death is a good or an evil, why should I propose a penalty which would certainly be an evil? **[37C]** Shall I say imprisonment? And why should I live in prison, and be the slave of the magistrates of the year—of the Eleven? Or shall the penalty be a fine, and imprisonment until the fine is paid? There is the same objection. I should have to lie in prison, for money I have none, and I cannot pay. And if I say exile (and this may possibly be the penalty which you will affix), I must indeed be blinded by the love of life if I were to consider that when you, **[37D]** who are my own citizens, cannot endure my discourses and words, and have found

them so grievous and odious that you would fain have done with them, others are likely to endure me. No, indeed, men of Athens, that is not very likely. And what a life should I lead, at my age, wandering from city to city, living in ever-changing exile, and always being driven out! For I am quite sure that into whatever place I go, as here so also there, the young men will come to me; and if I drive them away, their elders will drive me out at their desire: and if I let them come, **[37E]** their fathers and friends will drive me out for their sakes.

Someone will say: Yes, Socrates, but cannot you hold your tongue, and then you may go into a foreign city, and no one will interfere with you? Now I have great difficulty in making you understand my answer to this. For if I tell you that this would be a disobedience to a divine command, and therefore that I cannot hold my tongue, you will not believe that I am serious; **[38A]** and if I say again that the greatest good of man is daily to converse about virtue, and all that concerning which you hear me examining myself and others, and that the life which is unexamined is not worth living—that you are still less likely to believe. And yet what I say is true, although a thing of which it is hard for me to persuade you. Moreover, I am not accustomed to think that I deserve any punishment. Had I money I might have proposed to give you what I had, **[38B]** and have been none the worse. But you see that I have none, and can only ask you to proportion the fine to my means. However, I think that I could afford a minae, and therefore I propose that penalty; Plato, Crito, Critobulus, and Apollodorus, my friends here, bid me say thirty minae, **[38C]** and they will be the sureties. Well then, say thirty minae, let that be the penalty; for that they will be ample security to you.

The jury condemns Socrates to death.

Not much time will be gained, O Athenians, in return for the evil name which you will get from the detractors of the city, who will say that you killed Socrates, a wise man; for they will call me wise even although I am not wise when they want to reproach you. If you had waited a little while, your desire would have been fulfilled in the course of nature. For I am far advanced in years, as you may perceive, and not far from death. **[38D]** I am speaking now only to those of you who have condemned me to death...

[39C] And now, O men who have condemned me, I would fain prophesy to you; for I am about to die, and that is the hour in which men are gifted with prophetic power. And I prophesy to you who are my murderers, that immediately after my death punishment far heavier than you have inflicted on me will surely await you. Me you have killed because you wanted to escape the accuser, and not to give an account of your lives. But that will not be as you suppose: far otherwise. **[39D]** For I say that there will be more accusers of you than there are now; accusers whom hitherto I have restrained: and as they are younger they will be more severe with you, and you will be more offended at them. For if you think that by killing men you can avoid the accuser censuring your lives, you are mistaken; that is not a way of escape which is either possible or honorable; the easiest and noblest way is not to be crushing others, but to be improving yourselves. **[39E]** This is the prophecy which I utter before my departure, to the judges who have condemned me.

Friends, who would have acquitted me, I would like also to talk with you about this thing which has happened, while the magistrates are busy, and before I go to the place at which I must die. Stay then awhile, for we may as well talk with one another while there is time. **[40A]** You are my friends, and I should like to show you the meaning of this event which has happened to me. O my judges— for you I may truly call judges—I should like to tell you of a wonderful circumstance. Hitherto the familiar oracle within me has constantly been in the habit of opposing me even about trifles, if I was going to make a slip or error about anything; and now as you see there has come upon me that which may be thought, and is generally believed to be, the last and worst evil. **[40B]** But the oracle made no sign of opposition, either as I was leaving my house and going out in the morning, or when I was going up into this court, or while I was speaking, at anything which I was going to say; and yet I have often been stopped in the middle of a speech; but now in nothing I either said or did touching this matter has the oracle opposed me. What do I take to be the explanation of this? I will tell you. I regard this as a proof that what has happened to me is a good, and that those of us who think that death is an evil are in error. **[40C]** This is a great proof to me of what I am saying, for the customary sign would surely have opposed me had I been going to evil and not to good....

[41D] Wherefore, O judges, be of good cheer about death, and know this of a truth—that no evil can happen to a good man, either in life or after death. He and his are not neglected by the gods; nor has my own approaching end happened by mere chance. But I see clearly that to die and be released was better for me; and therefore the oracle gave no sign. For which reason also, I am not angry with my accusers, or my condemners; they have done me no harm, although neither of them meant to do me any good; **[41E]** and for this I may gently blame them. Still I have a favor to ask of them. When my sons are grown up, I would ask you, O my friends, to punish them; and I would have you trouble them, as I have troubled you, if they seem to care about riches, or anything, more than about virtue; or if they pretend to be something when they are really nothing,—then reprove them, as I have reproved you, for not caring about that for which they ought to care, and thinking that they are something when they are really nothing. And if you do this, **[42A]** I and my sons will have received justice at your hands.

The hour of departure has arrived, and we go our ways—I to die, and you to live. Which is better God only knows.

Questions

1. **Why does Socrates deny that he is eloquent?**
2. **Why is he more afraid of his old critics than of the formal accusers at his trial?**
3. **In what way does he think himself wise?**
4. **How does he say he became unpopular?**
5. **What does he claim his teaching consists of?**
6. **How does he defend himself against charges of a political nature?**
7. **Why do you think the jury convicted him and condemned him to death? Do you think they were right in doing so?**

3.   MEMORABILIA

Xenophon was a contemporary of Plato and also an admirer and associate of Socrates. In his own brief *Apology of Socrates* and in his recollections, however, he presents a very different picture of the philosopher. He is chiefly concerned to explain Socrates' lofty tone with the jury and to defend him against charges of irreligion and of truly corrupting enemies of the democracy like Alcibiades and Critias. This latter was part of a defense against an essay, now lost, called the "Accusation of Socrates," written by a certain Polycrates, who says that Socrates was tried and condemned for political reasons. Xenophon refers to him as "the accuser."

1.1.1 I have often wondered by what arguments those who drew up the indictment against Socrates could persuade the Athenians that his life was forfeit to the state. The indictment against him was to this effect: Socrates is guilty of rejecting the gods acknowledged by the state and of bringing in strange deities: he is also guilty of corrupting the youth.

1.1.2 First then, that he rejected the gods acknowledged by the state—what evidence did they produce of that? He offered sacrifices constantly, and made no secret of it, now in his home, now at the altars of the state temples, and he made use of divination with as little secrecy. Indeed it had become notorious that Socrates claimed to be guided by "the deity": it was out of this claim, I think, that the charge of bringing in strange deities arose. **[3]** He was no more bringing in anything strange than are other believers in divination, who rely on augury, oracles, coincidences and sacrifices. For these men's belief is not that the birds or the folk met by accident know what profits the inquirer, but that they are the instruments by which the gods make this known; and that was Socrates' belief too.

1.1.16 Such, then, was his criticism of those who meddle with these matters. His own conversation was ever of human things. The problems he discussed were, What is godly, what is ungodly; what is beautiful, what is ugly; what is just, what is unjust; what is prudence, what is madness; what is courage, what is cowardice; what is a state, what is a statesman; what is government, and what is a governor;—these and others like them, of which the knowledge made a "gentleman," in his estimation, while ignorance should involve the reproach of "slavishness."

1.1.17 So, in pronouncing on opinions of his that were unknown to them it is not surprising that the jury erred: but is it not astonishing that they should have ignored matters of common knowledge? **[18]** For instance, when he was on the Council and had taken the counsellor's oath by which he bound himself to give counsel in accordance with the laws, it fell to his lot to preside in the Assembly when the people wanted to condemn Thrasyllus and Erasinides and their colleagues to death by a single vote. That was illegal, and he refused the motion in spite of popular rancour and the threats of many powerful persons. It was more to him that he should keep his oath than that he should humour the people in an unjust demand and shield himself from threats.

1.2.1 No less wonderful is it to me that some believed the charge brought against Socrates of corrupting the youth. In the first place, apart from what I have said, in control of his own passions and appetites he was the strictest of men; further, in endurance of cold and heat and every kind of toil he was most resolute; and besides, his needs were so schooled to moderation that having very little he was yet very content. **[2]** Such was his own character: how then can he have led others into impiety, crime, gluttony, lust, or sloth? On the contrary, he cured these vices in many, by putting into them a desire for goodness, and by giving them confidence that self-discipline would make them gentlemen.... **[6]** He held that this self-denying ordinance insured his liberty. Those who charged a fee for their society he denounced for selling themselves into bondage; since they were bound to converse with all from whom they took the fee. **[7]** He marvelled that anyone should make money by the profession of virtue, and should not reflect that his highest reward would be the gain of a good friend; as though he who became a true gentleman could fail to feel deep gratitude for a benefit so great.

1.2.9 But, said his accuser, he taught his companions to despise the established laws by insisting on the folly of appointing public officials by lot, when none would choose a pilot or builder or flautist by lot, nor any other craftsman for work in which mistakes are far less disastrous than mistakes in statecraft. Such sayings, he argued, led the young to despise the established constitution and made them violent....

1.2.12 Among the associates of Socrates were Critias and Alcibiades; and none wrought so many evils to the state. For Critias in the days of the oligarchy bore the palm for greed and violence: Alcibiades, for his part, exceeded all in licentiousness and insolence under the democracy. **[13]** Now I have no intention of excusing the wrong these two men wrought the state; but I will explain how they came to be with Socrates. **[14]** Ambition was the very life-blood of both: no Athenian was ever like them. They were eager to get control of everything and to outstrip every rival in notoriety. They knew that Socrates was living on very little, and yet was wholly independent; that he was strictly moderate in all his pleasures; and that in argument he could do what he liked with any disputant. **[15]** Sharing this knowledge and the principles I have indicated, is it to be supposed that these two men wanted to adopt the simple life of Socrates, and with this object in view sought his society? Did they not rather think that by associating with him they would attain the utmost proficiency in speech and action? **[16]** For my part I believe that, had heaven granted them the choice between the life they saw Socrates leading and death, they would have chosen rather to die. Their conduct betrayed their purpose; for as soon as they thought themselves superior to their fellow-disciples they sprang away from Socrates and took to politics; it was for political ends that they had wanted Socrates....

1.2.24 And indeed it was thus with Critias and Alcibiades. So long as they were with Socrates, they found in him an ally who gave them strength to conquer their evil passions. But when they parted from him, Critias fled to Thessaly, and got among men who put lawlessness before justice; while Alcibiades, on account of his beauty, was hunted by many great ladies, and because of his influence at Athens and among her allies he was spoilt by many powerful men: and as athletes who gain an easy victory in the games are apt to neglect their training, so the honour in which he was held, the cheap triumph he won with the people, led him to neglect himself....

1.2.29 Nevertheless, although he was himself free from vice, if he saw and approved of base conduct in them, he would be open to censure. Well, when he found that Critias loved Euthydemus and wanted to lead him astray, he tried to restrain him by saying that it was mean and unbecoming in a gentleman to sue like a beggar to the object of his affection, whose good opinion he coveted, stooping to ask a favour that it was wrong to grant. **[30]** As Critias paid no heed whatever to this protest, Socrates, it is said, exclaimed in the presence of Euthydemus and many others, "Critias seems to have the feelings of a pig: he can no more keep away from Euthydemus than pigs can help rubbing themselves against stones." Now Critias bore a grudge against Socrates for this; **[31]** and when he was one of the Thirty and was drafting laws with Charicles, he bore it in mind. He inserted a clause which made it illegal "to teach the art of words." It was a calculated insult to Socrates, whom he saw no means of attacking, except by imputing to him the practice constantly attributed to philosophers, and so making him unpopular. For I myself never heard Socrates indulge in the practice, nor knew of anyone who professed to have heard him do so. The truth came out. **[32]** When the Thirty were putting to death many citizens of the highest respectability and were encouraging many in crime, Socrates had remarked: "It seems strange enough to me that a herdsman who lets his cattle decrease and go to the bad should not admit that he is a poor cowherd; but stranger still that a statesman when he causes the citizens to decrease and go to the bad, should feel no shame nor think himself a poor statesman." **[33]** This remark was reported to Critias and Charicles, who sent for Socrates, showed him the law and forbade him to hold conversation with the young....

4.7.6 In general, with regard to the phenomena of the heavens, he deprecated curiosity to learn how the deity contrives them: he held that their secrets could not be discovered by man, and believed that any attempt to search out what the gods had not chosen to reveal must be displeasing to them. He said that he who meddles with these matters runs the risk of losing his sanity as completely as Anaxagoras, who took an insane pride in his explanation of the divine machinery…

4.8.4 I will repeat what Hermogenes, son of Hipponicus, told me about him. "When Meletus had actually formulated his indictment," he said, "Socrates talked freely in my presence, but made no reference to the case. I told him that he ought to be thinking about his defence. His first remark was, 'Don't you think that I have been preparing for it all my life?' And when I asked him how, he said that he had been constantly occupied in the consideration of right and wrong, and in doing what was right and avoiding what was wrong, which he regarded as the best preparation for a defence. **[5]** Then I said, 'Don't you see, Socrates, that the juries in our courts are apt to be misled by argument, so that they often put the innocent to death, and acquit the guilty?' 'Ah, yes, Hermogenes,' he answered, 'but when I did try to think out my defence to the jury, the deity at once resisted.' **[6]** 'Strange words,' said I; and he, 'Do you think it strange, if it seems better to God that I should die now? Don't you see that to this day I never would acknowledge that any man had lived a better or a pleasanter life than I? For they live best, I think, who strive best to become as good as possible: and the pleasantest life is theirs who are conscious that they are growing in goodness. **[7]** And to this day that has been my experience; and mixing with others and closely comparing myself with them, I have held without ceasing to this opinion of myself. And not I only, but my friends cease not to feel thus towards me, not because of their love for me (for why does not love make others feel thus towards their friends?), but because they think that they too would rise highest in goodness by being with me. **[8]** But if I am to live on, haply I may be forced to pay the old man's forfeit—to become sand-blind and deaf and dull of wit, slower to learn, quicker to forget, outstripped now by those who were behind me. Nay, but even were I unconscious of the change, life would be a burden to me; and if I knew, misery and bitterness would surely be my lot.'"

4.8.9 "'But now, if I am to die unjustly, they who unjustly kill me will bear the shame of it. For if to do injustice is shameful, whatever is unjustly done must surely bring shame. But to me what shame is it that others fail to decide and act justly concerning me? **[10]** I see that posterity judges differently of the dead according as they did or suffered injustice. I know that men will remember me too, and, if I die now, not as they will remember those who took my life. For I know that they will ever testify of me that I wronged no man at any time, nor corrupted any man, but strove ever to make my companions better.'"

4.8.11 This was the tenor of his conversation with Hermogenes and with the others. All who knew what manner of man Socrates was and who seek after virtue continue to this day to miss him beyond all others, as the chief of helpers in the quest of virtue. For myself, I have described him as he was: so religious that he did nothing without counsel from the gods; so just that he did no injury, however small, to any man, but conferred the greatest benefits on all who dealt with him; so self-controlled that he never chose the pleasanter rather than the better course; so wise that he was unerring in his judgment of the better and the worse, and needed no counsellor, but relied on himself for his knowledge of them; masterly in expounding and defining such things; no less masterly in putting others to the test, and convincing them of error and exhorting them to follow virtue and gentleness. To me then he seemed to be all that a truly good and happy man must be. But if there is any doubter, let him set the character of other men beside these things; then let him judge.

Questions

1. **How does the picture of Socrates painted by Xenophon compare with those of Aristophanes and Plato? Which do you find most credible?**
2. **If Socrates had made his defense along the lines of Xenophon's do you think he would have been more successful?**

OPINIONS OF MODERN SCHOLARS

1. Mogens Hansen, Reader in Classics at Copenhagen University, here attempts a reconstruction of the trial and emphasizes its political aspects.

FROM MOGENS HERMAN HANSEN, *THE TRIAL OF SOKRATES — FROM THE ATHENIAN POINT OF VIEW*

A Reconstruction of the Trial

IN THE ARCHONSHIP OF LACHES (400/399), and more precisely during the winter of 399, Sokrates was indicted by Meletos the son of Meletos of Pitthos Lykon of an unknown deme and Anytos Anthemion's son of Euonymon. He was brought to trial by a *graphé asebeias*, a public action for impiety, submitted to the King Archon by Meletos. Thus it was Meletos who was liable for being fined 1,000 drachmas if he obtained less than a fifth of the votes of the jurors. The text of the indictment has survived and runs as follows: "under oath Meletos the son of Meletos of Pitthos has brought a public action against Sokrates the son of Sophroniskos of Alopeke and charged him with the following offences: Sokrates is guilty of not acknowledging the gods acknowledged by the state and of introducing other new divinities. Furthermore he is guilty of corrupting the young. Penalty proposed: capital punishment." The action was heard by a panel of 501 jurors chaired by the King Archon. Being the principal prosecutor Meletos made the first speech and charged Sokrates with having corrupted the young by discussing and propagating the natural philosophers' critical views about the gods, and with having acted as an unauthorized oracle, invoking his daimonion. Lykon and Anytos appeared as synegoroi for Meletos.

What Lykon said we do not know, but Anytos must have accused Sokrates of corrupting the young by his subversive criticism of the democratic institutions: Sokrates had formerly influenced Alkibiades and Kritias, two of the most dangerous enemies of the people. Because of the amnesty he could no longer be called to account for what he had done before 403, but since he still held the same views and aired them unabated, there was a risk that his followers might join a third attempt to overthrow the democracy. The prosecutors called a number of witnesses, partly some who discussing with Sokrates had felt that they had been ridiculed, and partly some who had attended such discussions.

Sokrates' speech in his own defence conveyed the impression of being an off-the-cuff performance in which he concentrated on refuting the charges brought by Meletos. He denied that he had taken any interest in natural philosophy, and he invoked his daimonion as evidence that he was not an atheist. Furthermore, the purpose of his discussions with the young, mostly sons of the rich, had been to make them better not to corrupt them. The Delphic oracle's response, that no man is wiser than Sokrates, was a major point in the defence put forward by Sokrates, and since Chairephon had passed away, Sokrates had it witnessed by Chairephon's brother. The charges brought by Meletos were further refuted by a cross examination of Meletos, during which he involved himself in self-contradictions. The charges brought by Lykon and Anytos, however, were passed over in silence, and Sokrates countered the political accusations only indirectly by reminding the jurors of his constitutional behaviour during the trial of the generals and his opposition to the Thirty by refusing to assist in the arrest of Leon.

After Sokrates' own speech some of Sokrates' friends came forward as his synegonti and they may have countered the charges made by Lykon and Anylos, especially the accusation that Sokrates had propagated undemocratic views.

When the hearing was over the jurors voted and, since we are told that Sokrates would have been acquitted if 30 of the jurors had voted differently, Sokrates must have been found guilty by a majority of 59 or 60 votes. If the figure 30 is correct, the inference seems to be that the votes were 280/221, or, perhaps, 280/220, if one of the jurors abstained from voting.

The indictment stipulated capital punishment and in a short speech Meletos must have put it to the jurors that Sokrates be sentenced to death and executed. In his reply Sokrates first refused to come up with a realistic alternative to capital punishment. He may even have suggested entertainment in the Prytaneion for the rest of his life as an appropriate penalty.

He then proposed a fine he could afford, i.e. half a mina, but eventually, when some of his friends including Plato promised to go bail, he proposed a fine of 30 minas = half a talent. When the vote on the penalty was taken, Meletos' proposal was passed by an even greater majority than the verdict of guilty.

With the second vote the trial was over, but, on his own initiative, Sokrates delivered a third speech to the jurors (or at least to those who cared to listen) in which he reflected on the meaning of death in general and in particular on the death sentence he had just incurred.

The Political Accusations

After the reconstruction of the trial I will examine the charges brought against Sokrates, both the charge of impiety and the political charges. I will look for parallels and for sources that can shed light on the Athenians' view of impiety related to freedom of conscience as well as their view of antidemocratic beliefs related to freedom of speech.

The indictment of Sokrates was not the only one of its kind that was heard in Athens in those years. A few months earlier the Athenians had acquitted Andokides of a charge of impiety, and in the very same year Nikomachos was charged with *asebeia* in connection with his codification of the laws of Athens. The year 400/399 seems to have bristled with law suits concerning religious offences, and there is no reason to assume that the trial of Sokrates was provoked by some specific activity in which he had been involved. Sokrates was found guilty because of what he believed about the Gods and probably also because of his critical view of the Athenian democratic institutions. There is a very interesting fragment of Hypereides, which is mostly overlooked by those who write about the trial of Sokrates. In his speech against Autokles, Hypereides reminded the Athenians that their fathers had punished Sokrates for his words, *epi logois*, i.e. not because of anything he had done. This fragment, and the verdict itself shows that the Athenians would not grant Sokrates what we today

call freedom of speech and of conscience, either because freedom of speech and of conscience were not ideals accepted by the Athenian democrats, or because Athenian democracy in this respect resembles modern democracies: freedom of speech and conscience are cherished as ideals central to democracy, but democrats do not always live up to their own ideals, not even in states that regularly take pride in being democracies.

I will begin with a discussion of freedom of speech, which is often called *parresia* in our sources. I find it superfluous here to argue that Athenian *parresia* was as close to modern democratic freedom of speech as any ancient concept can be to its modern equivalent. And all sources show that freedom of speech was an ideal cherished by the Athenian democrats. It suffices to mention that the Athenians had a trireme called *parresia* and to refer to Demosthenes' remark that a basic difference between Spartan oligarchy and Athenian democracy is that in Athens you are free to praise the Spartan constitution and way of life, whereas in Sparta it is prohibited to praise any other constitution than the Spartan.

Nevertheless, praise of the Spartan constitution may well have been what offended the Athenians and what the prosecutors held against Sokrates during the trial. As argued above one of the political accusations made against Sokrates must have been that he preferred election of magistrates to selection by lot and said that sortition was silly. Now, Isokrates, for example, emphasized that a basic difference between the Athenian and the Spartan constitution is that magistrates are elected in Sparta but selected by lot in Athens. And in Plato's Gorgias, when Sokrates criticizes the Athenian democracy, Kallikles retorts that Sokrates' criticism is an echo of what is said by those with cauliflower ears; but "having cauliflower ears" was a well known epithet used about those who admired and imitated the Spartan way of life. The sources form a synthesis when we add that Polykrates apart from his *Kategoria Sokrates* was the author of a lampoon of the Spartans, entitled *Kategoria Lakedaimonion*.

To sum up: Freedom of speech was probably the most cherished of the Athenian democratic ideals, and in Demosthenes it was exemplified by the right to praise the Spartan constitution at the expense of the Athenian. We know that many citizens and metics availed themselves of this freedom of speech without ever being brought to trial. Plato, Isokrates and Aristotle are the three most prominent figures, but there are many others. The trial of Sokrates is, in fact, the only attested case of an Athenian having been put on trial for what he thought and said. In all other cases of antidemocratic behaviour the defendant is charged with conspiracy, treason or corruption. But there is one important difference between Sokrates and the three others I have mentioned. Plato, Isokrates and Aristotle were teachers, but they taught only those who frequented their schools. Sokrates was probably more prominent and better known. Aristophanes' choice of Sokrates to impersonate the sophist in the *Clouds* is a strong indication that Sokrates was a well-known figure in Athens. What was dangerous about Sokrates was not the views he had about democracy, but his propagation of such views to anyone who cared to attend his daily discussions in the Agora.

The condemnation and execution of Sokrates demonstrates that the Athenians did not always live up to their own ideals; but that those ideals were not just empty words is apparent both from the presumption that the trial of Sokrates was unique in Athenian history, and from the fact that Sokrates, after all, lived to be seventy although he must have criticized the democratic institutions regularly throughout his adult life. As George Grote rightly remarked: if Sokrates had been a citizen in one of Plato's Utopias, he would never have reached the age of seventy....

I now turn to the charge officially brought against Sokrates, the charge of impiety. In this case too it is appropriate to ask: is the trial of Sokrates unique in the Athenian administration of justice or can parallels be found? To come up with an answer to that question, however, is difficult since our sources have been muddled by the myth that grew up around Sokrates. The *graphé asebeias* against Sokrates has made it almost impossible in later sources to tell historical lawsuits from anecdotal ones. The most admired general in the ancient world was Alexander the Great. He was crook-shouldered and because of that innumerable generals after him walked around with their head on a slant. Again, the admired philosopher Sokrates had been convicted of impiety. After Sokrates it was an accolade for a philosopher to have been charged with impiety, and the Hellenistic biographers were eager to bestow the honour on quite a few of Sokrates' contemporaries and successors: Anaxagoras, Protagoras, Prodikos,

Stilpon, Theodoras, Aristotle and Theophrastos. Anaxagoras may have been put on trial, but the evidence for all the other public prosecutions of philosophers for impiety is anecdotal and dangerous to rely on without further information. Even the trial of Anaxagoras is not above suspicion. If we can trust our sources, in order to have a law that warranted a suit of that kind, a certain Diopeithes had to propose and carry a decree that public action be brought against atheists and astronomers, probably a hendiadys for atheistic astronomers. In any case, the urgent need for a decree in order to have Anaxagoras put on trial indicates that the Athenians did not normally interfere with what people thought about the gods as long as they did not profane the mysteries or mutilate the Herms or commit other acts of impiety.

It is still a common belief that the trial of Sokrates was warranted by Diopeithes' decree. But we must not forget that the Athenian law code was revised in 403/2 and that laws not included in the revised code were no longer valid. Diopeithes' decree against atheistic astronomers, if genuine, was certainly tailored to suit the trial of Anaxagoras. Consequently it is most unlikely that it survived the codification in 403/2 and was included in the revised code.

Apart from the trial of Anaxagoras there is only one other attestation of a *graphé asebeias* having been brought against an atheist, namely the trial of Diagoras, called *ho atheos*. But even Diagoras was not charged with being an atheist but with having revealed the mysteries to some uninitiated persons. So let us remember that Meletos, when cross-examined by Sokrates, almost automatically refers to Anaxagoras. And the reason may well be that the trial of Anaxagoras (if it took place) was the only precedent of a person being charged with not believing in the traditional Gods.

The second and third part of the indictment are, in fact, more serious than the first. "Sokrates introduces other new divinities and corrupts the young." The Athenians granted their citizens a certain freedom of conscience privately, but could not tolerate that a person, without proper authorization, introduced new cults and attempted to proselytize the younger generation. It is amply attested how the Athenians dealt with such behaviour.

Phryne, the mistress of Hypereides, was brought to trial through a *graphé asebeias* for having introduced a new divinity and surrounded herself with a group of young proselytes. She was found not guilty at the trial.

Menekles brought a *graphé asebeias* against Ninos, the priestess. She was charged with having administered a potion, probably an aphrodisiac, to her devotees of young people. Menekles obtained a conviction against her and she was sentenced to death.

Theoris of Lemnos was charged with the same offence as Ninos. She was likewise put on trial and a sentence of death was passed on her and her entire family.

I would like to stress that it is Sokrates himself who connects the charge of impiety with the charge of corrupting the young. Both in Plato's *Apology* and in *Euthyphro* Sokrates says that the Athenians do not care about what he himself thinks, but they take him for a teacher, and that they will not tolerate. Here is a clear difference between the Athenian and the modern concept of freedom of conscience. The Athenians would not allow private unauthorized religious communities. From a juridical point of view the most serious of the charges brought against Sokrates was undoubtedly that he corrupted the young who surrounded him by acting as a private oracle, namely by giving them the advice of his *daimonion*. Sokrates was not charged with being an atheist, but with being a missionary.

To sum up: Sokrates was sentenced for not sharing the ordinary Athenian's views about the gods, and probably also for having criticized the democratic institutions. As said before a trial of a person who had his own views about the gods was rare, and a trial of a person who criticized the democratic institutions is unique. The presumption is that Sokrates was not put on trial for having such views, but rather for having propagated them to his followers every day, year in, year out. In that case the pertinent question must be: who were the persons who gathered around Sokrates and listened to his discussions in the Agora? In Plato's *Apology* Sokrates tells the jurors that most of his followers were young and rich, because they had the spare time required to frequent the agora on weekdays. It is worrying that Sokrates' criticism of the Athenian democratic institutions was aired among the rich and the young. On the whole a rich man would prefer oligarchy to democracy, and the young were notorious for being prone to revolutionize the established society. Remember that the Greek word

for revolution is *neoterismos*. So let us have a closer look at the circle round Sokrates.

In Plato's dialogues we meet about sixty named persons. I have concentrated on those who contribute to the discussions. The cast could be somewhat extended by including the mutes and those mentioned, but not present. And the list could made even longer if we included the persons we meet in Xenophon's Socratic dialogues.

Thus, the group I study here is the cast known from Plato's dialogues. It comprises sixty persons of whom thirty are unknown to us in the sense that Plato provides us with no information about who they are and what they are, nor are they known from any other source. Again, half of the remaining thirty persons are either travelling sophists (like Protagoras, Gorgias, Hippias and Prodikos), or foreigners staying in Athens (like Menon), or poets (like Aristophanes and Agathon). So we are left with fifteen persons known not only as participants in the discussions conducted by Sokrates but also as participants in Athenian politics. Of those only five are loyal democrats; the other ten are black sheep and disreputable persons whom the Athenians sentenced to death, often in absentia.

Let us start with a presentation of the five democrats. First comes Chairephon, who asked the Delphic oracle whether any person was wiser than Sokrates. He was among the democrats who had to go into exile in 404 during the rule of the Thirty. Next come the generals Nikias and Laches, whom we meet in Laches, and Kallias, in whose house Sokrates met Protagoras. He served as strategos in 391/0 and was one of the Athenian envoys sent to Sparta in 371. Finally there is Anytos who in Meno is persuaded to join the discussion, which he does until he becomes so cross that he leaves. He cannot properly be called a follower of Sokrates, in which case the circle around Sokrates counts, not five, but just four good democrats.

It is much easier to find crooks and traitors among Sokrates' friends and followers: In Parmenides we are introduced to Pythodoros, who served as strategos in 425/4 but was deposed, charged with treason and sentenced to death in absentia. In 415 no less than five of Sokrates' friends were convicted of having profaned the mysteries and/or mutilated the Herms. They are: Phaidros known from the dialogue that bears his name, the doctor Eryximachos from Symposion and his father Akoumenos, referred to in Phaidros,

Axiochos known from the dialogue that bears his name, and last but not least Alkibiades, who in addition to profaning the mysteries offended the Athenians several times later on. If we move ahead a few years we meet Kleitophon both in the *Republic* and in the dialogue Kleitophon. He has, with considerable confidence, been identified with the political leader who proposed and carried the rider to the decree that set up the oligarchy of the Four Hundred in the spring of 411. And in Laches appears Melesias, the son of Thukydides, who was one of the Four Hundred and undoubtedly exiled when the oligarchs were overthrown in the autumn of 411. Going down to the oligarchy of 404–03 we come across the two most notorious of Sokrates' friends: Kritias, the leader of the extremistic wing among the Thirty, and his relative Charmides who was the leader of the executive committee set up by the Thirty in the Piraeus. They were both killed in the Battle of Mounichia and thus avoided being held responsible when the democracy was restored in 403.

There can be no denying that the trial of Sokrates is thrown into relief by the gallery of characters found in Plato's dialogues. The Athenians may have known that Sokrates had no intention himself of overthrowing the democracy. But Sokrates aired his critical views of the democratic institutions among blasphemers, oligarchs and traitors. We all know the saying "tell me who your friends are, and I will know who you are." As many other sayings it is of Greek origin and found for example in a fragment of Euripides' lost play *Phoinix*.

Many a time ere now have I been made
the judge in men's disputes, and oft have heard
for one event conflicting witnesses.
And so to find the truth, I, as do all
wise men, look sharp to see the character
that marks the daily life, and judge by that.
The man who loves companionship of knaves
I care not to interrogate. What need
is there? I know too well the man is such
as is the company he loves to keep.

It is telling that this fragment of Euripides is known from Aischines' speech against Timarchos. After a detailed account of Timarchos' lecherous life Aischines refers to Timarchos' friends and followers as a further reason for finding him guilty, and it is in that context that he quotes the Euripides passage.

We know that those who prosecuted Sokrates must have adopted the same line of argument since they stressed that Kritias and Alkibiades had been taught by Sokrates. It is Xenophon in particular who takes great pains to refute any attempt to throw suspicion on Sokrates in this way. He pleads that Sokrates was a loyal democrat and performed his sacrifices to the gods as everybody else. But even if he is right—as he may well be—the followers of Sokrates still cast a shade upon their master: his criticism of the democratic institutions provided his oligarchic friends with the arguments they wanted, and Sokrates may have performed his sacrifices in public, but so did those of his friends who had profaned the mysteries in secret. Who could know what Sokrates did during the night in company with his young and rich friends? The profanation of the mysteries and the two oligarchic revolutions took place before the amnesty of 403, but Sokrates kept on having the same views, and the Athenians may have entertained a lurking suspicion that Sokrates' friends might venture a third attempt to overthrow the democracy.

Perhaps the best and least biased source for the trial of Sokrates is Aischines' terse and brief reference to it in his speech Against Timarchos:

> You, Athenians, had Sokrates the sophist
> executed because he was shown to have
> been the teacher of Kritias, one of the
> Thirty who overthrew the democracy.

Sokrates might have avoided the trial if he had been more cautious, and he might have incurred a milder punishment if he had been more modest. The Athenian administration of justice rested on private prosecution. If you had an enemy, there was a permanent risk of being taken to court by him. Now, what is it that Sokrates, year after year, had told the Athenians in the Agora and repeated before the jurors when he was tried? The Delphic oracle has found that I am the wisest of all men. I have put the oracle's response to the test and found that it is true. What punishment is appropriate for such behaviour? to be entertained at public cost in the Prytaneion for the rest of my life.— A philosopher's humility is often indistinguishable from arrogance. Sokrates' behaviour irritated first Anytos so that he joined the other prosecutors and later the jurors so that they passed a sentence of death on him. Sokrates took the conviction boldly and did nothing to evade the consequences of having associated with disreputable citizens and suspicious foreigners. Was the condemnation of Sokrates judicial murder or even miscarriage of justice? No law prohibited an Athenian to speak his mind and to criticize the democratic institutions. On the contrary the Athenians took pride in their freedom of speech and extended it even to metics and slaves. Similarly, there was probably no law against private religious associations, if only they had been authorized by a decree of the people. So there may have been no law to warrant the sentence passed on Sokrates. But in the heliastic [judicial] oath the jurors were instructed, where no law existed, to act as in conscience bound. In the trial of Sokrates the jurors must have made use of that passage of the heliastic oath, at least as far as the political accusations are concerned. Our sources are insufficient to determine whether the sentence passed on Sokrates was unforgivable or understandable or even justifiable, since the case for the prosecution cannot be reconstructed with sufficient certainty. But we have no evidence to refute the argument that in condemning Sokrates the jurors voted honorably, believing that they were protecting the democratic institutions of Athens. Therefore this investigation of the trial of Sokrates must end in Socratic ignorance with a query.

> **2.** Paul Cartledge emphasizes the religious character of the charges brought against Socrates and the inseparability of politics and religion in the minds of the ancient Athenians.

FROM PAUL CARTLEDGE, *DEMOCRACY REAFFIRMED*

THE TRIAL OF SOCRATES is a subject that arouses a high degree of moral involvement in many scholars, sometimes at the expense of maintaining an appropriate distance from the historical object. Let us fervently hope that I shall not fail to maintain such a distance here, though this is a notoriously challenging subject, not least because it involves centrally the value of freedom: one that, it has been well said, we tend to forget—until we have lost it. Freedom is, moreover, an essentially contested concept. But there would be widespread assent, I think, to the proposition that, for the West, freedom of speech is the fundamental civil liberty. Without it there can be no others—or at any rate only in a distinctly weakened sense. There is, however, a price to be paid for free speech, the price of offence, even though arguably feelings of being offended can never by themselves justify any kind of official, state-imposed or state-directed censorship. The trial of Sokrates, it has been often thought, constitutes a standing insult to that democratic civil liberty principle. One modern interpreter indeed has gone so far as to claim that in trying and then condemning Sokrates, a man of politically directed speech rather than political action, the democratic Athenians sinned against their own free-speech credo.

Stone was himself a major supporter of the Athenian style of democracy in general, as he understood it; but actually most intellectuals from Sokrates's own day onwards have not been; indeed, they have pretty often been the reverse of supportive. One thinks, at once and above all, of Plato and his pupils, not excluding Aristotle, though the Stagirite was far more tolerant than his mentor had been of the majoritarian principle of decision-making and government as such. Thus the trial and death-sentence of Plato's own mentor Sokrates have been regularly seen and portrayed as the supremely awful act of censorship by an intolerant, unenlightened democracy. Even J.S. Mill, who was in general a defender of the Athenian Many against its right-wing oligarchic critics, saw the trial of Socrates as exemplifying what in his libertarian tract *On Liberty* (1859) he most feared, namely the tyranny of the majority.

But are Stone and Mill quite correct in their objections, criticisms and fears? This is not an easy matter to decide. Not only because it is never easy to revisit and re-imagine the hothouse atmosphere of a court of law operating under quite different norms and codes from those with which we today might be familiar. But also because the evidence for making a retrospective re-judgment is systematically skewed. Sokrates is quite probably the most famous philosopher ever to have lived, at least within the Western tradition. This is not a bad achievement for a man about whose life (469–399) we know very little indeed for certain, and who apparently never wrote down a word of his philosophy! However, it also causes first-order problems of deciding what were "his" views, let alone correctly interpreting them. Moreover, as regards his trial, we hear only the case for the defence; and that case is conveyed to us only indirectly, with doubly or trebly forked tongue. Nevertheless, with hand on heart and heart in mouth, I shall venture to argue the following case: that the Athenian jury in 399 BCE, and thus the Athenian Demos as such, were indeed right to convict Sokrates. And, more especially, I shall argue that they did so on the basis of the main charge, that of impiety.

It may seem odd that it is felt necessary to argue the latter point at all, since the action brought against Socrates was a *graphé asebeias*, a writ of (sc. alleging) impiety heard within the court presided over by the Basileus, the archon responsible for the oversight and enforcement of major religious law. Here is the text of the indictment lodged against Socrates, as preserved, surely accurately, by the 3rd-century CE doxographic biographer Diogenes Laertius in his *Lives of the Philosophers* (II.40):

> Meletus, son of Meletus of the deme Pitthos, has brought this charge and lodged this writ against Socrates son of Sophroniskos of the deme Alopeke. Socrates has broken the law by [1a] not duly acknowledging the gods whom *the polis* acknowledges and by [1b] introducing other new divinities. He has also broken the law by [2] corrupting the young. The Penalty proposed is Death.

However, Socrates's own defenders at the time, and probably the majority of interpreters since, have thought or claimed that the real charge against him, the one that effectually sent him down to his death, was the second, that of "corrupting the young," which they have typically interpreted as a claim that Socrates was in effect a traitor to or—at best—an enemy of the democracy. But in ancient Athens religion was itself not just politicized but—as I shall argue again—political, part of the essence of "the political" indeed; and it would be viciously anachronistic therefore to distinguish a "political" from a "religious" charge.

I shall start my attempted defence of the Athenian Demos by setting out a series of four "Articles" concerning religion in the ancient Greek city in general, not only or specifically in the democratic city of Athens in 399. I shall then present a further series of four "Propositions" regarding the specific circumstances of the city of Athens at that time. The heuristic purpose of the distinction is this: whereas, according to the four "Articles," Classical Athens was a normal Greek city, on the contrary according to the four "Propositions," not only was Athens a highly abnormal Greek city, but the circumstances in 399 were also highly abnormal when seen within the history of Classical, democratic Athens as a whole.

Article 1

The Greek *polis* was a city of Gods as well as of Men, or rather of Gods before Men. Being properly Greek was, crucially, knowing your place in the world economy, knowing that you were by unalterable nature not divine and inferior to the divine universe. As Louis Gernet once put it, the Greek city was a "concrete and living entity under the sure protection of the Gods, who would not abandon it as long as it did not abandon them." Religion therefore was implicated with everything, and everything was imbricated with religion—even though the Greeks did not happen to "have a word for" religion and often used some such periphrasis as "the things of the gods" (to *ton theori*). Religion either determined (or occasioned) human behaviour, above all ritual practice, or gave to behaviour that was not primarily or exclusively religious a religious dimension, association or at least flavour. For example, a meeting of the Athenian Assembly began with the ritual slaughter of a piglet, with the blood of which the seats of the fifty Presidents of the Council and Assembly were splattered and thereby considered purified.

Article 2

Greek *polis* religion was not a religion much like those in which (I assume) the vast majority of my readers were brought up, or with which they are at any rate more than vaguely familiar: one or other version of Judaism, Christianity or Islam. Ancient Greek religion, that is, was not a purely spiritual monotheism, revealed and dogmatic, nor essentially a matter of personal faith, or of sacred books interpreted and administered by a professional, vocational, hierarchical priesthood. The distinction and opposition may be summed up as follows: according to the unquestionable dogma of Judaism, followed by Christianity and Islam, God (singular) created the world; whereas according to the mythology of the pre-Christian Greeks, the world preexisted the gods (and goddesses) whom it in some sense created.

Article 3

Greek religion was not separable from politics in the broadest sense of communal self-determination and government. In the narrow sense of politicking or political infighting, Greek politics may indeed be separated from religion, though even here, by most modern liberal-democratic standards, the link between them was pretty tight. For example, a regular Greek term for a revolutionary political conspiracy was *sunômosia*, which means literally a joint oath-fellowship, and oaths were by definition religious, being sworn in the name of the gods (as witnesses and guarantors). And, much more than just formally speaking, Meletos's indictment of Socrates was an *antômosia*, a counter-oathswearing: Meletos swore against Socrates in the sight of the gods that what he alleged against him was true. Our Latin-derived English term "affidavit" is the equivalent *of antômosia*, but it has lost the powerful original spirit and essence of the Greek term.

Article 4

Greek *polis* religion down to and beyond Socrates's time was essentially, of its nature, a public matter, expressed primarily by collective ritual action undertaken in common under communal civic direction. The typical expression *of polis* religion, its beating heart, were its feasts or festivals (*heortai*), which were observed systematically in accordance with an ultimately meteorologically based calendar, the regulation of which was an important part of the *polis's* business. Greek religious ritual implied, took for granted, faith, which itself was not some more or less explicit intellectual or emotional attribute but something experienced and affirmed implicitly in and through action (including words as well as nonverbal behaviour). Hence, our modern dichotomies or polarities, such as Action as opposed to Belief, or Ritual as opposed to Faith, were not operative in the Classical Greek city.

In terms of those four "Articles," Classical democratic Athens was thoroughly normal and typical, only even more so in one respect, in that Athens managed to celebrate annually more festivals than any other Greek city. It was very much otherwise with the following four "Propositions," the combined effect of which is to reveal Athens as both an abnormal Greek city in key ways and undergoing in 399 a time of such abnormality within the framework of its own history as befits the justified use of the often overworked term "crisis."

Proposition 1

Athens in 399 was a democracy (People-Power), as most Greek cities then were not. It was, moreover, a radical or thoroughgoing democracy, as most Greek democracies were not (either then or later). Yet only five years earlier Athens had ceased to be a democracy at all, for the second time within a decade. This was thanks to a Sparta-backed oligarchic coup that brought to power in 404 a small cabal or junta of extreme anti-democrats who thoroughly earned themselves their hateful nickname of the "Thirty Tyrants." Socrates's relations with this regime are, as we shall see, very material to the case against him.

The lessons to be drawn from this topsy-turvy decade are twofold. First, Athens more than any other Greek city gave genuine power to the mass of the ordinary, poor citizens; and that *kratos* included religious power, the power to determine legally as well as normatively what was, and what was not, right and proper behaviour *vis-a-vis* the gods whom the city recognized. Second, democracy, however long established (and Athens had had versions of democracy since 508/7 . . .), was vulnerable and fragile, so that the price of continuing democratic self-government was eternal vigilance. In 399 that need for democratic vigilance was perceived, rightly, to be paramount.

Proposition 2

Democracy was exercised by the People in courts of law no less than in the Assembly. Indeed, according to Aristotle's persuasive definition (*Pol.* 1274b31–78b5, esp. 1275b 19–20), being a Greek citizen, regardless of the city's constitutional complexion, meant "sharing in office (*arkhe*) and in judicial judgment (*krisis*)." Though not himself a citizen of Athens, Aristotle was an acute observer of the Athenian scene, and it was probably with Athens in mind that he added the observation that his general definition applied more especially to being a citizen of a democracy. Certainly, the democratic Athenians took the notion of popular jurisdiction in their People's Court as far as it could reasonably go; and they knew nothing—and would have wanted to know less-about the early-modern and still widely accepted liberal doctrine of the separation of the powers of government (legislative, executive and judicial).

Athenian-style ancient democracy was direct, participatory democracy in more than one sense. The citizen volunteer (*ho boulomenos*, "he who is willing") who, like Meletos in 399, brought a public legal action against another citizen was doing so overtly, ideally, indeed ideologically on behalf of the city as such, thereby fulfilling the role played by the Director of Public Prosecutions in states where government is not so conceived and conducted. Athens, of course, had no DPP, because it chose not to need one.

Prosecutors like Meletos were therefore bound (in more than one sense) to invoke in their support and justification what they represented to be the communal interest: not only what was allegedly in the community's best interests at the time, but what they claimed to be traditionally and conventionally understood as the community's best interests. In other words, they claimed to have on their side *nomos* (custom and convention), as well as to be publicly defending *nomos* in the sense of statute, or law and legality more generally. This was in full accord with the dominant ideological conception of what litigation was, and was for, in democratic Athens. In practice, it was often enough not so much—and sometimes not at all—about finding out the truth of what had actually happened in regard to the breach or otherwise of the city's laws. It was rather a matter of dispute-settlement involving individuals, of course, the prosecutor and defendant at the least, but also the good of the community as a whole, in the interests of citizen harmony and solidarity. This was particularly the case in high-profile political trials like that of Sokrates. Such dispute-settlement could acquire strong religious overtones, like those of a ritual cleansing and purification of the city's Augean stables polluted by alleged criminality, even where the overt content of the court case was not religious— as of course it was in the trial of Socrates.

Proposition 3

This generally recognised and accepted social function of litigation at Athens made particularly good sense in the specific context of 399. For Athens was then in crisis—in the modern sense of that Greek-derived term: economic, social, political, and, not least, ideological (including religious) crisis. Athens had recently lost a uniquely long, costly and debilitating war, the Atheno-Peloponnesian War of 431–404. Athens had then immediately suffered the second of two exceptionally nasty and brutal bouts of *stasis*—that is, civil discord boiling over into outright civil war and political revolution. On top of Athens's purely military disasters—such as those in Sicily (413) and at Aegospotami in the Hellespont (405)—the city had suffered also what we call a major "natural" disaster, the Great Plague of 430 and later (this took off perhaps as much as one third of the citizen population). We sometimes call such disasters "acts of god," figuratively speaking; but for the ancient Athenians they were literally that. Even Pericles the supreme rationalist (who himself died in 429 from its effects) is made by Thucydides (2.64.3) to refer to the Plague as *daimonion*, "heaven-sent" or supernatural. Ordinary, non-intellectual, conventionally believing Athenians would have had no difficulty, or hesitation, in regarding so huge, unexpected, uncanny and unbeatable an accident (*sumphora*, which also meant "disaster") as the work in some sense of a *daimon* or *daimones* (plural), a supernatural, superhuman power or powers.

On top of that *daimonion* disaster, the Athenians had also been made to suffer during the Atheno-Peloponnesian War two man-made disasters involving relations with the gods. First, in 415, there occurred a widespread mutilation of the Herms (stone figures of the god Hermes, sporting an erect phallus) that adorned both private houses and civic shrines. This deed was a darkly ill-omened manoeuvre, as it coincided, no doubt deliberately, with the despatch of the Athenian and allied naval expedition to Sicily, the mightiest armada yet to emerge from a single Greek city, and Hermes was among his other divine attributes the god of travellers. Around the same time, secondly, Alcibiades, the leading promoter of the Sicilian expedition and a former ward of Pericles, was arraigned for profaning the sacred Eleusinian Mysteries: not exactly parodying them (as is often misleadingly said), but holding unauthorized celebrations of the secret rites within private houses that fell outside the control of the hereditary Eleusinian priesthood, not to mention the control of the Athenian People as such—who legislated regularly, most recently in about 422, to try to ensure that the benefits of this near-panhellenic shrine on Attic soil should accrue differentially to the Athenians and the Athenian state. Most Athenians were Eleusinian initiates (*mystai*)—hence Aristophanes's use of a chorus composed of initiates for his main chorus in the *Frogs* of 405. Hence too the arraignment of Alcibiades by his enemies on that particular charge in 415. Most relevantly for our purposes, though, is that this was a kind of anticipation of the charging of Socrates, not coincidentally a teacher of the young Alcibiades, with religious crimes that almost all Athenians would unhesitatingly and unthinkingly deem to be heinous and capital crimes.

In the extraordinarily aweful circumstances of 399, ordinary pious Athenians were practically bound to ask themselves the following questions: since the gods (or "the god," "the divine") were manifestly angry with the Athenians, causing them to lose the Atheno-Peloponnesian War and experience the horrors of civil war, was this because the Athenians had omitted to honour duly (some of) the established gods, or because there were unestablished gods whom they ought to be propitiating and honouring but for some reason were not? Put that another way: had the gods deserted the Athenians—or had the Athenians deserted the gods? Or both? This is the framework within which to consider my final Proposition.

Proposition 4

The Athenians provided the social and political context within which open speculation, not excluding questioning the very existence of the gods, could be taken to the limits—though not beyond them: there were set limits. And the limits of official toleration of such intellectual speculation were quite clearly set by public ordinances, which indeed were drawn more tightly as the fifth century proceeded. We do not know when the *graphé asebeias* under which Socrates was prosecuted was first introduced, nor what exactly the Athenians understood the charge to cover. For the Athenian democratic justice system dispensed with jurisconsults and professional lawyers, so that the legal definition or specification of crimes was deliberately left constructively vague. But we do know that at some time during Socrates's adult lifetime the seer (*mantis*) Diopeithes, a self-styled religious expert, successfully proposed a decree before the Assembly "relating to the impeachment of those who do not duly recognize the divine matters (*nomizein ta theia*) or who teach doctrines relating to the heavens"—meaning incorrect and untraditional doctrines, especially perhaps atheistical ones. There are problems concerning the historicity of all but one of the trials allegedly held under the auspices or within the ambit of this decree, for example that of Pericles's non-Athenian associate Anaxagoras of Lampsacus; the one exception is of course the unambiguously historical trial of Socrates. In order to explain the force, significance and applicability of Diopeithes decree, we must first anatomise its main target: the thinkers lumped together as *sophistai*.

The Sophists (capital S) were a movement, not a school, of thought. Some were generalists, some specialised in one particular area of learning or thought. But all were—or claimed to be—experts in and teachers of *sophia* in some sense: wisdom, most generally, or a specific skill or technique or knack. *Sophistes* (the agent noun, masculine in gender, of the verb *sophizomai)* seems originally to have meant simply a "wise man"; Solon of Athens (flourished c.600) is so labelled by Herodotus (1.30), for instance. But by the time of Plato (c.428–347) it was used just as often to mean a purveyor of false or fake wisdom, someone who claimed to be able to teach true wisdom but who, actually (in the opinion of the author), was a charlatan, an intellectual conman. My mention of Plato was deliberate: it was thanks to him, above all, that the negative sense *of sophistes* won out, and not only in ancient Greek but also in the European languages somehow descended from or borrowing from ancient Greek. Hence English's unambiguously negative terms "sophistry" and "sophistical," and its ambivalent term "sophisticated."

Plato's responsibility for giving the Sophists a bad name was first demonstrated in modern times in the famous 67th chapter of George Grote's *History of Greece* (1846–1856). The explanation is quite straightforward. So desperately keen was Plato to refute the contemporary Athenian perception—purveyed, for example, by Aristophanes in the *Clouds* (423 BCE)—that his revered mentor was a Sophist, in the bad sense, that he emphasised above all that Socrates—unlike the purely or largely mercenary Sophists—did not practise his art for sordidly materialistic reasons. Rather, his was a pursuit of genuine wisdom and a disinterested quest for the truth, or at least self-enlightenment, even or especially if that came at the cost of creating greater perplexity or bafflement (*aporia*) both in himself and in his interlocutors and auditors. Socrates, Plato's Socrates, was thus keen to deny that he *knew* anything, in any strong epistemological sense: if he was indeed the wisest man on earth, as the Delphic Oracle (fount of all religious wisdom) was said to have announced, that was (only) because he knew he knew nothing. An overstatement, no doubt, or perhaps strictly a logical contradiction, but one that was entirely consistent with the famous Delphic injunction "know yourself" *(gnothi seauton)*—as indeed was the burden of Socrates' philosophising as a whole, as that is represented by Plato.

Plato's defence of Socrates in particular proved less successful than his attack on the Sophists in general. During a famous show-trial over half a century after Socrates's death, the leading politician Aeschines (Aesch. 1, *Against Timarchus*, 173) referred back to him and his condemnation as follows: "Athenians, you had Socrates the Sophist put to death because it appeared that he was the teacher of Critias, one of the Thirty who destroyed the democracy." However, it is important to remember that in Socrates' own lifetime by no means all the Athenians had always shared and endorsed Plato's negative view of all Sophists. Athens, the "city of words," was full of officially authorized public forums for agonistic debate. The Theatre of Dionysos served for this purpose as well as the Assembly and Lawcourts. If we may believe Thucydides's Kleon in the Mytilene Debate of 427 (Thuc. 3.37), among other sources, ordinary Athenians also loved listening to informal public debates between Sophists, where the outcome would be purely personal enjoyment or instruction, not decisive public action. In other words, merely being thought to be a Sophist would not necessarily have been a disaster for Socrates—in ordinary, happy circumstances.

In 399, however, Athens was not any longer a happy place of free and open speculation and free and uninhibited debate. It had become precisely the sort of place that Pericles, in the version of his Funeral Speech of 430 attributed to him by Thucydides (2.37), had proudly proclaimed Athens was *not:*

We do not get into a state with our next-door neighbour if he enjoys himself in his own way, and we do not give him the kind of black looks which, though they do no real harm, do hurt people's feelings. We are free and tolerant in our private lives.

In actual fact, "we" (the Athenians) were by 399 acting uncomfortably like stereotypical traditional Mediterranean villagers—suspicious, conservative, superstitious, irrational. Indeed, rather more so even than that stereotype suggests: for in 399 the Athenians did not any longer content themselves with shooting black looks they took fellow-citizens to court and prosecuted them on major capital charges, such as impiety. In 400/399 there were to our knowledge no fewer than six major public trials, all relating in some way to the disastrous events of the last years of the Athene-Peloponnesian War and its aftermath.

In spirit at least, if not also in the letter, these trials breached the oath of *amnestia* sworn in 403 between the Athenians and the Spartans. This had been a conscious public act of forgetting the "bad," that is anti-democratic, deeds of 411–10 and 404–3. The oath had been sworn by all Athenians on the restoration of democracy after the tyranny of the Thirty, and, for the most part, the oath had been conspicuously observed—but not in 400/399. Moreover, at least two of these six trials—those of Socrates and of the tricksy politician Andokides (for his role in the Mysteries and Herms scandals of 415)—explicitly involved religion. In so far as the defendants could be portrayed as irreligious free thinkers, the trials thus also constituted a popular, anti-Sophistical reaction. For the volunteer prosecutors were seeking, in the name of the Athenian People, to exact revenge for the religious pollution that the Athenians felt they had or might have incurred by harbouring in their midst men who either by word or by deed had violated the city's most basic religious norms and code. Men such as Socrates. It is to the precise details of his accusation that we must now turn.

Meletos's affidavit as preserved (above) constitutes a twofold charge, with the first main charge being further subdivided into two sub-charges, and possibly also the second too. Charge **1a** is negative, an accusation of omission expressed in language very similar to that of Diopeithes's decree: Socrates has not duly recognized the gods which the city recognizes. The clue to what Meletos was getting at is provided for us by the far less sophisticated—but for that very reason far more instantly comprehensible—of the *two Apologies* (Defence Speeches) of Socrates that are extant: that composed by another of Socrates's upper-class Athenian disciples, Xenophon. In actual fact, Socrates seems not to have delivered any sort of coherent *apologia* at his trial, but rather to have employed, unconventionally, his usual everyday technique of question-and-answer and directed it to the chief prosecutor, Meletos; an at least partly fictionalized sample of such cross-questioning is preserved in Plato's *Apology*. But Xenophon, by far the more conventional thinker of the two disciples, predictably offers a standard set-speech defence, integral to which is Socrates's defence that he has indeed duly acknowledged the gods. For he has performed regularly all the sacrifices (*hiera*) that the city requires and enjoins.

Sacrifice, especially in major public festivals, was simultaneously a political and a religious act in the ancient Greek city. Performing, that is sharing in, sacrifice whether public or private was a key demonstration of good citizenship, and it was the prime means of registering both one's communion with and one's distance from the gods. It was of the essence of Greek religious politics and political religion. However, from Socrates's other main apologist, Plato, may perhaps be derived an idea of why the mere fact of Socrates's sacrificial participation might not have been considered an adequate response to the main religious charge against him. For it seems that Socrates demanded an added ingredient from worshippers, over and above the mere fact of participation, for the act of sacrifice to be efficacious, namely a good mental disposition. It was not enough for him, apparently, that worshippers merely went through the motions, as it were. That added value is somewhat reminiscent of Socrates's equally unconventional construction of the divine, of what it was truly to be a god: for him, a god properly so called had by definition to be morally good. Perhaps, though, we are being too demanding. Maybe all that Meletos needed to do in order to win over a majority of the jury was persuade them that Socrates was the sort of person who might have adopted such an unconventional stance, who could therefore have cast doubt in words on the validity of what ordinary conventional Athenians assumed to be proper, efficacious, pious deeds. That might indeed not only sufficiently account for the effectiveness of the charge; but it

might also explain why Plato in his *Apology* makes Socrates refer back to the *Clouds* of Aristophanes staged in 423. The Athenians were generally very keen on the theatre, if not theatre-mad, and they had long memories—or effective gossip-networks at any rate. The Socrates of the *Clouds* had been portrayed as an archetypal Sophist, and, as such, an atheist, in the sense that he wished to replace Zeus as divine governor of the cosmos with a god of his own fabrication, Dinos (Vortex or Whirlpool). That, not coincidentally, takes us on to charge **Ib:** of "introducing *hetera kaina daimonia*."

Even if those three italicized Greek words were not in fact the actual words used by Meletos, they surely should have been, since they precisely capture the required nuances. Greek had two words for "other": *heteron* and *allon*. *Heteron* means "other of two," in this case two kinds of divinities, the good and the bad, a black-white polarization thoroughly typical of Greek habits of thought touching the most basic features of their culture. The Greek language also had more than one word for "new": the deliberate choice of *kainon* would have been designed to convey the sense of "*brand new*," that is, unprecedented. To the Greeks' ways of thinking, any form of novelty was considered in and of itself to be potentially threatening to the established order Their expressions for political "revolution" were *neoterismos* (innovationism) and *neotera pragmata (too* new affairs). The polar opposite of new in these senses was traditional, and traditional in Greek was *patrion*, "ancestral." Greek or Athenian official religion could be glossed or even paraphrased as *ta patria*, "the things of the ancestors." It was not at all accidental or coincidental that the recently completed tidying up and publication of Athens's laws (initiated in 410, after the first restoration of democracy) had included a transcription of "ancestral rites."

Daimonia, thirdly, meant supernatural powers generally and was not in itself an unambiguously negative term, though the diminutive *-ion* was probably meant to imply a lower grade of divinity than *daimon*, while *daimon* was itself of a lower status than *theos* ("god"). So perhaps Meletos intended the jury to think of the sort of indistinct, unseen and potentially entirely harmful powers that frequented the Greek underworld rather than of the manifest anthropomorphized gods who inhabited the sunlit peak of Mount Olympus. At any rate, it is not at all certain that Meletos intended them to think of what Socrates himself, according to Plato's *Apology*, spoke of as his *daimonion:* this was a sort of hotline to the divine, an inner voice, that Socrates said only ever told him when not to do something, and never positively advocated any particular course of action. Yet even that by itself would not have been reassuring news to the jury, since it implied the existence of a power outside the regulatory control of the People, and that is just what was at stake in the verb used next by Meletos to describe what Socrates allegedly did with his *hetera kaina damonia.*

This was to "introduce" (*eishegoumenos*) them. Here perhaps was Meletos's most brilliant stroke. For there was nothing remotely odd or untraditional, let alone impious in "introducing" new divinities at Athens—provided the introduction was done properly that is, formally, publicly, and above all democratically. In the course of the fifth century, several new official cults had been "introduced" into the pantheon of divinities officially worshipped by the Athenian state: among others, those of Pan, Asklepios, and Bendis, the latter (a Thracian goddess) being not only non-Athenian but non-Greek by origin. By implication, therefore, not only had Socrates' *daimonia* not received the seal of official approval. They were also not the sort *of daimonia* that would have been likely to receive it had Socrates attempted—as of course he had not—to "introduce" them officially.

In short, the religious charges brought against Socrates were as weighty as they well could have been, both in general terms—that is, as judged by the normal standards of Athenian piety and its official policing by the democracy—and specifically in the highly charged, highly unstable political circumstances of 399. They would in my opinion probably have been sufficient by themselves, if persuasively enough argued, to persuade a majority of the 501 jurors to vote Socrates "guilty." However, just in case there was a significant number of "floating voters" on the jury, citizens who were either more tolerant of religious deviance on principle or more robust in the face of adversity, or who were not persuaded that Socrates had been impious in the past or that he constituted a genuine religious threat to the community for the future, charge 2 was added as a supplementary for insurance purposes. This was possibly done at the instigation of one of Meletos's two *sunegoroi* (supporting litigants), the prominent politician Anytus.

Charge 2 was a "political" charge in the narrow sense. It breached the 403 Amnesty in spirit, if not formally, since its burden was to accuse Socrates of politically motivated anti-democratic behaviour in the lead-up to, and during, the regime of the Thirty. This was a breach that the prosecution team knew they would be able in the climate of opinion to get away with. Without accusing Socrates himself in so many words of being an anti-democratic traitor, it implied that Socrates was at the very least guilty by association. For "corrupting the young" was a euphemistic, allusive way of saying that Socrates had been the teacher both of Alcibiades, a proven traitor, and of Kritias, leader of the Thirty Tyrants; and it implied that what Socrates had taught them was to be anti-democratic traitors. The implied syllogism—Socrates taught them, they were traitors, therefore Socrates taught them to be traitors—was logically false, but it was none the less persuasive for that. Even if jurors could not decide what impiety was, or whether Sokrates was guilty of impiety as charged, they knew a traitor and an enemy of the Demos when they saw one. What they knew, or thought they knew, of his views on majority rule and of his behaviour under the Thirty would have made him appear to be not a huge friend of the Demos and democracy.

However, though Socrates's defenders and opponents alike at the time were quick to claim that this was the real charge against him, and the real reason why he was convicted, we should, I think, hesitate before leaping to assent to that reading. In all major Athenian public political trials, the issue in question on which the outcome revolved was typically not so much the defendant's guilt on the alleged, past technical grounds, but rather the future good of the community as that was perceived by the majority of ordinary juror-citizens. Precise voting figures are uncertain, but it looks as though something like 280 or 281 out of the 501 jurors voted "guilty"—a smallish but sufficiently clear cut majority over the 220 or so against. In religious terms, I suggest, the trial of Sokrates, like that of Andokides, was akin to a rite of purification and reincorporation. At all events, by the Athenian democracy's own standards, Socrates was indeed justly condemned by due legal process.

But need the jury also have gone on to condemn Socrates to death? This is a separate question, in the literal sense. For the kind of trial Sokrates underwent (an *agon timetos*) was divided procedurally into two parts. In the first, the issue was guilt or innocence. In the second, if the majority vote was for "guilty," the issue was the nature of the penalty (*time*), and prosecutor and defendant again spoke to that.

Meletos, of course, argued strenuously in favour of the death penalty for Sokrates. Impiety of this sort was after all a heinous political crime, and the Athenians had no scruples about inflicting the death sentence in cases where they felt that major public crimes had been committed that threatened the good of the whole community.

Sokrates himself, not unnaturally, demurred. Yet instead of making a plausible counter-proposal of a truly heavy penalty (exile or a large monetary fine), it seems that at first he in effect claimed he ought to be treated as a public benefactor and feted (like an Olympic victor) with free dinners at the city's hearth for the rest of his days. This did not go down well with the jury. Nor was his eventual final offer—to pay a substantial, but by no means substantial enough, monetary fine—a winning move. So, if Socrates would not himself offer either to pay a really seriously large fine or to remove himself into permanent exile, then he would have to be removed forcibly and irremediably from the Athenian community by act of the People. In the event, more jurors (perhaps 360 or so in all, a ratio of 2.5:1) voted for his death sentence than had voted for his guilt in the first place. And yet, even then Socrates need not have died as he did, by a self-administered draught of hemlock in the state prison. He could still have gone into exile, as his loyal friends like Kriton urged.

To them, however, Sokrates is said to have replied magnanimously, if also somewhat puzzlingly, that he owed it to the city under whose laws he had been raised to honour those laws to the letter. There is no denying his bravery. He can even be seen as a hero: a new kind of intellectual hero, a martyr to freedom of thought and conscience, who believed—in the famously ringing words attributed to him by Plato (*Apol.* 38a)—that "the unexamined life was not worth living for a human being". But he was in an important sense a voluntary martyr, and it is only in retrospect and, often enough, under very different political circumstances and from very different political standpoints than those obtaining at Athens in 399 that the guilt for the manner of his death has been transferred from Sokrates to the Athenian People. Wrongly so, as I have tried to show. But whatever the rights or wrongs of "l'affaire Sokrates," by his conviction Athenian democracy had been reaffirmed.

Consider

1. What were the charges brought against Socrates? What lay behind them?
2. Why were the underlying complaints concealed?
3. How did Socrates answer the charges, open and concealed?
4. What alternatives did Socrates offer in place of the death penalty? Why did he choose these?
5. What is the significance of the evidence of Hypereides?
6. How did Socrates' views on the relative merits of the Athenian and Spartan constitutions come into the picture?
7. Why does Hanson think Socrates was especially dangerous?
8. Why is the trial of Anaxagoras important?
9. What does Hansen think was the true religious charge against Socrates?
10. What is the significance of the evidence of Aeschines?
11. What sort of people surrounded Socrates? How did they affect the case against him?
12. How would you have voted? Why?
13. What charges have modern critics made against the Athenian democracy's condemnation of Socrates?
14. How does the place of religion in ancient Athens compare with that in the modern democratic state?

15. What did the Athenians think about the relative value of tradition as opposed to change?

16. How did political events from 411 to 399 BC affect the thinking of the Athenian people? What part did the courts play in the life and government of the Athenians?

17. How did the course, events, and conclusion of the Peloponnesian War connect with their religious ideas?

18. How did attitudes toward the Sophists affect the trial of Socrates?

19. How did the charges accuse Socrates of violating or threatening Athenian religion and tradition?

20. To what extent was Socrates responsible for his own fate?

21. Which consideration, political or religious, was more important in the trial and condemnation of Socrates? Why do you think so?

CHAPTER 12
DEMOSTHENES VERSUS PHILIP OF MACEDON

THE FOURTH CENTURY witnessed the attrition of the power and prosperity of the Greek city-states. Constant warfare, poverty, and civil strife increased disunity. Sparta and Thebes attempted to achieve hegemony but, like Athens, each failed. After the Battle of Mantinea in 362 BC, as Xenophon says, "there was more confusion and disorder in Greece than before." Into the power vacuum stepped Philip of Macedon, who embarked upon a vigorous, ingenious, and ultimately successful campaign to put Greece under Macedonian control. In this effort he was most vigorously opposed by the Athenian politician and orator Demosthenes. He advocated a policy of Athenian patriotism and panhellenic resistance to Macedon. His efforts produced the coalition which opposed Philip and which was finally smashed at Chaeronea in 338 BC. Demosthenes and his policy remain the subject of much debate. Was he a sincere patriot or a self-seeking politician? Was his policy a good one? Was it practical, given the "degenerate" nature of the Athens of his time? Was he a man of narrow vision or a defender of liberty and autonomy at any cost?

Ancients Sources

1. Plutarch, *Demosthenes*, 12–21, DEMOSTHENES
2. Demosthenes, *Third Philippic Oration*, translated by A. W. Pickard-Cambridge, DEMOSTHENES' THIRD PHILIPPIC ORATION

Opinions of Modern Scholars

1. Johann Gustav Droysen, *Geschichte des Hellenismus,* translated by Donald Kagan
2. A. W. Pickard-Cambridge, *Demosthenes*
3. George Cawkwell, *Philip of Macedon*

ANCIENT SOURCES ON DEMOSTHENES AND PHILIP OF MACEDON

1. DEMOSTHENES

The following selection tells of Demosthenes' public career at the battle of Chaeronea in 338 BC.

12. However once he had found a noble cause to engage his political activity, that is the defence of the Greeks against Philip, he fought for it with admirable spirit. He quickly became famous and his reputation was enhanced by the courage of his speeches, so that he was admired in Greece and treated with respect by the king of Persia. King Philip took more notice of him than of any other

Athenian statesman, and even his enemies were forced to agree that they were dealing with a man of distinction: both Aeschines and Hypereides admit as much, even in their denunciations of him…

16. Demosthenes' political position was clear enough even while peace still prevailed, for he allowed no act of Philip's to pass un-criticized, and seized upon every occasion to incite and inflame the Athenians against him…

17. At length the course of events began to move inexorably towards war, since Philip was incapable of sitting quietly at home, and the Athenians were constantly being stirred up against him by Demosthenes. First of all he urged his countrymen to invade Euboea, which had been subdued and handed over to Philip by its local tyrants, and as the result of a resolution passed in his name the Athenians crossed over to the island and drove out the Macedonians. Next, when Macedonia was at war with the citizens of Byzantium and Perinthus, Demosthenes persuaded the Athenians to lay aside their grievances and forget the wrongs they had suffered from these peoples in the Social War, and to dispatch a force which succeeded in relieving both cities. After this he set off on a diplomatic mission, which was designed to kindle the spirit of resistance to Philip and which took him all over Greece. Finally he succeeded in uniting almost all the states into a confederation against Philip. The result of these efforts was to raise a mercenary army of fifteen thousand infantry and two thousand cavalry besides the local forces of each city, and the allies readily agreed to pay these soldiers. It was on this occasion, according to Theophrastus, when the Greek states requested that a quota should be fixed, that the Athenian demagogue Hegesippus, who was nicknamed Crobylus ("top-knot"), remarked, "War has an appetite that cannot be satisfied by quotas."

Greece was now wrought up to a high pitch of expectation at the thought of her future, and her peoples and cities all drew together, Euboeans, Achaeans, Corinthians, Megarians, Leucadians and Corcyraeans. But there remained the most important task of all for Demosthenes to accomplish, namely to persuade Thebes to join the alliance The Thebans had a common frontier with the Athenians and an army ready to take the field, and at that time they were regarded as the finest soldiers in Greece. But it was no easy matter to persuade them to change sides: moreover during the recent Phocian war Philip had rendered them a number of services and cultivated their goodwill,

and the various petty quarrels which arose because of their proximity to Athens were continually breaking out afresh and exacerbated the relations between the two cities.

18. Meanwhile Philip, encouraged by his success in dealing with Amphissa, marched onto take Elateia by surprise and proceeded to occupy Phocis. The news stunned the Athenians. No speaker dared to mount the rostrum, nobody knew what advice should be given, the assembly was struck dumb and appeared to be completely at a loss. It was at this moment that Demosthenes alone came forward and urged the people to stand by the Thebans. Then in his usual manner he put heart into his compatriots and inspired them with fresh hopes, and he was then sent off with others as an ambassador to Thebes. At the same time Philip, as we learn from Marsyas the historian, sent Amyntas and Clearchus of Macedonia, Daochus of Thessaly, and Thrasydaeus to oppose the Athenians and put the case for Macedon. For their part the Thebans could see clearly enough where their interests lay, but each of them could also visualize the horrors of war, for the sufferings they had endured in the Phocian conflict were still fresh in their memories. Yet in spite of this Demosthenes' eloquence, so Theopompus tells us, stirred their courage, kindled their desire to win glory and threw every other consideration into the shade. As if transported by his words, they cast of all fear, self-interest or thought of obligation towards Macedon and choose the path of honour. So complete and so glorious was the transformation wrought by his oratory that Philip promptly dispatched an embassy to ask for terms of peace: just then all Greece seemed to have recovered her confidence and was up in arms to support Demosthenes for the future—so much so that not only did the Athenian generals take their orders from him, but also the Boeotarchs. At this moment he could control all the meetings of the Theban assembly as effectively as those of the Athenian, he was beloved by both nations, and exercised supreme authority; moreover he never used his position unconstitutionally nor did he go beyond his powers, so Theopompus tells, but acted with complete propriety.

19. However it seems that at that very moment some divinely ordained power was shaping the course of events so as to put an end to the freedom of the Greeks: this fatal destiny opposed all their efforts in the common cause and produced many portents of what was to come. Among these were the ominous prophecies uttered by the Pythian priestess and an ancient oracle which was quoted from the Sibylline books:

Let me fly far from the battle at Thermodon, let me take refuge
Watching from high in the clouds, as I soar with the wings of an eagle.

* * *

20. It is difficult to discover the exact truth about these prophecies, but certainly Demosthenes is said to have had complete confidence in the Greek forces and to have been elated by the strength and spirit of so many men, all of them eager to engage the enemy: in consequence he would not allow his countrymen to pay attention to the oracles or listen to the prophecies. Indeed he even suspected that the Pythian priestess was on the side of Philip, and he reminded the Thebans of the example of Epaminondas and the Athenians of Pericles, both of whom acted only on the promptings of reason and regarded prophecies of this kind as mere pretexts for faint-heartedness. Up to this point, then, Demosthenes acted like a brave man, but in the battle of Chaeronea which followed, so far from achieving anything honourable, he completely failed to suit his actions to his words. He left his place the ranks and took to his heels in the most shameful fashion, throwing away his arms in order to run faster, and he did not hesitate to disgrace the inscription on his shield, on which, according to Pytheas, were engraved in letters of gold the words "With good fortune."

In the first flush of victory Philip felt insolently exultant at his success. He went out with a party of companions to look at the bodies of the dead, and drunkenly sang the opening words of the decree which had been passed on Demosthenes' initiative dividing it according to the metre, and beating the time.

Demosthenes, son of Demosthenes, of Paeania, moves *as* follows:

> But when he came to himself and understood the magnitude of the dangers that had surrounded him, he trembled to think of the power and skill of the orator who had forced him to risk his empire and his life on the outcome of a few hours in a single day. For the fame of this speaker had travelled even to the Persian king, who had sent letters to the satraps on the coast ordering them to offer money to Demosthenes and to pay more attention to him than to any other Greek, since he could create a diversion and keep the king of Macedon busy at home by means of the troubles he stirred up in Greece....

21. However, at this moment when the news of the disaster to Greece became known, the orators who opposed Demosthenes attacked him and prepared indictments and impeachments against him. But the people not only acquitted him, of these charges, but continued to honour him as a loyal citizen to remain in public life. Consequently when the bones of those who had fallen at Chaeronea were brought home to be buried, they chose him to deliver the panegyric in honour of the dead. So far from displaying a cowardly or ignoble spirit in the hour of disaster (as Theopompus implies in his exaggerated description of the scene) they made *it* clear by the special honour and respect which they paid their counsellor that they did not regret the advice he had given them. So Demosthenes delivered the funeral oration, but henceforth he would not put his own name to any of the decrees he proposed in the assembly: instead be used, those of his friends, one after the other, and avoided his own as being ill-omened, until he once more took courage after Philip's death. And in fact Philip died soon afterwards and survived his victory at Chaeronea by less than two years...

Questions

1. **What does Plutarch consider to be the strengths and weaknesses of Demosthenes as a leader? How does he represent Philip's attitude towards him?**
2. **What was the Athenians' judgment?**

2.   DEMOSTHENES' THIRD PHILIPPIC ORATION

In 341 BC Demosthenes delivered his *Third Philippic*, in which his over-all policy is described. It is usually considered the greatest of his speeches.

[1] Many speeches are made, men of Athens, at almost every meeting of the Assembly, with reference to the aggressions which Philip has been committing, ever since he concluded the Peace, not only against yourselves but against all other peoples; and I am sure that all would agree, however little they may act on their belief, that our aim, both in speech and in action, should be to cause him to cease from his insolence and to pay the penalty for it. And yet I see that in fact the treacherous sacrifice of our interests has gone on, until what seems an ill-omened saying may, I fear, be really true—that if all who came forward desired to propose, and you desired to carry, the measures which would make your position as pitiful as it could possibly be, it could not (so I believe), be made worse than it is now. [2] It may be that there are many reasons for this, and that our affairs did not reach their present condition from any one or two causes. But if you examine the matter aright, you will find that the chief responsibility rests with those whose aim is to win your favour, not to propose what is best. Some of them, men of Athens, so long as they can maintain the conditions which bring them reputation and influence, take no thought for the future [and therefore think that you also should take none]; while others, by accusing and slandering those who are actively at work are simply trying to make the city spend its energies in punishing the members of its own body, and so leave Philip free to say and do what he likes. [3] Such political methods as these, familiar to you as they are, are the real causes of the evil…

[4] For though our position is very bad indeed, and much has been sacrificed, it is still possible, even now, if you will do your duty, to set all right once more. [5] It is a strange thing, perhaps, that I am about to say, but it is true. The worst feature in the past is that in which lies our best hope for the future. And what is this? It is that you are in your present plight because you do not do any part of your duty, small or great; for of course, if you were doing all that you should do, and were still in this evil case, you could not even hope for any improvement. As it is, Philip has conquered your indolence and your indifference; but he has not conquered Athens. You have not been vanquished—you have never even stirred…

[8] Now if it is possible for the city to remain at peace—if the decision rests with us (that I may make this my starting-point)—then, I say that we ought to do so, and I call upon any one who says that it is so to move his motion, and to act and not to defraud us. But if another with weapons in his hands and a large force about him holds out to you the name of peace, while his own acts are acts of war, what course remains open to us but that of resistance? Though if you wish to profess peace in the same manner as he, I have no quarrel with you. [9] But if any man's conception of peace is that it is a state in which Philip can master all that intervenes till at last he comes to attack ourselves, such a conception, in the first place, is madness; and, in the second place, this peace that he speaks of is a peace which you are to observe towards Philip, while he does not observe it towards you: and this it is—this power to carry on war against you, without being met by any hostilities on your part—that Philip is purchasing with all the money that he is spending.

[10] Indeed, if we intend to wait till the time comes when he admits that he is at war with us, we are surely the most innocent persons in the world. Why, even if he comes to Attica itself, to the very Peiraeus, he will never make such an admission, if we are to judge by his dealings with others. [11] For, to take one instance, he told the Olynthians, when he was five miles from the city, that there were only two alternatives—either they must cease to live in Olynthus, or he to live in Macedonia: but during the whole time before that, whenever anyone accused him of any such sentiments, he was indignant and sent envoys to answer the charge. Again, he marched into the Phocians' country, as though visiting his allies: it was by Phocian envoys that he was escorted on the march; and most people in Athens contended strongly that his crossing the Pass would bring no good to Thebes. [12] Worse still, he has lately seized Pherae and still holds it, though he went to Thessaly as a friend and an ally. And, latest of all, he told those unhappy citizens of

Oreus that he had sent his soldiers to visit them and to make kind inquiries; he had heard that they were sick, and suffering from faction, and it was right for an ally and a true friend to be present at such a time. Now if, instead of giving them warning and using open force, he deliberately chose to deceive these men, who could have done him no harm, though they might have taken precautions against suffering any themselves, **[13]** do you imagine that he will make a formal declaration of war upon you before he commences hostilities, and that, so long as you are content to be deceived? Impossible! **[14]** For so long as you, though you are the injured party, make no complaint against him, but accuse some of your own body, he would be the most fatuous man on earth if he were to interrupt your strife and contentions with one another—to bid you turn upon himself, and so to cut away the ground from the arguments by which his hirelings put you off, when they tell you that *he* is not at war with Athens.

[15] In God's name, is there a man in his senses who would judge by words, and not by facts, whether another was at peace or at war with him? Of course there is not. Why, from the very first, when the Peace had only just been made, before those who are now in the Chersonese had been sent out, Philip was taking Serrhium and Doriscus, and expelling the soldiers who were in the castle of Serrhium and the Sacred Mountain, where they had been placed by your general. **[16]** But what was he doing, in acting thus? For he had sworn to a Peace. And let no one ask, "What do these things amount to? What do they matter to Athens?" For whether these acts were trifles which could have no interest for you is another matter; but the principles of religion and justice, whether a man transgress them in small things or great, have always the same force. What? When he is sending mercenaries into the Chersonese, which the king and all the Hellenes have acknowledged to be yours; when he openly avows that he is going to the rescue, and states in it his letter, what is it that he is doing? **[17]** He tells you, indeed, that he is not making war upon you. But so far am I from admitting that one who acts in this manner is observing the Peace which he made with you, that I hold that in grasping at Megara, in setting up tyrants in Euboea, in advancing against Thrace at the present moment, in pursuing his machinations in the Peloponnese, and in carrying out his entire policy with the help of his

army, he is violating the Peace and is making war against you;—unless you mean to say that even to bring up engines to besiege you is no breach of the Peace, until they are actually planted against your walls. But you will not say this; for the man who is taking the steps and contriving the means which will lead to my capture is at war with me, even though he has not yet thrown a missile or shot an arrow. **[18]** Now what are the things which would imperil your safety, if anything should happen? The alienation of the Hellespont, the placing of Megara and Euboea in the power of the enemy, and the attraction of Peloponnesian sympathy to his cause. Can I then say that one who is erecting such engines of war as these against the city is at peace with you? **[19]** Far from it! For from the very day when he annihilated the Phocians—from that very day, I say, I date the beginning of his hostilities against you. And for your part, I think that you will be wise if you resist him at once; but that if you let him be, you will find that, when you wish to resist, resistance itself is impossible. Indeed, so widely do I differ, men of Athens, from all your other advisers, that I do not think there is any room for discussion today in regard to the Chersonese or Byzantium. **[20]** We *must* go to their defence, and take every care that they do not suffer [and we must send all that they need to the soldiers who are at present there]. But we have to take counsel for the good of all the Hellenes, in view of the grave peril in which they stand. And I wish to tell you on what grounds I am so alarmed at the situation, in order that if my reasoning is correct, you may share my conclusions, and exercise some forethought for yourselves at least, if you are actually unwilling to do so for the Hellenes as a whole; but that if you think that I am talking nonsense, and am out of my senses, you may both now and hereafter decline to attend to me as though I were a sane man.

[21] The rise of Philip to greatness from such small and humble beginnings; the mistrustful and quarrelsome attitude of the Hellenes towards one another; the fact that his growth out of what he was into what he is was a far more extraordinary thing than would be his subjugation of all that remains, when he has already secured so much;—all this and all similar themes, upon which I might speak at length, I will pass over. **[22]** But I see that all men, beginning with yourselves, have conceded to him the very thing which he has been at issue in every Hellenic war during the whole of the past. And what is this? It is the right to act as he pleases—to mutilate and to strip the Hellenic peoples, one by one, to attack and to enslave their cities. **[23]** For seventy-three years you were the leading people of Hellas, and the Spartans for thirty years save one; and in these last times, after the battle of Leuctra, the Thebans too acquired some power: yet neither to you nor to Thebes nor to Sparta was such a right ever conceded by the Hellenes, as the right to do whatever you pleased. [Far from it! **[24]** First of all it was your own behaviour—or rather that of the Athenians of that day—which some thought immoderate; and all, even those who had no grievance against Athens, felt bound to join the injured parties, and to make war upon you. Then, in their turn, the Spartans, when they had acquired an empire and succeeded to a supremacy like your own, attempted to go beyond all bounds and to disturb the established order to an unjustifiable extent; and once more, all, even those who had no grievance against them, had recourse to war. **[25]** Why mention the others? For we ourselves and the Spartans, though we could originally allege no injury done by the one people to the other, nevertheless felt bound to go to war on account of the wrongs which we saw the rest suffering.] And yet all the offences of the Spartans in those thirty years of power, and of your ancestors in their seventy years, were less, men of Athens, that the wrongs inflicted upon the Greeks by Philip, in the thirteen years, not yet completed, during which he has been to the fore. Less do I say? They are not a fraction of them. A few words will easily prove this. **[26]** I say nothing of Olynthus, and Methone, and Apollonia, and thirty-two cities in the Thracian region, all annihilated by him with such savagery, that a visitor to the spot would find difficult to tell that they had ever inhabited. I remain silent in regard to extirpation of the great Phocian race, what is the condition of Thessaly? Has he not robbed their very cities of their governments, and set up tetrarchies, that they may be enslaved, not merely by whole cities, but by whole tribes at a time? **[27]** Are not the cities of Euboea even now ruled by tyrants, and that in an island that is neighbour to Thebes and Athens? Does he not write expressly in his letters, "I am at peace with those who choose to obey me"? And what he thus writes he does not fail to act upon; for he is gone to invade the Hellespont; he previously went to attack Ambracia; the great city of Elis in the Peloponnese is his; he has recently intrigued against Megara; and neither Hellas nor the world beyond it is large enough to contain the man's ambition. **[28]** But though all of us, the Hellenes, see and hear these things, we send no representatives to one another to discuss the matter; we show no indignation; we are in so evil a mood, so deep have the lines been dug which sever city from city, that up to this very day we are unable to act as either our interest or our duty require. We cannot unite; we can form no combination for mutual support or friendship; **[29]** but we look on while the man grows greater, because everyone has made up his mind (as it seems to me) to profit by the time during which his neighbour is being ruined, and no one cares or acts for the safety of the Hellenes. For we all know that Philip is like the recurrence or the attack of a fever or other illness, in his descent upon those who fancy themselves for the present well out of his reach. **[30]** And further, you must surely realize that all the wrongs that the Hellenes suffered from the Spartans or ourselves they at least suffered at the hands of true-born sons of Hellas; and (one might conceive) it was as though a lawful son, born to a great estate, managed his affairs in some wrong or improper way;—his conduct would in itself deserve blame and denunciation, but at least it could not be said that he was not one of the family, or was not the heir to the property. **[31]** But had it been a slave or a supposititious son that was thus ruining and spoiling an inheritance to which he had no title, why, good Heavens! How infinitely more scandalous and reprehensible all would have declared it to be. And yet they show no such feeling in regard to Philip, although not only is he no Hellene, not only has he no kinship with Hellenes, but he is not even a barbarian from a country that one could acknowledge with credit—he is a pestilent Macedonian, from whose country it used not to be possible to buy even a slave of any value.

[32] And in spite of this, is there any degree of insolence to which he does not proceed? Not content with annihilating cities, does he not manage the Pythian games, the common meeting of the Hellenes, and send his slaves to preside over the competition in his absence? ... **[33]** Does he not write to the Thessalians to prescribe the constitution under which they are to live? Does he not send one body of mercenaries to Porthmus, to expel the popular party of Eretria, and another to Oreus, to set up Philistides as tyrant? And yet the Hellenes see these things and endure them, gazing (it seems to me) as they would gaze at a hailstorm—each people praying that it may not come their way, but no one trying to prevent it. [34] Nor is it only his outrages upon Hellas that go unresisted. No one resists even the aggressions which are committed against himself. Ambracia and Leucas belong to the Corinthians—he has attacked them: Naupactus to the Achaeans—he has sworn to hand it over to the Aetolians: Echinus to the Thebans—he has taken it from them, and is now marching against their allies the Byzantines—is it not so? [35] And of our own possessions, to pass by all the rest, is not Cardia, the greatest city in the Chersonese, in his hands? Thus are we treated; and we are all hesitating and torpid, with our eyes upon our neighbours, distrusting one another, rather than the man whose victims we all are. But if he treats us collectively in this outrageous fashion, what do you think he will do, when he has become master of each of us separately?

[36] What then is the cause of these things? For as it was not without reason and just cause that the Hellenes in old days were so prompt for freedom, so it is not without reason or cause that they are now so prompt to be slaves. There was a spirit, men of Athens, a spirit in the minds of the people in those days, which is absent today—the spirit which vanquished the wealth of Persia, which led Hellas in the path of freedom, and never gave way in face of battle by sea or by land; a spirit whose extinction today has brought universal ruin and turned Hellas upside down. [37] What was this spirit? [It was nothing subtle or clever.] It meant that men who took money from those who aimed at dominion or at the ruin of Hellas were execrated by all; that it was then a very grave thing to be convicted of bribery; that the punishment for the guilty man was the heaviest that could be inflicted; that for him there could be no plea for mercy, nor hope of pardon. [38] No orator, no general, would then sell the critical opportunity whenever it arose—the opportunity so often offered to men by fortune, even when they are careless and their foes are on their guard. They did not barter away the harmony between people and people, not their own mistrust of the tyrant and the foreigner, nor any of these high sentiments. Where are such sentiments now? [39] They have been sold in the market and are gone; and those have been imported in their stead, through which the nation lies ruined and plague-stricken—the envy of the man who has received his

hire; the amusement which accompanies his avowal; the pardon granted to those whose guilt is proved; the hatred of one who censures the crime; and all the appurtenances of corruption. [40] For as to ships, numerical strength, unstinting abundance of funds and all other material of war, and all the things by which the strength of cities is estimated, every people can command these in greater plenty and on a larger scale by far than in old days. But all these resources are rendered unserviceable, ineffectual unprofitable, by those who traffic in them.

[41] That these things are so today, you doubtless see, and need no testimony of mine: and that in times gone by the opposite was true, I will prove to you, not by any words of my own but by the record inscribed by your ancestors on a pillar of bronze, and placed on the Acropolis [not to be a lesson to themselves—they needed no such record *to* put them in a right mind—but to be a reminder and an example to you of the zeal that you ought to display in such a cause]. What then is the record? [42] "Arthmius, son of Pythonax, of Zeleia, is an outlaw, and is the enemy of the Athenian people and their allies, he and his house." Then follows the reason for which this step was taken—"because he brought the gold from the Medes into the Peloponnese." Such is the record. [43] Consider, in Heaven's name, what must have been the mind of the Athenians of that day, when they did this, and their conception of their position. They set up a record, that because a man of Zeleia, Arthmius by name, a slave of the King of Persia (for Zeleia is in Asia), as part of his service to the king, had brought gold, not to Athens, but to the Peloponnese, he should be an enemy of Athens and her allies, he and his house, and that they should be outlaws. [44] And this outlawry is no such disfranchisement as we ordinarily mean by the word. For what would it matter to a man of Zeleia, that he might have no share in the public life of Athens? But there is a clause in the Law of Murder, dealing with those in connexion with whose death the law does not allow a prosecution for murder but the slaying of them is to be a holy act: "And let him die an outlaw," it runs. The meaning, accordingly, is this—that the slayer of such a man is to be pure from all guilt. [45] They thought, therefore, that the safety of all the Hellenes was a matter which concerned themselves—apart from this belief, it could not have mattered to them whether any one bought or corrupted men in the Peloponnese; and whenever

they detected such offenders, they carried their punishment and their vengeance so far as to pillory their names for ever. As the natural consequence, the Hellenes were a terror to the foreigner, not the foreigner to the Hellenes. It is not so now. Such is not your attitude in these or in other matters. **[46]** But what is it? … And what counsel? Do you bid me tell you, and will you not be angry if I do so?

[He reads from the document.]

[47] Now there is an ingenuous argument, which is used by those who would reassure the city, to the effect that, after all, Philip is not yet in the position once held by the Spartans, who ruled everywhere over sea and land, with the king for their ally, and nothing to withstand them; and that, none the less, Athens defended herself even against them, and was not swept away. Since that time the progress in every direction, one may say, has been great, and has made the world today very different from what it was then; but I believe that in no respect has there been greater progress or development than in the art of war. **[48]** In the first place, I am told that in those days the Spartans and all our other enemies would invade us for four or five months— during, that is, the actual summer—and would damage Attica with infantry and citizen-troops, and then return home again. And so old-fashioned were the men of that day—nay rather, such true citizens—that no one ever purchased any object from another for money, but their warfare was of a legitimate and open kind. **[49]** But now, as I am sure you see, most of our losses are the result of treachery, and no issue is decided by open conflict or battle; while you are told that it is not because he leads a column of heavy infantry that Philip can march wherever he chooses, but because he has attached to himself a force of light infantry, cavalry, archers, mercenaries, and similar troops. **[50]** And whenever, with such advantages, he falls upon a State which is disordered within, and in their distrust of one another no one goes out in defence of its territory, he brings up his engines and besieges them. I pass over the fact that summer and winter are alike to him—that there is no close season during which he suspends operations. **[51]** But if you all know these things and take due account of them, you surely must not let the war pass into Attica, nor be dashed from your seat through looking back to the simplicity of those old hostilities with Sparta. You must guard against him, at the greatest possible distance, both by political measures and by preparations; you must prevent his stirring from home, instead of grappling with him at close quarters in a struggle to the death. **[52]** For, men of Athens, we have many natural advantages for a war, if we are willing to do our duty. There is the character of his country, much of which we can harry and damage, and a thousand other things. But for a pitched battle he is in better training than we. **[53]** Nor have you only to recognize these facts, and to resist him by actual operations of war. You must also by reasoned judgement and of set purpose come to execrate those who address you in his interest, remembering that it is impossible to master the enemies of the city, until you punish those who are serving them in the city itself. **[54]** And this, before God and every Heavenly Power—this you will not be able to do; for you have reached such a pitch of folly or distraction of—I know not what to call it; for often has the fear actually entered my mind, that some more than mortal power may be driving our fortunes to ruin—that to enjoy their abuse, or their malice, or their jests, or whatever your motive may chance to be, you call upon men to speak who are hirelings, and some of whom would not even deny it; and you laugh to hear their abuse of others. **[55]** And terrible as this is, there is yet worse to be told. For you have actually made political life safer for these men, than for those who uphold your own cause. And yet observe what calamities the willingness to listen to such men lays up in store. I will mention facts known to you all.

[56] In Olynthus, among those who were engaged in public affairs, there was one party who were on the side of Philip, and served his interests in everything; and another whose aim was their city's real good, and the preservation of their fellow citizens from bondage. Which were the destroyers of their country? Which betrayed the cavalry, through whose betrayal Olynthus perished? Those whose sympathies were with Philip's cause; those who, while the city still existed brought such dishonest and slanderous charges against the speakers whose advice was for the best, that, in the case of Apollonides at least, the people of Olynthus was even induced to banish the accused.

[57] Nor is this instance of the unmixed evil wrought by these practices in the case of the Olynthians an exceptional one, or without parallel elsewhere. For in Eretria, when Plutarchus and the mercenaries had been got rid of, and the people had control of the city and of Porthmus, one party wished to entrust the State to you, the other to entrust it to Philip. And through listening mainly, or rather entirely, to the latter, these poor luckless Eretrians were at last persuaded to banish the advocates of their own interests. **[58]** For, as you know, Philip, their ally, sent Hipponicus with a thousand mercenaries, stripped Porthmus of its walls, and set up three tyrants—Hipparchus, Automedon, and Cleitarchus; and since then he has already twice expelled them from the country when they wished to recover their position. . . .

[59] And why go through the mass of the instances? . . . **[63]** How for what reason, you may be wondering, were the peoples of Olynthus and Eretria and Oreus more agreeably disposed towards Philip's advocates than towards their own? The reason was the same as it is with you—that those who speak for your true good can never, even if they would, speak to win popularity with you; they are constrained to inquire how the State may be saved: while their opponents, in the very act of seeking popularity, are co-operating with Philip. **[64]** The one party said, "You must pay taxes"; the other, "There is no need to do so." The one said, "Go to war, and do not trust him"; the other, "Remain at peace,"—until they were in the toils. And —not to mention each separately—I believe that the same thing was true of all. The one side said what would enable them to win favour; the other, what would secure the safety of their State. And at last the main body of the people accepted much that they proposed—not now from any such desire for gratification, nor from ignorance, but as a concession to circumstances, thinking that their cause was now wholly lost. **[65]** It is this fate, I solemnly assure you, that I dread for you, when the time comes that you make your reckoning, and realize that there is no longer anything that can be done. May you never find yourselves, men of Athens, in such a position! . . .

A noble recompense did the people in Oreus receive, for entrusting themselves to Philip's friends, and thrusting Euphraeus aside! **[66]** and a noble recompense the democracy of Eretria, for driving away your envoys, and surrendering to Cleitarchus! They are slaves, scourged and butchered! A noble clemency did he show to the Olynthians, who elected Lasthenes to command the cavalry, and banished Apollonides! **[67]** It is folly, and it is cowardice, to cherish hopes like these, to give way to evil counsels, to refuse to do anything that you should do, to listen to the advocates of the enemy's cause, and to fancy that you dwell in so great a city that, whatever happens, you will not suffer any harm. **[68]** Aye, and it is shameful to exclaim after the event, "Why, who would have expected this? Of course, we ought to have done, or not to have done, such and such things!" The Olynthians could tell you of many things, to have foreseen which in time would have saved them from destruction. So too could the people of Oreus, and the Phocians, and every other people that has been destroyed. **[69]** But how does that help them now? So long as the vessel is safe, be it great or small, so long must the sailor and the pilot and every man in his place exert himself and take care that no one may capsize it by design or by accident: but when the seas have overwhelmed it, all their efforts are in vain. **[70]** So it is, men of Athens, with us. While we are still safe, with our great city, our vast resources, our noble name, what are we to do? . . . We ourselves, in the first place, must conduct the resistance and make preparation for it— with ships, that is, and money, and soldiers. For though all but ourselves give way and become slaves, we at least must contend for freedom. **[71]** And when we have made all these preparations ourselves, and let them be seen, then let us call upon the other states for aid, and send envoys to carry our message in all directions—to the Peloponnese, to Rhodes, to Chios, to the king [of Persia]; for it is not unimportant for his interests either that Philip should be prevented from subjugating the world; that so, if you persuade them, you may have partners to share the danger and the expense, in case of need; and if you do not, you may at least delay the march of events. . . . **[73]** But I do not mean that we should call upon the other states, if we are not willing to take any of the necessary steps ourselves. It is folly to sacrifice what is our own, and then pretend to be anxious for the interests of others—to neglect the present, and alarm others in regard to the future. I do not propose this. I say that we must send money to the forces in the Chersonese, and do all that they ask of us; that we must make preparation ourselves, while we summon, convene, instruct, and warn the rest of the Hellenes. That is the policy for a city with a reputation such as yours. **[74]** But if you fancy that the people of Chalcis or of Megara will save Hellas, while you run away from the task, you are mistaken. They may well be content if they can each save themselves. The task is yours. It is the prerogative that your forefathers won, and through it **[75]** each of you is to sit and consult his inclinations, looking for some way by which he may escape any personal action, the first consequence will be that you will never find anyone who will act; and the second, I fear, that the day will come when we shall be forced to do, at one and the same time, all the things we wish to avoid move. **[76]** If the proposal is carried out, I think that even now the state of our affairs may be remedied. But if anyone has a better proposal to make, let him make it, and give us his advice. And I pray to all the gods that whatever be the decision that you are about to make, it may be for your good.

Questions

1. **What danger to Athens does Demosthenes identify?**
2. **Whom does he blame for it? Why is each to be blamed?**
3. **What policies does he recommend to meet the danger?**

OPINIONS OF MODERN SCHOLARS

THE FUTILITY OF THE POLICY OF DEMOSTHENES

1. Droysen was a Prussian patriot who championed the unification of Germany under Prussian leadership. Like other Germans of his day he saw the Macedonian conquest of the autonomous Greek states as the unification necessary for achieving the great deeds of Philip's son Alexander. Here he indicates his disapproval of Demosthenes, who resisted these great developments.

FROM JOHANN GUSTAV DROYSEN, *GESCHICHTE DES HELLENISMUS, TRANSLATED BY DONALD KAGAN*

IN HELLAS THE THOUGHT OF A NATIONAL STRUGGLE against the Persian power was never forgotten; it was for the Greeks what the struggle against the infidels was for western Christendom centuries later. Even Sparta for a time had sought to clothe its rule and greed with this mask; Jason of Pherae saw a justification for the tyranny which he had established in the national struggle for which he prepared. The clearer the weakness and internal disorder of the gigantic empire became the easier and more profitable appeared the task of its destruction, the more general and confident became the expectation that it would happen and must happen. Plato and his school might try to find and realize the ideal state; Isocrates, from whom a still brighter and more popular operation emanated, always came back to this: that the struggle against Persia must be begun, such a war would be a festive procession rather than a military campaign. How could one bear the disgrace that these barbarians wished to be the guardians of peace in Hellas while Hellas was in a position to accomplish deeds which were worthy, which were bidden by the gods? And Aristotle said the Greeks could rule the world if they were united in a single state.

The one thought lay quite close to the other, the union of Hellas and the struggle against Persia, and as a combined operation; one should not be allowed to wait until the other was accomplished. But how might such thoughts be realized?

King Philip of Macedon undertook it. He had to do it, one may say, if he wanted to restore and secure the confused kingship of his house. The policy of Athens, Sparta, Olynthus, Thebes, the Thessalian rulers had always fostered quarrels in the royal family, supported usurpations by princely chieftains of the land, and induced the barbarians to launch incursions and raids against Macedonia. If they all had no other legal claim for their proceedings than the weakness of the Macedonian monarchy, only the establishment of a sufficient power was required to prove that right against them. And they had no claim on the consideration of the Macedonian monarchy since for so long they had pursued their own interests against it.

Philip's success was based on the secure foundation which he knew how to give to his power, on the movement of his policy, going forward step-by-step in the face of the Greek states, now alert, now sleeping, but always self-seeking in its means or ends. Above all it rested on the unity, the secrecy, the speed and consequence of his undertakings which were for so long considered impossible by those who were to meet them, until it was no longer possible to elude or to withstand him. While Thessaly sank into disorder with the murder of Alexander, while the Athenians turned all their attention to the Social War, the Thebans to the Sacred War which compelled the partition of Phocis, the Spartans tried to preserve some influence in the Peloponnese, Philip pushed his borders so far to the south and east that he held the pass to Thrace with Amphipolis, the gold mines with Mount Pangaeus, the Thermaic Gulf and access to the sea with the coast of Macedonia, the road to Thessaly with Methone. Then the Thessalians called upon him for help against a very serious threat from the Phocians. He came. He had a difficult position in the face of the well-led military force of the temple robbers. First he threw them back by moving up reinforcements; he stood at the pass of Thermopylae he placed a Macedonian garrison at Pagasae, and with this he was master of the Thessalian harbor and the road to Euboea. Now the Athenians opened their eyes. Under Demosthenes' leadership they began the struggle against the power which so it appeared, stretched its hand out for the command of Hellas.

No one will doubt the patriotism of Demosthenes and his zeal for the honor and might of Athens, and with the fullest right is he admired as the greatest orator of all time. Whether he was great in the same measure as a statesman, whether he was the statesman of the national policy of Greece, is another question. If the decision in this struggle had been victory over Macedonia what would the further fate of the Greek world have

been? At best the establishment of Athenian authority in the same way as the one which had just collapsed a second time: either an alliance on the basis of the autonomy of the allies which would not have been able to check the barbarians in the North, nor to defy the barbarians in the East, nor to take upon itself the defense of the declining Hellenism of the West. Or else it might be an Athenian domination over subject territories, as Samos, Lemnos, Imbros, and Scyros were already, in part in the form of cleruchies, or, as in a looser form Tenedos, Proconnesus, the Chersonese, and Delos were in the possession of Athens. To the extent that the Athenians extended their dominion, they would have encountered greater jealousy, a stronger opposition from rival states; they would only have increased the already deeply corroded split and disunity of the Hellenic world; they would have welcomed any assistance, even from the Persians, the Thracians or Illyrian barbarians, tyrants, wherever it could be found, in order to hold their own. Or would Athens only have warded off the incalculable changes which the power of Macedonia threatened to bring to Hellas, only have preserved conditions as they were? They were so miserable and shameful and were becoming more untenable and explosive the longer they were left in that carelessness and crippling of the petty existence in which one member after another of the Greek world was withering away.

If the Athenian patriots believed or pretended they were leading the struggle against Philip in the name of freedom, autonomy, Hellenic culture, national honor, none of these benefits would be secured by the victory of Athens or preserved by the renewed dominion of the Athenian demos over allies or subject territories, by the threadbare and exhausted democracy, its sycophants, demagogues, and mercenaries. It was an error of Demosthenes, who perhaps deserves respect for his heart, certainly not for his wisdom, if he could believe that with that babbling, unwarlike, banausic citizenry of Athens— even if he could carry it along to glorious decisions with the power of his rhetoric, even if he could galvanize it to action for a moment—he could still make a great policy, still carry through a long and difficult struggle. It was a still more serious error if he could believe that he could halt the growing power of King Philip by means of an alliance with Thebes, Megalopolis, Argos, and other such states tossed together in a moment of danger. Even if a treaty was obtained from him he would return with redoubled force while the Hellenic alliances came to an end with the first defeat. Demosthenes must have known what it meant that he himself, who recommended political projects, was not the military hero who carried them out, that he must entrust them, and with them the fate of the state, to generals like the willful Chares and the dissolute Charidemus. He must have known that even in Athens just as he won influence the rich, the indolent, the self-seeking would find themselves together against him, that his personal enemies, supported by them, would use every trick and delaying tactic provided by the constitution to cross his plans, plans whose value was summed up by an Athenian after the battle of Chaeronea with the bitter words: "if we had not lost, we would have been lost."

THE CHARACTER OF DEMOSTHENES

2. In the nineteenth and the first part of the twentieth-century opinion in the French and British democracies tended to favor the attempt of Demosthenes and Athens to preserve the independence and liberty of the Greek city-states against the authoritarian, expansive monarchy of Macedonia. A. W. Pickard-Cambridge was Fellow of Balliol College, Oxford. He was a particularly fervent admirer of Demosthenes.

FROM A. W. PICKARD-CAMBRIDGE, *DEMOSTHENES*

THE QUESTION HOW FAR DEMOSTHENES was justified in the policy which he pursued has been discussed … in relation to each of the principal crises of the struggle in which he played so large a part. His vindication of himself in the *Speech on the Crown* is more convincing than any discussion at the little more need be said. The claim of Demosthenes to be ranked among the heroic men of the past rests above all on the constancy and sincerity with which he defended the noblest cause known to the Greeks—that of Hellenic liberty; and only those who have failed to recognise that most of what was best in the Greek, and, above all, in the Athenian character sprang from and was bound up with political liberty, can seriously censure his choice. If any cause was, to a Greek, worth fighting for to the death, that for which Demosthenes fought and died was pre-eminently so. Polybius indeed, writing two centuries later, declared that the "crop of traitors" in the Greek cities, whom Demosthenes so vehemently denounced, deserved no such name, and that they were pursuing the true interest of their several countries in submitting to Philip and Alexander, and finding in subjection to a common master that freedom from strife with one another which they had failed to find so long as they were autonomous.

Yet such a solution of their political problems can hardly be called an honourable one; nor did these States ever bring forth fruits comparable to those achievements by which the Athenians, when they were most fully inspired by the spirit of freedom, won the admiration of humanity.

Moreover, it is plain that the test by which Polybius tried the policy of the statesmen of the fourth century was simply that of success. Demosthenes' policy, he said, led to the disaster of Chaeroneia, whereas the Arcadians and Messenians enjoyed the blessings of peace. If success is the true and only test of statesmanship, Polybius was doubtless right. But if political liberty had proved itself so precious that without it the whole of life would have seemed to be lived on a lower plane, success was an altogether unworthy criterion by which to judge the actions of those who were dominated by such a sentiment. Demosthenes was convinced that such was the persuasion of the Athenians, if not of all other Greek peoples, and that by struggling to the end for the freedom of Athens, and causing the Athenians to struggle for the freedom of the Hellenes, he was fulfilling their noblest instincts.

If, however, success is seriously taken to be the proper criterion of merit, it must not be forgotten that the policy of Demosthenes very nearly did succeed. Philip was actually discomfited before Byzantium; and the defeat of Chaeroneia was due to nothing which it was in Demosthenes' power to provide against, nor even to the inferiority of the forces which he had brought together, but simply to bad generalship. Whether, supposing that Philip had been defeated at Chaeroneia, the struggle would have been at an end, no one can say; and it is idle to speculate upon such questions; but at least the defenders of Hellenic liberty came near enough to success to justify their attempt, even from the narrow standpoint assumed by Polybius and by some modern critics. Nor is it without significance that Aristotle (who had no special liking for Demosthenes), when he desires to illustrate a common form of fallacy, finds a conspicuous illustration in the statement that the policy of Demosthenes was responsible for all the evils that befell his country.

The principal causes of the failure of Demosthenes' plans have long been plain to us— the unsteadiness of the Athenian people; the lack of generals comparable in ability to the statesmen of the time; the disunion of the Greek States. For the second of these causes, no blame attaches to Demosthenes, and it is not certain that he could have been aware of the inferiority of the Athenian commanders until they were put to the test. The disunion of the States he strove hard to overcome, and to a very remarkable extent he succeeded. The alliance of Thebes and Athens was a thing of which the most sanguine prophet could never have dreamed a few years before.

But ought Demosthenes to have recognised that his fellow-countrymen were no longer equal to the strain to which he desired to subject them? Is he to be blamed for taking too generous a view of their character? Certainly he was not unaware of their defects. No one ever pointed out more candidly than he, how far they fell short of the traditional ideal of Athenian citizenship, or realised more clearly their unwillingness to sacrifice pleasure and ease, and to undertake great personal risks for the sake of the national honour. The fickle and spasmodic nature of their patriotism, their liability to be carried about by alternate gusts of courage and alarm, were constantly before him. Yet even so, incapable of sustained effort and prolonged sacrifices as the Athenians were, it was a nobler thing to attempt to revive in them the spirit which they had lost, than to acquiesce in their degeneracy and levity, and to "despair of the

Republic." Nor must it be forgotten that in this attempt also Demosthenes came nearly enough within reach of success to justify his policy in the judgment of any large-minded critic.

Demosthenes' ideal and his determination to maintain it, as the ideal not of himself alone but of his nation, stand in no need of vindication; and he well deserves our admiration for the courage with which, in pursuit of this ideal, he contended against those desires and prejudices of his fellow-countrymen which were inconsistent with it. In three important points at least, his policy ran directly counter to popular sentiment—in his demand that the festival-money should be given up for purposes of war; in his far-sighted desire to bring about an alliance with Thebes; and in his attempt to obtain the co-operation of the Persian King against Philip. Yet all these aims he pursued without faltering in face of attack and misrepresentation; and there can be little doubt that he was wise, as well as courageous, in so doing.

The question whether liberty and preeminence are political ideals which possess a universal value and need no justification is too large to discuss here. There are many who believe (as Plato and Aristotle probably believed) that these are secondary in importance to the good life of the individual in a peaceful society, and to whom militarism and imperialism are consequently abominable. There is something to be said for this view. But it must not be forgotten that in the Athens of Demosthenes' day it was a view which had not made its way into the region of practical politics, but was peculiar to philosophic circles. There is no evidence that it was desire for the good life, or for the refined enjoyment of art, literature and philosophy, that made the majority of the Athenians unwilling to fight; or that any higher motives than business, pleasure, and love of ease were the cause of their reluctance. Nor is it an absurd contention that the life of the individual is itself greatly ennobled by membership of an imperial nation. It may at least be doubted whether more than a handful of Athenians thought otherwise; and if so, it is a mistake to judge Demosthenes by a standard which is out of relation to the political life of his times.

The faults which sullied the character of Demosthenes as a public man are not only conspicuous, but are such as tend in many ways to alienate the sympathies of the modern world from him. The worst, perhaps, was an indifference to truth, which, while it was not incompatible with the larger sincerity manifested in his constancy to the supreme objects of his; life, led him to deal very unfairly with his opponents, to falsify history, and to repudiate his own share in transactions which were perfectly proper, but which had come in time to be viewed with disfavour by the majority of the Athenians. Doubtless some of the blame for this should be assigned to the People itself; and Demosthenes' attempts to deceive the People in regard to the past are in some degree excusable when we consider that if he had spoken or admitted the whole truth, his policy in regard to the present and future would certainly have been imperiled. It may be that absolute truthfulness is not possible for the leader of a democracy. But it is difficult not to feel that the misrepresentations of which Demosthenes was guilty sometimes went beyond anything that such considerations can justify; that one who could lament over the calamities of the Phocians, which he had done nothing to prevent, and could ascribe them to the man who (if anyone had done so) had helped to mitigate them deserves the severest reprobation; and that his scandalous inventions in regard to his rival's history and morals are utterly atrocious. There was also a certain intransigence — amounting at times almost to ferocity — in his absolute refusal to consider even the most reasonable offers which Philip might make, and in the steps which he took to exacerbate the relations between Athens and the King of Macedon. No doubt he was whole-heartedly convinced that even if a compact, as favourable to Athens as possible, were made with Philip, it would mean at best that Athens would be sure only of the second place in the Hellenic world; and that whatever compact were made, it would only be observed by Philip until such time as he desired to break it. Yet Demosthenes, however sincere and patriotic he may have been, is sometimes repellent in the hatred which he displays, and at times this hatred led him to make false charges and to commit acts of cruelty which admit of no justification.

In his money-dealings he did not always observe the standard of correctness which a modern statesman is expected, as a matter of course, to observe. There is not, however, an iota of evidence that will stand criticism to show that he profited personally by any of the transactions that were alleged against him; and the worst of these transactions, the appropriation of Harpalus' treasure, was probably dictated, just as his receipt of the gold from Persia had been, by public spirit so intense as to render him unscrupulous about means. Judged by the standard of his times, he is almost beyond reproach. It is not unworthy of notice that within a few months of condemning Demosthenes for taking some of Harpalus' money, the People themselves took all that was left of it to pay the cost of the Lamian War. No one now asserts that the policy of Demosthenes was in the smallest degree influenced by considerations of gain or of gratitude for presents received. It is doubtful whether this could be said of some of the orators who opposed him.

To the enumeration of his faults as a statesman, it must be added that he seems to have been a man of an unsociable and unfriendly temperament, and a bitter and relentless enemy; in all that we learn about him from the ancients or from his own writings, there is no hint of any intimate friendship or domestic affection. So wholly was he identified with political aims that he almost seems to have had no private life. He was, moreover, deficient in humour and in gentlemanly feeling; and both these faults reveal an unattractive narrowness of imagination.

But against these faults, public and private, is to be set a devotion to a great ideal, absorbing the whole man; a capacity for work unrivalled in the history of great statesmen; a thoroughness in all that he did, which cared for every detail, and left nothing to chance; a gift of language, penetrated and transformed into eloquence of the very highest order by the passion for a great cause; and a courage which rose superior to all physical weakness, and was not daunted by failure or danger. The greatness of his character in these respects more than redeems its unloveliness.

3. George Cawkwell's study of the Greek poleis' conqueror is characteristic of more recent judgments of Demosthenes' career than of older studies. It is highly critical for reasons different from those of Droysen and others, focusing instead on a critique of the alleged ineffectiveness of his policies rather than the vision and purpose that underlay them. George Cawkwell is a Fellow and Praelector in Ancient History of University College, Oxford.

FROM GEORGE CAWKWELL, *PHILIP OF MACEDON*

EXPERIENCE HAS TAUGHT ME that if one does not join the chorus of encomiasts of Demosthenes someone will darkly ascribe dissent to wickedness in one's political views. The connection may not be obvious to outsiders nor is it necessary in fact. It is true that there have been those who have seen in Philip one of those great unifying figures of history that men of vision welcome with hero-worship, and who have supposed that since Demosthenes chose to oppose rather than to submit, he was an impediment to progress. It will, I trust, be evident from my book that that is not my view of either of these men. Since, however, professional Greek historians are sometimes animated by passions that enable them to see in black and white much that is grey, I may as well spell out my villainy. While I hold what I conceive to be a Thucydidean view of politics, viz. that men will always seek to have and extend power over others and so empire in the broad sense is inevitable, I also hold liberty to be one of the greatest of goods and therefore regard it as one of a statesman's prime duties to defend it. In so far as I have criticized Demosthenes as a defender of liberty, it is not because he sought to defend it, but because he did it badly. Likewise, I regard Philip as a great man and so a great menace to the liberty of Greece.

* * *

Judgement of Philip has varied. To a recital similar to that of Alexander's speech, Ephorus who was Philip's contemporary and a major historian added that "his achievements were not due to luck but to his own excellence; for this king was outstanding for the sharpness of his strategic sense, for his courage, and for the brilliance of his personality." Another major historian, Theopompus, engaged on a History of Greece for which it would appear he had collected material for at least the first four decades of the fourth century, was so impressed by the rise of Philip that he cut short his projected history at a somewhat unlikely point and turned to writing the *History of Philip*, a huge work which ran to fifty-eight books and made the reign of Philip the central fact of fourth-century history. In the Proem he declared that Europe had never produced anyone to match Philip and in his *Encomium of Philip*, which must have been written at much the same time as the Proem, he predicted that, if Philip continued to comport himself as he had begun, he would become king of the rest of Europe as well. Although Theopompus tempered his admiration after seeing Philip and his court for himself, both these historians took a view of Philip markedly opposed to that of Demosthenes, for whom Philip succeeded almost entirely because Greeks were corruptible. Generally speaking, the Demosthenic view prevailed. At Rome the speeches of Demosthenes were studied and imitated; histories had less appeal. Although a Polybius might dissent, and others follow Theophrastus, on whom the mantle of Aristotle fell, in favourably contrasting Philip with his murderous son, the Romans generally accepted that Philip "much more bought the Greeks than beat them."

Thus Demosthenes the orator had his way in antiquity. In modern times it has been Demosthenes the champion of liberty and democracy over whom historians have differed, reflecting attitudes to contemporary events. For some, Philip was the Philip of Demosthenes and those whom Demosthenes denounced as traitors to liberty were traitors. For others, Philip was the unifier and saviour of Greece, the great leader who saved it from itself, despite the efforts of Demosthenes to prevent salvation.

This dichotomy is crude. To be sceptical about Demosthenes does not necessarily argue indifference to liberty or hero-worship of great men. Demosthenes was not necessarily the only or the wisest champion of liberty, and historical judgement need not follow what he said of himself and his opponents. Yet if Philip was not the contemptible figure Demosthenes made of him, that does not mean that Philip should not have been resisted.

It is the theme of this book that Philip transformed the ancient world, confronting the city-states of Greece with the national state of Macedon, that he was therefore a serious menace to the liberty of Greece, but that the policies of Demosthenes were almost entirely misconceived and caused Philip to be opposed less effectively than he might have been.

* * *

Athenian policy and the opposition of Demosthenes

When Philip turned back from Thermopylae in 352, Athens seemed to have cause for great satisfaction: Philip could in future be kept out of central Greece, provided Athens did not involve herself in unprofitable military ventures far from Greece. In November came a new crisis. Philip was reported to be besieging Heraeum Teichos in Thrace ... For Athens that was dangerously close, and a decree was promptly passed despatching a fleet of forty ships manned by citizens of ages between twenty and forty-five, and to be financed by a capital levy of sixty talents. Then came word that Philip was seriously ill. The naval expedition was stayed. The Chersonese remained untroubled, and the decision not to proceed with the expedition seemed justified. Not until September 351 did a force leave Athens for the Hellespont and that was a mere ten ships manned by mercenary crews. The commander was Cersobleptes' former general Charidemus, now an elected Athenian general. He took with him to the place he knew well a mere five talents. He would have to live on his wits, but, since Cersobleptes needed all the help he could get, he could be expected to pay.

In all this there was policy—to act strenuously in a crisis in defence of vital interests, but for the rest to leave the war to run itself. There was at Athens no government in our sense of the word, but politicians with a policy could be of great influence over a number of years. Two were preeminent in the second half of the 350s, Diophantus and Eubulus. Another, Demosthenes, has been made to seem important, because literary preference preserved a number of his speeches and buried those of almost all whom he attacked. He played a very minor part, and must be considered after the important people.

At the end of the Social War in 355, Athens had lost a large part of the probably not very substantial income she had received from the Second Athenian Confederacy and her own city revenues were down to a mere one hundred and thirty talents, that is about a quarter of what had been normal in the fifth century. The resident aliens (metics) had left in large numbers and there were many vacant properties in the city. Clearly all but the most necessary wars were luxuries and the nearly hopeless war for Amphipolis

was the wildest luxury of all. Only in peace could the city's fortunes be restored, but a peace that abandoned Amphipolis was unthinkable. It was this dilemma that Diophantus and his associate Eubulus resolved.

Athenian finance was essentially a matter of a number of separate accounts earmarked for specific purposes, but any money in these accounts unused by the end of the year was available for the People to use in other ways. The regular method of financing wars, at Athens as generally in the Greek world, was to impose a capital levy (*eisphora*). In the fifth century the tribute had made such levies rare, and in the fourth, perhaps from the early days of the Second Athenian Confederacy onwards, the contributions of the members being comparatively small, a military fund, the so-called Stratiotic Fund, was created to which were devoted the annual "surpluses" from the various accounts. Diophantus and Eubulus changed all that. A law was passed creating a new fund, the Theoric Fund, which received these "surpluses" and which was used in very small measure for distributions at the theatre and in very large measure on "developing" the city and its port, the Piraeus, for the purposes of trade. Most importantly, the "surpluses" could only be used for other ends if the law was repealed, a process possible once a year but not on the spur of the moment or of some sudden military necessity. The policy succeeded handsomely. The law was not repealed until 339/8 after the outbreak of the final war with Philip, and enabled Athens to face the war with confidence in its resources. In 351 the Theoric Fund was not worth Demosthenes' thinking about; by 349 it was. The city's revenues had risen to 400 talents by 346 and whereas in the mid-350s the richest citizens had to be combined in groups of up to sixteen persons to provide the running costs of a single trireme, by 339 one man might be called on to fund two ships by himself. Demosthenes in 349 denounced the Theoric Law as a disgraceful impediment to the city doing what it ought to do, but by 341, when he was pressing hard for all-out war with Philip, he advocated the maintenance of the law.

The real bite of this law was in foreign policy. The war for Amphipolis had to be left to run itself; small forces of the sort sent out under Charidemus in September 351 were all that would confront Philip as he built up his power. There was obviously good sense in the policy elsewhere. For instance, Eubulus opposed, successfully, Athenian help in 351/0 for the democrats of Rhodes when they were seeking to regain control of the island; which was all very sensible, for Athens had nothing to gain and much to lose including the cost of help. But was it not the policy which allowed Philip the maximum opportunity for his aggressive designs? That was at any rate the view of the young Demosthenes, to which we may now turn. Before doing so, however, one must point out the important corollary of this policy. Where vital interests were involved, Athens could and must act with a will: hence in 352 the swift move to Thermopylae and the large preparations to stop Philip attacking the Chersonese, and in 348 the prompt defence of Euboea. Nor did it stop there. On a number of occasions Eubulus and his associates responded to dangerous situations by seeking to bring the Greeks together in a sort of national organization that would confront an aggressor with united military action. The policy as a whole might be summed up thus: "avoid imperialist dreams in pursuit of which we would inevitably fight alone and beyond our means, and keep our power for wars in which our vital interests are challenged and for wars in which all Greece is endangered."

It was the view of Demosthenes that this policy was ruinous in that it left Philip free to build up his power, and, although before 348 when Demosthenes became a supporter of Philocrates he was of little importance, it is vital to consider his criticism. If he had had his way, could the growth of Philip's power have been checked?

In 351 when Demosthenes attacked Philip for the first time in The First Philippic, he was only thirty-three, probably well known as a man who could write an effective speech for someone else to use in the courts but little regarded for the speeches he himself made in the assembly. Attacking Eubulus and his policy was perhaps bound to be unpopular, but two of his speeches suggest a serious lack of judgement. Thebes was Athens' main enemy in Greece itself, and it was all-important that Thebes be checked by Phocis in Central Greece and by Sparta in the Peloponnese, but in his speech For the Megalopolitans of spring 352 he could advocate Athens opposing Sparta in the Peloponnese but entirely neglect to consider the effect on the balance of power in Central

Greece; his policy would have been disastrous and it was rightly rejected. Later in 352 the speech *Against Aristocrates* was argued in the belief that Cersobleptes, not Philip, was Athens' enemy in the north. As has been already pointed out, Aristocrates, who moved the decree honouring Cersobleptes' general, and those who supported it, saw things more clearly. Admittedly the speech was written for someone else to deliver, but it is inconceivable that the Demosthenes of The *First Philippic* could have written it, if he had appreciated what was happening. What he lacked in judgement he made up for in morose severity, to judge by the familiar, admittedly stylized representation of him. Unlike the genial Aeschines he did not drink wine, and was an unsociable and slightly comic figure. Those who disagreed with him were in his view "corrupted." It is instructive to read his concluding remarks in the speech *On the Liberty of the Rhodians*, a matter far removed from the passions aroused by Philip and the bribery of which he was constantly suspected, and in which there seems very little indeed to be said in favour of Demosthenes' proposed course of action; his opponents have "chosen to act contrary to the interests of the city." Some found him lacking in common modesty, and it no doubt caused general satisfaction when in 348 before a theatre audience he was punched in the face by an exasperated supporter of Eubulus. His whole temperament was nervous. During his audience with Philip in 346 words literally failed him. He was generally regarded as ill-humoured and ill-mannered. A difficult character surely enough, but such a man can sometimes be right; especially if he was, as Theopompus asserted, inconsistent. Was he right about the war for Amphipolis?

Philip's campaign against Cersobleptes of later 352, in which he laid siege to Heraeum Teichos, was at least partially successful to judge by the fact that Cersobleptes surrendered his son as a hostage. If he intended to turn and attack the Chersonese, he was prevented by illness and 351 was a fallow year as far as operations against the Athenians were concerned. But it was to be feared that in the autumn he might again approach the Chersonese, and as a precaution the small force of ten ships under Charidemus was sent out in September. Before that, possibly in June, there was a debate in the Athenian assembly, perhaps on a proposal quickly to send out a force before the Etesian winds made it impossible—indeed it could have been the proposal to send Charidemus, who did not manage to leave before the weather worsened. In this debate Demosthenes delivered his *First Philippic* in which he expounded his views on how the war for Amphipolis should be conducted.

Demosthenes made two main criticisms of what was happening. First, Athens was always too late; Pydna, Potidaea, and Methone had all been taken before the relieving expeditions could get there. Second, she had put her trust in mercenary forces ill-supplied with money; to supply themselves, they had what she still had. It would have been best to accept that Amphipolis was lost forever, but, since the Athenians could not face that fact, the policy that Demosthenes attacked was the best that could be done. By miracle Amphipolis might fall into their hands but there was no sense in impoverishing the state while they waited. (It may be added that the miracle would have to be the collapse of the new Macedonian state; otherwise if Athens ever did chance to get Amphipolis, Macedonian siegecraft would be likely to take it and all its defenders.) The great *First Philippic* was greatly wrong-headed.

Throughout 351 and 350 Philip left the Greek cities alone. In mid-349, when the Etesian winds were due, he began to attack Olynthus and a new phase in Athens' war opened.

* * *

Demosthenes' views are only partially known to us. His three Olynthiac Orations were all delivered, it would seem, in the early months of the war. The first urged the Athenians to send forces to help the Chalcidians (although he always referred to them as the Olynthians) and was perhaps delivered as part of the debate on the first appeal. In it he revived the idea of The *First Philippic*—one force "to save the cities for the Olynthians" and another to ravage Macedonia; if Athens would not use the monies devoted to the Theoric Fund, there would have to be a capital levy. In The *Second Olynthiac* there were no precise proposals. It was merely to encourage the Athenians; Philip, who had deceived everyone, would now pay the price; without his allies Macedonian power was weak and his allies could now be got to desert him. In The *Third*

Olynthiac (also delivered probably in the very early days of the Attic year 349/8, as is shown by his demand for the repeal of laws, a process which could only be initiated early in the year) he demanded that Athens help "with all her might to the best of her ability" and to that end the law about the Theoric Fund and other unspecified laws about military service be all now repealed. All three speeches seem inspired by the idea tentatively advanced in The *First Philippic* and now confidently asserted. Either Athens must fight Philip in the north or she must fight him within Greece.

Unfortunately Demosthenes in the Olynthiac Orations never said exactly what he wanted. A force to ravage Macedonia would have done no more in 349 to distract Philip from his objective than it could have done two years earlier, and may be dismissed here again. But was he right in thinking that Athens could "save the cities"? That could hardly have been done by occupying them. They were mostly inland, and any forces that Athens could conceivably have sent would have been besieged and captured. He must have been thinking of his large force cooperating in the field with the Chalcidians, and defeating the Macedonian army. But the dangers were immense. If the Macedonian army dealt with the Chalcidians as it had dealt with the Phocians at the Battle of the Crocus Field, the cause would have been lost and a large part of the Athenian army as well. If the Chalcidians were at first successful, Philip, near to his base, could attack again. The initiative lay with him, and there was a serious danger, if not a likelihood, that Athens would so greatly weaken herself that she would be very much less in a position to keep Philip out of Greece. Far from it being the truth that if she did not fight Philip in the north, she would have to fight him in Greece, the position was that if she did heavily commit herself to the defence of the Chalcidians, she would fight him less effectively in Greece.

Athens did finally vote a very large force. The expedition to the Peloponnese of 362 excepted, 2,000 hoplites was two-fifths of the largest number of hoplites Athens ever sent out in the fourth century before the battle of Chaeronea in 338. Three hundred cavalry was three-tenths of her total cavalry force. It might be argued that if this force was to be sent at all it should have been sent in 349 when Demosthenes appears to have demanded it. But that would be an argument based on the presumption that Philip's strategy would have been the same no matter what happened. If Athens had sent this large force in the early days of the war, Philip could have delayed his attacks on the Chalcidian cities and let the Athenians wait and pay. His army was large enough to act elsewhere without endangering the security of Macedon, to attack the Chersonese or even to march south.

The unpalatable strategic fact was that the Chalcidians could not be saved and the Athenians were fortunate that no large number of their citizens was ever landed to attempt the impossible. The only hope for Athens was that they could unite the Greeks in defence of Greece itself, and Demosthenes was here as elsewhere without the true statesman's strategic sense. But, it will be asked, were those whom he opposed any better? A substantial force was finally sent. If it was useless, why was it sent at all? If it could accomplish something, why was it not sent earlier? Was not the policy of Eubulus exposed as at least inconsistent? The answers to these questions can only be given in terms of the crisis at Athens in 348 over Euboea.

The island of Euboea was of vital strategic importance to Athens in its war with Philip. Thermopylae and the Phocian alliance were a barrier sufficient to keep him out of Central Greece if he approached by land, but if he were able to get an army across into Euboea, there was a serious danger of his being able to cross into Boeotia where he would be welcomed as Thebes' ally in the Sacred War and thence to march into Attica. It depended largely on the attitude of Chalcis which controlled the bridge across the strait, and it was important for Athens to do all she could to make sure that those in power at Chalcis were not hostile to her. In February 348 Athens was suddenly confronted by a serious deterioration in her influence in Euboea. The leading politician of Chalcis, whom we shall meet later, Callias, was seeking to unite the cities of the island in some sort of Pan-Euboean League. Since that would inevitably mean that they would leave the Second Athenian Confederacy, their independence might work badly for Athens. As early as 351, Philip had been sending letters to "the Euboeans" and, although he had no part in the events in Euboea of 348, he would be expected to exploit any

decline in Athenian influence; the danger of Philip controlling this island was therefore considerable. Opposed to Chalcis under Callias was, by age-old rivalry, her neighbour Eretria, and when Chalcis sought to coerce Eretria to join in her plans, Eretria appealed to Athens for help. A small force went and won a minor victory, but, when Chalcis gathered mercenaries, a larger force was needed. Thus in the spring Athens was in no position to send a large citizen force to help the Chalcidians of Olynthus, and there is no need to ask why it was not sent earlier than it was. But the war in Euboea also explains why it was sent too late to be of use. This war appears to have been the especial concern of Eubulus and his supporters. It turned out disastrously, with the Athenian commander taken prisoner. A lame peace had to be concluded with the Euboeans. The island was lost to Athens, and the friendship with Philip grew. In these circumstances it would not be surprising if the influence of the Eubulus group which had insisted on the war was for the moment diminished and the final appeal of the Chalcidians answered in a way that all good sense should have counselled against. The Chalcidians could not be saved. Athens must keep her strength to meet the real danger of Philip intervening in Greece.

Demosthenes took the contrary view of the Euboean War, counselling the assembly against it, presumably because he was pressing for a large force to be sent to the north. Since Euboea was so vitally important to Athens, his view was paradoxical. He claimed to have been unsupported in his opposition. Since, however, the war turned out badly, one might wonder whether there was not something to be said for his policy. One may note that Euboea could only be useful to Philip if he could cross to it by sea. He did not attempt to use it in 346 when, although the Euboeans were no less friendlily disposed to him, the Athenian general Proxenus was stationed at Oreos in the north-west of the island with a squadron of ships. So did it matter who controlled Euboea, if Athens controlled the sea? But control of the sea required a base and where other than on Euboea could Athens base a force that would guard the narrow crossing? Control of the sea but not of Euboea would not suffice to keep Philip out. So Demosthenes' policy here too was ill-conceived and it is no wonder that no one supported him. It may be added that in all these debates he was a very minor participant, as is shown by the fact that, when in 330 Aeschines reviewed his political career, he began with the year 346. Prior to that Demosthenes did not count.

* * *

The Athenian War-party

From the moment that the news arrived in Athens in mid-346 that Philip was within the Gates, Demosthenes was looking for an opportunity to resume the war. In late summer 346, when in his speech *On the Peace* he counselled against provoking Philip and the Amphictyons, he alluded to the possibility of "resumption of war over Amphipolis or some such grievance which does not concern others," and he ended by pointing out the folly of "going to war against all the Amphictyonic powers over the shadow in Delphi at this moment." There would be war, but at the right moment.

He was not alone in what his critics termed "war-mongering." Hegesippus, who delivered the seventh speech in the Demosthenic Corpus, and Hyperides, the celebrated orator, accuser of Philocrates in 343, played leading parts in breaking up the Peace, with Polyeuctus and the future financier Lycurgus in support. All shared with Demosthenes the honour of being demanded by name by Alexander in 335 after the suppression of the revolt of Thebes—save Hegesippus, whom perhaps death rather than repentance excepted. Demosthenes, however, was their leader thanks to his rhetorical gifts. As Aeschines was later to remark, "those who were at war against the peace of the city were pleased to call Demosthenes to the speaker's platform, saying that only his name was untouched by bribery; Demosthenes would come forward to speak and set them on to cause war and confusion ... He brought things to the point that if Philip did not send ambassadors he said that Philip despised the city and if he did send them he called them spies, not ambassadors." His method was simple and effective. He kept hammering away at untruths until enough Athenians came to believe them. For instance, the city of Cardia, which lay on the neck of the Gallipoli Peninsula and had been in the fifth century part of the Athenian-controlled

Chersonese, had firmly refused to have anything to do with Athens in the fourth. In the 350s it had sided first with Cersobleptes, and then with Philip in a formal alliance, and thus had participated in the Peace of Philocrates explicitly as his ally, as Demosthenes acknowledged in 346. In 341 the city was spoken of without argument as belonging to Athens and usurped by Philip, and this despite the fact that both Philip and the Cardians themselves had frequently called on the Athenians to settle their differences by arbitration. Clearly truth had ceased to matter in such details, the achievement of Demosthenes and the war-party.

Caution was necessary. Early in the Attic year 346/5 Demosthenes and his political ally, Timarchus, both having been members of the Council in the previous year, joined in an attack on Aeschines who then rounded on Timarchus with a charge of immoral conduct. The case was heard very early in 345, and, despite the assistance of Demosthenes and Hegesippus, Timarchus was deprived of civil rights. The Athenian people were clearly in no humour yet to pay heed to the war-party. So throughout 345 they confined themselves to attacking Philip while he was away fighting against Pleuratus.

The following year, 344, gave them a chance to widen the sphere of their criticism. With Philip seemingly preoccupied with the affairs of his own kingdom, the Spartans judged once again that the time had come to resume control of Messenia. Philip was appealed to by both the Messenians and the Argives (though we do not know how precisely they were involved) and he responded by sending a rescript to the Spartans warning them off. Presumably he wrote as Amphictyon and threatened Amphictyonic action. There was excited reaction in Athens. Demosthenes proposed an embassy to the Messenians and Argives to expostulate with them for giving Philip the chance to intervene in the Peloponnese, and was himself appointed ambassador. His embassy was by no means successful in persuading the Peloponnesians, but it was a start. Both in Athens and abroad, from 344 onwards Demosthenes and his associates were relentless in arousing hostility to Philip.

* * *

Demosthenes' Reasons for Seeking to Destroy the Peace

Were Demosthenes and the war-party right to reject the proffered chance to negotiate a more satisfactory peace? Was Philip wholly untrustworthy?

The theme is constant in Demosthenes' speeches that Philip was constantly breaking the Peace. Much of what he says is demonstrably untruthful—concerning Cardia and the Thracian forts once held by Cersobleptes. But there were incidents in Greek cities, for which he claimed Philip was really responsible, and one must inquire whether in the very period that Philip was protesting blamelessness he was infringing the spirit, if not the letter, of the Peace. One such incident was at Elis where in the course of 344/3 there was a bloody revolution at the end of which those who supported the cause of peace with Philip were established in control of the city; Elis remained neutral in 339/8 in the campaign of Chaeronea, and the "Philippizers" were later named by Demosthenes in his Black List in the speech *On the Crown*. In Megara, on Athens' very doorstep, in 343 a leading citizen was alleged to have brought mercenary soldiers from Philip and just failed in an attempt to force his way into the city—a detailed story. So was Philip, blatantly or secretly, doing all he could to see that his friends came to power in the cities of Greece?

The history of most of the city-states of Greece in the fourth century is a melancholy procession of violent expulsions and expropriations. Both before and after the bloodshed of 344/3 Elis was no exception. Megara too continued to be troubled; shortly after, perhaps in 341/0, the illustrious Athenian general Phocion intervened by force of arms to prevent the Boeotians gaining influence in the city; the alleged "Philippizer," Perillus, named in the Black List, was nonetheless later "thrown overboard" by Philip or Alexander; in the 320s violence continued. Despite the men on the Black List, Megara fought against Philip at Chaeronea. In such confusion Demosthenes could without difficulty make "the facts" suit his case. In fourth-century Athens one had to rely on rumours and some of Demosthenes' confident assertions were proved incorrect. In 344 he declared "Philip is sending mercenaries" to help the Argives and Messenians, but no more was heard of them. In 343, Philip was said to be 'continuing to plot against Geraestus, the cape at the south of Euboea which was of vital importance for the safety of the corn-supply of Athens from the Black Sea: no more is heard of that charge either, and no corn-ships were molested before the outbreak of war in 340. Any stick was good enough or bad enough with which to beat Philip's reputation. The Megara story is suspect if for no other reason than that, if it had indeed been the case that mercenaries from Philip were used in 343, the acquittal of Aeschines is, in the terms of Athenian political trials, inexplicable.

So even if one had only Demosthenes' speeches, one should hesitate to assert that Philip was infringing the Peace between 344 and 342. But there is also a powerful indication that he was not. When Hegesippus in early 342 delivered the final answer to Philip's proposal to negotiate the Peace, he claimed as proof of Philip's insincerity that he had installed in Pherae in Thessaly a Macedonian garrison, had incorporated in the Molossian kingdom three inland cities of north-western Greece, and was campaigning against Ambracia. If Philip had done the dastardly deeds of which Demosthenes had accused him, why should Hegesippus have been scraping the bucket for these remote and debatable matters? Why is there nothing said about Megara or, even more serious for Athens, Euboea, a bridge into Greece? Demosthenes vaguely asserted in 343 "there are soldiers in Euboea," by implication Philip's, but not a word on this subject passed Hegesippus' lips. It would be confidently alleged in due course that Macedonian soldiers were in Euboea, but in 343 there were almost certainly none. Otherwise Hegesippus would have said so. He did not refrain from the empty Demosthenic claptrap about the Thracian forts. Why should he have renounced his real "proofs"?

The truth is that between 344 and 342 Philip did not intervene in Greece or infringe the Peace. Demosthenes lied. Perhaps in a good cause, but he lied. So should not the Athenians have taken Philip's offer seriously?

But, it might be asked in Demosthenes' defence, had not Philip in 346 refused to entertain the notion of a Common Peace? Why should the Athenians have taken the offer seriously in 344? The Synod of the Second Athenian Confederacy in

346 had proposed a peace that all Greeks could join, a Common Peace, and Aeschines had vainly sought to advance it, but their purpose was to make it possible for Phocis to join and so secure safety. Philip would not have peace with Phocis, as Demosthenes knew, and the idea of a Common Peace was dropped in hopes of saving Phocis by other means. But in the two following years Philip had perhaps learned that he had been too optimistic. If he was himself to offer security against aggression by Sparta or any other states, he would be accused of seeking to dominate Greece. Some other system must be tried, and a Common Peace with a sanctions clause may have seemed to him worth attempting.

No Athenian, of course, in the crucial assembly of 343 could be sure of what exactly Philip would accept. It was to be presumed that Philip would require some share in the joint arrangements. By the League of Corinth of 337 Macedonian power was, as we shall see, enthroned within Greece itself. After the disaster of Chaeronea nothing else was possible. But in 344 something was to be expected more akin to the Common Peaces established under the influence of the Great King. Outrageous as they had been to Panhellenist sentiment, they had served Greece well enough. At any rate the hegemon, the Great King, had never sent military forces into Greece, and even Isocrates had come to see some virtue in the peaces dictated by Persia; in 355 he even advocated that the system of the King's Peace be restored. Under that system the Greeks had been left to keep order amongst themselves under the patronage (prostasia) of either one or two leading states, and the hegemon need never intervene. Would Philip have tolerated such a state of affairs? No one could tell until negotiations began. Yet there was the possibility, even the hope. Aeschines cherished it. Demosthenes and the war-party destroyed it—an act of great political folly.

For Demosthenes had no alternative other than a war, which Athens could not win. The war for Amphipolis had proved that she could not succeed in containing Philip in Macedon even before the great increase in Macedonian strength which the eastward extension of the kingdom had brought, let alone succeed in destroying him. Demosthenes however had learned nothing— Athens, he supposed, could return to plundering

and ravaging much of Philip's land, and "a multitude else." It had all been tried before and found ineffective. Worse still, since 346 Philip had kept a garrison in Nicaea, the town that dominated Thermopylae, and had open access to Greece. How was he to be kept out of Attica itself?

It is the axiom of apologists for Demosthenes that he had in mind that, come Armageddon for Athens, she would not fight alone, that he could count on the support of the leading military power of Greece, the Thebans. Demosthenes was the so-called *proxenos* of Thebes at Athens (i.e. the Greek equivalent of a consular representative), who not only provided hospitality for Theban ambassadors to Athens but also could be counted on to speak on their behalf whenever the interests of Athens did not plainly forbid him. In his speech *On the Crown* Demosthenes began his defence of his conduct in making the Theban alliance in 339/8 by declaring that despite the influence of "Philippizers" in Thebes and Athens he had continually sought to prevent the two cities becoming embroiled with each other; in early 352 in the speech For the Megalopolitans he had envisaged in extreme circumstances alliance with Thebes; and at Pella in 346 he had tried to prevent Aeschines attacking the Thebans in his speech to Philip. So was Demosthenes so blind strategically? Or did he in 344 foresee the alliance of Chaeronea, confident that Athens would not fight alone?

It might be comforting to be able to think more highly of Demosthenes' strategic sense, but study of the speeches does not permit it. If we did not know that Demosthenes was Theban *proxenos*, we could never guess it from the speech On the Megalopolitans; alliance with Thebes is envisaged only as a wild paradox; elsewhere he argues that Athens' advantage lay in the weakening of Thebes. In the case of The Second Philippic, far from suspecting that Demosthenes was Theban proxenos, one would suppose that he was a bitter opponent of Thebes; Thebes was on Philip's side which was only to be expected from the state that had betrayed Greece to Persia in 480; there was nothing to be said for the restoration in 346 of the captured Boeotian cities; any suspicions of trouble between Thebes and Philip were to be discredited; the Thebans were being nurtured out of hostility to Athens. All this would have been very curious if in the act of preferring the path to war Demosthenes was hoping for Theban alliance. In 343 in his attack on Aeschines he played on the theme of Theban hubris, a mixture of insolence and violence. In the speeches of 341 the slanderous references to Thebes are not to be found, but there is no break in the ice. The Thebans are thought of as on Philip's side, which they increasingly were not, and when Demosthenes calls for embassies to be sent all over the Greek world, he lists a number of places, ending with the paradox of appealing to the Great King, but there is not a word of Thebes. It may be countered that Thebes was so hated at Athens that he dared not reveal his ultimate plans. There is indeed a time and a place for revealing plans, but, if Demosthenes had been nurturing hopes of the Theban alliance, he missed the vital moment. Early in 339 the Thebans seized control of Thermopylae, a very serious blow against Philip, but events of the following months were to show that there was a strong party in Thebes not prepared to fight Philip, and the making of the alliance was a close-run thing later in the year. The moment to act was when Thermopylae was seized, but Demosthenes uttered not a word of his alleged great hope until the news came that Philip had marched into Phocis. In that perplexed moment, when no one rose to speak, when there seemed nothing to say or to be done, Demosthenes came forward and proposed the Theban alliance. A curious hope indeed to have nurtured, if it could not be advanced by a single word until the moment of despair had come. The truth is that either he did not nurture it but conceived it at the very last moment, or it was so utterly impracticable that it could not be unveiled.

If one studies Demosthenes' answer to Philip's declaration of war in late summer 340, a solemn truth emerges. Demosthenes was not putting his trust in a Theban alliance. Thebes is declared to have become lukewarm towards Philip; there is no suggestion that she should be stimulated to seize Thermopylae or in any way become hot for the liberty of Greece. Demosthenes' real hope lay in his city's good Fortune. "For Fortune is of great weight, nay, is all important in all the affairs of men"—a theme echoing what he has often enough declared before. In 341 he let out an illuminating comment about choosing "a policy in which Fortune prevails more than reasoned judgements." His hope was in the name of Fortune, and "Fortune" echoes through his great apology, *On the Crown*. The word occurs there no less than twenty-six times. "Fortune" was to blame for what had happened. He had thought all and done all that could be thought and done, but Fortune had failed them. He had bet on Fortune and had lost.

Demosthenes was, in a sense, the hero of a tragedy of his own making. The end of his policy was, as Polybius pointed out, the disaster of Chaeronea. But a defence might be made in these terms. It is better to die in liberty than live without it. There was a greater danger to Greece than any danger ever mentioned in the speeches of Demosthenes. It was the danger that Greece would be passed by and the assault on Persia succeed. Every step that a Macedonian king took on the road to the heart of the Persian Empire was that much more territory and power for Macedon. If Phoenicia, the seat of Persian naval power, were to be taken, Athens and her fleet would be irrelevant and dispensable. So perhaps it was better to have sudden death in Greece than to suffer the long strangulation of any sort of Macedonian peace? That is a hard question indeed. But, if Philip attacked Persia, there was hope that Greece might yet be free—not so much that Persia alone would destroy the Macedonian power, but that preoccupation with war against Persia would afford the opportunity for Greece to revolt. United in and by a Common Peace, they might have succeeded. As it was, the revolt of Thebes in 335 and of Sparta in 331 were unsupported. The great land-powers were destroyed one after the other. The final revolt of the Lamian War on the death of Alexander put an end to Athenian naval supremacy forever. All might have been different if Demosthenes and the war party had tempered their plans in 344 and explored Philip's offer to consider amending the Peace. The Greek cause was not hopeless. Demosthenes' policy was.

Consider

1. Why does Droysen think Philip sought to dominate Greece and make Macedon a great power? On what grounds does he criticize Demosthenes?
2. How does he view the consequences of an Athenian and Greek victory over Macedon? In what ways would it have been unsatisfactory?
3. What is Pickard-Cambridge's chief reason for praising Demosthenes?
4. What does he say was Polybius' argument against Demosthenes' complaints against the Greeks who cooperated with Philip?
5. How does he defend Demosthenes?
6. How does he explain the failure of Demosthenes' policy?
7. What made his policy unpopular in Athens?
8. What faults does he find in Demosthenes? How does he weigh them against his virtues?
9. How does Cawkwell evaluate Philip's purposes? Those of Demosthenes?
10. How does his critique of Demosthenes differ from that of Droysen?
11. How does he characterize the policy of Eubulus? Why did Demosthenes object to it?
12. What were Demosthenes' complaints in the *First Philippic*?
13. How does Cawkwell treat Demosthenes' proposed response to Philip's actions in the Chalcidice involving Olynthus?
14. What problem did Athens face in regard to Euboea?
15. What was Demosthenes' proposed policy in regard to Euboea? How does Cawkwell criticize it? On what does Cawkwell say Demosthenes relied for Athenian success? Is he right? Are there alternate explanations?
16. What course does Cawkwell think would have been better than the one urged by Demosthenes? Can you think of any objections to it?
17. What were Philip's goals in Greece?
18. If Philip's goals were not aggressive from the beginning; how did it happen that Philip conquered the Greek city-states and subjected them, ending their independence forever?

CHAPTER 13
ALEXANDER THE GREAT

❧

FEW, IF ANY, FIGURES have had as great an impact on the course of history as Philip II's son Alexander III. For the past two centuries, scholars have debated what type of man was Alexander the Great. For example, was he a philosopher, a pragmatic politician, or a humanitarian hoping to establish universal peace? Or was he a megalomaniac driven by a strong desire (*pothos*) to rule a world empire? Did Alexander really believe he was a god?

Alexander became king of Macedon at the age of 20 after Philip was murdered in 336 BC. He inherited not only the throne but also his father's ambition to conquer Asia Minor from the Persian Empire. Whatever the ultimate aims of Philip might have been, Alexander led his army as far south as Egypt, to the north of Bactria/Sogdiana and east to the Indus River. During his proclaimed quest to avenge the Greeks against Persia for the Trojan War and Xerxes' invasion of Greece in 480 BC, he did not suffer a single defeat. When he died at the age of 32, he had already conquered nearly the entire known world east of Greece. Had he lived long enough, it seems certain that Alexander would have advanced West to subdue Italy and Carthage. He saw himself as a second Achilles and attained the status of a god during his campaign. By the time he had reached the Hyphasis River, Alexander had changed the world irrevocably. He had spread the Greek language and civilization over the vast area he had conquered and had caused a radical cultural change in the Near East. He created a model for the later Hellenistic kings to emulate. Romans such as Julius Caesar and Augustus measured their success next to that of Alexander. And the spread of Christianity would have been difficult to imagine without him.

Despite or maybe because of the magnitude of his achievements students of Alexander have come up with a remarkable range of assessments of him. The first major modern study of the meteoric career of Alexander was the biography by Droysen. The events of Droysen's era in mid-nineteenth-century Germany heavily influenced him. For Droysen, Philip and Alexander had unified the quarrelling Greek city-states through conquest, just as he strove for the unification of the German peoples under the strong leadership of Prussia. Alexander was the ideal figure who had fused Greek and Oriental cultures and spread the civilizing force of Hellenism throughout the world. Perhaps the most famous and certainly the most debated of the many Alexanders inspired by Droysen in the twentieth century was that of Tarn. Badian describes Tarn as "Droysen translated into the King's English." But the Alexander of Tarn, who wrote in the wake of the League of Nations, not only unified Greece and diffused Hellenic culture but also sought to establish world peace and unity. This visionary Alexander rejected the advice of Aristotle to rule the Greeks as free men but the barbarians as slaves. Instead, Alexander had a divine mission to harmonize men in general and act as a reconciler of the world. On the other hand, Nazi Germany influenced the Alexander of Badian. He portrays Alexander as a paranoid and ruthless tyrant who ruled by terror. Even a brief sketch

Alexander and Darius. King Darius III looks back in distress as Alexander advances against his vanguard during the battle of Issus, as depicted in a Roman mosaic from the first century BC.

of scholarship on Alexander seems to validate Ulrich Wilcken's suggestion that "every student has an Alexander of his own." This chapter presents some of the relatively recent work on Alexander and examines how it tends, following Badian's lead, to reject the hero worship of Droysen and Tarn.

Ancient Sources

1. Arrian: *History of Alexander*, 4.9–19, THE INTRODUCTION OF *PROSKYNESIS*
2. Arrian: *History of Alexander*, 7.4.4–7.6.5, THE SUSA WEDDING (324 BC)
3. Arrian: *History of Alexander*, 7.8.1–3; 7.10.5; 7.11.1–7.12.4, THE MUTINY AT OPIS
4. Plutarch: *Moralia*, 329AD, THE POLICY OF FUSION
5. Fragments of the Lost Alexander Historians

Opinions of Modern Scholars

1. From W. W. Tarn, "Alexander the Great and the Unity of Mankind"
2. From W. W. Tarn, *Alexander the Great* 1
3. From A. B. Bosworth, "Alexander and the Iranians"
4. From Peter Green, *Alexander of Macedon, 356–323 B.C.: A Historical Biography*
5. From Paul Cartledge, "Alexander the Man"

ANCIENT SOURCES ON ALEXANDER THE GREAT

There are two main problems in dealing with the literary sources for the reign of Alexander. First, all the accounts written during his lifetime or shortly after his death have perished. Second, the surviving narratives were not only written centuries after the events they describe but also reflect widely different moral viewpoints.

Historians generally divide the ancient sources for Alexander into two groups. On the one hand, the writings of Diodorus, Trogus, and Curtius comprise the Vulgate tradition. Cleitarchus, a contemporary but not an eyewitness of Alexander's campaigns, is the ultimate source for the Vulgate writers. On the other hand, Arrian is the main extant source that represents the alternative tradition on Alexander. He based his account on the writings of three of the historians who travelled with Alexander on campaign: Ptolemy, Aristobulus, and Nearchus. In addition to the two groups of writers is Plutarch who stands apart from both the Vulgate tradition and the alternative sources.

In order to attempt an overall assessment of Alexander it is helpful to examine first his policies. Scholars think certain events in the career of Alexander the Great help demonstrate whether or not he aimed at a policy of racial fusion and universal brotherhood. The following are the most remarkable examples.

1. THE INTRODUCTION OF *PROSKYNESIS*

Persian kings traditionally required that their subjects prostrate themselves before them. Alexander, as Lord of Asia, attempted to introduce this practice at Bactra in 327 for both Macedonians and Persians.

4.9.7. Some say that Anaxarchus the Sophist came by summons to Alexander to offer consolation [to Alexander, who regretted his killing of Clitus], and finding him groaning on his bed, laughed at him and said that he had not learnt why the old philosophers made Justice sit by the throne of Zeus, because whatever is determined by Zeus is done with Justice; so too the acts of a great King should be held just, first by the king himself and then by the rest of mankind. **[8]** These words are said to have consoled Alexander for the time, but I say that he did Alexander even greater harm than the affliction he then suffered from, if indeed he gave this opinion as that of a sage, that the duty of the king is not to act justly after earnest consideration, but that anything done by a king in any form is to be accounted just. **[9]** The fact is that the report prevails that Alexander desired people actually to do him obeisance, from the underlying idea that his father was Ammon and not Philip, and as he was now expressing his admiration for the ways of the Persians and Medes, both in his change of dress and in addition by the altered arrangements for his attendance, and that even as to obeisance there was no lack of flatterers to give him his wish, among whom the most prominent were Anaxarchus and Agis of Argos, an epic poet, two of the sophists at his court.

4.10.1. It is said that Callisthenes of Olynthus, a past pupil of Aristotle, and with something of the boor in his character, did not approve of this, and here I myself agree with Callisthenes; on the other hand I think Callisthenes went beyond reason, if the record is true, in declaring that Alexander and his exploits depended on him and his history; **[2]** it was not he who had come to win fame from Alexander, but it would be his work to make Alexander renowned among men; and again, that Alexander's share in divinity did not depend on Olympias' invention about his birth, but on the account he would write and publish in Alexander's interest. **[3]** Some too have recorded that Philotas once asked him whom he thought to be held in highest honour by the Athenians; and he replied, Harmodius and Aristogiton, because they slew one of the two tyrants, and destroyed the tyranny...

4.10.5. As to Callisthenes' opposition to Alexander regarding obeisance, the following story is also prevalent. It had been agreed between Alexander and the Sophists and the most illustrious of the Persians and Medes at his court that mention of this topic should be introduced at a wine party. **[6]** Anaxarchus began the subject, saying that it would be far more just to reckon Alexander a god than Dionysus and Heracles, not so much because of the magnitude and nature of

Alexander's achievements, but also because Dionysus was a Theban, and had no connection with Macedon, and Heracles an Argive, also unconnected with Macedon, except for Alexander's family, for he was descended from Heracles; **[7]** but that Macedonians in their turn would be more justified in paying the respect of divine honours to their own king; in any case there was no doubt that when Alexander had departed from men they would honour him as a god; how much more just, then, that they should give him his due in life rather than when he was dead and the honour would profit him nothing.

4.11.1. When Anaxarchus had said this and the like, those who shared in the scheme approved his argument and were actually ready to begin doing obeisance, but the Macedonians for the most part were opposed to it, though silent. **[2]** Callisthenes broke in and said: "Anaxarchus, I declare Alexander unworthy of no honour appropriate for a man; but men have used numerous ways of distinguishing all the honours which are appropriate for men and for gods; thus we build temples and erect images and set aside precincts for the gods, and we offer them sacrifices and libations and compose hymns to them, while eulogies are for men; but the most important distinction concerns the matter of obeisance. **[3]** At greeting men receive a kiss, but what is divine, I suppose because it is seated above us and we are forbidden even to touch it, is for that very reason honoured by obeisance; dances, too, are held for the gods, and paeans sung in their praise. In this distinction there is nothing surprising, since among the gods themselves all are not honoured in the same way; and what is more, there are different honours for the heroes, distinct again from those paid to gods. **[4]** It is not, therefore, proper to confuse all this, by raising mortals to extravagant proportions by excesses of honour, while bringing the gods, as far as men can, down to a demeaning and unfitting level by honouring them in the same way as men. So Alexander himself would not endure it for a moment, if some private person were to thrust himself into the royal honours **[5]** by unjust election or vote, and the gods would have far better cause to be displeased with any men who thrust themselves or permit others to thrust them into divine honours. Alexander both is and is thought to be above all measure the bravest of the brave, most kingly of kings, most worthy to command of all commanders. **[6]** As for you, Anaxarchus, you above all should

have expounded these arguments and stopped those on the other side, as you are attending on Alexander as philosopher and instructor. It was improper for you to take the lead in this topic; you should rather have remembered that you are not attending nor advising a Cambyses or Xerxes [i.e., a Persian despot] but a son of Philip, a descendant of Heracles and of Aeacus, whose forefathers came from Argos to Macedonia, and have continued to rule the Macedonians not by force but in accordance with custom. **[7]** Even Heracles himself did not receive divine honours from the Greeks in his own lifetime, nor even after his death till the god of Delphi gave his sanction to honouring him as a god. If, however, we must think like barbarians, as we are speaking in their country, even so I appeal personally to you, Alexander, to remember Greece, on whose behalf you made your whole expedition, to annex Asia to Greece. **[8]** Consider this too; when you return there, will you actually compel the Greeks as well, the freest of mankind, to do you obeisance, or will you keep away from the Greeks, but put this dishonour on the Macedonians, or will you yourself make a distinction once for all in this matter of honours and receive from Greeks and Macedonians honours of a human and Greek style, and barbarian honours only from barbarians? **[9]** But if it is said of Cyrus son of Cambyses that he was the first of men to receive obeisance and that therefore this humiliation became traditional with Persians and Medes, you must remember that this very Cyrus was brought to his senses by Scythians, a people poor but free, Darius too by other Scythians, Xerxes by Athenians and Lacedaemonians, and Artaxerxes by Clearchus, Xenophon and their Ten Thousand, and Darius by Alexander here, who does not receive obeisance."

4.12.1. By these and the like words Callisthenes greatly provoked Alexander, but pleased the Macedonians, and realizing this, Alexander sent and told the Macedonians to think no more of obeisance. **[2]** When, however, a silence fell after these words, the senior Persians arose and did obeisance one by one. Leonnatus, one of the Companions, thinking that one of the Persians made his obeisance ungracefully, mocked his posture as abject; Alexander was angry with him at the time, though reconciled later. The following story has also been recorded. **[3]** Alexander sent round a loving cup of gold, first to those with whom he had made an agreement about obeisance; the first who drank from it rose, did obeisance, and received a kiss from Alexander, and this went round all in turn. **[4]** But when the pledge came to Callisthenes, he rose, drank from the cup, went up to Alexander and made to kiss him without having done obeisance. At the moment Alexander was talking to Hephaestion, and therefore was not attending to see whether the ceremony of obeisance had been carried out by Callisthenes himself. **[5]** But as Callisthenes approached to kiss Alexander, Demetrius son of Pythonax, one of the Companions, remarked that he was coming without having done obeisance. Alexander did not permit Callisthenes to kiss him; and Callisthenes remarked, "I shall go away short of a kiss."

4.12.6. In these incidents I do not at all approve either of Alexander's arrogance at the time or of Callisthenes' tactlessness, but in fact I think it enough for a man to show moderation in his own individual conduct, and that he should be ready to exalt royalty as far as practicable, once he has consented to attend on a king. **[7]** So I think that Alexander's hostility to Callisthenes was not unreasonable in view of his untimely freedom of speech and arrogant folly, and on this account I infer that Callisthenes' detractors were readily believed that he had a part in the plot laid against Alexander by his pages…

Questions

1. **Why did Alexander introduce the practice of *proskynesis* at his court?**
2. **What points did Anaxarchus make in his speech in favor of deeming Alexander a god?**
3. **Detail the arguments Callisthenes made against the proposal of Anaxarchus. What is Arrian's opinion on the matter?**

---

2.   THE SUSA WEDDING (324 BC)

7.4.4. He [Alexander] also held weddings at Susa for himself and for the Companions; he himself married Darius' eldest daughter Barsine, and, as Aristobulus says, another wife as well, Parysatis, the youngest daughter of Ochus. He had already taken to wife Roxane, the daughter of Oxyartes the Bactrian. **[5]** To Hephaestion he gave Drypetis, another daughter of Darius, sister to his own wife (for he desired Hephaestion's children to be cousins to his own); to Craterus, Amastrine daughter of Oxyartes, Darius' brother; to Perdiccas, a daughter of Atropates, satrap [governor] of Media; **[6]** to Ptolemy the bodyguard and Eumenes the royal secretary, the daughters of Artabazus, Artacama and Artonis respectively; to Nearchus the daughter of Barsine and Mentor; to Seleucus the daughter of Spitamenes the Bactrian, and similarly to the other Companions the noblest daughters of Persians and Medes, numbering about eighty. These weddings were solemnized in the Persian style; **[7]** chairs were placed for the bridegrooms in order, then, after the healths had been drunk, the brides came in and each sat down by the side of her bridegroom,

and the men took them by the hand and kissed them, the king setting the example, for all the weddings took place together. None of Alexander's actions was thought to show more affability and comradeship. **[8]** After receiving his bride each bridegroom led her home. Alexander gave them all dowries. All other Macedonians who had married Asian women had their names registered by Alexander's orders; they proved to be more than ten thousand, and Alexander gave them too wedding gifts.

7.5.1. He thought this a convenient moment to discharge all the debts any of his soldiers had incurred and ordered each man to register what he owed, on the basis that they would receive the money. At first only a few registered their names in the fear that Alexander had merely tried an experiment, to see which soldiers had not lived on their pay and which had been extravagant; **[2]** but when he was informed that most were not registering their names but concealing any bonds, he reproved the troops for not trusting him; the king, he said, must always speak the truth to his subjects, and none of the subjects must ever suppose that the king speaks anything but the truth. **[3]** He set up tables in the camp with gold on them and instructed the persons who were to administer the grants to discharge the debts to all who produced a bond, without any further registration of names. As a result they actually came to believe that Alexander was speaking the truth, and they were more gratified by the concealment of their names than by the extinction of the debts. This grant to the army is said to have amounted to twenty thousand Talents...

7.6.1. [Alexander] was also joined by the satraps from the new cities he had founded, and the other land he had conquered, bringing about thirty thousand boys now growing up, all of the same age, whom Alexander called Epigoni (Successors), dressed in Macedonian dress and trained to warfare in the Macedonian style. **[2]** It is said that their arrival aggrieved the Macedonians, as if Alexander was actually contriving every means of reducing his dependence on Macedonians in future, that in fact they were greatly pained to see Alexander wearing the Median dress, while the marriages celebrated in the Persian style did not correspond to the desires of most of them, including even some of the bridegrooms, despite the great honour of being raised to equality with the king. **[3]** They were also aggrieved at the adoption by Peucestas, satrap of Persia, of the Persian apparel and language because Alexander approved of him going barbarian; at the incorporation of the Bactrian, Sogdianian, Arachotian, Zarangian, Areian and Parthyaean cavalrymen and of the Persian troopers called Euacae in the Companion cavalry, in so far as they seemed to be specially distinguished by rank, physical beauty or any other good quality; **[4]** at the addition to these of a fifth hipparchy [cavalry unit], though it was not entirely barbarian, but when the whole cavalry force had been augmented, barbarians had been enrolled for the purpose; at the further enrolment in the *agema* [royal guard] of Cophen, son of Artabazus, Hydarnes and Artiboles, sons of Mazaeus, Sisines and Phradasmenes, Sons of Phrataphernes, satrap of Parthyaea and Hyrcania, **[5]** Itanes, son of Oxyartes and brother of Alexander's wife, Roxane, and Aegobares and his brother, Mithrobaeus, at the appointment of Hystaspes the Bactrian as their commander, and at the issue to them of Macedonian lances in place of barbarian thonged javelins. All this aggrieved the Macedonians, as they thought that Alexander was going utterly barbarian at heart, and treating Macedonian customs and Macedonians themselves without respect.

Questions

1. **What do you think Alexander was aiming at with the wedding at Susa?**
2. **Was each of his actions described above consistent with that policy? Explain why or why not.**

---

3. THE MUTINY AT OPIS

Alexander held a banquet of reconciliation after the mutiny at Opis in 324. It was here that he prayed for harmony among races.

7.8.1. On reaching Opis, [Alexander] summoned his Macedonians and announced that he was discharging from the army and sending home men unfit for active service because of old age or physical disability. He would give those who remained with him enough to make them objects of envy to those at home, and stir up the rest of the Macedonians to readiness for sharing the same dangers and hardships. **[2]** Alexander said this, no doubt, to show his favour to the Macedonians. But they supposed that they were by now objects of his contempt and that he thought them wholly useless in his wars; they were, not without reason, aggrieved once more by the speech he had delivered. In the whole of their expedition they had had many sources of discontent; on many previous occasions they had been vexed by his Persian dress, which suggested the same thing, by the equipment of the barbarian Epigoni in Macedonian style and the introduction of foreign horsemen in the ranks of the Companions. [3] Consequently, they did not endure in silence, but called on him to discharge them all from the army, and to campaign himself in company with his father, referring in mockery to Ammon. Hearing this Alexander, who had become by this time quicker-tempered and, courted as he now was in the barbarian manner, had ceased to be so kindly as in old times to the Macedonians, leapt down from the platform with the officers round him and ordered them to arrest the most conspicuous of the popular agitators, personally pointing out to the hypaspists [elite infantry] with his finger whom they were to arrest; they numbered about thirteen. He ordered them to be led away to execution but, as the others were stunned and remained in dead silence, he remounted the platform and spoke as follows…

7.10.5. "And now it was my intention to send away only men unfit for war, to be the envy of those at home but, as you all desire to go, let all of you begone, return to your homes and report that your king, Alexander, defeated Persians, Medes…and that when you returned to Susa you deserted him and went off, handing him over to the protection of the barbarians he had conquered. This is a report that will perhaps win you a fine reputation with men and will doubtless be holy in the sight of heaven. Begone!"

7.11.1. After his speech he leapt down swiftly from his platform and, passing into the palace, paid no attention to his bodily needs, and was not seen by any of the Companions, not even on the following day. But on the third day he summoned inside the picked men among the Persians and divided the commands of the battalions among them and restricted the right to kiss him to those he declared his kinsmen. [2] The Macedonians had been immediately stunned by his speech, and stayed in silence there by the platform, none following the king when he left except for the attendant Companions and bodyguards; but the mass, though they stayed behind, had nothing to say and yet were unwilling to depart. [3] But when they heard about the Persians and the Medes, and the commands given to the Persians, and the Oriental force being drafted into the units, and the Macedonian names—an *agema* called Persian, and Persian "foot companions," and *astheteroi* [royal guard] too, and a Persian

battalion of "silver-shields," and the cavalry of the Companions which now included a new royal *agema*—[4] they could no longer contain themselves, but all ran together to the palace and, throwing down their arms there before the doors as signs of supplication to the king, they themselves stood shouting before the doors begging to be let in. They said they would give up the instigators of the late disturbance and those who began the clamour; they would depart from the doors neither by day nor by night unless Alexander would have some pity on them.

7.11.5. When this was reported to Alexander, he quickly came out, and seeing them so humble, and hearing most of them lamenting loudly, he too shed tears. He came forward as if to say something, while they stayed there in supplication. [6] One of them called Callines, a man distinguished by age and hipparchy in the Companions' cavalry, said something like this: "What grieves the Macedonians, Sire, is that you have now made some of the Persians your kinsmen and that Persians are called 'Alexander's kinsmen,' and permitted to kiss you, but no Macedonian has yet enjoyed this privilege." [7] On this Alexander broke in: "But I regard all of you as my kinsmen, and from this time forth I shall give you that name." When he had said this, Callines approached and kissed him, and so did any other who wished. So they took up their arms again and returned to the camp shouting and singing their victory song. [8] On this Alexander sacrificed to the gods to whom it was his custom to sacrifice, and gave a public banquet, seated all the Macedonians round him, and next to them Persians, and then any persons from the other peoples who took precedence for rank or any other high quality, and he himself and those around him drank from the same bowl and poured the same libations, with the Greek soothsayers and Magi initiating the ceremony. [9] Alexander prayed for various blessings and especially that the Macedonians and Persians should enjoy harmony as partners in the government. The story prevails that those who shared the banquet were nine thousand, and that they all poured the same libation and gave the one victory cry as they did so.

7.12.1. And now such of the Macedonians as were unfit for service from old age or any other circumstance were ready to leave him; they numbered about ten thousand. Alexander gave them the pay due not only for the time already served but also for that of their journey home; in addition he also gave each man a gratuity of a Talent. **[2]** If they had children by Asian wives, he ordered them to leave them behind with him, and not take home to Macedonia a source of conflict between foreigners and children of foreign wives and the children and mothers they had left behind them; he promised personally to see that they were brought up in the Macedonian way, particularly in military training; when they were grown to manhood, he would take them back himself to Macedonia and hand them over to their fathers. **[3]** While making these vague and uncertain promises to them at their departure, he also thought fit to give them the most solid proof of his love and affection for them by sending with them Craterus, his most loyal follower, whom he loved as dearly as his own life, to protect and lead them on their march. So then having bidden them all farewell, with tears in his eyes, and tears in theirs, he dismissed them. **[4]** Craterus was not only appointed to be their leader but, after conducting them back, he was to take charge of Macedonia, Thrace, Thessaly and the freedom of the Greeks, while Antipater was to bring drafts of Macedonians of full age to replace the men being sent home. He also despatched Polyperchon with Craterus, as the officer next in seniority to Craterus, so that in case of harm coming to Craterus on the way, since he was an invalid when sent off, they should not want a general on their route.

Questions

1. **Why did Alexander dismiss his troops?**
2. **Discuss the intention of Alexander's speech in the context of each of his actions in Arrian's account of the mutiny at Opis.**

4. THE POLICY OF FUSION

MOREOVER, THE MUCH-ADMIRED *Republic* of Zeno, the founder of the Stoic sect, may be summed up in this one main principle: that all the inhabitants of this world of ours should not live differentiated by their respective rules of justice into separate cities and communities, but that we should consider all men to be of one community and one polity, and that we should have a common life and an order common to us all, even as a herd that feeds together and shares the pasturage of a common field. This Zeno wrote, giving shape to a dream or, as it were, shadowy picture of a well-ordered and philosophic commonwealth; but it was Alexander who gave effect to the idea. For Alexander did not follow Aristotle's advice to treat the Greeks as if he were their leader, and other peoples as if he were their master; to have regard for the Greeks as for friends and kindred, but to conduct himself toward other peoples as though they were plants or animals; for to do so would have been to cumber his leadership with numerous battles and banishments and festering seditions. But, as he believed that he came as a heaven-sent governor to all, and as a mediator for the whole world, those whom he could not persuade to unite with him, he conquered by force of arms, and he brought together into one body all men everywhere, uniting and mixing in one great loving-cup, as it were, men's lives, their characters, their marriages, their very habits of life. He bade them all consider as their fatherland the whole inhabited earth, as their stronghold and protection his camp, as akin to them all good men, and as foreigners only the wicked; they should not distinguish between Grecian and foreigner by Grecian cloak and targe, or scimitar and jacket; but the distinguishing mark of the Grecian should be seen in virtue, and that of the foreigner in iniquity; clothing and food, marriage and manner of life they should regard as common to all, being blended into one by ties of blood and children…

> **Questions**
>
> 1. **What advice did Aristotle give Alexander about dealing with Greeks and barbarians?**
> 2. **In what ways does Plutarch's account of Alexander agree with that of Arrian?**
> 3. **How do you account for the differences between the two writers?**

5. FRAGMENTS OF THE LOST ALEXANDER HISTORIANS

87. Chares of Mytilene says that once at a banquet Alexander, after drinking, handed the cup to one of his friends, and he, on receiving it, rose up so as to face the household shrine, and when he had drunk, first made obeisance to Alexander, then kissed him, and then resumed his place upon the couch. As all the guests were doing this in turn, Callisthenes took the cup, the king not paying attention, but conversing with Hephaestion, and after he had drunk went towards the king to kiss him; but Demetrius, surnamed Pheido, cried: "O King, do not accept his kiss, for he alone has not done thee obeisance." So Alexander declined the kiss, at which Callisthenes exclaimed in a loud voice: "Well, then, I'll go away the poorer by a kiss" (**Chares, *FGrH* 125 F 14a = Nut. *Alex.* 54.4–6**).

88. The following account has also been given: Alexander drank from a golden goblet the health of the circle of guests, and handed it first to those with whom he had concerted the ceremony of prostration. The first who drank from the goblet rose up and performed the act of prostration, and received a kiss from him. This ceremony proceeded from one to another in due order. But when the pledging of health came to the turn of Callisthenes, he rose up and drank from the goblet, and drew near, wishing to kiss the king without performing the act of prostration. Alexander happened then to be conversing with Hephaestion, and consequently did not observe whether Callisthenes performed the ceremony completely or not. But when Callisthenes was approaching to kiss him, Demetrius, son of Pythonax, one of the Companions, said that he was doing so without having prostrated himself. So the king would not permit him to kiss him; whereupon the philosopher said: "I am going away only with

the loss of a kiss" (**Chares, *FGrH* 125 F 14b = Arr. 4.12.3–5**).

89. But Alexander...neither laid hands upon these women, nor did he know any other before marriage, except Barsine. This woman, Memnon's widow, was taken prisoner at Damascus. And since she had received a Greek education, and was of an agreeable disposition, and since her father, Artabanus, was son of a king's daughter, Alexander determined, at Parmenion's instigation as Aristobulus says, to attach himself to a woman of such high birth and beauty (**Aristobulus, *FGrH* 139 F 11 = Plut. *Alex.* 21.7–9**).

90. And Chares, in the tenth book of his *History of Alexander*, says: "When he took Darius prisoner, he celebrated a marriage feast for himself and his companions, having had ninety-two bedchambers prepared in the same place. There was a house built capable of containing a hundred couches; and in it every couch was adorned with wedding paraphernalia to the value of twenty minae, and was made of silver itself but his own bed had golden feet. And he also invited to the banquet which he gave, all his own private friends, and those he arranged opposite to himself and the other bridegrooms; and his forces also belonging to the army and navy, and all the ambassadors which were present, and all the other strangers who were staying at his court. And the apartment was furnished in the most costly and magnificent manner, with sumptuous garments and cloths, and beneath them were other cloths of purple, and scarlet, and gold. And, for the sake of solidity, pillars supported the tent, each twenty cubits long, plated all over with gold and silver, and inlaid with precious stones; and all around these were spread costly curtains embroidered with figures of animals, and with gold, having gold and silver curtain-rods. And the circumference of the court was four stades. And the banquet took place, beginning at the sound of a trumpet, at that marriage feast, and on other occasions whenever the king offered a solemn sacrifice, so that all the army knew it. And this marriage feast lasted five days. And a great number both of barbarians and Greeks brought contributions to it; and also some of the Indian tribes did so. And there were present some wonderful conjurors—Scymnus of Tarentum, and Philistides of Syracuse, and Heraclitus of Mitylene; after whom also Alexis of Tarentum, the rhapsodist, exhibited his skill. There came also harp-players, who played without singing—Cratinus of Methymne, and Aristonymus the Athenian, and Athenodorus the Teian. And Heraclitus the Tarentine played on the harp, accompanying himself with his voice, and so did Aristocrates the Theban. And of flute-players accompanied with song, there were present Dionysius of Heraclea, and Hyperbolus of Cyzicus. And of other flute-players there were the following,

who first of all played the air called The Pythian, and afterwards played with the choruses—Timotheus, Phrynichus, Caphesias, Diophantus, and also Evius the Chalcidian. And from this time forward, those who were formerly called Dionysio-colaces, were called Alexandro-colaces, on account of the extravagant liberality of their presents, with which Alexander was pleased. And there were also tragedians who acted—Thessalus, and Athenodorus, and Aristocritus; and of comic actors there were Lycon, and Phormion, and Ariston. There was also Phasimelus the harp-player. And the crowns sent by the ambassadors and by other people amounted in value to fifteen thousand talents" (**Chares, *FGrH* 125 F 4 = Athen. 12.538b–539a**).

91. In Susa also he celebrated both his own wedding and those of his companions. He himself married Barsine, the eldest daughter of Darius, and according to Aristobulus, besides her another, Parysatis, the youngest daughter of Ochus (**Aristobulus, *FGrH* 139 F 52 Arr. 7.4.4**).

Questions

1. **What do you think were the aims of Alexander in each of the actions described above?**
2. **Did Alexander strive for the brotherhood of man?**
3. **Were both the introduction of *proskynesis* and the wedding at Susa part of the same policy? Explain.**
4. **For what reasons might Alexander have adopted Persian dress and manners?**

OPINIONS OF MODERN SCHOLARS

ALEXANDER AND THE "UNITY OF MANKIND"

1. In his 1933 Raleigh Lecture "Alexander the Great and the Unity of Mankind," W. W. Tarn argued that in addition to his conquests Alexander deserves credit for a revolution in human thought. W. W. Tarn was a Fellow of the British Academy.

FROM W. W. TARN, "ALEXANDER THE GREAT AND THE UNITY OF MANKIND"

I MAY NOW SUM UP. We have followed down the line of kingship the theory that it was the business of a king to promote Homonoia among his subjects—all his subjects without distinction of race; and we have seen that this theory ought to be connected at the start with

some king, who must be later than Philip and earlier than Demetrius; and there is a definite tradition which connects the origin of the theory with Alexander. We have further seen that the intention to promote Homonoia among mankind, attributed in the tradition to Alexander, is certainly not a projection backwards from Stoicism, or apparently from anything else, while it is needed to explain certain things said by Theophrastus and done by Alexarchus. Lastly, we have seen the idea of the kinship or brotherhood of mankind appearing suddenly in Theophrastus and Alexarchus; their common source can be no one but Alexander, and again tradition supports this. Only one conclusion from all this seems possible: the things which, in the tradition, Alexander is supposed to have thought and said are, in substance, true. He did say that all men were Sons of God, that is brothers, but that God made the best ones peculiarly his own; he did aspire to be the harmonizer and reconciler of the world—that part of the world which his arm reached; he did have the intention of uniting the peoples of his empire in fellowship and concord and making them of one mind together; and when,

as a beginning, he prayed at Opis for partnership in rule and Homonoia between Macedonians and Persians, he meant what he said—not partnership in rule only, but true unity between them. I am only talking of theory, not of actions; but what this means is that he was the pioneer of one of the supreme revolutions in the world's outlook, the first man known to us who contemplated the brotherhood of man or the unity of mankind, whichever phrase we like to use. I do not claim to have given you exact proof of this; it is one of those difficult borderlands of history where one does not get proofs which could be put to a jury. But there is a very strong presumption indeed that it is true. Alexander, for the things he *did*, was called The Great; but if what I have said to-day be right, I do not think we shall doubt that this idea of his—call it a purpose, call it a dream, call it what you will—was the greatest thing about him.

2. Tarn interpreted the policies of Alexander in light of what he believed were his philosophical beliefs.

FROM W. W. TARN, *ALEXANDER THE GREAT* 1

The Susa Wedding

At Susa too a great feast was held to celebrate the conquest of the Persian empire, at which Alexander and 80 of his officers married girls of the Iranian aristocracy, he and Hephaestion wedding Darius' daughters Barsine and Drypetis. It was an attempt to promote the fusion of Europe and Asia by intermarriage. Little came of it, for many of the bridegrooms were soon to die, and many others repudiated their Asiatic wives after Alexander's death; Seleucus, who married Spitamenes' daughter Apama, probably an Achaemenid on her mother's side, was an honourable and politic exception. At the same time 10,000 of the troops married their native concubines. Alexander undertook to pay the army's debts, and invited all debtors to inscribe their names. It is significant of the growing tension between him and his men that they at once suspected that this was merely a trick to discover those who had exceeded their pay; he thereon paid all corners in cash without asking names. But the tension grew from another cause. The governors of the new cities came bringing for enrolment in the army the 30,000 native youths who had received Macedonian training; this inflamed the discontent

already aroused among the Macedonians by several of Alexander's acts, the enrolment of Asiatic cavalry in the Hipparchies and of Persian nobles in the *agema*, and the Persian dress worn by himself and Peucestas. Alexander, they felt, was no longer their own king, but an Asiatic ruler.

The Mutiny at Opis

It was soon afterwards, at Opis, that the discontent in the army came to a head. Alexander was not trying to oust the Macedonians from their ancestral partnership with him, but they thought he was; he only wished to take it up into something larger, but they distrusted the changes entailed by a new world, and especially his Persian policy. The occasion was his proposal to send home with Craterus any veterans past service. The Macedonians took this to mean that he intended to transfer the seat of power from Macedonia to Asia, and the whole army except his Guard, the *agema* of the Hypaspists, broke into open mutiny; all demanded to go home, and told him to go and campaign with his father Ammon. Alexander's temper rose; after ordering his Guard to arrest the ringleaders, he passionately harangued the troops and ended by dismissing the whole army from his service. "And now, as you all want to go, go, every one of you, and tell them at home that you deserted your king who had led you from victory to victory across the world, and left him to the care of the strangers he had conquered; and no doubt your words will win you the praises of men and the blessing of heaven. Go." Then, after shutting himself up for two days, he called the Persian leaders to him and began to form a Persian army, whose formations were to bear the old Macedonian names. This broke down the Macedonians; they gathered before his quarters, crying that they would not go away till he had pity on them. He came out and stood before them, with tears running down his face; one began to say "You have made Persians your kinsmen," and he broke in "But I make you all my kinsmen." The army burst into wild cheers; those who would kissed him; the reconciliation was complete. Those veterans who desired (10,000) were then sent home with large presents under Craterus' leadership.

But before they went, Alexander's reconciliation with the army had been followed by a greater reconciliation. He made a vast banquet—traditionally there were 9,000 guests—to celebrate the conclusion of peace; at his own table there sat Macedonians and Persians, the two protagonists in the great war, together with representatives of every race in his Empire and also Greeks, who were part of his world though not under his rule. The feast ended, all at his table drew wine for the libation from a huge silver crater which had once belonged to Darius, the crater which Eratosthenes or his informant was to figure as a loving-cup of the nations, and the whole 9,000 made libation together at the sound of a trumpet, as was Macedonian custom, the libation being led by Greek seers and Iranian Magi. The libation led up to, and was followed by, Alexander's prayer, in which the ceremony culminated. A few words of summary, and a brief allusion, are all that have reached us; but he prayed for peace, and that Macedonians and Persians and all the peoples of his Empire might be alike partners in the commonwealth (i.e. not merely subjects), and that the peoples of the world he knew might life together in harmony and in unity of heart and mind—that *Homonoia* which for centuries the world was to long for but never to reach. He had previously said that all men were sons of one Father, and his prayer was the expression of his recorded belief that he had a mission from God to be the Reconciler

of the World. Though none present could foresee it, that prayer was to be the crown of his career; he did not live to try to carry it out.

The Policy of Fusion

Next, Alexander's policy of the fusion of races. It was a great and courageous idea, which, as he planned it, failed. He might indeed fairly have supposed that his experiment in mixed marriages would be successful, for he only applied it to Asia and it only meant marriage between different branches of the white race. Greek blood had once been mixed with Anatolian with good results in Miletus and many other cities, as with Libyan (Berber) blood in Cyrene; Herodotus and Themistocles were half-breeds, while the intermarriage of Macedonian and Iranian was to produce that great organiser Antiochus I; but speaking broadly, the better-class Greeks and Macedonians now refused to cooperate. And it is doubtful whether, even had he lived, he could have carried out his idea of a joint commonwealth; for his system of Iranian satraps had broken down before he died. Of eighteen appointed, two soon died, one retired, and two are not again heard of but ten were either removed for incompetence or executed for murder of subjects or treason, and were replaced by Macedonians. The three who alone held office when Alexander died were doubtless good men; nevertheless Atropates certainly, and Oxyartes possibly, ended by founding independent Iranian kingdoms, while from Phrataphernes' satrapy of Parthia-Hyrcania came later the main Iranian reaction. In fact, Alexander had come into conflict with the idea of nationality, which was exhibited, not merely in the national war fought by Sogdiana, but in the way in which, even during his lifetime, independent states like Cappadocia and Armenia under Iranian rulers arose along the undefined northern limits of his empire. But of course, owing to his death, his policy never had a fair trial. The Seleucid kings indeed, half Sogdian in blood, were a direct outcome of that policy, and they did carry out parts of it; they transferred Europeans to Asia, employed, though sparingly, Asiatics in high position, and produced a marvellous mixture of east and west. But it was not done on Alexander's lines or in his spirit; the Macedonian meant to be, and was, the dominant race. What Alexander did achieve was again done through the cities, both his own and those which he inspired Seleucus to found, and it was a great enough achievement; the cities radiated Greek culture throughout Asia till ultimately the bulk of the upper classes over considerable districts became partially hellenised, and Demetrius of Bactria led Greeks for a second time beyond the Hindu Kush, to succeed for a moment where Alexander had failed and rule northern India for a few years from Pataliputra to Kathiawar. What Alexander did succeed in ultimately giving to parts of western Asia was not political equality with Greece, but community of culture.

* * *

The real impress that he left on the world was far different; for, whatever else he was, he was one of the supreme fertilising forces of history. He lifted the civilised world out of one groove and set it in another; he started a new epoch; nothing could again be as it had been. He greatly enlarged the bounds of knowledge and of human endeavour, and gave to Greek science and Greek civilisation a scope and an opportunity such as they had never yet possessed. Particularism was replaced by the idea of the "inhabited world," the common possession of civilised men; trade and commerce were internationalised, and the "inhabited world" bound together by a network both of new routes and cities, and of common interests. Greek culture, heretofore practically confined to Greeks, spread throughout that world; and for the use of its inhabitants, in place of the many dialects of Greece, there grew up the form of Greek known as the *koiné*, "common speech." The Greece that taught Rome was the Hellenistic world which Alexander made; the old Greece counted for little till modern scholars re-created Periclean Athens. So far as the modern world derives its civilisation from Greece, it largely owes it to Alexander that it had the opportunity. If he could not fuse races, he transcended the national State; and to transcend national States meant to transcend national cults; men came to feel after the unity which must lie beneath the various religions. Outwardly, this unity was ultimately satisfied in the official worship of the Roman Emperor, which derived from the worship of Alexander after his death; but beside this external form there grew up in men's hearts the longing for a true spiritual unity. And it was Alexander who created the medium in which the idea, when it came, was to spread. For it was due to him that Greek civilisation penetrated

western Asia; and even if much of the actual work was done by his successors, he broke the path; without him they would not have been. Consequently, when at last Christianity showed the way to that spiritual unity after which men were feeling, there was ready to hand a medium for the new religion to spread in, the common Hellenistic civilisation of the "inhabited world"; without that, the conquests made by Christianity might have been as slow and difficult as they became when the bounds of that common civilisation were overpassed.

But if the things he did were great, one thing he dreamt was greater. We may put it that he found the ideal State of Aristotle, and substituted the ideal State of Zeno. It was not merely that he overthrew the narrow restraints of the former, and, in place of limiting men by their opportunity, created opportunities adequate for men in a world where none need be a pauper and restrictions on population were meaningless. Aristotle's State had still cared nothing for humanity outside its own borders; the stranger must still be a serf or an enemy. Alexander changed all that. When he declared that all men were alike sons of one Father, and when at Opis he prayed that Macedonians and Persians might be partners in the commonwealth and that the peoples of his world might live in harmony and in unity of heart and mind, he proclaimed for the first time the unity and brotherhood of mankind. Perhaps he gave no thought to the slave world—we do not know; but he, first of all men, was ready to transcend national differences, and to declare, as St Paul was to declare, that there was neither Greek nor barbarian. And the impulse of this mighty revelation was continued by men who did give some thought to the slave world; for Zeno, who treated his slave as himself, and Seneca, who called himself the fellow-slave of his slaves, would (though Alexander might not) have understood St Paul when he added "there is neither bond nor free." Before Alexander, men's dreams of the ideal state had still been based on class-rule and slavery; but after him comes Iambulus' great Sun-State, founded on brotherhood and the dignity of free labour. Above all, Alexander inspired Zeno's vision of a world in which all men should be members one of another, citizens of one State without distinction of race or institutions, subject only to and in harmony with the Common Law immanent in the Universe, and united in one social life not by compulsion but only by their own willing consent, or (as he put it) by Love. The splendour of this hopeless dream may remind us that not one but two of the great lines of social-political thought which until recently divided the world go back to Alexander of Macedon. For if, as many believe, there was a line of descent from his claim to divinity, through Roman Emperor and medieval Pope, to the great despotisms of yesterday, despotisms "by the grace of God," there is certainly a line of descent from his prayer at Opis, through the Stoics and one portion of the Christian ideal, to that brotherhood of all men which was proclaimed, though only proclaimed, in the French Revolution. The torch Alexander lit for long only smouldered; perhaps it still only smoulders to-day; but it never has been, and never can be, quite put out.

ALEXANDER AND THE IRANIANS

3. A. B. Bosworth, Professor of Classics and Ancient History, University of Western Australia, finds unconvincing Tarn's notion that Alexander aimed at racial fusion to achieve his vision of world harmony. Instead he argues that Alexander sought pragmatic solutions to the various challenges of his reign.

FROM A. B. BOSWORTH, "ALEXANDER AND THE IRANIANS"

THE LAST TWO DECADES have seen a welcome erosion of traditional dogmas of Alexander scholarship, and a number of hallowed theories, raised on a cushion of metaphysical speculation above the mundane historical evidence, have succumbed to attacks based on rigorous logic and source analysis. The brotherhood of man as a vision of Alexander is dead, as is (one hopes) the idea that all Alexander sources can be divided into sheep and goats, the one based on extracts from the archives and the other mere rhetorical fantasy. One notable theory, however, still flourishes and has indeed been described as one of the few certainties among Alexander's aims. This is the so-called policy of fusion. As so often, the idea and terminology go back to J. G. Droysen, who hailed Alexander's marriage to Rhoxane as a symbol of the fusion (*Verschmelzung*) of Europe and Asia, which (he claimed) the king recognised as the consequence of his victory. At Susa the fusion of east and west was complete and Alexander, as interpreted by Droysen, saw in that fusion the guarantee of the strength and stability of his empire. Once enunciated, Droysen's formulation passed down the mainstream of German historiography, to Kaerst, Wilcken, Berve and Schachermeyr, and has penetrated to almost all arteries of Alexander scholarship. Like the figure of Alexander himself the theory is flexible and capable of strange metamorphoses. In the hands of Tarn it developed into the idea of all subjects, Greek and barbarian, living together in unity and concord in a universal empire of peace. The polar opposite is an essay of Helmut Berve, written in the heady days before the Second World War, in which he claimed that Alexander, with commendable respect for Aryan supremacy, planned a blending of the Macedonian and Persian peoples, so that the two racially related (!) *Herrenvölker* would lord it over the rest of the world empire. On Berve's interpretation the policy had two stages. Alexander first recognised the merits of the Iranian peoples and placed them alongside the Macedonians in his court and army hierarchy. Next came the "*Blutvermischung*," the integration of the two peoples by marriage.

Most scholars have tacitly accepted Berve's definition and take it as axiomatic that Alexander did recognise the merits of the Iranians and did try to integrate them with the Macedonians. The extent of the fusion is disputed, some confining it to the two aristocracies, but few have denied that Alexander had a definite policy. The loudest voice crying in the wilderness has been that of Franz Hampl. Hampl has repeatedly emphasised the arbitrary and speculative nature of most discussions of the subject and the absence of concrete evidence in the ancient sources, and he categorically denies the existence of any policy of fusion. The protest is a valuable warning but in itself it is insufficient. The fact that there is no reliable ancient attestation of the policy of fusion does not prove that no such policy existed; it merely makes the case more complex. The attested actions of Alexander may still be explicable only on the assumption that he had some definite policy of integration. This is a viable hypothesis, but it must be tested rigorously. We need to examine precisely what the ancient sources say and not interpolate them with our own interpretations or wishful thinking; and above all the evidence needs to be treated in its historical context, not thrown together haphazardly to buttress some abstract concept which attracts us for sentimental reasons.

There are two passages in the sources that suggest that Alexander had some ideas of fusing together the Macedonians and Persians. Foremost comes the famous prayer of reconciliation after the Opis mutiny (late summer 324). According to Arrian Alexander held a sacrifice at which all participants, Macedonians, Persians and representatives of other nations, sat around Alexander while he and his entourage poured libations from the same vessel. The king made a prayer whose main burden was "concord and community in empire for Macedonians and Persians" (*homonoia te kai koinonian tes arches Mekedosi kai Persais*). The two concepts, concord and community, are tied together grammatically and contextually. The background of the prayer was mutiny, a mutiny caused in part at least by Macedonian resentment of Persians and crushed by Alexander turning towards his Persians and creating a new court and army structure composed totally of Persians. The stratagem had been entirely successful and the Macedonians capitulated as soon as Alexander began his distribution of army commands to notable Persians. There was certainly Macedonian fear and resentment of the Persians around Alexander and the king played upon these emotions to destroy the mutiny. There was every reason under the circumstances for a ceremony of reconciliation and a prayer for concord. Concord is associated with community in empire, and there is no doubt that Arrian means the sharing of command in Alexander's empire. The terminology is vague and imprecise, as so often with Arrian, but there is no reason to give the prayer a universal significance. Alexander may be referring to the satrapies of the empire which had been and were to continue to be governed both by Macedonians and Iranians. There may even be a reference to the army commands recently conferred upon Persians and a covert threat that he would repeat his action if there were further trouble. The prayer and its context are primary evidence for bad blood between Macedonians and Iranians and Alexander's desire to use some at least of both races in the administration of the empire. They do not give any support for a general policy of fusion.

Diodorus is more explicit. In the context of the notorious *hypomnemata*, the alleged last plans of Alexander presented to the Macedonian army by Perdiccas, came a proposal to synoecise cities and transplant populations from Europe to Asia "to bring the continents to common unity and friendly kinship" by means of intermarriage and ties of community. We have here two things, a proposal to found cities and transplant populations, and an interpretation of that proposal. The interpretation is unlikely to have been embodied in the original plans submitted by Perdiccas, and like the puerile note a few sentences later (that the Pyramids were accounted among the Seven Wonders) it is most probably a comment either by Diodorus or his source. Now there is little or no evidence that Diodorus had a personal interest in Alexander as an apostle of international unity and the overwhelming probability is that the comment comes from his immediate source, Hieronymus of Cardia. Hieronymus was a contemporary of Alexander but his history was written towards the end of his prodigiously long life and covered events at least to 272. His recollections of Alexander were now distant and his views of the king's motives perhaps affected by fifty years of experience and reflection. He may have considered that Alexander's shifts of population were designed to bring about greater community between races, but nothing suggests that Alexander shared his views. What is more, the authenticity of the *hypomnemata* is a notorious crux. It is certainly possible that Perdiccas included fictitious proposals which he knew would antagonise the army in order to induce them to revoke the whole of Alexander's *acta*. If so, those proposals would have been couched in the most provocative terms. There is, then, no certainty that even the original proposal to transplant populations emanates from Alexander, let alone the parenthetical comment. And the force of the comment is that Alexander envisaged a general spirit of unity among all his subjects, Greek and barbarian; it is not in any sense a plan to combine Macedonians and Persians as a joint ruling class. The only connection with the Opis prayer is the fact that the concept of *homonoia* occurs in both passages!

The next relevant observation comes from Eratosthenes, who observed that Alexander ignored advice to treat the Greeks as friends and barbarians as enemies, preferring to welcome all possible men of fair repute and be their benefactor. On the surface Eratosthenes' comment has nothing to do with any policy of fusion: it is merely the just observation that Alexander was catholic in his benefactions and did not treat the conquered peoples with hostility. There is no hint here of a proposed union of races. But discussion has been unforgivably confused by the belief that Eratosthenes lies at the base of Plutarch's exposition in the first of his speeches *de Alexandri fortuna*. As is well known, this essay is the prime source for the view of Alexander as the reconciler of mankind. In a famous passage of rhetoric Plutarch tells of the rejection of Aristotle's advice to treat the Greeks *hegemonikos*; Alexander blended all men together, mixing their lives, marriages and ways of life in a *krater* of friendship and making his only distinction between Greek and barbarian a man's virtue or vice. After the recent analyses by Badian and Hamilton there should be no question that the whole shaping of the passage is Plutarch's own, designed to show that Alexander achieved in fact the single polity which Zeno advocated. He may have drawn on Eratosthenes, but nothing suggests that the passage as a whole is an extract or summary. In particular there is no reason to believe that Eratosthenes used the metaphor of mixing.

There is still a tendency to argue that Eratosthenes described a policy of fusion.... Plutarch explicitly cites him on the subject of Alexander's court dress, a mixture of Persian and Macedonian elements. He goes on to explain that the object was to win the respect of the subject peoples and further the aim of a single law and polity for all mankind. But there is nothing to suggest that Plutarch's interpretation of the mixed dress comes from Eratosthenes. The whole passage is designed to buttress the paradoxical thesis that Alexander was a philosopher in arms and seeking the reconciliation of mankind which was merely preached as an ideal by conventional philosophers. The concrete examples of the Susa marriages and the adoption of mixed court dress are chosen as examples of his achievement of *koinonia* and the choice is Plutarch's own. The reference to Eratosthenes seems thrown in as a passing remark ... he interlaces his exposition with casual references to Onesicritus, Aristobulus, Anaximenes and Duris. Eratosthenes, we may be sure, described Alexander's court dress, but we cannot assume that he gave it an ecumenical significance. What matters is Plutarch's mode of procedure. His task is to prove the thesis that Alexander was a philosopher in practice and both the examples and their rhetorical embellishment are carefully geared to that end. His general view may derive ultimately from Onesicritus' story of Alexander and the gymnosophists, but, if so, the original is totally transformed. Onesicritus' view is of an Alexander who still has sympathy for the search for wisdom even in

the cares of empire; but for Plutarch Alexander not only sympathises with philosophical theories, he embodies and perfects them in his actions. In the same way the interpretation he gives to the Susa marriages and the assumption of court dress need owe nothing to previous writers. Once he had propounded his theme he was limited in his choice of material and his interpretation was predetermined. Other rhetoricians with other theses to prove would adapt their viewpoint accordingly. One need only compare Aelius Aristides' *Roman Oration*. Here Rome is exalted as Plutarch exalts Alexander. She is the civilising power, breaking down the old distinction of Hellene and barbarian by the conferment of citizenship upon all deserving men. Against that background Alexander can only be presented as a meteoric failure, who acquired empire but had no time to establish a permanent system of law, taxation and civil administration. If Rome was the great reconciler, Alexander could only appear as an ephemeral conqueror. In these pieces of epideictic rhetoric it is the thesis adopted for debate which determines both the choice of material and the interpretation put upon it, and it is a possibility, if no more, that the whole topic of racial fusion in Alexander's reign was a creation of the rhetorical schools of the early Empire. In Plutarch himself there is only one reference in the *Life of Alexander* (47.3) to Alexander's efforts to achieve *koinonia* and *anakrasis*, and the examples he chooses are different from those in the earlier speech—the creation of the *Epigoni* and the Marriage to Rhoxane. And there is virtually no reference to racial fusion outside Plutarch. Only Curtius places in Alexander's mouth a speech commemorating the Susa marriages as a device to remove all distinction between victor and vanquished. This speech was allegedly delivered to the Iranian soldiers during the Opis mutiny, and once again the circumstances determine the content of the speech. The subject matter, as often in Curtius, may be derived from his immediate source; but the speech is composed in generalities with none of the interesting points of authentic detail found in other Curtian speeches, and it seems to me that the observations on the fusion of Macedonian and Iranian tradition are most likely to be embellishments by Curtius himself. Even so, it is interesting that the idea of fusion occurred to Curtius as a natural theme for a speech of Alexander during the Opis crisis. The *topos* of fusion existed in the early empire and there were regular *exempla*—court dress, dynastic marriages, and the assimilation of Iranians in the national army. Not surprisingly these are the areas in which modern discussion of the "policy of fusion" has tended to centre—and there is the possibility that the rhetoricians of the early empire and modern scholarship are correct in their interpretation. But forensic eloquence is no substitute for analytic evaluation of the evidence, and the various *exempla* need to be assessed both in their historical detail and historical context.

We may begin with the assumption of Persian court ceremonial. This is most fully described by the vulgate sources, especially Diodorus who mentions five aspects. Alexander introduced court chamberlains of Asiatic stock (*rabdouchoi Asiageneis*) and a body-guard of distinguished nobles including Darius' brother Oxyathres. Secondly he adopted some aspects of Persian court dress—the diadem, the white-striped tunic and the girdle. Next he distributed scarlet robes and Persian harness to his companions, and finally took over Darius' harem of 360 concubines. Curtius has much the same detail but adds that Alexander used Darius' ring for his correspondence in Asia. The sources assess these moves variously. The vulgate sources unanimously regard them as a decline towards barbarian *tryphé* as indeed does the normally uncritical Arrian (later he suggests on his own initiative that the adoption of mixed dress was a *sophisma* to win over the barbarians). Plutarch in his life represents the mixed dress as either an adaptation to native custom or anticipation of the introduction *of proskynesis*. It is only in the *de Alexandri fortuna* that he represents it as a means to bring about friendship between victor and vanquished. There is no indication that any of the ancient sources had direct information about Alexander's motives for the innovation.

It should be emphasised that the adoption of Persian court protocol was fairly extensive, not confined to Alexander's choice of a mixed court dress. On the one hand he used Persians in ceremonial positions, but he also issued his hetairoi with the traditional purple robes of the Achaemenid courtiers. The new king had his *purpurati*, but they were Macedonians. As yet there was no attempt to integrate the two nobilities. Diodorus implies quite clearly that they formed separate groups. The Persians might be given posts as chamberlains and selected nobles formed into a corps of *doruphoroi*, but Alexander showed clearly by his distribution of purple that the courtiers of the new Great King were his Macedonians. In his dress and court ceremonial Alexander adopted Achaemenid practices but he kept Persians and Macedonians distinct and the Macedonians were in a privileged position.

The date of the innovation is also important. Plutarch states explicitly that Alexander first assumed mixed dress during the rest period in Parthia after the Hyrcanian expedition, that is, in autumn 330. It is precisely at this point that the vulgate sources place the episode, and we cannot doubt the accuracy of the chronology. Now Alexander's claims to be the legitimate king of the Persian empire go back at least to the Marathus correspondence of early 332, when he demanded that Darius acknowledge him as overlord. After Gaugamela he was solemnly pronounced King of Asia and furthered his claims by solemnly occupying the throne of Darius in Susa. It is possible (though it cannot be proved) that Alexander was never formally consecrated in Pasargadae, and he seems never to have used the title "King of Kings" in his dealings with the Greek world. But his claims to be the legitimate king of the Persian empire were absolute. Yet, even so, Alexander did not adopt Achaemenid court protocol until at least six weeks after the death of Darius. What was the importance of the period in Parthia? The answer is that Alexander now had a rival. It was precisely at the time that he returned to Parthia that Alexander learned that Bessus had declared himself Darius' successor, assuming the jealously guarded royal prerogative, the *kitaris* or upright tiara, and also the regnal name Artaxerxes. The news, according to Arrian, reached Alexander on his return to Parthia and the vulgate sources place Bessus' usurpation in the context of Alexander's new court protocol. Now the threat from Bessus should not be underestimated. He was related by blood to Darius and could be seen by some as his legitimate successor. He also commanded the resources of Bactria and Sogdiana, whose cavalry had retired practically undefeated from the field of Gaugamela. It was also a period at which Alexander's military resources were at a low ebb. The Greek allied troops had been demobilised from Ecbatana, probably at the news of Darius' death. More seriously Alexander had left behind 6,000 of his phalanx troops at the Median border for the escort of his vast bullion train, and they were to remain detached from his main force until he entered Arachosia in early 329. He had also transferred his Thracian troops and a large body of mercenaries for the garrison of Media. Alexander was caught with a greatly reduced army and he suffered for it. Satibarzanes, once a regicide and Alexander's first governor of Areia, immediately revolted and forced Alexander to return from his march on Bactria. His intervention brought only temporary relief. No sooner had he moved south to Drangiana and Arachosia than Satibarzanes returned with reinforcements from Bessus, and his uprising was not crushed until the summer of 329. At the same time Bessus' forces invaded Parthia and tried to establish a certain Brazane as satrap. The disaffection was widespread and it lasted almost a year. It was late 329 before Bessus was captured and the last rebels were brought from Parthia and Arcia to meet the judgement of Alexander. There had been almost a year of challenge and insurrection, and it is difficult to believe that Alexander did not foresee trouble when he first heard of Bessus' usurpation.

The adoption of court protocol had an obvious propaganda value in these circumstances. Alexander demonstrated that he was genuinely King of Kings, not a mere foreign usurper, and the bodyguard of noble Persians was crucial to his claim. At his court in a position of high honour was none other than Oxyathres, brother of the late king. Not only was Alexander the self-proclaimed successor to Darius, but Darius' brother recognised the claim and supported Alexander's court ceremonial. This had been one of Alexander's assertions as early as 332, when he boasted that the Persians in his encourage followed him out of free choice. At the same time Alexander adopted some items of Persian court dress, not the more obtrusive regalia (the tiara, and the purple trousers and long-sleeved *kandys*) but the diadem, the royal tunic and girdle, which he wore with the broad-brimmed Macedonian hat (*kausia*) and the Macedonian cloak.

Even this caused serious discontent among the Macedonian army—and Macedonian resistance to things oriental is one of the persistent factors of Alexander's reign. All sources stress the hostility to Alexander's adoption of mixed dress and it is prominent in the list of grievances which led to the Opis mutiny in 324. The cleft widened among Alexander's officers, and the disagreements between Craterus and Hephaestion were notorious; Craterus, we are told, steadfastly adhered to Macedonian tradition. Now the popularity of Craterus is one of the best-attested facts of the period after Alexander's death. His short marriage to Phila made the lady a desirable bride for Demetrius. So strong was the devotion of the phalangites that Eumenes in 321 went to extraordinary lengths to conceal the fact that Craterus led the opposing army, in the belief that no Macedonian would fight against him. The reason Plutarch gives (excerpting Hieronymus) is that Craterus often

incurred Alexander's hatred by opposing his inclination to Persian excess and protecting ancestral customs from erosion. Now it is notable that in the latter years of Alexander's reign Craterus was sent repeatedly on lengthy missions away from court, almost assuming the mantle of Parmenion. In particular he led the army division of Macedonian veterans first from India to Carmania in 325/4 and then from Opis to the coast. The veterans were the men most closely bound to him but his popularity was universal and the reason was his championship of ancestral custom. Macedonian kings were said to rule by custom rather than force (*oude bia alla nomo*) and the sight of a Heraclid and Argead in the trappings of the Great King, the paradigm of despotism, must have been deeply shocking. All the more so since the march from Babylon, which had been a triumphal progress, marked by the sacking of Persepolis and the burning of the palace and finally the ignominious death of the last Achaemenid at the hands of his subjects. Now the victor was assuming the protocol of the vanquished, acting the part of Great King and declaring his intentions of remaining as lord of Asia—a matter of weeks after his troops had come near mutiny in their desire to end the campaign and return home.

The autumn of 330 was a time of crisis when Alexander was under strong and conflicting pressures. On the one hand the challenge from Bessus and his temporary shortage of troops forced him to propaganda, demonstrating to his subjects that he was not merely a foreign conqueror but the true Great King, supported by the old nobility of Darius. On the other he could not antagonise his Macedonians by too outrageous a breach of custom. The mixed dress was a compromise, taking on the very minimum of Persian attire compatible with his pretentions: and at the same time Alexander's Macedonian companions were given the purple robes of courtiers. This involved them in some of the odium of breach of custom and at the same time marked them out as the friends and satraps of the Great King. It was a limited experiment, and Diodorus is probably right that Alexander used the new ceremonial fairly sparingly. We hear little of it in the years after 330. The Persian ushers figure among Cleitus' complaints at Maracanda, but only in Plutarch's version and then only as a peripheral attack. The complaints re-emerge in Curtius' speeches on the occasion of the Pages' Conspiracy (327). They are raised briefly by Hermolaus and answered by Alexander. The material may come from Curtius' sources, as do several details in these speeches, but the formulation is vague and consistent with the limited experiment implied by Diodorus. Polyaenus also indicates that Alexander reserved his Persian ceremonial receptions of his barbarian subjects during the campaigns in Bactria, Hyrcania and India, but, as we shall see, his information is garbled to some extent and mostly refers to the last years of the reign. Nothing, however, contradicts the pattern of the evidence, which suggests that Alexander's first introduction of Persian ceremonial was a limited gesture, designed to capture the allegiance of his barbarian subjects at a time of crisis.

* * *

Some degree of integration had taken place by the end of the reign. After the great mutiny of 324 Alexander introduced 1,000 Persians into the court guard of hypaspists. Both Diodorus and Justin agree on the fact but differ over whether it came after or during the mutiny. Either it was part of Alexander's moves to bring his Macedonians to heel or it was a consequence of the mutiny, a permanent reminder of his threat to recruit his guard from Persians alone. But even so there is no evidence that the two races were intermingled in the guard and some that they were not. The panels on Alexander's sarcophagus portrayed the elaborate progress of the king in the last part of his life. Alexander rode in a chariot, preceded by an advance guard and surrounded by his regular court guard. This guard was divided into two separate bodies, one Macedonian armed in Macedonian style and the other Persian *melophoroi*. Now the two races stood side by side, but they were brigaded in separate and identifiable corps. There was no attempt to integrate them into a unified body; if anything, it looks like deliberate design to balance one against the other.

It is clear that Alexander's court had become much more pretentious in the last two years of his life. The mixed dress was a more permanent feature and there was an increasing use of Persian *melophoroi* as court guards. The pomp and circumstance fits well the increasing megalomania of Alexander's last years which, as is well known, rose to a climax after the death of Hephaestion. The increase in Persian ceremonial was doubtless caused by the fact that in 325/4 Alexander was travelling consistently between the old Achaemenid capitals (Persepolis, Susa, Ecbatana and Babylon) and needed to display himself to his oriental subjects as the new Great King. What is more, his absence in India between 327 and 325 had brought renewed insubordination and insurrection. The satraps of Carmania, Susiana and Paraetacene were executed when Alexander returned to the west and replaced by Macedonians. More seriously, when he reached Persia proper he discovered that Orxines, apparently a lineal descendant of Cyrus the Great who had commanded the Persian contingent at Gaugamela, had established himself as satrap without any authorisation by Alexander. There had also been trouble in the inner satrapies, for Craterus needed to arrest an insurgent, Ordanes, during his progress through southern Iran; and in Media a certain Baryaxes had assumed the upright tiara and laid claim to the throne of the Medes and Persians. Alexander must have felt that there was widespread reluctance among his Iranian subjects to accept his regal authority, and his parade of all the magnificence of the Achaemenid court including the old bodyguard of *melophoroi* is perfectly understandable. But while Alexander increased the Persian complement in his immediate entourage he appears to have reduced their political influence away from court. The end of the reign saw only three Iranians governing satrapies—Alexander's own father-in-law in distant Parapamisadae, the impeccably loyal Phrataphernes in Parthia/Hyrcania, and Atropates in Media, the satrapy with the most formidable garrison of Hellenic troops. There are many aspects to Alexander's behaviour. We may plausibly argue a desire to flaunt ostentatiously the splendour of his court, to impress his Iranian subjects with his military power and legitimacy as Great King; and there are signs that he used his promotion of Iranians to crush discontent among his Macedonian army. What we cannot as yet assume is any serious policy of assimilating and fusing the two races. The reverse seems the case.

We must now turn to the theme of mixed marriage, which was the original inspiration for Droysen's idea of "*Verschmelzungspolitik.*" For almost the first ten years of his reign Alexander avoided marriage with remarkable success. After Issus the majority of the Persian royal ladies were in his power. Alexander scrupulously cultivated the Queen Mother, Sisygambis as his "Mother" and promised dowries to Darius' daughters. Taking over Darius' functions as son and father he buttressed his claims to be the genuine King of Asia. But he stopped short of actual marriage, contenting himself with a liaison with Barsine, the daughter of Artabazus and descendant of Artaxerxes II. This liaison was protracted and from it came a son,

Heracles, born in 327, but there was no question of marriage until the last days of Alexander's campaign in Bactria/Sogdiana. Then came his meeting with Rhoxane and almost immediate marriage. The circumstances whereby Rhoxane came into his hands cannot be elucidated here, for they involve one of the most intractable clashes of authority between Arrian and the vulgate tradition, but fortunately there is unanimity about the date of the wedding (spring 327) and equal unanimity that it was a love match. There is, however, no suggestion of a policy of fusion. Curtius merely accredits him with a statement that it was conducive to the stability of the empire that Persians and Macedonians were joined in marriage; the arrogance of the victors and shame of the vanquished would both be reduced. This is a far cry from the symbolic union of races which many have seen in the marriage.

* * *

Finally we come to the palladium of Alexander's alleged policy of fusion—the mass marriage at Susa at which Alexander and 91 of his Companions took Iranian brides. The weddings were celebrated with the utmost splendour in the Iranian mode and Alexander commemorated the event by distributing gifts to Macedonian soldiers who had taken native wives, to the number of 10,000. Without doubt this was a ceremony of unparalleled pomp with important political implications, but the sources leave us totally uninformed of those implications. In the speech *tie Alexandri fortuna* Plutarch represents the marriage as a means of uniting the two imperial peoples, as does Curtius in the speech he attributes to Alexander; but, as we have seen, both statements reflect the rhetorical interpretations of the first century A.D. rather than any authentic tradition from the time of Alexander. But if we look at the recorded facts, one feature stands out starkly—so starkly that it is incredible that it was first noted by Hampl in 1954. The marriages were totally one-sided. Persian wives were given to Macedonian husbands, but there is no instance of the reverse relationship.

Admittedly Alexander's court was not well endowed with noble ladies of Greek or Macedonian extraction, but, if his aim was really to place the two imperial races on an equal footing, it would have been relatively easy for him to import the necessary brides from mainland Greece and delay the ceremony until they arrived. In fact there is nothing attested except

Persian women married to Greco-Macedonian men. The names as recorded are striking. Alexander and Hephaestion both married daughters of Darius, Craterus a daughter of Darius' brother, Oxyathres. The other wives whose names are recorded came from prominent satrapal families—daughters of Artabazus, Atropates of Media, and even Spitamenes, the leader of the insurgent Sogdians during 329 and 328. This was an integration of sorts, but its effect was to mark out Alexander's Companions as the new rulers of the Persian Empire. They already had the scarlet robes of Persian courtiers; now they were married into the most prominent satrapal families. Nothing could have made it clearer that Alexander intended his Macedonians to rule with him as the new lords of the conquered empire.

* * *

It is difficult to trace any admission of Persian nobles into the Macedonian court hierarchy. Before 324 the only certain example is Oxyathres, brother of Darius, who was admitted to the ranks of the *hetairoi* immediately after his brother's. It is hazardous to argue from silence, given the defective nature of all Alexander histories, but there is some evidence that Persians were initially excluded from the court hierarchy. In 329 Pharnuches, apparently an Iranian domiciled in Lycia, found himself in titular command of a force of mercenaries thanks to his competence in the local dialects. When his force was ambushed, he attempted (so Aristobulus claimed) to cede his command to Macedonian officers on the grounds that he was a barbarian while they were Macedonians and *hetairoi* of the King. The account in general is confused and tendentious, but the clear distinction between barbarians and *hetairoi* is fundamental to it. Admittedly the text does not state that there were no barbarian *hetairoi*, but it does support the argument from silence. Nearchus' list of trierarchs for the Indus fleet takes us further. The Macedonians of Alexander's court are listed according to their domicile, as are the Greeks. There are two representatives of the regal families of Cyprus, and finally one solitary Persian—Bagoas, son of Pharnuches. The rarity of the patronymic virtually guarantees that Bagoas was the son of the Lycian Pharnuches. Unlike his father, he achieved a status commensurate with the Macedonian *hetairoi*, and he was probably the Bagoas who entertained Alexander at Babylon. But at the time of the Indus voyage he was the only Persian among the *hetairoi* (Oxyathres had retired to Ecbatana to supervise Bessus' execution);

otherwise it is inconceivable that his fellow Iranians did not compete as trierarchs.

* * *

The evidence so far has produced little or nothing that suggests any policy of fusion. Alexander's actions when viewed in their historical context seem rather to indicate a policy of division. There was no attempt to intermix the Macedonian and Persian nobilities, if anything an attempt to keep them apart. In particular the Macedonians seem to have been cast as the ruling race. It is they who monopolise the principal commands, civil and military, they who marry the women of the Persian aristocracy, they who dominate court life. Even when Alexander adopted Persian ceremonial his Macedonians were marked out as his courtiers and his chiliarch (or grand vizier) was no Persian but his bosom friend Hephaestion. By contrast apart from a small, carefully chosen elite the Persians had no positions of power at court and the Iranian satraps were inexorably reduced in numbers as the reign progressed. The factor which dominated everything was Alexander's concept of personal autocracy. From early 332 to the end of his life he declared himself King of Asia. He acknowledged no equal and all were his subjects. Against that background the traditional recalcitrance of the Iranian satraps was totally unacceptable and, I believe, Alexander's actions can largely be explained as a demonstration of the fact of conquest. His court ceremonial underlined that he alone was the Great King and the mass marriages made it patently obvious that he and his nobles were the inheritors of the Achaemenids. As for the Persians, they were gradually extracted from the satrapies in which they had been prematurely confirmed in the years after Gaugamela and only a small group was left, tied by marriage to the Macedonian conquerors and with sons virtual hostages at court. This is a far cry from any policy of fusion. The only counter evidence comes from the Opis mutiny, when Alexander turned to his Iranians in order to crush disaffection among the Macedonians. Afterwards Alexander was able to pray for community of command, but the prayer was demonstrably affected by the recent events. In effect there is no hint that Alexander gave positions of power to Iranians during his last year; the hierarchy of command remained stubbornly Macedonian.

If there is no trace of any planned integration of the Macedonian and Persian aristocracies, it might be thought that the fusion took place at a lower level. By the end of his reign Alexander certainly possessed a mixed army, in which Persians and Macedonians fought side by side both in the phalanx and Companion cavalry. But did the mixture come about by policy or by military necessity? And how rigorous was the fusion? Were the two races divided into separate sub-units or did they fight side by side in integrated companies and with common weaponry? These questions are fundamental and once again require close examination of the evidence.

According to orthodox dogma Alexander began to use oriental cavalry at an early stage. In his description of the Hyrcanian campaign (late summer 330) Arrian notes that the king now had a body of mounted javelin-men (*hippakontistai*). These troops were used repeatedly in the campaign in central Iran and Bactria, and it is universally assumed that they were a select Iranian squadron, recruited to give extra flexibility to his cavalry. But there is no hint in any of the ten references in Arrian that these troops were Iranians. In fact they are invariably grouped with regular units of the Macedonian army, the Agrianians, and the Companions. What is more, *hippakontistai* formed the nucleus of the garrison of Areia in 330 and they were massacred during Satibarzanes' first revolt. It is surprising that Iranians were chosen for such an exposed position, more surprising that they remained loyal. One should certainly admit the possibility that these troops were Macedonians. Now one of Alexander's principal cavalry units, the Scouts (*prodromoi*) is not mentioned after the pursuit of Darius. Instead the *hippakontistai* appear precisely in the role formerly cast for the Scouts, and in Sogdiana they are used alongside *sarissophoroi*, who previously belonged to the Scouts. It is possible that Alexander reorganised the Scouts in the year after Gaugamela and turned them into two formations, one using the ponderous *sarisa* and the other light missile javelins. At Gaugamela the Scouts had been mauled by the cavalry of the eastern satrapies, and Alexander perhaps thought it prudent to variegate his cavalry before moving east. The year 330 was one of reorganisation, the year that hipparchies are first mentioned in Ptolemy's campaign narrative, and it is perfectly credible that Alexander trained some of his Scouts as a unit of javelin-men. There is no reason to assume that he was using an Iranian squadron in conjunction with his Macedonian troops as early as 330.

The first unequivocal reference to use of oriental troops comes in the Sogdian revolt of 328/7, when we are told that Bactrians and Sogdians fought in the satrapal forces of Amyntas. When he left Bactria for India Alexander had with him large numbers of Iranian cavalry, from Bactria, Sogdiana, Arachosia and Parapamisadae. There were also Saka cavalry from the northern steppes. These troops fought alongside the Macedonians at the Hydaspes but they were brigaded in separate formations and outside the battle narrative they are not individually mentioned. There is one exception, the squadron of horse-archers (*hippotaxotai*) which first emerges during the march on India and is mentioned repeatedly in Arrian's campaign narrative. The horse-archers are usually employed alongside Macedonian units in relatively light formations, performing the same functions, it seems, as did formerly the Scouts and *hippakontistai* (who are mentioned once only after the invasion of India). These horse-archers seem to have been recruited from the Dahae, who are specifically designated the horse-archers at the Hydaspes, and it looks as though they formed a *corps d'élite* corresponding to the Agrianians in the infantry. The first appearance of these Iranian troops is significant. After the protracted campaign in Bactria/Sogdiana Alexander was leaving the area altogether and moving to invade India. The Iranian cavalry were being employed outside their home territory where there was little chance of disaffection. Alexander could safely draw upon them to strengthen his own cavalry, and at the same time they served as a great pool of hostages, exactly as had the troops of the Corinthian League during the first years of the campaign. They fought in national units and there was as yet no attempt to combine them with his Macedonian troops.

* * *

If the evidence of Arrian is strictly interpreted, it indicates that, apart from one hipparchy, Macedonians and Iranians served in separate units within the body of the Companion cavalry. In other words, the Iranian cavalry shared the title of *hetairoi*. This has often been doubted, but Arrian's terminology seems unambiguous: they were assigned to the Companion cavalry.

Alexander's actions at Opis are not contrary evidence. There he began to create new formations of Persians bearing the Macedonian names, including a fresh cavalry *agema kai he ton hetairon hippos*. This does not imply that all Companions had previously been Macedonians, rather that in future he intended to have a corps of Companions who were exclusively Persian. That is quite compatible with a situation before the mutiny in which Macedonians and Iranians served together in a single body of Companions. And the single reference in Arrian to Macedonian Companions does not exclude there having been Persian Companions also. A curious picture therefore emerges. The Iranian cavalry largely served in separate hipparchies, and they retained their national weapons (it is only the group of nobles in the *agema* who are said to have exchanged their javelins for Macedonian lances). Nevertheless they served in the Companion cavalry and presumably bore the title hetairoi. It would seem that Alexander was using the traditional policy of Macedonian kings. The title *pezhetairoi* (Foot Companions), as a name for the entire phalanx infantry, appears to have been introduced as a deliberate measure to place the infantry on terms of equality with the cavalry. The King named all his infantry his Companions and emphasised their close ties to him, thus setting them up as a group parallel and opposed to the aristocratic cavalry, the group which had previously monopolised the title of Companion. Alexander, it seems, did the same with his cavalry, establishing a body of Iranian Companions in the same organisation as the Macedonians. This development fits well into the period after the Hyphasis mutiny, when Alexander was faced with disaffection or, at best, lack of enthusiasm among his own troops. The admission of Iranian Companions made it clear that he was not limited to his Macedonians and could find support elsewhere. It was an implicit threat, which was nearly fulfilled at Opis. There is, then, no trace of a policy of fusion. Once again the tendency seems to have been to keep Iranians and Macedonians separate and even mutually suspicious. Each served as a check and balance on the other.

The pattern is further exemplified in Alexander's use of Iranian infantry. First and foremost is the formation of 30,000 *Epigoni*, Iranian youths armed in Macedonian fashion and trained in phalanx discipline. All sources agree that the *Epigoni* arrived during Alexander's stay in Susa and aroused the jealousy and fear of the Macedonians by their brilliant display. Plutarch alone says that the institution was designed to promote a mixture (*anakrasis*) and harmony; the vulgate sources see much more sinister motives. For Diodorus the formation was Alexander's reaction to the recalcitrance of his Macedonian troops ever since the Hyphasis mutiny (he speaks of the Ganges!). The king needed an *antitagma* for his Macedonian phalanx. Pierre Briant has recently elucidated the sense of *antitagma*; it was a counter-army, "*face a une phalange macedonienne et contre elle.*" Elsewhere Diodorus uses the word to describe the force of mercenaries raised by Thrasybulus of Syracuse to counter his citizen forces and Plutarch describes as an *antitagma* the force of cavalry which Eumenes in 322/1 built up to counter and crush the phalanx infantry of Neoptolemus. When applied to Alexander's *Epigoni* the word has a sinister ring. Alexander intended the Persians not only to balance his Macedonian forces but also to be thrown against them if necessary.

* * *

So far the evidence has indicated that Alexander kept Iranians and Macedonians separated in both cavalry and infantry and that he used the two races to counterbalance each other. There is, however, one instance of a combined force of Persians and Macedonians. Shortly before Alexander's death Peucestas arrived in Babylon with a force of 20,000 Persians, reinforced with mountaineers from the Zagros and Elburz. The king commended this new force and assigned them to the Macedonian ranks (*katalegein es tas Makedonikas taxeis*). The details of this reorganisation are given, for once, and they are interesting. This new composite infantry was organised into files (*dekades*) of sixteen, twelve Persians to four Macedonians. Each file was commanded by a Macedonian, backed by two other Macedonians in second and third place. The Persians then filled out the centre of the phalanx and a Macedonian brought up the rear. The four Macedonians were armed in traditional style (with the *sarisa*) and were given preferential rates of pay, whereas the Persians retained their native bows and javelins. The result was a curiously heterogeneous phalanx, packed with Persians untrained in Macedonian discipline. The Macedonians formed an elite, the first three ranks using *sarisae* and bearing the brunt of any attack. Even in the old phalanx there was hardly space for more than the first three ranks to use sarisae in

couched position. In Polybius' day, when *sarisae* were longer, only the first five ranks were able to thrust with their weapons; the rest added weight and held their *sarisae* vertically as a screen against missiles. The Persians in the new phalanx added weight and numbers and no doubt they were intended to shoot arrows and javelins over the heads of the Macedonian ranks, much in the same way as the *logchophororoi* were to operate in Arrian's legionary phalanx of A.D. 135. This new phalanx could only be used in frontal attacks. There was no possibility of complex manoeuvres or changes of front and depth on the march which had been the hallmark of the old Macedonian phalanx and had been displayed so prominently in the Illyrian campaign of 335 and the approach to Issus. This reorganisation was in fact a means to make the best use of untrained manpower and also to husband the trained Macedonian phalangites. It is strong *prima facie* evidence that Alexander's native Macedonian troops were in short supply by 323.

There is every reason to believe that the main army was drained of Macedonians. Curtius (x 2.8) implies that Alexander was thinking of leaving a moderate holding army in Asia after the departure of Craterus' veterans, an army comprising 13,000 infantry and 2,000 cavalry. These are superficially high figures, but none the less misleading. There is no reason to think that only Macedonians are understood. The explicit context is the size of the force to be left in Asia (he had recently threatened to attack Athens and the Arabian expedition was in preparation); it is specifically a holding force and presumably contained a relatively small proportion of Macedonians. After Opis Alexander deliberately drained his infantry forces, sending with Craterus 6,000 of the veterans present at the Hellespont in 334 and 4,000 of the troops conveyed in later reinforcements. There is no statement how many remained, but one may assume that the fighting in India and the Gedrosian desert march took a heavy toll of life, and there is little trace of reinforcements. Only Curtius speaks of 8,000 *Graeci* sent to Sogdiana in 329/8 and 5,000 cavalry (*sic*) sent from Thrace in 326. There is no trace in the sources of Macedonian reinforcements and it seems that Antipater did not have the necessary manpower resources to cater for Alexander's demands. Diodorus says explicitly that Macedonia was drained of national troops in 323 because of the numbers of reinforcements sent to Asia, so that he could not cope with the initial crisis of the Lamian War. The forces who remained in Babylon can only be guessed at. The *argyraspides*, 3,000 in number, were present in Perdiccas' invasion force in 321, and, since their baggage train contained their wives and children, we can assume that they were not sent with Craterus' column in 324. Alexander must have retained them in Babylon together with an unspecified number of *phalingites*. They were also veterans for the most part. The evidence for the *argyraspides* is unanimous that they had all fought through the campaigns of Philip and Alexander. The statement that the youngest of the corps were sixty years old may be an exaggeration, but it is common to Diodorus and Plutarch and presumably derives from Hieronymus. And we should not forget the exploits of Antigonus at Ipsus and Lysimachus and Seleucus at Corupedium: *in hac aetate utrique animi juveniles erant*. It seems then that Alexander was left with a nucleus of Macedonian veterans. He had ordered Antipater to bring prime troops from Macedonia to replace Craterus' army column but they could not be expected for some time after Craterus reached Macedon—and he was travelling with prudent slowness. But Alexander was about to embark on the Arabian expedition, and shortly before his death the advance orders for the departure of both land and naval forces had been given. There was no alternative but to make the best of his Macedonian veterans—to distribute them among the front-rank positions and fill up the phalanx in depth with Persian infantry. The mixture was patently forced upon Alexander by military necessity. Had the fresh levies from Macedon ever arrived, he would certainly have removed the Iranian rank and file and replaced them with the trained manpower from Macedon.

Nothing remains of the policy of fusion. As regards his military organisation Alexander was reacting to a series of problems. To begin with, his use of Iranians from the central satrapies was determined by his need for auxiliaries in the Indian campaign and the obvious desirability of removing crack fighting men from their native satrapies, where they would be fuel for any revolt against his regal authority. The next stage was to use his Iranian auxiliaries as a counter-weight to his increasingly mutinous Macedonian troops, and finally, when the Macedonians were decimated and cowed, they were used as a pool of manpower to supplement the trained Macedonian cadres. There is nothing here remotely resembling a deliberate policy to fuse together the two peoples into a single army. If there is any policy it is *divide et impera*. We have seen Alexander at work at two levels. Firstly the continuous and traditional recalcitrance of his Iranian nobles forced him to proclaim his pretensions as the heir of the Achaemenids with increasing pomp and splendour and to make it increasingly obvious that his Greco-Macedonian nobles had in fact supplanted the Iranians as a ruling class. On the other hand the increasing disaffection of his Macedonian rank and file forced him to rely more on Iranian infantry and cavalry. If there is any consistent element it is Alexander's categorical claim to personal autocracy and the reciprocal demand for total obedience from his subjects at all levels of society. The resistance to that claim appeared in different forms and Alexander's response was accordingly different. There is little that can be said to approximate to careful premeditated policy: rather Alexander seems to have reacted promptly to the various challenges confronting him during his reign. The result is piecemeal and certainly less romantic than a visionary policy of fusion and conciliation but it is far truer to the evidence as it stands.

ALEXANDER OF MACEDON

4. In this section of his famous biography, Peter Green discusses the sources for Alexander from antiquity to modern times. He concludes with his own assessment of the conqueror.

FROM PETER GREEN, *ALEXANDER OF MACEDON, 356–323 B.C.: A HISTORICAL BIOGRAPHY*

ALEXANDER MAY HAVE DEMANDED deification in his own lifetime, but by a kind of ironic rough justice he got mythification after he was dead. While his physical remains, smoothly hijacked by Ptolemy to Alexandria, lay on view in a glass coffin, a tribute to the local embalmers' art, his legend took root and flourished. When Aristobulus could concoct pure fiction about recent and known events, to be recited in the presence of their actual protagonist, what would later romancers not achieve, once freed from the fear lest Alexander himself should pitch their effusions into the nearest river, and threaten to deal with them in similar fashion? Immediately after his death, the king's character, reputation, and career were taken in hand by endless propagandists, would-be monarchs, historians, and a whole series of interested parties with some axe or other to grind.

He was not popular in Hellenistic times (though in art his portraiture, especially that by Lysippus, started a widespread iconographic trend, and rulers were fond of using his head on their coinage as a species of political endorsement), which may partially account for the fact that none of our main surviving accounts of him was written less than three hundred years after his death. By the time world-conquest came into fashion again, with Augustus, Alexander was already well on the way to becoming a giant, a demigod, the superhuman figure of romance who figured during the Middle Ages as Iskander the Two-Horned (a description which started from coin-portraits showing him wearing the ram's horns of Zeus Ammon).

Nothing did more to accelerate this process than the so-called "Alexander-romance." Perhaps in the second century A.D., perhaps much earlier—some details suggest propaganda of a date not long after the king's death—an anonymous writer who borrowed the name of Callisthenes wrote a sensational-ized, semi-mythicizing version of Alexander's career which at once ousted all the more sober versions, and spread like wildfire not only through the Greek and Roman world, but far into the East. In this work, for example, Alexander was alleged to have been sired on Olympias by the Egyptian Pharaoh Nectanebus, himself changed into a magician for the occasion. By the fifth century A.D. Syriac and Armenian versions of this weird farrago were in circulation. Arabic and Persian poets drew on it, with the result that cities like Secunderabad in the Deccan preserve Alexander's name although he never came anywhere near them.

Yet the uncomfortable fact remains that the Alexander-romance provides us, on occasion, with apparently genuine material found nowhere else, while our better-authenticated sources, *per contra*, are all too often riddled with bias, propaganda, rhetorical special pleading, or patent falsification

and suppression of the evidence. Arrian drew for the most part on Ptolemy and Aristobulus, who both (as we have seen) had powerful motives for preserving a *parti pris* version of the events in which they had taken part. No one has yet worked out a satisfactory analysis of the eclectic tradition on which Plutarch and Diodorus drew. Curtius, for all his tedious rhetorical hyperbole, contains valuable material not found elsewhere, and not all of it can be written off as hostile material invented by Cleitarchus or the "Peripatetic tradition," as Tarn would have us believe.

The truth of the matter is that there has never been a "good" or "bad" source-tradition concern-ing Alexander, simply *testimonia* contaminated to a greater or lesser degree, which invariably need evaluating, wherever possible, by external criteria of probability. This applies to all the early fragmen-tary evidence quoted in extant accounts as well as, *a fortiori*, to the authors of those accounts them-selves. A. E. Housman's strictures, in the field of textual criticism, against "the reigning fashion of the hour, the fashion of leaning on one manuscript like Hope on her anchor and trusting to heaven that no harm will come of it" could equally well be applied, *mutatis mutandis*, in the field of Alexander studies, where until recently Arrian received similar treatment. This was due, as Borza acutely noted, to a process whereby scholars formed a rigid estimate of Alexander's character, and then "began to reject or accept evidence depending upon whether that evidence was consistent with their characterization."

Such a circular process of argument will also leave judgement very much at the mercy of contem-porary fashions and preoccupations, a fate to which Alexander (who has always tended to involve his interpreters' emotions at least as much as their reasoning faculties) is, to judge by the record, peculiarly prone. Everyone uses him as a projection of their own private truth, their own dreams and aspirations, fears and power-fantasies. Each country, each generation, sees him in a different light. Every individual biographer, myself included, inevitably puts as much of himself, his own background and convictions, into that Protean figure as he does of whatever historical truth he can extract from the evidence. The power and fascination of Alexander's character are undeniable, and operate as strongly on modern scholars as they did on his Macedonian veterans. The king's personality is so strong, so idiosyncratic, that it comes through despite all the propaganda, pro or con: the smears, the eulogies, the star-struck mythologizing.

Something can be done, by careful analysis, to sort out truth from propaganda and legend. But this is where the real difficulties begin, since each student inevitably selects, constitutes criteria, according to his own unconscious assumptions, social, ethical or political. Moral conditioning, in the widest sense, plays a far greater part in the matter than most people—especially the historians themselves ever realize. So, indeed, does contemporary fashion. To the Romans of Augustus' day Alexander was the prototype of fashionable world-conquerors; they could call him "the Great" without any sense of creeping inferiority, since their own Princeps had so signally eclipsed his achievements, both in scope and durability. Juvenal, writing slightly later, at a time when imperial pretensions had become something of a cliché, saw Alexander rather as a supreme instance of the vanity of human wishes.

The medieval world, which enjoyed Juvenal's savage sniping at wealth and ambition, developed much the same theme. "And where is Alisaundir that conqueryd al?" asked Lydgate; many other poets echoed his rhetorical question. With the Renaissance came a reversion to the Augustan picture. Great Captains—as the popularity of Plutarch's *Lives* demonstrates—were once more in the ascendant: the prevailing mood was summed up for all time by that marvellously evocative line of Marlowe's:

Is it not passing brave to be a king, and ride in
    triumph through Persepolis?

Such an attitude survived largely unchallenged until the early nineteenth century. One event which then heralded a change in Alexander's reputation was undoubtedly the Greek War of Independence, following close on the French Revolution and the American War of Independence. The climate of educated liberal opinion had swung sharply round against the concept of imperialism; the fashion now was to endorse all subject races struggling for liberty, an ideological programme into which it would be hard to fit Alexander's career without some fairly thorough-going (not to say casuistic) reappraisal of the evidence.

This trend reached its logical climax in the famous—and still eminently readable—*History of Greece* by George Grote, a professional banker and passionate liberal, two things less mutually exclusive then than they have, it would seem, since become. Grote's hero in the fourth century is Demosthenes, whom he sees as embodying the true spirit of independence in the face of brazen and calculated imperialist aggression. He writes off both Philip and Alexander as brutalized adventurers simply out for power, wealth, and territorial expansion, both of them inflamed by the pure lust for conquest. Earlier historians, of course, had said much the same thing, but without Grote's note of moral censure.

Committed liberalism, however, was not a universal feature of nineteenth-century scholarship. European history moved in various channels, some more authoritarian than others: as usual, Alexander's reputation varied according to context. One milestone in Alexander studies was the publication of Johann Gustav Droysen's still immensely influential biography, *Alexander der Grosse* (1833). It has often been said, with justice, that this is the first work of modern historical scholarship on Alexander: Droysen was, undoubtedly, the first student to employ serious critical methods in evaluating our sources, and the result was a fundamental study. Once again, however, Droysen's own position largely dictated the view he took of his subject. Far from being a liberal, he was an ardent advocate of the reunification of Germany under strong Prussian leadership and after 1848 served for a while as a member of the Prussian parliament.

Thus we have a biographer of Alexander imbued with a belief in monarchy and a passionate devotion to Prussian nationalism: how the one aspect of his career influenced the other is, unfortunately, all too predictable. For the aspirations of independent small Greek states (as for their German counterparts) he had little but impatient contempt. In his view it is Philip of Macedon who emerges as the true leader of Greece, the man destined to unify the country and set it upon its historical mission; while Alexander carried the process one step farther by spreading the blessings of Greek culture throughout the known (and large tracts of the unknown) world. Plutarch's early essay on Alexander had made much the same point, contrasting the untutored savage who had not benefited from the king's civilizing attentions with those happy lesser breeds who had, the result of their encounter being that blend of Greek and oriental culture which Droysen, perhaps rather misleadingly, christened Hellenism.

As one contemporary scholar says, " 'Droysen's conceptions were propounded so forcefully that they have conditioned virtually all subsequent scholarship on the subject." Whatever their views on the nature of his achievement, most subsequent biographers tended to see Alexander as, in some guise or other, the great world-mover. This view held up surprisingly well until after the Second World War. The late nineteenth century, after all, saw the apogee of the British Empire, and scholars who got misty-eyed over Kipling in their spare time were not liable to argue with Droysen's view of Alexander. But this was also the heyday of the English gentleman, and much of that fascinating if often legendary figure's characteristics also now began to figure in their portraits—Alexander's becoming lack of interest in sex, his chivalrous conduct to women, his supposed ideals and aspirations towards the wider and mistier glories of imperialism.

The climax of this trend was, of course, the famous and enormously influential biography by the late Sir William Tarn, first published in the *Cambridge Ancient History* (1926) and then again in 1948, the narrative more or less unchanged, but this time supported by an immense volume of specialist research on various key topics. Tarn's basic picture resembled that of Droysen, but he added something new: a social philosophy, a belief on Alexander's part in the Brotherhood of Man. Why he took this line is clear enough. Tarn had an ethical dilemma to solve when he set about his task. By the time he came to write, imperial expansionism was no longer a tolerable programme in the minds of progressive intellectuals unless it had some sort of idealist or missionary creed to underwrite it. Tarn could not possibly, therefore, treat Alexander as a conqueror pure and simple and still regard him with unqualified approval. He had to find some ulterior goal for this imperial adventurer to pursue, and duly did so.

His solution, as it happened, lay conveniently ready to hand. The early 1920s were the heyday of the League of Nations, and as a gentlemanly late-Victorian liberal Tarn—along with Sir Alfred Zimmern, Gilbert Murray, and many others— was instantly swept away on a wave of international idealism. As in the case of Droysen (though with rather different results) Tarn's personal political convictions strongly affected his subsequent treatment of his hero. The League of Nations was proclaiming the Brotherhood of Man. Tarn brooded over the feast at Opis, laced it with some hit-and-miss proto-Stoicism, added a pinch of dubious early rhetoric from Plutarch, and duly evolved what I have always thought of as the League of Nations Alexander.

We can, if we so wish, criticize Tarn on the grounds of political naivety, and this is, of course, the most significant and damaging weakness in a *magnum opus* which, by any standards, remains a major scholarly achievement. But in this connection there are two important points we should remember. The first, and perhaps the most important, is that his version proved immensely popular. True or not, it was what a vast majority of people actively *wanted* to believe, and they therefore believed it, despite the critical small-arms fire with which various hardheaded historians, both at the time and later, riddled Tarn's central thesis. The second consideration to bear in mind is this. Tarn passed his formative years at the close of a century of peace and affluence, which enjoyed a stability—financial, social, political—such as the world had seldom seen since the days of the Roman Empire under the Antonines. This epoch, which those who lived through it regarded as the climax of a rational process with its roots in the eighteenth century, we now know for the unique phenomenon it was. This awareness, it goes without saying, has profoundly modified our attitude to the problems of history.

Tarn and those like him held that the devils of emotion and irrationalism had been chained and tamed forever. They believed in the supremacy of human reason, the essential goodness of human nature. The grim events of the past sixty years have taught us that man's life, alas, remains much the same as Thucydides or Thomas Hobbes saw it: nasty, brutish and short. The optimistic idealism characteristic of so much Victorian thinking bears little relationship to the overall sweep of human history. Towards the end of his life Tarn, in a groping way, began to realize this. The final paragraph of his original study in the *Cambridge Ancient History* was an impassioned plea for the ultimate indestructibility of the Brotherhood of Man as a perennial concept. In his 1948 edition, however, he appended a footnote which read: "I have left the latter part of this paragraph substantially as written in 1926. Since then we have seen new and monstrous births, and are still moving in a world not realized; and I do not know how to rewrite it."

There we have the humanist's *cri de coeur*, the last despairing utterance of an idealist mind at the end of its tether. Behind the clumsy abstractions there stalk ghosts not laid but merely sleeping: horrors like the gas-chambers and the hydrogen bomb, the world of double-think and ruthless power-politics and Orwell's *1984*, things which Thucydides and Alexander and Augustus understood very well in their own terms, but which Western Europe or America in the early years of this century simply could not conceive. Tarn further suffered from a sternly *simpliste* attitude to the psychological facets of morality: in his eyes murder was wrong, promiscuity was wrong, homosexuality was especially wrong, pure aggression without justification was wrong. Alexander, as a great man and a great hero, *had* to be cleared of such imputations as far as possible. It was only a short step from this axiom to the corollary that those traditions which presented Alexander in a morally good light were sound, while hostile testimony could be with confidence dismissed as false propaganda.

In short, the rise of psychology as a scientific discipline, combined with the return of totalitarianism as an instrument of politics, left Tarn's approach almost totally bankrupt in principle, if still a most impressive achievement over matters of detail (e.g. Alexander's eastern foundations) where ethical considerations did not apply. It is impossible to have lived through the middle decades of this century and not apply its lessons to the career of Alexander, which in so many ways shows remarkable parallels with those of other would-be world-conquerors who used propaganda as a deliberate tool and believed that truth was a commodity to be manipulated for their own ends.

Our picture of Augustus, as those who have read Sir Ronald Syme's classic work *The Roman Revolution* will be well aware, has been altered out of all recognition by this traumatic modern experience. It was hardly to be expected that the old rose-tinted view of Alexander would remain unaltered either. For post-war historians the king has once more become a world-conqueror *tout court*, the act of conquest being regarded not as a means to an end but an end in itself carried out by a visionary megalomaniac serving the implacable needs of his own all-consuming ego. At the same time, perhaps inevitably, a Freudian element has crept into the study of Alexander's personality during recent years. Critics now point out that his distaste for sex,

the rumours of his homosexual liaisons—in particular his lifelong friendship with that rather lumpish character Hephaestion and the sinister but beautiful young eunuch Bagoas—coupled with his partiality for middle-aged or elderly ladies and the systematic domination of his early years by that formidable matriarch Olympias, all suggest the presence in his nature of something approaching an Oedipus complex.

It hardly needs saying that this generation is no more free from the influence of its own overriding assumptions than any previous one; that perhaps once again we are reading into that chameleon personality what we ourselves fear or desire or find of obsessional concern in our own lives and society. As I suggested earlier, the Freudian interpretation of Alexander's motives can easily be overdone: an Adlerian power-complex would seem to fit the facts better. The real virtue of the new approach, it seems to me, is its basic pragmatism: it at least begins by looking at the historical facts without trying to fit them to a preconceived moral theory based on some arbitrary assessment of character. The picture which emerges in the course of such an investigation is hardly one to please idealists; but it makes a great deal of political and historical sense. To strip away the accretions of myth, to discover—insofar as the evidence will permit it—the historical Alexander of flesh and blood: this must be the task of any contemporary historian, and to the best of my ability I have attempted it.

For me, in the last resort, Alexander's true genius was as a field-commander: perhaps, taken all in all, the most incomparable general the world has ever seen. His gift for speed, improvisation, variety of strategy; his coolheadedness in a crisis, his ability to extract himself from the most impossible situations; his mastery of terrain, his psychological ability to penetrate the enemy's intentions—all these qualities place him at the very head of the Great Captains of history. The myth of the Great Captains is wearing rather thin these days, and admiration for their achievements has waned: this is where we too become the victims of our own age and our own morality. Viewed in political rather than military terms, Alexander's career strikes a grimly familiar note. We have no right to soften it on that account.

Philip's son was bred as a king and a warrior. His business, his all-absorbing obsession through a short but crowded life, was war and conquest. It is idle to palliate this central truth, to pretend that he dreamed, in some mysterious fashion, of wading through rivers of blood and violence to achieve the Brotherhood of Man by raping an entire continent. He spent his life, with legendary success, in the pursuit of personal glory, Achillean *kleos;* and until very recent times this was regarded as a wholly laudable aim. The empire he built collapsed the moment he was gone; he came as a conqueror and the work he wrought was destruction. Yet his legend still lives; the proof of his immortality is the belief he inspired in others. That is why he remained greater than the measurable sum of his works; that is why, in the last resort, he will continue an insoluble enigma, to this and all future generations. His greatness defies a final judgement. He personifies an archetypal element, restless and perennial, in human nature: the myth of the eternal quest for the world's end, memorably summed up by Tennyson in the last line of *Ulysses:* "To strive, to seek, to find, and not to yield."

ALEXANDER THE MAN

5. Paul Cartledge in Chapter 10 of his 2004 book *Alexander the Great: the Hunt for a New Past*, examines what sort of man Alexander was.

FROM PAUL CARTLEDGE, "ALEXANDER THE MAN"

The scene of Alexander's recovery from the near-fatal wounding in India in 325, and his troops' fanatical reaction to it, prove that he was nothing if not extraordinary. But just what sort of a man was he, in so far as he *was* a man (and not a god or hero)? Was he the reasonable Alexander of Ulrich Wilcken? The gentlemanly and visionary Alexander of W. W. Tarn? The titanic and Führer-like Alexander of Fritz Schachermeyr? The homerically heroic Alexander of Robin Lane Fox? or the amoral and ruthlessly pragmatic Alexander of Ernst Badian and Brian Bosworth? Or was he none of these, or something of all, or some, of them? *Faites vos jeux, mesdames et messieurs.*

Following Alexander's death at Babylon in early June 323,...there was inevitably a period of confusion and uncertainty. Perdiccas, who had emerged as a marshal of the Empire and one of the leading Macedonian power-brokers produced what he claimed were Alexander's very own drafts for his "last plans" (the last that he would have been able to draw up, anyhow). These were written down allegedly in the *Hypomnemata* or "Notebooks," but the only preserved evidence for them is in Diodorus's far from wholly reliable *Library of History*. We cannot, therefore, be sure that any one item in the list of plans is accurate and authentic, though none of them is demonstrably a forgery.

There were, as reported by Diodorus, five main projects. The most important, politically and militarily, was one to construct a thousand warships for a campaign against Carthage (in modern Tunisia) and other inhabitants of the western Mediterranean (Libya, Sicily, Iberia). This campaign was, of course, to follow that against the Arabs of the Arabian peninsula, for which Alexander had already launched serious preparations before he died (or was killed). The other four major projects were, first, the erection of temples—three in Greece, three in Macedonia (including one to Zeus at Dium, the Macedonians' sacred city at the foot of Mount Olympus), and a particularly lavish and magnificent one to Athena at Ilium (New Troy). Second, a gigantic pyre to be completed at enormous cost (ten to twelve talents?) at Babylon as a memorial to Hephaestion, who had died at Ecbatana in the winter of 324/3 and been buried there with astonishing ceremony. Third, a pyramid to be constructed in honour of Alexander's human father, Philip. Fourth, significant population movements, including a transfer of peoples between Europe and Asia, and, finally, the formation of cities out of separate villages by the process the Greeks called "synoecism." Perdiccas, though, presented the supposed document to the army in order for the Macedonian soldiers to reject it as the sort of extreme projects they had been objecting to ever since their successful refusal to advance beyond the Hyphasis river in 325. In other words, even though the *Hypomnemata* may not have been drafted or dictated by Alexander, they contained projects that his soldiers believed he would or could have drafted. In their way, then, they can be said to bring us as close to Alexander the man, at a particular point in his career, as—in the absence of a truthful autobiography—it is possible for us to get.

Whatever we make of the authenticity or realism of these plans, Arrian's authorial comment at the start of the seventh and final book of the *Anabasis* is salutary:

> For my part I cannot determine with certainty what sort of plans Alexander had in mind, and I do not care to make guesses, but I can say one thing without fear of contradiction, and that is that none was small and petty, and he would not have stopped conquering even if he'd added Europe to Asia and the Britannic Islands to Europe. On the contrary he would have continued to seek beyond them for unknown lands, as it was ever his nature, if he had no rival, to strive to better the best.

To "seek...for unknown lands," "to strive to better the best": Arrian was clearly on to something here. It may be possible to detect in spiritual terms a progression in Alexander's choice of rivals. He started with Achilles the Homeric hero, went on to Heracles the universal hero who becomes a god, and climaxed with Dionysus the universal god of wine, transformation and spiritual release. Perhaps all that was left was to compete with himself as a god presiding over a universal empire? That would certainly have been "striving to better the best," a thoroughly modern version of the age-old Homeric aristocratic ideal.

Throughout Arrian's historical account the word *pothos* meaning a craving, yearning, longing or powerful desire—recurs in connection with Alexander's more adventurous undertakings. Thus in 335 he has such a craving to land on the further side of the Danube. In 333 he has a craving to visit the palace of the long-dead Phrygian king Gordius and his son Midas and to loosen the knot with which the yoke of Gordius's funeral wagon was fixed to its pole. In 332 he has a craving to found a city at the Canogic mouth of the Nile, the city that was to become the most famous and influential of his several Alexandrias. In 332/1 he has a craving to visit the oracular shrine of Ammon in Libya. In winter 327/6 he has a craving to capture the mighty rock of Aornus overlooking the River Indus. In 326 he

has a craving to visit Mount Merus near Nysa not far south of Aornus. In 324 he has a craving to sail down the Euphrates and Tigris out into the Persian Gulf. In 323, finally, he has a craving to explore the Caspian Sea.

This is a somewhat heterogeneous list, and it cannot be proved that the *pothos* motif is original to Alexander himself (as opposed to Arrian or one of his sources). The temptation to identify the dreamy look in the eyes of statues alleged to represent Alexander as an aesthetic visualization of this *pothos* should therefore be resisted. Yet there does seem to be the common element of seeking to do or to see the unusual, the daunting, that which is beyond the normal ken of most ordinary mortals. And in three of the eight instances cited, Arrian explicitly links the *pothos* motif to the motif of rivalry with Heracles and/or Dionysus. This does not mean that there were not also perfectly good secular or humanly rational motives for the various actions. But it does suggest or hint that such motives were not found entirely satisfying by Alexander himself. Or at least that he sought to project a persona of which a *pothos* for the out-of-the-ordinary was an integral component. That, to me, is the framework within which Alexander seems to have wanted and expected his personality to be assessed; an essentially larger-than-life framework.

Much is usually made of Alexander's physical, genetic inheritance from his parents, Philip and Olympias. His personal courage, outstanding generalship, quickness of decision and intellectual perceptiveness are qualities he shared with and so perhaps inherited from his father. To his mother's genes are attributed his strong will and passionate nature, stronger and more passionate even than Philip's, and his religiosity. But all this is mere speculation, since we are told so little in the surviving sources about Alexander's early life. In fact, more or less all we know is contained in the first seven chapters of Plutarch's *Life of Alexander*, which deal with his first twenty years. Still, there are embedded in these few chapters one or two bits of evidence that may give some clues as to the future course of his development: "Alexander seems actually to have despised the whole tribe of professional athletes. At any rate he founded a great many contests of other than athletic type: in tragic drama, in playing the *aulos* and lyre, in the recitation of poetry, in fighting with staves, and in various forms of hunting."

For all elite Macedonian men, the hunting of wild animals, especially the wild boar and the mountain lion, was more than just an excuse for an invigorating work-out or a pleasant diversion from more serious pursuits. It was itself a deadly serious calling. It made a man of a Macedonian youth, in the full social as opposed to the merely physical sense. In order to wear a distinguishing sort of belt, in order to be able to recline rather than sit at the symposium (the semi-formal elite male drinking party), one had to have killed a man and a boar in fair and open combat. Alexander triumphantly passed these manhood tests—so triumphantly, indeed, that it was as a huntsman that he was represented in eye-catching central position on the fresco adorning the front of the tomb at Vergina that has plausibly been identified as that of his father Philip. In choosing its iconographic repertoire, Alexander's known wishes would have been followed to the letter by the painter or painters.

Two famous hunting incidents became staple ingredients of Alexander lore. In one, the less creditable perhaps, he is saved by Craterus from a possibly fatal mauling by a lion in Syria. It is thought that this very scene is depicted in a beautiful pebble mosaic of the late fourth century from Pella. In the other, Alexander is enraged when a close companion, Lysimachus (not to be confused with the tutor below), interposes himself during a hunt near Maracanda (Samarkand in Uzbekistan) and dispatches the imposing lion that he had selected as his own kill. This is how the Roman author Curtius tells the story:

> In that part of the world there are no better indicators of the barbarians' wealth than the herds of fine animals that they enclose within spacious tracts of wooded grazing-land…Alexander entered one such wood…and ordered that the animals be beaten from their lairs throughout the area. Among these was an unusually large lion which came charging forward to pounce on the king himself. Lysimachus… happened to be standing nearby and started to aim his hunting spear at the beast. But Alexander pushed him aside, told him to get out of the way, and added that he was as capable as Lysimachus of dispatching a lion single-handed.

From all the evidence a consistent picture emerges of an Alexander passionately attached, almost addicted, to the thrills and spills of the chase. Butchering wild animals was by no means irrelevant to the career of a man moved on more than one occasion to treat "untamed" human enemies, such as the Cossaeans in 324/3, with unrestrained savagery.

Plutarch tells us that a great number of teachers were appointed to supervise Alexander's upbringing, but that in overall charge was one Leonidas, a relative of Olympias from Greek Epirus. Leonidas is said to have been a stern disciplinarian, but that he was much more than this is indicated by his being referred to as Alexander's foster-father and mentor. "Foster-father" is wholly appropriate, since his real father was away from home so often during Alexander's formative years that he is unlikely to have had the chance to develop any warmer or more intimate feelings for him than admiration and respect—unless we count jealousy as a warm and intimate feeling. Alexander's other main boyhood tutor, apparently his favourite, was another Greek, Lysimachus from Acarnania to the south of Epirus. Plutarch dismisses him loftily as "neither an educated nor a cultivated man" and refers with disapproval to his trick of likening the trio of Philip, Alexander and himself to the heroic Homeric trinity of Peleus, Achilles and Chiron (the half-man, half-horse centaur who tutored Achilles in Thessaly). But Lysimachus would appear to have tapped into a rich vein of symbolism and romance here, one that Alexander himself would mine to near-exhaustion in later life.

For Alexander, Achilles does seem to have been a hero in our sense of that word. And though it is possible to push the idea too hard or too far, Alexander frequently does appear to have acted in accordance with the aristocratic-heroic values of Homer. We note, for example, right at the end of his life, the "last plan" to build a temple for Athena at Ilium. This was Alexander's peculiar take on the general Greek notion of *philotimia*, or competitive seeking for honour and fame, that motivated figures in the public eye. Homer by himself, however, would have been an inadequate guide for a future king of Macedon, especially one who like Alexander was not naturally bookish. Besides the textual education provided by Leonidas and perhaps by Lysimachus, we must make full allowance for the education and self-education of Alexander outside the classroom, especially on the hunting field.

But not even a diet of Homer and hunting was considered wholesome enough by Philip for the prince who by the time he emerged into his teens was the only serious candidate for heir. So in about 343, when Alexander was thirteen or so, Philip decided to broaden his son's mind by appointing Aristotle his tutor. This choice reflects as well on Philip's discriminating judgement as it does on Aristotle's intellectual equipment. Philip might, after all, have selected Speusippus, Plato's nephew and chosen successor as head of the Academy at Athens, or Isocrates, founder of his own rhetorical school at Athens and a correspondent of Philip.

Aristotle was primarily a scientist, who specialized in zoology and botany, and there is no reason to doubt Alexander's genuinely scientific fascination with exotic flora and fauna, or the stories of his having specimens sent back from Asia to Aristotle at Athens (where he established his Lyceum institute for advanced study in the mid-330s). It was also Aristotle, so Plutarch believed, who did more than anyone to inspire the young prince's interest in the art of healing. But here Alexander typically combined a scientific approach with traditional piety. Among the countless local legends the religious traveller-scholar Pausanias picked up in the mid-second century CE is one concerning Gortys in Arcadia. Here, he was told, Alexander had dedicated a breastplate and spear to Asclepius, the universal Greek hero-god of medicine. Alexander, who was so often wounded or otherwise in need of medical attention, might well have thought it worthwhile to secure Asclepius's favour, even in this remote shrine.

Aristotle is also said to have instructed Alexander in the principles of politics and ethics, as well as in more secret, esoteric doctrines. We may, though, doubt just how deeply the political-philosophical teachings of the master sank into the pupil's consciousness. Not even he could lure Alexander very far away from Homer or tame his overriding passion for the *Iliad*, whose practical utility was strictly limited. So, resignedly, Aristotle gifted Alexander with a text of the poem that he himself had annotated—it would have been a very long papyrus scroll, or rather set of scrolls. Alexander is said to have carried this *Iliad* with him on the expedition to Asia, where it became known as the "casket copy." For among Darius III's personal effects captured after the Battle of Issus in 333 was a golden casket, and it was in this that

Alexander stored the precious Aristotle-annotated text. Indeed, he was so attached to it that at night he allegedly slept with it–and a dagger—under his pillow. But, despite this parade of book-learning, it is doubtful whether Alexander ever thought the stylus was mightier than the sword.

* * *

If sex did not thrill Alexander, religion certainly did. This facet of his character may well have been, in significant part, an inheritance from Olympias. In ancient Greek terms, Alexander was monumentally pious, verging on the superstitious. It was perhaps no mere coincidence that the Greek term meaning superstition, *deisidaimonia* (literally, a fear of demonic or supernatural phenomena), was coined in Alexander's own lifetime. And Aristotle's best pupil, Theophrastus, made the Superstitious Man one of his gallery of thirty shrewdly observed caricatures that together formed his famous and much-imitated *Characters*.

In order to discover or test the will of the gods or other supernatural powers, Alexander had with him constantly his own seer (*mantis*), Aristandrus. He came from Telmessus in a rough highland area of southwest Anatolia, a fertile breeding-ground of diviners. No major undertaking would be embarked upon without consulting Aristandrus, and there were occasions when his interpretation of an alleged omen or portent was decisive, directly affecting Alexander's course of action.

For example, when in 334/3 a plot against his life was reported to Alexander, he was undecided as to whether to give it credence. Then, while he was taking a nap during the siege of Halicarnassus, a swallow perched on his head and refused to budge. When Aristander declared that this portended a friend's treachery, Alexander acted to have that friend killed. Perhaps, as often was the case with omens and oracles in ancient Greece, the consultant did what he or she wanted to do anyway. But the support provided by an authoritative interpreter was vital for the course of action to be undertaken.

Alternatively, Aristander might merely make comforting predictions that would not affect Alexander's behaviour one way or another. For instance, when he was in camp on the River Oxus in the upper satrapies of central Asia in spring 328, a spring of water and a spring of oil (a gush of petroleum) rose up near each other close by his tent. Aristander duly declared that the spring of oil—the first certain mention of petroleum in all ancient Greek literature, incidentally—portended difficulties to come followed by eventual victory. Again, there are occasions on record when Alexander disregarded Aristandrus' interpretations, only for them to be proven correct in the event. It is quite remarkable that even the normally sceptical Arrian seems to have been convinced that Aristandrus had something special going for him, whatever exactly that rationally indefinable something may have been.

Nor was Alexander just monumentally superstitious. There was also a powerful streak of the religious mystic in him. This comes out most clearly during his visit to the Siwah oasis in 332/1. After it, he regarded himself as not merely descended from Zeus but actually in some sense Zeus's son. Yet it is important to stress that it was with Ammon, a non-Greek god, rather than with Zeus that Alexander contracted what we might call a "special relationship." When he made his curious detour to Ammon's oracular shrine at Siwah, he asked a question of the god and—so he said—was given the answer his heart desired. The exact nature of this answer he never divulged. Plutarch's report that Alexander wrote to tell Olympias that on his return he would reveal certain prophecies to her alone has, alas, to be treated with extreme scepticism. Undoubtedly, though, Ammon thereafter occupied a special place in Alexander's heart— hence in 328 Cleitus the Black's fatal accusation that Alexander had disowned Philip in favour of Ammon. For this, and other unfortunate suggestions, Alexander instantly killed the man who had saved his life at the Granicus river.

Arrian's reporting of Alexander's attitude to Ammon is impressively discriminating. He accepts that Alexander did indeed come to believe that he was a quasi-natural or naturalized son of Ammon, yet he does not include Ammon among the ancestral gods to whom Alexander was habitually disposed to offer sacrifice. Thus in November 326 at the River Indus he poured "a libation to Heracles his ancestor and to Ammon and to the other gods it was his custom to honour." Later on, in 325, he "offered sacrifice to those gods whom he liked to say Ammon had instructed him to honour"—perhaps a coded reference to instructions he had (he said) received in person from Ammon at Siwah. The clearest

proof of Alexander's special attachment to this exotic god was his accepting Ammon's response that Hephaestion should be worshipped as a hero rather than a god.

For his ancient contemporaries, Alexander was, like Hephaestion, a hero in the precise technical sense that after his death he was worshipped as such, privately, in Pella and doubtless elsewhere. But as we know, he also saw himself, famously or notoriously, as a Homeric hero in the mould of his alleged ancestor Achilles or, even better, of his alleged ancestor Heracles. For Heracles was both a Homeric-style hero, a super-achiever, and the son of a god (Zeus) and a mortal woman, who achieved the status of full divinity after accomplishing his famous twelve Labours. Alexander's heroic self-estimate has evoked widely varying reactions among historians and analysts both ancient and modern. Our current view of heroes, at any rate, is very different from that of Alexander and his contemporaries. For a view much closer to that of the ancients we would probably have to track back as far as Thomas Carlyle's nineteenth-century *Heroes and Hero-Worship*. But not even that Victorian paean can quite capture the full range and flavour of ancient hero worship.

Alexander's extreme reaction to the death of his best comrade raises the further issue of his character and its evolution. In ancient Greek a "character" meant a stamp; it was something innate, not socially constructed. At most, a person's natural birth character might be somewhat restrained or modified by education and experience. Otherwise the events of a person's life served only to reveal what that aboriginal stamped-on character truly was underneath the surface. The ancient literary sources for Alexander are unanimous that, in so far as his character changed, it underwent a change for the worse during the eleven years of his campaigning and rule in Asia. This view was echoed by the great eighteenth-century Scottish Enlightenment historian, William Robertson, who in his *History of India* noted "the wild sallies of passion, the indecent excesses of intemperance, and the ostentatious displays of vanity too frequent in the conduct of this extraordinary man." But Robertson also very properly added that these features "have so degraded his character, that the pre-eminence of his merit, either as a conqueror, a politician, or a legislator has seldom been justly estimated." We historians today, in our quest for that just estimate, are less overtly moralistic than Robertson, but we are no less passionately committed, both for and against.

Among the "anti" camp is Ian Worthington, who has argued that "the 'greatness' of Alexander must be questioned, and the historical Alexander divorced from the mythical, despite the cost to the legend." To which the American historian of Alexander, Frank Holt, has replied, "The danger now…is that the new orthodoxy—a reprehensible Alexander beset by paranoia, megalomania, alcoholism, and violence—may gather a deleterious momentum of its own."

My own view falls somewhere between these two and takes account of Lord Acton's dictum that "Power tends to corrupt, and absolute power corrupts absolutely." On top of the hugely self-indulgent mourning for Hephaestion, the following episodes seem to bespeak a diminishing self-restraint: the campaign of blood against native Indians such as the Mallian people after the mutiny at the Hyphasis in 326; the unnecessary forced march through the Gedrosian desert; the reign of terror (if that is really what it was) on his return to Iran in 324; and his severe, even callous reaction to his Macedonians after the Opis mutiny. But on the whole, historically rather than moralistically speaking, my Alexander is something of a contradiction—a pragmatist with a streak of ruthlessness, but also an enthusiast with a streak of passionate romanticism.

The finely balanced judgement of the French historian Claude Mossé, one of the sagest historians of all things ancient Greek, offers a fitting conclusion:

> He was no doubt neither the political and military genius that some have described nor the sage who derived total self-control from Aristotle's teaching. Nor was he the drunkard incapable of mastering his temper, nor the "savage" barbarian who razed Thebes and burned down Persepolis. He was a man of his times, no doubt affected by the contradictions implied by a Greek education, the extent of his conquests and the servility of part of his entourage. But perhaps, in the end, that is not what matters most. Should we not rather judge Alexander by his achievements and by the evolution of the empire that he conquered in just over one decade?

We surely should—but does Alexander's legacy (or legacies) permit us the luxury of objective and rational judgement?

Consider

1. If Tarn is correct about Alexander's philosophy regarding mankind, how might his beliefs have shaped his actions as a world conqueror? Discuss the Susa wedding and the mutiny at Opis in this light.
2. What was Alexander's policy of racial fusion according to Tarn? Compare Bosworth with Tarn on these issues.
3. What actions of Alexander seem to support the theory of racial fusion and how do they support it?
4. Discuss the historical circumstances for each of his policies.
5. How does Bosworth reconcile his view of Alexander's actions, such as introducing Persian court practice, with what the sources say?
6. Discuss how the evidence supports the interpretation of Bosworth and of Tarn regarding mixed marriage and the mass marriage at Susa?
7. How does Bosworth explain Alexander's use of Persian troops in his Macedonian army?
8. Does Bosworth convincingly refute Tarn's thesis about racial fusion? Why or why not?
9. Why did myth become such a prominent element in the story of Alexander after his death?

10. What is Green's stance on the "good" or "bad" source-tradition concerning Alexander?
11. How have historical circumstances and personal biases shaped the Alexanders of the historians Grote, Droysen, and Tarn?
12. What is Green's estimate of Alexander?
13. What relevance do the last plans (*hypomnemata*) of Alexander have for determining his character?
14. What role does Alexander's *pothos* play in assessing his personality?
15. Why does Cartledge stress the importance of hunting for the development of Alexander and of Homer, especially of Achilles as a model?
16. How does Cartledge view Alexander's attitude toward religion?
17. Of the four modern scholars, whose portrayal of Alexander do you find most convincing and why?
18. What prejudices might affect your judgment of Alexander?
19. Is it possible to know the historical Alexander? Why or why not?

PHOTO CREDITS

INDEX

Order ***Problems in The History of Ancient Greece: Sources and Interpretation*** with

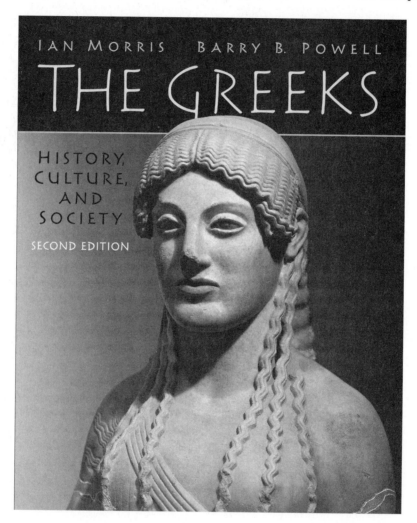

and receive a significant discount when the two titles are packaged together.

Please contact your Pearson representative for details or go to www.pearsonhighered.com for more information.